Dazzler

Dazzler

THE LIFE AND TIMES OF MOSS HART

STEVEN BACH

ALFRED A. KNOPF   NEW YORK   2001

THIS IS A BORZOI BOOK
PUBLISHED BY ALFRED A. KNOPF

Copyright © 2001 by Steven Bach

All rights reserved under International and Pan-American Copyright Conventions.
Published in the United States by Alfred A. Knopf, a division of Random House, Inc.,
New York, and simultaneously in Canada by Random House of Canada Limited, Toronto.
Distributed by Random House, Inc., New York.

www.aaknopf.com

Knopf, Borzoi Books, and the colophon are registered trademarks of Random House, Inc.

ISBN: 0-375-41150-X
LCCN: 2001087954

Manufactured in the United States of America

FIRST EDITION

Frontispiece:
Preparing *Camelot,* 1960
(Graphic House / Eileen Darby / NYPL)

FOR ROBERT DOGGETT
AND STANJA LOWE

Joie de vivre is the rarest phenomenon in the world.

S. N. BEHRMAN

CONTENTS

PART ONE

Outside

PART TWO

Inside

PART THREE

Solo

PART FOUR

Pro

"Huckleberry Hart"

These pages began when I was a student growing up in the dreary middle of a drearier nowhere and felt life suddenly given color and glow by the pages of Moss Hart's best-selling book *Act One*. I wanted to know more about the man who wrote that tantalizing memoir of apprenticeship in the theater, the craftsman who wrote *The Man Who Came to Dinner* and *You Can't Take It With You* and *Lady in the Dark* and *A Star Is Born* and—as if all that weren't enough—directed *My Fair Lady* and *Camelot,* too. The absence of any biography in the four decades since *Act One* first appeared and its author died convinced me that the only thing to do was write one, so I did, and this is it.

The change Hart made in my life was real. After some academic detours I entered the theater and related areas of show business, arenas that were creative and exciting and ruthless. The world of American show business breeds and betrays illusion, and its paradoxes—trivial and weighty—made me more curious than ever to understand a man who lived his life there with such apparent delight and easy grace. I knew, too, that I was not alone: *Act One* still changes lives. Ask any young (or not so young) actor, dancer, playwright, composer, or director making the rounds today and he or she will tell you: *Act One* is about him, about her.

Hart spoke to the stagestruck, but quickened aspiration on stages larger than the ones with footlights. He cast his beginnings as a romance and a fable: upward striving, rags to riches, the outsider triumphantly inside, a whole catalog of Horatio Alger virtues and rewards that can still inspire. No wonder he liked to call himself Huckleberry Hart.

He was writing about a Broadway that was vanishing in the late 1950s, even as he re-created it on the page. It was the end of the Golden Age, when New York was the place books and magazines and movies came from (all their corporate headquarters were there). It was the acknowledged center of American culture and no aspect of it was more dazzling than the theater, which was what New York meant for so many who wanted to be there and weren't. Broadway defined New York more than subways or skyscrapers or the Yankees. Broadway wasn't a street—it was the Great White Way, the Street of Dreams. Lights burned brighter there.

That Broadway is gone now, which is not an occasion for mourning. The daily rounds Hart's theatrical progeny make are as likely to be in Seattle, Denver, Los Angeles, or Newark as in and around Times Square. Broadway may always have been a state of mind, but it is real estate, too, and now a theme park. The New Amsterdam Theatre, where Hart began his career as an office boy called Mouse is now owned by one—called Mickey.

And, onstage, a lion! New creative standards and legends will emerge from Forty-second Street's renaissance, but Broadway, to the true believer, is about what is created there: the songs, stories, and plays that amuse, reflect, and sometimes reveal or shape us. Real estate sets boundaries; theater erases them.

Moss Hart was a storyteller, as all writers are, and a performer, as all playwrights must be. As I hunted and gathered for the facts of his life, I came to appreciate how artful a dramatist he was whenever he took up his pen, and how resourceful an entertainer. The man who rehearsed his dinner table bon mots while waiting for the guests to arrive was as incapable of not improving the story as he was of acting out a bad one. The differences between the life he lived and the one he told and performed are here (and there are notes at the end for those who need or want them).

His friends mostly recognized these differences at the time and accepted them. George Abbott told him he thought *Act One* had contrived a "truth-ier truth" about the world of the theater. Another friend from the early days was dismayed and "shocked." Still another smiled wryly at things "you omitted, but hell, you undertook to write 'Act One' and not 'Chapter and Verse.'"

Biographers, however, must deal with chapter and verse, and I have tried to do that, just as—after seven years of sharing my desktop and hours with the memoirist of *Act One*—I have taken him at his word when there seemed no reason not to. There was also the life after *Act One,* a life of success, fame, glamour, and money for which he became the glittering personification. There was darkness, too, hinted at but hidden. There were rumors that needed to be tracked down and were.

He dedicated *Act One* to his wife Kitty Carlisle Hart, who, for reasons of her own, chose not to cooperate in the pages that follow. In them I have tried to depict a life—"truth-ier truths" intact—without giving it more or less meaning than it had. It was a life of uncommon generosity in an often mean-spirited world, a life more painful than we knew, and maybe a braver one, too. He was cherished and mourned by friends and colleagues not only because of his success, but because of the man he became against such great odds and the man he aspired to be even when he seemed to have everything. I take that as reason enough to care about him now. And because he lifted spirits—not least his own—and made us laugh.

Outsíde

1

Broadway Baby

The residents of Manhattan are to a large extent strangers
who have pulled up stakes somewhere and come to town,
seeking sanctuary or fulfillment or some greater or lesser grail. The
capacity to make such dubious gifts is a mysterious quality of
New York. It can destroy an individual, or it can fulfill him,
depending a good deal on luck. No one should come to
New York to live unless he is willing to be lucky.

E. B. WHITE

"I was born on Fifth Avenue," Moss Hart liked to say. Then, when eyebrows had gone up all over the room, he would ricochet the very notion with a punch line: "The wrong end!" The joke always worked, but was never as self-deprecating as it sounded; he wanted you to know how far he'd come.

Wherever he was—in the precincts of the Shuberts and Ziegfelds or the playgrounds of the Thalbergs and Zanucks, on croquet lawns or in paneled drawing rooms—was Broadway. When he walked into the room, people say, the party got better, and because it did he loved to call himself "the Darling of Everyone there," no matter where "there" was. But the airy witticism floated oh so casually over cocktails or at Sardi's had been as carefully rehearsed in the shaving mirror as any actor's speech on any stage. He had a performer's timing and need for applause and a style so theatrical no mere actor would have dared pull it off. What made his grand manner easy to like was his unabashed love for the Broadway he came to personify. Even when his ardor for it was unrequited, he couldn't wait to entertain you with tales of his rejection, hilarious or heart-rending or both.

He was not born on any end of Fifth Avenue, but in a tenement at 74 East 105th Street, a neighborhood not of carriages and hansom cabs, but of dray wagons, pushcarts, and immigrants. It was an uptown version of the Lower East Side and not much farther from Broadway, he liked to quip, than, say, Yakima, Washington.

The tenement he was born in fell long ago to the wrecker's ball. In its place stands the DeWitt Clinton housing project, just where East 105th Street is interrupted by a hard-packed urban playground behind a chain-link fence. Aromas in the air today are not from the shtetl, but from the islands. Neighborhood wisdom comes not from rabbis, but from psychics and palm readers who hang neon promises in storefront windows. One suspects that few of them know or care that just a few blocks away a museum dedicated to the city of New York celebrates Hart as a son of this very neighborhood. What remains of him uptown is mostly behind glass: some glossy eight-by-tens, a tarnishing cigarette case, and dog-eared contracts that hint at the terms and conditions of fame and fortune on Broadway.

On the day Hart was born—October 24, 1904—this part of town was dominated not by nearby Central Park, but by the New York Central Railroad roaring north and rattling fire escapes all the way to the East River. The trains rumbled through a tunnel beneath what we now call Park Avenue and emerged into daylight, as they do today, at Ninety-sixth Street, where the tracks climb above ground to run in the channel of a stone viaduct. Those massive walls built to protect Upper East Siders from the railroad—and vice versa—must have looked like the walls of a prison in 1904. They still do, but modernity and mobility were popular issues early in the century and, to prove it, three days after Moss was born the New York subway system opened for business.

Hart's birthplace on East 105th Street drifted with railroad soot and smelled of failure and cigars. "Shabby gentility," he called it, though it was closer to bare subsistence. The flat was ruled by his grandfather Solomon, whose daughter Lillie was Moss's mother. Barnett—"Barney"—Solomon was a cigarmaker born in London in 1833, a man of "enormous vitality, color and salt" according to his grandson. He was also vain and a tyrant and a thwarted visionary outraged by life's injustices, so many of them visited on him. He had confounded immigrant cliché by working his way not up but down from comfortable respectability in England to near-penury in New York. For the rest of his life he fulminated with bitter tales of the wealthy and distinguished family he had left behind, and the stories were true.

The Solomons he came from were a generation removed from Holland, where they had been silversmiths in Amsterdam. The original spelling had been Salamon or Salaman. In England, Barney's older brother Joseph, a less mercurial and more prudent Solomon, worked his way from apprenticeship in a leather factory in Bermondsey to ownership of one of his own. He grew so affluent that he established night classes for his workers in keeping with his fervor for moral uplift and self-improvement. He improved himself into a London town house designed by John Nash, who had built Regent Street, Trafalgar Square, and Buckingham Palace. There he founded a small dynasty of Solomon sons (seven) and daughters (five), who would pursue and achieve distinction in the arts and professions even as his brother Barney raged at the social order that bestowed wealth on Joseph and hardship on himself. Just as well, perhaps, that Barney didn't live to know that a granddaughter of Joseph would play violin at Albert Hall with Mischa Elman; or that a painter son, grandly named Solomon J. Solomon, would become the second Jewish member of the Royal Academy, exhibiting his portraits of Members of Parliament and the aristocracy, and even of Mrs. Patrick Campbell, for whom Shaw wrote Eliza Doolittle, a character to return to these pages.

A Shavian family note was apt in any event, for Joseph Solomon declared himself a Shaw disciple and liked to quote the playwright's definition of a gentleman as one who tried "to put at least as much into life as [he] took out of it." Solomon put more Solomons into life, some of them eccentrics, including suffragettes, Zionists, and at least one hot-air balloonist. When young Moss was growing up in humble American obscurity, a British writer was noting among the Solomons in England "such a surprising number of persons who have won eminence in Art, Music, and the Drama as has probably created a record!" Their eccentricities would—much later and much Americanized—find life on Broadway, as they pursued their individual creative talents or whims without a worry in the world because, as one of them would put it, you can't take it with you.

On East 105th Street, by contrast, there was nothing but resentment and grievance, for Barney Solomon had never shared his brother's diligence and piety. Even as a youth he was deemed a "ne'er do well," a firebrand and malcontent. In his thirties he was "cast off to El Dorado," a family member recalled, to pursue his personal crusades out of sight and out of mind.

His bride, Rose Lewis, was not only uncultivated, she was illiterate. She may have been non-Jewish as well, a factor that probably did not recommend her to Joseph Solomon, by now a warden at London's Bayswater Synagogue. Whatever her shortcomings, by the time of Barney's expulsion from the family circle Rose had presented him with a family of his own: daughters Kate in 1868 and Lillie in 1870. Shortly thereafter the family set sail for America.

In El Dorado Barney pursued cigarmaking, which provided him with a job, a friend, and a cause. Samuel Gompers was London-born, too, and a fellow cigarmaker rolling tobacco leaves (family legend has it) at the very next bench. Gompers was unburdened by wife or family and had only the Noble Order of the Knights of Labor to worry about, a social club with ambitions to become a trade union. Gompers's slogan— "Reward Your Friends and Punish Your Enemies"—was just the sort of incendiary cry to appeal to Barney's own sense of injury and injustice.

Gompers was elected president of the American Federation of Labor in 1886, but if Barney was at his side he left no traces on union history, though family apocrypha had him marching with Gompers and even rivaling him for leadership. The story Moss told had something to do with who got to carry a briefcase into union meetings. In fact, Barney's reward as Gompers's friend was the picket line, where he and the other faithful punished Gompers's enemies (and themselves) with a thousand strikes a year until the end of the century.

Sometimes Barney was a passionate crusader and sometimes he merely sulked in the cramped quarters he shared with his wife and daughters. On occasions of nostalgia for England, when not locked in his private world of rage or depression, he used storytelling as an antidote to the dispiriting realities of the Land of Liberty. Moss wrote that the defeated cigarmaker read aloud serial installments of Dickens's latest novel (though Dickens had died in 1870, making them very back numbers indeed), thrilling his daughters with Victorian cliff-hangers and tutoring Rose with the only education she was ever to receive. When he detected or imagined flagging attention, he refused to continue reading, locked Dickens in the closet, and brooded in ominous silence for days on end. He would bequeath his love of stories and his unpredictable moods to his grandson.

During the strikes of 1892, which halted the production of iron and steel as well as cigars, Rose revealed that she had somehow salted away enough pennies to finance a family excursion back to England. Her husband, idle for months, erupted at the treachery of wherewithal withheld, before agreeing that an ocean voyage might relieve the frustrations of striking and brighten his mood, maybe even his prospects.

Rose may have had family assistance in mind, but Barney's hat would be on his head, not in his hand. He appropriated funds from her hoard to indulge a fit of extravagance and vanity. He dyed hair, mustache, and goatee jet-black, the better to set off the Panama hat and bravado with which he crowned the whole ensemble.

Joseph Solomon's children thought his sartorial pretensions "touchingly transparent," but they and some grandchildren named Bentwich and Montagu took a friendly interest in shy young Lillie, who was twenty-two and "buxom." Haughty young Kate, who was twenty-four and prematurely "wizened," took an interest in *them*.

She surveyed their comfort, culture, and the cornucopia of plenty that accomplishment had put on the table, and decided she had ripened on the wrong branch of the family tree. For the rest of her life she valiantly redressed fate's error by taking on airs and never again—or almost never—lifting a finger except to turn the pages of a novel or a theater program.

While Kate accustomed herself to a style of life to which her birthright should have entitled her, the more practical Lillie made friends with Solomons, Bentwiches, Montagus, and with working-class companions who gathered around her father. Among them was a bachelor seven years older than she who bore her father's first name and the surname Hart.

Born in London in 1863, Barnett Hart was a cigarmaker, too. He looked on Barney Solomon as a mentor who knew an old trade in a new world and shared not only his name but also his interest in trade unionism. Hart was a welcome acolyte to Barney, and his mild and passive manner may have attracted Lillie from the start. That and his jauntily ignored vulnerability, for he was lame, born with a bad leg.

Whatever warmth flickered between them dimmed as funds dwindled, dictating that Barney bundle his brood back to America. Barnett Hart proved a cautious suitor. It would take a full year before he mustered courage—or passage—to follow his future.

When the thirty-one-year-old Hart finally arrived in New York in 1894, he found the cigarmaker's trade as depressed as it had been in England. Workbenches not idled by strikes and boycotts were being removed to make room for machines. To further dampen his welcome, he discovered that Rose had died shortly after the family's return to New York. Lillie had taken her place as housekeeper for her father and as handmaiden to Kate, whose airs had grown loftier than ever in the absence of the illiterate mother whose very presence had been a denial of grandeur and a brake on delusion. If Hart felt romantic ardor for Lillie it was inhibited by his realization that her father had no intention of trading a diligent housekeeper for an indigent son-in-law.

Lillie continued with the cooking, laundry, and housecleaning, and had little leftover energy or time for Hart. The newcomer accepted this for most of a decade with no apparent loss of good humor before finally claiming the hand that, in the meantime, kept her father in clean collars and her sister in the loftier reaches of fantasy and pretension.

Barnett was thirty-eight in 1901 when he finally married thirty-one-year-old Lillie. The long courtship speaks feebly of passion or forcefully of patience. Whatever the case, it appears likely that Lillie's motivation for marriage was partly to get out of her father's domain and into lodgings of her own. The newlyweds set up housekeeping on West 118th Street until Lillie became pregnant two years later.

Left alone and to their own devices, Barney and Kate mixed with predictable volatility. Shortly before Lillie's delivery came due, Barney demanded that the Harts leave the West Side for his own dwelling in order to prevent his killing Kate or himself. The Harts did as they were told, which is how and why their first son was born within earshot of the New York Central's roar on East 105th Street.

They named him Moss, after his father's father.

Lillie was a caretaker because she had no choice. Marriage merely shifted the caretaking focus from one set of dependents to another. Barnett—like his father-in-law—subsisted mainly on vain hopes and the dole, and even that would vanish as union coffers emptied and industrialization further eroded his trade.

Barney Solomon grew more volatile, accumulating rage with years. When Lillie gave birth at thirty-four, Barney was past seventy and "monstrous," his grandson reported.

Moss's arrival changed everything from the family dynamic to the family address. They moved into lodgings a few blocks away at 14 East 107th Street, where Barney and Barnett seem to have shared superintendent chores and extra rooms were rented to boarders to supplement what income there was. Lillie cooked and cleaned and laundered for strangers in addition to caring for father, husband, sister, and an infant son who required more than routine attention.

The first year of Moss Hart's life was marked by eczema that required constant vigilance and a pharmacopoeia of remedies. It was a persistent, unsightly condition and until it went away Lillie smothered her son with creams and lotions and body wraps. She may have smothered him, too, with her own anxieties. Or maybe she withdrew into cold drudgery that substituted order for warmth. Maybe the food on the table, however meager, was easier to provide than other forms of nourishment.

Barnett Hart had already withdrawn. The birth of a son when he was past forty modulated hopes for the future into the resignations of middle age that he bore with what his son later called "unruffled self-preservation." His ship might come in, or not, or perhaps it already had and this was it. He would allow Lillie's hand to rock the cradle and steer circumstance by whatever rudder she could grab onto.

Moss was less his mother's or father's child than his grandfather's. He was "his sole and jealously guarded possession" who awakened an old man's exuberance. Barney chased butterflies in the park for his grandson, trying to snare them in his Panama hat as onlookers jeered. He unlocked the closet to retrieve the precious installments of *David Copperfield* or *Great Expectations.* He taught the boy to hear the spoken word, to memorize and recite.

Moss's later version was that before he saw the inside of any school he was awakened at night, hoisted from his crib by his grandfather, and deposited in the middle of the kitchen table to rub his eyes in the glow of a gas lamp, or candlelight if the meter had run out. Surrounded by the indulgent faces of Barney's Friday Evening Literary Society, Moss recited texts drilled into him by the old man—a passage from *A Christmas Carol,* perhaps, or even Shakespeare. His adult memory would credit his introduction to theater to another champion at another time and place, but surely it was there on that kitchen table—so very like a stage—that he first felt the warmth of approval by pretending to be someone he was not: Tiny Tim or Puck or Bottom.

The rest of what he remembered was an "unending drabness" in an "atmosphere of unrelieved poverty." It was not to be dispelled by the two Barnetts, rolling cigars in leather cuffs at the very kitchen table where Lillie prepared food for boarders. They cobbled together a newsstand and when that failed they tried selling cigars door-to-door and when that failed there was more injustice collecting and sulking and cursing of Fate and that failed, too.

Finally, in 1910, the seventy-seven-year-old despot and patriarch emerged from one of his depressions and stirred with a final burst of energy. He demanded funds from Lillie, heedless that they came from the bottom of the barrel, and herded his court—Lillie, Barnett, Aunt Kate, and six-year-old Moss—all the way to Brooklyn, to Brighton Beach.

It may have been literally mad, this excursion to the shore, but for Moss, whose memory this is, there was magic to it. The old man squandered the family capital on boardwalk vistas and music-hall tunes that maybe only he saw and heard, but Moss thought, looking back on it, that all the thunder and lightning had been "a cry from the heart." His grandfather was preposterous and a failure, a bully and a ne'er-do-well, but he rejected the humdrum, the prudent, the cautious, the joyless, and sometimes the foolish and often the wise. He defied his lot and his grandson would, too.

2

Poor Relations

To be brought up in a poverty-stricken household, to know nothing but poverty in childhood and adolescence, is not so bad while you are enduring it; it is quite tolerable in fact. . . . It is in later life that it takes its toll.

S. N. BEHRMAN

Moss's grandfather went back from Brighton Beach to East 107th Street, where he died of pneumonia on January 2, 1911, one month shy of seventy-eight. His death produced unmitigated grief in no one but his grandson.

There were distractions from mourning. Three months later, on April 1, Moss witnessed the birth of his brother and only sibling, Bernard. To the seven-year-old Moss "Bernie" seemed less a rival or companion than the victim of a cruel April Fools' joke or evidence of a family curse, for he was born with a withered arm, a counterpart to his father's crippled leg.

A different kind of distraction was P.S. 171 in Manhattan, which Moss hated from the start. He was enrolled in the first grade on his sixth birthday, but could not finish even his first term due to poor health, which caused him to miss more than a third of his classes. His teeth were so bad they merited a note in school records, with nutrition cited as a likely cause.

He began his first term over again in September 1911 when he was almost seven. He earned A's or B's when he attended classes, but he was there less than two-thirds of the time. He fell farther behind his age group when forced to drop out of third grade because of the family's move to East 156th Street in the Bronx. Transferring to P.S. 10 brought difficulties of adjustment in arithmetic and spelling (never a strong subject for him) and, surprisingly, reading. He fell behind again. No wonder he hated it.

His grades in the Bronx turned satisfactory as his attendance improved. There were renewed warnings about his terrible teeth (they would plague him all his life) and, again, nutrition. The A's and B's he received were some consolation for the full-year age difference that set him apart, but there was more to widen the distance he felt from his peers than merely being older.

He had that odd first name, he had no physical aptitude for athletics or boyish games, and he had inherited a faint English accent that sounded sissified and affected. This was especially so when a certain theatrical lilt acquired from his Aunt Kate bumped up against the dropped aitches of his father's Cockney, an accent whose usefulness lay almost entirely in the future of a girl not yet born named Julie Andrews.

Moss would all his life have an overpolished manner of speaking sabotaged by echoes of the Bronx in everyday words. He said orchest*er* for orchestra, chrysanthe*num* for chrysanthemum, and xylophone came out *zollo*phone. He pronounced "drama" to rhyme with Alabama and "dramatist" sounded like amethyst, but "again" always rhymed with the rain in Spain falling mainly on the plain. Sometimes the ordinary became weirdly posh, as with Yakima (YAK-i-maw), which came out Ya-KEE-ma. Friends retailed stories poking fun at his pronunciation, but the best anecdote was the one he told on himself about the time he got it right. At some point in the thirties he was arguing with Edna Ferber, who had written *Show Boat* and could churn through heavy waters as if she were one. Ferber maintained the word "squalor" was "squa*y*lor," not "squa*h*lor," as Moss insisted. Exasperated, he told her, "When I lived in it, it was squa*h*lor!"

It was never truly that. There were hardships, and they left scars, but they strengthened his character more than they stunted it, teaching him the endurance and persistence the theater demands of survivors. It was the humiliation of being the poor relation that was so terrible, that remained so sharply bitter to him to the end of his life. He invoked it endlessly, as if by doing so he could justify later extravagant prodigality and reassure himself and others he had truly escaped the poverty he had hated. Far more significant than any empty table was the emotional turmoil his grandfather Solomon left behind, in which Moss became a pawn.

Kate had been able to hold her own with her tyrannical father because she was so much like him, with "the same streak of iron," Moss recalled. Her eccentricity echoed his, her delusions mimicked his despair in reverse, and both were connoisseurs of injustice. Kate was "faintly grotesque" to her nephew, but she was also "immensely shrewd and sensitive . . . with some secret splendor within herself." She was willing to share that splendor with an appreciative audience and it didn't take her long to find one in Moss.

He later related (and may have believed) that Kate seized on her father's death to exploit the English relatives. She blackmailed them, he said, manipulating their sympathies for her as a spinster and orphan (of forty-three) to solicit a private dole that would keep her supplied with the novels and theater tickets that were as necessary to her as the sun to the day.

The truth is, she didn't have to. The Solomons had been helping the Harts out all along. They had fixed a sympathetic eye on their American cousins ever since that sabbatical to England in the 1890s. In 1906, Lillie's first cousin, Susannah Solomon Bentwich, sailed to America to help her newly married daughter Lillian settle in an apartment with her husband, Israel Friedlander, who had a teaching position at the Jewish Theological Seminary in New York. Susannah found something for them in the Jersey Palisades and then sought out her Uncle Barney and her cousins Lillie and Kate. She found them still at East 105th Street. The two-room flat with direct access to the fire escape was appalling to a woman raised in a London town house designed by John Nash. The Harts' mean circumstances aroused her compassion as did Lillie's firstborn. Susannah, who had eleven children of her own, examined the infant and wrote back to England about the sickly "new babe" called Moss.

From that point on the Solomons and Bentwiches contributed modestly to the Hart household; Lillian and Israel Friedlander would do so, too, as they prospered in America. Their help was never a windfall, but it kept the wolf from the door and Kate from spiritual deprivation. She knew that if she earmarked some of those funds for the pursuit of culture no Solomon was likely to object, so she took her allowance and herself to the theater.

She had a shrewd sense of timing. Moss was unhappy at home and school following his grandfather's death and his brother's birth, feeling as alien as Kate. She recognized a kindred spirit and moved in, seducing the boy into her conspiracy of superiority and significance. If she was the True Princess, he was the True Prince, deposited like her on the wrong fire escape or front stoop by capricious fate. There had simply been some terrible mistake, rectifiable with enough music, lights, and make-believe. She wrapped Moss in her fantasies and carted him off to the theater, where his unhappiness was dispelled with the force of an epiphany.

The location was the Bronx Opera House at 149th Street and Third Avenue. The play was a William A. Brady production called *Life,* a spectacle that did everything possible to live up to its title. It featured a cast of more than one hundred, not including the horses. Four acts depicted its hero's progress in a succession of naturalistic settings that must have been a stage designer's dream and a stage crew's nightmare. They included Yale, a "Stuyvesant mansion," Sing Sing Penitentiary, and St. Patrick's Cathedral. There was a detour to a desert in the American southwest and a stopover at the governor's mansion in Albany so the hero's best friend could explain away the dreadful misunderstanding that had led him—a Yale man!—to Sing Sing and Death Row, where the executioner was counting every tick of the clock.

Producer Brady had been a boxing promoter and was a movie mogul, too, which helped make *Life* as sweeping as any film well before anyone had seen *Birth of a Nation*. "The colossal, picturesque, human Bradydrama," as he grandly billed it, included—live and on stage!—the Yale-Harvard regatta, an automobile chase, a roof-garden restaurant, a debutantes' ball, and what the program called illustrated intervals during the many cumbersome scene changes. These lulls in the action were, in fact, little movies filmed by a Brady actor learning a new trade. His name was John Cromwell and he did so well at "intervals" that he went on to direct movies like *Of Human Bondage* with Bette Davis, *Abe Lincoln in Illinois* with Raymond Massey, and *Anna and the King of Siam* with Irene Dunne and Rex Harrison. Still later he would return to acting, working for a writer-director who was now, in 1911, just seven years old and in kneepants, perched in the upper balcony of the Bronx Opera House, thunderstruck.

Life may not have seemed very lifelike when compared to the Bronx or P.S. 10, but that, of course, was the point. It presented an enchanted world in which pluck was rewarded, adversity overcome, obstacles surmounted, and destiny gloriously fulfilled, all of it to the music of applause.

Kate plucked Moss from P.S. 10 whenever she could for Thursday matinees, or for vaudeville acts at the Alhambra on 126th Street and Seventh Avenue (Moss ever after called it the Al-AHM-bra), or for touring plays at the Bronx Opera House with a constantly changing pageant of stars from unimaginably distant Broadway itself: Ethel, John, and Lionel Barrymore; Mrs. Fiske; Leslie Carter; and E. H. Sothern and Julia Marlowe.

For Kate this was entitlement; for Moss it was "the beginning of a lifelong infection," incurable and contagious. He understood at once that the theater made possible "the art of being somebody else," somebody who was not a scrawny boy with bad teeth, a funny name, an odd way of talking, a father and brother who were crippled, and a mother who was a distant drudge. Like every stagestruck youth before and since he saw himself predestined "to be loved and admired; to stand gloriously in a spotlight [amidst] waves of applause that roll over the footlights." The theater was refuge, shelter, asylum; it was a haven for those who felt nowhere else at home.

There was not a moment to lose. On the first Thanksgiving of the Great War, when he was ten, he donned his mother's dress, hat, and shoes (or were they Kate's?) and went door-to-door doing impersonations of Fanny Brice and Nora Bayes, two of his favorites from the Alhambra. The youthful drag artist accepted pennies in tribute from admirers and got punished when Lillie found out about it. Singing for money was begging. But no punishment could be harsh enough—the theater itself would be full of them—to discourage a would-be thespian in a picture hat, cheered on by an eccentric aunt.

Kate was also, a cousin recalled, "insanely jealous of Lillie." Benevolent to her nephew, she was compulsively competitive with her sister and her boldness would tear the family apart. Fantasies flourish where needed and Kate's needs were real, vain, and deeper than anyone knew. She was tireless in expressing contempt for her companions in life, and of no one was she more scathing than her Cockney brother-in-law. Moss later related that Kate high-handedly gave away some books Barnett had received from a boarder and that this act precipitated catastrophe. But there was more.

Kate the haughty spinster lived a life empty of any romance not on a page or a stage. At some point she attempted to demonstrate her superiority over her surroundings by becoming sexually aggressive. "She made a brazen play for Barnett," a cousin remembered. Her bid to seduce Barnett—whether from malice, jealousy, or sexual need—appears to have failed. But if she could not steal Lillie's husband, she had already, in some unsettling way, appropriated her son.

However and whenever it happened, Kate overplayed her hand and Barnett, sick of being patronized and scorned, threw her out. Moss attributed it to the quarrel over books, thus avoiding issues of Kate's sexual aggressiveness that may have made him uncomfortable or worse as a boy, and he oddly omitted mention of Lillie from the story altogether. We don't know what role she played in Kate's banishment, but she had a lifetime of motives. All that is certain is that Kate had thrown herself at Barnett and was now forced to throw herself on the mercy of the world.

Her leaving may have been a narrow escape for Moss, but he felt it as calamity. Without her, there would be no more Alhambra or Bronx Opera House; her leaving deprived him of his real home and abandoned him to people too insensitive to care that they were expelling from his life the one source of joy it contained.

He later acknowledged Kate was "pathological," but gratitude and compassion led him to romanticize her even before he made her a heroine in the autobiographical pages of *Act One,* altering the story of her expulsion and the nature of her subsequent decline. When he became famous in the thirties and the press got curious about a series of bizarre incidents *The New Yorker* referred to as "the great family mystery," he glossed over them, dismissing them as the sort of fascinating things bound to happen to celebrities as interesting as himself.

What he concealed was that Kate had lost all reason. She pursued the family that had exiled her like an avenging fury, with curses she scrawled on walls and hexes and crosses she carved into doors and furniture, not just in the Bronx but later in Brooklyn and Manhattan. She set fires—at least one of them backstage in a major Broadway theater—driven by her relentless sense of having been wronged. "Beware!" was the mildest of her imprecations; most were violent and so obscene that no surviving relative who knew her would repeat them.

She made do mostly by folding laundry in the Home for Immigrant Girls on Second Avenue. When she died in the mid-thirties (not in the early twenties as Moss later wrote), her curses died with her. But she and her father had awakened in Moss an unsettling fear of mental imbalance that might be hereditary. If twisted limbs could be inherited, what about twisted minds?

Perhaps the most disconcerting footnote to Kate's unhappy story is that after her death and Lillie's, Moss allowed reporters to assume that the unstable figure responsible for "the celebrated bogey of the crosses," as *The New Yorker* called it, and the obscenities and the fires had not been his aunt, but his mother.

"I did not like her," Moss wrote about Lillie, and admitted feeling no sorrow at her death. She had kept the family afloat, but that had put him at her mercy, a cold and ambiguous place to be. His views of her were shared by some. The screenwriter Walter Bernstein, a boyhood friend of the family, remembers her as "a battle-ax." One of Moss's boyhood friends held Lillie in memory as a neighborhood landmark, trudging home from the library, arms laden with books for her son. A relative remains bewildered at Moss's lack of compassion for "a warm-hearted and remarkably resourceful woman."

The resourcefulness was real, but humiliating. Better-off relatives could admire her hoarding of melon seeds and lemon pips to make "jewelry," without grasping the resentment her son felt when given the seeds to dry, dye, and string at the kitchen table before selling them door-to-door with his younger brother.

Lillie worked for relatives to avoid the appearance of charity and so did Moss. The disparities between the haves and the have-nots were as apparent to him as they had been years before to Kate and he resented them just as deeply. Lillie cooked and catered for the Friedlanders and others and Moss dutifully helped deliver and serve the products of her kitchen. It brought in money, but confused identity: Was he a relative or a servant?

There is a surviving photograph that suggests this discomfort. It was taken in March 1922 when he was not yet eighteen. The occasion was the wedding of his mother's cousin, Carmel Bentwich, to young rabbi Louis Finkelstein. Carmel was a granddaughter of Joseph Solomon who left England after the Great War to study education at Columbia with John Dewey. Like every Solomon relative who crossed the Atlantic, she stayed first with Lillian and Israel Friedlander and there she met her future husband, a theology student of Israel's.

Moss is there in Carmel's wedding photograph, a tall, darkly handsome youth, his mouth closed and unsmiling to hide his crooked teeth. He stands mostly behind the other relatives and is utterly expressionless, as if he felt no connection to this world and its conventions. He does not look sullen or resentful: he just looks absent, elsewhere.

Moss admitted later that he was not merely unhappy growing up, but "deeply disturbed." Maybe so, but he was not as friendless as he later claimed. The streets and stoops near the Hart apartment in the Bronx teemed with boys of similar age and class and the evidence is that he got on well. Most of them belonged to "the Asphalt League" and lost or triumphed raucously at games with names like stickball, punchball, and boxball.

Moss mostly shunned athletics from lack of interest and aptitude, with one showy exception. He became in adolescence the owner of a tennis racket, an item of considerable exotic interest in the Bronx. He wielded it with such swank that the other boys asked if he was doing an impersonation of some silent film star he'd seen down at Colman's, the neighborhood picture palace.

Colman's was a haunt and so was the music store run by Pop Levenson, who taught violin and piano on the side, a black cigarillo dangling from the corner of his mouth. Moss went to school with Harold and Abe Levenson and at twelve got a job working for their father after school. He earned pocket money dusting shelves, running errands, and filing sheet music decorated with famous faces like those of George M. Cohan, Al Jolson, and Eva Tanguay. He learned to play the piano a little and the ukulele a lot.

The ukulele became part of the tap-dance act of Ho and Ko, performers better known to their mothers as Irving Haskell and Alvin Nussbaum. Ho and Ko entertained in St. Mary's Park and Moss was their choreographer, teaching them dance steps he remembered from the Alhambra and strumming his ukulele in accompaniment as he and another neighbor boy, Ben Feuerstein, sang duets.

When not performing in the park, Moss and the boys played poker at George Steinberg's house. George's parents ran the candy store on the corner, an establishment with a natural gravitational pull where Moss found a voice more gratifying than the ukulele's. Summer evenings were too hot and humid for much but listening to stories on the candy store stoop, and Moss had that knack of telling them he inherited from grandfather Solomon. He later remembered telling the story of Dreiser's *Sister Carrie* (which takes place partly in the theater and might have been a natural, if precocious, choice), but one of his wide-eyed listeners recalled fare less lofty and more satisfyingly chilling and lurid at the same time— Poe's "The Murders in the Rue Morgue" and "The Purloined Letter."

There was life beyond the Bronx. The Friedlanders now had two boys, Herzl, two years younger than Moss, and Ben, the same age as Bernie. The family had moved from the Palisades to nearer the Jewish Theological Seminary where Israel still taught and they had a summer cottage, too, in Pine Hill, New Jersey. Moss and Bernie joined them there every summer from 1914 to 1920 except for the polio-scare summer of 1916 when everyone stayed home.

The Friedlanders were the source of Moss's mystery tennis racket. They gave him his first typewriter, too, and his first portable phonograph and, in a moment of almost clairvoyant serendipity, Lillian Friedlander gave him a special gift: a volume of plays by George Bernard Shaw including *Pygmalion*.

In the spring of 1917, when Moss was twelve and America was just entering World War I, he took part in a public speaking contest at P.S. 51. He wrote and delivered an exhortation to buy War Savings Stamps and the speech he gave survives. It is full of rotundities about liberty and honor and full of outrage at that "beast and monster," the kaiser. Only "Old Glory" could defeat the atrocities and horrors of the Hun.

Moss must have delivered his four-minute declamation with fire, for he won first prize. He was awarded a handsome scroll signed by the principal that he saved for the rest of his life. The certificate was a memento of achievement after early stumbles, an earnest of promising things to come, too, until life dealt him a blow so cruel not even the kaiser could have thought of it. Barnett Hart could and did.

Moss had been promoted to the second term of the eighth grade in June of 1919, but never attended a single class. On October 20, four days before his fifteenth birthday, he was discharged forever from further schooling with a doctor's certificate of illness. The nature of his malady is not recorded, but health was almost certainly a pretext. Barnett withdrew his son from school so he could go to work.

They needed the money. The war had dried the flow of charity from England and Barnett, now in his fifties, had gone from obsolete to unemployable. He needed income more than he needed a son with a diploma. He could easily justify it to himself, for statistics tell us that hardly more than 10 percent of American youth graduated from high school before the 1920s. But statistics could not console Moss, who condemned his father's action as "staggeringly selfish" and never forgave him for it, any more than he ever forgave Lillie for not preventing it.

Moss had worked part-time at the music store and had catered with his mother from time to time, but now a steady paycheck was the whole point. It was Israel Friedlander, speaking to a Zionist friend, who got Moss a job in the garment industry.

He went to work at Neuburger Furs near Union Square, pushing carts in and out of the fur vaults. He was a fastidious boy who loathed the smell of the pelts, which clung to him on the subway rides to and from the Bronx, and he hated those, too. He got a better job, again with Israel's help, at the National Cloak and Suit Company on West Twenty-fourth Street. There he was a storeroom clerk, then a floorwalker, entrusted with seeing that company assets did not go home on the backs of fellow employees. He wore a suit and tie and could breathe air perfumed by patrons, not dead animals. He could take lunch breaks and wander about Manhattan and dream about his future.

Young ladies—in whom he had shown no interest—began to figure in his daydreams. They were up-to-the-minute, full of pep and zip and rhythm, and had enticing names: "Miss Melody," "Miss Plot," and "Miss Jazz."

Moss, not yet eighteen, was about to become an impresario.

3

"That Damn Kid"

*Anyone who will let anything on earth stop him from going on
the stage might better steer clear of the theater altogether.
For his own sake. And the theater's.*

ALEXANDER WOOLLCOTT

At seventeen, Moss had the restraint and diffidence of a lit firecracker. If
he looked absent in the wedding photograph of March 1922, it is a fair
guess that his mind was on a more festive occasion planned for late June,
a red-letter date for the National Cloak and Suit Company and a star-
spangled one for himself.

Now that the Jazz Age and Prohibition had set the tone for American
life, Moss's employers had a vital interest in being up-to-the-minute. To
show off the latest flapper fashions and (soberly) reward worker loyalty
at the same time, the owners hosted a dinner dance shortly before the
Fourth of July. It fell to Moss to make the event intoxicating. He cam-
paigned to turn the evening's entertainment into his version of *George
White's Scandals* or the *Music Box Revues* of Irving Berlin, writing and
staging the event himself and using employee talent as his cast. Persuaded by his enthusiasm—or just bowled over by his seventeen-year-old
chutzpah—the cloaks and suits agreed.

The curtain rose on June 26, 1922, on Moss Hart's first production,
"The 'National' Revue." It had two parts, one musical, one not. A prologue was set in "The Author's Study," where the Author (played by
Moss) consulted with "Miss Plot," "Miss Melody," and "Miss Jazz" about
the evening ahead.

The musical part of the evening followed, accompanied by "The
Broadway Harmonists," who also supplied fox-trot rhythms before and
after the show. An opener called "Coming Events Cast Their Shadows
Before" was set in the employees' lounge, where hopefuls twiddled their
thumbs or tapped their toes while waiting for that one big chance. "Miss

Melody" and "Miss Jazz" did their stuff with "Jazz Gems," followed by a whistling act, a Highland fling, a love duet, a Spanish tango by six boys and six girls clicking castanets, climaxed by trills from "The 'National' Songbird."

The second part of the evening featured Moss's debut as a playwright. "Clothes and the Man" was an eleven-character play in two acts or scenes. The text is lost, but the title nodded to Shaw and it is likely the dramatic events underscored the importance of being well dressed, a theme unlikely to displease the evening's sponsors. The scene was "A Country Post Office" where "John Hayseed" met "Yvette Sidonia Smith, the Vamp" and there, in full view of the postmaster, his wife, and some villagers, they did whatever it is they did.

No reviews survive the evening. Drama critics that night were mostly attending the Theatre Guild's premiere of the German expressionist drama *From Morn to Midnight* or the Players' production of *The Rivals,* or even *Strut Miss Lizzie* on Times Square, billed by the Minskys as "colored vaudeville."

This was the year the Moscow Art Theater came to town for a season that lasted until 1924, revolutionizing New Yorkers' ideas of what acting and theater could be and introducing them to Stanislavsky and Chekhov. That Moss's fledgling effort roughly coincided with such a turning point in the theater may account for his never mentioning "The 'National' Revue" again. But if he failed to threaten the Russians, he amply demonstrated his drive to make something of himself and his skill at persuading others to give him the chance.

Later he seemed to forget about the National Cloak and Suit Company itself. He remembered, instead, working (and reeking) in the Neuburger fur vaults for two and a half years until one day he slammed the steel doors shut in desperation and headed straight for Broadway. His purpose, he said, was commiseration from a boyhood chum who had a job in the theater district.

There was such a boy, George Steinberg, whose parents ran the candy store in the Bronx, and he did work as an office boy in the New Amsterdam Theatre Building. Once Moss got there, he said, he learned from the receptionist—George's aunt, who had gotten him the job in the first place—that George had quit that very day, leaving behind a crisis and an opening. Moss, like Ruby Keeler in *42nd Street,* fell into one of life's vacancies.

No one was ever better at romantically spinning the Broadway narrative than Moss. Slamming shut the doors on the fur vaults was a kind of magic metaphor at which Moss excelled and so was George's quitting the very day he came to call. It wasn't George's Aunt Belle (as Moss wrote) who was the receptionist, because Aunt Belle worked for producer John Cort at his namesake Cort Theatre on West Forty-eighth Street; it was Belle's sister Aunt Bea who worked for producer Augustus "Gus" Pitou, Jr., in the New Amsterdam. Moss confused the sisters because both had been on his list. If it hadn't been Aunt Bea at the New Amsterdam it would have been Aunt Belle at the Cort or Aunt Somebody Else wherever she was or he would have done it alone, but he would have done it. The question was never "if"; it was when and where and how.

There had, in fact, already been a breakthrough far more impressive than "The 'National' Revue," though it was another that Moss later forgot. "Clothes and the Man" had been only half an evening, but around the same time he wrote a full-length play. The text is (again) lost, but what remains provides a glimpse of an adolescent playwright of remarkable daring. Moss's first full-length play was about and was called *Oscar Wilde*.

Wilde has not been exhausted as a dramatic subject even today, but in 1923 he was a figure whose disgrace and death in 1900 were still a living, gaudy memory. "The love that dare not speak its name" was still whispering in code words, but the contours of Wilde's life were sensationally dramatic in every sense. That Moss tackled such a provocative subject while still in his teens is revealing, but the themes Wilde suggested were ones with which almost any young playwright could identify: the artist versus society; originality versus conformity; audacity versus convention; public versus private behavior; above all, the self as theater, something Moss had embraced since childhood. At eighteen or nineteen *Oscar Wilde* brought him his first sale.

The buyer was silent film producer Louis Burston, owner of a production company called Films Incorporated with offices in New York and California. Burston (né Lewis Burstein) produced movies on both coasts, including several with Oliver Hardy before the comedian joined with Stan Laurel to form a great comedy team. He produced "Super-Serials" with titles like *The Hawk's Trail* and *The Silent Mystery,* and he was a sometime partner of W. S. (Woody) Van Dyke, later famous as the director of *The Thin Man* movies at MGM.

Burston's theatrical background was sketchy, but his showman's sense may have drawn him to a celebrity scandal with literary overtones. He announced *Oscar Wilde* to the press for "immediate production" in the 1923–24 Broadway season, referring to Moss as if he were an established playwright and not an unknown teenager. The announcements made the New York papers, whereupon Burston left for California and drove his car into the path of a Southern Pacific railroad train. Moss's dreams of a Broadway production before the age of twenty ended—as did Burston—in a pile of wreckage just outside Pomona.

Then (as now) the New Amsterdam Building rose above the art nouveau theater of the same name on Forty-second Street. When Moss began to work there for producer Gus Pitou, the theater was home to Will Rogers, Gilda Gray, and Gallagher & Shean ("Positively, Mr. Gallagher; Absolutely, Mr. Shean") in Florenz Ziegfeld's longest-running glorification of American pulchritude, *The Ziegfeld Follies of 1922*. The theater was only a year older than Moss, but already a landmark with plaster angels peering out from garlands and vines, and boxes not numbered, but designated by color: Buttercup, Heliotrope, Violet.

Names on the office doors upstairs were colorful, too: Ziegfeld, of course, and George Tyler, producer of the comedies of George S. Kaufman and Marc Connelly; Al Woods, in whose Bronx Opera House Moss first saw *Life;* Aarons & Freedley, newcomers soon to present a string of musicals by young George Gershwin. On the roofgarden crowning the building was Ziegfeld's nightclub, where couples trying hard to be mistaken for Scott and Zelda Fitzgerald danced and romanced the twenties away.

Gus Pitou, whose offices were on the eighth floor, wasn't exactly a Broadway producer in spite of his address. Like his father before him (who once carried a spear in Edwin Booth's *Hamlet*), he produced touring shows and called himself King of the Road. Others smirked and tagged him King of the One-Night Stands, but he put six different companies on tour each year headlined by "stars" Broadway preferred to struggle along without.

In what was called *the* show business then, the stage still flourished wherever railroad tracks led. The shows Pitou assembled were welcomed in towns where no one had ever heard of the Moscow Art Theater (or maybe even Oscar Wilde) or cared about the New York critics. Pitou was less interested in what might please George Jean Nathan of *The Smart Set* or waspish Alexander Woollcott of the *Herald* than in what might go over in Dubuque, Fort Wayne, or Cedar Rapids. His Bible was not Shakespeare or *Variety;* it was the *Railway Guide*.

Pitou didn't ship out touring companies of New York hits, but road vehicles suitable for "the entire family" and tailored to actors he had under contract. His advertising assured patrons that whatever else the attraction of the moment might be, it was emphatically "Not a Picture!"

Pitou's players included his wife, Gertrude Coghlan, lesser light of a celebrated theatrical family; character actress May Robson, more famous ten years later as "Apple Annie" in Frank Capra's *Lady for a Day;* and his most reliable crowd-pleaser, Irish tenor Fiske O'Hara, successor to the senior Pitou's biggest star, Chauncey ("When Irish Eyes Are Smiling") Olcott. Rounding out the Pitou "stable" were the Henry Duffy Players, whose eponymous actor-manager was married to Pitou's house playwright, a onetime actress called Anne Nichols.

Just before Moss began working for Pitou, Nichols had a surprise success on the West Coast with one of her plays. She decided her name should now light up Broadway, the very street Pitou gazed down on from his office window and regarded as the sure road to ruin. When Nichols announced she was prepared to finance her Broadway debut herself but would sell Pitou 50 percent for $5,000, he declined. As a consequence, he lost out on millions when the curtain rose on *Abie's Irish Rose,* and he lost his house playwright, too.

He bore his fate philosophically, but a secret seed of Broadway temptation had been planted. Fortunately, its germination required no more than the two modest rooms in the New Amsterdam he had always rented. He shared the inner sanctum with his maps and *Railway Guide,* leaving the anteroom to Moss, who now held court as secretary, receptionist, typist, and gatekeeper.

Moss had learned early to recognize the flushed, pained look on Pitou's face that sent him dashing down the hall at unpredictable intervals trying to outrace the effects of a spastic colon. Pitou's malady gave Moss plenty of time to kibitz with anyone in the building who could furnish him with free passes. He could see—gratis—anything on Broadway for which there were unsold tickets. This was sometimes a mixed blessing, but an instructive one as to what worked and what didn't on the Great White Way. For the rest of his life he maintained that "You never learn anything from a hit," which only taught you what somebody else had already done so well that it didn't need doing again. Failure was the great teacher, and no ivied campus could have tutored Moss better than the half-empty houses noisy with coughs and humid with flop sweat.

His circle widened as he handled auditions and interviews for neophytes and veterans alike who were grateful that he was generous with tips about casting. He was known already for what an acquaintance recalled as "a gift for banter and a passionate devotion to all things theatrical." He made fans and friends, like future film director George Cukor, then fresh out of Rochester, New York, and looking for a job as a stage manager. Five years older than Moss, Cukor remembered him as looking like the young Tony Curtis then. Their friendship would be lasting.

A sprightlier anteroom acquaintance was a teenage actor-dancer from Detroit named Leonard Sillman, whose ear got bent by sketches Moss wrote and loved to read aloud. Sillman was as hungry for nightclub material as Moss was to hear it applauded. The teenager dubbed Moss "Goofus Feathers" because of hair that "climbed onward and upward until it looked like the crowning glory of a cockatoo." Sillman's sharp eye for undiscovered talent would eventually make him the producer of *New Faces,* the revues that showcased newcomers like Henry Fonda, Van Johnson, Imogene Coca, Eartha Kitt, Ronny Graham, Maggie Smith, and Madeline Kahn.

Higher-toned and higher-minded was a would-be playwright and director who had been deeply impressed by the Moscow Art Theater. Edward Eliscu was two years older than Moss and had a degree from City College, a distinction that inspired respect and awe. Eliscu remembered Moss as "theater mad," with a "fantastic appetite" and an alarmingly gap-toothed smile in need of orthodontia. They traded play ideas, though Eliscu's erudition gave him the edge. He would eventually wind up in Hollywood, writing pictures like *Flying Down to Rio* for Fred Astaire and Ginger Rogers, and lyrics for songs like "More Than You Know" and "The Carioca." In 1924 Moss thought enough of him to inscribe a photograph "To Edward Eliscu, —My Best Pal And My Severest Critic." In relaxed moments they agreed that, however profound their admiration for Chekhov and *The Cherry Orchard,* Kaufman and Connelly's *Merton of the Movies* was more in their line.

When the outer office was empty or its audience had already heard all of Moss's sketches or jokes, he carried them through the halls, not sparing the most opulent suite of all. The Ziegfeld office was ruled by the fabulous Goldie, whose day was incomplete, she later claimed, without something Moss "wanted me to have Ziggy read" before he became "a great playwright" and it was too late to hire him. "Ziggy would come in every damn time," she remembered, "and say 'What's that damn kid doing here again?' "

"That damn kid"—or "Mouse" or "Marcy" as Pitou called him—was learning the basics of the business and got his first lesson in star tactics in 1924. Pitou's leading moneymaker, Fiske O'Hara, began making demands fantastic even for an Irish tenor. Pitou refused to meet them. O'Hara walked out, taking with him the "harp play" (as Irish vehicles were called) in which he had spun gold for years on the road and which, it now turned out, he owned. Pitou had already booked an upcoming Irish-American tour and found a substitute tenor named Joseph Regan. But no matter how sweet Regan's voice, he could not win the hearts of the hinterland without a play. Moss was ordered to find one.

Opportunity was beating on Moss's door with a shillelagh. He knew the harp play formula by heart: equal parts melodrama, jokes, and sentiment ladled up in a stew of blarney and songs. If he had a harp play of his own he could, in one fell swoop, capture Pitou's undying gratitude and the fame he had hoped to win with *Oscar Wilde*.

But a formula was not a play. He asked Eliscu to come up with an idea they might work on as a team, promising that he would convince Pitou that Eliscu should direct it. Eliscu agreed and they dashed off a couple of acts about an "Irish Robin Hood" masquerading as a notorious bandit who "kidnaps" the daughter of a banker in order to bring her down to earth and win her heart. It began with the banker's daughter gaily announcing on board the Dublin Express bound for the countryside that "Anything might happen!" It ended in Hibernian hills with the revelation that her abductor is no bandit, but a famous opera star hiding out from his fans, which explains his bursting into song at the slightest provocation. The banker's daughter—surprise—knew it all along.

Moss and Eddie worked evenings "squeezing out the dialogue like toothpaste," Eliscu remembered, racing to finish before Pitou found something else. He did, in fact (*Heart O'Mine* it was called), but Moss submitted their incomplete draft anyway, claiming it was the work of a lawyer called "Robert Arnold Conrad," who wanted to be a dramatist.

Pitou read what Moss and Eddie had titled *Lad O'Laughter* and subtitled "A Rip-Roaring Comedy." He liked it. He wanted to meet Conrad.

Moss improvised and invented, claiming Conrad was busy with the law and could only be reached by letter. Pitou then and there insisted on dictating four pages of single-spaced comments and suggestions about the draft. Moss was to type everything up at once and deliver it.

Pitou's comments centered first on economy, which made putting the Dublin Express onstage impractical, but "I can see in the first act the breaking down of an automobile . . . off-stage." He focused secondly on Joseph Regan, who was "a great singer [but] suffers as an actor." If the play could be rewritten to minimize his suffering by emphasizing song, and by strengthening the banker's daughter—lifted so cleverly, Pitou realized, from *The Taming of the Shrew*—then *Lad O'Laughter* might work. It might work better if it borrowed even more from James M. Barrie's *The*

Admirable Crichton than it already did in the part about the pampered rich girl forced to be useful. "Marcy will explain to you about how this can be done," Pitou dictated, adding quickly, "without plagarism [*sic*]."

Pitou dictated his letter on September 24, 1924. It occurred to Moss and Eddie that very day that they had no agreement between themselves. Eddie thought the play was "claptrap" and didn't much care what happened as long as it got "sawed, hammered, and glued together" and he could direct it. He and Moss wrote up and signed a formal contract, agreeing to share author credit equally unless Eddie was hired to direct, in which case he would allow Moss to claim the writing credit alone. They worked out a scale for sharing royalties and, as it happened, that was the last Eliscu would hear about credit, and almost the last about money.

Pitou liked the "claptrap" of *Lad O'Laughter* and, even today, it is not hard to see why. The heroine's plucky "Anything might happen!" is a mood that enlivens every page, no matter how preposterous. The musical interpolations—"Yes, We Have No Bananas!" is indicated in one draft, along with Joyce Kilmer's "Trees" set to music and, of course, "Mother Macree"—made no more or less sense than many onstage outbursts of song in 1924. The play was nowhere original and its logic was riddled with holes, but it demonstrated an instinct for comedy and what Eliscu acknowledged as Moss's "uncanny ear for the rhythm of stage speech that would play." It even had a theme of sorts, in the opera singer masquerading as a bandit, tired of "mistaking the glamour of life, for life itself!"—a notion with a ring to it, even if it didn't quite make sense.

Pitou was no Ziegfeld, not even a humbug producer-playwright like David ("Bishop of Broadway") Belasco, but he wasn't a fool, either. He had spotted the lifts from Shakespeare and James M. Barrie right away, and when Moss at last confessed the deception about authorship— his part of it, anyway—Pitou received it in silence before responding. "Mouse," he said, "I don't know whether you know it or not, but when an author writes his first play he doesn't get the regular royalties."

As far as anyone could remember, Eliscu's name as coauthor or director never came up.

Retribution for this oversight came swiftly. As Eddie observed from his shelf of anonymity, "Our jerry-built wagon was suddenly hailed as a gilded chariot." Moss collected the advance of $250 against royalties of 2 percent of the box-office gross, plus $75 a week on the road, while *Lad O'Laughter* gained a new title. *The Hold-up Man* sounded to Pitou as if it emphasized the rip-roaring and commercial parts and downplayed the comedy. He communicated his enthusiasm to friends, including Mrs. Henry B. (Renée) Harris, a woman whose survival instincts were demonstrated for all time when she declined to go down on the *Titanic*. Her husband was last seen slipping under an iceberg, but he left his widow a yacht, some racehorses, and the Fulton Theatre on West Forty-sixth Street where, since 1922, *Abie's Irish Rose* had been raking in cash by the barrel. Pitou was not about to make the same mistake twice and Mrs. Harris was not about to let him. When she read *The Hold-up Man* she cheerfully declared herself his partner, if he would make the play his long-delayed Broadway debut.

One month after his twentieth birthday, Moss was rattling along on a train to Batavia, then Warsaw and Rochester, New York, en route to Chicago before heading back in triumph to Broadway. With him were eight actors, two producers, a director (a reliable former actor named Priestly Morrison), trunks of traveling props, and a carload of flats.

On his first night out, Moss wrote Eliscu from the Hotel Richmond in Batavia of discovering on their arrival that *The Hold-up Man* had no advance sale *"at all."* Not one ticket. He was exhausted and depressed. "I'm taking some more sleeping pills," he wrote, or "something will bust."

What busted was the dress rehearsal the following day. It was "the most unfunny performance . . . I ever sat through," Moss told his coauthor, now enjoying his position on the sidelines, far from the heat of Moss's "scorched and scalded" reports from the road. Royalties were at last in sight, Moss said, though an advance sale of twenty-eight tickets did not sound like a windfall. He was too worried about the rewriting he had to do as a result of the dress rehearsal to worry about royalties. "I'm absolutely thunk out!"

The play was booked into the Lyceum Theater in Rochester for the week beginning Sunday, November 23, with matinees on Wednesday and Thursday, which was Thanksgiving Day. Rochester was a picky theater town and Moss was relieved to find that the week's competition was nothing stronger than Clara Bow flickering on-screen in *Black Lightning*, two bills of vaudeville, and one of burlesque. After the deadly dress rehearsal and dismal business in Batavia and Warsaw, critics in Rochester were surprisingly generous.

"HOLD UP MAN" WINS FAVOR read a headline. Critic Beulah Brown admitted it "cannot be said to be exactly hilarious . . . but it succeeded—last night—in evoking a good many chuckles." A critic noted tactfully that "to build a play [around] the needs of a singing actor has always proven a difficult task," but it was "met in an admirable manner by Robert [Arnold] Conrad."

Encouraged, the company traveled by train to Chicago with guarded hopes. Joseph Regan revealed that he was not only a tenor but an amateur petomane, as well, and could sing from both ends. He spent the journey entertaining his companions with his personal impersonations of the Windy City.

They arrived in Chicago early Sunday morning. Moss moved into the Hotel Sherman on Randolph Street, just down from the Adelphi Theater where they would open that night and play until December 27 before heading on, Mrs. Harris assured him, to Broadway in the New Year. To save on expenses, Moss shared a room with Pitou.

Which may have been why Moss hated Chicago at first sight. He wrote Eddie that it was "a depressing town" where "the color of the buildings, from the lake smoke, is absolutely black." It was Moss's mood that was black, especially after the Chicago critics took aim at *The Hold-up Man*. He later wrote that Ashton Stevens, Chicago's leading critic, walked out early and, instead of reviewing the play, ran an obituary notice bordered in black that began, "There died last night at the Adelphi Theater . . ." and continued with a list of the names of everyone involved.

But Stevens wasn't there. He ignored the Adelphi, which was a former burlesque house. The critics who *were* there found the experience less funereal than Moss suggested. One headline ran LOVELY REGAN VOICE ENCHANTS AT THE ADELPHI.

Opinion about "Robert Arnold Conrad," however, ranged from indifferent to brutal. One reviewer summarily dismissed his play as "too awful for words."

"The play is a colossal failure," Moss wrote Eddie in despair. The day after the reviews the box-office take was a pathetic $34. Pitou wouldn't let Moss return to New York because he needed someone to moan to about business until two or three in the morning and, besides, the show couldn't just close. Pitou had believed in it so much he had guaranteed the Adelphi $3,500 a week to the end of December in order to secure the booking. They were trapped, even if they never sold another ticket.

"God knows I'm absolutely heart-sick," Moss wrote. "The atmosphere is so mournful you could cut it with a knife." On top of that, he was broke.

"Funny, isn't it. Here we have a play running, and one of the authors has to borrow money . . . each week from the box office to send home so that they get it by Saturday, and then pay it back when I get the royalty check." He hastily added, "About your share, Ed . . . . I will settle with you in New York."

The Hold-up Man was clearly not ready for Broadway. The acting company was released and Moss traveled back to New York with a dejected Pitou and an oddly rejuvenated Mrs. Harris. The woman who had survived the *Titanic* was undaunted by Chicago. That's what out-of-town was for, she pointed out. To inspire improvements.

Buoyed by Harris's enthusiasm, *The Hold-up Man* went through yet another metamorphosis. Because Regan's acting left nothing to desire but talent, Pitou rummaged around his stable to find someone who could sing *and* act, while Harris reconsidered the title. Maybe *The Hold-up Man* wasn't as rip-roaring as they thought. Romance might be emphasized by a title that would, as a side benefit, make it sound like a brand-new play. *The Beloved Bandit* seemed just right.

Pitou began consulting his *Railway Guide* for 1925–26.

Moss's black mood lifted in New York. By May he was positively ebullient about *The Beloved Bandit*. "Things are booming!" he told Eliscu, turning down his offer to help with the rewrite. "I'll surprise you," Moss predicted.

The surprise was allowing Pitou to bill *The Beloved Bandit* as "The New American Comedy by Moss Hart." What was new about it was mostly the star, an Irish tenor from Chicago named Gerald Griffin. He came with a brand-new sheaf of songs (by himself) to spice up *The Beloved Bandit,* which now took place in Arizona. Mother Macree was suddenly Mamaçita. Paddy had become Pedro.

Moss spent the summer of 1925 at run-throughs of the new cast in a sweaty rehearsal hall in the West Fifties, to which he invited envious friends. The new tour would concentrate on the sort of one- and two-night stands Pitou was king of. He had been burned by the Chicago critics and his publicity now fell back on old promises of "A Cyclone of Mirth and Music" that was full of "Speed and Pep." *The Beloved Bandit* was a "Sure Cure for the Blues" and was—audiences could rest assured—"Not a Picture!"

The tour began in September with two performances in Youngstown, Ohio, two more in Fort Wayne, Indiana, and others in Grand Forks and Dubuque, Iowa. Pitou's publicity did its job with small-town newspapers in which he bought advertising. The *Fort Wayne Journal Gazette,* for instance, alerted Indiana readers to "a fascinating play of American life in the West from the pen of the distinguished author, Moss Hart."

Business was weak. It wasn't that audiences didn't want a cyclone of mirth and music or a sure cure for the blues; it was that they could find all the speed and pep they wanted or needed in things that *were* pictures.

This was 1925, the year of Charlie Chaplin's *The Gold Rush,* Douglas Fairbanks's *Don Q, Son of Zorro,* Rudolph Valentino's *The Eagle,* and John Gilbert's *The Big Parade.*

The week *The Beloved Bandit* opened in Youngstown, Vincent Youmans's *No, No, Nanette* opened on Broadway. So did *Dearest Enemy* by Richard Rodgers and Lorenz Hart, whose *Garrick Gaieties* had been held over downtown from the previous season. The big holdover uptown was *Lady, Be Good!* with Fred and Adele Astaire dancing to a Gershwin score. The Theatre Guild was presenting Shaw, Molnár, and Pagnol, and if you didn't like the imported stuff, you could order the domestic: Eugene O'Neill's *Desire Under the Elms,* George Kelly's *Craig's Wife,* or Maxwell Anderson and Laurence Stallings's *What Price Glory?*

Mrs. Harris watched her Broadway career sink with *The Beloved Bandit,* but had no regrets. Later in life she fell on hard times and when she approached Moss for help in getting a job, she looked back on her fling as his producer and pronounced it "Fantabulous." Even "the King of the Road" was philosophical about it. His kind of theater had been designed to play Peoria and now had trouble getting bookings even there. He heard his cue to retire in the newly syncopated rhythms of Broadway—so different from "When Irish Eyes Are Smiling"—and bowed gracefully to the inevitable. He would no longer need offices in the New Amsterdam overlooking Times Square and the theater district, now turned garish in the glare of that new thing they called "neon." Nor would he need a secretary called "Mouse" or "Marcy."

It was the end of the road, and left Moss feeling like a has-been at twenty-one.

4

Mountain Greenery

Want to know what the Theater is? A flea circus. Also opera.
Also rodeos, carnivals, ballets, Indian tribal dances, Punch and Judy,
a one-man band—all Theater. Wherever there's magic and make-believe
and an audience—there's Theater. . . . It may not be your Theater,
but it's Theater for somebody, somewhere. . . .

JOSEPH L. MANKIEWICZ

Moss's having had a flop by twenty-one was some kind of show-business distinction, if not quite the grand disaster his story sense led him to claim. Theater was viable then. A young man or woman just off the bus and hoping to go places in the theater had a reasonable expectation there was someplace to go.

In some versions, losses on *The Beloved Bandit* mounted to $60,000, but the likely figure was half that, almost all of it due to Gus Pitou's open-handed guarantee to the Adelphi Theater, not to production costs. Thirty thousand dollars was not a negligible figure, but in 1925 a full-scale musical could have been mounted for not much more. Even Ziegfeld's lavish extravaganzas rarely ran to six figures and a hit musical like *Good News!* could recoup its entire investment within a month.

Theater was an affordable enterprise. Producers could self-finance their shows or find a couple of generous backers, like Mrs. Harris, to do it for them. The Theatre Guild, for years the most eminent production entity on Broadway, was capitalized in 1919 for $2,160 in start-up money collected literally from the pockets of its founders. Three years later, when the Guild flopped with its world premiere of George Bernard Shaw's *Back to Methuselah*—which took three nights to perform—they lost only $20,000.

The public could afford the theater, too. Even a church mouse like Moss could find a pew at the *Follies,* where the top ticket cost $3.50 and standing room could be had for the price of a hot dog at Nathan's. Ticket prices were not negligible (a parody of *What Price Glory?* was titled *Glory, What Prices!*), but they were within reach, costlier than tickets to the movies, but not prohibitive.

Because the economics made sense, so did everything from *Ladies' Night in a Turkish Bath* to Eugene O'Neill's *Beyond the Horizon* to Shakespeare in repertory, all on the same calendar page in 1920. And there were theaters to play them in. Twenty-six new theaters opened between 1924 and 1929, bringing the total in New York to ninety, housing an *average* of 225 new productions a year for the decade. Lehman Engel, the conductor and historian, tallied up 423 musicals produced in the 1920s, making sense of Alexander Woollcott's complaint about "Broadway's desperate plight" when a single season loomed "with only seventeen or eighteen musicals in view."

Broadway was the center of American popular culture and the commercial focal point but hardly all there was. Outsiders and newcomers were challenging what they saw there as slick, shallow, or complacent fare motivated solely by the box office. Commercial theater was at its peak, but there was a young, adventurous audience willing to go uptown to Harlem or downtown to Greenwich Village for stimulation not yet (or maybe ever) to be found on Broadway.

When Moss returned to New York "at liberty" after *The Beloved Bandit,* Broadway was heading for 264 new productions in one year. He and Broadway stood on the threshold of a justly heralded Golden Age, and not just commercially. Theatergoers and theater-makers were challenging each other, and that contrapuntal energy would result in the most creative decade the American theater had yet seen.

However keenly Moss felt the fate of *The Beloved Bandit* and the loss of his job, nothing about his style suggested defeat. Few of his companions knew much about his family, and even those who did, like Eddie Eliscu, were unaware of exceptional hardships. Pride concealed them and so did Moss's wardrobe, his style of self-presentation. Even on meager resources, he was a dandy, a haberdasher's dream.

He was dashingly handsome, tall, and slender, with a high forehead, dark wavy hair, expressive eyebrows, and a taste for the most flamboyant fabric on the rack. No stripe was too vivid, no plaid too vivacious. It would be years before he toned down the contents of his closet or before others did it for him.

Moss whiled away the hours smartly dressed over coffee at Rudley's Café or the Paramount Building coffee shop with other theatrical wanna-bes among whom being at liberty was no disgrace. It was even something of a badge of honor among those most stridently denouncing an entrenched theatrical system whose chief failing was that it did not entrench them.

His circle included office boys who would one day be producers like Freddie Kohlmar, who worked for Al Woods of the Bronx Opera House and (oh, irony!) the Adelphi in Chicago; Irving Morrison, gofer for George Tyler, producer of Kaufman and Connelly. There were the two Eddies: Eliscu and Chodorov, the latter another college-man playwright-to-be, whose degree from Brown gave him the self-esteem to pontificate knowingly about Ambrose Bierce and break into a soft-shoe routine at the same time. Ziegfeld's Goldie sometimes drifted by, lifting spirits with passes to the hottest seats in town for those interested in glorifying the American girl.

Some were; some weren't. The senior and most outspoken of this overcaffeinated fraternity was an acerbic gadfly named Lester Sweyd, who provided career guidance and cultural critique and frankly viewed Moss as his protégé. Twelve years older than Moss, Sweyd was a former dancer and actor with an encyclopedic knowledge of the theater. He dilated knowingly about great stars he had worked with like Tyrone Power, Sr., Lionel Atwill, and Marie Dressler. He had done everything, including a Gus Edwards kid act in vaudeville, tours of England and the Continent, and a featured role in the spectacular oriental wheeze *Chu Chin Chow,* which he liked to boast had "a cast larger than *Ben Hur.*" His arch opinions and air of certainty made him both annoying and an arbiter to Moss's circle. He was now making ends meet playing piano in silent-movie houses—which made him an authority on motion pictures, too—exasperating, but tolerated because of his plans to become a literary agent someday soon.

Moss met Sweyd through another mutual friend, an actor named Maurice Burke, who had been an understudy in Kaufman and Connelly's *Merton of the Movies.* Burke liked to display press clippings that described him as a "dangerously attractive young man" but his career was faltering because he called people "darling" and admitted to "a lack of masculine sex-appeal."

The theater was laissez-faire about sexual preference and so was Moss, who was flattered to be the center of Sweyd's attention. The older man's focus had been unswerving through rehearsals for *The Beloved Bandit* in the summer of 1925 and possibly even earlier. Sweyd was an obsessive collector who kept an elaborate scrapbook of Moss's career that went back to "The 'National' Revue" in 1922, suggesting that they met when Moss was still a teenager. The scrapbook was a labor of love and Moss contributed a handsome studio portrait to it: "Here's that picture—sleep with it next to your heart," he wrote. Sweyd added a caption of his own: "A Dirty Mind is a Perpetual Solace."

This sounds like a romantic involvement and may have been one. Moss had homosexual friends like Cukor, Sillman, and Burke and heterosexual ones like the two Eddies, but Sweyd's specific appeal was his willingness to play mentor to a young man looking for one. The professional standards Sweyd trumpeted were more stringent than any Moss had encountered working for Gus Pitou, and more sophisticated, too. His air of worldliness was underlined by the frequent presence at his side of a young man from England, a former acrobat now working as an actor for the Shuberts named Archibald Leach, who wasn't attracting much attention in spite of his looks, but would do better once he changed his name to Cary Grant.

The two Eddies, with their college degrees and the self-confidence that went with them, helped focus Moss's attention on theatrical experiments from abroad. Eliscu had long since roused curiosity about the Russians and, especially, Chekhov. Chodorov, who owed his job working backstage on *Abie's Irish Rose* to Moss, repaid the debt with expansive dissertations on Meyerhold and Germans like Max Reinhardt and expressionist playwright Georg Kaiser.

Both of the Eddies were intrigued by the then-burgeoning Little Theater movement, where theory and experimentation were lures in lieu of wages. A coffee-shop chum named Milton Krims had introduced Chodorov to a group called the Labor Temple Players, who were amateurs with high aspirations and a home in the Labor Temple Auditorium at Fourteenth Street and Second Avenue. They also had a toehold in the theater district itself.

The Players were managed by a would-be playwright named William J. Perlman, who was co-owner of the small Mayfair Theater just east of Broadway on Forty-fourth Street that began life as a cafeteria. Perlman would soon have plays of his own on Broadway, but was mainly involved in making the Mayfair pay and would do so later in the year with the American premiere of Sean O'Casey's *Juno and the Paycock*.

Moss, brought to the Labor Temple Players by Chodorov, began working with them shortly after he left Pitou. Krims was directing Ibsen's *Ghosts* there and offered Moss the part of the doomed Oswald, a juicy role for any stagestruck young man, and Moss grabbed it at once. Surprisingly enough, *Ghosts* was still an eyebrow lifter in 1926 because of its use of syphilis as a plot element. Ibsen had written the play more than forty years before and it had been produced downtown by the Washington Square Players (forerunners of the Theatre Guild) in 1917, but not on Broadway until the great actress-manager Mrs. Fiske presented it there the same year Moss acted in it on Second Avenue.

For all the genuine artistic daring of the 1920s, Broadway was still constrained by the conventions of Mrs. Grundy's moral watchdogs, determined to remain firmly rooted in the nineteenth century. That same year—1926—the New York Suppression of Vice Squad turned the lock on *The Captive,* a lesbian-themed drama from France that had been an international success, and turned the key again on Mae West when she appeared on Broadway in a play she claimed to have written called *Sex.* West boasted that the publicity about being suppressed and thrown in jail was worth millions, and she was right: it made her famous. Later in the year she and *The Captive* were parodied onstage as "Stars With Stripes" in the *Grand Street Follies.*

Ghosts at the Labor Temple was thus old enough to be a classic and new enough to feel daring and avant-garde. It was, for Moss, a leap from the *Railway Guide* to the theater of aspiration. He soon took on directing chores, partly because directors, unlike actors, got reimbursed for carfare. He began with George Kelly's one-act play *The Flattering Word,* which would become a staple of his repertoire. It would also become—with its tale of a worldly celebrity taking advantage of small-town innocents—a kind of template for one of Moss's most successful later works.

Moss cast himself as the "prominent dramatic star" slumming in Youngstown. Kelly might have written the role for him. "He is tall and thin [with] soft-looking black hair," reads the stage direction, "[and] wears a long, beautifully tailored coat . . . a perfectly cut, double-breasted sack suit . . . is quietly gloved and spatted; wears a gorgeous shawl scarf of steel-blue silk around his neck, and carries a snakewood cane, tipped with silver." Even the Ohio locale would reappear, perhaps in homage to this play Moss liked enough to stage over and over again.

Kelly was much more than the uncle of Princess Grace of Monaco, as he is chiefly remembered today. In 1926 he had just won the Pulitzer Prize for *Craig's Wife* after narrowly losing it the year before for *The Show-Off,* the classic comedy that Moss would soon add to his program. Kelly was a superior craftsman, whose dialogue, characters, and satiric themes provided Moss an immediate model for study, not least because Kelly's first big success as a dramatist (he had been an actor) was *The Torchbearers* in 1922, his satire about the artistic pretensions of the very Little Theater movement now occupying Moss's time and energies.

Kelly was also the first established playwright Moss got to know personally. He was an eccentric bachelor who lived more or less openly with his chauffeur in Philadelphia and granted rights to his plays not through an agent, but by personal application. To that end, he included his home address in the published versions of his plays. Moss sought and received permission to present Kelly plays repeatedly in the next few years and the usually cold, even misanthropic Philadelphian offered Moss encouragement and "Thinking of you" telegrams as his own writing career progressed.

Working with amateurs gave Moss confidence and forced him to stay one step ahead of them by burying himself in dramatic literature at the Fifth Avenue branch of the New York Public Library. Lester Sweyd and the two Eddies advised him on what to look for on the page; on the stage he needed no counsel. He satisfied his hunger for theater with passes from friends or by sneaking in at intermission to see the second act of something whose first act might remain forever a mystery.

In May 1926 the nucleus of the Labor Temple Players—led by Moss, Eddie Chodorov, an actress named Eleanor Audley, and an actor named Clarke Silvernail—persuaded William Perlman to turn the Mayfair over to them on Sunday nights when the theater was dark. Calling themselves the American Co-Optimists (a name borrowed from a popular English group), they published their credo: to provide "the intelligent New Yorker" with theatrical options beyond Broadway's "decidedly limited" offerings. Their opening bill (Moss's taste is evident) was a program of three short plays, one each by Oscar Wilde and George Kelly, plus a dramatization by J. Rosamond Johnson of "Water Boy," a "Negro Spiritual." Johnson was a member of the Co-Optimists and a measure of their democratic openness. He was the composer-lyricist of "Under the Bamboo Tree" and several hundred other "coon songs," as they were called. His sometime co-lyricist was his brother, James Weldon Johnson, an early NAACP leader.

The Co-Optimists were never heard of again. After they had come and gone, Moss faced an uncertain summer until he and Chodorov were rescued from "liberty" again by Perlman, who, in addition to managing the Labor Temple group and the Mayfair, was also managing director of a summer camp in Lackawaxen, Pennsylvania, in the heart of the Poconos.

Camp Greater Utopia was a summer camp for adults and an elaborate one on what was known as "the Borscht circuit" because of its mostly Jewish clientele seeking escape from New York's summer heat. This camp's staff included Dr. Will Durant, whose *Story of Philosophy* was published that year, making him famous. He and his wife Ada Kaufman (he would rename her "Ariel") were just beginning work on their monumental *Story of Civilization,* an enterprise that would make them rich, too, and forevermore strangers to summer camps and campers.

The spirit of Camp Greater Utopia was less philosophical than frisky. The paying guests expected entertainment and Chodorov was hired to provide it as social director. Moss cited his boyhood summers in New Jersey with the Friedlanders as proof that he could rough it and was hired as his assistant for the not-very-whopping sum of $30 a week.

They prepared for the great out-of-doors by looking in on shows around town for material they could steal and present to the campers as their own. Most of it came from the sprightly second edition of *The Garrick Gaieties,* which included, appropriately enough, Rodgers and Hart's hit number "Mountain Greenery." Armed with bootlegged songs and skits, they took along several members of the Labor Temple Players, including Chodorov's sister Belle, an agent-in-the-making, to help them entertain the civilians.

Moss packed up his tennis racket, his ukulele, and—fortunately, as things turned out—"Miss Melody," "Miss Plot," and "Miss Jazz."

The Utopian Follies of 1926 premiered on the Fourth of July weekend billed as "A Revue in Eighteen Scenes by Edward Chodorov and Moss Hart." Chodorov took first billing as social director, while Moss grumbled about procrastination "a la Chodorov," that is, languid musings about art while others did the heavy lifting.

This was not unfair. Chodorov was almost entirely absorbed by his plans for a trip to South Africa at summer's end, forcing Moss to pick up his friend's loose threads and wind them around spindles from the National Cloak and Suit Company. The *Follies*'s first scene had a familiar ring. It took place in "The Author's Studio" where the Misses Melody, Plot, and Jazz welcomed Mr. Harmony, Mr. Comedy, Miss Ingenue, and Miss Leading Lady. Telling them what to do for the rest of the evening were the Authors: Chodorov as playwright Owen Davis and Moss as Eugene O'Neill.

Moss also appeared onstage as Queen Elizabeth and as an opera singer called "Madame Garnischt," who was, one guesses, closely related to Fanny Brice. He and Chodorov borrowed from George S. Kaufman's *The Butter and Egg Man* and from his celebrated sketch "If Men Played Cards as Women Do," in which they portrayed "Miss Ed" and "Miss Moss." Other skits kidded icons like Ethel Barrymore and topics of the day like the newly invented radio networks, about which Moss wrote a skit called "The Microphone Hunters" that he would recycle in years to come.

The Utopian Follies kept the campers happy. It was lifted and derivative, but as high-spirited as the Fourth of July. It kidded the contemporary scene in a bright, impudent, and witty voice that can be imagined as Moss's even in the absence of a surviving text.

Moss returned to New York after Labor Day to work for Perlman at the Mayfair, soliciting theater bookings. Perlman must have liked him, or his loyalty. The manager had a play produced in New York that summer titled *My Company*. When the *New York Times* gave it a negative review, Moss wrote a long, irate letter to the *Times*'s critic then known as "J," Brooks Atkinson, denouncing him and defending the play without bothering to mention that he worked for its author. It was only another office-boy job, but one that returned him to the daily goings-on of the theater district and came with a bonus for an aspiring actor: an early look at casting notices.

Moss was almost immediately cast in the Mayfair production of O'Neill's *The Emperor Jones*. The revival starred Charles Gilpin, who had created the role in 1920 at the Provincetown Playhouse. O'Neill himself once called Gilpin the only actor he found wholly satisfying in any of his plays, which had not prevented his firing Gilpin for excessive drinking and replacing him in London with Paul Robeson, whose career then ascended as Gilpin's sank, mostly into a bottle. Author Ann Douglas tells us Gilpin was "considered the greatest [black actor] on the American stage," but by 1926 he was working as an elevator operator.

The offer to revive the role that made him famous came as a lifeline first thrown in the Village, where the Provincetown Playhouse had revived *The Emperor Jones* with Gilpin in February. Perlman was not just transferring the earlier production, however, but mounting a new staging with a new cast directed by Gilpin himself.

Gilpin was satisfied with Moss's Cockney accent (Barnett Hart's legacy) and cast him as Smithers, the seedy Cockney slave trader who had the only other sustained speaking part in the play.

The production opened November 10, 1926, at the Mayfair and notices were mixed, although almost all the critics reviewed Moss favorably. He portrayed "the cheap Cockney trader to perfection" and was "a delight both to the eye and ear."

Gilpin's drinking was serious but did not prevent a transfer to the Intimate Theater in the Bronx, where Moss went with him, identified in the program as "Marcy Hart." The run lasted fifteen weeks, during which Moss often felt "shattered" by the "inner violence" of Gilpin's performance when his "maniacal power" was turned outward, not inward in self-destruction. Four years later Gilpin was dead.

While *The Emperor Jones* was still running Moss tried out for other acting jobs. He auditioned unsuccessfully for a bit part in British director Basil Dean's production of *The Constant Nymph*, a play that Noël Coward—one of Moss's most lasting enthusiasms—had starred in in London understudied by John Gielgud. In New York the role went to Claude Rains, Gielgud's acting teacher in his American debut. Moss's audition amounted mostly to watching Dean tongue-lash another player, a spectacle that sharply increased his sensitivity to every actor's vulnerability. He knew from experience that, in the final and cruelest analysis, an actor has nothing to offer but himself. For the luckless that is an invitation to rejection and humiliation. For the incompetent or damaged, as for Gilpin, it could lead to what Moss called "the tragedy of those who did not turn away in time." Moss loved actors—their gifts and their foibles—and they loved him back. It wasn't just that he had been one, though that helped. It was that he believed in the "magic of personal chemistry" that was beyond prediction or manufacture. Actors would be the enduring love of his life, the subject and theme of his life's work.

Moss used his *Emperor Jones* celebrity to add directing jobs to his schedule. The first came through Lillie Hart's cousin, Carmel (Bentwich) Finkelstein, whose wedding Moss had attended in 1922. Her husband was now rabbi of the synagogue at Catona Park in Brooklyn where Moss became director of the "Park Players" of the Young Folks League. He added a new staple to George Kelly and his portfolio: "In 1999" by William deMille, which had been the curtain-raiser for *The Emperor Jones* at the Mayfair. He added, too, something called *Green Chartreuse* by someone named "John Doe."

By spring he had taken on two more groups: the "Y" Players at Brooklyn's YMHA and the Masquers, the YMHA's youth group. He directed more George Kelly and in late May introduced a "mystery-comedy" called "Anything Might Happen" by "distinguished author, Moss Hart," a recycling in one act of *The Beloved Bandit.*

Recycling became a necessity as he added the Center Players at the Jewish Center in Brooklyn, a like-named group at the Jewish Community Center in Jersey City, and, still later, the Newark Stagers. Each group meant a small but crucial paycheck and he crisscrossed Manhattan underground to get them. They also meant experience. In all he mounted fifteen productions of Kelly, six of Ibsen, four of the well-known prison play *The Valiant,* three of deMille, two of *The Emperor Jones,* and four of "Anything Might Happen." His total Little Theater output by the end of the decade can be documented as fifty-nine productions of twenty-nine plays and there may have been more.

This was work that demanded patience and stamina and benefited from youthful recklessness. He wasn't yet twenty-three and was taking texts apart and putting them back together again onstage to see how and if they worked. It was pragmatic work: theory withered when confronted by the only litmus test that mattered, the audience. With no mentor to guide him, he was like an apprentice watchmaker with a handful of wheels and springs, trying to put them together so he could know what time it was. When the jokes came and the audience laughed, he knew.

It was 1927. The Crescent Country Club on Lake Champlain in Vermont had the most beautiful natural setting of Moss's camp summers. There were four such summers that he later expanded to "six damnable years," probably because they felt that way.

One of the Crescent Country Club owners was an equestrian charmer called George Gold. On hiring Moss, Gold expansively sent him to Geller's Men's Wear on Eighth Avenue to select and charge a summer wardrobe of blazers, flannels, silk scarves, and tennis togs for delivery in Vermont. They never arrived. Geller's knew what Moss didn't about Gold's credit rating. It was an omen Moss had no inclination to heed. He was too busy turning his lack of wardrobe to creative account by dressing daily in whatever the camp's costume trunk yielded, turning himself into a one-man theme park. Today, Valley Forge; tomorrow, Gettysburg. It was humiliating, but a hit.

The Crescent deal Moss negotiated included camp jobs for sixteen-year-old Bernie and their father Barnett, now over sixty and as placidly resigned to defeat as ever. Bernie bussed tables in the dining room and worked on the stage crew, learning the basics of stage management. Barnett manned the canteen, oddly cheerful when dispensing cigarettes and sodas to campers even though he earned only room and board and a cut of the tip pool at summer's end. He had worked for less.

The Vermont summer allowed or forced the family to give up the old apartment in the Bronx and Moss expected to accumulate enough money, including the summer salary and tips he'd be paid on Labor Day, to rent another when they returned to New York. Lillie took a room with the Friedlanders in the meantime and, to Moss's astonishment, greeted the arrangement without a murmur. Perhaps she looked forward to her first vacation in twenty-five years and was too relieved to waste words on spelling it out.

Moss later wrote in his memoirs about the Crescent Country Club (disguised as the Half Moon Country Club) as if it were a condemned trailer park in one of hell's lower circles. In reality it was a noted camp that advertised itself as "A Summer School of the Theater" and offered courses ranging from history of the drama and playwriting to voice and body control, makeup, criticism, publicity, and pageantry. In charge of classes was Philip Gross, a graduate of George Pierce Baker's famous play-writing workshop at Harvard that had produced Eugene O'Neill and Philip Barry among others. Gross had founded one of the earliest impor-tant Little Theater groups, the Thalians, and was dramatic director of the Metropolitan League of YMHAs, which gave him the power to dispense Little Theater directing jobs citywide.

Moss assisted Gross at Crescent, donned blackface to direct himself in and as *The Emperor Jones,* and recycled material he had tested at Camp Greater Utopia. He grew closer to Bernie, whose withered arm proved no handicap to his good humor or the stage crew. He even played host to Rabbi and Carmel Finkelstein when they visited, organizing an excur-sion by boat across Lake Champlain.

The ostensible purpose of the trip was to visit a state fair on the New York side of the lake that turned out to be closed, but Moss had another, unannounced goal. He had arranged a men-only tour of the Dannemora state prison so he could pick up authentic color for *The Valiant,* the prison play that was one of his staples. Once they had crossed the lake, they tied up to the dock and the men proceeded to the prison. The ladies waited in the open boat, where they were pummeled by the pounding rains of a sudden summer squall. The downpour drenched them, but failed to drown out the obscenities and curses shouted at them from behind the prison walls. Only after their return to camp, bedraggled and too late for dinner, did they realize that the date—August 23—was that scheduled for the execution of Nicola Sacco and Bartolomeo Vanzetti, the Italian immigrant-anarchists sentenced to death for murder and robbery in spite of evidence establishing their innocence that the Massachusetts judge who had sentenced them refused to hear on appeal. The case aroused world-wide outrage, nowhere as vehement as inside prison walls.

Moss, sullenly resigned to his own miscarriage of justice, spoke of his work at the Crescent with scorn, but others were more impressed. Cres-cent was allied with a nearby camp for children who were allowed to attend shows at the Crescent. One of them, a boy from New York named Herman Wouk (who would later turn the summer to novelistic use), remembers it today as "Shangri-La" and Moss's shows as akin to the Folies-Bergère.

The summer came to a disastrous end when Gold (called "Mr. Axeler" in Moss's memoirs) mounted his horse just before Labor Day and rode into the sunset with their summer wages. Back in New York, Moss went directly to Gold's partner, Philip Gross. He extracted a portion of his wages by telling what Gross remembered as "a woeful tale" about his homeless, destitute family. Gross paid him what he could and added to it a directing job at the Brooklyn Jewish Center.

Gross was an important contact from that disastrous summer and there were others. As social director Moss had a small music staff and his piano player was a member of Gross's Thalians. John Brown was younger than Moss and given to hero-worship that continued beyond Labor Day and looked more and more like puppy love. Learning from Gross that Moss would be directing at the Brooklyn Jewish Center, he joined the group as its first and only gentile member.

Brown was competent enough as an actor that Moss cast him in the title role in George Kelly's *The Show-Off* in January of 1928, but his clinging was ambiguous enough to make Moss nervous. He didn't reciprocate Brown's interest or it was too threatening. Brown later became a character actor best known in radio. He appeared in films now and then and played a fussy schoolmaster in *Hans Christian Andersen,* a movie written by Moss at a time when the two were no longer in contact. For years after their initial closeness, Brown stayed in touch with Carmel Finkelstein, whom he had met on that stormy excursion to Dannemora. "You are," he told her, "as close to Moss as Moss will let me get." Her own friendship with Brown, she later observed, "separated, rather than linked me to Moss."

If Moss deflected some relationships, he was skilled at pursuing others. The most lasting contact of that summer was a paying guest at the Crescent, a thirty-year-old businessman named Joseph M. Hyman. Born in Cripple Creek, Colorado, Hyman had been stagestruck since high school and set out for the Great White Way as soon as he had his diploma in hand. The self-described "budding John Barrymore" encountered indifference from Broadway impresarios due, perhaps, to an appearance that suggested a "gorilla," the nickname used behind his back. Moss more gently described him as "a cross between a well-dressed gangster and the director of the Hoboken Technical Institute."

Hyman gave up his dreams of Broadway, got married, established a successful knits-and-woolens business, and indulged his yearning for the theater by staging amateur theatricals, though on a smaller scale than Moss did. At Crescent he was impressed with Moss's work and volunteered for the stage crew, where he got to know Bernie. He invited them to look him up in New York.

It is unlikely he expected a visit quite so soon. After Gold absconded, Moss couldn't relocate the family on the money he'd extracted from Philip Gross. Hyman loaned him $200 and called it an advance against plays Moss might someday write and that Hyman might someday produce. He found jobs in his woolens company for Bernie and Barnett, so Moss might have time to write. It was an investment that would pay off in spectacular fashion.

Moss moved the family into a three-room apartment the Friedlanders found for them a few blocks from Coney Island in Sea Gate. He resumed his Little Theater directing in Brooklyn and New Jersey, earning $12 to $15 a week from each of his groups, enough to keep him in suits and ties and to ensure Bernie's graduation from high school.

His reputation as a director of amateur groups had grown. He could now give paid dramatic readings at YM- and YWHAs around the boroughs on the strength of his name alone. Amazingly, he renewed relations with the Crescent Country Club, acting as master of ceremonies for a recruiting event disguised as a reunion in a hotel ballroom in midtown Manhattan. Enough had been forgiven—or guaranteed for the future—that he quietly returned to Vermont and the Crescent Country Club for a second summer.

His third year of camp social-directing led him back to Brooklyn and Newark, no closer to Broadway than he had been since leaving Gus Pitou. He concocted shows like "The Center Follies" at the Brooklyn Jewish Center that began (again) in "the Author's Studio" with Moss (again) as "the Author" and, at some point in the evening, he did his impersonation of Fanny Brice. He staged "Anything Might Happen" whenever he could fit it in.

His directing and the travel from borough to borough allowed him little time for writing, though he had a habit of announcing titles he intended to write. There was one he described as a boardinghouse play with roles suggested by his family, revolving around a tragic character modeled on his aunt Kate or grandfather Solomon or both. Living near Coney Island inspired an idea titled B.R.T. to Baghdad, and there was one about just plain folks called Married for Keeps. It's unlikely these plays ever got written; their absence from the playing schedules of Moss's theater groups suggests they didn't.

It was about this time that Moss admitted experiencing the depressions that would debilitate and plague him intermittently for the rest of his life. Insomnia had always been a problem; he had relied on sleeping pills at least since his days with Pitou, as he admitted to Eddie Eliscu in letters from the road. Now he experienced periods in which he did not sleep, shave, bathe, or brush his teeth. He broke out in boils, suffered asthma attacks, and was seized by an uncontrollable stammer. He ascribed his symptoms to despair over money, but they alternated with contrasting episodes of sudden extravagance and ebullience, extremes of behavior suggesting manic-depressive mood disorders before he or anyone he knew could recognize them as such.

Money worries were real enough, and frustration with his career grew more urgent at the coffee counters he still frequented during the day in New York. His contemporaries were no longer office boys; they were now young professionals with developing careers that provoked comparisons.

Among the new faces was the flamboyant Preston Sturges, whose background was Continental and monied and who had written a play called *Strictly Dishonorable* that would make him known and take him to Hollywood. Archie Leach was now on Broadway in *Golden Dawn* ("golden yawn," Walter Winchell called it), but would soon head west, too. Producing hopeful Oscar Serlin, later to strike it rich with *Life With Father*, now drank ten cups of coffee a day, carried a walking stick, and lived on credit extended by the Alvin Hotel. Some of Moss's friends lightened the hours with anecdotes, like theater manager and actor Frank Merlin with his picture-people gossip gleaned working at the Vitagraph Studios; or old Labor Temple and Co-Optimist colleague Clarke Silvernail, just returned from Hollywood with a fund of hilarious tales about the transition to the talkies.

Gossip and shoptalk were overseen—as always—by Lester Sweyd, now working for Frieda Fishbein, a play agent, and as possessively devoted to Moss as ever. Lester browbeat Moss about his scanty output, accusing him of "procrastination" on the Chodorov scale. He finally goaded Moss into turning over the first act of a play he had been working on, the title of which may have mirrored his emotional state in 1928. It was called *Panic*.

The play centered on a father-son conflict suggested by gossip about Douglas Fairbanks, Sr.'s gloom at the rise of Douglas Fairbanks, Jr., as a leading man and movie star. The elder Fairbanks, never an active father, was not about to sacrifice his own youthful image just because he had a son who was also a grown man. The play detailed the father's selfishness and its destructive effect on his son, a theme echoing Moss's feelings about the "staggeringly selfish" Barnett.

Sweyd may or may not have known about Moss's family history, but he knew a good commercial idea—even a first act—when he saw one. Sweyd was reluctant to show pages-in-progress, but Moss reasoned that if a star could see himself in the leading role of the father, who was a famous stage star in the play, that interest might be used to secure a producer. Stars, Moss pointed out reasonably, could often visualize themselves portraying stars.

Sweyd agreed. He gave the first act of *Panic* to Tyrone Power, Sr., and to Lionel Atwill, both of whom he had worked with in his acting days. The role of George Adrian (Fairbanks, Sr.) was not just a star, but an aging matinee idol, a tricky subject to submit to aging matinee idols, exactly what Power and Atwill were. Both actors feigned disinterest and—being actors—wanted to know where the rest of the play was. It was all Sweyd needed to persuade Moss to finish the play.

He completed his first draft of *Panic* in early 1929 and gave it to Sweyd for his comments. While waiting, he worked on *The Center Follies* and directed the Newark Stagers in yet another production of *The Valiant,* this time winning first prize with it in the New Jersey Federation Dramatic Contest. It was a small honor, but one watched closely by booking agents, and it attracted an offer of another summer camp job. He accepted it without hesitation.

On May 22 he directed his final Little Theater production of *The Emperor Jones* (playing Smithers) in Newark and went off to the Catskills, with Sweyd's notes for revising *Panic* under his arm.

Moss's summer job in 1929 was as social director at the Flagler Hotel in Fallsburg, New York. The Flagler—"Hebrew Tech," Moss called it— was, along with Grossinger's, one of two camps in the Catskills of such gaudy desirability that Moss could now style himself King of the Borscht Circuit and be taken seriously. These were legendary training grounds for dozens of well-known entertainment industry figures like Danny Kaye, Garson Kanin, and Phil Silvers. Moss had not an inkling how short his reign as "King" would be.

The distance from Vermont's Crescent Country Club to the Flagler could not be measured in salary alone, though Moss would earn a handsome $1,200 from Memorial Day to Labor Day at the Flagler. Its amenities were more resortlike than camplike and included a professional theater seating more than a thousand. As social director Moss was allowed an assistant earning $400 for the season, plus a staff of twenty-one including now eighteen-year-old Bernie as stage manager; tennis, golf, and swimming instructors; baby-sitters to look after guests' children; and a cameraman who made silent movies of each week's activities for projection on Movie Night. The Flagler orchestra had nine players who provided dance and show music for performing talent recruited from paying guests and the staff.

Chief among the latter was Moss's assistant and closest friend from the Newark "Stagers," Dore Schary, whom he called "Butch" and who called him "Bossy Mossy." Schary, in addition to being Moss's assistant, was the editor of the *Flagler News,* the daily newsletter that announced camp events and was larded with gossip about campers, staff, and visitors. Its mimeographed pages kept up a running commentary on Moss's dandyism, noting on July 8, for example, "Moss showed up last night with a lavender shirt and a tapestried tie. Now we ask you."

Moss's attire was not showier than his work. As the summer got under way he produced, directed, and acted in old standbys like *The Valiant* and "Anything Might Happen," and in musical entertainments "conceived and staged by Moss Hart" like *The Flagler Scandals of 1929,* or a "revuesical comedy" called *Let's Talk About You,* or a "fantastical musical revue" titled *Wake Up and Dream,* or a collegiate musical irresistibly called *SIS-BOOM-BARBARA* and described as "climaxes and more climaxes, singing, dancing and much general hell raising."

Some of the material was cribbed, adapted, or recycled, but there was also *Homeward Bound,* a "nautical musical comedy" set aboard an ocean liner that bore the stamp of its creator. It was the season's final show and in it Moss played a character called Robert Arnold, two-thirds of the pseudonymous author of *The Hold-up Man.* A matron on the ship was Mrs. Bentwich, the maiden name of Lillian Friedlander and Carmel Finkelstein, Lillie Hart's cousins. Lillie herself spent the Fourth of July weekend at the Flagler, a beaming guest of her son.

Nothing filled the summer as fully as *Panic.* Between the myriad activities Moss was fulfilling with dazzling success at the Flagler, he somehow completed the play and revisions and sent them off to New York. Manic energy seemed to be driving him forward, but he was convinced *Panic* was his breakthrough and wanted Lester Sweyd to share that conviction. His letters complained about the pay phone in the hall of Sweyd's Forty-second Street boardinghouse that no one ever answered. To suggest that their bonds had a future he constantly emphasized "we"—or even "WE."

"I won't forget," he wrote, and the promise reactivated Sweyd. Though working with play agent Fishbein, Sweyd decided to bypass her, submitting *Panic* instead to Richard Madden, Eugene O'Neill's agent, a clear indication of his opinion of the play's merits. He told Moss what he had done and Moss had no choice but to sweat it out in the Catskills while Madden read.

Looked at today, *Panic* reveals obvious talent, but it is overwritten and lacks focus. Still, it is the first of Moss's plays to deal directly with his love affair with the theater and there is a knowing sense of backstage reality to it. It draws strength from theater's rituals and myths: "the lucky break," the "poison" of failure, the gulf between being "in" the theater and "of" it, the "panic" of a fading star, and the frustration of newcomers desperate to get inside.

The father-son rivalry is, ironically, the weakest thing about it. The father is a Pygmalion in reverse, bent on keeping his "creation" unthreatening, under wraps, and in his place. The son is oddly obsequious, much too timid to be any kind of credible threat and too callow to inspire sympathy or admiration.

Subsidiary characters engage Moss's talents more fully, emerging with sympathy and strength. The most suggestive is Arthur Hadley, a playwright. He is witty, angry, and bitter about the humiliations of poverty. He supports his writing by directing amateur theater groups and is an obvious self-portrait. Nan, the young actress in love with the son, is clever, warm, and perceptive about the father's motives:

NAN: . . . *people are going to say: "Kenneth Adrian? Is that George Adrian's son? Why, my goodness, I never knew he had a son that old. . . ." And that will be the beginning of the end. Because, Ken, you have a spark . . . a fine, new talent . . . and he knows it. And he's afraid.*

By play's end, the son's rise to stardom is secured in spite of his father's treachery. The father graciously and cunningly leads the chorus of acclaim while adroitly turning the spotlight back on himself. This is expected, but there's a twist. As if accepting his son's autonomy, he begins spinning dreams of a series of plays—Shakespeare, perhaps—"starring" himself and "featuring" his son. In an unexpected reversal, the son agrees. He is his father's son, corrupted by success and greedy to ensure more, even at the cost of his own independence. When Nan realizes the awful truth, her sense of tragedy brings down the curtain with a plaintive, "We are lost."

The play is too self-conscious and too hastily composed to achieve more than a smart cleverness, but hints at Moss's own skepticism about the very obsession with success that was driving him to finish the play. A speech from the son goes:

KEN: *I want to spend . . . I want to know how it feels to go to the Plaza for tea. And buy a $150 overcoat. Maybe a raccoon coat. And pay for tickets. And have a car, perhaps . . . just to have it. Just to show off, I guess.*

There's irony in the dying fall of that speech. Could success—so elusive and so prized—amount to nothing more than showing off?

Richard Madden was businesslike and prompt. He read *Panic* and returned it on July 22, 1929, with a letter to Sweyd:

> *I wish Mr. Hart had utilized his splendid talents on a subject matter and theme that will afford a little more freshness or novelty. . . . Frankly, I don't think the conflict between father and son as show folks will be half as important to an audience of today as to people in and of the theater. If Mr. Hart has anything else I would certainly like to read it.*

Moss later claimed that Madden's letter praised his sense of comedy and inspired him to turn in that direction, but that wasn't true. What Moss turned to was the despair he always felt with negative reviews and then, snapping out of it, he changed the title. *Panic* became *No Retreat,* perhaps to mirror his own resolve.

No Retreat was in Sweyd's hands now. Moss needed to start all over again, even if he was "the glittering hero of us Borscht Belt showbiz aspirants," as one of them put it. The Borscht Belt wasn't where he wanted to glitter.

He returned to Sea Gate from the Flagler to face another season of Little Theater in Brooklyn and Newark. He unpacked his smart summer wardrobe and took pad and pencil to the shore. "It looks like a great season," he had written Sweyd in late July. "If ever the Theater offered great rewards its *[sic]* now—what with the talkies, etc." The talkies were, in fact, on his mind and an idea about them had begun to bubble. He wrote out a title: ONCE TO EVERY MAN. Not quite right. He tried another: EVERY MAN FOR HIMSELF. Well, why not? He began to write.

5

ONCE IN A LIFETIME

Dying is easy; comedy is hard.

EDMUND KEAN, on his deathbed

Sometimes pages seem to write themselves and they did with "Every Man for Himself." Characters, scenes, and gags fell into place even when scribbled on the subway or dashed off during breaks in yet another production of *Ghosts,* with Moss as Oswald. By October 7, after just a month of writing and reading scenes to Lester Sweyd on the telephone as soon as they were on paper, he had a draft he was ready to show. Sweyd, already the play's "most fierce and passionate champion," gathered a small group for a reading at the National Vaudeville Artists on West Forty-sixth Street.

The setting could hardly have been more apt. "Every Man for Himself" centers on a trio of vaudevillians thrown out of work by Hollywood and the talkies. The action begins when they decide to go to Hollywood and pass themselves off as elocution experts who can teach movie stars how to talk. Not for the last time, Moss was as topical as the headlines in the morning paper.

Actually, the talkies were so familiar by 1929 it is a wonder no one had seized on them before. *The Jazz Singer* had been released two years earlier and, by the time Moss read his draft aloud on the mezzanine of the vaudevillians' clubhouse, the transition to sound was virtually complete. But novelty lasted longer then. Magazines and gossip columns were slow to tire of stories about the talkies and the changes they were wreaking in Hollywood. The collapse of John Gilbert's career because his milquetoast tenor didn't go with the "great lover" image was common, if faulty, knowledge at soda fountains everywhere. Garbo hadn't talked yet, but everyone knew she was busy—somewhere—practicing, and the world would hold its breath until she did. Foreign stars who had never bothered to learn English had packed their bags for home, and great stars of the stage, once scornful of déclassé flickers, were dashing down Grand Central Station's red carpet to the westbound Twentieth Century Limited, enunciating their vowel sounds.

As usual, there are different versions of how the idea came to him. One was that, while sitting in a cheap balcony seat watching *June Moon,* Ring Lardner and George S. Kaufman's satire about songwriters, he was so inspired that he "started the first act that night," but the Lardner-Kaufman play didn't open until two days after the first reading of "Every Man for Himself" at the vaudeville club. If Moss's play owed a debt to *June Moon* it was in its wisecracking style and the notion that if a comedy kidding Tin Pan Alley could be a hit, why not one about Hollywood and the talkies?

The subject had been on his mind all summer, teased by *Variety*'s snappy headlines and focused by friends like Clarke Silvernail and Frank Merlin. Silvernail, Moss's former Labor Temple and Co-Optimists colleague, had moved into the Astor Hotel, where he was gallantly holding court while losing ground to cancer. Moss and Sweyd visited him there, listening to his anecdotes about writing scenarios for illiterates in Hollywood. Moss used him as the model for a New York playwright called Lawrence Vail whose struggle to maintain his sanity in Hollywood drives him crazy. Merlin, a struggling stage manager, contributed vignettes he'd observed at Vitagraph, trading anecdotes about vulgarian moguls for advice about a play of his own called *Hobo* that would soon open and close on Broadway.

Moss stirred these elements together with fantasies of what Hollywood must *really* be like and came up with a lampoon that put studio receptionists in evening gowns and ropes of pearls and installed boobs in the boardroom. The vaudevillians he invented to take advantage of them were May Daniels, a wisecracking "dame" who is smart, weary, and cynical; Jerry Hyland, the sharp dresser and wise guy who sells their act so they can afford train tickets to Hollywood; and George Lewis, the guileless dimwit who mostly cracks Indian nuts with his teeth and quotes *Variety.*

Jerry is the go-getter with big ideas about Hollywood, but it is May—who once ran an elocution school in Wilkes-Barre, Pennsylvania—who dreams up teaching movie stars to talk. On the train to Hollywood they bump into Helen Hobart, one of her former diction students, now Hollywood's most feared and courted movie critic. Hobart proposes, for a 50 percent stake in their elocution school's profits, to introduce them to studio czar Mr. Dahlberg, who—forbidden topic—turned down the Vitaphone and will now buy anything.

The scheme seems good until Dahlberg rejects the diction-school scam in his own barely comprehensible accent. Dumb George blurts out the awful truth: *You're* the man who turned down the Vitaphone. Dahlberg is astounded by this yes-man who says no. "He's right. He's absolutely right. I did turn it down. I thought it was rotten and I still think it's rotten. The movies are and should remain unspeakable."

George's wise-fool honesty causes Dahlberg to make him studio supervisor. Soon George has produced the worst picture ever made, which becomes a huge hit, adding to his appeal for Susan, a movie hopeful he met on the train to Hollywood whose sole talent is reciting Rudyard Kipling's "Boots" while marching in place.

Now an acknowledged genius, George steps before the cameras as the groom in the climactic wedding sequence of his latest Super-Colossal production (he's also the director) with Susan on his arm as the bride. As the curtain falls, he reigns at Dahlberg Studios as a sort of Irving Thalberg, Ramon Novarro, and Erich von Stroheim rolled into one, still cracking Indian nuts. And Susan is destined to become a star. As someone notes, "She is dumb enough."

The reading at the vaudeville clubhouse went so well that Sweyd cajoled a friend into typing Moss's first draft on credit, a favor earlier extended for *No Retreat*. When the typed version was delivered, Moss gave his original pencil draft to Lester with a poem about friendship on the cover so oozing with treacle that Sweyd nicknamed him "Marcella Hartowitz."

Sweyd quickly organized a fuller reading of the play by actor friends at his sister's apartment on West Seventy-second Street. The sound of laughter was so heady that Moss canceled a rehearsal of *Ghosts* in Newark and read the play aloud to the Newark Stagers, acting all the parts himself. Dore Schary, his closest friend in the group, insisted that Moss submit it to wunderkind producer Jed Harris, who had made the cover of *Time* the year before at only twenty-eight. Schary knew Harris's sister, who could get it to him, and Harris would have no choice but to produce the comedy at once.

But the play wasn't available for Harris or anybody else. Moss had impulsively given Oscar Serlin, still living on credit at the Alvin Hotel, a free option to produce it himself. Serlin would eventually make millions producing *Life With Father,* but in 1929 he couldn't finance a ticket, let alone a show. Meanwhile, "Every Man for Himself" was becoming shopworn and might need a new title, as *The Hold-up Man* once had. Moss waited for Serlin's four-week option to run out and, when it did, put a new title page on it. *Once in a Lifetime* it became, with a new subtitle: "A Comedy of Sound and Fury."

The author turned twenty-five on October 24. Five days later someone at *Variety* composed a memorable headline: WALL STREET LAYS AN EGG.

Moss took Sweyd's advice and went to agent Frieda Fishbein and read the newly retitled play to her from beginning to end. Impressed, she agreed to represent it and to try her best with *No Retreat* as well. She was not a master-agent like Richard Madden, but represented Elmer Rice's *Street Scene,* the Pulitzer Prize winner for 1929, which gave her entrée she was eager to use.

She submitted *Once in a Lifetime* and *No Retreat* widely, not neglecting the two Harrises: Jed the Wonder Boy and the more seasoned Sam H. Harris, former partner of George M. Cohan, now partnered with Irving Berlin in the Music Box Theatre. Sam Harris was in California at the moment, but Max Siegel, his twenty-nine-year-old general manager, took a look at the script himself.

In the meantime, Jed Harris (whose real name was Jacob Horowitz; he had renamed himself, oddly enough, after Sam) responded much as Schary had predicted and summoned Moss to his suite at the Madison Hotel on East Fifty-ninth Street.

Few producers ever glittered as brightly or dangerously as Jed Harris. At twenty-nine he was flush with prestige and profits from producing hits like *The Royal Family* and *The Front Page,* and would eventually stage Thornton Wilder's *Our Town* and Arthur Miller's *The Crucible.* He was brilliant and abrasive and lucky and as feared and hated as he was envied.

"I'm a master of espionage," he liked to say. "I know what's going on in every office," and it was probably true. Certainly he would have known that Fishbein had submitted *Once in a Lifetime* elsewhere and that producers David Belasco, William A. Brady, Gilbert Miller, and Brock Pemberton had all turned it down. His only real competition was the other Harris, who was still in California.

After making Moss wait days in the lobby of his hotel, Harris invited him up to his rooms. He spoke as if they were equals, ruminating about the state of the theater, his theories of comedy, his upcoming production of *Uncle Vanya* starring Lillian Gish—all of it stark naked.

While Harris was expatiating in the altogether, Max Siegel was reading. He liked *Once in a Lifetime* and telephoned Hollywood to say so. Sam Harris, who claimed he liked to hold a comedy script to his ear and shake it "to hear the laughs," trusted Siegel's judgment and told him to pursue it.

Sam Harris had reason to like Moss's subject. He had produced *The Jazz Singer* on Broadway, and thus played an indirect role in the sound revolution Moss's play satirized. Additionally, he was intrigued by some Tin Pan Alley song-pluggers writing movie songs in the first draft (later dropped), who suggested that this might be the basis for a musical. He was in Hollywood, in fact, working with Irving Berlin on a movie musical called *Puttin' on the Ritz.* The movie was being made with direct recording for musical numbers rather than playback, resulting in the kind of chaos Moss's script was full of. The musical idea seemed a natural, and a way to get Irving Berlin back to Broadway, too.

Moss claimed that he bristled "I do not write musical comedies" when Siegel proposed the idea in his office. "I'm a playwright. I write plays—*only* plays." Fishbein and Sweyd, Moss later wrote, looked at him "aghast" as he prepared to walk out of the Music Box Theatre in a huff. Both of them were, he wrote, "furious" at "my courage."

This is a wonderful scene, full of artistic principle as the author of such distinguished "plays—*only* plays" as SIS—BOOM—BARBARA turns down the chance to collaborate with an authentic American genius. It is also a scene that Sweyd claimed never took place and that Fishbein, considerably incensed when she heard about it, dismissed to Moss as "a figment of your imagination."

His later memory may have faltered, as it did regarding Eddie Eliscu and *The Hold-up Man,* but Fishbein's remained clear as an alarm bell. She resented being turned into a peripheral figure by Moss's memory lapses and with reason. She had, after all, attracted the attention of both Harrises to *Once in a Lifetime.* As she did, she was negotiating with producer Billy Rose for Moss to write sketches for Fanny Brice. She was also concluding a contract for him to rewrite a musical comedy—not a play and not by Irving Berlin—scheduled for a Broadway opening in the spring. If that were not enough, she was still working to sell *No Retreat.*

Siegel didn't know or care about any of that. He merely conveyed to Sam Harris that the youthful author—twenty-five, but claiming to be twenty-three—and his agent had said no to a musical. Harris was unperturbed and wondered if George S. Kaufman might be interested. If Kaufman wanted to get involved, Harris said from California, he would option the play. Siegel placed a call.

There were few men on Broadway with larger reputations than George S. Kaufman. He had become known as a drama critic on the *New York Times,* then as editor of the *Times*'s drama desk, and finally as a playwright and member of the group of wits who sat at a round table in the Algonquin Hotel on West Forty-fourth Street and traded memorable quips and insults. His successes as a playwright included *Dulcy, Merton of the Movies,* and *Beggar on Horseback,* all with Marc Connelly. He wrote *Animal Crackers* for the Marx Brothers with Morrie Ryskind, then *The Royal Family* with Edna Ferber, and *June Moon* with Ring Lardner. He had only one successful play on his own, *The Butter and Egg Man,* but as a director he had staged *The Royal Family* and *June Moon,* as well as *The Front Page* by Ben Hecht and Charles MacArthur, the huge success produced by Jed Harris.

Moss forever after maintained that he leaped at the suggestion of the man who would become his longtime collaborator, but he leaped in the opposite direction—toward Jed Harris, harboring the "secret illusion" that, in the end, the younger Harris would take charge of his play and career.

There was ambiguity in the situation. Nothing in the record suggests that Sam Harris, who still hadn't read the play, wanted Kaufman brought in on *Once in a Lifetime* as a writer. As director, Kaufman would contribute lines and bits of business, but that was all. Moss may well have thrilled to the idea of Kaufman as director, but Frieda Fishbein, on his behalf, was wary of anyone who might overshadow her young client, intentionally or not.

Moss called Jed Harris. Perhaps Harris would be so impressed by hearing about Sam Harris and Kaufman he would decide to produce Moss's comedy himself. Harris heard Moss out and allowed that Kaufman sounded like a good idea. He even volunteered Kaufman's home telephone number so Moss might call him directly and tell him Jed Harris said so. Moss placed the call. Kaufman coldly replied, "I would not be interested in anything that Jed Harris was interested in," and hung up.

Kaufman and Harris had had major hits together, but now detested each other. Harris was "compulsively devious," as his biographer Martin Gottfried admitted, and must have known and intended that Moss's phone call to Kaufman would backfire. Moss attributed the action to sheer perversity, but there had been more to it than malice. Harris had listened carefully to Moss and introduced the notion of a collaborator, even suggesting a candidate. Ben Hecht had "been all through that racket out on the Coast," he told Moss. Hecht had not only coauthored *The Front Page,* but had won an Academy Award for writing the gangster movie *Underworld.* He was an authority on a town and industry Moss was just guessing at.

What Harris was up to is unclear, but he may have hoped Moss would mention Hecht to Kaufman and that Hecht's name might lure Kaufman back to the Jed Harris fold, in spite of their mutual loathing. In any case, Kaufman hadn't read the play when he hung up on Moss, but it lay there on his desk and mention of Harris's name sparked his curiosity. He picked up the script. He found it fresh, funny, and brash and asked Max Siegel to arrange a meeting.

On January 17, 1930, Moss and Fishbein met Kaufman at the Music Box. The newcomer and the veteran cautiously agreed they could work together as writer and director. The next day the *Times, Variety,* and other publications reported Kaufman's signing on as director of *Once in a Lifetime,* and all reported that the young author was twenty-three years old. Moss signed a contract with the Sam H. Harris office that nowhere mentioned a cowriter or sharing credit in any way. What it mentioned was an advance against royalties of $1.69.

Jed Harris may deserve more credit than he has been given in establishing one of Broadway's most celebrated writing teams. Without his mischief or malice Kaufman and Hart might never have come together and he might have produced *Once in a Lifetime* himself, with Ben Hecht doing a rewrite. What is certain is that Harris had genuine interest in Moss. To prove it, a week after Moss signed his contract with the other Harris for *Once in a Lifetime,* Jed Harris took an option on *No Retreat,* calling it "the best back-stage play" he had ever read.

Kaufman's antipathy for Jed Harris revealed as much about himself as it did about Harris. Like Dorothy Parker, his witticisms were endlessly repeated and seldom examined. A famous example occurred at the *Times* where, in spite of his other successes, Kaufman had never given up his job as drama editor. A Broadway press agent asked Kaufman what he would have to do to get an actress's name in the paper. "Shoot her," Kaufman replied.

The anecdote has inspired laughter for decades, but the circumstances have faded from memory and are revealing. The actress was Helen Hayes, then in a hit comedy called *To the Ladies* written by Marc Connelly and none other than George S. Kaufman. Kaufman's "Shoot her" was not just a gratuitous zinger, but an attempt to avoid a blatant conflict of interest and self-promotion. He was a man of principle, as well as wit.

Similarly, Kaufman's aversion to Jed Harris was more than a theatrical feud and also went back to the *Times.* The flash point was an out-of-town review for a Harris production. Harris was outraged that Kaufman allowed a negative review from the *Philadelphia Inquirer* to be excerpted in the *Times* even though quoting out-of-town reviews was a policy of the paper. The play, Sam Behrman's *Serena Blandish,* turned out to be a hit in New York, but Harris was determined to punish. He described Kaufman and his wife around Broadway as "that fat Jewish whore and her withered cuckold of a husband," and made sure Kaufman knew it.

This was extreme even for the backbiting world of Broadway. The marriage of George and Beatrice Kaufman was unorthodox, but it was meaningful to them and Harris's remark was unforgivably vicious. Moss hadn't known any of that when he called Harris and then Kaufman. He hadn't even known Kaufman was married, though the complicated affections binding George and Beatrice would soon play a vital role in shaping his own affections and future.

Moss and Kaufman met to work together in late February at 158 East Sixty-third Street, the town house the Kaufmans rented from playgirl Peggy Hopkins Joyce.

Kaufman was not an easy man. Tall, gaunt, and remote, he wore horn-rimmed glasses that rode low on an awesome nose and had a smile that one of his employees at the *Times* called "hardly more than a baring of the teeth." He was a lifelong hypochondriac who shunned physical contact and consequently merely waved the long fingers of his bony hand in greeting. He would have been altogether intimidating were it not for the hair that rose from his lofty brow as if electrified, making him look oddly like Abraham Lincoln impersonating one of the Marx Brothers.

Kaufman's study was on the top floor, a former maid's room with a desk and a typewriter, a studio couch that doubled as a bed, an easy chair, and a portrait of Mark Twain. Perhaps not knowing what to make of Moss's youth or brashness, Kaufman called him Er. Moss registered the restraint, but assumed this was the way all great Broadway figures behaved. At least Kaufman was clothed.

They had very little in common at twenty-five and forty besides being tall, dark, and Jewish. Moss was exuberant; Kaufman, dour. Moss was handsome; Kaufman, homely. Moss was self-taught; Kaufman had studied law and playwriting at Columbia. Moss wrote purple poems to friendship; Kaufman cringed at displays of emotion and abhorred sentimentality. Moss was outside; Kaufman was as inside as one could get.

Even their senses of humor were different. Moss was the ingratiating charmer, transparently eager to please. Kaufman was the "master of the destructive jest," as Brooks Atkinson noted, his wit barbed, caustic, and feared. The contrasts were what suited them to each other. They meshed. One warmed while the other cooled. Finally they would become like a chessboard: you couldn't tell if it was black squares on red or red on black, and that's the way they wanted it.

Work was delayed by commitments on both sides. Moss's Little Theater chores in Newark and Brooklyn still claimed his evenings. He was trying to turn out sketches for Fanny Brice in Billy Rose's new revue *Corned Beef and Roses* scheduled for fall under the direction of none other than Jed Harris. Moss was cowriting the book for a musical called *Jonica* with Dorothy Heyward, wife of *Porgy*'s DuBose Heyward, which producer William Friedlander had scheduled for a Broadway opening in April.

Kaufman's plate was equally full. In addition to his chores for the *Times,* he looked after the January opening of *Strike Up the Band,* the anti-war satire with a score by George and Ira Gershwin that had been a failure on the road two years earlier. It had since been reworked in a jokier vein by Morrie Ryskind, who described the adaptation as "*War and Peace* for the Three Stooges." Kaufman continued to look in on *June Moon* and directed George Jessel in a flop called *Joseph,* about the wearer of the biblical coat-of-many-colors as a flippant wise guy.

When Moss and Kaufman at last knuckled down, there was pressure to do their work quickly. Sam Harris announced out-of-town tryouts in May, with a fall opening at the Music Box after a summer shutdown for fine-tuning. The pattern was that of *June Moon,* which had undergone major revisions on the road before emerging as a hit.

The editor in Kaufman cut away the talky underbrush that plagued all of Moss's early work. Aimless dialogue, irrelevant gags, whole scenes were excised. Details became more credible on things as minor as the cost of Pullman car travel to Hollywood. Moss had guessed; Kaufman knew.

Kaufman's style as a director was often characterized as "faster, louder, funnier" and was anything but tentative or cerebral. To move things along at once, May's backstory in Wilkes-Barre got cut. So did the Hollywood songwriters (one of whom Moss had given the family name of Solomon). Susan, the ingenue who can't stop reciting "Boots," remained, but her chaperones didn't, and Kaufman was willing to overlook Moss's lifting her Kipling recitations directly from George Kelly's *The Flattering Word,* where the poet had been Tennyson.

Certain things got added. Moss had underwritten the Hollywood scenes, or minimized their use as too expensive to stage. Kaufman expanded them for visual opulence to go along with the gags. The corner of a hotel nightclub in Moss's draft became the lobby of the Stilton Hotel, lavishly peopled with burlesques: movie stars with chauffeurs and Russian wolfhounds, Garbo and Gilbert look-alikes, all twelve of the movie-mogul Schlepkin brothers, even the studio czar Mr. Dahlberg, whose name was too close to Thalberg (he became Herman Glogauer of Glogauer Studios).

The most vital changes strengthened the play's structure. Moss's first draft had depended on merely escalating the absurdity. Kaufman knew that the comedy of caricatures couldn't hold for an entire evening and that the vaudeville trio's attempts to "take" Hollywood needed fresh obstacles and reversals.

Act one ended as it always had, with Glogauer's recognition of George's "genius" (he's been quoting *Variety* again) and buying the elocution school. The revised act two, however, began with a reversal in the reception room of Glogauer Studios, where uniformed pages carry signs announcing MR. GLOGAUER IS ON NUMBER FOUR or MR. GLOGAUER IS ON NUMBER SIX. Waiting to see Glogauer is Lawrence Vail, the New York playwright inspired by Clarke Silvernail, imported to write scenarios but unable to get an appointment with anyone who will tell him what to write. Breaking down, Vail delivers a diatribe condemning Hollywood idiocy and waste, not to a reporter, as in Moss's first script, but to nut-cracking George, about to be fired. Vail exits with a line from Moss's original draft that remained the biggest laugh in the play: "Listen, son. I'm going to the Men's Room [and] if [anybody] wants me, I'm in Number Three."

When Glogauer tries to fire him, George quotes Vail's diatribe about idiocy and waste in Hollywood. Glogauer again recognizes "genius" when he hears it and elevates George to supervisor, ensuring bigger and better fiascoes to come.

Kaufman's cuts and changes added structure to Moss's first draft and by late April it was clear that his contributions were more extensive than a director's touch-up; this was becoming a genuine rewrite. On May 9, contracts were redrawn, spelling out the writing collaboration for the first time. They gave Moss first billing and split the authors' royalties 40 percent to Kaufman and 60 percent to Moss.

What Kaufman brought to *Once in a Lifetime* were the skills of the editor and director. The characters and themes of vanity, pretension, moguls running amok, and idiocy rewarded had all been present in "Every Man for Himself," along with most of the wittiest and best-remembered dialogue. What Kaufman did was to structure Moss's scatter-shot effects with pace and precision. Moss had given it laughs here and audacity there; Kaufman gave it shape and rhythms that made the laughs grow from and with the audacity.

None of which meant anything without an audience. Sam Harris booked tryout theaters: the Apollo in Atlantic City in May, to be followed by the Brighton in Brooklyn.

Moss didn't stop working in Newark and Brooklyn. He did plays in January, February, and April. Whatever confidence he felt about *Once in a Lifetime,* he took the precaution of quietly signing with the Flagler for another summer as social director, nominating Dore Schary as his replacement if he should be needed elsewhere.

Jed Harris still held an option on *No Retreat* and Billy Rose was still nagging him for sketches for Fanny Brice, who needed material for a little girl act she was calling "Babykins." Most time-consuming of all was *Jonica.*

Jonica's story was by Dorothy Heyward, who had adapted *Porgy* for the stage with her husband two years earlier. *Jonica* was an innocent-maiden-goes-madcap story and the libretto Moss cowrote with her was the kind of thing Glogauer Studios might have released as a Super-Colossal and, if George Lewis had supervised, it might have been a hit.

What Moss knew about a convent girl (Jonica) hopping a train with a revolver in her purse (the gimmick) to get to a wedding on time (the plot) is unclear. It didn't make much sense and didn't have to. Shows like *No, No, Nanette* and *Oh, Kay!* had done fine without much more in the way of plot, but *Nanette* had Vincent Youmans and "Tea for Two" and *Kay* had the Gershwins and "Someone to Watch Over Me." All *Jonica* had was Joseph Meyer and William Moll and "If You Were the Apple (Then I'd Love to Be the Bough)."

The show opened at the National Theater in Washington, D.C., on March 25. Washington reviews were good on the whole, with the *Post* noting that the show had "almost as many scenes as *Show Boat.*" A week later at the Apollo in Atlantic City reviewers cited "smart cracks" and "high voltage." *Variety* found it "routine . . . but amusing."

When *Jonica* arrived at the Craig Theatre on West Fifty-fourth Street in New York on April 7 the *Times* rated it "Grade-B," while Walter Winchell dismissed it as "soggy" and "banal." Others liked it enough to allow *Jonica* to play a total of forty performances on Broadway, a run that was no disgrace in the first full year of the Depression, but not quite the dazzling debut Moss had in mind. Later, he could rely on short memories and deny he had anything to do with it if anyone should remember, which is just what he did.

By early May Kaufman had cast *Once in a Lifetime* with Aline MacMahon as May and Hugh O'Connell as George. The showy small role of Vail went to Kaufman himself. The Apollo in Atlantic City was close enough to Broadway that a prankish cheering section showed up for the first performance, including Groucho and Chico Marx and George Jessel. Banished from performances until Brighton Beach were Moss's friends and family except for Joe Hyman, who wanted an early look at the results of his post-Vermont investment in Moss's future.

The curtain went up on act one with Kaufman pacing furiously at the back of the auditorium, head down, listening to the rhythm of lines and laughs as if it were a radio show. Moss's stomach kept him sick in the men's room until the sound of steady laughter lured him back to take up the pacing while Kaufman prepared for his appearance in act two.

The curtain rose on the Glogauer reception room revealing Kaufman as Vail, billed in the program as Calvin Brown. The audience, led by Groucho and Chico, recognized him at once and exploded with laughter. His scene with George was fast and funny and his exit on "if anybody wants me I'll be in Number Three" got the biggest laugh of the evening.

But as the scenes got bigger, the laughs got smaller. George made his colossal Glogauer production all wrong and there was a premiere at Grauman's Chinese Theater and a return to the lobby of the Stilton Hotel that had been featured in act one. By play's end the laughter had mysteriously ceased altogether. The curtain came down and, in the absence of prolonged applause, Jessel leaped onstage to introduce himself and the two Marx Brothers, stimulating applause the play could not.

Sam Harris went to New York, leaving Moss and Kaufman to mull over an act and a half that worked and an act and a half that did not. Reviews were more enthusiastic than not, but demeaning to Moss. They assumed that George S. Kaufman would save this newcomer, at whose feet the evening's deficiencies were laid. Moss and Kaufman rewrote at night for the rest of the two-week Atlantic City engagement and moved on to Brighton Beach on June 2 with what seemed a tighter, sharper, funnier show.

Those who came expected nothing less than a rollicking hit. Lillie and Barnett were there with Bernie, Lillie promising to see every performance, alternating her two best dresses. The Friedlanders and Finkelsteins and most of Moss's amateur players from Newark and Brooklyn were there. So was the faithful Joe Hyman, assessing the progress since Atlantic City.

As before, the first act couldn't miss. Act two had been improved enough to keep them laughing until midway, when silence descended over all but the coughers. It descended over Kaufman, too. The midnight toil had improved too little. The opulent sets and extravagant action excited audible admiration, but few laughs. He and Moss continued rewriting at night, Kaufman fueling their sessions with fudge he made himself that energized him and sent Moss to the bathroom to flush it surreptitiously down the toilet while noting effusively how tasty it was. *Once in a Lifetime* needed more than glucose.

The final performance in Brighton Beach had not improved appreciably from the first performance in Atlantic City. Except for Lillie, who applauded even the light cues, hearty laughter was inexplicably followed by the hush of silence, attentive but rollicking not at all. After the final curtain, Kaufman diplomatically threw in the towel, telling Moss he had nothing more to offer. He should feel free to take *Once in a Lifetime* elsewhere.

Moss had been shoved off a cliff. However kind Kaufman was in delivering the death blow, he knew no producer would take a chance on a show that he and Sam Harris had abandoned after months of work and four weeks out of town. Moss knew that, too. Maybe somewhere, Jed Harris was smiling.

Moss had known desperation before and had been able to focus on his aspirations as an antidote, which is what he did that night on the streetcar back to Twenty-first Avenue in Brooklyn. If he could come up with something, it would have to be better and it would have to be fast. News of Kaufman's defection would be all over Broadway by sunrise and other offers would start pouring in.

Audiences wanted to like this play; you could hear it. There was goodwill in the laughter and affection, too, but some mysterious block to sustaining it. He pondered the gags, the sets, and the characters and, energized by desperation, tried to see things fresh.

It was early when he arrived at 158 East Sixty-third Street after a day of rethinking the play. Kaufman could hardly turn him away after the blow he had delivered two nights earlier. Before Kaufman could even think about *Grand Hotel*—the script was sitting on top of his desk—Moss began describing changes he wanted to make to *Once in a Lifetime,* acting out the scenes as he talked.

Later he was vague about his new approach to the play, noting that he "scribbled" out a "rough scenario of new second and third acts," but the play was much nearer its final form than that. The area that the collaborators had argued over—"bitterly," said one eyewitness—was characterization, and Moss seized on the issue now.

What they had argued about was May. Moss had wanted Aline MacMahon to play the part all along, but Kaufman wanted Jean Dixon, who had been a tremendous hit with her cynical Lucille in *June Moon*. But Dixon had turned May down, fearing she might be typecast forever as a wisecracking dame, and MacMahon had gotten the role over Kaufman's objections.

What if, Moss asked himself, Dixon had been right? What if May were just a smart-talking dame, cracking wise while George cracked Indian nuts? What if it were *all* too flippant and too mocking to satisfy anything but easy laughs that grew tired halfway through the evening? What if, say, May were vulnerable beneath the brittle surface and were sweet on Jerry? It might give them a grown-up romance to parallel the sillier one between George and Susan, and might engage the audience with something more solid than the Hollywood jokes they'd been piling on.

This was risky. Kaufman liked to claim he was not a cynic, just a realist, but he also suspected himself of some "lack of warmth and inventiveness" and avoided situations that might prove it. If he recoiled from sentimentality in his writing as in life, Moss did not. If May were in love with Jerry, it might make her a credible and sympathetic character and explain her hanging around so long with a second-rate vaudeville team. It might justify her going along with Jerry's Hollywood scheme. It might account for her remaining there when she hated the place.

What if she threatened to go back to New York? What if she traded some of the wisecracks that Dixon had found excessive for some cool but weary sanity about what was happening to her and to Jerry and to George? Hollywood was absurd, but it was also a place that did things to you if you weren't careful, not all of them funny. May could stop being a joke machine and become an anchor.

It is not known exactly what Moss said to Kaufman, but this is the direction the script now took. The comic exaggeration remained, but was tempered by a clear-eyed, acerbic guide who was still ready with a wisecrack, but wise, as well.

The first cast had already been dismissed. Maybe Kaufman had been right all along about MacMahon; there *was* something matronly about her. Maybe they could go back to Dixon with a less brittle May, one who was just tender enough to be more than a "dame." Maybe they could get her.

Kaufman listened attentively to Moss's arguments. He had more regard and respect for Moss than Moss knew. He had told the tough, competitive crowd at the Algonquin that "this new boy has so much talent" it frightened him. That talent reproached him now, by refusing to accept defeat. Kaufman called Sam Harris and asked him to reserve the Music Box for fall. They were going back to work.

Moss knew the odds against him. When Dore Schary, who had replaced him as social director at the Flagler, invited him there for a long summer weekend, Moss had to decline, but he wasn't burning any bridges. The Flagler owners kept after him in New York, probably knowing that others were making offers, too. In order not to sabotage Schary at the Flagler, Moss accepted an offer from Camp Copake for the following summer. Broadway might not work out.

He was close, but *Jonica* hadn't made him a Broadway figure, and Billy Rose's *Corned Beef and Roses* seemed doubtful. Now retitled *Sweet and Low,* the show was in Philadelphia in midsummer with Jed Harris directing and hating Moss's sketches for Fanny Brice as Babykins. He fired Moss just before Rose and Brice fired *him.* Audiences didn't find much that was sweet when the show opened on Broadway in November, but critics thought there was plenty that was low. Someone restrained Rose from titling a second edition *Sweeter and Lower,* but at least "Babykins" evolved, with no help from Moss, into "Baby Snooks," the mischievous brat Brice would fully realize in later editions of the *Follies* and play on the radio until her death in 1951.

Moss didn't make it to the Flagler that summer, but he sent constant bulletins to Schary about *Once in a Lifetime* and *No Retreat,* too, which had unexpectedly come back to life.

Jed Harris had dropped "the best back-stage play" he had ever read when he dropped Moss from *Sweet and Low.* Frieda Fishbein immediately sold a new option to Hungarian producer Bela Blau, formerly a bookkeeper with the Theatre Guild and now producing on his own. Blau had several plays for the new season, among them an antifascist play by journalist William Bolitho, who died suddenly in June, upsetting Blau's schedule and creating a gap for *No Retreat* to fill.

Blau hired H. C. "Hank" Potter to streamline *No Retreat* for mid-July tryouts in Southampton, Quogue, and East Hampton, New York. Potter, who would build a career directing stars like Fred Astaire, Margaret Sullavan, and James Cagney in Hollywood, was now directing the Hampton Players. He cut the cast of *No Retreat* in half, giving himself the role of a theater director named Morrison, Moss's gesture to Priestly Morrison, the director of *The Hold-up Man*. Albert Dekker of the Theatre Guild was cast as the actor-father and as Nan, Sally Bates, fresh from Broadway and Jerome Kern's *Sweet Adeline*.

The tryouts gave Moss an excuse to leave the city. He and Lester Sweyd borrowed a car and a road map and got hopelessly lost on the backroads of Long Island. Finally they found Southampton, where a glittering summer crowd was gathered at Parrish Memorial Hall, including Mr. and Mrs. Gus Pitou, wishing the onetime office boy well in another assault on Broadway.

Reviews were mostly social notes from the Hamptons, but among them was an assessment from humorist Finley Peter Dunne. He thought *No Retreat* "a most interesting comedy" marred by "a lush growth of dramatic weeds" that "made the going heavy." Dunne might have been amused to learn that twenty-five years later his son Philip would produce and direct a film written by Hart that was one of Moss's many reworkings of the very themes that the elder Dunne found such heavy going. They were not too heavy for Blau, who announced he was taking the play to Broadway.

Moss, however, was shaken by what he saw on Long Island. He wrote Schary that local papers had found it "marvelous," but that Potter had "butchered" it. It would never make it to Broadway—in its original form, anyway—and Moss decided that, like *Jonica,* it was better off forgotten, unaware how useful it would be in his future.

Moss returned from the Hamptons to East Sixty-third Street. Beatrice Kaufman had sailed for Europe for the summer and Kaufman offered Moss their adopted daughter Anne's room to save travel time as they reworked the script. The move was no hardship. Ravenous hunger was. Moss was too embarrassed to mention that, apart from the fudge he couldn't stomach, Kaufman's monkish diet left him famished. Fortunately, he discovered an all-night drugstore around the corner on Lexington Avenue that got him through the summer on a surreptitious diet of jelly doughnuts, fig newtons, and chocolate malteds.

There were other hungers. Shortly before Beatrice sailed she had given a "tea," as cocktail parties were called during Prohibition, and invited Moss to attend. It was something like walking into the pages of Frank Crowninshield's *Vanity Fair.*

George Gershwin played the piano. Algonquinites Dorothy Parker and Robert Benchley chatted up other Algonquinites like Edna Ferber and Heywood Broun. Ethel Barrymore traded shoptalk with Helen Hayes and baseball scores with Harpo Marx. Alfred Lunt and Lynn Fontanne glittered all over Robert E. Sherwood and publisher Herbert Bayard Swope. Alexander Woollcott was, as always, acerbic, owl-faced, and sufficient unto himself.

Moss was intoxicated. His later account of the "tea" was probably a composite of occasions, but the cast of characters and their levels of achievement made an indelible impression. If he felt like an impostor or intruder, no one seemed to notice and Beatrice had, after all, invited him: he must belong. Or shortly would belong. This was what it was like, being inside the world of the New York lucky, mingling with the rich and witty, brushing elbows with the accomplished and famous, none of whom knew who he was except Kaufman, of course, and Beatrice, who moved among her guests with such poise, smoke rising from her cigarette in its paper holder to curl around her smoke-colored hair, all the while smiling and studying him.

With Beatrice in Europe, Kaufman took Moss with him on his daily visits to the Music Box to approve cast, scenic designs, costumes, advertising, publicity, and other chores. He let Moss tag along to gatherings of the "Thanatopsis Literary and Inside Straight Club," the poker-table offspring of the Algonquin Round Table. There he met the idols he had not already met through Beatrice, including publisher Ralph Pulitzer, *The New Yorker* editor Harold Ross, newspaper columnist Franklin P. Adams (F.P.A.), and Sam Harris's real estate partner, Irving Berlin.

He was invited to join Kaufman at the Long Island estate of Otto Kahn, and wrote Schary that the financier of the Metropolitan Opera was stingy with the food and drink. He spent the first of many weekends at Neshobe, Woollcott's island retreat in the middle of Lake Bomoseen in Vermont. He wrote Schary about the demanding standards of the Woollcott crowd and how exhausting it was to have to be perpetually charming and witty among them.

Moss would later call these "the days of terror," but he was exhilarated and energized by them. He also knew that whatever happened with *Once in a Lifetime,* he had a parachute. When Frieda Fishbein agreed in May to negotiate the new contract allowing for the Kaufman collaboration, she did more than get first billing and 60 percent of the royalty for her client. She persuaded Harris to finance Moss's future, as well. In return for exclusive rights to his work for the next five years, Harris agreed to provide a guaranteed income as an advance against future royalties. Moss would have a top producer and a theatrical "home" no matter what the fate of *Once in a Lifetime.*

Which was not the same as having a hit.

. . .

Sam Harris announced the opening of *Once in a Lifetime* at the Music Box for September 24 and booked the huge Lyric Theater in Philadelphia for a three-week run beginning September 1. A new and expensive set was built to open act three with a new scene Moss hoped would introduce freshness to the long stretch after the second intermission that had, so far, drained laughs from the evening.

Even Kaufman was guardedly optimistic. When the company moved to Philadelphia, he was visited by Brooks Atkinson, who worked for him on the *Times*. Atkinson suggested tactfully that, what with acting every night in a show and earning "corpulent sums of money" on Broadway, this might be the moment to retire from the paper. After thirteen years at the *Times*, Kaufman wrote a dignified letter and resigned, possibly a sign of his confidence in the play and his new collaborator.

Jean Dixon had agreed to play May after all, admitting that she had seen the play at a run-through before Atlantic City and regretted having turned it down. Grant Mills came in as a new Jerry, and Hugh O'Connell stayed on as George.

When the curtain went up in Philadelphia it was clear that softening May and getting Dixon to play her gave both warmth and snap to the role. There was something unpredictable about her now that made the audience more attentive. The first two acts played without a hitch. At the end of act two George was made supervisor of Glogauer Studios and made the wrong picture from the wrong script, having confused the wastebasket for the script file. He forgot to tell the electricians to turn on the lights and cracked Indian nuts as the cameras turned, every bite recorded by the microphones. He got fired and Glogauer made a mogul decree: "After this I make a ruling—every scenario we produce, somebody has got to read it!"

The new set for act three was an extravagant nightclub called the Pigeon Coop, with waitresses in feathers and booths shaped like eggs. The audience greeted the set with applause, sat back to learn of Hollywood's reaction to George's disaster, and stopped laughing except for intermittent titters. Act three wasn't working.

There was no canceling Broadway now. Tickets were being sold and the New York papers were printing excerpts from the Philadelphia reviews. "It is smart. It is snappy. It is witty," they wrote. Many referred to "Mr. Kaufman's play," ignoring Moss altogether as Fishbein had feared. Minutes got trimmed; scenes got tightened. The hour was late for miracles.

Moss walked through the Lyric Theater depressed, wondering if he would ever be this close again. Would the glamorous throng of achievers at Beatrice Kaufman's "tea" remember him only as an "almost was"? He wandered over to join Sam Harris, relaxing and feeling philosophical at a nearby speakeasy. Harris had been a fight promoter before becoming a producer and knew nothing was over until the final bell. He liked Moss and assumed he would see a lot of him in the future now that he had signed that five-year contract, but he had hoped for a cheerier send-off from Philadelphia. He sighed about what a "noisy play" this was. "It tires an audience out," he said.

It had tired out Moss, too, and maybe exhaustion clouded his mind, for there were two versions of what he did next. In one version Kaufman joined him, but wandering into a Philadelphia playground in the middle of the night to ride a children's carousel (or the swings, in another version) doesn't sound much like Kaufman. What it sounds like is a metaphor for going in circles. Whatever it was, it gave Moss time to ponder Sam Harris's remarks and a reviewer's comment in *Variety* about "too much of a good thing." He knew that Beatrice hated the new third act and, though he couldn't have said why, this mattered to him and helped him focus.

He was too tired to write another word or come up with another idea or dredge up another inspiration or go to Kaufman with it and persuade him to make another change; except that he had to, so he did.

The Music Box has been everybody's favorite New York theater since it opened in 1921. It is intimate and formal, but friendly. September 24, 1930, was the first big opening night of the first season since the Crash, which didn't slow the stream of taxis and limousines pulling up to the curb. The first-nighters descended in their dress clothes, all the celebrities, socialites, taste and opinion makers, and critics.

And Lester Sweyd and Frieda Fishbein and Archie Leach and Lillie and Barnett and Bernie, stuffed with dinner Joe Hyman had treated them to at Dinty Moore's.

Backstage Moss read his telegrams. There was one from Lester:

WELL DARLING HERES THE NIGHT WEVE BEEN WAITING FOR

And one from somebody with a taste for puns:

ONCE IN A LIFETIME IT MOSS BE HART TO TAKE

There was one from George Kelly, whose plays had been important to Moss in learning how to write comedy. THINKING OF YOU, it read. Even

David Belasco, who had turned down the play, sent good wishes, and the simplest of all read: BEST WISHES and was signed "Mama, Papa, and Bernard."

That was the message in all the cables, however it was phrased. For all the competition and jealousies of Broadway, no one wanted to see a bad show. Everyone wanted to be in on a hit, and the word on *Once in a Life-time* was more hopeful than not.

When the curtain rose at 8:45 Kaufman was again pacing the back of the house and Moss, when not in the men's room being sick, was with him. The laughter started early in act one, as George cracked his Indian nuts while reading *Variety* in the vaudevillians' boardinghouse in the West Forties. May delivered her new dialogue about the toughness of the road, the lousy theaters, and audiences too dopey to realize that the vaudeville they were laughing at was already dead. The audience in the Music Box knew that May had a case on Jerry before he made his spiffy entrance all charged up about *The Jazz Singer.* Why else would she have put up with the two-a-day for so long?

The laughter mounted in the Pullman car as Spring Byington appeared as Helen Hobart, dripping with diamonds and furs. Roars greeted the Stilton Hotel lobby as the Hollywood grotesques slouched preposterously with Russian wolfhounds on jeweled leashes.

Kaufman left at intermission to prepare for his entrance. Moss listened to lobby talk that was bright and merry; people were eager to get back inside. The New York audience knew in advance that Kaufman was playing a part and his Vail proved funnier and more indignantly sane than ever, as if Broadway itself were telling upstart Hollywood where to get off. The second act hurtled from gag to gag and lampoon to lampoon and the laughter never really stopped except when the authors wanted it to or for the catching of breath.

Then came the third act, that stretch of silence that had plagued the playwrights since Atlantic City. They had tried everything and nothing had been enough or it had all been too much. Moss's new solution might work or not. The first-nighters would laugh or they wouldn't.

His new act three opened not in the expensive Pigeon Coop set, that "too much of a good thing" that Sam Harris paid for and then junked without complaint. Instead it opened on the movie set during the shooting of the big wedding scene that had been Moss's original ending for the play. Glogauer discovers that George is making the wrong picture and fires him. Jerry squirms while making excuses, saving his own skin to May's disgust.

Now came the major change, which was neither noisy nor tiresome, but calm. The scene returned to the same Pullman car that brought them to Hollywood in act one, and the same porter is still at work with the same whisk broom. There is a sole occupant, sadder but wiser May, going back where she came from. The audience understood without a word of dialogue. She had given up on both Jerry and Hollywood. They rewarded May's pensive silence onstage with surprise and satisfaction. They relaxed and settled back to find out what had happened and what would happen now. They seemed to care about it, too.

May's train stops briefly at Needles Point, Arizona. There's a sanitarium there, the porter explains, just for playwrights. Once in a while they let one loose to go back to New York. May asks the porter to find the Los Angeles papers and, as she waits, is joined by a boarding passenger: Lawrence Vail, just recovered from a nervous breakdown brought on by underwork in Hollywood.

The papers arrive with reviews of *Gingham and Orchids,* George's wrong movie from the wrong script. May reads; Vail reads. Hollywood critics declare the fiasco a masterpiece. That dark atmospheric lighting! Those curious sound effects, so reminiscent of the tom-toms in *The Emperor Jones*! And that old-fashioned script—so dated it's new!

After a moment, Kaufman as Vail looked up from the reviews and delivered an improvised line he had warned Dixon to expect. "The whole thing couldn't be a typographical error, could it?" The house came down. They stopped laughing just long enough to cheer May's return to Hollywood in response to a telegram from George. He needs her more than ever now that he practically owns the place.

May and Jerry reunite and George has not been resting on his diamond-studded laurels. The studio is panicked all over again: he has just bought a fleet of two thousand airplanes because you get one free with every fleet. Before Glogauer can fire him again the switchboard lights up. Aviation pictures are the next big trend. All Hollywood wants planes and only Glogauer Studios has them.

And when the bulldozers start tearing down the studio to make room for the planes, Glogauer welcomes them. If George says tearing down studios is another trend, it must be so. The wrecking ball falls, and so does the curtain.

Everyone in the theater knows the clichés and knows they're true. Applause is love and money and sweeter than any music. It breaks like thunder and rolls like waves and embraces with warmth and crowns with light, as it did that night. It can go on and on and even the best-prepared, most hopeful cast runs out of prerehearsed curtain calls and can only stand there, engulfed by cheers. The least sentimental cannot but be affected by tumultuous applause, the theater's ultimate approval and validation.

Which is why Kaufman finally stepped forward and begged for silence. When it came he said, "I would like this audience to know that eighty percent of this play is Moss Hart."

Moss may have wondered, then, why he was only getting *60* percent of the royalty, but what he did was turn to his mother. Lillie had heard the applause and the cheers and Kaufman's curtain speech and surely she understood now what had animated her son for all these years, all that toil she had dismissed as "homework."

He told her to name anything in the world she wanted, and it would be hers. She thought it over and allowed the sky to be her limit. What she wanted, she said, was a charge account at Macy's.

Insíde

6

"And Who, Pray Tell, Is Moss Hart?"

A hit show . . . is a share in a child's dream, for a hit is the world crowding your doorstep; it is the telephone ringing without stop; it is love come crashing through the window and under the door and breaking through the walls. And another thing so lovely about it is so often this love comes in the form of money.

JED HARRIS

George Kaufman's curtain speech was gracious and necessary. Since Atlantic City and Brighton Beach, headlines had read KAUFMAN'S NEW PLAY or KAUFMAN'S WITTY SATIRE, as if Moss did not have first billing or any billing at all. Most observers automatically assumed that if something was funny it was Kaufman's. Even Broadway insiders were confused. Alexander Woollcott announced he was awarding a pocket watch to the author of Broadway's funniest line of the year and "I'll be in Number Three" was the winner. When Woollcott presented the watch, Kaufman demurred, admitting the line was Moss's. "He's *your* collaborator," Woollcott sniffed. "*You* deliver the watch."

Almost before the curtain fell on opening night a headline in the *New York Times* asked AND WHO, PRAY TELL, IS MOSS HART? To satisfy curiosity Moss replied that he was just turning twenty-four, and had studied geometry and French composition at Morris High School in the Bronx and creative writing at Columbia University. This was judged fit to print by the *Times,* and why not? Reviews of *Once in a Lifetime* had been so uniformly enthusiastic that he could have said almost anything and been believed.

Daily reviewers were as jubilant as Walter Winchell, who told his readers to "see it and die—laughing!" Weekly voices were equally enthusiastic. Heywood Broun, the rumpled "one-man slum" who kept the Algonquin Round Table from looking too soigné, called it "gorgeous fooling" in *The Nation*. *The New Yorker* thought it "much more than just a comedy," while *Time* found it positively "Swiftian."

Seventy years later, *Once in a Lifetime* seems not so much dated as familiar because it has been borrowed from so often it can seem unoriginal to those discovering it for the first time. The over-the-top burlesque of Hollywood is a genre to itself by now, and *Once in a Lifetime* fixed its style and tone. Freshness is hard to recapture in a work whose influence has been so long apparent: *Boy Meets Girl* in the thirties, *Singin' in the Rain* in the fifties, and *Bullets Over Broadway* in the nineties are all direct descendants of *Once in a Lifetime*, whether their borrowings are admitted or accidental.

What is even harder to recapture than freshness is that *Once in a Lifetime* was not just a hit, but the first great comedy success of a Depression whose shadow was growing long on Broadway. It is hard to think of it as a Depression play, but that's what its contemporary viewers saw.

Once in a Lifetime took a look at American business (movies were the fourth largest industry in the nation) and guffawed out loud. The funniest line may have been Vail's crack about "Number Three," but the most biting was his more general assessment that "the whole business is in the hands of incompetents." It was a sentiment that indicted more than Hollywood. The movies were such an obvious target they could stand for every industry or institution that was top-heavy with boardroom boobs. Ridiculing Hollywood offended no one but the deserving: movie moguls and their more staid, but no less foolish, corporate cousins from sea to shining sea.

Needling high-level incompetents gave the play relevance and bite that accounted for a mere comic burlesque's attracting support at Pulitzer Prize time. It lost to Susan Glaspell's *Alison's House*, inspired by the life of Emily Dickinson, but poet and scholar Mark Van Doren protested the choice, suspecting the Pulitzer judges had mistaken *Once in a Lifetime* as "merely funny." Brooks Atkinson took on the committee in the *Times*. "There has been no more brilliant criticism of the American scene this season [than from] Moss Hart and George S. Kaufman," he wrote. The American idiom had a bright new voice and no one knew better than Kaufman that it simultaneously crackled and skewered mostly because of the young man critic Burns Mantle recognized as "a lad with a future, I hope, even though he begins it handicapped by a smashing success."

Success looked nothing like a handicap. It looked like confetti made of money. A month after opening night Moss was, at twenty-six, awash in the stuff, even in a depressed season in which the number of Broadway openings fell by more than 20 percent, to 190 from 250 the year before. The 60 percent of the authors' royalty that Frieda Fishbein negotiated for him amounted to $2,000 a week at capacity, roughly comparable to ten times as much today, and more in a week than Moss had ever made in a year.

Few weeks fell short of capacity, in spite of competition like the Gershwins' *Girl Crazy* with Ginger Rogers and a brass calliope called Ethel Merman. For those in search of poetry there was *Elizabeth the Queen* with the Lunts in blank verse. Sophistication oozed from every pore of Noël Coward and Gertrude Lawrence in Coward's *Private Lives,* a virtual two-hander for stars whose dazzle left young Laurence Olivier little to do onstage but seem dazed by their brilliance and hope it was catching. Katharine Cornell was playing Elizabeth Barrett Browning in *The Barretts of Wimpole Street* and, like an actor-manager of old, was producing it herself.

Not all the season's competition was so memorable, but stars were everywhere evident. Ethel Barrymore, Fanny Brice, George M. Cohan, Al Jolson, Fred and Adele Astaire, Jack Benny, Jimmy Durante, W. C. Fields, Clifton Webb, Marilyn Miller, and Helen Hayes were all on brief or extended exhibit. So, on integrated Broadway, were Ethel Waters and Bill "Bojangles" Robinson.

Nipping at the established stars' heels was a whole new breed of talent mostly trained in drama schools or the same world of Little Theater that had provided opportunity for Moss. A bumper crop of newcomers made debuts or very early appearances in New York theater that season, and their names would soon enter the almanacs: Bette Davis, Jessica Tandy, Katharine Hepburn, Rosalind Russell, Fred MacMurray, Melvyn Douglas, Burgess Meredith, Margaret Sullavan, and Shirley Booth, not one of whom came close to the success of the most brilliantly successful debut artist of 1930–31, Moss Hart.

Moss moved Lillie, Barnett, and Bernie from Bensonhurst to Manhattan, putting them up at the Hotel Edison on West Forty-seventh Street, two blocks from the Music Box, which Bernie dubbed "the Money Box." Moss soon found a worthier address for the family at the Ansonia Hotel, the opulent Beaux Arts landmark at Seventy-third and Broadway that was home at various times to Babe Ruth, Arturo Toscanini, Al Jolson, Enrico Caruso, and even, briefly, Sarah Bernhardt. Moss took a nine-room tower apartment with multiple fireplaces and a semicircular turret window that displayed the city below like an electric map in which all roads led to Times Square. It also had walls a yard thick to shield him from the trills of neighbor Lily Pons, just down the hall. He hated opera.

He began a lifelong habit of burnishing the bank accounts of New York interior decorators. His taste in furnishings, like his taste in clothes, was his own. His Ansonia phase was partial to gilt, red velvet, and heavily carved furniture of more-or-less Spanish derivation. His bedroom featured a black satin divan on a raised dais in the middle of the room surrounded by black walls and floors. Here and there were strategically placed eruptions of massed ostrich plumes or indoor rock gardens, and everywhere there were curtains: net under chiffon under satin under heavy black velvet, a cocoon to mitigate insomnia and insure privacy. "I never had any curtains when I was poor," he announced gaily, "so I thought I'd like to have plenty."

He spent to make up for his youth and then some. His spending was extravagant-to-profligate and went beyond his family. His habit of handing out too-expensive gifts for no reason at all caused recipients who knew about money and had plenty of their own to wonder if he really had that much. He did, but never for very long. He was spending his way out of the Bronx and Brooklyn and acting out a lifelong conviction that reckless generosity was one of the nicer perquisites of wealth.

The clotheshorse bred in the garment district moved uptown, too, showier than ever. He indulged a craving for English swank as epitomized by Noël Coward and Archie Leach, still knocking elegantly around Broadway. Moss was much given, an acquaintance recalled, to handmade shirts that were "much too stripe-y, showing a yard of cuff with monograms the size of billboards." He accessorized his raiment at Cartier's. He accumulated twenty-four-karat gold cuff links, garters, money clips, lighters, and buckles until he glittered like Fort Knox. He boasted about a solid gold cigarette case whose shape was molded exactly to the curve of his silk-clad bottom to perfect the line of the tailor-made garments draped over it.

His delight in conspicuous consumption was contagious. He was proof that the loom of the American dream still wove riches from rags, even as Wall Street kept a running score of its defenestrating brokers. It was suggested that Herbert Hoover needed nothing around the corner so much as young Moss. Prosperity would be sure to follow.

Many of Moss's contemporaries were wakened to social conditions they had never considered before but that Moss had known from birth and was happy now to ignore. The Group Theatre was just breaking off from its Theatre Guild parent and staging plays animated by social and political concerns far removed from the more trivial amusements that had driven the theater of the twenties.

Group Theatre firebrands like Harold Clurman, Lee Strasberg, John Garfield, and (soon) Elia Kazan were frankly political and strident in their search for new ideals, mostly radical. Some would pay heavily for their attraction to the organized left, but they were directing their views of the American theater past the proscenium and the box office to an audience bewildered by economic collapse and what seemed like a helpless or un-caring State.

Moss had long since internalized hard times as a private humiliation, and his success signaled how well the American dream worked, not how corrupt or flawed it was. He viewed himself as a connoisseur of hard knocks and was more than ready to move on. He struck it rich at exactly the right—or wrong—moment. He was perfectly poised to join the mer-itocracy of swank that came with Broadway success; he'd been rehearsing it for years and wasn't about to turn privilege away now. Still, he was a writer, a would-be satirist with something to say in danger of settling for wisecracks. In a period of intense social adjustment he would write dis-mayingly little that expressed any political viewpoint more profound or nuanced than Tin Pan Alley or Hallmark. If this troubled him, he gave no sign. He felt no need to justify anything to those who discovered the dark brown reality of the underclass just as he, at last, was leaving it. He'd been there; he'd paid those dues.

Where he hadn't been, ironically, was Hollywood, a situation about to be corrected. Legendary showman Sid Grauman had contracted to present the West Coast company of *Once in a Lifetime*. Moss would co-direct it there with Robert Sinclair, stage manager of the New York pro-duction, and would play Lawrence Vail in California before taking over for Kaufman on Broadway.

When Moss boarded the Twentieth Century Limited to the west in December 1930, it was with a fretful and defensive glance over his shoul-der at Newark. Burns Mantle's barb about success nagged at him as he wondered if the slight queasiness he was feeling was what he called "suc-cess poisoning" when it happened to others.

Dore Schary had fallen silent for some unknown reason since *Once in a Lifetime*'s opening. Now that the initial din of celebration had dulled, Moss noticed the silence and it bothered him. He wrote "Butch" from the Twentieth Century Limited and protested that he had not, as some seemed to think, forgotten his "money-grubbing" past or been changed by success. Being rich and famous was no reason for friends who were not rich and famous to deny him sympathy, he said, confessing to feeling depressed and having lost all "capacity for enjoyment." Nothing meant anything anymore. Except—he allowed—his luxurious parlor car with its bedroom and real bed, which he couldn't resist describing in detail. If anyone thought he had gone high-hat—well, maybe they never understood him to begin with.

Certainly Frieda Fishbein had not.

True, she had sold *No Retreat* to Jed Harris and then to Bela Blau, and *Once in a Lifetime* to Sam Harris. She had gotten Moss the jobs on *Jonica* and writing for Billy Rose and Fanny Brice. And she had made *Once in a Lifetime* the cornerstone of that five-year exclusive contract with Sam Harris, providing funds advanced on plays not yet written or even conceived. Moss accepted all that, but what he couldn't accept was that Fishbein should receive commission or compensation for it.

Fishbein saw her lawyer who saw a judge who saw things her way and she received an out-of-court settlement and short shrift forever after. "The moment you became a success," she wrote him, much more in anger than in sorrow, "you threw over those who helped you."

It was to deny such charges that he took such care in writing Schary as he traveled to the West Coast. He had been out of touch, perhaps, but had not forgotten where he came from. How could he? Why even Lester Sweyd remained loyal and adoring. It would take decades for Lester to realize that he, like Fishbein, had been left behind and spurned. Fury and outrage then would reach a boil, but that day was still distant.

Sid Grauman, a household name because of his Chinese and Egyptian Theaters in Hollywood, had turned his picture palaces over to his creditors and rented the Mayan Theater in downtown Los Angeles for what he announced was his return to the legitimate theater. His previous legitimacy was limited to a storefront nickelodeon with vaudeville-on-the-side back in San Francisco just after the earthquake and Great Fire of 1906, an experience that had taught him plenty about spectacle.

Hollywood had carefully charted the content and coffers of *Once in a Lifetime*. A rumor had circulated before the New York opening that the brothers Warner were feeling litigious about Moss's Schlepkin brothers, but someone pointed out that not even twelve Schlepkins could equal five Warners, and the lawsuit blew over.

Rumor had it that Douglas Fairbanks, Sr., and film producer Joseph Schenck had an interest in *Once in a Lifetime* and it may have been true. The two were partners in United Artists and Schenck, a childhood friend of Irving Berlin, was a silent partner with Berlin and Sam Harris in the

Music Box. The Fairbanks-Schenck rumor suggested to an alarmed Hollywood that United Artists might have the courage or gall to produce *Once in a Lifetime* as a movie attacking the industry. They didn't, but they shrewdly incited courage and gall in others.

Most of the big moguls had seen the play in New York but none had bid on the movie rights. The Hollywood press was more sensitive than usual to the gags of *Once in a Lifetime* and wrote about them in their columns as if describing poison gas attacks. Gossip columnist Louella Parsons (correctly) recognized herself as the model for Helen Hobart and managed to be insulted and flattered at the same time. To impress Lotus Land with the gravity of the situation, Grauman announced that Moss's train would be met at Union Station by bodyguards and a bulletproof car.

When the train arrived, Moss shared his first impressions before his foot hit the platform. *Once in a Lifetime* was "if anything, a slight understatement. Hollywood, in its own naïve way," he announced, "is a kind of opera bouffe *Cabinet of Dr. Caligari*." Reporters did double takes, but they scribbled. Grauman beamed.

Such remarks piqued interest in the play and the playwright. He went on after unpacking to analyze what he saw as "a sense of decay about present-day Hollywood," everything "outlined in neon lights but Sam Goldwyn." He told the locals that "the entire place is pervaded by a sneering provincialism that is alarming and more than a little bewildering to the uninitiated; and of glamour there is none." *That,* however, could be corrected, and there was a way for the cinema to pull itself out of its neon-lit swamp: movies must, he said, "attract the finest dramatists of the day to write for them." No one had to ask which dramatists he had in mind.

Offended to the quick, the moguls leaped to offer him jobs. He turned down Paramount's offer to write a talkie based on Kaufman and Connelly's *Merton of the Movies,* which had been filmed as a silent in 1924. He was chauffeured from studio to studio and hinted to the press that he would be signing an exclusive contract with some unnamed company. Even Parsons figured out which one as Moss showered unsolicited praise on no Hollywood executive but MGM's Irving Thalberg, whose penchant for remaining anonymous in the credits resulted in his being credited for everything. Moss admired Thalberg above all others in Hollywood and compared him in his ability to incite creativity to—of all people—Jed Harris.

He moved into a rented house at 709 South Mariposa in Hollywood and the whirl continued at luncheons, "teas," and dinners with every famous name and face, interrupted only when he and Bob Sinclair began casting and rehearsing. It was Moss's first time directing professional actors and Sinclair, stage manager of the show on Broadway, was a link to Kaufman's production. An even earlier link was Aline MacMahon, Moss's original choice for May, who had played the part in Atlantic City and Brighton Beach. She would play it now on the West Coast and make it permanently hers in the Universal movie version in 1932, opposite Jack Oakie as George.

After a successful tryout in Santa Barbara, *Once in a Lifetime* opened at the Mayan Theater on January 27. Grauman had not stinted. He made sure reviewers were augmented by fashion reporters to write about Gloria Swanson in chinchilla, Norma Shearer in sable, and Joan Crawford in ermine. They—and Constance Bennett, Lilyan Tashman, Jean Harlow, Laura La Plante, and the wives of Cecil B. DeMille, Michael Curtiz, and Jack Warner—were all outdone, the press reported, by Mrs. B. P. Schulberg of Paramount Pictures, who arrived in both ermine *and* sable.

The only thing Grauman failed to provide for the opening was Moss Hart. "Influenza," the papers said. "Under a nurse's care," they continued. Sinclair went on for him and Moss remained incommunicado until Valentine's Day, when he braved a matinee audience before his much delayed debut that evening.

Too much had happened too fast. The warning signs were present in the prickly and defensive letters he wrote Schary from the train with the hint about being depressed. Then came the bodyguards and bulletproof cars; the too outspoken interviews; the luncheons and dinners and "teas"; the strain of being bright and witty when introduced to Charlie Chaplin, John Barrymore, and Mary Astor; the hectic pace of keeping up with the Marxes and their brethren; the reunions with old faces like Leonard Sillman, who gave intimate parties that somehow turned vast and for which Moss was both guest of honor and floor show, always "on," burning bright, burning out. He had had a small but unmistakable nervous breakdown.

Schary had not answered Moss's letters. When his illness made national newspapers, Schary broke the silence with a get-well cable. Moss wrote back with relief, saying he felt "weak and wasted." He suspected he had caught some kind of bug from spending too much time in steam rooms with Fairbanks Senior and Fairbanks Junior. He may well have been laid low by microbes, he said, but allowed that "success poisoning" was going around.

He convalesced in Palm Springs, then as now a discreet place to recover from anything. The El Mirador Hotel was an oasis that satisfied his needs for privacy and style. His "siege," as he called it when writing Schary, was overseen by a team of starched-white jailers, including a genuine M.D., consulting specialists, and nurses around the clock. The opulence of the El Mirador did not go unremarked ("horribly expensive—but a fairyland"), hinting at a premium blend of self-indulgence and self-pity.

From his sickbed he filled seven pages with details of his social life with Chaplin, Barrymore, and others, the strain of which had led him to the isolation he now endured beneath palms that also sheltered—he added not very wanly—Ramon Novarro, Loretta Young, Jeannette MacDonald, and George Gershwin.

Self-dramatizing is always a possibility with a playwright, but Moss was confiding in Schary, not playing to the press when he confessed to "fearful depression." His mood sounded not very different from the despair he had suffered a few years earlier in Vermont and had hidden behind the mask of the social director. The mask now was very public and all but fixed. For all his protestations, however, success had changed him in ways he liked and wanted to make permanent. He had discovered a public persona and lifestyle that delighted him, one he would cultivate at considerable expense, not all of it monetary, for the rest of his life.

Success meant living in a spotlight for a young man who had, even in his days with Gus Pitou, concealed much about himself, from his family background to the details of his emotional life. People wanted to know who he was and why. No matter what he claimed, he was overwhelmed by his success and needed to deny it meant anything to friends like Schary, but it meant and changed everything. He had solved the surface aspects of becoming somebody else, somebody who was no longer in the Bronx or a subway car, always traveling and never arriving. The problem was a bit like the one May faced when she and Jerry and George got to Hollywood. We've arrived. Now what?

7

Facing the Music

I write plays . . . only plays.

MOSS HART

Moss played Lawrence Vail in Los Angeles, San Francisco, and then on Broadway without erasing memories of Barrymore or even George S. Kaufman. Jean Dixon, still sharp and funny as May in New York, thought his performance "poor." Eddie Chodorov had wryly crowned him "the complete ham" early in their Little Theater days and others, later, remembered a manner so theatrical it could seem "swishy." Sensitive to the danger of sounding affected since boyhood, he sometimes went to the other extreme, "pitching his voice in a monotone that made him sound," to *The New Yorker* at least, "like some kind of Chinese actor."

Acting and indulging his new celebrity in California had prevented much writing, even though Sam Harris was asking for something to justify the five-year deal he had made. Moss dug into the archives at the Huntington Hartford Library in Pasadena to oblige, researching an idea he called "Twentieth Century Limited"—about the era, not the train. He hinted it might deal with a family called Rockefeller.

In late April he sailed to New York from San Francisco via the Panama Canal. He reported that he spent the entire voyage turning his Pasadena research into an ambitious multigenerational play titled *Wind Up an Era* that, in the end, had nothing to do with the Rockefellers, though he would come back to them, and soon. The play chronicled instead a typical American family from the turn of the century to the Crash, an idea Harris greeted with enthusiasm.

When nothing came of *Wind Up an Era,* Moss said his plans had been dashed the moment he disembarked in New York after his Panama Canal journey and read in that morning's *Times* about Noël Coward's *Cavalcade,* which did for an English family what Moss wanted to do with Mr. and Mrs. Smith or Jones.

He probably did have an American chronicle play in mind and *Wind Up an Era* was as good a title as any, but if he ever started it, his abandoning it had nothing to do with *Cavalcade*. Coward hadn't even begun *Cavalcade* when Moss returned from California. The English star-playwright-composer-director was still selling out on Broadway in *Private Lives* and taking pains to keep the *Cavalcade* idea under wraps, knowing how easily it might be pilfered. In May he cabled his London producer, C. B. Cochran, just before beginning to write:

PLEASE TAKE CARE THAT NO DETAIL OF THIS SHOULD REACH
PRIVATE OR PARTICULARLY PRESS EARS

Moss's California breakdown and acting chores had, in truth, prevented his coming up with anything more than ideas. No one ever saw a word of *Wind Up an Era,* but he could claim that his sorrow at abandoning it made turning to anything else a "sheer impossibility." He was an established playwright with nothing to write and no mentor to coax him along. He and Kaufman had discussed working together again and had flirted with an idea for the Marx Brothers, but nothing came of it. Even before *Once in a Lifetime* opened, Kaufman was collaborating with Morrie Ryskind on a musical for the Gershwins to follow *Strike Up the Band.* They worked steadily on what they called *Tweedledee* when Kaufman wasn't onstage as Vail. By the time the Gershwins returned to New York from Hollywood, where they'd written songs for a Janet Gaynor musical movie called *Delicious,* Kaufman and Ryskind had completed a libretto. *Tweedledee* was becoming *Of Thee I Sing.*

At the same time, Kaufman was writing sketches for *The Band Wagon* with Howard Dietz, MGM's head of advertising and publicity who was better known as the lyricist partner of composer Arthur Schwartz. *The Band Wagon,* a revue to be produced by Max Gordon, would have songs by Schwartz and Dietz and be the last outing of Fred and Adele Astaire as a brother-sister act (she would get married and retire; he would drift west). Also in the cast were deadpan comedienne Helen Broderick and future Wizard of Oz Frank Morgan, who summed up the show's nonchalant attitude toward the Depression: "In a few years from now these are going to be known as the good old days. What is called down in the dumps today will be known as up in the dumps."

Moss may have been relieved that Kaufman was so busy. He confided to Jean Dixon his fears of becoming dependent on Kaufman or being known as just another collaborator. But apart from his contract to write for MGM—"But not on the lot," he assured the New York press; "I am permitted to do my writing in New York, and do it without the bane of studio conferences"—he had no new projects. He took over as Vail on May 4 while Kaufman turned his attentions to *The Band Wagon* and *Of Thee I Sing*.

Sam Harris was not a man to allow a contract or a talent to lie fallow for long. It was time to tighten belts, amortize investments, and forge ahead with his top priority: getting Irving Berlin back to Broadway. Harris had been pursuing this goal at least since suggesting that *Once in a Lifetime* become a musical. That had not worked, but something on the order of a *Music Box Revue of 1931*, say, would wrap Harris's interests neatly together: the Music Box Theatre, Irving Berlin, and his bright young playwright.

The triple-play sounds inevitable now but didn't then. Moss, in spite of his earlier disdain and lordly "I write plays" speech, wasn't the problem. It was Berlin, who was in a major career slump. He had suffered huge losses in the Crash, but they mattered little compared to his fear that he'd "gone dry," as his daughter Mary Ellin Barrett later wrote, his certainty that he was at "rock bottom."

That was where everything else on Broadway seemed to be. The Shuberts were in bankruptcy; Ziegfeld had been forced to accept backing from mobster Dutch Schultz for his last original show, *Hot-Cha!,* starring Bert Lahr and Lupe Velez (Schultz tastefully subtitled it "Laid in Mexico"); revered producer Charles Dillingham (who built what is today the Lunt-Fontanne Theatre) had been caught rifling the till to make ends meet; and Berlin, master songwriter of the teens and twenties, now sounded old-hat and passé to the crowds singing smart new songs by the Gershwins, Rodgers and Hart, and Cole Porter.

Berlin had not had a Broadway song hit since "Shakin' the Blues Away" in the *Ziegfeld Follies of 1927*. His having gone to Hollywood for *Puttin' on the Ritz* was symptomatic of his lack of direction, made worse by his experience on the soundstages that had seemed chaotic and resulted in what he called a "fiasco." His "dry spell" showed no sign of breaking and no one was less confident of his ability to break it than he was.

Harris had survived a difficult partnership with George M. Cohan and was not discouraged by Berlin's self-doubt. He reintroduced Moss and Berlin, who had met briefly through Kaufman at the "Thanatopsis" poker sessions. Berlin at forty-three was Kaufman's age (only a year older), but shared with Moss things that Kaufman didn't, like the New York Jewish-immigrant experience. Both had worked up and out of nothing; both were insomniacs given to depressions we would today recognize as clinical; and both needed a show.

Over lunch at Sardi's, Berlin glumly told Moss he was not interested in writing another *Music Box Revue,* though his earlier editions, for which the Music Box Theatre had been built, had all been huge hits. They were yesterday, just where so many observers already consigned him. Moss threw out some ideas. His ability to improvise was second nature after years of summer camp shows and he could spin ideas from anything—newspapers, magazines, maybe even menus. Berlin agreed that one or two had possibilities, but his mood was as gloomy as the economy. What he really wanted was a play, a book musical.

The opening of *The Band Wagon* at the New Amsterdam on June 3 did nothing to bolster Berlin's confidence that he could write for the new decade. *The Band Wagon* boasted songs with double-edged, timely titles like "Dancing in the Dark," and sophisticated showstoppers like "I Love Louisa," a Bavarian merry-go-round number staged on turntables by the gifted designer and director Hassard Short. Berlin and Short had worked together on the *Music Box Revues* but never achieved the praise inspired by *The Band Wagon.* Hardly anything ever had. Brooks Atkinson in the *Times* found it "brilliantly written . . . brilliantly staged . . . brilliantly acted . . . brilliantly scored" and added, as if salting Berlin's wounds, "it will be difficult for the old-time musical show to hold up its head."

Harris didn't seem to notice. He was a horseplayer and seconded Berlin's preference for a book musical. Harris had already scheduled *Of Thee I Sing* for the Music Box, thinking it "certainly different," but not at all sure that its musical mockery of American politics would keep the theater full for very long. What kind of song was "Wintergreen for President," anyway?

Moss and Berlin began working in June at the composer's apartment in the Warwick Hotel in Manhattan, but summer heat inspired a move to the Berlin estate at Sands Point, Long Island. There Berlin sat at the famous transposing piano he called "the Buick," built to compensate for his inability to play on any but the black keys of F-sharp. Then, "haunted by fear of failure," he made one false start after another.

To Moss's dismay Berlin liked to work from midnight to nine in the morning. Those were hours Moss usually spent tossing and turning anyway, but trying to sleep during the day, when Berlin drifted off like a baby, was impossible. When the composer was awake and working he was so anxious and jittery that Moss felt, in comparison, like "Buddha incarnate."

To imagine Berlin struggling at a low point in his career is difficult today. He seems in retrospect to have made an unbroken musical journey from Ellis Island to Tin Pan Alley to Broadway and Hollywood, with occasional pauses to dash off the odd anthem or pop hymn (still in the future in 1931) like "God Bless America," "White Christmas," "Easter Parade," or his hallelujah chorus for the business like no business he knew. He was a genius who, as Jerome Kern once remarked, *is* American music.

Berlin's greatest period lay ahead, not behind, but he didn't know that and neither did Harris. The irony was that Harris was relying on an insecure newcomer to rescue a seasoned veteran. It was obvious to Moss that he needed to do more than spin summer camp ideas if Berlin's repeated false starts were to bear fruit. More crucially, he needed to come up with something to confirm that he was not a one-shot wonder, but a dramatist of today who had a tomorrow.

He took a breather from Berlin that may have cleared his head. He and Max Siegel visited Lillie, Barnett, and Bernie at Camp Copake, where he had not had to serve as social director thanks to *Once in a Lifetime.* The Hart cabin at Copake was next to the one occupied by the Bernstein family, whose teenage son Walter was friendly with Bernie. Walter wanted to be a writer, and would later become one with a letter of introduction from Moss to Harold Ross at *The New Yorker.* All Moss could give now was an encouraging pat on the back, but being generous to a bright young newcomer seemed to restore him, like a bracing reminder of where and what he'd come from. He left Camp Copake, batteries recharged, and went back to Long Island and Irving Berlin.

Things suddenly fell into place. He had an idea or Berlin did or they had one simultaneously. What matters is that ink began to flow from Moss's pen and by August Berlin's fingers were racing over the keys (the black ones) with the old confidence. They called their show, with a merry touch of irony, *Face the Music.*

The new partners energized each other, Berlin as mentor, Moss more than willing to play the acolyte. They plunged into the vein of the vernacular that was a feature of the best work of both and came up with gold. *Face the Music* took place in the topical here and now, "naming names without mercy," as Brooks Atkinson would note in the *Times,* and as Mayor Jimmy Walker would note with chagrin as he squirmed in his aisle seat on opening night.

As *Once in a Lifetime* had targeted Hollywood, *Face the Music* took on New York City, full of broke millionaires, tapped-out Broadway impresarios, and crooked police. It took on Broadway itself, and—most daringly—the Seabury Commission, the then-ongoing investigation into New York City corruption that would result in Walker's resignation from office a year later. Moss's book was better structured than his original draft of *Once in a Lifetime* and was often just as funny and wickedly on target. Apart from romantic numbers like "Soft Lights and Sweet Music" and "On a Rooftop in Manhattan" for the obligatory young lovers, Berlin's score was equally sharp and strong.

Face the Music opens at the Automat, where high society meets to sing "Let's Have Another Cup o' Coffee" now that hard times have forced cancellation of tables at the Ritz. A threadbare Broadway producer (a near-ringer for Ziegfeld; he even has a secretary named Goldie) tries to raise money on the sidewalk in front of the Palace Theatre, where the marquee promises Ethel Barrymore, Al Jolson, the Marx Brothers, Rex the Wonder Horse, and Professor Albert Einstein, all for a dime—with free sandwiches thrown in at intermission. Nobody has any money but New York's Finest, living like lords in the then-new (and unrentable) Empire State Building, where they stash their graft in "little tin boxes."

Unifying all this with bawdy malapropisms is the wife of the chief of police, Mrs. Martin Van Buren Meshbesher, who is, she announces, "just lousy with money!" Played with saucy brio by grande dame Mary Boland, Mrs. Meshbesher is gorgeously vulgar, flashing with jewels ("on a clear day, you can see me from Yonkers!"). She gives away used diamonds as tips, sends lavish bouquets of "Pomeranians," has a revolving account with Rolls-Royce, and a weakness for show folk. "They're so loose!"

It is Mrs. Meshbesher's inspiration that prevents Judge Seabury's spoilsports from seizing the loot. She insists that her husband the police chief (Hugh O'Connell, the indomitably dim George of *Once in a Lifetime*) should lose it all in the Ziegfeld-like producer's extravaganza *Rhinestones of 1932,* in which she consents to appear in the big production number, "My Beautiful Rhinestone Girl." The number is set in Venice, "the biggest city in France," where everything is covered with rhinestones, from Mrs. Meshbesher to the gondolas to the Doges' Palace to the pigeons, who fly in, rhinestone wings flapping, with a rhinestone-encrusted wedding bell they drop on Mrs. Meshbesher, eclipsing her magnificence from view.

Rhinestones of 1932 is the money drain its impresario had promised, but a reversal in city finances means it must be saved in the only surefire way anyone can think of: making it dirty. Off come the crinolines in the nostalgic Dixie number, which is now performed by chorus girls who carry parasols and wear bonnets (that's *all* they wear) with chorus boys in nothing but top hats and canes. The upstage bows offer more "moons" to the audience than the Planetarium. Even Mae West walks out.

The show is padlocked by a judge who notes, "I've seen dirty in my time, but never anything like this!" Mrs. Meshbesher seeks reassurance: "You're not just being kind?"

The plot climaxes in a hearing in Judge Seabury's courtroom, where testimony is lively, thanks to the showgirls and Mrs. Meshbesher, making her entrance in pink chiffon and towering feathered headdress, riding on the back of an elephant.

It had been common gossip around Broadway that *Face the Music* was in so much trouble during the summer that it might never open. When it did, on February 17, 1932, it was a triumph. In addition to "Let's Have Another Cup o' Coffee" and "Soft Lights and Sweet Music," Berlin's score included "I Say It's Spinach (and I Say the Hell With It!)" and was judged "just about the best he's ever done."

Reviewers found Moss's work "hilarious," "sharp and deadly," "rich and racy," and "comparable to the rich buffoonery of his *Once in a Life-time*." Berlin's five-year-old daughter Mary Ellin liked it, too, but then she thought the elephant was real; so did Brooks Atkinson, though he felt obliged to tell readers of the *Times* how well the beast had been "trained to look like papier-mâché." What Sam Harris kept to himself was that it was an old *Follies* prop he bought at a Ziegfeld fire sale for the bargain price of $600.

There were larger ironies afflicting Harris. *Face the Music* had been meant as a Music Box show, but Harris's other musical of the season, the "certainly different" one that looked so dicey, had become a phenomenal success there. *Of Thee I Sing* opened the day after Christmas and was so firmly ensconced that it would set a new house record, bettering Berlin's own record of 440 performances for his *Music Box Revue of 1921* by playing for 441.

Of Thee I Sing's long run meant that *Face the Music* had to play the New Amsterdam, the show palace that formerly housed Ziegfeld and his *Follies* (and Gus Pitou and young Moss). The New Amsterdam was a bigger house requiring bigger effects than the Music Box and the physical production grew accordingly, especially in the lavish parody sets for *Rhinestones of 1932*.

Kaufman had agreed to direct the book scenes in *Face the Music,* but the major staging chores were left to the stylish Hassard Short, who seemed not to know there was a Depression on. He had mounted *The Band Wagon* on the same stage and was delighted to be able to reuse the revolving turntables he had installed for "I Love Louisa." The effects would be stunning, but the size and spectacle demanded by the New Amsterdam (and Short) shot the budget of *Face the Music* to a then astronomical $165,000.

Viewers didn't complain. The opulently garish Venetian number, meant to tweak not only Ziegfeld but Berlin's own *Music Box Revues,* regularly drew gasps of admiration from audiences who thought it the prettiest thing they'd ever seen. Or, if it wasn't, Short offered up "Soft Lights and Sweet Music" as a mirror number. Forty dancers swirled under chandeliers whose sizes diminished in forced perspective. Some couples danced before and some behind layered translucent scrims under ever-smaller chandeliers that produced a swooningly romantic optical illusion of endlessly receding mirrors. The program noted that the effect was "patented and protected" by Short, a legal warning that wasn't romantic and wasn't meant to be.

The satire of Moss's book occasionally bumped into the optimistic cheer of Berlin's song style, just as Kaufman's quick-paced direction of the comedy was at odds with Short's sweeping musical numbers. The show never achieved the unity that made *Of Thee I Sing* so seamless. The use of turntables and the preposterous circus of the courtroom scene were effects Moss (and Short) would reprise to stunning effect in *Lady in the Dark* a few years later, but here they seemed to discerning observers merely showy, can-you-top-this ways to bring down the curtain.

The inevitable irony was that *Face the Music* would forever suffer comparison to *Of Thee I Sing,* not just because both were political satires, but because the Gershwin show became the first musical to win a Pulitzer Prize, for the book by Kaufman and Ryskind and the lyrics by Ira Gershwin. George Gershwin's brilliant score went unrecognized under Pulitzer rules that had never contemplated a musical winner as Best Play. Some thought, not entirely in jest, that the Pulitzer Prize should have gone to Sam Harris for having dared to produce both shows.

Critics predicted *Face the Music* would run forever, and it might have, had it not been for Mary Boland, making a brilliant musical comedy debut after years of work that had failed to make her a true star. Short had first cast her in comedy in the mid-twenties, and in *Face the Music* she gave what John Mason Brown called "the performance of performances." No one dreamed she would leave her moment of triumph at the end of her standard six-month contract to go to Hollywood, but she did. On a clear day you could see her at Paramount.

Boland was so irreplaceable that Harris didn't even try. He closed the show after only 165 performances. When Boland was again free in the fall he sent *Face the Music* on the road and in January 1933 brought it back to Broadway, slightly updated to take note of the building of Radio City. But the freshness was gone; Mayor Jimmy Walker was gone; the fun was gone. An almost brilliant show sabotaged by a star's whim died in revival after only thirty-two performances. Harris lost $65,000, but Berlin was back on top and right there with him was Moss.

Moss took himself to Europe. *Once in a Lifetime* was opening in London in 1933 and he wanted to visit the land of the Solomons and Bentwiches. He traveled with Short and Short's companion, Billy Ladd, a former chorus boy who had startlingly bleached hair and spent his time making amateur movies. Short, who was always called Bobby, was English (his real name was Hubert Hassard-Short). A onetime actor, he had turned to directing after being cast as an effeminate homosexual opposite Lynn Fontanne in Kaufman's first Broadway play, *Someone in the House.* He made his greatest mark as a stager of musical revues, for which he also designed lighting and, often, sets and costumes, as for the *Music Box Revues.* Vastly innovative and influential in the theater, he kept a low profile out of it, perhaps because of his relationship with Ladd, though Mrs. Irving Berlin noted wryly that the Short/Ladd liaison was "the happiest marriage of the group," before adding, "my own excepted, of course."

Between *The Band Wagon* and *Face the Music,* Short had staged in London a show that originated in Vienna as a small curiosity with music by the Johann Strausses, father and son. He anglicized it and turned it into something more elaborate called *Waltzes From Vienna.* English lyricist Desmond Carter, who had written lyrics for George Gershwin, wrote words for the Strausses, their music adapted by a musical prodigy from Vienna named Erich Wolfgang Korngold. Short wanted Moss to see the show in London and assess its possibilities for America, though nothing on Moss's résumé suggested any expertise in the world of the Viennese waltz. He thought the show just operetta "folderol," and moved on to the Continent.

He went armed with letters of introduction. One of them, from dancer Georgie Hale, who choreographed *Of Thee I Sing,* led him to the Ritz Bar in Paris and to Cole Porter. Moss passed on the belated Christmas gift Hale had entrusted him to deliver: garters with initialed gold clasps from Cartier's. Porter lifted his pant leg and blithely removed the old ones, tossing them to the Ritz bartender as if imitating Mrs.

Meshbesher's solution to the problem of used diamonds. Porter invited Moss to dine the following evening at home in the rue Monsieur, where his wife Linda held regal court in the reflective shimmer of platinum-leaf wallpaper and walked on zebra rugs.

Moss was dazzled by Linda, though he may have found her intimidating. He later described her with a hint of the sexual ambiguity that drifted around both the Porters as a woman "as easily beguiled by a chorus girl as by a duchess and equally at home with both."

The marriage of Cole and the former Linda Thomas was as outwardly happy as that of Short and Ladd, and no less unconventional. Both Porters had money, and indulged themselves and their intimates on a luxurious scale with parties someone called "terrible in their grandeur." Both were tireless sightseers, as comfortable in Berlin, Biarritz, and Monte Carlo as in Venice and Paris, where they had celebrated houses.

Linda was socially prominent (she boasted a signer of the Declaration of Independence in her family tree), but her money had come in a divorce settlement from her first husband, publisher Edward Thomas, a sportsman whose rough-stuff athletics included, it was rumored, the sexual. If not herself lesbian (opinions differed) Linda seemed to have had enough of the physical side of marriage by 1918. It was then she met Porter, eight years younger than she and the very model of sophisticated urbanity. Linda was content to marry a man uninterested in her sexually in return for civilized, witty companionship. Unlike some Broadway and Hollywood marriages of convenience, theirs was not merely show or camouflage, but was grounded in respect and some unorthodox but authentic bond of affection best understood by themselves. Still, there were tensions, and when they erupted, as they would with Moss as a flash point, they could be painful.

What Moss knew about their unconventional life was what everyone knew, but "In those days people didn't talk about it," as a friend of Porter's, the singer and actress Benay Venuta, admitted. The code of the day, according to Steven Watson, a knowledgeable commentator on the arts of the 1930s, was not so much "Don't ask, don't tell" as it was "Do more, say less."

The Porters intrigued Moss. He had no known experience with women and his views of marriage had been conditioned by the drab one he had grown up with and the highly sophisticated and open Kaufman union, as unorthodox in its way as the Porters'. For his part Moss let it be known he simply was not in the marriage market. "At seven," he told a reporter, alluding to the song in *Face the Music,* "I swore off spinach. The only other wise thing I have done is to forswear marriage."

Still, he was drawn to Linda and Beatrice Kaufman as more than mother figures. They were sophisticated, independent women who accepted him mostly as the attractive, witty, and charming young man he worked at being. Both were unthreatening because unavailable, and neither thought of him as a once-sickly burden in the Bronx doing "homework." Linda was icily dazzling, but she didn't smother or restrict Cole any more than Beatrice did George. Both enriched the lives of their husbands, nurturing them professionally and expanding their social spheres, which almost always went hand in glove in the theater.

Moss was in awe of the Porters, and maybe of Short and Ladd, too. He hoped they all might be part of his future, professionally or not, and the wish seemed graciously reciprocated as he boarded trains for Berlin, Vienna, and Budapest before traveling on to Italy, all of which were fine places to go. They revealed to him a world beyond Broadway, but the ultimate destination of his Grand Tour was Hollywood and the world of MGM, where, no matter what he had told the press, he would endure "the bane of studio conferences." He could hardly wait.

8

Hollywood to Broadway

Writing a good movie brings a writer about as much fame as riding a bicycle.

BEN HECHT

Europe could only faintly compete with the allure of MGM, which emanated chiefly from Irving Thalberg. The studio chief had reminded Moss of Jed Harris as a generator of creative excitement and may have reminded him of himself, too. Thalberg was only five years older and he, too, had once toiled as a secretary, typing and taking dictation before he began his spectacular rise in Hollywood. He was now enthroned as the creative genius of MGM and would become, thanks to an early death and F. Scott Fitzgerald's *The Last Tycoon,* the most fabled production executive of them all.

Fabled, but his throne was already teetering when Moss arrived at MGM in the summer of 1932. Broadway had its own insecurities, its short runs, dry spells, and sudden deaths out of town or in; but there was a kind of continuity, if only the illusory but consoling one of fraternity and tradition. The theater world was changing faster than Sam Harris's benign paternalism let on, but Hollywood had few traditions more exalted than the assembly line. It was a factory town from the beginning, and foremen—fabled or not—were expendable. Within months of Moss's arrival at MGM, Thalberg would be sidelined by ill health and ill will. Louis B. Mayer's concern for his protégé's heart—so fragile, so much more admired than his own—would require sacrificing the crown prince in order to save him.

On Broadway, if you had a flop, only the audience could fire you from it; in Hollywood, if More Stars Than There Were in Heaven were no protection, what was? Hadn't Moss written the book—or the play—about that? Russian director Sergei Eisenstein acknowledged *Once in a Lifetime*'s accuracy about Hollywood when he secured the rights to it for the Soviet Union. A man who had survived revolutions and Stalinist purges but could not cope with the czars of Paramount, Eisenstein called Moss's play "the most morbid thing I ever saw." It wasn't a comedy at all, Eisenstein insisted. It was "grim realism."

Moss was not eager to play Lawrence Vail in real life, forced to linger unemployed while drawing down a weekly check. He was a New York celebrity with two Broadway hits to his credit and that was the part he intended to play. He moved into an apartment overlooking Los Angeles from Sunset Plaza Drive and smelled fame and money in the air. He knew little about screenwriting, but a lot about dialogue and wit and sophistication. Wasn't that why they had hired him?

To prove it, Thalberg turned Moss over at once to producer John Considine, then preparing a picture to follow Wallace Beery's Oscar-winning bathos as a broken-down boxer in *The Champ*. Considine had a story treatment about what *Variety* termed "the honorable profesh of grappling" that needed some dialogue. Moss knew as little about wrestling as he did about Viennese waltzes, but that was the profesh in *Flesh*. Beery was to play a German wrestler who goes downhill from Bavaria to Hoboken and finally to a cell on Death Row. Along the way he goes weak in the knees for bad-girl blonde Karen Morley, who strings him along for many reels before he figures out that Ricardo Cortez is not her brother, as she claims, but her lover. Beery, the Bavarian brawler, puts an end to that, and to Cortez, too. They might better have titled it *The Chump*.

Writers and directors for *Flesh* had fairly whirled through the revolving door that Thalberg installed to excite creativity. It was Thalberg's or Considine's wisdom that Moss could write pidgin-German dialogue for Beery and some tough-girl wisecracks for the ex-jailbird played by Morley.

Moss began writing in August and kept at it through shooting in October. John Ford directed in a perfunctory fashion and the picture's only distinctions were as Moss's first screen credit and as one of Ford's least. Reviewers expected *Champ II* when *Flesh* was released in December, and found it "a severe disappointment."

In spite of such reviews Moss had passed some kind of MGM or Thalberg test and it may have gone to his head. In mid-October he giddily told Dore Schary he had been promised *Tugboat Annie,* the successor to Beery and Marie Dressler's *Min and Bill*. Before the week was out, however, Thalberg came to his senses and shifted Moss to Joan Crawford and Clark Gable, marginally more in his line.

Crawford immediately sent over an autographed picture as inspiration, which Moss hung in his house at 602 North Maple Drive in Beverly Hills. He had moved from Sunset Plaza Drive (now that he had a screen credit) so that Lillie, Barnett, and Bernie could join him in California and leave the Hotel Ansonia's many-layered curtains and Spanish credenzas behind. Ensconced in Beverly Hills, Moss set to work on *Dancing Lady*, the tale of a chorine's rise to overnight stardom on Broadway based on a *Saturday Evening Post* story by James Warner Bellah. Here, at least, was a background he knew something about, on which he could lavish wit and sophistication.

His very first scene echoed long-ago adventures of Ho and Ko in St. Mary's Park in the Bronx. Janie, a bossy but high-spirited waif who will grow up to become Joan Crawford, tells her playmates how to play the game:

JANIE: *You all go over there—you're the crowned heads of Europe. I'm the famous Dancer—you're all at my feet. Soldiers are fighting duels outside over me, and the Prince has just committed suicide. . . . When I come on the stage, you all say: "Ah, How beautiful she is!" Then you, Ruthie, while I'm dancing, you say: "The greatest dancer in the world, gentlemen! I would give my throne for her!" Then I throw you a rose and I fall down dead.*

RUTHIE: *Yeah—we know.*

You can almost hear Crawford saying it, but dropping down dead was just what Crawford didn't need. She had done that only months before as Sadie Thompson in the disastrous *Rain* at United Artists and thought that was enough self-sacrifice for one career. Moss was swiftly replaced by playwright John Howard Lawson, Anita Loos, the team of Goodrich and Hackett, and even *The New Yorker*'s Robert Benchley. None of them got credit, though Benchley got a part in the picture. So did Nelson Eddy. So did the Three Stooges. So did Franchot Tone, soon to replace Douglas Fairbanks, Jr., as Mr. Crawford.

Dancing Lady was finally taken over, along with much else at MGM, by David O. Selznick. The big song was "Everything I Have Is Yours" by Burton Lane (his first hit) and Harold Adamson. It overshadowed a weak number by Rodgers and Hart and a dreadful one by Lane and Adamson that was homage to "I Love Louisa" in *The Band Wagon* or a brazen rip-off of it. Called "Let's Go Bavarian," it had the sole virtue of introducing Fred Astaire to movie audiences with tiny billing as dancing partner to Crawford's two left feet. "Janie" was maniacally cheerful in blond pigtails, while "Fred" was as debonair as anyone could be dancing in lederhosen.

Moss's abruptly terminated stint on *Dancing Lady* left him free for borrowing from MGM by Samuel Goldwyn, who hired him to dialogue *The Masquerader,* a vehicle for Ronald Colman that had been a novel in 1904, a play in 1917, and a silent movie in 1922. The story was a wheeze but gave Colman a double role: a drug-addicted Member of Parliament and his clean and sober cousin who stands in for him in public when the glassy-eyed look might be a giveaway. At the very moment that the M.P. fatally overdoses in his dope den, the cousin is impersonating him by giving a speech that brings the unsuspecting House of Commons to its feet. It dawns on the cousin that the M.P.'s sordid death means the masquerade must now become permanent—to save England. With stiff upper lip, he accepts the burdens of duty: rank, prestige, power, and Elissa Landi as Mrs. M.P., who wonders with a smile why her husband seems so different.

The story adaptation by Academy Award winner Howard Estabrook (for *Cimarron*) provided framework enough for Moss to fill in the blanks and get a "dialogue by" credit. Reviewers noted a "brittle" quality that didn't prevent Colman from giving an uncannily convincing impersonation of Colman. Neither version was very happy about it. *The Masquerader* marked the end of the star's long and bitter contract dispute with Goldwyn, and he spent the next two years off the screen rather than work for the producer again. He may have passed the time chewing over *Masquerader* reviews that sniffed at the mildew of "yesteryear."

Moss grew fond of Goldwyn, who, despite beginnings no less humble than Barnett Hart's, was his antithesis in accomplishment. Goldwyn won Moss's affection by being frankly paternal with him and there were other ties they shared in the cat's cradle of show-business relationships. Freddie Kohlmar, one of the old office-boy gang, would soon work for Goldwyn in New York, following Arthur Hornblow, Jr., translator of *The Captive* and son of the editor of *Theatre Magazine,* who would remain Moss's friend for life. The lawsuit Kaufman brought against Goldwyn to collect money he was owed for a screen story was no inhibition to Moss's personal friendship with Goldwyn, nor did it give Goldwyn pause. His curious reaction to the lawsuit was to insist that Beatrice Kaufman become his New York story editor.

Moss pleaded with Goldwyn to give twenty-two-year-old Bernie a job in his California offices. Bernie had been working in publicity for Broadway producer Max Gordon, a job that had ended with the family's move to California. Goldwyn explained that times were tough even for nepotists: Mrs. Goldwyn's brother-in-law had been on the hire list for three months without ever making it to the payroll.

Bernie's future remained undetermined even though, unlike Moss, he had received his high school diploma. That did not make up for a withered arm, but his eager-beaver puns made people forget the mild disability. Moss accepted a fatherly role in Bernie's life by default, while Barnett and Lillie enjoyed the palms and the sun. Beverly Hills was not the Bronx, they said, but then what was?

Goldwyn offered Moss another screenwriting job: *The Wizard of Oz*. Moss thought it should be a musical, as it had been on Broadway before he was born, and said he'd do it if Irving Berlin would do it with him. Berlin declined, and Goldwyn let the story and characters go, with famous results.

Moss and Goldwyn maintained their affection over the years, with Goldwyn investing in Moss's plays and Moss welcoming the support. He would repay it with something else from the world of fairy tales, *Hans Christian Andersen*, which was no less fanciful than *The Wizard of Oz*—or *The Masquerader*, for that matter.

After Moss finished off Ronald Colman for Goldwyn, longtime MGM supervisor Harry Rapf assigned him to the thankless task that landed on the desk of virtually every New York playwright who crossed the Culver City border. Three years earlier MGM had shelved nearly a million dollars' worth of footage, some of it in two-strip Technicolor, all of it featuring famous vaudeville acts now sinking daily deeper into obscurity. The project, known as "The March of Time" or "Show World" or "Just Kids," was to have been a follow-up to MGM's successful *Hollywood Revue of 1929* until 1930 came along and the overcrowded musical market was trampled to death by audiences fleeing the box office.

The revue format had been only fitfully successful on-screen, as in *Hollywood Revue* or Warner Bros.' *Show of Shows,* but left behind the only definitive visual records we have of vaudeville in its prime. The shelved footage for "The March of Time" was a virtual library of routines by headliners like Weber and Fields, Marie Dressler, Fay Templeton, DeWolf Hopper, and the Albertina Rasch Dancers doing a "Snow Ballet." Now that movie musicals had unexpectedly been revived by Warner Bros. and *42nd Street,* those miles of color footage Rapf kept trying to salvage might be worth something after all.

Rescue operations on "The March of Time" had been active since September 1930 with new titles to disguise or freshen the project like "Toast of the Town," which sounded upbeat, or "It's Gotta Be Big," which sounded, well, big. Playwright Donald Ogden Stewart was only one of many writers who worked on the project. So did Jimmy Durante, when Rapf decided the footage might benefit from patter by "the great Schnozzola." Another brainstorm focused on long-legged comedienne Charlotte Greenwood, who would presumably kick it back to life. It was a standing MGM joke that Rapf's grim determination to amortize his costly footage would sooner or later lead him to every writer on the lot and it inevitably led him to Moss.

In mid-December Moss turned in a jokey story for "The March of Time" about a desperate movie executive grimly determined to save old vaudeville footage by incorporating it into a movie called *The March of Time.* Moss's story featured writer suicides, cartoons (inspired by Disney) of the stars already on film, and old newsreel footage to indicate the passage of time. It all turned out to be a hideous dream, what lyricist E. Y. "Yip" Harburg once called a "Metro-Goldwyn-Nightmayer." The story may have been Moss's comment on what MGM did to writers, but it read like Hollywood Night at Camp Utopia and was quickly rejected.

Two weeks later Moss submitted a more conventional draft that neatly solved the footage problem. He invented a backstage story about "The Two Hacketts," a music hall couple who become "The Three Hacketts" with the arrival of a blessed event. The theatrical family provided a framework into which the filmed vaudeville acts could be intercut. The notion worked and got a new title: *Broadway to Hollywood.*

Moss turned in his outline three days before Christmas and the first draft of his screenplay on January 4, 1933. Over the holidays Thalberg suffered a heart attack and was replaced in the MGM hierarchy by Mayer's son-in-law, Selznick. Mayer's easy betrayal of Thalberg had an eerie parallel in Moss's script. Superficially Moss's story suggested a music hall version of his old *Wind Up an Era* generational idea, but the characters and conflicts came from an even earlier source, *No Retreat.*

Broadway to Hollywood's Hackett Senior attempts to sabotage his son's career with the same ploys of paternal betrayal Moss invented that summer at the Flagler. Hackett Junior's girl—named Nan, as in *No Retreat*—tells him the truth about his father in identical dialogue. Only the names were changed:

NAN: *People are going to say: "Ted Hackett? Is that Ted Hackett's son? Why, my goodness, I never knew he had a son that old . . ." And that will be the beginning of the end. Because, Ted, you have a spark . . . a fine, new talent . . . and he knows it. And he's afraid.*

No one at MGM had ever heard of *No Retreat* and this approach provided the Hackett family with a story and conflicts that were still fresh in Moss's emotional life. A father's failings—selfish and deliberate—provided the goad for a son's triumph. In Culver City that triumph would not degenerate to irony as in *No Retreat*. Nan would not utter "We are lost," not at MGM, where nobody on-screen but Garbo was ever lost.

Moss's story was strong enough to survive more than half a dozen scribes who followed him through MGM's ever-revolving writer door. The script got a final polish from director Willard Mack and MGM contract writer Edgar Allan Woolf, who had worked on "The March of Time" intermittently since 1930 without success. Rapf now rewarded them with screen credit that belonged to Moss, who provided the structure, characters, and themes that made *Broadway to Hollywood* possible.

That didn't matter in 1933. There were no guilds or unions to prevent a producer from arbitrarily assigning credits however he wanted. Rapf may have told himself, with assembly-line logic, that Moss's contribution was just cogs and wheels and Moss had been a Thalberg hire, anyway, which made him yesterday's spark, yesterday's fine new talent.

The MGM conveyor belt kept right on rolling. Rapf and MGM hired a total of thirty-six writers between 1930 and 1933 (including Moss) to save some old celluloid that, in the end, was hardly used. Apart from a Weber and Fields horse-and-cab routine, some (now lost) color footage of Fay Templeton, and the Albertina Rasch Dancers doing their "Snow Ballet," the rest of the footage was cut up into short subjects or ukulele picks.

The final version of *Broadway to Hollywood* added a third generation to the Hackett story, bringing it up-to-date and to the soundstages, where the picture could end on a musical number being filmed by Hackett the Third. Mother Hackett, called Lulu, was played by Alice Brady, who came from a famous theatrical family herself. She had been the original Lavinia in O'Neill's *Mourning Becomes Electra,* and her father, William A. Brady, had produced *Life,* the very first play Moss saw back in 1911 with Kate.

Her husband, Ted Hackett, was Frank Morgan, closer to being the Wizard of Oz than he had been in *The Band Wagon.* Hackett Junior was played as a boy by child star Jackie Cooper, who grew up in the film to become the talent-free Russell Hardie, a refugee from Mae West's stage career. As Hackett Junior, Hardie defied his father to become a star, a drunk, and finally cannon fodder in World War I. *His* son got raised by the grandparents, still hoofing away in the two-a-day. The youngest Hackett the Third was Mickey Rooney, a tornado of talent at not quite twelve, who in five minutes wiped everybody else off the screen. This was Rooney's introduction to Leo the Lion and remains the chief distinction of *Broadway to Hollywood*. That, and the curious fluke of being the movie in which child star Jackie Cooper played child star Mickey Rooney's father.

For Moss the best feature of the finished picture was not the opportunity to get *No Retreat* out of his system, but that the rewrite so muted the father-son treachery (was it too reminiscent of Mayer and Thalberg?) that he could lift it all over again if he had to.

Moss was a compulsive worker when not debilitated by depression and, unlike his earlier stay on the West Coast, his Hollywood schedule this time suggests balance and productivity. Between August 1932 and January 1933, he worked on four pictures and got screen credit on two of them. Almost all of it was hackwork.

He had been expensively imported by a production executive now stripped of power, only to be miscast or underused. Writing dialogue for story treatments already completed by more experienced hands was just connecting the dots. His work was quick and facile and allowed him to skate over flaws in structure and characterization that often weakened his plays. The one solid piece of work he turned in, *Broadway to Hollywood,* got appropriated by others who diluted it or moved commas from one place to another to satisfy Harry Rapf's daily or weekly page quota.

Major films would eventually bear Moss's name, but all would be adaptations and he preferred it that way. He told Goldwyn that his "own picture experience [was] not sufficient . . . to make a proper breakdown of [a] book," which "should be done by someone with more of a camera mind and camera eye." Then, of course, he would be "perfectly capable of doing the final script job with dialogue, etc." Like many New York playwrights who felt they were slumming on the West Coast, he assumed that Hollywood was indifferent to the quality of movies because *he* was, and because movies seemed indifferent to him. "If the picture was bad no one cared," he said, mistaking Hollywood defensiveness for indifference.

Moss liked the glamour and money of Hollywood but knew, as he admitted to Goldwyn, that he lacked any real flair for screenwriting. The proscenium and the theater's "fourth wall" kept things under control, safely at a distance, on display without danger of intrusion. The camera, on the other hand, was a kind of portable audience, intruding wherever it wanted at whatever distance or angle and dictating an architecture of images that took precedence over words. Faces thirty feet wide needed a different kind of dialogue, too, than did live actors projecting to box seats or balconies.

Moss knew and appreciated all this without ever finding the task important or congenial enough to master except once. The best screenplay of his career would be the remake of *A Star Is Born,* written to a pre-established blueprint by, among others, Dorothy Parker. It would touch and thrill with the intensity of images and music and the star power of Judy Garland, but by then Moss knew how to get out of the way and leave well enough alone.

The most telling evidence of Moss's casual attitude toward movies was that not even his adaptations (with a single exception) were of his own work. All but one of his plays, beginning with Universal's movie version of *Once in a Lifetime* in 1932, he left to others with no apparent regrets. This Hart's beat was Broadway.

Thalberg's fall—or shove—from grace in early 1933 cast a pall over MGM. Moss's own tendency to depression was averted by Harry Rapf, who had none of Thalberg's creative or personal glamour, but remained a dogged Louis B. Mayer loyalist, guarding the assembly line against power failure. After Moss turned in his script for *Broadway to Hollywood,* Rapf assigned him to work on a Hungarian play that Mayer hoped to turn into a musical for lyric songbird Jeanette MacDonald, newly poached from Ernst Lubitsch and Paramount.

Moss was enthusiastic about his coworkers, Richard Rodgers and Lorenz Hart (no relation, "except by mutual consternation," *The New Yorker* quipped). Their work on *Dancing Lady* had done nothing for any of them, but Rodgers and Hart had recently worked with MacDonald on *Love Me Tonight* at Paramount, and United Artists had just released their *Hallelujah, I'm a Bum!* with Al Jolson.

Moss and Rodgers and Hart were natural allies: refugees from Broadway in an atmosphere distracted enough by internal intrigues to let them go about their business. The trio set to work adapting their middle-European fantasy about a banker with a yen for an angel. Rodgers found

Moss "fairly bursting with ideas," and in little more than a month they turned in a script and score they called *I Married an Angel,* complete with rhythmic dialogue like that in *Love Me Tonight.*

Mayer was taken aback. Shocked. Not only were fantasies certain death at the box office, but the Legion of Decency would never permit a mortal to make love to a heavenly being, certainly not one as celestial as Jeanette MacDonald, whose bringing down to earth was a project Mayer was reserving for himself.

Tremors from on high, or from the 1933 Long Beach earthquake that occurred about the same time, were upheaval enough for Moss. He packed his bags and, leaving his family to live out the lease in Beverly Hills, went back to New York. He left Rodgers and Hart to rework *I Married an Angel* with Joshua Logan for Broadway five years later with Vera Zorina as the angel, choreographed for her Broadway debut by her then-husband George Balanchine. Brooks Atkinson called the whole thing "a miracle" in the *Times.* The real miracle was that Mayer saw it and liked it so much he bought it back from Rodgers and Hart and made it as a movie in 1942, with Jeanette MacDonald.

After Hollywood, Broadway—for all its unknowns and perils— seemed so logical. You got an idea and wrote it and it got produced or not and it worked or it didn't. A grateful or disgruntled audience told you *tonight,* not months later, after faceless minions in eyeshades had counted their beans on Wall Street. Hollywood was, finally, mechanical and defi- cient in magic, the compulsive, addictive kind Moss craved and found wanting under the all-too-sheltering palms.

"You were safe, there," he said of Hollywood. "You were miserable, but you were safe. . . . You sat at your typewriter and hated yourself, but in the evening you could leave the studio and forget it until the next morning. You didn't eat it and drink it and sleep it the way you did the theater."

Sam Harris and Irving Berlin understood that, which was why and how Moss found himself in April, leaning on the railing of the SS *Queen of Bermuda* beneath an azure sky. He puffed on the pipe he had lately taken up, so much more writerly than a cigar. Cigars reeked of 107th Street and the Bronx and Brooklyn and failure and everything he had worked to leave behind.

The ocean breezes, on the other hand, carried the tropical perfumes of the Caribbean toward which he was sailing with Berlin: heady, lush, and—unless inspiration failed—as green as money.

9

Cheers

I wanted a helluva success, and a modicum of glory.

MOSS HART

Moss and Irving Berlin wanted to work together again, in spite of Mary Boland's abrupt departure for Hollywood and the red ink she left behind. The failure of *Face the Music* to recoup costs inflated by the New Amsterdam's production wasn't entirely Boland's fault. The Depression was here to stay.

Ticket prices began at 25 cents for a balcony seat during the Shakespeare season at the Al Jolson Theatre and soared to $4.40 for the priciest loge at a smash like Noël Coward's new hit, *Design for Living*, starring Coward and the Lunts. Burns Mantle prematurely announced the end of high ticket prices, claiming that "the day of the $3, $4, $5 and $6 theater ticket is about over," but he predicted that the election of Franklin Delano Roosevelt was the harbinger of a "great rally," too.

The number of productions on Broadway plunged from a record high of 270 in 1927 to 180 in 1932 and would continue to decline. Almost a third of the shows were pared-down revivals of the Bard (fifteen of them), or Kaufman and Lardner *(June Moon),* or George Kelly *(The Show-Off).* Half the theaters were dark for all of 1933–34. Even so, you could still see Shakespeare for a quarter at the Al Jolson.

Moss had Depression blues of his own as he sailed for the Caribbean with Berlin. The income that had poured in from *Once in a Lifetime* and MGM and royalties from *Face the Music* had poured right back out again to rental brokers, tailors, shoe- and shirtmakers, monogram designers, goldsmiths, florists, headwaiters, decorators, drapery makers, travel agents, and to Lillie, Barnett, and Bernie for their general upkeep. Asking Goldwyn to give Bernie a job had not been merely big brotherly: Moss needed money.

Berlin had suffered his major reverses due to the Crash, but had all those copyrights and song royalties to keep the cupboard from going bare (and a rich wife, too). He loaned Moss $5,000 to tide him over and gave him pocket money for Bermuda on their working holiday.

Sam Harris had announced a title for their unwritten new show on Christmas Day of 1932 to stimulate interest in the revival of *Face the Music* that lasted for only thirty-two performances. *As Thousands Cheer* was a generic enough title for almost anything, but just as the SS *Queen of Bermuda* set sail for the Caribbean, a farce called *Man Bites Dog* opened and closed on Broadway. The hoary journalistic joke of the title may have inspired Moss and Berlin, for the curtain would rise six months later on their new revue and its opening skit and song would be called "Man Bites Dog."

The idea unifying *As Thousands Cheer* was so obvious one wonders why no one had hit on it before: a musical revue pretending to be a daily paper, with weather reports, political bulletins, human interest stories, society gossip, a Sunday rotogravure (picture) section, even comics.

Once in a Lifetime and *Face the Music* had lampooned contemporary events, but mostly at a safe distance. The new show would look closer up and more inside and would require adroit stepping. Moss's targets now that he was crowding thirty weren't the faraway famous they had been at Camp Utopia. Now they were mostly friends and rivals. He could take all the potshots he wanted, but would need to aim carefully. Today's target might be tomorrow's host, hostess, or backer.

Moss and Berlin wrote in Bermuda in a bungalow between those occupied by Dorothy Parker drinking on one side and playwright Philip Barry being aloof on the other, both neighbors providing Moss with inspiration for work to come. Accompanying Moss and Berlin were Hassard Short and Billy Ladd. Their presence or hibiscus perfume or something sent Moss a bit gaga when describing the tropical setting: "There, in the most idyllic land that one can possibly imagine," he gushed, "one designed by an all-embracing Nature for the convenience and inspiration of writers, we completed the first act and laid out the second in little more than a month."

To judge from the surviving manuscript, inspiration was lush. Moss wrote swiftly in a loose, rolling hand that raced with invention. If a sketch needed revision he dashed off another and another until one worked. He knew how to do sketches; he'd been doing them for years.

The revue format presented no character or structural problems that couldn't be solved with a blackout. The newspaper idea provided bones and allowed variety in short sprints, as in any lively daily. Moss and Berlin could even raid their trunks, and did. Moss reached all the way back to Camp Utopia for his sketch about radio, "The Microphone Hunters," and revamped it as a send-up of broadcasts from the Metropolitan Opera, where the commercials turned out to be longer than *Rigoletto*. His screenplay for *Broadway to Hollywood* had included newsreels to illustrate bygone days. One he especially favored that had been rejected by Rapf and MGM had called for an Easter parade on Fifth Avenue. That idea, coupled with a song Berlin had written fifteen years earlier called "Smile and Show Your Dimple," provided the show with a first act finale that simulated a sepia-toned rotogravure page in a tour de force of nostalgic design from Hassard Short. With a new lyric, it emerged as "Easter Parade." A decade later MGM would buy the rights to the song as the basis for a movie of the same name starring Fred Astaire and Judy Garland. Moss's old-timey idea would, in a roundabout way, come home again and cost MGM $500,000 when it did.

Moss invented sketches inspired by FDR, Noël Coward, the Rockefellers, Mahatma Gandhi, Aimee Semple McPherson, the end of Prohibition, and New York high society's roller-skating craze, the last two combined in a cocktail party on wheels. He even got tasty revenge for being dropped from *Dancing Lady* with a wicked sketch about the divorce of Joan Crawford and Douglas Fairbanks, Jr.

The newspaper format allowed Berlin equal latitude. In addition to "Easter Parade," he teased the many romances of five-and-dime heiress Barbara Hutton with the wry and wistful "How's Chances?" The weather report predicted a "Heat Wave." The advice-to-the-lovelorn column crooned a ballad called "Lonely Heart."

If melody couldn't quite handle, say, the romantic peregrinations of the then–Prince of Wales, Moss was ready with a skit about backstage life at Buckingham Palace. Nothing was sacred and no one was spared. Moss's long list of candidates for skewering was elastic, allowing for up-to-the-minute newsbreaks (or lawyers whose clients lacked senses of humor). On the back burner, just in case, were former secretary of state Henry Stimson and financier Otto Kahn, as well as Edna Ferber, Alexander Woollcott, Elsa Maxwell, Somerset Maugham, the Lunts, the Marx Brothers, and Lady Mendl.

Invention bubbled everywhere in *As Thousands Cheer*. Both creators were in top form, though Moss experienced occasional uncertainty due to Berlin's raspy singing voice and ham-handed technique at the "Buick." When he played and sang "Heat Wave," Moss despaired. The more he heard, the worse it got. Finally on a hunch he requested "Always," a personal favorite. "Always" emerged so tuneless that Moss decided "Heat Wave" might be all right after all.

By June they had returned from Bermuda and were working on weekends in the Long Island "cottage" built by McKim, Mead, and White that Berlin had rented for his family near the beach in Montauk. During the week they worked in town at Moss's place. Since he had given up the apartment in the Ansonia, Berlin rented him his own former bachelor flat in the building he owned at 29 West Forty-sixth Street.

Sam Harris announced a September opening at the Music Box. *As Thousands Cheer* would not fall victim to the grandiosity of *Face the Music.* This show was to be simpler and cheaper, unified by a show curtain on which "headlines" could be projected to announce sketches and songs. Hassard Short would stage the musical numbers; Moss, branching out, would direct the sketches.

As Thousands Cheer was Moss's first Broadway outing since *Jonica* without Kaufman looking over his shoulder. Hollywood had been frustrating or amusing, but had proven he could work alone and had given him social self-confidence as well. He had hobnobbed as a popular dinner guest and "extra man" on the West Coast with Joan Crawford, Irving Thalberg and Norma Shearer, and the Selznicks, David and his wife Irene, who was the daughter of Louis B. Mayer. "Moss was still polishing up the personality," Irene remembered, "but he was up to *here* with charm. As a congenital or confirmed bachelor—whatever the euphemism was—he was irresistible and unthreatening at the same time and very, very bright. He didn't need *dates.*"

Kaufman was busy, in any case, with *Let 'Em Eat Cake,* the sequel to *Of Thee I Sing.* Moss's independence was encouraged by Berlin, who had cooled on Kaufman during *Face the Music.* Kaufman had been inattentive to the score and Berlin took it personally. "George hated music so much," he grumbled, "that if I'd written 'Rock of Ages' he'd have thrown it out." Kaufman responded that he was just nonmusical and didn't know the difference between "Handel's 'Largo' and—well—Largo's 'Handel.'" Anyway, Hassard Short was staging the musical numbers, not he.

Whatever he thought of Kaufman, Berlin's curiosity about the Gershwin show got the better of him. During preparations for *As Thousands Cheer,* he wandered over to the Imperial to eavesdrop on rehearsals for *Let 'Em Eat Cake.* He liked what he heard so much that he traded Kaufman 5 percent of *Cheer* for 5 percent of *Cake.* The swap became a windfall for Kaufman and crumbs for Berlin when the Gershwin show quickly folded and *As Thousands Cheer* became a branch of the U.S. Mint.

. . .

The success of *As Thousands Cheer* had hardly been a sure thing. Most opinion-makers in 1933 had already buried revue, which had achieved a seemingly unimprovable peak with *The Band Wagon,* next to which anything else could only pale by comparison. They didn't know then that Berlin's score for *As Thousands Cheer* would have more hits than anything he would write until *Annie Get Your Gun* over a decade later. Nor could they know that the cast would make the title prophetic.

The principal star was Marilyn Miller, the undisputed queen of musical comedy since she introduced "Look for the Silver Lining" in Jerome Kern's *Sally* in 1920. The daughter of vaudevillians rather like the Hacketts in *Broadway to Hollywood,* Miller had been onstage with her parents from the age of six. A delicate blond beauty, she was primarily a dancer with a small voice, but was so captivating onstage that Jerome Kern wrote "Who?" for her and the Gershwins obliged with "How Long Has This Been Going On?" She had been a Ziegfeld star who married Mary Pickford's brother Jack, who may or may not have died of syphilis that he may or may not have passed on to her. She was dainty, but the Dresden doll was made of steel. When working for Ziegfeld she was told backstage that her then-husband, Frank Carter, had been killed in an automobile accident. "I've never missed a performance, and I'm not going to miss one now," she said, going into her dance.

Moss called her his "dream girl" and admitted that her air of unattainability was crucial to her charm. He claimed to have seen her thirty-seven times in *Sally,* where she had seemed "a fairy princess." He thought her "remote as a star" and would come to wish she had stayed that way.

Fairy princesses had gone out with the Crash and, as theater historian Ethan Mordden has noted, girls who once looked for silver linings were now digging for gold. Miller was equal to changing times. Though absent from Broadway since *Smiles* with the Astaires in 1930, her return in *As Thousands Cheer* would be triumphant, but a farewell to Broadway. She would die in 1936 at the age of thirty-eight, supposedly of a brain infection following surgery for a sinus condition, but stirring memories of Jack Pickford and his rumored fatal illness.

Opposite Miller was Clifton Webb, the suavely effete song-and-dance man whose mother Maybelle had pushed him onstage at the age of three. He remained a theatrical fixture as an eccentric dancer until 1929, when he became a star singing and dancing "I Guess I'll Have to Change My Plan" in Schwartz and Dietz's *The Little Show.* It is something of a shock to late-show addicts, who identify him with films like *Laura, Titanic,* or

the *Mr. Belvedere* series, to learn that he was once a musical star who introduced not only "Easter Parade" and "How's Chances?" but standards like
"I've Got a Crush on You," "Alone Together," and "Something to Remember You By." Not one of them is identified with him today.

Webb was a mother-fixated gay man (Moss called him "my blemish"), an exquisite so elegant and arch he was usually taken for English
though, like Miller, he was from Indiana. They had worked together, in
fact, in Kern's *Sunny* in 1925, under the direction of the same Hassard
Short putting them through their paces in *As Thousands Cheer* in 1933.

Rounding out the trio of above-the-title stars was Helen Broderick,
the deadpan comedienne Moss called "part vitriol and part my favorite
person in the world." Broderick got the plums originally intended for
Mary Boland, still busy in Hollywood and forgiven for her walkout on
Face the Music. Broderick's appearance in *As Thousands Cheer* would be her
own ticket to filmland, where she would add vinegar to the Astaire and
Rogers films and encourage the career of her actor-son, future Academy
Award winner Broderick Crawford.

The real sensation of *As Thousands Cheer* was below-the-title. Ethel
Waters had moved from Harlem to Broadway in all-black shows like
Africana and *Lew Leslie's Blackbirds of 1930.* Her presence in *As Thousands
Cheer* would prove historic and shape the writing of the show. Miller and
Webb could have been replaced (and were) without altering its contours,
but Waters could not, partly because she had the musical comedy skills of
"a dusky Charlotte Greenwood," as the *New York Times* put it, but mainly
because she was black. Without her verve—"There's nothing I like better
than workin' on a *hot* stage!" she said when following a showstopper by
Webb—things would have been much cooler. Without her color there
would have been no controversy.

The final element the naysayers were unaware of was the swift, brilliant attack of Moss's sketches, each one of which went significantly
beyond the tomfoolery of earlier revues. The headlines projected on the
show curtain were topical and tantalizing, but the twists that followed
made them funny and penetrating. "Man Bites Dog" was, unexpectedly,
exactly what it said: a Park Avenue swell took toothy revenge on his wife's
vicious little Pekinese. "Franklin D. Roosevelt to Be Inaugurated Tomorrow" was not about the new president, but the old. Mr. and Mrs. Herbert
Hoover bicker as they pack their bags before Hoover joins the ranks of
the unemployed. Mrs. Hoover, stripping the White House bare of portraits of George Washington and any spare lightbulbs she can lay her
hands on, reminds her husband that she might have married that fellow
who became such a big deal in knitwear back in Palo Alto.

"Joan Crawford to Divorce Douglas Fairbanks, Jr." was the headline for Miller (as Crawford) and Webb (as Fairbanks) arguing over who will get top billing in the publicity for "a divorce the Industry can be proud of!" as movie morals czar Will H. Hays calls it. They are upstaged by Mary Pickford and Douglas Fairbanks, Sr., announcing *their* divorce. "World's Wealthiest Man Celebrates 94th Birthday" featured Webb as the ancient Ur-Rockefeller, "wrinkled" by toothpick grooves traced into a quarter-inch layer of pancake makeup. When the nonagenarian learns his birthday gift is a family project called "Radio City," of which he has been uninformed, he goes after the younger generation with a carving knife, ordering them to take it back to the crook who sold it to them.

"Noël Coward, Noted Playwright, Returns to England" introduces a scene in the hotel suite Coward has just vacated. Webb as a room service waiter, Miller as a chambermaid, and Waters as a scrubwoman remain so dazzled by the Coward glamour that they carry on like characters out of *Design for Living,* with Miller's chambermaid swanning about like Lynn Fontanne with a feather duster. Broderick's housekeeper takes in the scene and deadpans, "Well, I'll be goddamned!"

"Prince of Wales Rumored Engaged" took Broderick to Buckingham Palace, where Queen Mary's tiara was blown sideways by hot headlines about the prince's goodwill trip to Latin America. The British Embassy complained to Sam Harris about Moss's tasteless invasions of privacy in this skit, even before the world had heard of the prince's affair with Wallis Simpson. Moss answered, "[Y]ou [British] have different ideas. We just don't regard it as bad taste," while Harris pointed out that director Short was English and asked, "What is the matter with you people?"

The difficulty with the Prince of Wales sketch had been finding a look-alike to play the part. None of the stars or chorus boys would do. It was Max Siegel, still working for Harris, who discovered young Thomas Hamilton at a drugstore lunch counter. Hamilton had gone unnoticed in a couple of New York flops, but so resembled the prince that Short was said to have cried out, "I'll teach him to act if I have to stay up all night for the rest of the week." Billy Ladd pointed out coolly that directing the actors was Moss's job.

Hamilton's resemblance to the prince inspired nightly applause and led to some modeling jobs, though his acting career faltered. The Music Box stage manager recalled that Hamilton "liked to party a lot." Moss was either smitten or being ironic when he told Hamilton that his uncanny resemblance to the future king (and Duke of Windsor) was "pale, fragile, cameo-like, a thing of beauty."

Waters was not pale and not fragile, but to many she was a thing of extraordinary, exotic beauty. In "Heat Wave Hits New York," she wore a satiny red and gold outfit that seemed to define spontaneous combustion. In "Josephine Baker Still the Rage of Paris," she punctured the usual notion of expatriate gaiety with the bluesy "Harlem on My Mind."

The most startling and controversial headline was "Unknown Negro Lynched by Frenzied Mob," for which Waters sang "Supper Time," the wrenching lament Berlin acknowledged as "the most unusual song in my whole catalogue." It was a bitter outcry that made many audiences and critics uncomfortable and moved others to tears. It had been only three years since the Scottsboro Boys went to trial, during which time an additional forty-two confirmed lynchings had been reported in the South. Waters's honky-tonk background (she had worked for Al Capone and claimed "I'm a child of the underworld," but what she was was a child of rape) played easily enough into songs like "Stormy Weather" and "Heat Wave." But with "Supper Time" she said, "I was telling my comfortable, well-fed, well-dressed listeners . . . the whole tragic story of a race." John Mason Brown agreed that it was tragic and—therefore—unfitting for Broadway. Brooks Atkinson was stunned by its "taste and humanity."

Liberal-minded Sam Harris had insisted the song remain until the Philadelphia tryouts, when it could be dropped if it proved too daring or jarring. It stopped the show and was said to have stopped Webb, too. Gossip circulates to the present day that he was being racist, but he was just being an actor and the incident had nothing to do with "Supper Time." Webb had a Walter Winchell sketch that couldn't follow Waters onstage except as an anticlimax. He rebelled, delivering himself of an ultimatum that he would not open in New York without a change in running order or a new and better number for himself.

Moss got involved when he returned to Philadelphia from New York, where he had gone to check Lillie, Barnett, and Bernie into a hotel on their arrival from California. Harris told Moss and Berlin, "It's your show, you know." They agreed to back Harris when he told Webb's agent Louis Schurr, "You go back and tell [Webb] that he not only doesn't have to open in New York on Saturday, he doesn't even have to play the show here tomorrow night. The show is closed."

An alternate version of the story has Webb, Miller, and Broderick refusing to share their curtain calls with Waters, a situation scotched by Berlin's telling them he thought the show did not need curtain calls. Harmony was restored to the City of Brotherly Love until Miller delivered a fairy princess's knock-down-drag-out tirade at Moss for his failure to come backstage and compliment her on an especially tricky costume change.

A new finale was substituted for the roller-skating cocktail party when Short discovered it was unstageable in Philadelphia without risk to life and limb. A new final headline announced: "Supreme Court Hands Down Important Decision." Webb and Miller then deconstructed the very form of revue by announcing that, by Supreme Court order, *As Thousands Cheer* would not close with the time-honored reprises, but with a brand-new song presumably from the international desk: "Not for All the Rice in China." The newspaper show curtain came down on the same exhilarating note of the unexpected with which the evening had begun.

As Thousands Cheer opened at the Music Box on September 30, 1933, and was an all-but-unqualified hit. Heywood Broun in the *Record* recoiled from all the scantily clad young men onstage (there was an underdressed "Revolt in Cuba" number headlined by dancer José Limon), but otherwise thought it "the best revue I've ever seen." Brooks Atkinson wrote that "no doubt some one will be able to suggest how *As Thousands Cheer* could be improved," but he offered only "meek approval to every item on the program."

Berlin's songs assumed their place in the American songbook and Short's magic with lighting proved unforgettable, especially in "Easter Parade," which he lit with a sepia glow in a reported fifteen minutes flat. "Ah, God, it was gorgeous," one backstage witness remembered.

Onstage victory attached itself firmly to Moss, though Brooks Atkinson thought him occasionally "venomous and vindictive," a judgment hard to understand today. Moss's theatrical voice was impertinent, but without malice. Even when skewering pomposity, he was having too much fun to leave tooth marks or tire tracks. His humor, unlike Kaufman's, was a means of embrace, not pushing away. He lacked the knack of being vicious.

As Thousands Cheer went on for a Depression-phenomenal four hundred performances, and as with almost any hit, there were those who preferred suing to cheering. Berlin was charged with plagiarism on "Easter Parade" by the copyright holders of "Put on Your Old Grey Bonnet" because of some common rhymes. The suit forced Berlin to open his trunk and show the *Times* his 1916 manuscript page of "Smile and Show Your Dimple." That proved that "Easter Parade" was no theft and that it was probably impossible *not* to rhyme "bonnet" with "on it."

The second suit went less widely reported, but had greater impact. In the Rockefeller sketch, the children had sung "Happy Birthday" to Webb's ancient patriarch. The jingle, long assumed to be a folk melody in the public domain, had been published in 1893 by its composer, Mildred

Smith, a schoolteacher from Louisville, Kentucky. She titled her tune "Good Morning to You" and included it in a children's songbook. After Smith's death, a sister extended the copyright and, unluckily for Sam Harris, Smith had yet another sister who was on the faculty at Columbia and understood copyrights. A federal court ordered Harris to pay a flat fee of $250 for each use of the song, which came to a whopping $100,750 over the long run of *As Thousands Cheer,* including road companies, explaining why characters onstage and on-screen rarely sing "Happy Birthday" to each other to the present day.

As Thousands Cheer was such a success that Moss and Berlin began at once to talk of a sequel. *More Cheers* was announced by Harris, and newspaper columns were peppered with items about it, but it never happened. Perhaps they were discouraged from pressing their luck by the Kaufman-Gershwin stumble with *Let 'Em Eat Cake,* which eked out only ninety performances.

To recover from the opening, Moss sailed to South America with Charles Lederer, the young MGM screenwriter who was the nephew of Marion Davies, mistress of William Randolph Hearst and star of Cosmopolitan Pictures, housed at MGM. Moss called the getaway "doing a Noël Coward," and still claimed to be reworking *Wind Up an Era,* though he had dropped it two years earlier.

The South American cruise got as far as Jamaica before Moss and Lederer left or were removed from the ship. The cause, according to press reports, was an unspecified illness afflicting both. Moss and Lederer went back to MGM.

"That city of dreadful night," Moss called Hollywood when waxing dramatic, but his post–*As Thousands Cheer* reputation was so glowing it turned night into day. In a nifty demonstration of waste-not-want-not, he plucked the Walter Winchell caricature he had written for Webb and dropped it into a romantic comedy he tailored for Davies called "Miss Pamela Thorndyke."

The Winchell character in Moss's story attempted to inject life into the same-old-columns-with-the-same-old-names by inventing a certain Miss Thorndyke, who would become a "New York Garbo," the girl everyone talks about and no one knows because she doesn't exist. Until, that is, little Elsie Griffith from New Haven decides to impersonate her to win back the campus hero she lost to New York high society. It was likable and untaxing and left plenty of room for Elsie to sing and dance.

"Miss Pamela Thorndyke" was the only original story Moss ever wrote for the screen that got made, and it would get the usual MGM revolving-writer treatment before becoming *Broadway Melody of 1936* with Jack Benny as Winchell. It made a star of tap sensation Eleanor Powell in the role Moss intended for Davies. Robert Taylor was pretty and callow as the leading man who put the throb in Powell's heart and the beat in her feet. Moss's story got rewritten by, among others, German refugee Robert Liebmann, screenwriter of *The Blue Angel,* the picture in which Marlene Dietrich sizzled her way to international stardom. Liebmann rewrote Moss in German, but the final script—in Broadwayese—was by comedian Sid Silvers (who played Benny's sidekick in the picture) and Jack McGowan. The Arthur Freed–Nacio Herb Brown score included "Broadway Rhythm" and "You Are My Lucky Star."

Broadway Melody of 1936 is the freshest of a series that had further editions in 1938 and 1940. Moss retained "story by" credit in spite of the many changes, a sign of MGM's appreciation of his heightened cachet, and he was nominated for an Academy Award he did not win. His credit at MGM soared, resulting in the *real* Broadway melody: the jingle of MGM's money financing Moss's plays.

Before Moss turned in "Miss Pamela Thorndyke," George Kaufman joined him in California, a locale Kaufman mostly regarded as akin to a leper colony. Moss, having proven himself on his own (without Kaufman, anyway), could now propose they work together as equals and had an idea he was willing to explore on MGM's time.

They checked into the El Mirador in Palm Springs to talk and work. There, in the shimmer of the desert, Kaufman realized how immoderately splendiferous Moss had become in Hollywood. He made an entrance in a cowboy suit so studded with glitter it rivaled a premiere at Grauman's Chinese Theater. "Hi-yo, Platinum," Kaufman deadpanned.

The line was widely quoted when they got back to New York in April (it still is). It was so funny that few heard the hint of caution in it. Kaufman and his wife, Beatrice, shared concern about Moss's extravagance and the showiness that success should have muted by now. They thought that at thirty he could afford to reduce the size of his monograms and tone down the glitter and they suspected that the prodigal displays were compensating for more than the deprivations of childhood. Irene Selznick had noted that Moss was "still polishing up the personality" but, as far as anyone could tell, the personality was quite alone. Beatrice, eager to demonstrate her fondness for him, took Moss in hand.

It was easy for her. Striking rather than beautiful, full-figured and possessed of brains and education (she had gone to Wellesley), Beatrice was nothing like the unattainable fairy princess of Marilyn Miller. She was from Rochester, ten years older than Moss, and had almost married a rabbi before Kaufman entered her life. "You will marry him over my dead body," her father had said of the rabbi, though Kaufman, a newspaperman earning $35 a week in 1917, the year they married, can hardly have seemed a greater catch.

Beatrice delivered a stillborn child (a boy) three days before the Armistice of 1918. The trauma of the event is said to have resulted in Kaufman's impotence with her, after which each pursued sexual satisfaction outside marriage, still bound by affection acknowledged as unshakable by all of their friends and most of their lovers.

"Promiscuity forced itself upon them," concluded Kaufman's most meticulous biographer, Malcolm Goldstein, though Beatrice's romantic liaisons seemed willfully centered on surrogates for her husband, something Kaufman only half-registered. He once remarked to Alexander Woollcott that "Beatrice is always picking up these sensitive, ambitious young Jews." Woollcott agreed, snorting, "Sometimes she marries them."

The Kaufmans adopted an infant daughter they called Anne in 1925, and the family assumed an apparent conventionality. Beatrice remained a complex, independent woman with a circle of accomplished friends and a widening one of admirers, lovers, and protégés she took under what one of them, playwright George Oppenheimer, called "her soft and healing wing." She collected people, he said, "the way a successful investor collects money, only with infinitely less effort." She had writing ambitions of her own, but her truer gift was inspiring or encouraging what Oppenheimer called "her brood."

In passages Moss deleted from his autobiography he wrote fervently about her, calling their companionship "intimate." There seems to have been no sexual or overtly romantic relationship between them, though Moss was the very picture of the "sensitive, ambitious young Jew" Beatrice was attracted to. Unlike some who followed, she seems not to have decided she was the woman who could redirect him from the "confirmed bachelorhood" Irene Selznick and others assumed was his preference and his future.

His appeal at thirty was obvious. He was still tall, dark, handsome, and, apart from some overweight encouraged by too-attentive headwaiters, was an alluring challenge to men and women who needed to test their own charms and welcomed "projects." Beatrice's attraction for Moss lay in the soul mate she was, always attentive, always accessible intellectually and emotionally. Bennett Cerf, Moss's publisher at Random House, shared the feeling, remarking, "Part of the fun of doing things was telling Beatrice about them."

Intellectual curiosity inevitably led her to Freud, then newly fashionable among progressive New Yorkers. In long-term therapy herself, Beatrice urged Moss to see her own analyst, Dr. Gregory Zilboorg, a Russian-born Freudian who had escaped the Bolshevik revolution of 1917 and had a practice focused on the New York creative community.

Zilboorg, who claimed to speak eight languages, had supported himself by translating while earning his medical degree at Columbia. His most celebrated work was Leonid Andreyev's drama *He Who Gets Slapped,* which he translated from the Russian for the Theatre Guild in 1922. The symbolic circus drama became a surprise hit and an MGM silent movie with Lon Chaney and Norma Shearer, though its star on Broadway, Richard Bennett, was not alone in claiming he never understood it.

With the Andreyev play on his résumé, Zilboorg had creative credentials of his own that he used in a single-minded pursuit of celebrity clients. He cultivated a theatrical air, swooping about in a black cape and wearing a flamboyant mustache one of his detractors dubbed the "lunatic fringe."

Zilboorg was George Gershwin's analyst, too, which sealed his desirability for Moss if his reputation as the most expensive doctor on Park Avenue had not already done so. When asked how much he charged, Gershwin quipped, "He finds out how much you make and then charges you more than you can afford." He competed for the spotlight with his patients, sometimes pitted them against each other, and seems to have resented the very artistic success he was entrusted with helping them achieve. Composer Kay Swift, also a patient, had suggested Gershwin see Zilboorg and later called it "the most unfortunate suggestion" she ever made.

Zilboorg's conduct finally resulted in charges of unethical behavior with "criminal intentions" brought by a former patient before the New York Psychoanalytic Association, the board of which found Zilboorg's behavior unprofessional enough to warrant censure. He threatened to sue anyone who voted against him in what he called a professional "knifing." Censure was narrowly avoided and the charges dropped partly because rumors of the matter had found their way into the daily papers. The Zilboorg case could damage the reputation of the entire profession, contended Dr. Karl Menninger, then president of the American Psychoanalytic Association (and a personal friend of Zilboorg), who agreed with a majority of his colleagues that allowing a patient to testify against an analyst was "one of the most dangerous and vicious precedents that I can think of." Censure was dropped.

The larger issue, of course, was medical malpractice in psychoanalysis, though warnings about psychiatric tyranny long predated Zilboorg. Ernest Jones, Freud's disciple and biographer, wrote a pioneering essay on the subject in 1913, "The God Complex," that warned against the sort of manipulation an opportunistic charlatan with psychiatric training might find hard to resist. Zilboorg was just such a dubious pilot for Moss, who was all too eager to undergo personal transformation. Geography would move Moss from Zilboorg to other analysts as he followed the footsteps of Gershwin to Hollywood, but the escape from Zilboorg was narrow and perhaps never really complete.

He always spoke freely of his analysis, sometimes reverently, sometimes facetiously, but never skeptically or with doubt. He would spend half his life in treatment with one of Zilboorg's most outspoken critics and rivals, psychoanalyst Lawrence S. Kubie, whose penchant for celebrity clients was subtler, if not a whit less avid than Zilboorg's. Therapy would have profound and life-altering consequences in the areas that mattered most to Moss: self-doubt, sexual identity, creativity, and in what remained for him the most essential self-measure of all, success.

10

Broadway Melodies

*Broadway always thinks in terms of Broadway; it finds Broadway motives
in every person it satirizes; when it goes through the elaborate ceremony
of unmasking a celebrity it only bares the Broadway heart.*

BROOKS ATKINSON

After *As Thousands Cheer,* when Moss went off to the Caribbean with
Charles Lederer and then to MGM, Hassard Short did a quick job of doctoring for producer Max Gordon. Short turned his wizardry of lights,
sets, and costumes on a troubled show Gordon had out of town. *Gowns by
Roberta* was notable for its Jerome Kern score, a young comedian named
Bob Hope, a saxophone-playing actor named Fred MacMurray, and a
dull story whose biggest moment was an onstage fashion show. The score
included "Smoke Gets in Your Eyes," which should have been enough
for any composer, but Kern had insisted on staging the show, too. To save
it—and Kern's ego—Short performed some uncredited out-of-town
magic that made the show a hit as *Roberta.*

Following his favor to Gordon, Short and Billy Ladd sailed for
England, where they looked in on *Waltzes From Vienna,* the operetta Moss
called "folderol." Short had staged it at the Alhambra in 1931, where it
was still going strong, and it would soon be turned into an anomalous
Alfred Hitchcock film with Edmund Gwenn and Jessie Matthews ("My
lowest ebb," Hitchcock called it).

Short was still determined to bring the musical to America and cer-
tain, after the two Berlin shows he and Moss had done together, that
Moss was the writer to enliven it with humor for the Broadway audience.
Gordon had taken an option at Short's insistence in 1931 and had forgot-
ten all about it in the swirl of producing a string of hits that included
The Band Wagon, The Cat and the Fiddle, Design for Living, and *Dodsworth.*
These were credits as prestigious as any on Broadway and they had taken
their toll. Gordon was now hospitalized, recovering from a nervous

breakdown. Short took advantage of his immobility to press the favor he had earned by saving *Roberta*. He persuaded the ailing producer that *Waltzes* could be "the most stupendous operetta in Broadway history." Not only that, it was "clean."

Short's taking advantage of Gordon was shameless, but inspired. Depression audiences would soon seek escape from harsh reality in the sentimental, and hardly anything was farther from reality than the story of father Strauss competing with son Strauss and the composing of "The Beautiful Blue Danube."

Moss meanwhile returned from California. When he heard the idea he announced gaily that it sounded "just a little mad," which was not the same as saying "no." Moss knew Gordon (Bernie had worked in his office), and while visiting at his bedside agreed to rewrite the English version of the Austrian original, even though "for years I have been dodging operettas in every shape, form or manifestation, [earning] a sort of second-string notoriety as the boy who had never seen *Rosemarie*." Perhaps it seemed a way to prove he was not venomous or vindictive, but could be as kitschy as anybody else.

Sam Harris agreed to let Moss work for Gordon, as the two producers were friendly and often invested in each other's shows, though Harris would steer clear of this one. Moss's helping Gordon would get Bernie a job as assistant stage manager. It would show gratitude to Short, who had added greatly to *Face the Music* and *As Thousands Cheer* and whose style would have a lasting effect on Moss that was markedly different from the "faster, louder, funnier" precision he learned from Kaufman. He renamed the play *The Great Waltz* and decided to get *No Retreat* out of his system and out of his trunk once and for all.

In the meantime, he did another favor. Chester Erskine, like Moss a graduate of the Office Boy and Coffee Shop School of Dramatic Arts, was preparing to direct a movie for RKO based on a play that, by coincidence, had opened on Broadway the night after *Once in a Lifetime* in 1930. *Frankie and Johnnie*, written by Jack Kirkland (who would soon hit the jackpot with *Tobacco Road*), told the story of the famous song and *Show Boat's* Helen Morgan was cast as Frankie opposite Chester Morris as the man who done her wrong. The "lady known as Lou" was Florence Reed (the lurid Mother Goddam in John Colton's *Shanghai Gesture*) and Nellie Bly was Lilyan Tashman, a film star on the skids who died just after finishing the picture.

Moss wrote the screenplay for Erskine, setting it mainly in a Mississippi bordello where Morgan could sit on a piano and warble torch songs. The picture was shot in February at the converted brownstone on 14th

Street in New York where D. W. Griffith had once hired little Gladys Smith and turned her into Mary Pickford.

Frankie and Johnnie was shot as a quickie but its release took two years and was greeted by *Variety* as "unusually slovenly entertainment." The picture had fallen afoul of Will Hays, the movies' censorship czar recently put onstage by Moss as the divorce referee between Crawford and Fairbanks, Jr. in *As Thousands Cheer.* Frankie's Mississippi bordello required so much sanitizing and cutting that, when RKO trade-screened it a year later, the picture was only seventy minutes long. Eager to be rid of the thing, RKO sold it to poverty row's Republic Pictures, which cut it even more and let it escape in 1936 at sixty-six minutes, with dialogue *Variety* called "inane." Tashman got the only good acting reviews, but Republic didn't bother listing her in the credits because she was already dead. Nobody noticed.

Moss put Mississippi bordellos behind him for Vienna, a place he'd at least been to. He dashed off *The Great Waltz,* retaining a Russian countess invented for the London version who diplomatically stage-managed the father-son conflict that Moss lifted more or less in toto from the play he had written in 1929 at the Flagler.

Nan of *No Retreat* (and *Broadway to Hollywood*) is now Resi and again loses her lover—young Strauss is called Shani—to worldly ambition, but she strikes some familiar chords along the way:

> *People are going to say, "Young Strauss? Is that Johann Strauss's son? Why, I never knew he had a son that old. . . ." And that will be the beginning of the end. Because, Shani, you have a spark . . . a fine, new talent . . . and he* knows *it. And he's afraid.*

Moss's recurring waste-not-want-not economy required only a little backdating. In *No Retreat* the son declared, "I want to spend" and "show off" a little and so does young Strauss, who puts it this way:

> *I want to spend. . . . I want to know how it feels to go to Doumayers for tea and buy an enormous overcoat, maybe fur-lined and with an astrakhan collar, and pay for my tickets to concerts, and have a carriage perhaps. With three horses . . . just to* have *it. To show off a little.*

Gordon claimed he had been "intoxicated by the lovely Viennese music" and wanted a lot of it but, when sober, the producer who was part showman and part hustler realized that, unlike Sam Harris, he didn't own his own theater. But the Rockefellers did, two of them.

The larger of the two theaters boasted of being the largest variety theater in the world with sixty-two hundred seats, most of them empty. Now that vaudeville was dead the Rockefellers realized the huge space was too vast for variety shows and turned it into the Radio City Music Hall, New York's premier venue for movies with stage shows and the Rockettes, a formula that would work for decades.

The Roxy, the smaller theater a block away on Sixth Avenue, sat slightly fewer than four thousand and it became a movie theater, too: the first-run showcase for RKO, struggling to compete with the splendors down the street at the Music Hall. Gordon knew the joke of the day that the Roxy couldn't be filled with "Mae West playing *Little Lord Fauntleroy*," but his inspiration was to save the Roxy for the Rockefellers by getting them to finance its salvation, a scheme that sounded almost like a sketch from *As Thousands Cheer*.

The Rockefellers agreed to reverse the policy that had saved the Music Hall, by revamping the Roxy as a legitimate theater for *The Great Waltz*. They renamed it the Center Theatre and committed an initial $50,000, a sum that, at the height of the Depression, elicited gasps from Gordon's friends, in whom admiration was indistinguishable from envy. Cole Porter found the Gordon-Rockefeller alliance so amusing he included it among his catalog of modern wonders in the lyrics of "Anything Goes."

Gordon assured everyone that Rockefeller confidence merely echoed his own. "I've got nine hundred dollars of my own money in it," he boasted.

If the Rockefellers were swayed by Gordon's confidence, they must have been bowled over by Short's. The director had no desire merely to repeat his London production. He began at once to inflate Vienna's chorus of six into something that, on the thirty-eight-foot-deep stage on Sixth Avenue, would require ninety-four stagehands, fifty-six musicians, and 136 actors wearing over five hundred costumes. The direct cost to the Rockefellers of refitting the theater with turntables, stage elevators, and ten tons of scenery was $141,000, which didn't include the chandeliers.

When Gordon saw his first one, sixty candles ablaze, he was awe-struck at what his $900 had bought. "Hassard, it's magnificent," he said. "What a stage effect . . . it makes me speechless."

"Max, there are eight of them," Short replied.

The Great Waltz finally had nothing to do with drama and everything to do with spectacle. The grand finale was preceded by a fireworks display simulated by five thousand tiny bulbs responding to one thousand tiny switches on a massive light control board especially designed and installed for the occasion. The finale featured the entire orchestra, in period costumes and wigs, lifted by elevator from the pit, up over the footlights and onto the stage. Once they were in place, hydraulic pins coupled the orchestra platform to wheels and rolled the entire contraption to the back wall of the stage while the conductor's baton (presumably) never missed a beat. At the same time, the eight chandeliers were lowered on winches while ten pillars, each bearing a fifty-armed candelabra, slid in on rollers from the wings to illuminate (with a total of 980 electric candles) a ballroom in which scores of bewigged, tailcoated, or ruffled dancers waltzed with abandon, vindicating young Strauss while his father stewed. "Danube So Blue," da-dum, da-dum . . .

"You never saw so much scenery," said one critic, who thought it "prodigiously dull [and] a monstrously beautiful bore" that should have been titled "'The Great Waste.'" Moss's libretto was "dull, dull, dull" and "puny to the point of boredom," with "the size of the show" only "magnif[ying] its essential emptiness."

The Rockefellers, however, loved it. Gordon loved it. MGM loved it so much they made it into a movie twice (in 1938 and 1972). The public loved it. Even Barnett Hart loved it (though its father-son theme eluded him) and thought he could explain its success. "Moss, it's the hand to mouth publicity that puts it over," he said.

Moss rid himself of *No Retreat* for the next twenty years, and acquired (or refined) a permanent taste for spectacle. He was spared ignominy and self-reproach by the long lines at the box office. *The Great Waltz* ran for more than three hundred performances and enriched everyone involved, including the Rockefellers.

Fortunately for Moss's reputation, another show of his opened at the Music Box two nights after *The Great Waltz* opened at the Center. It played only half as many performances, but redeemed him in Broadway's eyes. The subject was integrity, and not a moment too soon.

Integrity was a subject Moss could joke about with high spirits. His cocktail party on roller skates that got dropped from *As Thousands Cheer* had included society and show business names like Cobina Wright and George Gershwin (and a "Bentwich" for a family touch), all of them on wheels. One wisecracked while whizzing across the stage, "Something inside cries out. I guess it's integrity."

What was crying out was the desire for a hit, but the issue of integrity did not go ignored. He pondered it when he could during his aborted trip to South America, to Hollywood and back, to Charleston, South Carolina, with Short and Ladd to polish off *The Great Waltz,* and on a turnaround cruise to Naples with Irving Berlin (they stayed in Italy one day) working on the not-yet-canceled *More Cheers.*

He finally settled down in August with Kaufman to work on the play they had begun in Palm Springs the previous February, when Moss had shown up in his "platinum" spurs. Sam Harris announced an opening for the new play at the Music Box at the end of September and Moss and Kaufman settled down only a few weeks before that to address the issue of integrity in earnest and in isolation. They did so on Woollcott's island retreat in Vermont.

Since *Once in a Lifetime* Kaufman had been busy with hits and misses. He wrote *Dinner at Eight* with Edna Ferber and directed it, directed (and doctored) *Here Today* by George Oppenheimer, and collaborated with Woollcott on a play called *The Dark Tower.* In addition he had begun another comedy with Morrie Ryskind called *Bring on the Girls* (it would close out of town) and had concocted a screen story with Robert E. Sherwood for Eddie Cantor, the assignment that resulted in the lawsuit against Sam Goldwyn.

These were collaborators of consequence. It was a measure of Kaufman's regard for Moss, and of Moss's self-confidence, that they could return to each other for a second time after almost four years. It seems telling that what they wrote was a play about a playwright.

Merrily We Roll Along's most famous distinction was that it began in the present (1934) and ran to the past (1916). It would never be clear who was responsible for the inspiration or the gimmick, and both views had adherents. "Don't ask who wrote which or what," Moss warned the curious. "Neither Mr. Kaufman nor I can remember" because of "total collaboration" on "every single speech."

Nevertheless, Moss said that the idea of a play's running backward had come to him when he was a boy daydreaming in the Bronx. He further muddied the waters by announcing that *Merrily We Roll Along* was really, after all this time, the old *Wind Up an Era* project supposedly derailed by Noël Coward and *Cavalcade* and that Kaufman had taken to deriding as "Hartacade." The projects had nothing in common but a generous slice of time. Adding to the confusion about the sources of *Merrily We Roll Along* was Kaufman's practice of assigning top billing to the originator of the project. Thus *Once in a Lifetime* was "by Moss Hart and George S. Kaufman," while *Merrily We Roll Along* was signed "George S. Kaufman and Moss Hart."

It wouldn't much matter except that *Merrily* was such a departure from the usual styles of both writers and so far from the burlesque farce of their previous collaboration. It was a serious play about idealism, betrayal, and that very Depression-era topic, the corrupting effects of material success.

The reverse running order was so startling and novel it seemed either an innovation of importance or some kind of stunt. It is possible, of course, that Moss's boyhood inspiration had been real. In 1914, when he was ten, Elmer Rice's *On Trial* had pioneered flashback scenes, a device Kaufman imitated not long after in a youthful play called *Going Up* that was never produced. There had been a backward-running play in the early twenties called *The Varying Shore* by Zoë Akins, but it was a failure too little seen to be remembered. The reversal of time was something a boy of ten might have sparked to and remembered, and it retains a certain technical fascination. Harold Pinter used the technique in the seventies in *Betrayal,* and it remains intriguing mainly because of Stephen Sondheim's more recent attempts to make *Merrily We Roll Along* work as a musical.

The curtain rises on the present (1934), during a celebration in honor of fashionable playwright Richard Niles's latest Broadway hit, *Silver Spoon.* The guests resemble real-life figures like George Gershwin (who plays piano), Rudy Vallee (who sings songs), and Dorothy Parker (who drinks). Niles's producer is there with his wife, along with a cellophane tycoon and his spouse (pretty packaging is a leitmotif), and some aristocratic types who title-drop about "the Prince." Center stage are Niles's newest leading lady, who is also his mistress, and the glamorous Althea Royce, his former leading lady, who is his wife. We learn that Niles's rise to eminence was greatly aided by Royce. She was once the kind of star who could make things happen for a young playwright from Indiana if he would give up writing coal-mine plays for the Provincetown Playhouse in favor of Park Avenue comedies for her. Niles is, as a result, rich and famous and something of a moral pariah. Royce—now descending the grand staircase—is, well, mature.

Her entrance is a sensation. She delivers some bitter dialogue about adultery and artistic integrity, forgetting that she was born Annie Riley and got to Broadway from vaudeville with techniques not learned in drama school. She accuses Niles of being "a money-loving, social-climbing, second-rate hack" and throws iodine in the eyes of her rival and successor, bringing down the curtain on a spectacular theatrical climax.

This was just the first scene and was, by virtue of the play's design, the only climax of the evening. *Merrily*—which is anything but—deconstructs the stages by which Niles went wrong, betraying talent, friends, lovers, and ideals. It ends with young Niles in 1916, delivering a heartfelt valedictory speech concluding with heavily ironic uplift borrowed from an already established playwright: "This above all; To thine own self be true. . . ."

It was a provocative theme for a playwright of thirty who once aspired to the laurels of Ibsen, O'Neill, and Shaw and found himself recently writing vehicles for chandeliers. *Merrily We Roll Along* had brutal honesty written all over it in 1934, but it was also written in the neon glare of Broadway. It was so knowing and calculated for commercial success that it seemed cynical if not hypocritical. A drama about the loss of integrity seemed odd, dished up with so much Broadway gloss that the production groaned under its weight.

Jo Mielziner (whose brother Kenneth McKenna played Niles) designed nine separate settings ranging from Long Island luxe to a courtroom to a cold-water flat, a chic restaurant, a park, and a reverently hushed college chapel. The acting company was not much smaller than the one in *The Great Waltz*. The cast numbered ninety-five, including forty dress extras. It was the most lavish dramatic show ever staged at the Music Box (the publicity boasted about it), complete with songs like Irving Berlin's "You'd Be Surprised" to define period, and a leopard-skin rug to define lust.

Moss maintained that he and Kaufman wrote the play in chronological order to ensure its solidity and, if so, they may have realized they had little to tell beyond a clichéd chronicle of idealistic rags to corrupted riches. But going backward from dissolution to idealism heightened poignance of the theme for many and confused others, like Walter Winchell, who seemed to have missed the point entirely, calling it "big time amusement." No one dismissed it and most critics approved of it as an experiment, not a trick. Brooks Atkinson was awed by "a pitiless, painful dissection of character" that gave the American theater "stature" and made it "impossible to dismiss Mr. Kaufman and Mr. Hart as clever jesters with an instinct for the stage."

This was the sort of recognition Moss longed for as a playwright. It lifted him from the class of Hollywood pens-for-hire and musical comedy jokesters. Moss had been reading and corresponding with Atkinson since the 1920s, and could only have basked in the critic's admiration for his delineation of "the exalted impulses we lose when we connive to stay alive."

But conniving is what the commercial theater is often about. It was precisely the authors' clever-jester instincts for the stage that made *Merrily We Roll Along* theatrically effective when it was. Robert Garland passed the clearest-eyed critical judgment. "It could have been a good play," he wrote. "But, instead, it is a brilliant show."

The curtain call presented the cast of over ninety in four deep rows, making the play's references to the tiny Provincetown Playhouse seem quaint, indeed. The spot-that-celebrity topicality quickened audience response, but went no deeper than the caricatures in *As Thousands Cheer*, and perhaps less deep because more self-consciously "serious." Niles was transparently suggested by Moss's aloof neighbor in Bermuda, Philip Barry, who wrote fashionable comedies about the upper classes like *Holiday* and (later) *The Philadelphia Story*. *Silver Spoon* is just the kind of title he might have chosen. But Barry was an elegant and thoughtful writer with a streak of mysticism that particularly annoyed Kaufman. It was about Barry that Kaufman grumbled, in a remark almost always misattributed to Sam Goldwyn, "If you have a message send for Western Union."

Neither collaborator liked Dorothy Parker, Moss's other Bermuda neighbor, whose portrait as a sloppy, sharp-tongued drunk called Julia Glenn (she refers to herself as a "whore") is just cruel. This boomerangs when the authors call upon her late in the play to sound the first warning note of conscience as a younger version of herself. She can't recover from the vat of alcohol and venom they've been marinating her in since the opening scene. Her plea for artistic integrity sounds ludicrous coming from a writer too drunk and bitter to write. At least Niles gets words on paper.

The Gershwin portrait ("I'm a genius. It's got nothing to do with me—I just am.") has a knowing feel, but only introduces a showy turn at the Steinway. The Rudy Vallee cartoon adds a warble or two, but is a stooge-with-a-megaphone. There are caricatures of producers Gilbert Miller and Charles Dillingham, easily recognizable to playgoers of the day, but thinly drawn and of only generic interest, spear-carriers à clef. What these characters contributed to the lowdown on the high life was vitiated by the authors' highly publicized offstage camaraderie with them, which suggested the playwrights might be equally shallow and superficial, just more clever at exposing their friends in public.

The play's reverse running order, which would later defeat Sondheim, required melodrama, a series of shockers to substitute for forward dramatic action. Royce's blinding of her husband's young mistress was a shocker, as was the Parker character's drunken lurch into a table that sends the glassware flying. There was a shocker of a fistfight in a swank restaurant between Niles and his oldest, truest friend. This character was a painter unsullied by compromise who seems to have completed only two (shocking) Dali-esque canvases: Althea as an octopus, and Niles embracing Althea and a cash register. (Someone suggests Niles should have married the painter, "you like him so much," a notion that might have been worth exploring.) The suicide of Althea's first husband is a shocker and so is the courtroom testimony about adultery on a leopard-skin rug. The rug, of course, is trotted out as if it could talk.

There was a deeper, more vexing issue that revealed the authors' ambivalence to their material: the need to retain audience sympathy for the leading character while detailing his descent. They addressed the issue by absolving him almost every step of the way. The issue is never character—his, anyway—it is always somebody else's. It isn't he who chased Royce; she chased him. He didn't succumb to her wiles; he was pushed at her by his first wife, who was tired of being a plucky drudge and by his in-laws, who were sick and tired of sharing their kitchen table. His capitulation to commercialism was precipitated by false friends who urged him to get away from himself (and Althea's husband's lawyers) on a cruise, as if sailing to Egypt and India might restore idealism and inspire fresh eloquence about coal miners. Niles was never the "prostitute" Althea called him or, if he was, the others were all pimping for him. He was the Niles he was forced to be by everyone else. Selling out is what he was *supposed* to do.

Ibsen might have found Niles the symptom or personification of corruption; O'Neill might have delved into his unconscious; Shaw might have made him a witty or perverse panderer giving the public just what it deserved. Kaufman and Hart, who must have related to him on some level, made him a victim and weakling to whom they and their audiences could feel sympathetic but superior. There was considerable posing in their writing and the surprising but unmistakable whiff of sanctimony rose from the drying ink.

Their friend Herman Mankiewicz defined *Merrily* in a famous, often-quoted summary: "Here's this wealthy playwright," he said, "who has had repeated successes and earned enormous sums of money, has mistresses as well as a family, an expensive town house, a luxurious beach house and a yacht. The problem is: How did the son of a bitch get into this jam?"

Paradoxically—or predictably—Broadway shrewdness paid dividends. MGM bought the movie rights to *Merrily We Roll Along*, though they never filmed it. It played for a respectable 155 performances; it was selected one of the ten best plays of the year by a critic who originally confessed himself "bewildered" by it, and, because of the movie sale, turned a small profit. The most satisfying outcome was that the aura of elevated purpose would cling to the authors even when they returned to comedy, and the challenge to play Hamlet—de rigueur among clowns—would continue to nag and beckon Moss.

Brooks Atkinson, who had been so moved when *Merrily* opened, reconsidered it when both authors were gone (they had been personal friends of course) and passed cooler judgment. He decided it was "not a contribution to thought or literature" and "came with ill-grace from two of Broadway's most successful playwrights." A sermon scorning the box office sounded tinny when delivered by the cash register.

It is uncertain what emotional autobiography might be present in *Merrily We Roll Along,* but many details came from life. Moss brought back the Levensons from the Bronx, the family whose father had given him the part-time job in the music store. There was a ukulele, and a cold-water flat like the ones Moss had grown up in.

The most ironic life-parallel was involuntary, a kind of flash-forward that concerned Kaufman. Near the center of *Merrily We Roll Along* is the courtroom where Niles, Althea, and the leopard-skin rug are on trial for adultery. The scene was written in Palm Springs, where Moss and Kaufman socialized with Mr. and Mrs. Richard Rodgers, who had taken a house in the desert with Mary Astor as a weekend houseguest.

Moss already knew Astor. He had met her on his *Once in a Lifetime* trip to Hollywood and wrote Dore Schary then that she was "the smartest gal in California." She was smart and beautiful and had a husband and a child and a career as John Barrymore's leading lady and lover when she was only seventeen.

Kaufman first met her in New York in 1933, and Moss and Richard and Dorothy Rodgers were effective cover for the affair that began in Palm Springs and continued in New York when Astor followed Kaufman east and looked in on rehearsals for *Merrily.* She hoped—an irony as sharp as any on the stage—to play Althea in the West Coast productions that eventually played Los Angeles and San Francisco, or even to star in the movie that never got made.

She documented her affair with Kaufman in a diary that played an explosive role in a 1936 trial for the custody of her child. The diary was read aloud in court, and what was taken to be coded detail about Kaufman's sexual endurance inspired headlines and smutty jokes from coast to coast. Hansom cabs in Central Park became as symbolic of illicit passion as leopard-skin rugs (or blue dresses from the Gap in a later day).

Something was prefigured in *Merrily* for Moss, too. There was a young actor who appeared among the extras on the crowded stage of the Music Box. He was the half brother of Max Siegel, Sam Harris's stage

manager. His name was Irving Schneider and he would become indispensable to Moss as secretary and shadow for the next decade. "Pale Irving,"
someone close to them observed, "was like Moss in many ways—without
the charm and without the talent." To others he was a Rock of Gibraltar,
steady and reliable. He would become part of the family when he later
married Anne Kaufman.

With *The Great Waltz* and *Merrily We Roll Along* both running, Moss
took another cruise, this time around the world. It may have been a way
of silencing or ignoring a question *Merrily We Roll Along* touched on but
never explored. "You think these plays mean anything to me?" Niles asks
Althea about what she calls his "powder puff" hits. "I do them," he tells
her, "because I can't do anything else."

"I did not like her"—
Moss's mother, Lillie Hart, in
the Bronx, about 1920 (NYPL)

Above: Moss's view of *Life* from the
balcony in 1915 changed his own. (SB)
Left: Moss's war effort of 1917:
First Honors in the P.S. 51 oratorical
contest—ironically, almost the end
of his formal education (WISC)

THE THREE BIGGEST THINGS IN THE WORLD

William A Brady's Production of

LIFE

By Thompson Buchanan

The Fate of the Financier
LIFE . . . Act III

THE UNITED STATES OF AMERICA
JOHN D. ROCKEFELLER'S FORTUNE

DO NOT FAIL TO SEE
LIFE
IT WILL AMPLY REPAY YOU
IT WOULD PAY YOU TO GO A LONG WAY SPECIALLY TO SEE "LIFE"

⊕ MINUTE MEN ⊕

To all who shall see these presents greeting.

This is to certify that

Moss Hart

has won First Honors in the

Junior Four Minute Men Speaking Contest

and has been selected as

Junior Four Minute Speaker
for The Third Liberty Loan

at *Public School 51, The Bronx*

Committee on Public Information:
The Secretary of State
The Secretary of War
The Secretary of the Navy
George Creel

By authority of the Government of the United States of America

Above: "To Edward Eliscu—My Best Pal And My Severest Critic," Moss wrote in 1923, which was not the same as giving his cowriter credit. (David Eliscu) *Below left:* Irish tenor Joseph Regan, who could toot from both ends, in costume for *The Hold-up Man* at the Adelphi in Chicago, 1923 (NYPL) *Below Right:* Gerald Griffin, in the revamped *The Beloved Bandit*, inscribed this sheet music "To Marcy Hart . . ." (WISC)

Left: Mrs. Henry B. Harris, coproducer of *The Beloved Bandit*, Moss's first failure, nevertheless found it "fantabulous!" (NYPL)
Below: Moss and his amorous mentor, Lester Sweyd, circa 1928–29 (WISC)

Above: Charles Gilpin in *The Emperor Jones,* which costarred Moss (NYPL)
Left: Dore "Butch" Schary, Moss's enduring confidant from Newark to Hollywood, without mincing words (NYPL)

Above: Moss and his brother Bernie at the Flagler, summer 1929 (WISC) *Right:* It wasn't Gershwin, but it got published. . . . (WISC)

ABOVE: Moss's first Broadway credit, for *Jonica*, 1930 (WISC)

Above: The collaborators: George S. Kaufman and Moss, 1930 (NYPL)
Below: Oh, Hollywood! May (Jean Dixon), Jerry (Grant Mills), and George
(Hugh O'Connell) get the cold shoulder from studio chief Herman Glogauer
(Charles Halton) in *Once in a Lifetime*. (NYPL)

The career-making hit . . . (WISC)

Moss with Max Siegel, the man who introduced Moss and *Once in a Lifetime* to
George S. Kaufman, at Camp Copake, summer 1931 (NYPL)

Left: Everybody's favorite producer, Sam H. Harris (NYPL)

Right: Everybody's favorite composer, Irving Berlin (NYPL)

11

Cruising

Technique is really personality.

OSCAR WILDE

"To thine own self be true" was a good curtain line, but easier to write than to emulate. What it meant exactly was not a simple matter to determine or articulate, even when paying $100 an hour to the flamboyant Dr. Zilboorg.

Moss's early psychoanalytic sessions piqued his intellectual curiosity and provided him with a fashionable pastime in 1930s New York. He joked about it regularly, boasting that he wore a letter sweater with an *F* for Freud. Therapy catered to narcissism and self-absorption, but was liberating. Free-associating and expressing the unexpressed stimulated a sense of discovery less narrow than navel-gazing. After Zilboorg, Moss's explorations into his unconscious would become more highly directed with a different man at the head of the couch and the process would become more painful as his bouts with depression worsened. Introspection would become a kind of addiction and the guided tour of his psyche a daily, sometimes twice-daily, necessity just to keep him on his feet.

For now his career was his main concern. Five Broadway shows in a row—two of them huge hits—meant he was no longer anything like a beginner. Still, the eternal question loomed: what next? The answer, as always, was work, but this time it was work that looked like play and would be conducted on a floating stage.

Cole Porter had fascinated Moss since 1933 when he nonchalantly disposed of those solid gold garters at the Ritz Bar in Paris. Porter had been born rich and had risen above it through ambition and industry. He was the only gentile among the big five composers of Broadway's golden age

(Berlin, Gershwin, Jerome Kern, and Richard Rodgers were all Jewish) and the only homosexual. He had degrees from Yale and Harvard, polish acquired on three continents, and a style that reflected his personality: elegant, risqué, and entirely his own.

Porter personified the born hedonist, though he applied his gifts assiduously, mining gold from talent with the perseverance of the forty-niner his maternal grandfather had been. The grandfather struck it rich enough to buy up a major portion of Indiana and it was there, among the cornfields, that Porter was born and raised.

When Moss and Porter met in Paris, the older man viewed the younger with amused condescension. He told a friend that Moss's brash-ness masked "timidity among the great," and tried to make him as com-fortable as a young man with the flavors of the Bronx still on his tongue could be in a Paris town house famous for Linda Porter and platinum walls. There had been talk of working together and, in November 1934, just after the cancellation of *More Cheers* and the opening of Porter's hugely successful *Anything Goes,* Moss invited the composer to lunch at "21."

Porter was a challenge. He had a notoriously low threshold of bore-dom and was ruthless in evading the old ennui. He had a habit, when monotony threatened, of raising a hand in farewell and vanishing from nightclub, drawing room, or continent with nothing so dreary as an explanation. A condition of his friendship was to be gifted, entertaining, and—preferably—young, attractive, and male. At thirty Moss was all of these. At forty-three, Porter found him amusing enough to add to his entourage.

Though *Anything Goes* had taken the town by storm, Porter had been unhappy with its development. The book had been drafted by veteran librettists Guy Bolton and P. G. Wodehouse, famous for their Jerome Kern musicals, and had featured a comedy shipwreck. The story was deemed unusable after the sinking of the *Morro Castle* with numerous fatalities. Casting was already complete. Ethel Merman from *Girl Crazy,* and William Gaxton and Victor Moore from *Of Thee I Sing* and *Let 'Em Eat Cake,* were a trio so hot they sizzled, but not without pages to rehearse. The show's director, Howard Lindsay, saved the day by concoct-ing a new book with the Theatre Guild's Russel Crouse, initiating a partnership that would eventually produce landmarks like *Life With Father, Call Me Madam,* and *The Sound of Music.*

Their book for *Anything Goes* was a shipboard comedy tailored to an already composed score and well-known stars. Though *Anything Goes* became Porter's biggest hit to date, the eleventh-hour salvage operation had disturbed his fastidious sense of how things ought to be done. His next show might better be constructed organically, songs developing hand in hand with the book. Moss, who had worked just that way with Irving Berlin on two memorable shows, seemed an ideal candidate.

Over lunch at "21" Moss stalled and feinted, complaining of fatigue after a year of writing several movies and two Broadway shows—one musical, one not—and claimed that he wanted to take a vacation now that *More Cheers* had fallen through. Porter suggested he embark on a holiday and a new show at the same time.

Moss later said they left "21" and went directly to a travel agent to book passage around the world, but it wasn't all that nonchalant. The original plan was to sail to London and outline there a musical set in Saudi Arabia about Americans in the oil business. With a workable story outline they could proceed to Morocco to do the actual writing, composing, and merrymaking.

There were the usual differing versions of who suggested what, but the round-the-world cruise sounded more like Porter than Moss. It was the kind of gesture that was second nature to a cosmopolite. Besides, Porter's good friend William B. Powell, an intimate since their student days at Yale, was a public relations man (mostly for Johnson's Wax) reputed to have invented celebrity endorsements and skilled at promoting staterooms in return for testimonials. Powell approached the Cunard White Star Line and traded passage on the SS *Franconia* for the authors' appearances in advertisements exclaiming what a kick one could get from Cunard. The ads would plug their show in return.

The *Franconia* was generous. The Porter party included not only the Porters and Moss, but also "Little Bill Powell," as everyone called him, and two of Porter's closest friends from Yale, Howard Sturges and actor-director Monty Woolley.

The four-and-a-half-month cruise set sail from New York on January 12, 1935, and seemed the nautical essence of *Anything Goes*. A brass band blared "You're the Top" as a flurry of Powell-engineered headlines informed the envious that the show to be written on board would be such an event it would require Sam Harris *and* Max Gordon to bring it to Broadway. This wasn't just hyperbole; it was contractual. Porter was committed to Gordon and Moss was still under contract to Harris. The producers had earlier presented *Rain* and *The Jazz Singer* together and were willing to reinstate their sometime partnership for a Porter-Hart bonanza.

Embarkation confetti had barely fluttered to earth when Harris and

Gordon booked the Imperial Theatre on West Forty-fifth Street for a show that had yet to be written. The *Franconia,* meanwhile, cruised south to Jamaica and through the Caribbean to the Panama Canal en route to stops in Hollywood and Honolulu. From there they would sail to the South Seas, Asia, Africa, and South America. The itinerary sounds like lyrics in a Porter list-song: Samoa, Kalabahi, Bali, Fiji, Pago Pago, Mombasa, Zanzibar, and Madagascar. Moss made a date to meet Noël Coward in Bombay. Anchors aweigh.

Harris and Gordon's immediate booking of the Imperial suggests the comparative ease of Broadway production even at the height of the Depression. The number of new productions for the 1935–36 season would fall to a new low of 120 from the pre-Depression high of 270, and only twelve of those would be new musicals. Even so, a show by name talents could find backing based entirely on reputation. Money and fists tightened with every down tick of the stock market, but Moss was maturing in a theatrical climate in which every show he worked on, from *Once in a Lifetime* until well into the 1940s, had a virtually guaranteed production before it was written. This was enviable, but creatively booby-trapped. He benefited economically by joining Kaufman as a silent partner in all of Harris's shows and most of Gordon's. But certainty that the show would go on encouraged flippancy and precluded the reflection, refinement, or real *bite* that might have resulted without that comfortable guarantee of an opening-night curtain.

What was guaranteed for producers and angels was an audience. Broadway remained a center of popular culture in spite of radio and the movies, though Hollywood was draining not just spectators, but the talent Broadway needed to continue thriving. Robert E. Sherwood lamented what he called "the fearful devouring of talent by the insatiable studios," even as he cashed his paychecks from Sam Goldwyn. Hollywood had its own woes in the mid-thirties, but knew that turning the bottom line from red to black was in some mysterious, never predictable way dependent on talent, which was—and is—why talent is both prized and resented there.

Irving Thalberg had been as rapacious as any robber baron, but made his genuine regard for talent the foundation of his success. At exactly the moment Moss was sailing to the Caribbean, Thalberg (dethroned but not deported) was doing his best to persuade Kaufman to sign on as a film director. Kaufman was then on the lot with Morrie Ryskind writing *A*

Night at the Opera for the Marx Brothers, and it was a temptation he found resistible for another decade. If Thalberg hadn't died, Kaufman might have succumbed earlier, and Moss, too. Hollywood would keep knocking at the door.

The movie moguls were doing more than poaching talent. They had recently begun buying Broadway material before it opened and became too expensive to acquire. In doing so, they were directly subsidizing Broadway, filling the gap left by Wall Street in distress. Production costs in the 1930s were still reasonable enough to make a flyer on Broadway attractive. *The Great Waltz* had cost $256,000, including the remodeling of the theater, but less fabulous shows could still be mounted on budgets that today seem minuscule. Warner Bros. in the thirties gave George Abbott $25,000 to produce and direct three shows of his choosing in return for the movie rights. Abbott went $2,000 over budget (for an average of $9,000 per show) and delivered *Three Men on a Horse, Boy Meets Girl,* and *Brother Rat,* all solid hits in the theater and later as movies.

In the same spirit, MGM, already enamored of Moss because of *Broadway Melody of 1936,* and already the owners of *Merrily We Roll Along* and *The Great Waltz,* agreed to finance the new show before it even had a title.

The *Franconia* was a pleasure ship that had been built for cruising. Moss told a friend who saw him off that he expected the trip to be nothing but "fun, fun, fun" and he boarded with plenty of his and his tailors' ideas of what the well-dressed young salt should wear on the high seas. This was a period in which Moss's wardrobe reflected, according to Lucius Beebe, a "penchant for diaphanous garments of blue polka-dot silk in the daytime." A world cruise required many such getups, as well as pith helmets to block the noonday sun and white dinner jackets to reflect the tropical moons.

Never able to resist a new and costly gadget, he brought along up-to-the-minute photographic equipment and dozens of rolls of film. The photograph album he produced would justify the expense, full of flora and fauna, some of the latter colorfully bedecked by the former and some of it not bedecked at all.

His shutter would capture celebrities along the way, like Helen Hayes and Robert Montgomery in costume for something at MGM during a stopover to introduce Porter to Louis B. Mayer. Edna Mae Oliver posed for his camera, as hatchet-faced on a Honolulu beach as she was on the screen. There would be studies of surfers in Hawaii, rugby players on Hilo, divers in New Zealand, and what Moss called "magnificent specimens of young Samoan manhood" that moved him more than he "cared to admit." There were temples in Bali, lawn parties in Java, rickshaws in Singapore, and elephants in Ceylon.

Porter was a more seasoned traveler and packed for work. He took along a butler, two maids, a metronome, a portable piano-organ, a typewriter, a phonograph with recordings from *Anything Goes,* quantities of black pencils and music paper, and three cases of Grand Chambertin champagne, vintage 1887.

He also brought along Linda to play den mother to the others. Moss was being initiated into the Porters' movable family, all of them from Yale and all of them gay. Powell was not just a passage facilitator, but the lover of Leonard Hanna, Porter's closest classmate at Yale and the son of Cleveland industrialist Mark Hanna. Before he and Hanna became a couple, Powell had lived at 412 West Forty-seventh Street, the famously bohemian residence shared by Alexander Woollcott with *The New Yorker's* Harold Ross and his wife Jane Grant. Powell occupied a third-floor apartment decorated, Grant recalled, with silk poufs in "tones of pink and purple and cerise."

Howard Sturges ("an exquisite from Providence, Rhode Island," Woollcott styled him) was now unattached, but had been the lover of the son of Shaw's original Eliza Doolittle, Mrs. Patrick Campbell. When that young man was killed in the Great War, Sturges took to drink. Linda Porter discovered him literally in a gutter in Paris and made a project of drying him out. His love life, Yale, and some music studies in Paris, where Cole had also studied, sealed the Porter friendship. Sturges lived with the Porters in a kind of ménage à trois in Venice, Paris, and elsewhere, though he and Porter were never lovers. Now in his late forties, Sturges maintained strict sobriety, noting cheerfully that alcohol had already "cost me two fortunes. Luckily I had a third."

The most outrageous and flamboyant of the quartet was the one known as "the Beard." Edgar Montillion Woolley was a forty-seven-year-old former teacher of drama at Yale and boon companion of Porter's ever after. He was a New Yorker so native that he had been born at the corner of Fifth Avenue and Forty-second Street in the Hotel Bristol, owned by his father. He left Yale when Professor George Pierce Baker came there from his renowned 47 drama workshop at Harvard, reducing Woolley's eminence and muting his thunder. He began directing professionally with two Porter musicals, *Fifty Million Frenchmen* in 1929 and *The New Yorkers* in 1930. He went on to direct *Champagne Sec,* an Americanized version of *Die Fledermaus* in 1933, in which a young soprano in pants named Kitty Carlisle made her Broadway debut as Prince Orlofsky. It was under Woolley's sheltering wing that Thomas Hamilton found refuge after his moment of fame as the Prince of Wales in *As Thousands Cheer.*

Moss was the newcomer to a crowd he dubbed "Miss Linda's School for Young Gentlemen," uncertain if he was a fifth musketeer or a fifth wheel. He was no stranger to the sexual smorgasbord of New York and the theater, but had never been part of such an openly gay, high-profile circle. Friends speculated that he and Cole Porter were having an affair or a fling, but there is no solid evidence one way or the other and taste argues against it. Porter was attracted to sailors and rough-hewn types (he and Woolley cruised New York together for sexual partners—the Greenwich Village docks for Porter, Harlem for Woolley), while Moss seems to have had a weakness for men younger than himself. The diary Moss kept during the trip may provide clues, but it is sealed for the lifetime of his widow.

Porter was "deeply concerned to encourage friendship between his lovers and Linda," as biographer William McBrien has noted, and his solicitude extended to new friends and associates like Moss, whose calling her "Miss Linda" hinted at respectful wariness. She seemed to relish being the only woman among five men, four of whom were openly homosexual, but she was still someone friends described as "old-fashioned, not modern at all," the kind of woman who "didn't know how to open a door," said one. "She'd just stand and wait for someone else to do it for her."

She knew how to protect her interests, however, and proved it during the voyage. At some point she startled passengers and crew by throwing Moss's fancy wardrobe overboard. One Porter biographer suggested her gesture was just a vivid fashion statement. She thought sandals and Bermuda shorts more appropriate cruisewear than the diaphanous silk pajamas Lucius Beebe so admired. Moss was reportedly "beside himself" and the behavior seems out-of-character for a woman like Linda Porter, no matter how stylish she was.

There is another possible explanation: Cole Porter routinely auditioned new songs for Linda before anyone else heard them. According to Kitty Carlisle, he first played "Begin the Beguine" for Moss, who inadvertently let this slip at the lunch table, reducing Linda to tears. Her junking of his wardrobe may have been retaliation for this trespass on her territory. If so, it suggests that her patience with Cole's young men and her freedom from jealousy had its limits. Whatever the case, Moss remained permanently diffident around the Porters. He later told Cole, "For some reason or other, I am always rather shy in your presence."

When not retrieving his clothes from the drink, Moss was free as the tropic breezes as he and the *Franconia* sailed on in a thirty-four-thousand-mile itinerary. The 250 other passengers were giddily aware that a show was being written in their midst. One of them accosted Moss as he tried to write on deck. "Do you get your ideas first and then write, or do you write first and then get your ideas?" she asked. It was a line he liked so much he would put it in the mouth of a bigoted matron from Darien when he wrote a screenplay about anti-Semitism a dozen years later.

Before the ship reached the West Indies, Moss had begun the Saudi Arabian musical, which he titled *Ball of Wax*. He also began his trip diary, later rewritten and published privately as "My Trip Around the World by Moss Hart," a chatty travelogue that reads like one of his letters to Dore Schary lamenting the burdens of la dolce vita. Copies of "My Trip," handsomely leather-bound and gold-stamped, were distributed to friends on his return, one of them to the still-faithful Lester Sweyd.

Moss's research for *Ball of Wax* came from copies of *Life, The New Yorker, The Reader's Digest,* and the annual reports of the Aramco Oil Company. He sketched characters, including an Oxford-educated sheik, a rebellious crown prince, and various American oil employees who could make clashes of class and culture amusing. He noted that the Americans might put on a show for Bedouins and Arab princes: Camp Utopia in the Sands. There might be a couple of dream ballets, a fat girl thrilled to find herself voluptuous in a burnoose, and so on. He wrote a first scene: Americans waiting for the company plane and its news from home in the glow of a desert sunset.

By the time the *Franconia* reached Kingston on January 16, the Saudi Arabian musical had been junked in favor of what amounted to an elaboration of the Buckingham Palace sketch from *As Thousands Cheer.* Instead of the Prince of Wales cutting loose in South America, Moss created an entire royal family bored by thrones and ceremony, aching to have wild and abandoned flings like ordinary folks.

The king could then indulge his hobby of string tricks in the park; the queen could read her movie magazines in peace and, with any luck, meet her favorite movie star, a Johnny Weissmuller caricature called Rausmiller, better known in his loincloth as "Mowgli." ("If he's the man I think he is," she exclaims, "God save the Queen!") The crown prince could pursue an American nightclub dancer resembling Ginger Rogers; the princess could indulge her infatuation with actor–playwright–composer Eric Dare, a Noël Coward parody so obvious that Moss's stage direction pointing it out was superfluous.

Getting them out of the palace was left to the kid brother of the crown prince, who just wants to visit Radio City. He and a cousin throw a stone through a palace window with a note threatening revolution and the stuffy kingdom rocks. The queen, who insists on being called "Butch" (homage to Dore Schary?), is assured by the prime minister (she calls him "Fruity") that the revolution is on. In the ensuing panic the royals make their incognito escape as "the Smiths."

Moss finished his first act as the ship passed through the Panama Canal. This was very quick work on material that was promising, but thin. Once the audience discovered that the crown prince had a yen for the nightclub dancer and the queen wanted to ogle her scantily clad hunk at close range, it was obvious where things were going. There would be songs, of course, to ease the way.

The princess (called "Diana") wonders at the outset of her newfound freedom, "Why Shouldn't I? (Take a Chance When Romance Passes By)." The crown prince and nightclub entertainer Karen O'Kane would dance to the insinuating "Begin the Beguine." And so on. The only real climax was the unmasking of the princely pranksters and bundling everybody safely back to the palace.

Moss's scenes moved along. They rollicked now and then, were occasionally witty, sometimes sentimental, but they lacked the bite he brought to his Berlin musicals. He was still shaky on structure but was saved by two elements that almost overcame the flimsiness of the premise. The first was Eric Dare, his Coward stand-in, who was dashing, witty, and incandescent with self-esteem. It is one of the showiest parts in any 1930s musical, written with perfect pitch. Two of the songs in Porter's score—"When Love Comes Your Way" and "The Kling-Kling Bird in the Divi-Divi Tree"—suggest Coward's "Someday I'll Find You" and "Mad Dogs and Englishmen" with a mastery beyond parody. Porter was so expert at imitating Coward's style that he would do it again as a favor to Moss and Monty Woolley when Moss brought Coward back yet again as a character in *The Man Who Came to Dinner.*

The second, more lowdown focus of the show was Moss's burlesque of that "tireless tugboat" of 1930s café society, Elsa Maxwell. Short, round, and ruthlessly self-promoting, Maxwell was constantly in the press thanks to lavish theme parties she gave that were really lucrative publicity assignments, like the one from the Italian government to make Venice's Lido fashionable again. Friends like the Porters gilded her guest lists and fueled her celebrity, though Linda reportedly found her pushy. To many she was already a caricature and Moss, egged on by Porter, laced into her with glee.

He called her Eva Standing and let her discover the king as "Mr. Smith" doing string tricks in a municipal park. She invites him to perform at the Come-As-Your-Favorite-Book-of-the-Month-Club party she is giving for several hundred of her most intimate friends. One of them, she says, is George Gershwin, who has created a sensation by promising *not* to play the piano.

The party gave Porter a chance to raid his trunk and use a song he had written in the 1920s for a birthday party for the real Elsa Maxwell. It lampooned her claim that every celebrity freeloading at her table was "My Most Intimate Friend." More important, her party served as the big finish toward which the show might build and provided an occasion for the royal runaways to reunite for a happy ending.

The whole thing sounded lively and likely to sell tickets, especially as this was the year that King George V of England was celebrating twenty-five years on the throne. The *Franconia* toasted that milestone as the ship crossed the equator in the Pacific and it gave Moss and Porter a title: *Jubilee.*

When the *Franconia* docked in New York on May 31, Lillie Hart was dockside to greet her son, having made the acquaintance of Cole Porter's mother, in from Indiana on a similar mission. The two women talked and Lillie announced to Moss that she found Mrs. Porter "very nice, very, very nice for a country woman."

Lillie may have had more urgent news to impart, for his aunt Kate's long-dormant vandalism seemed suddenly to have resurfaced. The Hart woodwork was again being whittled and carved by knives, as was the apartment Moss still rented from Irving Berlin. This time the damage added the ominously repeated "Kill!" to the usual profusion of X's or crosses.

Moss shrugged the whole thing off to reporters as he always did. He stayed only briefly in New York before accompanying Porter to California for *Jubilee* auditions. The primary goal was to secure from MGM the services of Mary Boland to play the queen. Though she had proven unreliable on *Face the Music,* she was perfect for a role that needed majesty spiced with vulgarity—Mrs. Meshbesher in ermine and a tiara.

Auditions at the Beverly-Wilshire Hotel in Beverly Hills, conducted by a composer and playwright *both* clad in silk pajamas, yielded Boland as the queen and British actor Melville Cooper as the mild-mannered king. Also signed was a Leonard Sillman *New Faces* discovery, dancer and future film director Charles Walters as the prince. June Knight would play the nightclub dancer and the prankster kid-brother prince, cast in New York, would be a teenager named Montgomery Clift.

The important role not cast in Los Angeles was that of the princess Diana. A possible candidate for the role was working at MGM on *A Night at the Opera.* Kitty Carlisle was the ingenue in the picture, playing an opera singer who couldn't stop singing "Alone" with or to Allan Jones. She later said she was introduced to Moss and Cole Porter on the set and was so excited she tripped over electrical cables and "fell flat at Moss's feet."

In spite of her pratfall, she related, she was invited to audition at the Beverly-Wilshire. She sang several songs and may have been so distracted by not being offered the part (it went to Margaret Adams) that her memory tricked her into thinking she'd sung a song that hadn't yet been written.

That unwritten song hinted that *Jubilee* was not as ready or problem-free as it had seemed on the high seas. The book problems would become clearer during rehearsals in September, but the need for one more song was already apparent. Moss and Porter had known from their first run-through for Harris and Gordon that their score was unusually rich, but songs like "The Entrance of Eric" and "Ev'rybod-ee Who's Anybod-ee" and "When Me, Mowgli, Love"—delicious songs all—were so character dependent that they made little or no sense outside the show. "Why Shouldn't I?" and "Begin the Beguine" and a list-song called "A Picture of Me Without You" had hit potential, as did a rousing music hall num-ber for the king and queen called "Me and Marie." But one more song was needed to compete with the expectations aroused by Porter's still running *Anything Goes.*

Following nine days of auditions in California, Moss spent the balance of the summer on Fire Island as houseguest of the Gershwins as George Gershwin completed work on the orchestrations for *Porgy and Bess,* which would open on Broadway two nights before *Jubilee.* Then in mid-August, Moss and Porter joined Woolley and Woolley's then-companion Derek Williams (who would play Eric Dare in *Jubilee*) for a prerehearsal holiday at Leonard Hanna's farm outside Cleveland. Moss again raised the need for another new song and by morning Porter had completed the words and music to "Just One of Those Things," one of the wittiest and most enduring songs he ever wrote. Only one word, describing a trip to the moon, eluded him. "Gossamer" was supplied by another houseguest, an architect named Ed Tauch who was part of their circle and gave up lyric writing while he was ahead.

Rehearsals in September revealed the weaknesses of the book. Monty Woolley had been signed to direct dramatic scenes and immediately clashed with Hassard Short, who was staging the musical numbers but left no part of the book "unscathed," Moss admitted. The British Embassy, alerted by the title and Moss's previous act of lèse-majesté in *As Thousands Cheer,* officially raised objections to portrayals of the royal family. Off came Melville Cooper's beard, which made him too closely resemble George V; Buckingham Palace was redubbed "Feathermore"; and Mary Boland's Queen Mary became Queen Kate, solutions that mollified the embassy and fooled nobody. Moss told the press, "There'll be no war if I can help it," and, claiming again to be broke, said the only royalty he cared about was the kind he could put in the bank.

Irene Sharaff was one of two costume designers who declared the Book-of-the-Month-Club party impossible to costume. A white-and-gold "Greek masque" was substituted, which allowed for chorus boys and girls in mini-togas to watch June Knight dance to a "Sapphic ode" recited in Greek. A swimming-pool scene was rewritten for the beach when Boland's appearance in a one-piece bathing suit proved a mistake. Songs were dropped at the last minute, including one called "Waltz Down the Aisle" that would re-emerge in *Kiss Me, Kate* as "Wunderbar."

More troubling even than the frantic last-minute rewriting were the outbreaks of vandalism backstage. A torn costume here or a missing prop there escalated to threatening letters warning Harris and Gordon to cancel the show. The letters pursued the company to tryouts in Boston and so unnerved Boland that she took to her bed and her bottle, missing the final dress rehearsal.

The threats followed them to New York. So did backstage fires on three separate occasions. Sam Harris was alarmed but, at Moss's request, informed neither the police nor the insurance company in spite of an estimated $20,000 in damage. Harris hired a private detective who revealed what Moss already feared: the source of the mischief was Aunt Kate. A story was given to the press that a disgruntled stage mother—who could not be identified because of "libel laws"—had confessed to arson. No insurance claim was ever filed.

Kate died not long after. Moss could ameliorate her fate only with his pen, and did so twenty years later by allowing her a fictional death off-stage when he was on the road in Chicago with *The Beloved Bandit.* It was a story improvement that served as a kind of benediction, loving and generous, perhaps, though—except as a literary device—he is not known ever to have mentioned her name again.

Jubilee opened on October 12, 1935, shortly before Moss's thirty-first birthday. Brooks Atkinson found it "a rapturous masquerade" and "a tapestry of showshop delights." Other critics generally followed suit, though there was considerable comment about an excessively inside aura and an odd tendency to pull satiric punches. Most notably, the publicity surrounding the writing of the show boomeranged. *Theatre Arts* sniffed at "what elaborate pre-production publicity can do" and Robert Garland wondered sourly why there hadn't been "more travail and less travel."

A legend has grown up that *Jubilee*'s two most enduring songs, "Begin the Beguine" and "Just One of Those Things," were ignored by critics, but this is untrue. Among the songs, "Me and Marie" became a hit for a while, but many critics singled out "Begin the Beguine," including Atkinson, who noted its "exotic originality."

But "Beguine," with its difficult 108–bar structure, had to wait for Artie Shaw and 1939 to insinuate its way into the American standard folio, aided by Fred Astaire and Eleanor Powell dancing to it on a black-mirrored floor in MGM's *Broadway Melody of 1940*. "Just One of Those Things" entered the book of standards at an unobtrusive pace, with no less permanent results.

In spite of publicity and selling reviews, *Jubilee* was a failure. The show lost money—and so did Cole Porter, who personally invested in it, his first and last such venture. The major cause was again Mary Boland. After four months on Broadway, she succumbed to boredom and the bottle and was replaced by Laura Hope Crews, soon to achieve screen immortality as Aunt Pitty-Pat in *Gone With the Wind*. The dithery Crews was wrong for "Butch" and could not draw Boland's crowds. The show closed after 169 performances, barely more than *Merrily We Roll Along*. MGM lost interest in it as a film, and it has never had a full-scale revival. The whole thing may have been, finally, too rarefied and inside for the general audience. Not many of them, really, cared all that much about Greek masques and Sapphic odes or Elsa Maxwell.

Moss took himself on another cruise with Cole and Linda Porter and Monty Woolley. They sailed to Bermuda with Mrs. Herman Oelrichs and bunked at the home of Vincent Astor. Moss's adventures among high and café society had been exhilarating and exposed him to a kind of swank that Hollywood and Broadway could not. But blood that was blue failed somehow to excite him. It flowed without the hot beat of Broadway and Times Square and, however genteel, seemed thin, not quite the real thing. Years later Agnes de Mille said Moss characterized Cole Porter as "the greatest amateur he'd ever met," by which he meant "that Porter wasn't a man of the theater."

Moss *was,* and was eager to return to it, back to earth, to work on something less exotic and inside than *Jubilee.* He wanted to go back to work on a real play again. And he had an idea, suggested, oddly enough, by the characters in his Porter musical. The notion of a family devoted to individual pursuits, however eccentric or downright loony, might be theatrical in a way that was less rarefied and a good deal warmer. Kaufman might like the idea, too.

12

Heart

[T]he way to live and be happy is just to go ahead and live,
and not pay attention to the world.

GEORGE S. KAUFMAN

During the year Moss sailed around the world and opened *Jubilee,* George
Kaufman worked mostly at MGM, writing *A Night at the Opera* with
Morrie Ryskind and directing a few uncredited scenes of the picture as a
favor to Irving Thalberg. On his return to New York, he discovered he
was a notorious tabloid Casanova, forced to duck journalists pursuing
him about the revelations of Mary Astor's diary by hiding out in Lillie and
Barnett Hart's apartment. In a less sensational vein, he collaborated on a
minor failure called *First Lady* and a major hit called *Stage Door.* The latter
he wrote with Edna Ferber, his spinster colleague at the Algonquin
Round Table who was, gossip had it, in love with him. Their collaboration had ended sourly on *Dinner at Eight* but the success of *Stage Door* on
Broadway with Margaret Sullavan (and on film with Katharine Hepburn
and Ginger Rogers) helped heal old wounds or ease unrequited longings.

Meanwhile, Moss returned from his post-*Jubilee* jaunt to Bermuda
with the Porters and Monty Woolley and resumed analysis with Gregory
Zilboorg. At Zilboorg's suggestion he purchased the dramatic rights to
a weighty Teutonic novel by Jakob Wassermann called *The Maurizius
Case* that had already been filmed in Germany. The novel told a near-
Dostoyevskian detective tale in which a boy proves that his rigidly
authoritarian father, a judge, has condemned an innocent man to death.
Righting the wrongs of a cold and heartless parent was a theme that
appealed to the patient.

Moss considered adapting a political novel by Dalton Trumbo called
Washington Jitters and proposed it to Kaufman for collaboration. He dick-
ered with Sam Goldwyn over Eddie Cantor and *Kid Millions* at Cantor's
request, but it isn't certain how serious he was about any of these projects.

He may have been floundering as he sank into an extended depression like the one that had hospitalized him in Palm Springs in 1931. He told the press he was working on *The Maurizius Case,* but he wasn't. He gave it to Walter Bernstein, the young writer he knew through Bernie and Camp Copake, asking Bernstein to adapt it and offering to look over the young man's shoulder as he wrote. What Bernstein wanted was a job at *The New Yorker* and, with Moss's letter of introduction to Harold Ross, he got it, the start of a writing career of distinction that lasts to the present day.

By early 1936 depression had overtaken Moss so completely he could not work at all. To escape New York he traveled to California, where he rented screenwriter Frances Marion's Beverly Hills house complete with tennis court and seven dogs. He entered into daily therapy sessions with Zilboorg's colleague Dr. Ernst Simmel, formerly of Berlin. Simmel was already treating George Gershwin, whose presence in Beverly Hills may have inspired Moss's move there. Oscar Levant and Herman Mankiewicz were Simmel patients, too, easing any doubts Moss had over Simmel's status as a refugee unable to obtain a license to practice in the state of California. Moss's confidence would not be shaken until the following year when Simmel, consulting with Zilboorg, would diagnose Gershwin's headaches as psychosomatic. The error contributed to delay in discovering the brain tumor that killed Gershwin, dealing Moss a double blow: a temporary crisis of confidence in analysts and grief for a man he openly idolized.

For now, however, Simmel's treatment was supportive and, supplemented by the sun and social life of Beverly Hills, seemed to have a positive effect. As Moss's depression lifted he asked Kaufman to join him and begin work on a new play. When Kaufman arrived in late May he wrote Beatrice with evident relief that Moss was "well again—that's all I can say. I asked him in detail, and didn't get a lot—he says he is back where he was two years ago. . . . He looks marvelous, and to me that's that."

The two men got down to business by rejecting the Trumbo novel (Kaufman dismissed it as "the political thing") and returned to an idea Moss had proposed two years earlier in Palm Springs. They had put the idea aside then in favor of *Merrily We Roll Along,* but it had an engaging, wholesome quality that lingered in memory and seemed appropriate to Moss's newly sunny spirits.

Carmel Bentwich Finkelstein, Moss's cousin, later insisted that the play about "a slightly mad family," as Kaufman described it, whose characters were each caught up in pursuit of some eccentric but harmless enthusiasm, was inspired by the tales Moss heard as a boy about the multi-talented Solomons in England. She may have been right, though the eccentrics Moss and Kaufman turned them into were unmistakably American, more artless and down-to-earth than their English "cousins." Each member of the household pursued a special interest—"no questions asked"—and what they "put back into life," to apply the standard of Moss's great-uncle Joseph Solomon, was the simple pleasure of pleasing themselves in a world that, beyond the front door, was reeling from one crisis to another, no shadows of which were allowed to darken their threshold.

Kaufman called the idea "a pip" when Moss proposed it in 1934, and told his wife Beatrice that it was "like nothing ever seen on land or sea." A stage direction refers to the characters' "mild insanity," but it is their idealized ordinariness that makes them so easy to like and so different from the oversized theatrical characters in most of the authors' work together. They toyed with title ideas and rejected "Foxy Grandpa," "Money in the Bank," "They Loved Each Other," "The King Is Naked," and (their favorite) "Grandpa's Other Snake." Beatrice dissuaded them from the last on the sensible grounds that it sounded more reptilian than amusing. The final title came from a line of dialogue in what Kaufman now referred to frankly as "the Hart play." The patriarch of the clan observes that "Life's pretty simple if you just relax" before adding lightly, "you can't take it with you."

Presiding over *You Can't Take It With You* and the Sycamore household of New York's Morningside Heights is Grandpa Martin Vanderhof, and it's his living room—"the every-man-for-himself-room"—that is the scene of the action. Penny Sycamore, his daughter, writes plays there, like her current war drama *Poison Gas*, or the one set in a monastery called *Sex Takes a Holiday*. She's been writing plays ever since a typewriter was delivered by mistake. Her married daughter Essie makes candy-to-sell in the kitchen and studies ballet with an excitable Russian refugee whose favorite American word is "stinks," usually to describe Essie's dancing. Essie wears her tutu to practice *tours jetées* in the living room while her husband Ed accompanies her on his xylophone. Besides being musical, Ed is an amateur typesetter. He prints up slogans that he adapts from Trotsky pamphlets left lying around the house and slips little messages like "God is the State; the State is God" into the boxes of Essie's "Love Dreams" when he sells her sweets door-to-door. Paul Sycamore, Penny's husband, is a former architect. Paul and Penny met long ago at a fireworks display of "The Last Days of Pompeii" and he now spends his time manufacturing fireworks in the basement with Mr. De Pinna, the boarder, who came to deliver ice six years earlier and never left, like the now-dead milkman before him. Mr. De Pinna stayed on because Penny needed him to pose in a toga as a discus thrower when she was still a painter, before she became a playwright. Grandpa Vanderhof dispenses wry patriarchal wisdom, collects snakes, and attends commencement exercises at Columbia, usually regretting not having brought along some ripe tomatoes to throw at the speaker.

The Sycamores' younger daughter Alice—the pretty, "sane" one—works as a secretary on Wall Street and tries vainly to introduce reality into the rambunctious Sycamore universe that slightly embarrasses her. She is in love with the boss's son, Tony Kirby, and introducing his stuffy parents to her family is the fulcrum of the plot.

Alice is right to be apprehensive. When the Kirbys arrive for dinner on the wrong night, they are exposed to the rowdy Sycamores at full, uninhibited throttle. The zanies are at their most appealing and appalling. Pickled pigs' feet hastily assembled for dinner, a word-association game in which Mrs. Kirby dryly pairs "honeymoon" with "dull," and an explosion of fireworks in the basement lead to pandemonium, a night in jail, and a second-act curtain.

The Sycamore household is the kind of place where "comic booby traps" (as Frank Rich calls them) are left lying around in plain sight. They don't have to be surprising to satisfy; they just have to go off on schedule, and they do, like those fireworks. It thus develops to no one's surprise (offstage) that Tony deliberately brought his parents on the wrong night, hoping they would unbend when confronted with this "whole different world" of tolerant people who love each other and have produced the Alice he hopes to marry. His embrace of her family disarms Alice, making her realize that "there's a kind of nobility about them." The lovers unite and Mr. Kirby, the Wall Street tycoon who had boyhood dreams of becoming a trapeze artist (and still hides a saxophone in his closet), lightens up and learns something about enjoying life, too.

To furnish a play so dependent on mood and character that one contemporary critic has called it "Chekhovian," the household includes Rheba the maid and her shiftless boyfriend Donald, both black, comic, and politically incorrect anyplace but Chez Sycamore. A deposed Russian grand duchess, who works as a waitress at Child's and hasn't had a good meal since the revolution, comes in late to spark the final moments and prepare blintzes. There's an actress Penny met on a double-decker bus who might want to appear in one of her plays if she ever comes out of her drunken stupor. There are visitors from the IRS and the FBI who would like to know more about Grandpa Vanderhof's failure to file tax returns and about Ed-the-Red-Menace, whose Bolshevik candy-box slogans have come to their attention. And what is the purpose of those explosives in the basement?

To go off, of course, as well-set booby traps do. Ed is too naïve to be anything but innocent; and Grandpa Vanderhof—after some debate about the necessity of taxes—slips off the IRS hook when Penny remembers that they buried the milkman as "Martin Vanderhof" when he died because they never quite caught his name and needed to call him *something*. A resident of the cemetery owes no taxes, and may even be entitled to a refund.

The extended family, including Mr. Kirby, sits down to the grand duchess's blintzes and Grandpa delivers grace as always. "We want to say thanks once more for everything You've done for us. Things seem to be going along fine. Alice is going to marry Tony, and it looks as if they're going to be very happy. Of course the fireworks blew up, but that was Mr. De Pinna's fault, not Yours. We've all got our health and as far as anything else is concerned, we'll leave it to You. Thank You." The curtain falls.

Moss and Kaufman began discussing the play on Memorial Day. Three days later they had sketched the characters and by June 26, less than a month after they had begun, a draft was on Sam Harris's desk in New York. So confident were they of success that they asked Harris to book a theater for November. They attached a list of actors for the principal roles, headed by the sweetly vague Josephine Hull for Penny. They cast character actor Henry Travers as Grandpa Vanderhof in California, where he was working in movies. Margot Stevenson came over from the touring company of *Stage Door* to play Alice opposite a young actor named Jess Barker as Tony.

Confidence in the Sycamores was not misplaced. *You Can't Take It With You* opened in New York on December 14 at the Booth Theatre and differed from the original draft only in that Tony and Alice didn't actually move in with the Sycamore family at the end. It was the swiftest, most trouble-free writing Moss and Kaufman ever did.

And the warmest. Neither Moss nor Kaufman had written—or would ever write again—characters so warm or openly affectionate with each other. If the Solomons were their prototypes, they were distant enough to be idealized and Moss kept it to himself, but other real-life models were freely admitted. Rheba the maid was based on Mary Campbell, a Jamaican woman known as "Big Mary" who worked for Lorenz Hart's family. Asked one day why she was single, she replied, "I don't have no man because the kind I want, I don't git, and the kind that want me, *I* don't want." Her best-known remark was her sassy reply to Josephine Baker, who came to visit and requested *"café au lait, s'il vous plaît."* Big Mary told her, "Speak with the mouth you was born with!"

The personality of the grand duchess Olga was inspired by a phony Russian prince who ran a fur salon in Beverly Hills, but Russian émigrés were ubiquitous in 1936, most visibly in the season's hit import from France, Jacques Duval's *Tovarich.* The word-association game the Sycamores played with the Kirbys was based on one Moss and Kaufman had learned to play at a Beverly Hills party.

It may be that Moss's analysis had brought him to a more relaxed acceptance of the eccentricities of his own family. Or that Kate's fate found a response in Grandpa Vanderhof's musings about "How many of us would be willing to settle when we're young for what we eventually get? All those plans we make . . . what happens to them?" Whatever the source or reason, there is a feeling of elegiac embrace to this play. It stands alone on the Kaufman-Hart bookshelf—"the Hart play," as Kaufman called it—in generosity and warmth.

Kaufman biographers detect elements of his cherished and contemplative father in Grandpa Vanderhof but his revered Mark Twain is there, too, in the speeches about government and taxes. When told by the IRS man that Congress, the president, and the Supreme Court need to be paid, Grandpa Vanderhof snaps back, "Not with my money—no sir." National defense doesn't move him, either. "Last time we used battleships was in the Spanish-American War, and what did we get out of it? Cuba—and we gave that back." But Moss's Grandfather Solomon is present, as well, his fierce distrust of institutional authority softened to "The world's not so crazy. . . . It's the people in it."

Barnett Hart may be guiding Ed door-to-door selling candy and in his "composing" Beethoven on the xylophone as Essie dances. Ever since Moss's first success, Barnett had taken to writing a song for each of the plays and was as eager as any tunesmith to perform "Merrily We Roll Along" or "Jubilee" to anyone who would listen. When Moss persuaded Irving Berlin to publish one of these ditties as a favor, Berlin made suggestions. "Now, listen, boy," Barnett told him. "You tend to your song writing and I'll tend to mine."

Name-dropping, that trademark of Kaufman-Hart plays, here seems tailored to personality, as when Ed frightens Essie with his Mrs. Roosevelt mask. Or when Penny notes with a nod to the Lindbergh tragedy that Ed isn't around and there's a lot of kidnapping going on lately. "Yes, but not of Ed," Grandpa Vanderhof replies. It's a joke, but it feels like Grandpa Vanderhof's joke, not one imposed on him by Broadway wits, and the restraint was deliberate. The first draft of the play was peppered with the names of Hitler, Stalin, and Mussolini but the references—all later removed—were too knowing, alien to the Sycamores and their self-sufficient world. And apart from Rheba's boyfriend Donald, who is on relief, only an offhand remark survives about the Depression in a play that is widely considered to define Depression-era comedy.

The case can be made, and often is, that the Sycamores live in a never-never land, a screwball variation on the boardinghouse comedies (like Harry Delf's *The Family Upstairs*) that Moss used to direct in Newark and Brooklyn. The first-scene direction supports this view, describing the Sycamore house as "just around the corner from Columbia University, but don't go looking for it." Escapist avoidance of darker issues was not the play's weakness so much as its strategy and point. We'll come through, *You Can't Take It With You* seems to say, and—in the heyday of the Group Theatre, agitprop, and the plays of Clifford Odets—it propagandized for nothing but the heart. As Kaufman told Beatrice, "the Hart play" asserted a simple point, "that the way to live and be happy is just to go ahead and live, and not pay attention to the world."

The critics were surprised and mostly delighted. Brooks Atkinson thought it "a much more spontaneous piece of hilarity than was their *Once in a Lifetime*"; *The New Yorker* thought it "the season's best comedy."

There were spoilsports. Chief among them was literary arbiter Clifton Fadiman, writing in *The Stage,* who acknowledged the "gorgeous wit" and "amiable goofiness" but lectured that all the money-isn't-everything moralizing depended on Grandpa Vanderhof's having a comfortably independent income (the Sycamores do, after all, have a live-in maid). "As usual," Fadiman chided, "when our best comic dramatists put on their thinking caps, the caps assume a vaguely conical shape."

Notwithstanding (or ignoring) Fadiman's critique, Columbia University announced in May that *You Can't Take It With You* had been awarded the 1937 Pulitzer Prize for drama, beating out Maxwell Anderson's heavily favored *High Tor,* which had earlier been given the top nod of the Drama Critics' Circle. The prize was a notable achievement, something worth boasting about, and Moss finally abandoned the whopper about having studied creative writing at Columbia. How far he'd come on a seventh-grade education made more colorful copy.

If there was any concession to the Depression in *You Can't Take It With You* it was in the economics of the production. It was the first Kaufman and Hart play to have a single set after the elaborate multiple sets of their earlier plays. It had fewer characters, as well, only eighteen compared to the ninety-five of *Merrily We Roll Along*. The trim operating costs permitted four separate companies to tour America while it was still selling out on Broadway and before the Pulitzer was announced. There were companies in Chicago, Boston, and Los Angeles–San Francisco, as well as one in the South that would continue to attract audiences for the next two years. In a graceful and grateful nod to times past, the Boston company featured as Grandpa Vanderhof an actor named Priestly Morrison, the long-ago director of *The Beloved Bandit*.

You Can't Take It With You spun gold that not even Moss's visits to Cartier's could exhaust, especially when Hollywood took notice. Sam Harris and his playwright-partners decided to sell the play to the first Hollywood bidder to offer $200,000. The figure was widely touted as the highest ever paid for a play, though *Abie's Irish Rose* had bettered it by $50,000 in 1928. Still, the price was more than any studio was willing to pay until Frank Capra threatened to leave Columbia Pictures over a contract dispute with his boss, Harry Cohn. Capra was in New York for the premiere of his Shangri-La epic *Lost Horizon* when Alexander Woollcott suggested he take in a performance of *You Can't Take It With You*. He loved it and made its purchase by Cohn a nonnegotiable condition of his return to the Gower Street studio. The asking price for the play was, in fact, double Capra's own fees for producing and directing, which made it, for Cohn, a very serious investment and a very bitter pill. Cohn swallowed.

The picture Capra made starred Jean Arthur as Alice, Lionel Barrymore as Grandpa Vanderhof, Jimmy Stewart—in the role that made him a star—as Tony, Ann Miller as Essie, Spring Byington as Penny, and Edward Arnold as Mr. Kirby. It was dismissed by some as "Shangri-La in a frame house" but it landed Capra on the cover of *Time* and became the most successful picture he or Columbia had ever made. It won Best Picture and Best Director Academy Awards for 1938 when it was released under the curious title of *Frank Capra's You Can't Take It With You*.

It was, in fact, the first time that Capra's name had appeared above the title in advertising and on the screen, an indication of his importance to Columbia. But the possessory credit also signaled how thoroughly he had appropriated the material. In his autobiography, *The Name Above the Title*, he discussed the picture in a way that suggested he had forgotten it was based on material by Moss and Kaufman, and the picture suggested the same thing.

Capra inflated the modest virtues of *You Can't Take It With You* into what he loftily called "an evolution from the brutal past to the compassionate future." That meant turning stockbroker Kirby into an armaments broker at the center of a struggle in which evil captains of industry got converted by "Capra-corn" (as *Time* called it) into warmhearted mush. Capra's biographer, Joseph McBride, called it "artistic regression" in which "doing one's thing [was] elevated to a spiritual value." It was a pretentious, sanctimonious affair, almost universally admired as the 1930s drew to a close to the sound of tanks warming up in Europe. It is excruciatingly labored today, while a filmed version of the 1983 Broadway revival by Ellis Rabb, with Jason Robards as Grandpa Vanderhof and Colleen Dewhurst as the grand duchess Olga, retains warmth and comedy that may approximate the original production. If there is a feeling of formula to *You Can't Take It With You*—and there is—it's a durable one, honored in imitation by every television situation comedy that derives from it. It is hard to name one that doesn't.

With the Pulitzer-crowned success of *You Can't Take It With You,* Moss and Kaufman rushed to follow with something completely different, trying their hands together on a musical. Before they could begin, they agreed to look in on Clare Boothe Luce's *The Women,* her all-female play that became a major hit and movie. Both authors invested in it if only as a favor to Max Gordon, who was producing, or to Robert Sinclair, who was directing and had been their stage manager on *Once in a Lifetime.* It may also have seemed politic to invest in any play written by the wife of Henry Luce, whose *Time, Life,* and *Fortune* made him the great media titan of the day. Boothe bashers, of whom there have been many, insist that the men made major changes to *The Women,* but apart from unknowable suggestions at rehearsals by either or both, Boothe's biographer, Sylvia Jukes Morris, established their input as a "typed list of 15 suggested amendments from Kaufman." Still, when MGM prepared to make the film version, Kaufman was asked to direct it. He declined and George Cukor took on the assignment.

With *You Can't Take It With You* doing SRO business at the Booth, Moss dashed off a sketch for the Shuberts' new revue, *The Show Is On,* which opened on Christmas Day 1936 at the Winter Garden. Staged by Vincente Minnelli, *The Show Is On* was a follow-up to Minnelli's hit (and first full show) of the previous season, *At Home Abroad,* which had been loosely structured around a world tour. The new show offered a tour of the theater, each scene lampooning a different area of show business, with Beatrice Lillie and Bert Lahr as comically inspired guides.

Lahr introduced "Song of the Woodman," which would become a signature number. Carrying a lumberjack's ax, clad in boots and plaid shirt and a toupee of possibly canine origin, Lahr reduced to belly-laugh absurdity the he-man tenors of the day like Nelson Eddy and Lauritz Melchior. He bellowed his way through a song that rhymed "Chaliapin" with "choppin'" and capped the recital with "ung-ung-ungs."

Lillie contributed her impersonation of a manic rhythm singer called "Gogo Benuti." In a harvest moon number, she swung over the audience from a papier-mâché crescent moon, tossing garters to the gentlemen down front and crying out that "I ain't had no lovin' since January, February—Gawd knows when!"

The Show Is On was awash in distinguished contributors. The Gershwins sent over "By Strauss," a fake-Viennese number kidding *The Great Waltz* that Minnelli would resurrect fifteen years later for Gene Kelly and *An American in Paris.* Rodgers and Hart checked in with "Rhythm." Vernon Duke, Ted Fetter, and E. Y. "Yip" Harburg all made contributions, though it was Hoagy Carmichael's hayseed valentine to a "Little Old Lady" that became the show's hit song.

Moss supplied the funniest sketch, "Mr. Gielgud Passes By." This was the season in which Broadway saw concurrent productions of *Hamlet,* one with Leslie Howard and one with John Gielgud. In Moss's sketch Reginald Gardiner impersonates Gielgud, barely audible from the stage above the chatter of a noisy late-arrival played by Lillie. She takes her seat down front announcing how "livid" she is about everything, including the usher. She goes to opening nights, she announces, because it's the one place she can count on meeting and chatting up her friends. "Gielgud" resorts to shouting his lines merely to be heard above her prattle. Finally, driven to desperation, he comes down front and offers her a free ticket to the Leslie Howard production down the street. Oh, she couldn't accept that, she tells him. Leslie Howard gave her the ticket to *this* production. Blackout.

Moss and Kaufman's musical idea, their first together, might have been fascinating had it been realized, a sort of Pirandello-in-spangles experiment. *Curtain Going Up* was to have been a musical about the making of a musical called *Curtain Going Up.* Casting was settled from the start. A character called "Moss" would be played by Moss. "George" would be played by Kaufman and "Sam Harris" would be impersonated by the original. Another "George," a composer, and his lyricist brother "Ira" would be played by the Gershwins, who would compose the score for the show and the show-within-the-show. The stars would be Moss's old "blemish" Clifton Webb and Ina Claire, the onetime *Follies* girl and high comedienne who had just made a dazzling Broadway comeback in Sam Behrman's *End of Summer.*

The idea of acting again quickened Moss's heartbeat; so did the chance to work with George Gershwin instead of merely inserting him into the script as he had done in show after show. Gershwin's unabashed delight in performing might have made *Curtain Going Up* historic as well, but Ira was far too modest and consented only to be an offstage voice. Harris flatly refused to appear onstage at all, but plans went forward once Webb and Claire agreed to star.

The sole obstacle appeared to be Sam Goldwyn, who had signed the Gershwins to write the score for *The Goldwyn Follies* over the summer, but *Curtain Going Up* was a spring project anyway. It is everywhere recorded that it was abandoned because of George Gershwin's death at the age of thirty-nine in July, but that isn't true.

Moss had been in California since January, just after the opening of *The Show Is On.* He had an assignment from MGM to write a comedy for Greta Garbo, whose European box office was contracting as Hitler's Germany was expanding. Moss was eager to make Garbo laugh, but almost at once plunged into another depression similar to the one of the year before. This time Dr. Simmel's ministrations were ineffective. Moss withdrew into his rented house in Beverly Hills and, after three weeks of a kind of emotional paralysis, repaid MGM the money already advanced and began plotting suicide.

He confided his plans to "Yip" Harburg in February. Harburg was in California to work with Harold Arlen on the same *Wizard of Oz* that Moss and Irving Berlin had once turned down and that would now make Judy Garland a star. "The subject of our conversation was suicide," Harburg later acknowledged. "I came very close to putting an end to it all," Moss wrote Dore Schary not long after, "but I threw the stuff away."

He managed to write a few letters while at his lowest ebb, several of them to "Prince Chap," as he sometimes called Clifton Webb. In mid-March he wrote as if *Curtain Going Up* would soon be under way, but by mid-April he gave up any pretext of working at anything. On April 17 he confessed abjectly that he had asked Kaufman and the Gershwins to release him from the project. There was no way he could write something so lighthearted, now or even in the autumn when the Gershwins would at last be free of Goldwyn. The project was dead before Gershwin was.

Moss had recovered many weeks before that and was at Cedars of Lebanon Hospital when Gershwin died. The composer's agent, Arthur Lyons, was in the operating room at the time of death, while Moss, Oscar Levant, Sam Behrman, and others paced the lobby with Ira Gershwin and his wife Leonore. Behrman was as overwhelmed by the composer's death as Moss, but angry, too. He dismissed the Beverly Hills passion for Freud as merely fashionable. He knew Gregory Zilboorg personally, thought him "boorish," and blamed him for the misdiagnosis that had delayed discovery of the fatal brain tumor. He was exasperated by those who defended Zilboorg, as Moss did, especially because Moss, in the first days of Gershwin's dramatic decline, had witnessed and recounted Gershwin's alarming clumsiness with a fork and his shocking inability to distinguish between his mouth and his ear at the dinner table. Such behavior suggested motor problems, not neurotic symptoms. But Moss's defense of Simmel and Zilboorg continued even as Gershwin lay dying. "I myself," Moss rattled on, "have had many suicidal impulses—I have been helped over them." Behrman was enraged, telling Moss that his suicidal impulses were, in the present tragic circumstances, irrelevant.

Moss's propensity for self-dramatization was never slight. Kaufman knew this and was willing to indulge it if it would get him back to work. He had been in California for almost three weeks when Moss begged off the Gershwin musical and may have concurred in his decision or even prompted it. He had been so alarmed by Moss's condition when he arrived on April 1 that he felt helpless beyond agreeing that Moss should turn to any idea that attracted him. Moss's newest notion may simply have been more congenial to him (he was juggling ideas) than *Curtain Going Up,* but grew out of his analysis and promised to pull him out of three months of despondency.

Behrman and others may have felt uncomfortable or bored listening to Moss talk about analysis at dinner, but such table talk yielded an idea for dramatizing the analytic process onstage. Moss turned his focus from Garbo to Marlene Dietrich, who was having box-office difficulties of her own. Dietrich had been a stage actress in Berlin and was looking for a Broadway vehicle to revitalize her faltering movie career. She and Clifton Webb had almost appeared together in a Cole Porter musical based on Gertrude Lawrence's old vehicle *Candlelight,* but that fell through and it may have been Webb, complaining about Dietrich's defection from the project, who triggered the new notion.

In early April Moss and Kaufman began to write a musical for Dietrich about a woman in analysis. It was an extension of the word game in *You Can't Take It With You,* based on the analytic process of free association. By the end of the month they had written a full act of the book and Rodgers and Hart had agreed to write the score. Then, suddenly, this project, too, fell victim to Moss's depressed inability to work and was abandoned to simmer on his back burner. He would return to it three years later without Kaufman and without Dietrich, but with spectacular results.

Having jettisoned the Gershwin and lady-on-a-couch musicals by early May, Moss suddenly emerged from the bleakness of the previous months and responded to still another musical idea with Kaufman, one that also appealed to Rodgers and Hart. It was a return to familiar territory for all four: a musical about the president of the United States. Moss had put Herbert Hoover onstage in *As Thousands Cheer,* Rodgers and Hart had done the same with Calvin Coolidge in *The Garrick Gaieties,* and Kaufman had written two presidential musicals, *Of Thee I Sing* and *Let 'Em Eat Cake.* This time, however, they would write a musical whose leading character—and star role—was the present occupant of the White House, Franklin Delano Roosevelt, a man all the participants admired and supported and were perfectly willing to kid for the sake of a show.

Moss's recovery from months of haunted fear of failure brought on by his depression was so rapid and complete that the FDR musical would open on Broadway in less than six months. The one thing they overlooked in their enthusiasm was casting. Only a star could play FDR. They would think of someone and, when they did, would rue the day.

Moss's dramatic swings from incapacitation to feats of copious creative output were almost certainly manifestations of manic-depressive disorder. The pattern was one he suffered all his life and was probably genetic in origin. The vacillations from ebullience to contemplation of suicide had been occurring since his early twenties and mirrored, in striking ways, the temperament he later described as having afflicted his grandfather Solomon.

The bursts of creativity that produced *Once in a Lifetime* and *You Can't Take It With You* were hugely gratifying but unpredictable. So were the spells of depression that arrived without warning and produced terror in him. Work was his means of earning a living and the source of his identity. Without his work there *was* no Moss Hart. Recycling material like the father-son conflict of *No Retreat* sometimes had thematic importance to him; at other times it was a matter of husbanding the inventory, as a songwriter guards the trunk of unused tunes that might yet sing. Moss never had a large repertoire of ideas and he stockpiled those he had against the day depression might render him unable to work at all, should he fall victim to the curse that afflicted his grandfather and his Aunt Kate.

The precise nature of the therapy he received from Zilboorg and Simmel is unknown, though questions of sexual identity played a role and may have become confused with his manic-depressive symptoms. His later treatment is less speculative because he was so open about it and it is less distant in time. But we know that he was plagued with insomnia and relying on sleeping pills even in his early twenties, as he had revealed during the *Beloved Bandit* tour. Still, pharmaceuticals in common use today were unknown fifty years ago and those that were were regularly denied him as part of a therapeutic process that eschewed reliance on chemicals in favor of shock therapy and patient-analyst dependence. The results may have been literally life threatening.

What is not conjecture is that in 1937 he roller-coastered from winning the Pulitzer Prize for the biggest success of his career to being unable to write, abandoning three promising projects—for Garbo, Dietrich, and the Gershwins—only to turn, inexplicably renewed and elated, to new projects with no apparent explanation but his own inner dynamic. Daylight and darkness arrived without warning, and both had treacherous aspects.

Kay Redfield Jamison of Johns Hopkins University has written with unusual sensitivity about depression from the unique vantage point of one who is both doctor and patient. In her book *An Unquiet Mind* she vividly characterizes the kind of depression Moss almost certainly suffered from (the italics are hers): "*. . . to be old and sick, to be dying; to be slow of mind; to be lacking in grace, polish, and coordination; to be ugly; to have no belief in the possibilities of life, the pleasures of sex, the exquisiteness of music, or the ability to make yourself and others laugh.*"

Moss's letters to Dore Schary and others mirror just such feelings in dreadful detail. But the insidiousness of manic-depressive mood swings is that the highs can be so seductive they seem to justify the terrible lows. According to Jamison, their attractions include "heightened energy and perceptual awareness, increased fluidity and originality of thinking, intense exhilaration of moods and experience, increased sexual desire, expansiveness of vision, and a lengthened grasp of aspiration." She stresses that "for many individuals these intoxicating experiences [are] highly addictive in nature and difficult to give up."

Moss's spells of runaway creativity were, from this point of view, enormously reassuring to him and to those he worked with. They were a source of wonder to collaborators who, again and again, cite his energy and powers of invention, as in Richard Rodgers's portrait of an exhilarated

Moss "fairly bursting with ideas" at MGM, or Kaufman's more recent, almost fatalistic relief that "[h]e looks marvelous, and to me that's that."

The heightened creativity and ruinous extravagance were twin aspects of the manic upswings, the "Hi-yo, Platinum!" exuberance that delighted some and appalled others. His inner states could almost be charted by his shopping expeditions, profligate spells that are symptomatic, Jamison tells us, of "bi-polar disorder," the clinical term she dislikes because it obscures the deeply human cost of such illness.

How Moss's manic-depressive states combined with issues of his sexual makeup isn't clear; perhaps there was no connection. What is clear is that no evidence indicates any romantic female involvement to this point in his life. He knew and liked women, but his relationships with them were friendly or maternal rather than romantic or sexual. That was part of what made him such a welcome social figure on both coasts. Beatrice Kaufman satisfied certain intellectual needs in New York as Irene Selznick supplied business connections and social entrée in California. Edna Ferber found herself a professional colleague cast in a surrogate maternal role. Moss wrote frank, sometimes agonized letters to her of his concerns about sexual ambivalence and his fears that he might be unable, finally, to fall in love with anyone at all, of either sex.

Moss's interest in men was active at this time. Jess Barker, who played Tony Kirby in the New York production of You Can't Take It With You (and would later gain a kind of fame when he married Susan Hayward), felt his performance was adversely affected by Moss's attraction to him. He related that during the run of the play he found it difficult to act because of Moss's habit of sitting in a box seat overlooking the stage "night after night" and staring at him with "frank sexual interest."

Perhaps there was something about the role of Tony, the idealized juvenile. The role was virtually indistinguishable from all the young male parts Moss wrote in other plays, and its oddly generic quality of harmless attractiveness may have encouraged him to focus on actors who played it, like the young man who played Tony in the touring company of You Can't Take It With You that featured Priestly Morrison as Grandpa Vanderhof and played its longest run in Boston.

Glen Boles was young and handsome and blond. Hollywood born, he had been in movies before coming to New York, playing his most notable role as the juvenile lead in Warner Bros.' film of Sinclair Lewis's Babbitt with Aline MacMahon and Guy Kibbee. He had toured with Mary Pickford in her attempted stage comeback in Coquette in 1935 and had toured in the title role in Langston Hughes's sensational Mulatto. Some minor Broadway assignments led to his being cast in You Can't Take It With You.

Moss and Glen Boles met at auditions, pursued their relationship through rehearsals, and lived together briefly. Moss followed Boles to Boston, where the pair took time from the play's run to vacation at Marblehead with an antique dealer named Laura Voss, a racy friend of Boles's who was "living in sin with her lover," as Boles recounted sixty years later. They traveled to California during the period of Moss's debilitating depression and Boles was with Moss at Cedars of Lebanon the night George Gershwin died.

According to Boles, "Moss was consumed with efforts to find his sexuality. He was sexually active but also confused and may have been experimenting. Sexuality per se was less important to him than wanting to love and be loved. He used to say," Boles remembered, "'If I could love somebody, I wouldn't care if it was a man, a woman, or a pig.'"

Boles was privy to details of Moss's analysis in New York and Los Angeles. They stimulated the younger man's intellectual curiosity and led to his later career as a psychiatrist in New York City. Following service with the Navy in World War II, Boles gave up acting and got his medical degrees on the G.I. Bill. His practice, lasting well into the 1990s, centered mostly on young gay men trying to adjust to their sexual orientation in a still hostile social atmosphere. He credits his career as an analyst to Moss's fascination with and openness about psychiatric issues, and the two men continued to see each other off and on until shortly before Moss died.

The sexual confusion Boles sensed is unlikely as the cause of Moss's suicidal impulses, but it can't have eased them. A man who began his career writing about Oscar Wilde could hardly have been insensitive to the legal and moral issues raised by a homosexual life at a time when it was criminalized and condemnation was widespread, if not universal. The world of the theater was more relaxed, as the Cole Porter–Monty Woolley circle demonstrated. It allowed a range of behavior with no apparent stigma. It was the theater, after all, and many people Moss worked with there assumed he was primarily homosexual all of his life, including some who knew him socially as well, like Agnes de Mille and Celeste Holm.

Another young actor Moss knew and worked with in the 1930s gives support to this view in a published literary portrait. The actor, Gordon Merrick, was "the handsomest young man on Broadway" in the 1930s and would appear in two Kaufman and Hart plays still to come. After he gave up acting for writing, he published a novel in which Moss was the model for a character who regarded sexual favors as a kind of initiation rite of the theater. Still in print, *The Lord Won't Mind* was first published in 1970, almost a decade after Moss's death, and was said by its publisher to be the first openly gay novel to win a place on the *New York Times* bestseller list.

The character based on Moss is a playwright named Meyer Rapper and the young actor who is the novel's protagonist "knew him from a hundred photographs—the swooping hairline, the Mephistophelian features, the elegantly tailored figure. He seemed to glitter with gold."

The playwright lives tended by a manservant in opulent splendor at the Waldorf-Astoria, as Moss did when Merrick knew him. He calls people "chappie," as Moss did. He tells the young actor, who is audition-ing for his latest play, "I'm afraid you'll have to learn right from the start what a sordid business the theater is. I want to go to bed with you." The approach is forthright and has an amusing and matter-of-fact explanation. "I'm sorry to make it sound so cold-blooded," the playwright says. "But my analyst would never speak to me again if I went into rehearsal with this situation unresolved. I might easily have a breakdown. It wouldn't be fair to my backers."

Rapper is fictional but was deliberately based on Moss, as Merrick admitted before his death to his longtime companion, Charles Hulse. He claimed the portrait was a fair one, Hulse recalls, "though Gordon denied personally having had a physical or romantic relationship" with Moss. "But then, he would."

Merrick was close to Woolley and his writing may be colored by that friendship. Others, including Otis Bigelow, a friend of Merrick's who would act under Moss's direction in *Dear Ruth* in the 1940s, echoed Mer-rick's impression of the erotic transactions that occasionally made Broad-way go round. "We wanted work and we weren't naïve or unavailable," he said.

It is unlikely Moss was ever as coolly manipulative as Merrick's fic-tional version of him. Glen Boles remembered that, in later life, Moss was distressed by the occasional involuntary attraction he felt around young actors, especially after he married. Boles recalled Moss's concern about the young Canadian actor-singer who played Lancelot in Moss's final Broadway show. "Thank God I had my heart attack and could get out of *Camelot,*" he told Boles. "It was the only way I could keep from being tough on Robert Goulet and taking out on him how much I resented him for being so attractive."

If sex was one of his demons, it was one he seemed able to control.

13

Grease Paint

*. . . in the old days, you know, we had what you might
call favorite scenes. There was the scene where the mother puts
a candle on the window sill while she waits for her long-lost boy
to come home. They loved that scene. We put that scene in one play
after another. You can't do things like that anymore.*

JOHN GOLDEN, 1954

Moss's emergence from depression in the spring of 1937 was as swift as it was unforeseen. He had been in virtual seclusion from January to April, but by May was sunnily ubiquitous on the Beverly Hills social circuit. He was the charming extra man at dinners given by the Selznicks and the Thalbergs; gave parties of his own, including a surprise party for Sam Harris at the Sunset Strip's chic Trocadero; and was seen tanned and resplendent in white on the courts of the Beverly Hills Tennis Club.

Members of the club were taken aback by Moss's smooth net technique, especially when he informed them he'd never played tennis in his life, except for four lessons just last week. Richard Rodgers was as amazed as everyone else and said so to Robert Sinclair, who promptly "exploded" that Moss had taken daily tennis lessons from a pro the entire previous summer when he had rented Frances Marion's house with the tennis court and the seven dogs. Moss was now so pleased with himself at being the tennis club's "miracle boy" that Rodgers couldn't bring himself to spoil his fun.

His recovery burst the creative block. Only days after withdrawing from *Curtain Going Up* and putting aside the Dietrich musical, he and Kaufman had an almost finished outline for the one about FDR. Rodgers wrote his wife on April 27 with an account of the plan to date: "very briefly," he wrote, "it concerns a boy and girl who are terribly confused by the modern scene and are taken up in friendship by President Roosevelt."

It's hard to think of a simpler notion: Boy meets Girl meets New Deal. The boy and girl were indispensable for a musical, or "revue," as they called the show, affirming that love still swept the country no matter how hard the times or who was in the White House. Young lovers would keep things from getting polemical and justify a ballad or two.

Putting FDR onstage in 1937 made this show "the most daring political satire of them all," Moss and Kaufman told Rodgers and Hart. Maybe so, but low comedy inspired their first title, "Hold On to Your Hats, Boys!," the punch line to a dirty joke then current (and not dead yet).

The daring was in naming names of an entire administration, cabinet members and all, and putting a sitting president onstage to sing and dance. That the real FDR needed a wheelchair to get around was largely unknown and irrelevant. What counted was that there had probably not been a presidential incumbent so able to arouse passionate feeling since Abraham Lincoln. Though Roosevelt had won a second term the previous November, he was at an all-time low of public confidence—or an all-time peak of public indignation—which made rumors of his running for a third term in 1940 so preposterous they became an obligatory element of the show.

All four of the collaborators were "ardently pro-FDR," according to Rodgers, but none was a deep political thinker. Roosevelt's policies and the man himself were the focus of strident daily debate as the Depression continued. He had introduced programs like Social Security that were so new even his supporters weren't sure how they felt about them. The alphabet agencies like the WPA (Works Progress Administration), the CCC (Civilian Conservation Corps), and especially the FTP—the Federal Theater Project—were subjects that begged for skits or numbers, particularly from disgruntled Broadway insiders unsubsidized by anything but the box office. Roosevelt's battles with the "nine old men" of the Supreme Court and his attempt to pack the court with six additional appointees of his own had come close to creating a constitutional crisis and suggested all kinds of onstage lampoonery. Not until the 1990s would an administration offer so many obvious song cues.

Less worrisome than who was sitting on the Supreme Court was the question of who would be sitting in the sixth row center on Broadway. Ticket buyers might easily be FDR boosters, offended at satirical views of their hero, or Republicans incensed at a singing-dancing protagonist their sputtering outrage defined only as "That man!" No matter how the playwrights treated him, there was the possibility of alienating half the audience. They decided to play Solomon of Broadway and straddle the fence.

Their show became a one-set fantasy, set entirely in a highly stylized Central Park that turned out, in the end, to be a dream. The plot was so simple that almost any song or sketch would fit: Young lovers Peggy and Phil arrive in Central Park for a Fourth of July concert and come across the president, gathering his thoughts for an Independence Day radio address. They explain to him that they can't get married until Phil gets a raise, and he can't get one until the budget is balanced. Couldn't FDR take care of that—for them?

He'd like to, he says, consulting the budget itself, which he carries around in a pocket ledger where he jots down the price of the ice-cream cones he buys them (25¢) and that of battleships ($150 million).

This cozy beginning set the tone for an Art Deco midsummer night's dream. Supreme Court justices in beards and dancing girls in much less popped out from behind bridges or boulders only to vanish again when their songs were finished. The cabinet magically appeared for a musical session under the trees and FDR lectured the wandering press and got lectured by his patrician mother, who just happened to be passing through with her butler, who just happened to be Alf Landon, the Republican Roosevelt had trounced the previous November.

Social Security, the Supreme Court, a hostile Congress, and the alphabet agencies all came in for ribbing. The big bipartisan topic was taxation. Since the cabinet will not sit still for any cuts in programs or patronage (Postmaster General James Farley devotedly dispenses jobs onstage to loyal Democrats under whatever park rock they may lurk), taxes are the only way to balance the budget, but how? Proposals are floated and shot down: since taxation shouldn't be *felt,* how about an official pickpocket? or taxing the government itself, with all that real estate and all those buildings? or asking the women of America to give up beauty for a year and contribute the $3 billion they spend annually on cosmetics to the national emergency?

All this, personalized as boy-girl dilemma, made the satire amusing and sweet, but bland; more fooling around than earnest effrontery. FDR was still the controversial focus and center, demanding an above-politics star without whom there could be no show. Moss and Kaufman approached Charles Winninger, who had been a beloved Cap'n Andy in *Show Boat,* but he was too contented in Hollywood to risk a return to Broadway.

Someone mentioned the need for old-fashioned flag-waving to make it clear that no one was being unpatriotic, some numbers like the ones George M. Cohan used to write and sing—like "You're a Grand Old

Flag" and "I'm a Yankee Doodle Dandy." Of course! Cohan! Mr. Born-on-the-Fourth-of-July (he wasn't). Mr. "Give My Regards to Broadway" himself.

Cohan was exactly the kind of star-spangled personality to appeal to Moss. He was the last of a breed of great popular stars up from the ranks that bridged yesterday and today, the kind of outsized figure Moss would have idolized from the balcony of the Alhambra or the Bronx Opera House. Moss and Kaufman immediately urged him on Rodgers and Hart, both of whom thought Cohan a star-spangled horror.

"I must have turned at least a dozen shades paler," Rodgers said of the suggestion. "Didn't they know that he was a disgruntled man with no respect for anyone's work but his own? Didn't they realize what they were getting themselves into?"

Just before Moss worked with Rodgers and Hart at MGM, the song-writers had worked with Cohan at Paramount. They wrote the songs for *The Phantom President,* Cohan's talking picture debut that included the first ditties he'd ever performed that he hadn't written himself. The picture costarred Claudette Colbert and Jimmy Durante in a story in which Cohan played the double roles of a shy candidate for president and the extroverted look-alike who campaigns for him.

He was the first great musical comedy star of the modern era and was not used to Hollywood or the lack of deference with which Paramount treated him. According to Rodgers he created "tension right from the start. There was never anything overt, simply a curtness and a disdain that he displayed . . . to everyone who had anything to do with the picture. One just knew that he felt he could direct better than the director, write a script better than the scriptwriters, and write music and lyrics better than Rodgers and Hart." In short, he thought he had written the musical comedy book and, in many ways, he had. It's just that his version of the book seemed tired and dated to most observers of the thirties.

The Phantom President was a failure in 1932—"Hoover got more votes," quipped Rodgers—and Cohan would never become a film star. Ironically, it is a film about him, rather than with him, that keeps him alive for modern audiences: *Yankee Doodle Dandy,* for which James Cagney won the 1942 Academy Award strutting his stuff as Cohan.

Changing times had not left Cohan a relic; he was still a beloved name for audiences in spite of a series of recent failures. Though he had not sung and danced onstage for a decade, he had given a memorable acting performance in Eugene O'Neill's only comedy, *Ah, Wilderness!*, in 1933.

Moss seemed blithely oblivious to Rodgers and Hart's gloom over the idea of tangling again with a man they viewed as arrogant and resentful that Broadway had passed him by. In early July, between the hospital deathwatch over George Gershwin and playing tennis at the club, Moss bent his charm to persuading the songwriters that they were wrong and that only Cohan could credibly—and commercially—play FDR.

He applied a mixture of snake oil and soft soap. He told Rodgers that Cohan had nothing but the highest regard for him and for Hart, that it was not working with them, but with shameless Paramount that had caused him to seem arrogant and haughty. The studio had treated him shabbily, but that was all.

"This [is] going to be different," Moss promised Rodgers. "This [will] be Cohan returning to Broadway in a musical comedy after an absence of almost ten years, and he [is] anxious and grateful to be getting back to work. Besides," Moss said, adding the clincher, the show would be produced by Sam Harris, who was Cohan's closest friend and former partner. Rodgers agreed "Sam was one of the sweetest men on Broadway . . . just about the only person in the world who could keep Cohan in line."

In July (while Moss was still in California) Kaufman and Harris broached the idea to Cohan in New York and Cohan voiced "no objections whatever." Rodgers was so "relieved," he told his wife, Dorothy, that he proposed a new title, "Hooray for Our Side!" but Mrs. Rodgers suggested a venerable line from American history and Henry Clay, "I would rather be right than president," and the show became, with a mild political pun, *I'd Rather Be Right*.

Moss and Kaufman peppered their script with inside jokes. FDR would muse at one point, "You can't take it with you," and when Social Security cards were distributed to ordinary citizens, they were named after *The New Yorker*'s new employee, Walter Bernstein, and Harold Levenson, the son of the Bronx music-store owner Moss worked for as a teenager. There were brazen plugs for Marx Brothers movies and even one for *The Great Waltz* in a parody number about a $675,000 Federal Theater Project called "Spring in Vienna" to be sung and danced in Central Park by a chorus of girls obliged by the FTP to put on a show whenever an audience of three turned up.

Rodgers and Hart wrote spirited numbers with titles like "Sweet Sixty-Five" about Social Security, "Labor Is the Thing" about capitalists and unions, "We're Going to Balance the Budget" about spending limits, and "A Baby Bond for Baby" about saving for the future. The important ballads were "Have You Met Miss Jones?" (heroine Peggy's last name was Jones) and the title song.

By early September the playwrights and songwriters were ready to present the entire show to their star in New York. They assembled in neutral territory at the home of Cartier executive Jules Glaenzer, who was an investor friendly with Rodgers. The composer and a rehearsal pianist played the score and Moss warbled the songs ("He didn't have a trained voice, of course, but he had excellent enunciation and an oddly charming way of putting over a song," Rodgers recalled). Cohan listened quietly to the entire score, patted Rodgers on the back, said, "Don't take any wooden nickels," and walked out.

Notice had been served. Cohan subsequently insisted that the love ballad that served as the title song be rewritten as a political patter number for himself, and it was. Another love song was dropped. He never spoke to Rodgers and Hart through rehearsals, treating them instead with what Rodgers called "contempt," and referring to them behind their backs as "Gilbert and Sullivan," even to the press.

What none of the writers of the show knew was that, in addition to resenting having to sing songs he had not written himself, Cohan hated Franklin Delano Roosevelt. His hatred was so intense that, on opening night in Boston, he interpolated some lines into a song FDR sings to the press called "Off the Record," making his political sympathies unmistakably clear to the out-of-town crowd. To make things still clearer, he then ad-libbed breezily that he would probably be fired for doing so, just so the audience would know what he thought of the show as well as of Roosevelt. He then repeated every word to the press.

Kaufman and Harris blew up. They read the riot act about unprofessional behavior to Cohan, who, by this time, knew that the show—ad-libs and all—was an enormous hit and was thoroughly confident who had made it one.

He wasn't wrong. The New York opening at the Alvin Theatre on November 2, 1937, was the most highly anticipated event of the season largely because he was in it. It had only one hit song ("Have You Met Miss Jones?"); its young lovers were such cardboard characters they would have disappeared had they turned sideways; but Cohan as FDR proved irresistible.

One of the sources of his appeal was the strong whiff of Grandpa Vanderhof built into the role by the authors. He never balances the budget, but he convinces Peggy and Phil to marry anyway, and delivers a culminating speech of uplift that made audiences feel swaddled in red, white, and blue banality:

We fought for our freedom, we fought among ourselves, we've had bad presidents and good presidents; we've had panics and depressions and floods and strikes and wars. But it seems there's something in this country that always sees us through.

He then affirmed the patriotic appropriateness of kidding the government, a note repeated by almost every critic:

[A]t least this is a country where you can come out and talk about what's wrong. And there aren't many left like that nowadays. . . . There's only one thing that really matters in this country, or ever will.

Whereupon he gestured broadly to the cast and audience. "You!"

The words might have been lifted from Moss's prizewinning schoolboy oration back in 1917 when Cohan was still singing "Over There."

I'd Rather Be Right went on to play 290 performances and became the longest-running topical show of the 1930s, a safe, inoffensive hit that pulled its punches, its gibes too toothless to dent any but the most sensitive skin. The sharp, biting satire Moss brought to *As Thousands Cheer* had been replaced by political bromides. Something was mellowing: the times or the teller of the tale, now an investor, an entrepreneur, a ticket taker.

The one voice Moss could not hear in praise of *I'd Rather Be Right* was that of the woman who had attended every Brighton Beach performance of *Once in a Lifetime,* who had visited the Flagler in the summer to see his revues and sketches, and who had followed his career with an avid if unsophisticated delight, though he never acknowledged her pride in his achievements.

Lillie Hart died on September 6, 1937. She and Barnett—and her sons—had drifted so far apart that she was vacationing alone when she succumbed to a coronary thrombosis in a tourist hotel in Asbury Park, New Jersey. She was buried two days later at Riverside Chapel in Manhattan. Joe Hyman, Moss's business manager and benefactor from Vermont, handled the arrangements. Moss stayed in California, nursing resentments that were years beyond redress. Twenty years later he would coolly write, "I did not like her." He was a man who could dramatize almost anything, certainly including himself, who could display his bereavement like a banner at the death of a Gershwin; but the death of a parent produced a calm, almost eerie sense of detachment and self-control and no regrets. Now Lillie, later Barnett.

• • •

Coming on the heels of the Pulitzer Prize for *You Can't Take It With You,* *I'd Rather Be Right* had the effect of uniting Moss and Kaufman so thoroughly in the public mind that, henceforth, "Kaufman and Hart" would be permanently linked, as American as ham 'n' eggs. They were eager to capitalize on their commercial viability and, with money flowing in from both productions, decided to become producers in name as well as silent fact.

The impetus was friendship with Max Gordon, for whom Bernie Hart still worked and who had presented shows for both men, with and without Sam Harris. Gordon's last successful production was *The Women,* but he had been hit hard by more recent failures. He now hoped to balance his books with a musical revue by the neophyte authors of the phenomenally successful downtown revue *Pins and Needles,* which had been presented by the International Ladies Garment Workers Union and would become, with *Hellzapoppin,* Olsen and Johnson's inane slapstick revue, one of the two longest-running musicals of the decade.

The new show, *Sing Out the News,* would be a much more pointedly liberal affair than *I'd Rather Be Right* and Moss and Kaufman would, for the first time, put their names on it as producers in association with Gordon.

While *Sing Out the News* was being prepared, however, the two playwrights turned again to another notion of Moss's. *I'd Rather Be Right* had been mostly Kaufman's idea and the credits signaled that by putting his name first. This time, as with *You Can't Take It With You,* Moss would take first honors. Or brickbats.

It is unlikely there was ever a playwright so ardently enamored of Broadway as Moss. He loved everything about it, the songs, the stories, the people, even its shabby business practices, always good for a quip or a punch line. If he pondered much the gulf that existed between the art of the theater and that of the box office, he never let on. He was content to bask in nostalgia for the shows of his youth and the stars who made them. Cohan, however difficult he was to work with, reawakened in Moss his love for theater gone by, as did a little-noted event the same year that had personal meaning.

Early in 1937 the New Amsterdam Theatre, fabled home of Ziegfeld and the *Follies,* and the less fabled one of Gus Pitou, was turned into a movie theater. The New Amsterdam was the most legendary name on the list of once-proud legitimate houses falling victim to Hollywood and the deterioration of Forty-second Street. The roar of the greasepaint had grown raucous and vulgar; the smell of the crowd had risen to high heaven.

Moss had never quite lost his enthusiasm for his old *Cavalcade* idea, the one he called *Wind Up an Era.* The sad fate of the New Amsterdam suddenly suggested a way to turn that never-written notion to advantage. It may be that his work on MGM's *Broadway to Hollywood* lent a page, too. Though that movie had been just a salvage job reworking the father-son conflict of *No Retreat,* it ended as a theatrical cavalcade from music hall to vaudeville to musical comedy to the movies.

The same general plan might lend itself to a tribute to the theater itself as Moss had experienced it, directly or through the scented reminiscences of Kate. The leading character would be a theater—a single theater—as subject of a biographical play with music and color. For its title he and Kaufman would coin a phrase by which the theater has been known ever since: *The Fabulous Invalid.* That title would be the most enduring thing about it.

Kaufman fell in with Moss's plan at once, which was curious, for Kaufman had never been known to wax sentimental about the theater, and if *The Fabulous Invalid* wasn't sentimental, it wasn't anything. Irving Schneider, Max Siegel's half brother who had appeared in *Merrily We Roll Along* and had since become Moss's right hand, was present at a meeting in which Kaufman presented the plan for the new show. Schneider told Kaufman's biographer, Malcolm Goldstein, that the senior member of the firm was as enthusiastic about the theatrical cavalcade idea as he had been about *You Can't Take It With You* and *I'd Rather Be Right.*

Perhaps it was that no other recent idea had sparked either writer. Moss, in the interim, had worked briefly on another movie in Hollywood on which he would receive no credit. He had checked in with Irene Selznick's husband, David, for a quick bit of doctoring on Selznick's and Ben Hecht's *Nothing Sacred.* The story of a newspaperman (Fredric March) overly eager to make a national heroine of a girl from Vermont called Hazel Flagg (Carole Lombard) who is dying of radium poisoning (only she's not) desperately needed a resolution that wouldn't alienate audiences from either of its stars. Moss was asked to supply an ending that had already defeated Hecht and every other writer who tackled it. Moss couldn't do any better than Hecht, but Ring Lardner, Jr., and George Oppenheimer came up with an ending that, if it didn't work either, didn't keep the picture from being a hit.

Kaufman had been offered, and toyed with the idea of, directing the Marx Brothers in *A Day at the Races,* their MGM follow-up to *A Night at the Opera,* but in the end returned to New York, where he memorably staged his adaptation of John Steinbeck's *Of Mice and Men.*

The one project the two worked on that held special interest was a curiosity. Before they returned from California to New York through the Panama Canal, Moss had begun remining his past. This may have been the result of his analysis or not, but they began work on a musical about Moss's apprenticeship in the theater and his triumphant success with Kaufman and *Once in a Lifetime*. It was a good idea, as Bennett Cerf and Random House would discover when Moss finally put it in book form twenty years later. It is still a corking idea for a musical.

The Fabulous Invalid, as every critic would point out, was more pageant than play, and though there were characters for the audience to sympathize with, they were (literally) ghostly guides through the fictional Alexandria Theatre, from its gala opening to its degraded, but—at the last minute—hopeful present.

It was a scrapbook culled lovingly by Moss from his memories of the past and old copies of *Stage* magazine that opened at the Broadhurst Theatre on October 8, 1938, with a cast of seventy-three. It was, in principal, a one-set show, much as Elmer Rice's *Street Scene* or the more recent . . . *one third of a nation* . . . by Arthur Arent had been, the main set being the Alexandria and the street before it. The stage pictured the theater's exterior as it degenerated from the age of gaslight and hansom cabs to become a movie theater featuring "SCREENO night," then a burlesque house, and finally a derelict firetrap occupied by a bunch of young idealists from something very like the Federal Theater Project the authors had satirized in *I'd Rather Be Right.*

The single set, however, had to be supplemented with interiors by set designer Donald Oenslager, together with a lighting scheme to accommodate a parade of vignettes from old shows that made *The Great Waltz's* fireworks and chandeliers seem child's play in comparison. *The Fabulous Invalid* was, in its curious pre-*Follies* way, the story of the decline and fall of a piece of real estate, but it insisted on showing the audience what seemed like every theatrical moment of note that occurred from curtain's rise in 1900 to its fall in 1938. This was very much in the style of the Living Newspaper shows then current, and brought a spurious kind of documentary flavor to what was essentially a valentine dipped in treacle.

The play began with an opening night on which the leading lady is so thrilled she dies of a heart attack backstage and her leading man and partner shoots himself rather than go on without her. With such a beginning, it wasn't surprising that the stage doorman turned out to be a ghost and a kind of heavenly gatekeeper as well. He tells them they needn't go to heaven—where there is no theater—as long as theater survives right here on earth. They have the choice, of course, whereupon the actress's ghost exclaims that the theater "*is* heaven!" From there, it is all downhill.

The ghosts stick around, joined at one point by a figure in doublet and hose who calls himself Bill and reassures them that audiences were just as undiscriminating in his day as they are in modern times. There have always been competing distractions. "One season it was cock-fights," he says, "the next season it was punting on the Thames," but nothing compared to the opening night of *Hamlet,* when "Burbage had laryngitis."

The ghosts watch the years go by, and the audience watches with them. They see excerpts from twenty-six plays, including bits from Eugene O'Neill's *Anna Christie,* Noël Coward's *The Vortex,* Maxwell Anderson and Laurence Stallings's *What Price Glory?,* an homage to Moss's George Kelly with *The Show-Off,* John and Lionel Barrymore in *The Jest,* and Fred and Adele Astaire in *Lady, Be Good!* There were glimpses of Ethel Barrymore in *Captain Jinks of the Horse Marines,* Mrs. Fiske in *The New York Idea,* Maude Adams in *Peter Pan.*

Musical numbers under the direction of Oscar Levant in the pit included (this is a partial list): "Rosie, You Are My Posy," "Glowworm," "The Merry Widow Waltz," "Every Little Movement Has a Meaning All Its Own," "The Tickle-Toe," "Alice Blue Gown," "Mandy," "Look for the Silver Lining," "Limehouse Blues," "Manhattan," "Make Believe," "Is It True What They Say About Dixie?" and—inevitably—a facsimile of George M. Cohan singing "Give My Regards to Broadway."

Copyright acknowledgments in the program listed ninety-two different sources for material presented onstage. Not only did the audience have to sit through all this, they had to watch it being performed by actors and actresses who were doubling and tripling in parts in which they couldn't hope to approximate the living memories of, say, the Barrymores or the Astaires or Cohan, who was so recently visible right down the street in another theater with fresher material.

One of the unknown actresses in the show was a beautiful young Toronto woman named Dora Sayers who played Ethel Barrymore, Eva Le Gallienne (in *The Sea Gull*), and a chorus girl. She learned to impersonate Barrymore by listening to her voice on records, but no amount of sincerity could turn secondary players into the great stars they were asked to impersonate. Iris Adrian, later famous for chewing gum as the prototypical floozy in Hollywood, did as well as anybody playing a stripper named (irresistibly) Daisy LaHiff, bumping and grinding the Alexandria's way into burlesque.

Finally, not even the ultimate fan, "The Man From Up There," can rustle much life from his black robes and his heavenly exhortation that somehow, somewhere the theater must continue to evolve and renew itself. Miraculously on cue, in comes a baby-faced director who is a dead ringer for the young Orson Welles, the enfant terrible of the Mercury Theatre, all set to light a fire under his generation of idealists with a speech of wind:

> They'll tell you that it isn't important, putting makeup on your face and playacting. I don't believe it. It's important to keep alive a thing that can lift men's spirits above the everyday reality of their lives . . . you're going to be kicked around, and a lot of the time you're not going to have enough to eat, but you're going to get one thing in return. The chance to write, and act, say the things you want to say, and do the things you want to do. And I think that's enough.

Critics weren't so sure and neither were audiences. The show expired after a mere sixty-five performances, the shortest run Moss and Kaufman would ever have.

The critics took deep breaths and expressed disbelief mingled with sympathy. It was impossible to doubt the sincerity behind the endeavor or, as John Mason Brown wrote, that it was "incredibly naïve," ultimately "laughable."

Sam Harris found a few quotes to run in ads, but resorted to Bill Powell's celebrity testimonial technique, publishing quotes from the authors' friends, and running them in full-page ads with caricatures identifying "Famous First-Nighters" like Cole Porter, Edna Ferber, Irving Berlin, and Harpo Marx, all of whom found the show just dandy. This was logrolling on a major scale, but even Porter's claim that "From now on I go to *The Fabulous Invalid* once a week" couldn't help.

Two weeks before *The Fabulous Invalid* opened at the Broadhurst, *Sing Out the News,* produced by Moss and Kaufman with Max Gordon, had opened at the Music Box. The show was conceived as what theater historian Stanley Green called "the uptown sister of *Pins and Needles,*" still a hit downtown. *Sing Out the News* boasted the same creative team as the earlier show, writer Charles Friedman and composer-lyricist Harold Rome, but somewhere on the journey from the Labor Stage to the Music Box something got lost, and Moss and Kaufman quietly took over the writing.

Though they awarded themselves no program credit, their emergency room doctoring was hinted at everywhere in the press.

They redeemed their liberal credentials with *Sing Out the News,* which was frankly leftist and antifascist, as 1938 drew to a close with headlines about Munich and Neville Chamberlain that worried America and the heavily Jewish theatrical community. The show utilized the talents of many who were left of center or fellow travelers, like Will Geer, later to find himself the apple-pie darling of television as a folksy Grandpa. Another of the stars, Philip Loeb, would later kill himself after being blacklisted by Senator Joseph McCarthy's cohort.

The great hit of the show was in keeping with the creators' sympathies. It was a joyous Harlem block party, in which Rex Ingram sang to welcome a new arrival to his family, the baby boy christened Franklin D. Roosevelt Jones. "F.D.R. Jones" swept the country.

Moss and Kaufman contributed a sketch that borrowed from the old *I Married An Angel* project, which Rodgers and Hart had, in the meantime, made a Broadway hit. In the Kaufman-Hart version, "I Married a Republican," Hiram Sherman played an angel sympathetic to the New Deal. When he is persuaded to vote Republican, his wings fall off.

Moss's strongest contribution was a sketch that returned him to Hollywood and the terrain of *Once in a Lifetime* with the assurance of one who now knew the plays and players. "Gone With the Revolution" was about Norma Shearer and Tyrone Power making *Marie Antoinette* for director W. S. (Woody) Van Dyke at MGM, with Robert Morley as a fussy Louis XVI. The studio is thrown into a panic when Van Dyke reads the script for the next camera setup and discovers that, in addition to the all-important Shearer-Power screen kiss, there's a revolution in this picture. Before long Louis B. Mayer is on the set shouting his horror that such a thing could happen at MGM. How? Why? Shearer wonders why Marie Antoinette couldn't lead the revolution to keep it sympathetic. Power is worried about looking young through the hurly-burly of the guillotine. Morley is just incensed. He's been told he is supposed to be impotent in this picture, and has been practicing ever since.

All ends happily when four thousand extras hired to play revolutionaries are reduced to four, so as not to be so obviously revolting. They rush across the soundstage during the Shearer-Power smooch and, inspired by the MGM style, wind up kissing each other. It was one of the funniest sketches Moss ever wrote.

The reviews for *Sing Out the News* were everything those for *The Fabulous Invalid* were not. John Mason Brown was most enthusiastic, finding it "uproarious," and "news which merits being sung out with pride." But *Pins and Needles* was still available downtown at cheaper prices and as war clouds darkened audiences grew thin uptown. The new show closed after 105 performances. Moss and Kaufman and Gordon lost every penny they had invested in it as sole backers of the show. Moss ever after referred to it bitterly as "Swing Out the Jews."

14

Americana

*There are times, I think, when [Moss] is not completely
sure whether the curtain is up or down.*

GEORGE S. KAUFMAN

Moss returned to New York in the fall of 1937 rich but homeless. Having traded Irving Berlin's bachelor flat on West Forty-sixth Street for Hollywood, he now needed a place to work and hang his hat. Town and country beckoned with separate but equal allure and he was soon well domiciled in each. In town he moved into the Waldorf-Astoria Hotel on Park Avenue; in the country, he bought a farm.

Moss's apartment was in the Waldorf Towers, the private sector of the Art Deco high-rise that sequestered 106 private suites and was then one of the most glittering addresses in America. Former president Herbert Hoover lived there; so did Cole and Linda Porter in separate apartments on the same floor. Moss's rooms, installed for him by New York decorator Mac Alper, vied with the others in opulence. His designer had persuaded him to switch from the Spanish look of the Ansonia to English antiques, whose quality and cost were underlined by understatement. The whole was accented by a "small yet authentic collection of antique Chinese ceramics," according to a reporter, who noted that the apartment-proud bachelor showed off his décor wearing that staple of the soigné, "an elegant but subdued dressing gown." Domestic chores were seen to by Charles Matthies, Moss's rather grand, fashion-plate butler who believed it a mark of loyalty to his employer to patronize the same tailor and, when economically feasible, the same goldsmith.

In the country Moss acquired property less formal but more spacious. He bought eighty-seven acres of Pennsylvania that spread out and around a two-story house built in 1710 of local fieldstone in Aquetong, not far from New Hope in Bucks County, about an hour and a half from New York.

The house was set back from what had been the York Road in pre-Revolutionary times, the stagecoach route from Philadelphia to New York. About a mile or so down the same two-lane country artery was Barley Sheaf Farm, the fifty-nine acres plus house and outbuildings in Holicong that George and Beatrice Kaufman had purchased the previous year and that inspired Moss to go rustic in the first place.

He dubbed his property Fairview Farm and had stationery made in which the name was whittled onto the slats of a swinging gate. He had a detailed historical map painted in Pennsylvania-Dutch sampler-style by a local artist, and researched the headless ghost who, it was said, had haunted the place since 1810. The nearly 230-year-old farmhouse needed renovation and, in Moss's pursuit of better homes and gardens, economy was not the watchword.

He added a swimming pool to rival the one the Kaufmans had down the road. He built on a screened-in porch, installed a modern kitchen, a central heating system, and several up-to-date bathrooms. The house seemed to cry out for new and expensive gadgets that would come to include the first television set in Bucks County, and an electric toothbrush against which, he boasted, he had "merely to *lean* his teeth."

Landscaping, decorating, and remodeling would continue as his Broadway and Hollywood earnings helped end the Depression in Bucks County, bringing delight to friends and contractors, not to mention well-diggers, who finally struck water on their seventeenth try.

Fairview Farm soon boasted a tennis court to complement the pool. The house expanded to include a two-story wing with a forty-by-thirty-foot living room, a study, and four double bedrooms for guests. The dining room featured a massive stone fireplace twelve feet wide and four feet deep that was too large for any but five-alarm fires and was filled instead with plants, surrounded by an assortment of andirons, kettles, ladles, axes, and guns that had once collected dust in local antique shops.

"My Pennsylvania extravagance, my appalling little dream-farm, my beautiful white elephant," he exclaimed, tearing open his checkbook. His extravagance, he maintained, was a form of benevolence to objects usually thought of as inanimate. "When I go into a store," he said, "I'm convinced that every piece of merchandise on every shelf is trembling with desire to belong to me." Brooks Atkinson dubbed him "Gold-plated Hart" after a weekend at Fairview Farm, and told readers of the Sunday *Times* that "whenever [Hart] has a moment he hurries to New Hope and buys something."

He was delighted to find that the colonial accessories he was snapping up at out-of-the-way shops were increasing rapidly in value. It finally dawned on Beatrice Kaufman, with whom he shared shopping expeditions, that not only were he and she in on the ground floor of a rising market, they *were* the rising market. George Kaufman stayed home at Barley Sheaf to read and write and raise the occasional eyebrow when pressed to admire the shoppers' loot.

Moss's early-American cabinets soon groaned beneath the weight of once undervalued treasures. A partial inventory made later enumerated: early American antiques, American primitive oils, paintings on satin, frackturs, gaudy Dutch spatterware, soft paste, tin tole ware, candle stands, spice cabinets, copper luster ware, appliquéd quilts, stitch-dated coverlets stored in their own hand-hewn pine blanket chests, grandfather clocks, yellowed farm ledgers, and a collection of local eighteenth-century blown glass. Chintz billowed; Windsor chairs cradled; other people's heirlooms added verisimilitude to the country-gentleman atmosphere. Windows, paned nine-over-six, overlooked undulating lawns that gently rolled where bulldozers pushed them at Moss's command. Grazing sheep decorated the lawns and pigpens were installed (out of sight) to keep the local caretaker happy. The sheep wandered and the pigs wallowed, but they were secondary to the star livestock, an Old English sheepdog, the first of many. When male, he was called Skipper; when female, Duchess. Moss bred puppies that he thought looked like "Baby Pandas," and distributed them with paternal pride to friends and colleagues. John Steinbeck got one. So, later, did Kurt Weill and Lotte Lenya.

The farm was a stage set; the tractor drivers and nurserymen were stagehands. Stone fences were built to redirect the eye and create false perspectives, as if designed by Hassard Short. Moss imported enough full-grown trees to satisfy Joyce Kilmer, and positioned them so they (and the deer statuary they sheltered) were artfully framed by the windows of the rooms that looked out on them. The cost of landscaping was said to have ranged anywhere from $35,000 to a then-astronomical high of $100,000. The total number of seedlings, shrubs, and mature trees climbed to 3,685, including pines, spruces, elms, and maples, all of them as quiveringly eager to belong to him as the merchandise on local shelves. They may have been props, but they had purpose. "When I order a tree at nine a.m.," he announced, "I want to be sitting in its shade by five p.m."

He styled himself the "Jewish Ethan Frome" and encouraged weekend guests to troop down by train or car from New York to witness the marvels of earth moving. There were the predictable theatrical in-jokes about *The Cherry Orchard* and *The Petrified Forest* and some acerbic wit coined one of the era's most memorable wisecracks while observing the improvements made to Mother Nature's drab plan: "Shows you what God would have done if He'd had the money."

The line was good enough to be claimed by or attributed to almost everybody. Credit usually goes to Alexander Woollcott or Kaufman, though Bennett Cerf, who knew Moss and Fairview Farm as well as anybody, claimed it originated with Wolcott Gibbs of *The New Yorker.* Glen Boles, who was still involved with Moss and spent frequent weekends at Fairview Farm, claimed the quip was the brainchild of the home owner himself. "Moss leaned out the window and said it as we watched them trucking in the trees," he recalled.

Moss and the Kaufmans designed a routine to share the demands and needs of weekend freeloaders. The Kaufmans entertained their own guests and Moss's at Saturday dinner, with Moss reciprocating on Sundays. Or it was Friday night at Barley Sheaf and Saturday night at Fairview. Both houses were spacious enough to accommodate crowds and inhibit work. Kaufman simply isolated himself in his study while Beatrice entertained below. Moss, like Beatrice, was stimulated by company and welcomed distraction. He was as likely to be found writing in longhand on a lapboard by the pool or in a lounge chair on the lawn as in his study. He was especially delighted to be disturbed by the thwack of mallet on wooden ball when a game of croquet was joined—for blood if possible—at any hour of the day or night. There was, of course, outdoor lighting, too.

Guests to Fairview Farm were made to feel at home by familiar faces—their own—greeting them in photographs hung like ancestral portraits in the living room. Edna Ferber, Katharine Cornell, and Woollcott shared wall space with Irving Berlin and the late George Gershwin. It was inevitable that restoring the property from dilapidation to faux-rustic splendor should suggest a play, and it soon would. The guests, too, were colorful and histrionic enough to put onstage, and the visit of one of them would shortly inspire a classic.

Fairview Farm was the first residence Moss had ever owned and, apart from rentals in California or Berlin's flat in New York, the first he had not shared with his family. Now that Lillie was dead, Barnett was eager to move to Florida, which Moss was willing to finance. Barnett styled himself "the Commodore" in Miami, or Moss, like any good casting director, anointed him with the moniker. He dressed in white flannels and yachting cap, and looked every inch the seagoing playboy of seventy-five, his eye for the ladies as keen as his wardrobe was rakish. He reveled in playing the Lothario with actresses who platonically decorated his son's arm at openings. His Cockney charm had its effect on more than one aspiring actress who decided that an aging but ardent Hart was better than none at all. When not in Palm Beach, Barnett shared a Central Park apartment with perennial bachelor Bernie, who was working steadily as a stage manager on Broadway, no longer dependent on Moss for the roof over his head.

Moss had hoped his mother's death would free him of the insomnia he associated with her. But his sleeplessness remained torturous, much more than tossing and turning. He confided to Boles that he was terrified of sleep at the same time he longed for it. "Whenever I try to fall asleep I'm panicked awake by a big black blob, starting in the ceiling, and descending slowly to smother me," he told Boles, who interpreted the complaint as "Basic Freud." The insomnia followed him to the country, where he fluctuated between ebullience and despair. He wrote Dore Schary often from Fairview Farm, sometimes dramatically detailing his despondency, sometimes waxing effusively about the simple life he was spending a fortune to simulate.

Schary was now in Hollywood, where he received an Academy Award for the story of *Boys Town,* the Spencer Tracy–Mickey Rooney movie about Father Flanagan, the same year *You Can't Take It With You* won awards for Frank Capra. Moss's letters bubble with euphoria at trimming his very first Christmas tree at the farm and feeling what he called "a kind of peace in one's flesh at last!" Life had turned to "sheer enchantment," he wrote, that "scares me a little—I'm not used to being happy."

Enchantment was of short duration. By the time *The Fabulous Invalid* and *Sing Out the News* were in simultaneous rehearsal in late 1938, he was forcing himself through the motions as if in "one of those dreams when you are being chased." Schary, who had listened to the catalog of Moss's highs and lows since Little Theater days, warned him about being so ostentatiously depressed that *The Fabulous Invalid* might sound like the title of an autobiography. Moss reacted with shock and chagrin, "unaware that I was suffering so publicly." Still, to indicate how truly dark his moods had become, he admitted to a professional indifference his buoyant public manner concealed from everyone except, perhaps, the Kaufmans: "I can't tell you whether the plays are any good or not. I don't know. What's more, I don't give a good goddam whether they are or not."

The failures of both productions in which Moss had invested heavily left him, he claimed, "finally broke," but his belt-tightening was modest. He abandoned the Waldorf Towers and leased a town house just off Sutton Place at 461 East Fifty-seventh Street. He moved in with nothing more than his electric toothbrush, butler Charles Matthies, and Skipper the sheepdog, and decorated his new domicile, floor by floor, in the velvets and furbelows of high Victoriana.

For all Moss's vacillating moods, his level of activity remained high. In mid-1938, before either *The Fabulous Invalid* or *Sing Out the News* had gone into rehearsal, he and Kaufman began work on yet another play, this time at the urging of Beatrice. She insisted they write a play affirming the fundamental strengths of American life, now that Europe was clearly headed for armed conflict and the world would need, once more, to be made safe for democracy.

As Jews, Moss and Kaufman were painfully aware of anti-Semitism and fascism in Germany, which would erupt in the violence of the infamous *Kristallnacht* in November. They at once began to talk out the play they would call *The American Way*. Kaufman assigned himself first billing and the title page announced, "This play is for Beatrice," a first dedication for either author, though not the last.

Each partner was used to working independently or with others, but they were so comfortable working together that turning out an annual play was by now routine, requiring no significant period of incubation. This mostly worked well with comedies; the jokes came easily and farcical mischief seemed second nature. With *The American Way*, however, they were striving for something very like the kind of message for which Kaufman once advised Philip Barry to employ Western Union. They chose to dramatize and celebrate the American Dream as experienced by an immigrant German (not Jewish) family over forty years in small-town America. The passage of years would demonstrate the resilience of democratic ideals in the face of social change. Ending in the present would add contemporary relevance, stressing the ongoing need for defense of freedom. The theme was worthy, sincere, and timely. Tanks were warming up in Europe. It was commercially timely, as well: the New York World's Fair was warming up, too, scheduled to open on April 30, 1939, and bringing with it hordes of patriotic tourists.

The Broadway of Kaufman and Hart depended more on commercial strategy than inspiration, but *The American Way* needed both. Inspiration on serious themes was not their forte, and they embarked on an intimate drama with an epic theme at a time when they were creatively overextended by their writing and producing chores on *The Fabulous Invalid* and *Sing Out the News*. Their confidence in the chronicle or scrapbook style of the yet-to-open *Invalid* must have been secure, for they used it for *The American Way,* too, as if it were an all-purpose template for big subjects. The chief difference in their nosegays to the theater and to democracy was that, in the latter, they would place their characters within the narrative, rather than allowing them to comment on it from the sidelines or backstage.

The pattern was that of the old *Wind Up an Era,* Moss's bid to challenge Noël Coward's *Cavalcade* and even Coward, himself, as Man of the Theater. Coward fascinated him. Moss had already written him into *As Thousands Cheer* and *Jubilee,* and would write him into a third play before the decade was over. Coward was a role model for Moss (accounting for his voguing about in elegant but subdued dressing gowns). He referred to Coward in conversation as "the English Moss Hart" with no apparent irony, though Coward was not only a hugely successful composer and playwright, but a film and stage star as well. While Alexander Woollcott had snidely branded Moss a poseur or dilettante as a playwright by calling him "the Clyde Fitch of yesteryear," he had dubbed Coward "Destiny's tot." It was a distinction that rankled and spurred rivalry.

Even without Coward and *Wind Up an Era,* the panoramic idea had roots in Moss's boyhood theatergoing experience, when spectacular shows like William A. Brady's *Life* manufactured theatrical excitement from pageantry and props rather than motivation. *Cavalcade* had been a throwback for Coward, too, to his own childhood of English pantomime and pageantry, and both men had a taste for nostalgia that softened and sentimentalized the otherwise bright and brittle façade. An American *Cavalcade* was what Beatrice Kaufman seemed to be suggesting when she asked for a patriotic play. It was precisely the sort of project with which Moss could fulfill his theatrical ambitions, validate his democratic convictions, and create a whopping big hit all at the same time.

Meanwhile, back at the Center Theatre on Sixth Avenue, the Rockefeller family was experiencing anxiety over the mammoth house they had converted from a cinema to a playhouse for Moss's *The Great Waltz.* Since that popular extravaganza, the Center had been home to musical offerings of similar outsized appeal, including *The White Horse Inn,* the German operetta a New York critic ranked among "the most profound musical bores of the century." *The White Horse Inn* featured the pretty trilling of Kitty Carlisle, back on Broadway in a dirndl after some strained duets with Bing Crosby at Paramount and *A Night at the Opera* at MGM. The charm of operetta imports was wearing thin, now that sophisticates like Porter and Rodgers dominated Broadway musically and the hit parade was swinging all the way to Carnegie Hall thanks to Benny Goodman and his clarinet.

The Center's size made it unsuitable for most dramatic plays, but the panoramic pageantry of *The American Way* was impossible in any other kind of theater. The Center's availability, in turn, encouraged ever more panoramic pageantry, though a vast canvas was not essential to its theme. At about the same time Kaufman and Hart began working on it, Thornton Wilder was shaping a similarly affirmative play about American life on so intimate and unprepossessing a scale that *Our Town* needed no canvas at all. No sets, anyway, though its folding chairs and bare walls would come to represent, for millions, an entire universe of feeling.

Not that intimacy of scale or approach was necessary or even desirable, as *Gone With the Wind* was proving from border to border. Americana was box office; patriotism was on a roll. Two plays about Abraham Lincoln opened in 1938, *Prologue to Glory* and Robert E. Sherwood's *Abe Lincoln in Illinois,* which would win the Pulitzer Prize. Away from Broadway, another Pulitzer winner, Southern playwright Paul Green, produced the first of his outdoor pageants like *The Lost Colony* and *The Common Glory,* folk dramas that paraded American history before tourist audiences in Roanoke and colonial Williamsburg so successfully that they continue to the present day.

Nostalgia for the American past was counterbalanced by a contemporary theater born from the distress of the present. The Federal Theater Project was challenging the conventions of Broadway with frankly radical fare; the Living Newspaper offerings used headlines to far different effect than Moss had ever done. They fashioned agitprop theater from news of the Dust Bowl and breadlines that was provocative and propagandistic, never just trendy. The thousands cheering now weren't roller-skating with cocktails; they were carrying placards and crying out for social change.

Kaufman and Hart's theater was commercial and conventional, but they had nodded in a friendly way to Orson Welles and the FTP in *The Fabulous Invalid* and, by its very nature, *The American Way* was recognition of the national mood. No one thought the Center could or should host anything remotely didactic, but even a feel-good-about-democracy show built around immigrants from Germany raised issues of torn loyalties any such family might have felt during the war of 1914–18 and the one darkening the immediate horizon. American isolationism, encouraged by ever-louder goosesteps, acknowledged the inevitability of another German war only twenty years after the last one had ended. Combating isolationism and homegrown fascism onstage with *The American Way* might be an opportunity to influence national debate and become more than Fourth of July pageantry for out-of-towners.

The Center Theatre and the Rockefeller family fell into Max Gordon's bailiwick, but he needed a partner for something as vast as *The American Way* was becoming even before it was written. Sam Harris, as on *Jubilee,* agreed to share the production. The false rumor circulated that the Rockefellers themselves were financing the show. The money, however, came from Harris's usual backers, including Moss and Kaufman, plus Gordon's sources, like RKO Pictures in Hollywood, Darryl Zanuck of 20th Century-Fox, and William S. Paley of CBS. The total budget would come to $250,000, making it the most expensive nonmusical show of the decade in a theater seating nearly four thousand at a top ticket price of $3.30.

To attract the World's Fair audiences, a Hollywood star was essential as the archetypal immigrant who climbs the ladder of the American Dream from carpenter to furniture manufacturer and family patriarch. Fredric March, a friend from Hollywood and *Nothing Sacred,* seemed an ideal all-American choice, highly regarded as an actor and familiar to every American who attended the movies. He had starred on-screen in roles ranging from Jekyll and Hyde to Vronsky opposite Garbo in *Anna Karenina* to the alcoholic Norman Maine in *A Star Is Born.* March and his wife, Florence Eldridge, had ambitions to challenge the Lunts in the theater and the previous season had made their Broadway debut as a couple in a play that closed as soon as it opened. With plucky good humor they had taken an ad in the trade papers picturing themselves as trapeze artists missing each other in midair. "Oops, sorry," the caption read. *The American Way* seemed an opportunity to recoup prestige. So confident was March of his box-office appeal that, according to *Variety,* he invested $50,000 in the production.

Moss and Kaufman quickly found that structuring forty years of American experience was a daunting assignment. History suggested an impossibly sweeping array of obligatory events: the rise of the automobile, flight, labor unions, women's suffrage, world war, global depression, and so on, including such changes in social mores as smoking, divorce, and flappers. Balancing an intimate foreground drama against a background of such scope required some unifying theatrical principle that proved frustratingly elusive.

Finally, in the late summer of 1938, facing a production deadline and an opening announced for January, Moss and Kaufman fled New York and Bucks County for Alexander Woollcott's island in Vermont in hopes of getting some work done.

Neshobe Island was in the middle of Lake Bomoseen, not far from the small town of Castleton, and accessible only by rowboat. A local boatman ferried guests to and from the wooded island when summoned by a flag run up a pole at the house or on the shore. This Yankee stalwart proved indifferent to the literary or theatrical celebrity of his passengers, which was just how they wanted it. They came mostly in search of privacy and the sort of peace and quiet guaranteed only when Woollcott himself was not in residence. Moss and Kaufman, as it happened, arrived to fill the just-vacated bunks of Ben Hecht and Charles MacArthur, who had written their screenplay for Emily Brontë's (and Sam Goldwyn's) *Wuthering Heights* there.

Moss had visited Neshobe off and on since Kaufman (who was a part owner with Woollcott) had taken him there for a break from *Once in a Life-time* in the summer of 1930. Unhappily, their host was present in 1938, and a relentlessly cranky distraction.

To escape Woollcott's kibitzing, Moss fled the island for the nearest railroad connection to New York, a few miles away in the town of Rutland. While looking for the depot he happened upon the town square, a swath of green surrounding a white wooden gazebo suitable for brass bands, Sunday orators, and schoolchildren playing hooky.

He was struck. The town square was Americana as pure as the *Saturday Evening Post* covers Norman Rockwell was painting a stone's throw away in the Vermont village of Arlington. The square was spacious, suggesting community, and defined, assuring intimacy. Moss recognized at once that it solved the technical problems of the production, providing a central setting around which characters and historical events might revolve. The square itself could remain unchanged through the decades, an emblem of enduring values, while details around it could signal time's passage. The bank and the courthouse might remain fixed, but an Irish bar could become a soda fountain; a stable, a movie theater. The passing parade could segue from bustles to bloomers to bobby socks, all of it around a village green as homely as Main Street, as starred and striped as John Philip Sousa.

Moss hurried back to Neshobe Island, where Kaufman agreed to the notion and they sat down to hurried, if productive work. The town square and other sets would be realized by Donald Oenslager, who had designed the stages of *I'd Rather Be Right* and *The Fabulous Invalid*. The square would be the heart of the play, while interior scenes—the family home, a carpentry shop, a factory, a country club—would be staged on platforms to the right or left. Covering the orchestra pit would make the stage even vaster than it already was, allowing room for a Fourth of July picnic and a fireworks display of the "Last Days of Pompeii"—the very one that had introduced Paul and Penny Sycamore in *You Can't Take It With You*. Lighting could instantaneously direct attention from one part of the stage to another in an almost cinematic flow. The props and sets for the Ellis Island scene that introduced the play could be simply flown in and out, making way for the town square and its changing yet permanent backdrop.

They located their small American town in Ohio and dubbed it Mapleton, after a quick look at an atlas failed misleadingly to reveal the existence of any such place with that name. Later, letters would pour in announcing that there was, indeed, a Mapleton, Ohio, and its population was 130, half the number of actors and extras required to bring the fictional Mapleton to life at the Center.

Getting them there required seven full-time stage managers supervising sixty-eight stagehands moving thirty tons of scenery. Squadrons of wardrobe personnel organized three thousand costumes; a special backstage crew activated industrial noisemakers including horns, bells, sirens, and whistles with the aid of compressed-air machines; a full orchestra conducted by Oscar Levant in a studio seven floors above the auditorium was alerted to the action onstage by flashing lights. Enough popular songs for a full-length musical established period, forty song cues in all. They marked immigration procedures at Ellis Island ("My Country, 'Tis of Thee"), a Fourth of July picnic ("Take [*sic*] Me to St. Louis, Louis"), youthful high jinks ("I Picked a Lemon in the Garden of Love"), or an engagement ("Peg O' My Heart" and "You Made Me Love You"). More songs signaled the outbreak of war ("Tipperary" and "We'll Hang the Kaiser From a Sour Apple Tree") or its end ("Over There"). Lindbergh's landing was danced by flappers and their beaux ("Ramona" and "Yes, Sir, That's My Baby"). An anniversary roused the old folks ("The Blue Danube" and "The Wedding March"), and all of them were piped in and broadcast over amplifiers specially designed for the production the orchestra never saw. To coordinate activity behind the scenes, where thirty-eight child actors were chaperoned by their thirty-eight stage mothers at every performance, a backstage public address system was installed, introducing a now-standard theatrical practice.

Keeping 250 actors and extras from bumping into each other required two directors. Kaufman took charge of the dramatic scenes. Pace, not panorama, was his strength. Because reviewers had found his staging of *The Fabulous Invalid* clumsy, Kaufman enlisted Hassard Short's expertise at lighting and crowd control, which created beautiful tableaux from what might have been chaos.

Assembled with precision rivaling the installation of the World's Fair itself, *The American Way* raised its curtain revealing Ellis Island as the young German carpenter Martin Gunther arrives in 1896 to seek freedom and fortune in America. In vignettes chock-full of name-dropping (everybody from Mark Twain to Admiral Dewey, the Wright Brothers to Charles Lindbergh), Gunther and his wife Irma grow rich, send a son to his death in the Great War, watch their grandchildren grow up, lose their fortune in the Crash, but remain comfortable and dedicated to democracy.

At the play's present-day climax, the Gunthers' out-of-work grandson is attracted to the fiery rhetoric of a gang of brown-shirted thugs preaching violence for what ails the world. The now-aged Martin Gunther (on his fiftieth wedding anniversary) cries out against them in the name of democracy, prompting them to beat him to death.

His murder jolts the grandson—and presumably the audience—to an awareness of a homegrown fascist threat. The curtain falls on the old man's flag-draped coffin and a 250-voice chorale singing "The Star-Spangled Banner."

When *The American Way* opened on January 21, 1939, much of the Center Theatre was sodden with tears. Walter Winchell declared himself so moved that he had seen only part of the play, "for the eyes would not stay dry." General critical hosannas attracted lines at the box office of up to sixty people, despite subzero January weather.

Winchell did not weep alone. John Anderson of the *Journal-American* reported, "No audience that I can remember in my time on the aisle has been so shaken with emotion." He noted, "[N]early 4,000 playgoers were on their feet . . . too choked to move." Brooks Atkinson in a friendly review in the Sunday *Times* could not help noting that it simplistically "misrepresent[ed] twentieth-century experience," in which democracy remained a promise less fulfilled than the sentimental pieties onstage hoped to suggest. But the *World-Telegram*'s Heywood Broun, one of many negative voices, wrote that the authors had "fallen flat upon their separate faces" in mounting what he acidly called "the greatest thing in the American theater since *Hellzapoppin*."

On balance, tears at *The American Way* were unearned. They were inspired not by the inner life of the drama, but by the sentimental conditioning of an audience guaranteed to choke up at "Oh, say, can you see" in a theater or at Yankee Stadium. They were feel-good tears at a feel-bad time.

It is one of the few plays Kaufman and Hart wrote about "civilians," and the ones they put onstage are so one-dimensional you wonder if either author knew any outside of the Algonquin or Bucks County. They are all white-bread (and white) and middle class in sentiment and station, even the factory workers Martin Gunther treats so well that they wouldn't dream of organizing, and the panicky townspeople he tries to dissuade from rushing his benefactor's bank to protect their life savings. This at a time when Walker Evans and Dorothea Lange were capturing on film the faces of dispossessed Americans, the kind unlikely to make World's Fair excursions or grow misty-eyed at the reassurances of Broadway.

Only two characters in *The American Way* are livelier than diorama figures, and both are Broadway types. One is the amusingly eccentric suffragette (a Jean Dixon part filled by Ruth Weston), the first to drive, smoke, wear bloomers, be a divorcée, and operate a beauty parlor, slapping on every mud pack with a wisecrack. The other is the Gunther family's comic-relief maid (played by Edna Ferber's niece Janet Fox), seduced and abandoned by a fireman. When asked how she met him, she deadpans, "I went to a fire." Her fatherless son grows up to become a crooner-bandleader under contract to MGM at $10,000 a week. Thus is democracy validated: even the son of a maid can make it in Hollywood.

The rest are more slogans than characters and being American is defined in terms of material success. "I have got everything that I wanted from America," the patriarch tells his grandson. "I came over here a poor boy, with nothing, and I got from America riches and years of happiness." There's freedom, of course, "and that *does* matter," which is why "you, and the young people like you, should take over this country, and keep it what it has always been."

It was all just chauvinistic hokum, perhaps, but playing to the largest possible audience and the lowest common denominator approached pandering. The play pulled the one solid punch it had, the climactic confrontation between Gunther and the fascist thugs. The authors bafflingly make them as generic as everybody else onstage, bewildering even critics predisposed to flag-waving.

Burns Mantle, the longtime arbiter of best plays (he would include *The American Way* among the year's top ten), was offended most by the sight of a real coffin onstage in the final scene. To satisfy his objections and the many complaints about the brownshirts, Moss and Kaufman continued revising the play after it opened, but the Nazis never became out-and-out Nazis. Isolationists bought tickets, too. But not enough; lines at the box office soon shrank and vanished.

All was not lost. Thanks to Max Gordon's deal with RKO, the movie rights to *The American Way* were sold for $225,000. Broadway regulars had flocked to the Center Theatre in the first weeks of 1939, but by the time the World's Fair opened in April those who wanted to see it had seen it, and the hoped-for influx of tourists failed to materialize. There was plenty to see at the fair that was just as spectacular and considerably livelier. After 164 performances, *The American Way* closed down for the summer, reopening in the fall for another eighty waves of the flag.

The enormous operating costs precluded profit, even with the movie sale. Harris had planned a road tour, but before he could load the buses and trucks, Hitler's tanks rolled into Poland. Mantle explained in the *Daily News* that Kaufman and Hart's still vague brownshirts were "certain to irritate borderline patriots and those who are German nationalists under their skins. No one thought the chance of rousing even a small race conflict was worth such box office profits as might come from it."

RKO told *Variety* that in the film version the "anti-Nazi angle in the play will be written out." Instead, the movie would emphasize "the American success story and emancipation of womanhood," but that wasn't enough to get the film made. In the end, the canvas was too big and the drama too small.

Kaufman, though he had taken primary billing on *The American Way* and dedicated the play to his wife, was not amused or gracious. In a rare moment of irritation for attribution, he seemed to blame things on Moss's taste for spectacle. "I wouldn't be surprised," he told a reporter when asked about their future plans, "if Moss wouldn't want us to join together in the writing of a little thing calling for 800 actors, three camels, and a herd of llamas." Kaufman said he would prefer something simpler, with "two actors and one set, possibly a telephone booth."

Kaufman was also annoyed by his cast. Not long after the play's closing, Alexander Woollcott reported gleefully to Lynn Fontanne that Kaufman had been so brutal to Florence Eldridge at a dinner party given by Edna Ferber that the leading lady of *The American Way* left the table in a flood of tears.

Moss retreated to his own private slice of Americana in Bucks County. He had neither the education nor the life experience to make him a subtle or profound commentator on political affairs and, in ducking the Nazi issue, he demonstrated that he lacked the daring to be a bold one.

Sobered by a third failure in a row, he sat down at the farm and composed a letter to Dore Schary. "We must all," he wrote, "be very nice to our careers." The way to do that was obvious. It was, in fact, staring at him from his living-room wall.

15

Prince Charming

See how rude and eccentric I can afford to be.
Dear, dear, how amusing I am, to be sure.

ALEXANDER WOOLLCOTT

Alexander Woollcott was the first big-time media celebrity. As a man-of-letters-and-more, he was all but inescapable on newsprint, in hardcover, at the lectern, on the airwaves, and occasionally on celluloid or before the footlights.

Woollcott's descent from ubiquity then to obscurity now may be its own comment on the shelf life of modern fame, but in his day he helped define high noon. He inspired portraits by novelists like Charles Brackett, who lampooned him as Thaddeus Hulbert in *Entirely Surrounded,* and filmmakers like Otto Preminger and Joseph L. Mankiewicz, who put him on-screen as (respectively) the erudite and lethal Waldo P. Lydecker in *Laura* and the merely treacherous Addison DeWitt in *All About Eve.*

He inspired rancor and ridicule and what a baffled James Thurber called a "Woollcott cult." Kaufman, challenged to define him in a single word, finally found one: "improbable."

"Insufferable," others said. Harold Ross of *The New Yorker,* who for a time shared a house with Woollcott, asked Thurber, "Have you ever been to one of his *famous* Sunday morning breakfasts? . . . He sits there like a fat duchess, holding out her dirty rings to be kissed." Edna Ferber declined to kiss the rings even when they were posthumous. When his biographer approached her for an interview, she showed him the door with "I want no part of Woollcott, dead or alive."

Woollcott began his rise to national celebrity when he was ten years old and rejected the usual small boy's ambitions to become a fireman or cowboy. "I would rather be a Fabbulous [*sic*] Monster," he declared in writing, and was off and running.

He first came to widespread attention as drama critic for the *New York*

Times, where colleagues referred to him as "God's big brother," a designation he did not contest. He won a famous battle with the Shuberts, who tried to bar him from their shows, and elevated the once-lowly station of the drama critic in America. He wore the reputation for integrity this gave him like the cape he donned for opening nights, with the flourish of a grandee. His passion for the theater carried him eventually from the *Times* to the *Herald,* the *Sun,* and the *World.*

Fellow critic John Mason Brown thought him by turns a "scorpion" or "an overdose of saccharine," but Woollcott justified his enthusiasms and aversions by noting serenely and not entirely in jest that the critic "grows delirious about the best in the theater because he alone knows the worst."

His favor was courted, his disdain feared. He gushed as often as he skewered. He delighted in being contrary and unpredictable. An early defender of Eugene O'Neill against the commercial contraptions dominating Broadway, he could nevertheless rhapsodize over *Abie's Irish Rose* and airily dismiss *Anna Christie* as "rubbish."

Woollcott was a caricaturist's dream: Broadway's owl-on-the-aisle. His resemblance to the fattest and wisest of birds was uncanny, and his Coke-bottle spectacles and unkempt mustache somehow augmented the resemblance. He charged furiously about in public—jowls and midsection wobbling—in opera hat and walking stick, with "cape flowing and sparks flying," as one observer noted. At home in Vermont or in the Manhattan apartment that Dorothy Parker dubbed "Wit's End," he held court—Ethel Barrymore to Harpo Marx, Walter Lippmann to Walt Disney—in pajama bottoms and a coffee-stained bathrobe strewn with cigarette ash.

He was a perennial bachelor of unknown sexual persuasion. He had suffered mumps as a young man and was presumed to be asexual as a result, though no one was sure. He confounded those who scorned him as "Louisa May Woollcott" by braving perils in World War I from which his eyesight might easily have exempted him. He served a medical unit in France with distinction and contributed to the army newspaper *Stars and Stripes,* where his doughboy colleagues included Heywood Broun and Harold Ross.

After the war, Broun and Ross joined him—and Kaufman and the others—at the Algonquin Round Table, which he more or less invented with humor columnist Franklin P. Adams. With him "the vicious circle" earned its reputation. Without him, it might never have existed.

When Ross founded *The New Yorker* in 1925, Woollcott was on the masthead, though he was still reviewing theater in the dailies and acting as an adviser to *Vanity Fair* as well. He contributed profiles to *The New Yorker* and an opinion and trivia column titled "Shouts and Murmurs," a heading the magazine retains to this day. He wrote weightier pieces for *The Atlantic Monthly* and lighter ones for the likes of *Good Housekeeping, Cosmopolitan,* and *The Reader's Digest.* He was a gleeful connoisseur of murder and the macabre on the one hand; on the other he was a tireless promoter of the then-new use of Seeing Eye dogs.

Radio made him a household name. The great networks had just formed in 1926, and by 1929 Woollcott was before the microphone— "This is Woollcott speaking"—inventing book chat. On the Mutual network he was "The Early Bookworm," creating overnight best-sellers like *Lost Horizon* merely on his say-so. It would take sixty years and Oprah Winfrey for this phenomenon to recur. On CBS he was "The Town Crier," recycling old anecdotes and tales of murder, sharing what he called his "incurable triviality" with millions of listeners on behalf of Cream of Wheat.

He was second in the ratings only to Kate Smith and radio fame stimulated coast-to-coast lecture tours. No audience was too remote or provincial to be denied his presence. Great universities dusted off their honorary degrees for him. Billboards and magazine pages (even *The New Yorker*'s, to Ross's fury) carried his endorsements for Muriel Cigars or Seagram's Whiskey. MGM put him on-screen in trailers urging his fans to hie themselves to the local Bijou for Robert Donat and Greer Garson in *Goodbye, Mr. Chips,* or Judy Garland and Mickey Rooney in *Babes in Arms.*

Woollcott was even on Broadway. He collaborated on two plays with Kaufman, *The Channel Road,* an adaptation of a story by de Maupassant in 1929 (immediately before *Once in a Lifetime*), and *The Dark Tower,* a murder-melodrama in 1933 (just before *Merrily We Roll Along*). Both were flops that Brooks Atkinson called "amiable but amateurish." Failure as a playwright, however, was a mere hiccup. Woollcott had played Puck in *A Midsummer Night's Dream* at the age of four and had been mulling a comeback ever since.

His opportunity arose unexpectedly in a summerhouse in the Hudson River Valley that he and Beatrice Kaufman shared with playwright Sam Behrman. Behrman was much admired for his glittering comedies *Biography* and *The Second Man,* and, in the summer of 1931, was completing another within earshot of Woollcott's chatter, which spilled onto the page. The play was called *Brief Moment* and contained a character who "somewhat resembles Alexander Woollcott, who conceivably might play him," Behrman wrote.

Woollcott did play him, lolling on a sofa for three acts and firing off wisecracks like poison darts. The play was flawed, but critics reported that the corpulent star "runs away with the evening's honors." *Brief Moment* continued on Broadway for 129 performances and Woollcott went on the road with it, adding to his renown. No one thought he could play anyone but himself, but nightly applause convinced him he was destined for thespic laurels. Between radio broadcasts and lecture tours, he waited for the offers to roll in. Producers, most of them stung at one time or another by his tongue or pen, rolled only their eyes.

Behrman, in the meantime, returned from Hollywood, where he had been writing screenplays for Garbo at MGM. Under his arm was *Wine of Choice,* another play with a part for Woollcott. As fate would have it, the play tried out in Philadelphia at the end of 1937, a short drive from Bucks County.

Woollcott's visits to the country were rare, for he preferred Neshobe Island, where he could set the rules and call the tunes. As 1937 drew to a close, however, he took a recess from Philadelphia and *Wine of Choice* to spend New Year's Eve with the Kaufmans at Barley Sheaf Farm. He left them on New Year's Sunday to stay overnight at Fairview with Moss on his way back to Philadelphia.

He was in high prima donna mode, petulant and demanding. Most of the holiday weekend he spent vilifying Behrman and his play, and was especially annoyed to find he was not the only guest at Fairview, for Moss had invited Max Gordon, too. Gordon's table manners were so distasteful to Woollcott that he fled to the Kaufmans for dinner before coming back to spend the night. By the time he did, Gordon had departed for New York, but Woollcott's high dudgeon refused to subside. He demanded Moss's bedroom, as well as a milk shake and a freshly made chocolate cake to be served bedside by Moss's butler, the grand Charles, whom Woollcott denounced as insolent and dishonest even as he was being tucked in.

Before nodding off, he wrote in a guest book Moss kept, in which guests vied at writing the wittiest testimonials to the hospitality of their host: "I wish to say that on my first visit to Moss Hart's house I had one of the most unpleasant evenings I can ever recall having spent."

The next morning, he insisted Moss make up for the hardships he had suffered by chauffeuring him back to Philadelphia. Moss later said, "I would have gone to Alaska to get him out of the house," but once behind the wheel, he agreed to view Woollcott's Philadelphia performance and discuss it over supper.

Moss offered polite praise for the acting, which precipitated Woollcott's brandy-laced complaints that he had been forced to rewrite his part "from beginning to end" because Behrman's "dialogue simply cannot be spoken." Moss may have pointed out that Behrman's dialogue—for which he was famous—had seldom tied the tongues of Ina Claire, the Lunts, Noël Coward, or any other of the stars who had spoken his lines to widespread acclaim. More likely, he just listened to Woollcott's diatribe, grateful not to be its target. Finally, Woollcott came to the real point, the one he had journeyed all the way to Bucks County to deliver in the first place.

What he really wanted, he announced over dinner—admitting to "a strong streak of exhibitionism"—was to be the star of a play Kaufman and Hart would write especially for him. He "yearned," he said, "to tour the country in the central part, so that if I could succeed in being funny it wouldn't disturb the other actors."

Moss nodded that it sounded like a good idea and returned to Bucks County, where he and Kaufman were still working on *The Fabulous Invalid*. Kaufman had collaborated with Woollcott already, and knew the perils of yielding to his preposterous vanity. No monster was "fabbulous" enough to justify the *tsouris*.

Moss later said he and Kaufman were struck at once by the appalling notion of what might have happened had Woollcott become indisposed and a more or less permanent houseguest in Bucks County. Thus was born, he said, *The Man Who Came to Dinner*, but the idea had other sources and was a long time in coming.

Moss's relationship with Woollcott had never been easy. He correctly felt that Woollcott, with his erudition and education (always a sensitive subject for Moss), treated him with condescension, but he treated everybody that way. Moss's easy charm and dashing good looks nettled Woollcott, who called him "Repulsive" while everybody else called him "Mossy." Then there were the flops Woollcott wrote with Kaufman, each annoyingly followed by a Kaufman hit written with Moss. Though both were sexually ambiguous, they vied for the platonic affections of Beatrice Kaufman, adding to the petty jealousies that thickened the atmosphere. It is hardly surprising that Moss was relieved that he and Kaufman had their hands full with *The Fabulous Invalid* and *Sing Out the News* when Woollcott announced his brainstorm.

Time passed. *The American Way* came round. It was their difficulties with that play that took them to Woollcott's island nine months later. Woollcott was incensed then to discover they had come to Vermont to write something for Fredric March and not for him. It was Woollcott's nagging about "his" play—"in the manner of the Dowager Empress of China receiving . . . a couple of coolies," Moss remembered—that finally drove Moss from the island.

When he returned, there was no avoiding Woollcott's divalike ire. The playwrights agreed to concoct a vehicle for him once they were free of other commitments.

They did no such thing. After *The American Way* opened, Woollcott's lecture schedule kept him out of sight and out of mind and they began work on another play that came to nothing. They also started a musical (of which nothing survives) for the unlikely duo of Cole Porter and W. C. Fields. When Woollcott returned unexpectedly to New York, Moss admitted they had written not a word of the promised play. Woollcott attacked.

He pointed out that his schedule—as big as Rand-McNally—had to be worked out many months in advance and had been held hostage to their irresponsibility and broken promises. He accused them of having "prostituted [their] talents in the most cheap and vulgar way imaginable." Moss was a "groveling slum gutter" and Kaufman "a second-rate hack with the ethics of a Storm Trooper."

Fuming, he went off to Canada to appear in a movie with the Dionne quintuplets, but not before proposing privately to Kaufman that if Moss were unable or unwilling to live up to his word, then he would take up his pen with Kaufman in Moss's place. The nightmare notion put an end to procrastination.

Goaded into action, Moss and Kaufman set to work in a spirit not entirely free of malice. Though their star had charged them with writing a role "as different from me as possible," they knew Woollcott could play no one but Woollcott. Making a virtue of his limitations, they launched into a full-blown portrait of him. He was exactly the kind of celebrity Moss had been honing his talents for parody on for years, and he threw himself at the target with relish. Kaufman recognized the accuracy of his mimicry by giving him, again, first billing.

The portrait would be Woollcott with warts, wattles, and wicked one-liners. Later, when a plagiarism suit arose, Moss would claim they only wrote "Woollcott as the public knew him," an assertion that quashed the lawsuit but was absurd. Woollcott-as-the-public-didn't-know-him was the whole delicious point.

They began a draft they titled "Prince Charming" with a monstrously egocentric radio star and lecturer they named Sheridan Whiteside. Recalling the notion of an indisposed Woollcott as a permanent Bucks County houseguest, they sent Whiteside to a small town in Ohio to give a lecture and go to dinner at the home of perfectly ordinary locals who happen to have an icy front porch. Whiteside would slip on the ice and be confined in their home to recuperate from his fractures. At the end of the play, after turning his hosts' world to pandemonium, the houseguest from hell would depart, only to slip on the ice again, bringing down the curtain on the appalling prospect of more of the same.

They wrote as swiftly as usual, putting Whiteside in a wheelchair and modeling his every word and action on Woollcott. By the time Woollcott returned from Canada and the quints, they had finished an act and a half and Woollcott insisted on hearing what they had. They agreed to read and Woollcott wondered why they were so "guilty-looking."

Whatever else he was, Woollcott was neither fool nor hypocrite. He recognized at once that Whiteside—described in their pages as a "portly and Falstaffian" presence who "looks like every caricature ever drawn of him"—was unmistakably himself. He had traded on his own eccentricities too shamelessly to be offended by Moss and Kaufman's doing so now. He later claimed that "I was considerably taken aback to find they had done a cartoon of me," adding with characteristic self-appreciation, "They had found it so easy and entertaining that they could not resist."

If he had been taken aback, he had also laughed. "I thought the play very funny," he admitted, and "had a sneaking notion that [it] would be a success." Still, he wanted time to think it over.

A week later he gave them his blessing to continue with the play, but surprised them by announcing that he would not play Whiteside. Appearing as himself "would be alienating and even offensive," he said, though not enough to prevent audiences clamoring for him to the extent that "I might have to stay in New York for two years."

No, he would withdraw in favor of the only actor he could think of who could do him justice—John Barrymore.

Woollcott was serious about Barrymore, and so would Warner Bros. be when it came time to make the movie, but Barrymore was in severe alcoholic decline, able to work only with the aid of cue cards, which were invented for him. Whiteside was a part that would require timing, rapid-fire delivery, and a certain grandiloquence, which Barrymore could certainly muster, but only if he could remember what he was supposed to be saying. Woollcott could memorize; he just couldn't act.

His withdrawal was not total (he would play Whiteside on the road), but in some ways was the making of the play. It allowed Moss and Kaufman to write a bravura role without having to tailor it to Woollcott's narrow talents. His blessing allowed them, at the same time, to take dramatic advantage of his every foible and eccentricity without seeming to attack the original.

To make sure no one thought they were exploiting a friend and colleague—and to make clear that was exactly what they were doing—they dedicated the play "TO ALEXANDER WOOLLCOTT. For reasons that are nobody's business."

That Woollcott sparked *The Man Who Came to Dinner* (the final title suggested by a stage manager) has always been a given, but other, less well-known sources gave it shape. The most useful was George Kelly's one-act comedy, *The Flattering Word,* which Moss had staged and acted in repeatedly from his Little Theater days to the Catskills. Whenever Moss staged it he cast himself in the leading role of Eugene Tesh, "a prominent dramatic star." Tesh, a showy, second-rate actor, comes to small-town Ohio and upends the middle-class morality of provincials who disapprove of the theater by flattering them that they, too, should be on the stage. The flattery is cynical and has an ulterior motive (he's after the minister's young wife), but neatly exposes local hypocrisy.

Tesh was in Ohio for a one-night stand, while Whiteside's stay would go on forever, a theme suggested by *That's Gratitude,* a play by actor Frank Craven, a Woollcott intimate. *That's Gratitude* dramatized the discomfort caused by a houseguest who couldn't be dislodged by dynamite and was a hit on Broadway the same season as *Once in a Lifetime.*

Minor borrowings included a nursery jingle Charles Brackett had invented for his 1934 novel *Entirely Surrounded.* There, his Woollcott lampoon sang out:

I'se des' a 'ittle wabbit in de sunshine,
I'se des' a 'ittle bunny in de wain,

which Kaufman and Hart lifted virtually intact for use as a first-act curtain.

Woollcott himself inspired Whiteside's pratfall just before the final curtain. He had told and retold an anecdote about George Bernard Shaw's breaking a leg and then, when his injury was mended and he was in hasty retreat from the advances of an amorous nurse, breaking it again.

If George Kelly and Frank Craven were making points about vanity and gratitude in their plays, so were Moss and Kaufman, but they were also exploiting a headline personality for a late-Depression audience that wanted laughter more than insight. Whiteside's outrageously insulting behavior was not just witty, it was barbed-wire hostile, as was Woollcott's, and avoiding hostility in the playing is still a trap for actors. But *The Man Who Came to Dinner* was character farce, not character study. Plumbing Whiteside's depths didn't go with exploiting his dazzling surface. The insecurity masked by arrogance could be hinted at by parodying Woollcott's habit of lapsing suddenly into baby talk (he cutely referred to himself as "Acky Wooky"), and he could show an appreciation of "little people" with the Stanleys' cook and butler, a married couple he unconscionably persuades to leave Ohio to work for him in New York. However "fabbulous," Whiteside would require comeuppance and get it.

Minor characters existed only in a centrifugal spin around him, but sparked vignettes like those that had livened almost all Kaufman and Hart plays. Famous names crop up with the regularity of a metronome.

Whiteside's tumultuous personality needed the blandness of his captive hosts, Mr. and Mrs. Stanley of Mesalia, Ohio (a town first mentioned in *The American Way*), for contrast and relief. Their twenty-something children, Richard and June, are targets for Whiteside's meddling to prevent their going middle-class ("Suppose your parents *are* unhappy—it's good for them."). His nurse, Miss Preen ("You have the touch of a sex-starved cobra!"); his physician, Dr. Bradley ("the greatest living argument for mercy killings"), with his manuscript *Forty Years an Ohio Doctor* ("Am I to be spared nothing?"); the club-lady fans who arrive with plants and calf's-foot jelly ("Made from your own foot, I have no doubt.")—all are little more than straight men for his bombast.

Two characters are more than objects of his withering scorn: Maggie Cutler, his longtime secretary, remains unflappable, immune to rages she's heard before; and Bert Jefferson, the local reporter, is a levelheaded, likable idealist who has written a play. He provides Whiteside with a literate chess partner and becomes the love of Maggie's life.

Maggie is the heart and anchor of the play, able to handle Whiteside until she, too, becomes his victim. When she falls in love and announces her intention to marry Jefferson and settle down, Whiteside sneers at the "temporary insanity" of a "flea-bitten Cleopatra."

To thwart Maggie's romance and focus the farce, Whiteside summons mantrap actress Lorraine Sheldon to snatch play and playwright from Maggie. Sheldon, a caricature of Gertrude Lawrence, collides with dashing composer-playwright Beverly Carlton and Hollywood's madcap Banjo, dead ringers for Noël Coward and Harpo Marx, who come to Mesalia to cheer up the great man in his time of trial. Carlton sings his latest song at the piano (the perfect Coward parody written by Cole Porter); Banjo dementedly stalks Preen. Maggie, comprehending at last the dimensions of Whiteside's selfish conniving, tells "Big Lord Fauntleroy" the jig is up. She resigns.

With the help of Carlton, Banjo, and a most unlikely mummy case fortuitously sent Whiteside as a Christmas gift by the Khedive of Egypt, Sheldon is dispatched to Nova Scotia without Jefferson or his play. Allowing true love to flourish redeems Whiteside, but he is hardly reformed. His final stunt is to trump the Stanleys' having called the sheriff to eject him by announcing that he has finally placed the face of Mr. Stanley's sweetly vague old-maid sister, who is none other than the long-sought axe-murderess Harriet Sedley, Mesalia's answer to Lizzie Borden.

The Man Who Came to Dinner is a well-made play in the now-denigrated sense, but the artifice acts as a reminder that the kidding is all in fun. Plot contrivances work like slow-burning fuses—those comic booby traps, again—lit now to explode later. The axe-murderess and the mummy case, not to mention the cockroach colony, the octopus in the basement, and the penguins in the library, are absurdly improbable, but whisked on- and offstage so deftly they add to the sense of comic chaos. The well-madeness of the play was reassuring and the parodies drawn with style, wit, and accuracy.

It has been suggested that *The Man Who Came to Dinner* is about success, but it isn't. It is about celebrity, something that mattered greatly to Moss. The play doesn't satirize celebrity or celebrity worship; it revels in the fun of celebrity, the privileges of fame, the giddy sense of being a somebody among nobodies, and the immunity from convention that allows the famous to get away with almost anything. Celebrity license was central to Woollcott and has changed very little over the years, which is why the play strikes chords with audiences today, in spite of the mostly forgotten names it drops: ZaSu Pitts, Haile Selassie, Chauncey Depew, and Admiral Byrd.

When the play was revived on Broadway in 1980, Frank Rich noted in the *New York Times* "as these names cease to be household words, the once-snappy lines that contain them begin to wilt." They do, but audiences still laugh, as their merriment proved in the revival of 2000 with Nathan Lane. They don't understand the allusions, but they understand the kind of celebrity they stood for. In *The Man Who Came to Dinner* it isn't superficial and spurious; it is what it was for Moss, something to be prized. It justifies almost anything, but requires comeuppance, as the authors felt Woollcott did. The put-him-in-his-place speeches are the funniest and, tellingly, the most satisfying in the play.

When the much-put-upon Nurse Preen resigns her post, she stops the show cold with her aria of grievance:

> *I am not only walking out on this case, Mr. Whiteside, I am leaving the nursing profession. I became a nurse because all my life, ever since I was a little girl, I was filled with the idea of serving a suffering humanity. After one month with you, Mr. Whiteside, I am going to work in a munitions factory. From now on anything that I can do to help exterminate the human race will fill me with the greatest of pleasure. If Florence Nightingale had ever nursed you, Mr. Whiteside, she would have married Jack the Ripper instead of founding the Red Cross.*

It's the best single speech in the play and can still bring down the house, followed closely by Maggie's more somber denunciation:

> *Shall I tell you something, Sherry? I think you are a selfish, petty egomaniac who would see his mother burned at the stake if that was the only way he could light his cigarette. I think you'd sacrifice your best friend without a moment's hesitation if he disturbed the sacred routine of your self-centered, paltry little life. I think you are incapable of any human emotion that goes higher up than your stomach, and I was the fool of the world for ever thinking I could trust you.*

Whiteside is rebuked, but still Whiteside. "Well," he huffs with righteous indignation, "as long as I live, I shall never do anyone a good turn again."

The Man Who Came to Dinner opened at the Music Box on October 16, 1939, and played for 739 performances on Broadway, almost as long as *You Can't Take It With You*. Brooks Atkinson in the *Times* found it "the funniest comedy of the season." Wolcott Gibbs, who knew everybody concerned, wondered in *The New Yorker* how anyone who did not dine frequently at the Algonquin could identify Sheridan Whiteside with "anything in life."

Everyone approved the actor playing the title role. When Woollcott withdrew from the play and abandoned the notion of Barrymore, his candidate was Robert Morley, a recent success as *Oscar Wilde*. Morley rejected the part (though he would play it in London and name his son, critic Sheridan Morley, after the role). It was next offered to Hollywood's

Adolph Menjou, who said no, and finally to Monty Woolley, Moss's erstwhile shipmate on the *Franconia.*

Woolley had been acting in New York and Hollywood, but was still known chiefly for his association with Porter musicals and as an eccentric character-about-town, as openly gay among the Broadway community as anyone in the 1930s. *The Man Who Came to Dinner* was his personal triumph and established him permanently as an actor in Hollywood.

Woolley was not Moss's only friend to be cast in *The Man Who Came to Dinner.* The small role of Sarah, the Stanleys' cook, was played by Mrs. Priestly Morrison (that was her stage name), the wife of the director of *The Beloved Bandit,* who had himself played Grandpa Vanderhof in the Boston company of *You Can't Take It With You.* A newcomer, Mary Wickes, established her long career deadpanning in Hollywood with Nurse Preen.

Another newcomer played Richard Stanley, the photographer-son encouraged by Whiteside to defy his family. Moss met him on *The American Way,* where he had played a village youth. His name was Gordon Merrick, and he would one day write *The Lord Won't Mind,* with its fictional portrait of Moss.

Merrick may never have yielded to Moss's charm, but there was someone else in the cast of *The Man Who Came to Dinner* who wanted to. Edith Atwater played Maggie Cutler on Broadway and on the road and became highly visible on Moss's arm during the play's long run. Janet Fox, who was in *The American Way* and close to Moss, had studied with Atwater at the American Academy of Dramatic Arts and remembered that "she was known as 'Moss's girl,' for a while." Atwater was "slick and smart and from a good family in Chicago," Fox said. "Moss had never met anyone quite like her. She wasn't a society girl, exactly, but a girl of education, and that intrigued him."

Nothing permanent developed, but friends wondered if marriage might not, after all, be lurking in the back of Moss's mind. Cole Porter was married. Alfred Lunt was married. Guthrie McClintic was married. Why not Moss? Woollcott was certain the Hart-Atwater romance had no future. The story circulated that, seeing Moss enter a restaurant with her, he chirped, "Here come Moss Hart, and the future Miss Atwater."

Woollcott could have been depended on, in any case, to get the last word. He got it when *Time* asked him for his opinion of *The Man Who Came to Dinner.* "I only review plays for money," he snapped.

16

Property

The success or failure of a show is settled when somebody says,
"Wouldn't it be a great idea . . ."

HOWARD LINDSAY

The Man Who Came to Dinner was such a crowd pleaser that Warner Bros. paid $250,000 for the movie rights, equaling the record set in 1928 by *Abie's Irish Rose* and establishing a new one for Kaufman and Hart. Warners earmarked the project for its top female stars, Bette Davis as Maggie Cutler and "Oomph Girl" Ann Sheridan as Lorraine Sheldon. Davis reawakened the John Barrymore question by insisting he play Whiteside. She reportedly wept when Warner executives showed her the screen tests Barrymore made for the part. Woolley, Davis agreed, would be fine on film, with third billing after herself and Sheridan, both in smaller roles than his.

Moss and Kaufman showed unusual interest in the movie version, agreeing not only to write the screenplay, but also to codirect the picture. Moss had no camera experience and Kaufman's was limited to a few days on *A Night at the Opera,* but the notion of writing and codirecting had appeal. Whatever Hollywood wisecracks Moss fashioned for the press, he enjoyed life there, where the steady stream of Broadway transplants made it seem more and more like Sardi's with bougainvillea.

He checked into a bungalow at the Garden of Allah on Sunset Boulevard in January 1940. He and Kaufman would write the script there, enjoying distractions like Charles Laughton, Robert Benchley, Dorothy Parker, and her husband, Alan Campbell, all of them in neighboring bungalows. Dominating life around the pool and everywhere else was Woollcott. He had agreed to Hollywood rehearsals for his stint onstage as Whiteside in the West Coast touring company. He found Hollywood "completely loathsome," he said, but only by rehearsing there could Kaufman (and Moss) direct him and write the screenplay at the same time. Woollcott's tour—"the amateur company," Moss called it—would begin in Santa Barbara, move on to San Francisco and Los Angeles, and eventually tour the Eastern seaboard.

Like almost everyone who dealt with Woollcott, Warner Bros. discovered they had more on their plates than Cream of Wheat. Moss and Kaufman had given Woollcott a percentage of the play in recognition of his contribution to it, which made him legally part owner of the property. His share of the movie sale came to $12,175, a tidy sum in 1940 dollars, not to mention his weekly share of the Broadway box office, still selling out with Woolley, and the one in Chicago, where the company was headed by Clifton Webb.

When reviewing documents, one of the studio lawyers asked if Moss and Kaufman had secured a legal release from Woollcott. It had never occurred to anyone that a release would be necessary, but surely it was simply a matter of form and probably would have been with anyone but Woollcott.

He was annoyed at not having been considered for the leading role on-screen and was worried, he told Kaufman, that Woolley might portray him as a "pansy." He suddenly decided that Whiteside was not just a friendly "cartoon," but a "libelous caricature," doing him irreparable damage. His reputation would require economic soothing before he could allow the picture to go forward. Furthermore, even though every critic who reviewed *The Man Who Came to Dinner* had identified him as the model for Whiteside, the movie could not do so on-screen or in advertising or publicity. The fact that Woollcott was preparing to play the part onstage himself was irrelevant, he said.

Warner Bros., where the phrase "you ain't heard nothing yet" originated, listened to his demands with equanimity and agreed to pay him $25,000 for the privilege of not mentioning his name.

Moss and Kaufman finished their screenplay. Any serious hopes they had of directing the picture were dashed when the studio rejected their script, believing it needed writers with more film experience to "open it up." The studio assigned the Epstein brothers, Philip and Julius (whose next picture would be *Casablanca*), to prepare a new draft. The Epstein script went into production quickly under director William Keighley, with Davis, Sheridan, and Woolley supported by Reginald Gardiner as Beverly Carlton, Jimmy Durante as Banjo, and Billie Burke as Mrs. Stanley.

Moss and Kaufman went back to New York, where their continuing windfall from *The Man Who Came to Dinner* got invested in more real estate.

The Lyceum Theatre, east of Broadway on Forty-fifth Street, was and is a medium-sized house built in 1903 by producer Daniel Frohman, whose career began with minstrel shows shortly after the end of the Civil War. Frohman's death in 1940 at age eighty-nine left the Lyceum vacant and vulnerable to demolition. Moss and Kaufman joined Sam Harris and Max Gordon to acquire it and save it for posterity and profits. Real estate investment had worked splendidly for Irving Berlin and Harris in the Music Box and might reward playwrights, too, guaranteeing them stage space that—full of hits—could amortize the costs of pens and paper and the upkeep on farms and town houses.

Moss and Kaufman agreed to launch the Lyceum's 1940–41 season with a new play as soon as they thought one up. "We just arbitrarily said we'd meet June first and do a play," Moss told Dore Schary, adding, "we haven't got even the remotest idea at the moment."

Moss was restless, however. Taking a leaf from Woollcott's date book, he briefly considered a lecture tour of his own. The restlessness was professional. He and Kaufman had written seven plays in just ten years and he was eager to break the routine for something different, without being sure what that might be. He didn't need money, for cash was flowing in from *The Man Who Came to Dinner,* though the West Coast tour was stopped dead in its tracks in May. Woollcott, never a dainty eater, had almost fatally overindulged at a restaurant in San Francisco. The menu, as recorded by his biographer, included "bisque of clams, baby squid, snails a la Bourgogne with fondue of truffles, alligator-pear salad, sweets, all washed down with a heavy Burgundy and uncounted cups of coffee." After dinner Woollcott collapsed. Doctors ordered him hospitalized and off the stage for the duration. In true trouper fashion, Woollcott declared the show would go on, but not without him. After six months' rest and ruthless dieting to clean out his arteries, he and the tour resumed on the Eastern seaboard with New Year's performances in Washington, D.C., where the audience included Eleanor Roosevelt. The first lady invited Woollcott to make himself at home in the Lincoln Bedroom, from which he wrote letters on White House stationery complaining about his lodgings, rather like Whiteside might have done.

Woollcott's heart attack may have caused Moss to reflect on the rigors of the road, for he canceled his lecture tour and went instead to Fairview

Farm. Bucks County was not so remote that he could avoid news of war in Europe, which unsettled and depressed him. "Evil is on the march and it pollutes everything for me," he wrote Schary in May, the day the German army seized the Channel ports, leaving him "no heart" for anything as trivial as yet another comedy. His grasp of military science was modest, but his sensitivity to the "ridiculous" figure he would cut as a soldier was acute. Denouncing the kaiser with oratory at twelve was one thing; slogging through trenches with a rifle at thirty-five was another. Schary—safely draft exempt with his lapful of children—scolded him for melodrama and vanity.

Almost as if avoiding another annual collaboration with Kaufman, Moss tried to interest Rodgers and Hart in a musical based on *The Road to Rome,* Robert Sherwood's 1926 play about an earlier juggernaut through Europe, conducted not in tanks but on elephant back. Rodgers and Hart declined to write tunes for Hannibal, as they were already busy with an eponymous nightclub heel called *Pal Joey.*

Moss emerged from seclusion in Bucks County to attend the Allied Relief Ball at the Astor Hotel in New York on May 10, where Noël Coward was master of ceremonies, introducing Ethel Merman, Bert Lahr, Eddie Cantor, and other Broadway headliners. But it was the Brits—Coward himself, braced by Gertrude Lawrence on one side and Beatrice Lillie on the other—who gave the evening focus, bringing "a European war" to the edge of Broadway's footlights for Moss, the theater community, and the FBI.

Foreshadowing things to come, FBI informants were among the crowd at the Astor. This was mid-1940 and they were taking down names of those the House Un-American Activities Committee (already formed) would later accuse of having been "premature anti-Fascists." Moss's name would be included on their lists simply because he was there.

As the Nazis occupied Paris, New York's newest theater owners tried to come up with a play. They toyed with the notion of a comedy set in a village barbershop, but the idea seemed episodic and expensive, calling for too many actors to drift across the small stage of the Lyceum. They worked mostly in Bucks County, where Moss followed news of the war in Europe and wrote alarmed letters to Schary full of what he called the "stress of emotion." Seeking calm by surveying Mother Nature's (and his own) handiwork at Fairview Farm, he was at last struck with a comedy idea so obvious it was surprising it hadn't written itself.

He had long entertained dinner parties and the press with anecdotes about going broke while going rustic. He and the Kaufmans had precipitated a rush of celebrities to the sticks that had become an all-out fad.

Cole Porter would tweak the trend on Broadway the following season with "Farming," a ditty in which Katharine Cornell, Lady Mendl, and Mae West could be found (lyrically) shelling peas, climbing trees, or making merry in the hay. "Way down upon the Soignée River," someone wisecracked.

Moss's inspiration was to write "a very simple little play, with a nice warm quality," all about urbanites restoring a dilapidated farmhouse with (to add a patriotic note) a Revolutionary War pedigree. It wasn't autobiographical, though Brooks Atkinson, a frequent houseguest in Bucks County, later noted that the huge fireplace and Dutch doors on the Lyceum's stage might have been carted in whole from Fairview Farm.

Moss and Kaufman titled the new play *George Washington Slept Here*. Protagonist Newton Fuller was "the kind of average man you meet every day of the week," said Moss, to whom "average" meant having a country house with a cook and a maid and a historical tie to the Father of His Country. Renovation and restoration of a derelict Pennsylvania farmhouse seem utterest folly to the average man's wife, Annabelle, whose tongue is sharp enough to split rails.

This "very simple little play" soon has the Fullers chasing livestock from their tumbledown kitchen so as not to lose their servants to modernity and plumbing. They dig for water—and dig and dig again, just as Moss had. They patch, refloor, and reroof. They decorate with cunning colonial touches. The simple life—still plumbing-free—gets complicated when the Fullers' daughter falls in crush with an actor slumming in local summer stock, but she gets over it. A hateful neighbor refuses access to his road, the only route to the Fuller front door. Money flows out as water refuses to flow in. The bank account dwindles. The mortgage comes due. The only hope is rich but miserly Uncle Stanley, who comes to freeload and, when pressed, confesses he's been flat as Kansas ever since the Crash.

In 1940 the spectacle of urbanites going rustic was fresher and more topical than it sounds today, and sparked a whole home-owner or fixer-upper genre that included Betty Macdonald's *The Egg and I* and Eric Hodgins's *Mr. Blandings Builds His Dream House*. City mice in the country have appeal (think Martha Stewart). Television's hugely successful *The Beverly Hillbillies* was just a reversal of the formula, sending country mice to town, where in no time at all they spun off something very like the original premise of the Kaufman-Hart play called *Green Acres*.

Topicality had been their stock-in-trade for a decade, but the jokes were getting mechanical and they were writing themselves into a rut. Domesticity seemed to drain energy and defeat wit, as common-folk drama had done in *The American Way*. They almost never wrote civilians with the flair they brought to theatricals, and *George Washington* was generic situation comedy, as television's recycling would prove. Or perhaps it was just that cobbling together a play to meet an arbitrary date at the Lyceum resulted in more carpentry than comedy.

Kaufman and Hart were a name brand by 1940. They had disappointed before, but *Merrily We Roll Along* had been ambitious and *The Fabulous Invalid* was a love letter from the heart. Even *The American Way* had had a thematic reason for being, but the raison d'être for *George Washington Slept Here* seemed, even to sympathetic Brooks Atkinson, "nothing in particular except the annual necessity of writing a play."

The production tried out to moderate success in Boston in late September. The rush to the Lyceum incurred problems right up to the opening. The most serious was the death of Berton Churchill, the actor playing Uncle Stanley. The veteran character actor died in his hotel room the day before the scheduled Broadway opening of October 11, causing a week's postponement and recasting with the better-known Dudley Digges.

Fuller was played by Ernest Truex, an actor who scampered onstage in 1894 at the age of five and had been stealing scenes ever since. His disruptive antics out of town were his response to discovering that his lines had fewer laughs than those of the caustic Annabelle. To compensate, Truex introduced acrobatic stage business, including a leap onto a farmhouse tabletop, a bit of upstagery that inspired the rest of the cast to threaten rebellion. Truex's falling to the stage and wrenching his knee, to the muted sympathy of his fellow actors, averted mutiny.

Jean Dixon, who had been the acerbic May of *Once in a Lifetime* and, before that, the acerbic Lucille of Kaufman and Lardner's *June Moon,* played the acerbic Annabelle. Dixon had accepted her role on faith, without reading the script. "For all I knew," she said (sounding acerbic), "it might very well have been a bit part of a Sicilian streetwalker." Instead, it was the same wisecracking dame she'd been playing for years.

The only other notable member of the cast was the little-known Percy Kilbride as the local handyman. Kilbride perfected here his quintessential hayseed half a dozen years before he achieved stardom with it opposite Marjorie Main in the movie of *The Egg and I,* which spun Ma and Pa Kettle into a low-budget, high-profit series of ten movies.

The real stars of *George Washington Slept Here* were the authors, who seemed to be underly ambitious, even as they cast a trademark nod to their real home turf, the theater. The wife of the actor philandering with the Fullers' daughter complains to Annabelle not about the affair, but that:

> *These hams come down here, work their cans off for a dollar-eighty a*
> *week, live in places that a cockroach would turn up his nose at—and for*
> *what? Just to* act. *So help me God, actors will act* anywhere, in *anything,*
> *and* for *anything . . .*

To the alert, such lines seemed to comment not all that obliquely on the anything at hand.

The average-man ordinariness of the Fullers didn't inspire sympathy and recognition; it just seemed average and ordinary. The Fullers were as one-dimensional as their predicament, their one-liners strained and by-the-numbers. The action was predictable the moment the word "mortgage" was pronounced. The hateful neighbor was a stock villain undone by an antique deed-from-the-blue giving the Fullers title to everything in sight, including the neighbor's road, water, and a fat parcel of his property. The wryest development among the few was the exclamation point designed to bring down the curtain in all their comedies. The deed-ex-machina revealed that the house's footnote to the American Revolution was real, after all: It wasn't George Washington who had slept there, but Benedict Arnold. Curtain.

The critics zeroed in. Brooks Atkinson acknowledged that the play was "labored and empty"; the almost always approving Burns Mantle found it "forced"; another thought it "dated" and "remote."

About the only thing that amused critics was a third-act slapstick free-for-all that may have been inspired by *Hellzapoppin* and came too late to matter. The Fullers, thinking the house they have painstakingly restored during the previous two acts is to be repossessed, destroy it in a drunken protest against foreclosure, returning it—as per the mortgage—to its "original condition." Some found the mayhem "riotously funny" and on "the real level of Kaufman and Hart," but there was something malicious about it that made the first two acts seem even more mechanical than they were.

George Washington Slept Here ran at the Lyceum for 173 performances. That was more than *Merrily We Roll Along* or *The Fabulous Invalid* had achieved, but less than *The American Way* and very small potatoes compared to the first-rate comedies whose authentic pleasures made it seem so dull. The length of the run was less telling than the modesty of the aspiration, which had been no more than to fill a theater and inspire a movie sale.

Warner Bros. had invested in *George Washington* on the stage and secured the movie rights for a comparatively meager $83,000, casting Jack Benny and Ann Sheridan as the Fullers the following year. Neither Moss nor Kaufman had anything to do with the movie, which reversed the roles of husband and wife, giving Jean Dixon's sarcastic attitude and lines to Benny, whose trademark slow burns made the role reversal work and pointed up how little the play or dialogue depended on character. Sheridan, much less showy than as Lorraine Sheldon, was appealing as the antique-loving spouse who—in the movie—bought the country property and got stuck with the lines Ernest Truex had found so bland onstage.

George Washington Slept Here was inferior stuff from the inventors of Grandpa Vanderhof and Sheridan Whiteside, characters who had accustomed audiences to expect more. There was something thin and tired about it, like a comedian going through the motions to get to a punch line that wasn't all that funny anyway.

And it was a punch line. *George Washington Slept Here* was the final full-length play by Kaufman and Hart, a collaboration that had so brightened times that were otherwise grim. Their separation seemed to many on Broadway to spell the end of an era, but the era was ending all by itself, as events in Europe and at home would soon prove.

The affinities Moss shared with his mentor had enriched him materially and creatively in ways he had only dreamed of before Sam Harris's inspired hunch that they might work well together. Their comic spirits had been genuinely complementary. Moss's sunny ingratiation was balanced by Kaufman's cool skepticism. On a nonprofessional level, too, there was a dynamic that answered old needs without creating new ones.

Kaufman was a cool and undemonstrative man whose approval was more often expressed by silence than by praise. Moss understood that, could interpret the affection behind the silences—or the barbs—at the same time that he needed unalloyed applause to feel equal. He felt, like most sons, the need to prove himself, even if that meant challenging the man responsible for his career.

There were those among their colleagues for whom the separation seemed overdue. Marc Connelly, a Kaufman collaborator himself, put it most bluntly by remarking that "Moss is in such a state of genuflection toward George all the time that I don't [know] how they ever get a play written. Moss really wants to be George's son."

Moss was acutely aware of the ambivalence in their relationship, but would always claim he owed everything to Kaufman. In terms of luck, timing, stagecraft, and serendipity it was true. But Kaufman's celebrated gifts are often stressed at the expense of his many partners because he alone seems the constant. Apart from *The Butter and Egg Man,* his one solo effort in the twenties, Kaufman never worked alone. He was the critic and collaborator par excellence who edited and sharpened and sometimes structured others—Ferber, Lardner, Connelly, Woollcott, and Moss—all of whom created original work without him.

Who did what is the enduring collaborator question, and Kaufman and Hart claimed never to remember, which is both disingenuous and just. The only surviving original draft that gives definitive clues is Moss's first version of *Once in a Lifetime,* in which the wit and originality were apparent before Kaufman became involved. Kaufman sharpened and polished *Once in a Lifetime* to Broadway standards and did the same with Moss. Their best work together was more than the sum of their parts; it was a whole in which wit joined feeling, and it produced two enduring comedies, *You Can't Take It With You* and *The Man Who Came to Dinner.* Kaufman gave Moss first billing on both of those plays (and on *Once in a Lifetime*), which speaks to professional fairness, and to Moss's sometimes inspired contribution to their best work.

They were not personally close. Moss was closer to Dore Schary, in whom he confided, and Joe Hyman, to whom he had entrusted his business affairs ever since Vermont. He was closer to Beatrice Kaufman, too, who was not embarrassed by personal revelations or displays of affection, as her husband was. But as writers Kaufman and Hart were better with each other because of each other. They would remain wedded in spirit to the ends of their lives, events that would almost coincide.

PART THREE

Solo

17

Going It Alone

No one would undertake the intricate,
painful, gargantuan, hysterical task of putting on a
musical play unless he had more enthusiasm than
most people have about anything.

BROOKS ATKINSON

Moss burned no bridges. He and Kaufman spoke daily on the telephone, remained partners in the Lyceum, invested in each other's plays, sharpened each other's pencils when asked, and would collaborate in the future on the odd skit or sketch. Mutual affection remained steady, if largely unexpressed. Kaufman, supportive but never fully reconciled to losing his most congenial collaborator, sought a full schedule by agreeing to work on a new play with Edna Ferber, but his plans were derailed almost at once.

Moss had been approached earlier in the year for advice by the young writing team of Joseph A. Fields and Jerome Chodorov. The two had written a comedy about sisters from Ohio out to conquer Greenwich Village on a bankroll of $40. The play, based on autobiographical sketches by Ruth McKenny in *The New Yorker,* was called *My Sister Eileen* and needed revision, but Moss thought it had exceptional Broadway promise.

The authors were newcomers, but not outsiders. Fields was the son of Lew Fields of the legendary comedy team of Weber and Fields (lyricist Dorothy Fields and librettist Herbert Fields were his siblings). Chodorov was the younger brother of now-successful playwright Edward Chodorov, who, as Eddie, had introduced Moss to the world of Little Theater and Camp Utopia in the twenties.

Moss was generous with advice when Jerry Chodorov brought him a draft of *My Sister Eileen,* recommending the play to Max Gordon and suggesting that Kaufman direct. *My Sister Eileen* would give Kaufman an immediate project, and give Gordon one, too. The producer desperately needed rescue from a string of flops and huge losses incurred in Hollywood, not helped by RKO's cancellation of the movie version of *The American Way*. Gordon's hopelessly large debt (including sums he owed the IRS) brought on a breakdown and suicide attempts. He was now hospitalized with "appendicitis," and Moss knew that a gesture of confidence in him as a producer might return him from the brink. Sam Harris generously agreed that Gordon should be given *My Sister Eileen,* and invested in it, too, as his own show of faith. Harris was the superior and more prestigious producer, but was busy, in any case, with Moss's first solo effort, which would be Harris's last production.

Moss's gesture was designed to benefit everyone, but especially Kaufman, who suffered not only the loss of his writing partner in 1940, but also that of both parents within five months of each other. Staging a finished comedy with eager newcomers, no matter how extensive the re-writes, would be more therapeutic than writing a new one with the demanding Ferber. Moss helped Kaufman postpone the commitment to her (her feathers eventually unruffled), tipped off Fields and Chodorov to Kaufman's sweet tooth (they stocked up on cheap candy), and turned *My Sister Eileen* over to Gordon complete with a list of investors, including himself, the authors of the play, the Kaufmans, Harris, and even Woollcott, who loathed Gordon but knew a good thing when he saw it. The only loser was the Lyceum. *George Washington Slept Here,* mediocre as it was, would run just long enough to prevent *My Sister Eileen*'s opening there. It played the Biltmore, instead, whose owners raked in the profits as it brought Gordon back in spirit and solvency, becoming the ninth longest running show in Broadway history.

Chodorov and Fields concluded later that Moss had urged *My Sister Eileen* on Kaufman to keep him at arm's length as Moss embarked on his solo venture, but it is equally likely that the opposite was true: that Moss was ensuring Kaufman's proximity—busy but not overtaxed by Ferber—should he need or want help while trying his wings. He was approaching independence with a show of confidence, but his nonchalance masked uncertainty. He confided to Schary that the writing of the new play was "pure torture" when it went well, and worse when it didn't.

Some of this was art-is-hard dramatics, some of it was the realization that solitary writing was lonely, and some was simple fear of failure. Still, ego and ambition demanded a solo spotlight. He wanted to direct, too, which he could not do while partnered with Kaufman. Nor could he pursue old aspirations to emulate Ibsen, O'Neill, and Shaw as a serious dramatist of big subjects, or challenge Noël Coward. If "the English Moss Hart" could wear all those hats, the American one could, too.

In any event, Moss's new project dealt with a subject more likely to raise Kaufman's eyebrows than his creative interest, except as satire. Psychoanalysis was the theme and Moss was approaching it with the zeal and reverence of a true believer, encouraged by a new psychoanalyst, Dr. Lawrence S. Kubie. In some measure, Kubie displaced Kaufman as Moss's mentor, for he was both the principal catalyst in Moss's declaring his independence and, because of his own ambitions, something like an uncredited collaborator, so much so that Moss would dedicate the new play to him.

Moss had turned to Kubie after George Gershwin's death and his disillusionment with Zilboorg in New York and Simmel in California. Kubie was an orthodox Freudian specializing in what he termed "neurotic distortion of the creative process," the title of his best-known book. He cultivated creative and artistic patients and, though he had been one of Zilboorg's harshest critics, appeared determined to outdo him in a client list of the famous.

Celebrity and pedigree seemed to influence Kubie's prognoses for treatment. Author Frederic Bradlee, brother of *Washington Post* editor Ben Bradlee, saw Kubie briefly in the early 1940s, not long after Moss began treatment with him. Bradlee was an actor then, appearing as the son in the Chicago company of *The Man Who Came to Dinner* with Clifton Webb, a Kubie patient who recommended him to Bradlee, as he had to Moss. Bradlee was convinced that Kubie "was a money snob and a celebrity snob." He was distant and disinterested until Bradlee let slip that he was related to an old New England banking family and to Frank Crowninshield of *Vanity Fair,* which seemed to enhance dramatically the young man's long-term potential in analysis. The patient quickly became an ex-patient. "Kubie was a star-fucker," Bradlee declared years later, "and I was on to him like that."

Kubie's interest in celebrities was, itself, celebrated. He had a much-discussed run-in with Ernest Hemingway in 1934, attempting in print to analyze the author whom he had never met. He wrote an article for the *Saturday Review* based on his reading of Hemingway. "Cyrano and the Matador" asserted that the well-known hairy-chested persona concealed Oedipal fixations and latent homosexuality. The *Saturday Review* blanched and elected not to publish the article, but Hemingway obtained a copy of it and threatened to sue for libel. As a result, Kubie's theoretical essay was not published until 1984, when both he and Hemingway were dead, but it made news at the time, as Kubie may have hoped. His thesis publicized his views on neurosis as a block to creativity and stressed his conviction that homosexuality was both pathological and treatable.

"Curing" homosexuality was mainstream psychiatric practice of the period, notwithstanding Freud's observation in a famous letter to an American mother worried about her son that such an approach was futile or misguided. Homosexuality in 1940 was socially condemned, criminal, and officially classified as a mental disorder by the American Psychiatric Association, a designation not lifted until 1973.

Kubie made curing homosexuals a primary focus of his practice, and later treated Vladimir Horowitz and Tennessee Williams. He insisted that the pianist and the playwright divorce themselves from manifestations of their sexual orientation on the grounds that yielding to temptation or entertaining even random thoughts would dilute or mask their neurotic symptoms. He persuaded Horowitz to lock himself in a room when stray impulses surfaced, with the unintended result that Horowitz gave up playing the piano altogether until discontinuing treatment. Similarly, Kubie ordered Williams to quit writing, which, Kubie asserted, was dissipating his symptoms by transforming them into drama. Williams declined, but bowed to Kubie's demand that he abandon his longtime companion Frank Merlo, a man many considered the most stabilizing element in Williams's life, at precisely the time Merlo was dying of cancer.

Kubie's autocratic technique struck many of his patients as dictatorial or angry. Even his daughter, Ann Rabinowitz, remembers her father as "a professional intellectual with a temper," and admits, "It was not always easy living with God."

Being treated by God, however, and having God sift through one's dreams and unconscious was immensely gratifying. As a result, Moss embraced Kubie's influence in every area of his life, professional, personal, and even social. Kubie's degrees from Harvard and Johns Hopkins validated his scientific authority, and his wide-ranging erudition echoed the German-Jewish high culture Moss had envied in the Solomon branch of his family when still an adolescent.

Moss joked about Kubie publicly, referring to him as "Herr Doktor." He repeated the jokes about the letter-sweater with the *F* for Freud. He waxed enthusiastic to any reporter who would listen and made the couch sound like one of the rewards of success. He explained what he called "going it alone" to the press by noting, "I've literally sabotaged every serious idea I've had [until] my psychiatrist made me resolve that the next idea I had, whether it was good or lousy, I'd carry through."

It sounded so easy, but his closest friends knew the despondency and depression he had suffered for years and indulged his belief that analysis—or Kubie—was literally keeping him alive. When not in Bucks County he could be found five times a week in Kubie's Upper East Side office in sessions that lasted from fifty minutes to two and a half hours. Sometimes he began and ended his day on the couch. Marathon therapy would come to include shock treatments every other day that caused friends to express dismay, but they accepted the intensity of his commitment to Kubie because *he* did.

Kubie responded with enthusiasm when Moss escorted women like Edith Atwater or, later, Paula Laurence or Dora Sayers. There was even a whirlwind pursuit by the English actress and onetime showgirl Binnie Barnes, until she abruptly sensed she was on the wrong track and went to Hollywood, where she had better luck and landed a studio head. At least one of "Moss's girls," as friends called them, was an actress he directed in a play he didn't write. According to Janet Fox, who knew them both, the actress gave up in frustration and turned her attentions instead to another Hart, the near-octogenarian "Commodore."

Encounters with young men like Boles elicited Kubie's immediate censure and "sabotage" (Boles's word), expressed with what Frederic Bradlee remembered from his own encounters with Kubie as "a rabbinical fury." To Boles, Kubie was just an opportunist with an agenda and a trophy patient. "Moss desperately wanted approval from Kubie," Boles remembers, "as well as from his friends in the theater. Finally he cared more about that than he did about who was in his bed. Kubie encouraged that and played on it."

Kubie's attentions to Moss went so far beyond the passive indirection of most analysts as to appear indiscreet, if not improper. Kubie shared his professional feuds with Moss, forwarding copies of his correspondence with Anna Freud, for instance, to whom he felt superior in his grasp of her father's work. He attached cover letters, carefully explaining to Moss exactly why and how he was right and Anna was wrong.

Marriage was a Kubie goal for Moss, but a distant one for the patient. The pleasures of the single life had not yet worn thin. There were drinks at the Oak Room of the Plaza or Sardi's, dinners at "21" or Voisin, suppers at the Stork Club or the Starlight Roof, shopping expeditions at Cartier's or Bergdorf's, snapping up colonial gewgaws for Fairview Farm or loose amethysts to strew on the Victorian tabletops in the city. He kept busy. He told Dore Schary that every time he thought about marriage he realized "what a pleasant, selfish, indulgent life I lead and [then I] run like hell."

Work, he concluded, was his life's "only saving grace," and, with Kubie's support, he plunged into it. The play he called "pure torture" was vetted at every stage by his new analyst and something of a tribute to him. Boles was certain that "it grew directly out of the sessions with Kubie as an extension of the therapy, a reinforcement of it."

Moss at first titled it with a phrase Kubie used: "I Am Listening." When it was finished and published, Moss inscribed a copy to Boles: "You always wanted to know what goes on inside me," he wrote. "Here it is." By then, "I Am Listening" had become something of a sensation, and had fulfilled almost every hope Moss had for his new solo career. It also had a better title—*Lady in the Dark*—and was, of all things, a musical.

Moss later claimed *Lady in the Dark*—"the next idea"—began as a drama for Katharine Cornell, but it was, of course, an outgrowth of the Dietrich musical Moss and Kaufman had worked on briefly in 1937. Two years later, when the idea resurfaced as something for Cornell, it featured a Kubie-like doctor treating a patient unable to choose among suitors or find fulfillment in a successful career. A song from her childhood would function as an associative device to unlock the repressed memory that thwarted her happiness as an adult.

Moss approached Cornell about the play in September 1939, when he was in Boston with *The Man Who Came to Dinner* and she was there trying out Sam Behrman's *No Time for Comedy*. Cornell liked the idea and, though not a singer, thought she could handle a simple song at the end of the evening. The role of a successful but troubled career woman could add to the gallery of roles that had made her a Great Lady of the American Theater, portraits that ranged from the glamorously doomed Iris March in *The Green Hat* to *Candida* to Elizabeth Barrett Browning in *The Barretts of Wimpole Street*.

Moss began working on the play as soon as *The Man Who Came to Dinner* opened in New York in October. In November he attended a birthday party for Walter Huston, where he was introduced to Kurt Weill. The German composer was enjoying Broadway success with *Knickerbocker Holiday*, which starred Huston as Peter Stuyvesant singing Weill's haunting "September Song."

Weill was a recent émigré from Nazi Germany, whose European collaborations with playwrights Georg Kaiser on *Silverlake* and Bertolt Brecht on *Mahagonny* and *The Threepenny Opera* were only vaguely known in America, if at all. He had composed a score for fellow émigré Max Reinhardt's production of *The Eternal Road*, a pageantlike spectacle that was an admired failure. So was *Johnny Johnson*, his antiwar musical for the

Group Theatre. The success of *Knickerbocker Holiday* followed an unhappy stint in Hollywood and he was eager to work again in the theater.

Moss was just putting "I Am Listening" on paper when he met Weill and it was Weill who took the next step. He asked their mutual friend Hassard Short to arrange a meeting with Moss to discuss a project that interested him but needed a new book. Over lunch, Weill revealed that the project was called *The Funnies*, essentially an elaboration of the "Funnies" number that Moss, Irving Berlin, and Short had put together six years earlier in *As Thousands Cheer*. Moss was uninterested in revisiting yesterday's newsprint, and conversation turned to the limitations of the American musical theater.

"We were both completely disinterested in doing a show for the sake of doing a show," Moss claimed later, perhaps because he and Kaufman were getting ready to do just that for the Lyceum. He maintained "the tight little formula of the musical comedy stage held no interest for either of us." What interested them was the kind of innovative musical gaining ground with, most notably, *Pal Joey*, "in which the music carried forward the essential story and was not imposed on the architecture of the play as a rather melodious but useless addenda."

Berlin and Porter probably hadn't viewed "Easter Parade" and "Begin the Beguine" as "useless addenda" in the shows Moss wrote with them, but the lament that songs took on lives of their own while librettos were quickly forgotten was (and is) standard among librettists. The so-called integrated musical had been evolving steadily ever since *Show Boat*, and even *Jubilee* had been more or less integrated: What it hadn't been was "serious."

As Moss and Weill talked, the notion arose that the dreams Moss's character related to her doctor in "I Am Listening," which threatened to become static monologues, might be treated musically. They might then contrast dream-logic with the naturalistic scenes in a highly theatrical way, taking the curse off what was the clinical case history of a woman who couldn't make up her mind.

Moss was seized with enthusiasm for "a new technique and a new musical form," making music and lyrics "part and parcel of the basic structure of the play [to] carry the story forward dramatically and psychologically." This was not song and dance; this was, he insisted, "a musical play." More important, it might make for one helluva spectacular show, with a whopping great part for a musical star, which was just what Katharine Cornell was not.

Moss agreed in November 1939 to collaborate with Weill, sketching out dreams the composer could then set to music in "little one-act operas" built from songs, recitatives, chorale numbers, love ballads, patter songs, parodies, and whatever else would work or fit. Both wanted Ira Gershwin to write the lyrics, but Gershwin had remained in California after his brother's death and was thought to be retired. Unknown to Moss, he had already returned to work on some songs with Jerome Kern and cut short Moss's elaborate arm-twisting with an unhesitating "Yes" on New Year's Day 1940.

Moss finished his draft of "I Am Listening" before he began work on *George Washington Slept Here,* which may explain the desultory work he did on the latter. His enthusiasm was heightened in March, when he heard Weill's first song, the childhood refrain meant to end their show. Without lyrics to work from, Weill had composed a dream-melody haunting enough to thread through the evening in fragments before emerging fully at the end, when childhood memory was restored and indecision resolved. With lyrics from Gershwin to convey love as life's most precious cargo, it became "My Ship."

By May 1940, Moss turned back to Kaufman and the Lyceum's need for a show. They had still not settled on an idea by June, when Ira Gershwin had already arrived in New York to work with Weill. As the two labored on the dreams from Moss's notes (vetted by Kubie), Weill quipped, "What does he mean, 'go it alone'? Now he's got *two* collaborators."

Weill and Gershwin completed their score by August, while Moss worked on *George Washington Slept Here* until October. By the time its disappointing reviews appeared, he may not have cared, for he was fully engaged by the musical, scheduled to open in Boston barely two months later. It was the kind of schedule he could handle only if free of depression, and he was clearly highly productive in rewriting and directing, as well as sharing producing decisions with Sam Harris, who was now sixty-nine and seemed unwell. Pressure energized Moss, his moods fueled and lifted by caffeine, adrenaline, and—he believed—by Kubie.

Moss didn't have two collaborators on *Lady in the Dark,* but many. Foremost among them was Hassard Short, who assumed responsibility for staging the elaborate musical dream sequences. Moss would handle the book scenes in the psychiatrist's office and the offices of *Allure,* the *Vogue*-like fashion magazine edited by the woman, now named Liza Elliott. It is unlikely that even Short could have met the demands of *Lady in the Dark* without the genius of a twenty-eight-year-old Czech émigré introduced to Moss by Weill.

Harry Horner had been an actor in Europe. He had followed Max

Reinhardt to America in flight from the Nazis and worked as assistant director on *The Eternal Road,* the ambitious Reinhardt failure for which Weill wrote the score. He was a slight and gentle visual genius with an ingratiating personality that made him one of the best-liked men on Broadway and, later, in Hollywood. He combined his training with Reinhardt (who had turned European circuses and cathedrals into theaters) with an architect's eye to achieve visual effects of originality seldom seen on Broadway. What Short couldn't do with lights, Horner could do with turntables and a new kind of see-through plastic called Lucite. The dream sequences of *Lady in the Dark* would have been impossible without him.

Weill was unique in doing his own orchestrations, giving his scores a complexity and color unlike anything else on Broadway. Choreography for a corps de ballet with dancers poached from Martha Graham was created by Albertina Rasch, whose work had graced Moss's Berlin and Porter musicals and added the swirl to *The Great Waltz*. Fashion world chic was provided by Hattie Carnegie, while costumes for the dreams were designed by Irene Sharaff, who had been involved with every Hart musical since *As Thousands Cheer.* Sharaff's chores were guided by insight into Moss. She confided to Weill that Moss could write no character but himself and, therefore, *was* Liza Elliott—or Liza's dream version of herself, more glamorous and ready for love than anyone knew. Weill concurred. Later, when Moss talked about a project he had in mind for Garbo, Weill recognized the Garbo role as yet another version of Moss, though he wasn't certain Moss knew it.

No matter how vital these collaborators were to *Lady in the Dark,* the indispensable one, the one without whom the rest could stay at home, was the star, and Moss had made a serious error in offering the part to Cornell.

In a Sunday piece he later wrote for the *New York Times,* Moss said that once Weill became involved he immediately explained the growing musical demands of the show to Cornell ("veritable Traviatas" of song, he said), and that she graciously bowed out. He did no such thing, as his unedited manuscript for the article reveals. Cornell was a very major star and Moss, fearing confrontation and crashing peals of great-lady thunder, kept her on the hook until he knew the little one-act operas would work and he had secured a musical star who could give them fireworks and glamour.

Noël Coward unwittingly came to Moss's rescue by inviting him to the Hotel Astor for that Allied Relief Ball in early May. The evening had included the appearance by Coward's old chum and costar Gertrude

Lawrence, on brief hiatus from a long-run tour in Samson Raphaelson's *Skylark.* One look at Lawrence persuaded Moss: She was his "irrevocable" choice for Liza, the very personification of allure and *Allure.*

Moss threw caution—and Cornell—to the winds and offered the part to Lawrence over drinks at the Oak Room. He used Cornell's interest as warning or bait, which bothered Lawrence far less than the title "I Am Listening," which seemed to refer insufficiently to her. Might it not be more appealing, she suggested to "Mossy Face" (as she called him), a bit more focused and risqué and *much* more appealing to call it, say, *Lady in the Dark*?

Cornell was a lady and an actress, but Lawrence was unalloyed glamour from toe to crown and had been, apparently, since birth. She was forty-two in 1940, only six years older than "Mossy Face," but had been a star in London's West End and on Broadway when he was still poring over railroad timetables for Gus Pitou.

Like Marilyn Miller, Lawrence is a legendary figure whose star quality is all but irretrievable today. No film or recording reproduces the qualities with which she ravished audiences on both sides of the Atlantic. She was not conventionally beautiful, was an indifferent dancer and an uncertain singer, but was easily the most glamorous theater star of her generation. Her love affairs were legion; her extravagances, and the bankruptcies they occasioned, were common knowledge. Her stage presence—by every account—was magical.

When she first appeared on Broadway in 1923, Percy Hammond forecast that "every man in town is, or will be, in love with her," a remark that proved prophetic. Chorus boys up and down the Rialto referred to her, reverently and campily at once, as "Myth Lawrence." She projected an aura of beauty more beguiling than the real thing. With a true star's attention to every detail that went into her self-presentation, she perfumed the hems of her gowns to ensure her charm would go to the heads of audiences (and critics) down front. She took the stage with such authority and presence that she achieved fame as a musical performer on both sides of the Atlantic in spite of her notoriously wavering key: Cole Porter, Noël Coward, and the Gershwins all wrote musicals for her, and her shaky voice did not prevent songs like "Do, Do, Do" and "Someone to Watch Over Me" from becoming standards.

Playwright John Van Druten spoke of her "radiance, indefinable but intensely vivid, that comes from something other than the human or technical talents of the actress." At her death in 1952, when she was starring on Broadway in *The King and I,* the lights of the Great White Way, the West End, and even Hollywood—where she had never really been successful—were dimmed in honor of that rare thing: a true star.

Moss still had not told Cornell about the music pouring from Weill's pen in every conceivable style, and certainly hadn't mentioned Lawrence. Feeling guilty, he enlisted Weill's aid in intimidating Cornell with the musical challenges of the role. "The play fairly reeks of music," he tardily admitted. Maybe Cornell had taken singing lessons or knew all about Lawrence (there are few secrets in show business) and wanted to make Moss squirm, but she announced gaily that she was far more musical than anyone suspected and couldn't wait to audition and prove it. Next Tuesday, perhaps?

Moss knew defeat when he heard it. He confessed his guilt and, after gorging on humble pie, finally secured Cornell's withdrawal, a story he decided to commit to his drawer rather than to the *Times*. One suspects Cornell was relieved, but breaking the bad news to her was nothing compared to getting Lawrence from "yes" to making it legal by signing a contract.

In fairness to her, Lawrence first heard Moss read an unfinished draft of *Lady in the Dark* when "My Ship" was the only completed song. No star—or myth—in her right mind would commit to a show that would rest almost entirely on her shoulders without hearing more. Her signature, however, seemed to depend on approval of everyone from her astrologer to Coward, who came, once again, to the rescue.

Moss read the play aloud to Coward, who exclaimed, according to Moss, "Gertie should pay you to play it." That was helpful, but in addition to Coward and the heavens, Lawrence listened to her lawyer, Fanny Holtzmann. Moss described Holtzmann as "a small delicate mouse-like creature" who was "as helpless as the Bethlehem Steel Company and as delicate as Jack the Ripper." He had used the same line about Elsa Maxwell in *Jubilee* (he even applied it to himself on occasion), but of Holtzmann it was gospel. She was a tiny bully-in-a-chapeau with a razor for a mind, and so intimidating that Moss fleetingly considered writing a play about *her*.

As Weill and Gershwin continued working, Moss turned what little attention he had to *George Washington* and Lawrence took a holiday from her *Skylark* tour. She visited Cape Cod and, to the astonishment of everyone who knew what promiscuous meant, got married.

Moss, still annoyed and concerned at having no firm commitment, cabled her groom, Richard Aldrich: "CONGRATULATIONS, AND ARE YOU SURE GERTIE SAID 'YES'?" Coward sent a slyer telegram that became a classic:

DEAR MRS A. HOORAY HOORAY
AT LAST YOU ARE DEFLOWERED,
ON THIS AS EVERY OTHER DAY
I LOVE YOU, NOËL COWARD

Moss took Weill and Gershwin to Bucks County in August so they could work far from the city heat and he could hover over Duchess, the Old English sheepdog who was expecting puppies. Duchess was safely delivered. Not so Lawrence, who was expecting, it developed, the moon.

Holtzmann drove a hard bargain, complete with codicils and riders. As it turned out, Lawrence would not sign a final contract until July 1941, six months after *Lady in the Dark* opened and she was so indispensable to it she could not be replaced and never was. By then Moss and Sam Harris were helpless to counter her demands, which included, Moss claimed, "my farm, the Music Box Theatre, Sam Harris's house in Palm Beach, half of Metro-Goldwyn-Mayer, a couple of race horses, and five thousand dollars a week."

Even without hyperbole the contract was unprecedented. It granted Lawrence $2,000 a week in base salary as a guarantee against 15 percent of the box-office gross, plus 10 percent of the show's profits, including all income from movie, television, radio, recordings, and amateur rights. It almost certainly ensured her recording her songs and performing a version of the show on radio (she did), but also entitled her to 10 percent of the motion picture and television sales, whether she starred in them or not (she didn't).

Despite Moss and Harris yielding to almost every demand Lawrence and Holtzmann made, and despite Coward's urging her to sign, Lawrence malingered until Moss abruptly stopped threatening and acted. He sent the script to Irene Dunne in Hollywood with a firm offer and a rush deadline, and made sure Lawrence knew he'd done so. Lawrence signed, though renegotiations would continue for the better part of a year.

There was a bitter surprise wrinkle. Lawrence's contract for the now-ended *Skylark* tour for John Golden (he modestly named the Golden Theatre on West Forty-fifth Street after himself) ran until the end of 1940. Moss had gone to him to make sure there were no conflicts and had even offered him a piece of the show and a line in the program noting that Lawrence's appearance was "by arrangement with John Golden."

For reasons unexplained, Golden decided that, even though the *Skylark* tour was finished, his contract bound Lawrence to him until mid-December, when *Lady in the Dark* was already booked in Boston. Moss raged that Golden behaved "with all the charm of a Gestapo agent and the manners of a dead-end kid." Moss and Harris took the matter to Actors' Equity, which ruled in their favor, possibly because Equity's president, Bert Lytell, had been cast in *Lady in the Dark* as Kendall Nesbitt, the older lover who financed Liza's magazine.

Equity's nick-of-time decision permitted the company to travel to Boston to install the most extravagant Broadway production since *The American Way*. Thanks to Harry Horner's ingenuity, *Lady in the Dark* cost only half as much at a still lavish $127,715.

Weill's "little one-act operas" were now big: a Glamour Dream, a Wedding Dream, a Hollywood Dream (later cut), a Childhood Dream (Liza is—of course—from Mapleton, Ohio), and a culminating, all-stops-out-on-the-calliope Circus Dream (an echo of the Circus Court that ended *Face the Music*). They were as intricate to operate as anything on Broadway since the swooping chandeliers and orchestra-on-wheels of *The Great Waltz*. Horner's most inventive contribution was the four revolving turntables—doubles: small ones inside larger ones—on which Liza's and her psychiatrist's offices could rotate out of sight to reveal the props, settings, dancers, and actors in the dreams with no delays for scene changes. The show required five stage managers and a stage crew of fifty-one to organize a cast of fifty-six, including more than a dozen children.

Apart from Bert Lytell as Liza's older, married lover, the men in her life were newcomers. Macdonald Carey began his long career by playing down-to-earth Charley Johnson, the advertising manager of *Allure* who sets Liza's teeth on edge because, she will realize by curtain's fall, she is in love with him. (He knows her childhood song, too, and helps her sing it.)

Victor Mature was the twenty-four-year-old slab of heavy-lidded beefcake cast as Randy Curtis, a movie star smitten with Liza precisely because of her severe, businesswoman aspect. He is looking for a mother or, at any rate, the antithesis of the Hollywood glamourpuss Liza visualizes herself as in her dreams. Mature, who had just become something of a throb as a loincloth-clad caveman in *One Million B.C.*, seems a startling choice today, but he had learned to walk across a stage at the Pasadena Playhouse and had even appeared in a movie version of *No, No, Nanette* opposite Anna Neagel.

Moss had wanted the Mowgli-like Buster Crabbe for the part, who proved unable to sing, dance, *or* act. Ira Gershwin suggested Mature, who was in New York to sign with Harold Clurman and the Group Theatre for a new play by Irwin Shaw. He jumped the Group ship for the one with Gertrude Lawrence, causing Clurman to threaten a lawsuit. Mature got his way and *Lady* got Mature—"Courtesy Hal Roach Studios, Inc.," as the program read, reminding audiences that he was a real movie star.

Mature could flex and go weak in the knees for Liza, but couldn't sing. Weill had written "This Is New" as a love duet, but Lawrence sang it alone and made it a soaring star turn without a partner. A line from Moss's script entered the vernacular: "A beautiful hunk of man," someone in the *Allure* office sighs, a description that clung to Mature for the rest of his life.

The newcomer who would emerge a star was Danny Kaye, the only member of the cast whose role was written for him. Twenty-seven-year-old Kaye, né David Daniel Kominski in Brooklyn, had been working as a singing comic on the Borscht Circuit since 1933. He had made some short films to no professional effect, but had scored briefly in *The Straw Hat Revue* on Broadway in 1939 and more strongly in a nightclub act at New York's Martinique in 1940.

Moss had seen Kaye perform "in some cellar on 57th Street," he said, and "was very taken with him." The young comedian came to Moss's table after the performance to be told how "electric" he was and that Moss was writing a new play that would have a part in it for him. To confirm his judgment, Moss took Brooks Atkinson to see Kaye when he opened at the Martinique, having already fulfilled his promise and created Russell Paxton, the "Cecil Beaton of *Allure,*" for him. The character was a fashion photographer who was flighty, biting, and, as Moss described him, "mildly effeminate in a rather charming fashion." He was, in fact, the only frankly gay character Moss ever wrote. Kaye made him so obvious that it was clear he was more interested in Randy Curtis than Liza was. Men? "I give *that* lecture with stereopticon slides!" he announces in an early draft.

Kaye transcended what *Variety* called "a pansy" in his one solo musical number. In dream sequences he appeared in various guises, as did all of Liza's "real life" figures, and his most memorable moment came late in the evening as the ringmaster of the Circus Dream, a moment he almost didn't survive to play.

Kaye had been hired solely on Moss's recommendation. Neither Lawrence nor Harris had ever seen him perform, and they watched him rehearse week after week with growing dismay. "About the second week of rehearsal," Moss recalled, "Miss Lawrence and Mr. Harris came to me and asked me to let him go. He just wasn't going to make it. I said I was sure he was and they were just as certain that he wasn't. And they said—quite rightly—that sometimes nightclub comedians disappear when the footlights light up. Well," he continued, "the only thing that gave me the courage to insist was that I had seen him before an audience. I *saw* his electric effect on an audience."

That electricity would course through *Lady in the Dark,* making Kaye a star and, ironically, stimulating Lawrence's own best-remembered moment when Kaye's performance goaded her into it.

Lawrence's star shenanigans were as well known and as large as her legend. They had already inspired Lorraine Sheldon, *The Man Who Came to Dinner's* manipulative mantrap. She was used to getting what she wanted, and though Moss effusively praised her gifts in public, privately he became "hysterical" with agitation, according to Weill. He would take revenge with his pen at a later date, but Lawrence's demands during *Lady in the Dark* might have sunk the show had her whims and judgment prevailed. Moss found repeated grounds for accusing her of trying to "run the show" in New York and, later, on the road. Finally, he threatened to close it down altogether "just to punish Gertie," which fazed her not at all.

The most critical moment occurred on opening night in Boston and was caused by Kaye. The Circus Dream was triggered by Liza's inability to decide between a circus cover and an Easter cover for her magazine, and her climactic number in it had never met with Lawrence's approval. Weill and Gershwin had written a meditative number for the spot called "Song of the Zodiac" that nodded to Lawrence's own annoying reliance on astrology. The song made clear, Gershwin helpfully explained, that "she'd done what she did because she couldn't help doing whatever she did do."

Moss and Harris worried that the zodiac song might be "dour and oppressive" so late in the evening and asked for something more rousing. Moss knew Weill and Gershwin were disappointed, but "each day after rehearsal I would go to [them] and say, 'Please, for goodness sake, get the song for Gertrude Lawrence!'"

Still nursing the scars of getting his star to sign her contract, Moss urged them to write a song about a woman who couldn't or wouldn't make up her mind. They reversed the notion in what Gershwin described as "a sort of bordello blues" called "The Saga of Jenny," about a woman who *always* made up her mind, with catastrophic but racy results. When they delivered the song, Lawrence glanced at it and dismissed it with, "This is not a song for me. This is Ethel Merman, and it's not very funny anyway."

Moss exploded. "You must do it," he told her. "We have a right to hear it. We're going out of town and if it's no good it'll be cut, but you have to sing it." Lawrence did what disgruntled stars do, according to Moss. "She just says, 'Yah, yah, yah, yah, mumble.' "

In Boston the show was too long on opening night, running three and a half hours. "The Saga of Jenny" came at the end of the Circus Dream, after Kaye's only solo number, the one that produced the electric effect Moss had predicted. His lyric was a bit of light verse Gershwin dug out of the trunk, something he had published in 1924 before hitting his stride as a lyricist. It was titled "Tschaikowsky" and was just the names of forty-nine Russian composers strung together in a tongue-tying list that Kaye was to deliver inside of a minute to a driving rhythm set by Weill. He did it in thirty-nine seconds and stopped the show cold.

During Kaye's number, Lawrence was onstage, sitting on a swing and passively watching him kidnap her audience. Gershwin was at the back of the orchestra, where Moss and Harris wore the carpet thin with their pacing. As the audience exploded with its approval of Kaye's tour de force, the lyricist felt a hand clutch his arm and heard Moss's strangled croak, "Christ, we've lost our star."

Moss remembered, "they kept applauding and applauding, and in the back of the theater I was saying 'SHHhhh,' trying to quiet them, knowing that the more they applauded the more likely the song was to be cut, and [Danny] kept bowing to Gertie as if to indicate she would sing next, and the more he bowed generously the more they applauded, and Gertie just *looked* at him. And finally . . . she saluted and walked to the footlights and then sang 'Jenny' as she had never rehearsed it. She did it with bumps, grinds, [like] a strip tease, and completely topped him."

Gershwin called it "complete devastation of the audience" and noted that the ovation for "Jenny" lasted twice as long as the one for "Tschaikowsky." *Lady in the Dark* had been stopped twice in a matter of minutes, just as it neared its climax. Lawrence's triumph with "Jenny" would make the cover of *Time* with "Gertie the Great" radiating star power as Kaye looked on, ironic and unidentified.

Opening night's three and a half hours required immediate surgery. Moss had made sure Kaufman was in Boston to help and they cut a full half hour before the second performance, still leaving the show too long. Excess running time hardly mattered to New Yorkers who had trained to Boston to see what Moss could do on his own. He called professional curiosity seekers "the wrecking crew," but they could spread good news, too. Word circulated quickly about the two successive showstoppers, and within days the press excitedly picked up the story, which, in turn, picked up ticket sales for the January opening at the Alvin Theatre in New York.

In Boston the show was already SRO after reviews verging on the rapturous. Bostonians could be forgiven for not noticing that the same night *Lady in the Dark* bowed, there had been another opening in town, one that prefigured things to come. Tennessee Williams watched his first Broadway-bound show, *Battle With Angels,* starring Miriam Hopkins, sink without a trace except for the one reviewer who noted, "The youthful author might well have important things to say in the theater a little later on."

Moss was preoccupied by the here and the now. The *Boston Globe* hailed *Lady in the Dark* as "the most fascinating, unconventional theater piece in years," but he was taking no chances. Aware that the evening's length might interfere with morning edition deadlines in New York, he imported the most influential New York reviewers to Boston. He paid the travel and other expenses for Atkinson of the *Times,* Richard Watts, Jr., of the *Herald-Tribune,* and two others so they might remain in their seats with no deadlines to rush to until "My Ship" had brought down the final curtain.

He needn't have worried. The annals of Broadway are full of stories about shows that opened well out of town only to crash and burn in New York, but *Lady in the Dark* had all the want-to-see elements for success Broadway could demand of its toughest. It had not one, but two chic subjects in psychoanalysis and the fashion world of *Allure;* it had in Lawrence a major star absent from the musical stage for a decade; it had a new star in Danny Kaye; it had a Hollywood star in Victor Mature. It also had a Pulitzer Prize–winning playwright publicly stepping away from a celebrated partnership to risk failure on his own; lavish production married to serious intent; a kaleidoscopically eclectic score graced with lyrics of wit and precision; and it had Broadway's most prestigious producer.

Still, nothing was certain and *Lady in the Dark* moved into the Alvin in the middle of an early-January flu epidemic that put Lawrence in bed, voiceless and under a doctor's orders to stay there. Harris postponed the opening by a week, relieved to have extra time for ironing out the show's technical demands until he realized there was no understudy prepared to play Liza during the vital tech rehearsals for the multiple turntables and for musical numbers as complex as any ever presented on Broadway.

A volunteer stepped forward. Moss would play Liza for the tech rehearsals, beginning to end, and did. He reclined on the psychiatrist's

couch in the book scenes, went sophisticated and languid for The Glamour Dream, and bumped and ground his way through "The Saga of
Jenny." The reaction of the New York stagehands is unrecorded, but
Danny Kaye remembered it as "the greatest performance, I think, ever
done on the New York stage."

Lady in the Dark opened in New York on January 23, 1940, with a
fully recovered Lawrence eager to reclaim her role. When she did, the
New York and national press were of one voice in praising the production
and the star. Atkinson, representatively, thought the production "a work
of theater art" and, as for Lawrence, she was "a goddess; that's all."

The ecstatic tone extended to all Moss's collaborators in virtually
unqualified praise. What is curious, in view of *Lady in the Dark*'s reputation as a landmark musical, is that Moss—its principal architect and
creator—was the only object of critical disapproval.

There were nitpicks about minor matters, like dream sequences that
were new only to those who hadn't been paying attention when Rodgers
and Hart used them in *Peggy-Ann* back in 1926. Or the weaving together
of the show with fragments of "My Ship" and revealing its full import
only at evening's end, a trick that went all the way back to *Naughty Marietta,* where "Ah! Sweet Mystery of Life" had done much the same thing.
Complaints that psychoanalysis was less fresh a subject than Moss thought
were widespread, and his repeated insistence that *Lady in the Dark* was a
"musical play," rather than a spectacular show, attracted dismissal verging
on ridicule. Even Atkinson, almost alone in praising the book's "taste and
artistic integrity," hinted that the "musical play" label was just semantics
or marketing. Other comments ranged from unimpressed to scathing.

No one was more dismissive than Louis Kronenberger in *PM,* the
progressive daily where Beatrice Kaufman was now writing the occasional piece. Kronenberger found the "superficial" book "clumsily written, and utterly uninspired." Scorning the box-office lines around the
block, he asserted that Moss's "play is too serious to have any life and not
serious enough to have any meaning." It should have been "either a better
show or a better play."

Moss the playwright had apparently fallen victim to Moss the showman, which was both fair and not. It was unjust because, apart from
Atkinson, hardly anyone credited Moss as the originator and organizing
force behind the very merits they were busy applauding in his collaborators. Moss had been the *auteur* of *Lady in the Dark,* if that now fashionable
word had been available then to describe the source of a unifying vision.
Today we would call *Lady in the Dark* "a concept show"—it was certainly

one of the first—but boasting about a "new musical form" had been an invitation to rebuttal.

Criticism was fair in that the structure of *Lady in the Dark,* the earnestly talky book interrupted by those little one-act operas, was too one-of-a-kind ever to have the influence Moss claimed for it. The score overflowed with sophistication, with Weill's brilliant range of styles and the most literate and sparkling lyrics Ira Gershwin ever wrote. The very aptness of the songs denied the show any real hits (Huxley and Stravinsky are not the stuff of jukebox refrains), but they were less "integrated" than artfully juxtaposed to the book scenes in a dream vs. reality counterpoint. The same juxtapositions made it hard not to find Moss's book banal in contrast.

Most harshly condemned was the very center of the play, its treatment of psychoanalysis. Serious reviewers found it simplistic and naïve even for 1941. Streamlining Liza's onstage "cure" was acceptable for Broadway, but her three sessions on the couch would have seemed record time had Freud himself been the analyst.

Moss was acutely sensitive to criticism, however much he denied it, and especially so for a subject in which he had such a vested emotional interest. For all his talk to Schary about the "pure torture" of writing *Lady in the Dark,* his original draft reveals none of the telltale signs of hesitation or uncertainty that mark manuscripts on which he had creative difficulties. Great chunks of "I Am Listening" survive with only minor changes in the version of the play that opened on Broadway.

Apart from a deleted scene in a swank Manhattan restaurant called Le Coq d'Or, in which the characters waste time in sit-down comedy that is irrelevant and not very funny, the structure of the play remains unchanged from the original draft, including dreams placed as they were in the final product. There was a much-too-easy caricature of Salvador Dalí called "Miguel Santos." When he contemplates painting the offices of *Allure,* Santos suggests "in the corner a cup of coffee crying. In the middle of the room a piece of liver playing the piano."

Moss cut all that, tightening the script with help from Kaufman and clarifying the speeches of Liza's analyst, "Dr. Brooks," with help from Kubie. Otherwise, it is hard to find evidence of rewriting a play that was what it was from the very beginning. It was just too long.

To defend himself against his critics, Moss called on Kubie to write a preface for the play when Random House published it in book form. The introduction, signed by "'Dr. Brooks,'" is an essay by Kubie—to whom Moss dedicated the play as "L.S.K."—validating the action. "From the technical psychiatric point of view," he wrote, it was "accurate in the subtlest detail." Dramatic compression made things clearer, simpler, and less threatening to the uninitiated but "the essential spirit of what was done and how it was achieved would not have been basically altered" with a more "literal version of the analytical procedure." The widely ridiculed speed of Liza's "cure" was merely, "Dr. Brooks" assured readers, "the license due a poet."

Nothing reduces the sting of bad reviews or induces amnesia about them like a roaring box office, and *Lady in the Dark*'s was deafening. It set a record for movie sales, surpassing even the amount paid for *The Man Who Came to Dinner*, when Paramount Pictures coughed up $283,000 for the right to base a terrible movie on it.

Paramount starred Ginger Rogers as Liza. Arlene Croce, in *The Fred Astaire and Ginger Rogers Book*, points out that Rogers, in following Lawrence as Liza, suffered attacks of great lady–itis and filled the Technicolor screen like "a walking identity crisis." The movie cut almost all of Weill's songs, including "My Ship," though Rogers got to sing "The Saga of Jenny" and "instead of being alluring and potent," Croce observes, "was garish and monstrous."

Lady in the Dark glittered for almost five hundred performances on Broadway and toured successfully. It established itself as one of the most sophisticated examples of American musical stagecraft ever to appear on Broadway, a reputation it retains today. And it made Moss a major Broadway figure. He didn't collaborate with others now; they collaborated with *him*. He wrote and directed and produced and owned part of his own theater and was a household word all by himself.

What seems slighted by those who write or talk about *Lady in the Dark* is the extent to which Irene Sharaff may have been right: that Liza Elliott was a version of Moss, at least in the sense of an unrealized personality seeking recognition that would overcome the past and alter the present. The yearning to be somebody else that had directed him since childhood had not yet been assuaged.

There's another motif seldom noticed in Moss's first great solo success, one that echoes a theme in *Merrily We Roll Along*. It is, oddly or appropriately, the failure of success. Moss now had more success than he knew what to do with, and it exhausted him. He told a reporter as the money and applause rolled in, "Right now I have no ideas at all. I'm going to take a rest."

18

Taking Wing

*A man who is a failure complains about fate, about bad breaks
and you can understand it. But when you're completely successful
and you're unhappy, it becomes a mystery. Most of the
successful people I know are unhappy.*

MOSS HART

In early 1941 Moss had three shows running at once on Broadway: *Lady
in the Dark* was selling out, *The Man Who Came to Dinner* was still prompting laughter, and *George Washington Slept Here* was winding down. Two
were runaway hits, all had sold to the movies, their aggregate income
would run into the millions, and present success only ignited fears about
the future.

Moss once confessed, "Just a few days after winning the Pulitzer, I
practically had to be carried feet first to my analyst's couch," which only
sounded like a joke. He was consumed by the fear that "every success was
a combination of luck and a modicum of skill, and that with each new
play the luck [was] bound to run out."

Some of this was postpartum blues now that *Lady in the Dark* was
completed. Some was reaction to criticism he had received as a playwright. Kubie helped privately in therapy and defended his patient publicly in press interviews that promoted his own expertise at the same time
that it validated Moss and the character of Liza Elliott.

Moss's self-administered antidote to depression was work, which
combated self-doubt and courted luck. Until he died he called each new
challenge "the toughest one I've ever had," a kind of mantra signaling
that success wasn't as easy as it looked to the envious, and a sign to a fickle
muse that he was knuckling under. For now, however, as he told Schary,
"I have no play ideas, and if I can help it, I don't intend to have."

The work he turned to after *Lady in the Dark* was his "book about the
theater," the story of his beginnings and Gus Pitou and *The Beloved Bandit*

and *Once in a Lifetime*. It was the narrative he and Kaufman had tried to build a musical around in 1937 and again he made little headway. It was an idea whose time had not yet come and he consoled himself by enumerating his other talents. "I'm an excellent director," he told himself (and Schary), "and a surprizingly [*sic*] good executive."

News of the war in Europe followed him to Bucks County, now that Hitler had invaded Russia and swastikas adorned the Champs Élysées. He wrote Schary in May that if the news got any worse he would not be surprised "to find either you or myself the social director of some cheap concentration camp."

He continued to voice fears about the kind of soldier he might make, without revealing that a year earlier he had applied for and received a draft deferment from the Selective Service. He was days shy of thirty-six at the time, an age that would have made him ineligible for active duty, but age restrictions might change in the event of American entry into the war. He registered with New York Draft Board No. 40 on October 16, 1940, two days before *George Washington Slept Here* opened, and just as he was putting *Lady in the Dark* into rehearsal. According to Department of the Army records, he requested and was granted a deferment "because of a dependent father and his claim that he had a breakdown and had been under psychiatric treatment for six years."

He kept his draft status to himself and claimed to be watching the mails for his induction notice. In January 1942, shortly after Pearl Harbor, he told the Associated Press that America's declaration of war had sent him immediately to an enlistment office for the Navy, where he was rejected, he said, "because of insufficient education."

Before labor and materials grew scarce, he added a guest wing and study to the house in Bucks County. He justified it as "my little gesture of defiance" against Hitler, but it made country entertaining easier during *Lady in the Dark*'s summer hiatus for Gertrude Lawrence's vacation. He invited Danny Kaye and his wife, Sylvia Fine, to keep him company and help divert the stream of New York and Hollywood visitors, as constant as ever to Fairview and to the Kaufmans' Barley Sheaf Farm.

When *The Man Who Came to Dinner* finally closed, the management of the Bucks County Playhouse decided that the amateur rights should be initiated close to home. The playhouse, without strenuous coaxing, rounded up George Kaufman as Whiteside, Moss as Beverly Carlton, and Harpo Marx as Banjo. Edith Atwater—"Moss's girl"—returned as Maggie Cutler, and Janet Fox stepped into Nurse Preen's white oxfords, not for the last time. Acting honors, according to Atwater, went to Harpo playing himself.

Playacting, croquet, tennis, and sun worshiping around the pool in the altogether (men only) were interrupted for mourning the death of Sam Harris in early July. Harris's uncertain health during the mounting of *Lady in the Dark* had been revealed as cancer by exploratory surgery in March, a diagnosis kept from him by family and friends.

Harris's dignity and respect for his colleagues had made him a revered figure in the theater. His early, often contentious partnership with George M. Cohan was being memorialized on film even as Harris lay dying in his apartment at the Ritz Towers. *Yankee Doodle Dandy*, with James Cagney as Cohan, featured future director Richard Whorf as Harris, and the movie's finale was Cagney-as-Cohan-as-FDR doing the "Off the Record" number from *I'd Rather Be Right*. The cause of Harris's death was off the record, too, officially "appendicitis," like Max Gordon's breakdown.

Harris had been as responsible as anyone for Moss's career, producing every show he had written since *Once in a Lifetime* except *The Great Waltz*. He had—perhaps even more than Kaufman—set the tone for Moss's mentoring that began with giving young Walter Bernstein advice and a letter to *The New Yorker*. Moss's guidance of newcomers was not promiscuous or fuzzy. "They had to be professionals, they had to be dedicated to what they wanted to do," a friend explained. "But if you had talent, you didn't have to be important. You didn't have to be a big name. You could go to Moss if you thought he could help, and he would." Sponsoring Jerry Chodorov and Joe Fields on *My Sister Eileen* was only the most current instance of his professional generosity, and its dividends would include a project to occupy the balance of the year.

My Sister Eileen's success inspired Chodorov and Fields to turn again to *The New Yorker*, which had published some wryly amusing sketches by Sally Benson about adolescence just off Fifth Avenue. In book form, *Junior Miss* sold over a quarter of a million copies and encouraged the authors to put teenager Judy Graves and her best friend, Fuffy Adams, onstage. Judy had charmed readers in sunny, often touching vignettes in which she tottered on trainer-heels and the brink of adolescence, not having quite abandoned dolls for boys. She and Fuffy were about as far from the neurotic luxe of Liza Elliott as it was possible to get, which may have been their chief appeal.

Teenagers and family life were big business. This was the era of Deanna Durbin, Mickey Rooney, and young Judy Garland on-screen, and of Rodgers and Hart's *Babes in Arms* on Broadway. MGM's Andy

Hardy and radio's Henry Aldrich (born on Broadway in 1938 in *What a Life*) were household names with fictional households as familiar as the real ones down the street.

The most familiar of all was from *The New Yorker* (again) to which Moss's old coffee shop chum Oscar Serlin had a subscription. Clarence Day, Jr.'s *Life With Father* was now on Broadway, adapted by Howard Lindsay and Russel Crouse, and two years into its run as the (still) longest-running nonmusical in Broadway history. A decade earlier, after Serlin had failed to raise money for *Once in a Lifetime,* he had sunk into near poverty in Greenwich Village. Now he was the producer of *Life With Father* and would never have to work again, though he would, presenting—what else?—*Life With Mother.*

Families whose personal dramas rarely exceeded the suspense of a daughter's date to the prom were a relief after the rigors of the Depression and the now constant war news. There was comfort in the familiar, as Thornton Wilder's *Our Town* had demonstrated with an innocent simplicity that seemed to distill values worth preserving or defending. It wasn't the posturing that had inflated *The American Way;* it was as modest and quiet and affirmative as a Norman Rockwell magazine cover.

When Chodorov and Fields finished *Junior Miss,* Kaufman was busy with his postponed Edna Ferber project and not free to direct, as he had *My Sister Eileen.* Moss eagerly agreed to do so, his first staging of someone else's work since Camp Utopia and the Flagler: the beginning of a new career.

Chodorov and Field's translation of *Junior Miss* ("play-giarized," a *Variety* wit remarked) was broader than Benson's sketches, which were so delicately crafted they seemed to float right off the page. Benson's version included just Judy; Judy's big sister, Lois; Mr. and Mrs. Graves; and "bosom friend" Fuffy. There were allusions to Hilda the maid and a long-lost uncle. The play's authors invented scenes and incidents for them, bringing them onstage without losing the charm of Benson's originals.

They added an improbable but harmless subplot about Judy's over-heated imagination and her determination to make life as interesting as the movies. She plays Cupid to her suddenly resurfaced uncle and her father's secretary, a romance that causes her father, in a related development, to lose his job. The twists blunt the light touch of Benson's original but keep the audience amused until Judy, wearing her first corsage, is ready to cross more than one threshold on her way to the prom.

Junior Miss is reminiscent of Kaufman and Hart in mechanics and jokes, but the tone is sweeter-natured and less knowing. There is even a convincing love scene between two lonely people finding each other that owes nothing to Benson and nothing to Kaufman and Hart, either. Conventional wisdom holds that Kaufman couldn't write love scenes and left them to Moss, but there *are* no love scenes in their plays. Alice and Tony spoon a bit in *You Can't Take It With You,* but tenderness and sentimentality weren't in Kaufman's inventory and frank sexual attraction wasn't in Moss's. To a notable degree, the collaborative comedies are free of any romance not directed at success or the theater.

Moss's pencil almost always made improvements to whatever he directed, but his contribution to the text of *Junior Miss,* according to Chodorov, "was forcing us back to the typewriter to try for better material." The authors acknowledged their debt by dedicating the play to him "with gratitude and affection." Chodorov, particularly, would become close to Moss and continue to hold him in near-reverential memory for his theatrical generosity, know-how, and loyalty.

Moss had never directed so uncynical a comic work and, surprisingly enough, credited Kaufman with enabling him to do so. "Everything I know, whatever I know, I learned from the best teacher in the world—Kaufman," he said. Directing was largely a question of pace and honoring the text with what he called the "hidden hand that has been the custodian of the proceedings on the stage, not the star of them."

He was intuitive as a director of other people's work, never doctrinaire, never adhering to any method, especially not to *the* Method. He was content not to preblock, but to let scenes arrange themselves as they felt comfortable to the actors and looked right as "pictures" onstage. Having worked so often with amateurs and been an actor himself, he was clear and he was kind. Clarity was administered with steel, and kindness made the steel endurable for the vulnerable creatures he knew actors to be, especially in auditions.

Junior Miss had a string of auditions in a production without stars (Gertrude Lawrence was enough for the time being), and in search of teenagers who could play Judy and Fuffy convincingly. Irving Schneider spoke of Moss's audition technique as "graciousness itself." He was "decent," and worked to "put people at their ease."

Gordon produced *Junior Miss* and marveled at Moss's intuition, especially with a sixteen-year-old girl reading for sixteen-year-old Lois, Judy's sister. After an only fair reading, Moss asked the young actress—"on a hunch," Gordon said—to read Judy's lines instead. Without Lois's high heels and lipstick, Patricia Peardon so perfectly read Judy that she won the part and landed on the cover of *Life* magazine. Lenore Lonergan, daughter of a well-known acting family, played Fuffy with "a voice like a frog"; Judy's beau was played by a gangly stalk of teenager named Billy Redfield, who would become William on Broadway (Cole Porter's *Out of this World*) and in Hollywood *(One Flew Over the Cuckoo's Nest)*.

The most vivid member of the cast was Paula Laurence, a nightclub singer and comedienne cast as the Graveses' maid Hilda. The character barely existed in Benson, but Chodorov and Fields gave her moments of comic sarcasm in the style of Jean Dixon. Laurence's deadpan humor was equally vivid in life. When Edith Atwater got married and dropped out as "Moss's girl," Laurence briefly dropped in.

Junior Miss opened on November 18, 1941, at the Lyceum, where it was an immediate hit that would tally 710 performances, almost as long as *The Man Who Came to Dinner.* Wolcott Gibbs in *The New Yorker* acknowledged its "considerable charm" and praised Moss's "extraordinary delicacy of touch." *Variety* yawned. The show-biz bible found the evening thin and uneven, directed "to the hilt," with "numerous over-obvious, threadbare bits."

Hollywood came calling in the person of a Junior Miss of yesteryear named Mary Pickford, but the rights bounced in ever-escalating increments from Warner Bros. to 20th Century-Fox, which secured them for a whopping $450,000, almost doubling the record set by *Lady in the Dark.*

Moss can hardly have minded. In addition to his percentage as part owner of the Lyceum, he collected as director and investor. *Junior Miss* eventually had four productions running simultaneously in New York, Chicago, Philadelphia, and London, where audiences were mostly perplexed by the precocity of American teenagers. London by then was being blitzed by more than Judy and Fuffy, and three weeks after *Junior Miss* opened on Broadway, America was at war, too. If Moss lied to the press about his draft status, he did not shrink from the writers' war.

"I'm on about several hundred War committees, it seems to me," he told Schary, but this was nothing new. He had often lent his name or presence to liberal political causes in the 1930s. His endorsement added visibility to fund-raising appeals for refugees of the Spanish Civil War and other victims of fascism, but none engaged him as fully as the European Jews whose fate was still unfolding in 1942. Moss had reason as a Jew to be concerned, but his friendship with Weill added a personal sense of urgency. Weill's former associates and colleagues were, like himself and Lotte Lenya (Jewish only by marriage), either in flight, exile, or concentration camps.

It is sobering to recall that neither the president of the United States nor American religious leaders spoke out in the early days of the war.

Their silence was worsened by an immigration policy whose "neutrality" effectively abandoned the Jews and others to Hitler's will. The details of his Final Solution may not have been known, but evidence of widespread murder had been there to see since the mid-thirties.

Out of frustration over American policy and outrage at Hollywood's fear of offending its European markets, Ben Hecht organized a dinner in January 1942. He invited thirty leading Jewish writers and people in the arts and urged them to help focus attention on what would come to be known as the Holocaust.

Incredibly, only Moss and Weill immediately volunteered their services. "I thought I'd tell you," Moss told Hecht that evening, "that if I can do anything definite in the way of Jewish propaganda, call on me." Weill added, "Please count on me for everything."

Their first attempt to mount a show called *Fight for Freedom* failed for lack of funds. Finally, on March 9, 1943, Madison Square Garden hosted forty thousand spectators for two performances of *We Will Never Die*. Hundreds of voices were raised in prayer and song at the Garden to remind the world of Jewish contributions to the arts and sciences and the terrible fate engulfing Jews now.

We Will Never Die was a pageant produced by Billy Rose and (uncredited) Hollywood's own Berlin-exile, Ernst Lubitsch. Hecht wrote it, with music by Weill and staging by Moss. Two hundred rabbis and two hundred cantors invoked prayers, including the Mourners' Kaddish, the Jewish prayer for the dead. Narrators at various performances included such well-known Jewish actors as Edward G. Robinson, Paul Muni, Sylvia Sidney, and John Garfield, with non-Jews like Ralph Bellamy, Frank Sinatra, and Burgess Meredith joining the cause.

The production was too modestly subtitled: "A Pageant Memorializing the Two Million Murdered Jews of Europe." Hecht, a militant Zionist, took little comfort from the apparent success of *We Will Never Die*, even as it went on with rotating narrators to presentations in Chicago, Philadelphia, Boston, Washington, and at the Hollywood Bowl in Los Angeles. "The pageant has accomplished nothing," he told Weill. "Actually all we have done is make a lot of Jews cry, which is not a unique accomplishment."

The Lyceum, with *Junior Miss* playing downstairs in a long and trouble-free run, turned its offices for the duration over to the American Theatre Wing, the organization best known for the annual Tony Awards. The Wing undertook to provide a series of morale-boosting entertainments for defense workers during their noon lunch-breaks.

"The Lunchtime Follies," as these revues were called, were organized with Moss's help in the Lyceum offices, and Kaufman joined him to write a couple of sketches for the first show. *Fun to Be Free* was presented at the Todd Shipyard in Brooklyn when the lunch whistle blew on June 22, 1942. The Kaufman-Hart sketches were "The Man Who Went to Moscow," in which David Burns (the original Banjo in *The Man Who Came to Dinner*) slapsticked Hitler in Russia, and "Washington, D.C.," which satirized doing business in the wartime capital.

Neither was more than a skit, and the authors wrote three more during the war for army camp shows, including "The Paperhanger," another Hitler burlesque; "The Ladies," about distaff warriors; and "Dream On, Soldier," a send-up of G.I. fantasies about postwar life. Kaufman and Hart first presented "Dream On, Soldier" on April 5, 1943, at Madison Square Garden in a Red Cross benefit. The actors were Kaufman and Hart.

That same week, Moss "enlisted."

First Lieutenant Irving Paul Lazar of the Army Air Corps was a diminutive and aggressive thirty-five-year-old desk jockey, assigned to the Pentagon and to Lt. Col. Dudley Dean, officer in charge of the Air Corps branch of Army Emergency Relief. Dean ordered Lazar to come up with a show that would do for the Air Corps what Irving Berlin's *This Is the Army* was doing for the infantry. Berlin's show had opened on July 4 of the previous year and had already been turned into a Warner Bros. movie (with Ronald Reagan). The stage version continued to churn money for the Army with Berlin himself onstage singing "Oh, How I Hate to Get Up in the Morning."

A month after the first performances of *We Will Never Die* and only days after Moss's appearance in "Dream On, Soldier," Lazar found himself in the Oak Room of New York's Plaza Hotel. He was accompanied by Lt. Benjamin Landis, who had been deputized with him to beat the Broadway bushes for creative talent. Across the room enjoying a drink with Edith Atwater was Moss. Lazar had no way of knowing Moss's draft status, but was shrewd enough to know that any man out of uniform in his thirties would be sensitive about that fact and possibly eager to do something about it. He marched to Moss's table and said, "My name is Lieutenant Lazar, and would you like to do a play about the Air Forces?"

Moss later said he replied, "Certainly," in order to get rid of the intruder, but the query piqued his interest. So did Lazar. Moss asked for something more formal than a barroom come-on, and within the week received a telegram from General H. H. ("Hap") Arnold, Commanding General of the Army Air Forces and a member of the Joint Chiefs of

Staff. Arnold later admitted he had never heard of Moss Hart, but was willing to be guided by Lazar and Landis, both of whom had show-business experience, Lazar as a booker of bands and singers for MCA, and Landis as a production manager.

The telegram instructed Moss to present himself at the Pentagon a few days later. He did as he was told and was surprised to find himself "completely tongue-tied." The four stars on Arnold's shoulders and the Pentagon itself were enough, he said, to make you "so damn impressed you feel that to even open your mouth would directly impede the War effort."

Moss allowed he would be delighted to put together a show if he could be "the boss"—and if he had the first idea what went on in the Air Corps, which he did not. Arnold suggested that a tour of airfields and training camps would provide everything a writer—or "boss"—might need in the way of background. Three days later Moss, who hated flying, found himself strapped into an Army plane on a white-knuckle flight to Fort Worth, Texas, his first stop on a tour of airfields and camps that would carry him twenty-eight thousand miles in the next eight weeks.

He flew from Fort Worth to Keesler Field in Mississippi (home to forty thousand would-be pilots) and on to the College Training Program at the University of Missouri in Columbia. At almost thirty-nine, Moss was painfully aware of the youth of the "Eager Beavers" (as they were called) among whom he was billeted, and said that their gung ho enthusiasm and energy reminded him of "Apple Blossom Time in Puberty."

It was the most physically demanding eight weeks of his adult life. He was outfitted in Air Corps suntans and fatigues, given papers with a false identity so he could pass as a recruit, and subjected to more or less the same tests and military discipline as the younger trainees from 4:30 a.m. until 8 p.m. each day. In eight weeks he hurtled through a training program designed to last fifteen months, submitting to pressure chamber and reflex tests, P-38 acrobatics and hair-raising night flights, taking notes on technical matters, military turns of speech, and personalities. He ate in chow lines, drank beer, and jitterbugged to jukebox jive surrounded by boys half his age before collapsing on a barracks cot. He complained jokingly, but admitted privately that the supercharged, hypermasculine atmosphere intimidated him. He also felt like Christopher Columbus discovering America. "In eight short weeks in the Air Force," he said, "I learned more about my country in terms of people than I had ever learned before," adding, "I got religion."

He learned, less happily, the military precision with which Arnold did things. The general wanted an opening date for the show Moss had not yet written and he got one. Opening night would be November 2, 1943, at Broadway's 44th Street Theatre and that was that.

Moss, fifteen pounds lighter than he had been in the Oak Room in April, dug himself into a foxhole in Bucks County in late June and hammered out a show in six weeks that, unlike *This Is the Army,* would be a real play. He titled it *Winged Victory,* not after the statue, but after an actual plane then fulfilling combat missions. His crew of characters would borrow the name for their own Flying Fortress onstage.

The play would open in (where else?) Mapleton, Ohio, and follow three young cadets (a barber, a banker, and a chemist) from that town and one each from Texas, Brooklyn, and Oregon through their Air Corps training to an island somewhere in the combat zones of the South Pacific. One would die in a training accident, another would wash out and become a bombardier, and another would be badly wounded. The central Mapleton boy would end the play on a pile of rubble under a palm tree, writing a letter to his newborn son just before flying off into the wild blue yonder.

It owed much to *The American Way.* Mapleton, Ohio, was by now a Moss Hart signature, and *Winged Victory* would set intimate moments against a panoramic background as the earlier play had done, but with a tighter time span. Simplicity and universal emotions, rather than characterization, were the keys to conveying the patriotism and sacrifice of the airmen. It was home-front propaganda—agitprop meets Uncle Sam—but epic in intent and fervent in attitude.

As in *The American Way* (and almost everything Moss wrote), music underlined emotion and sometimes substituted for it. Songs ranged from the predictable "Air Corps Song" to "Mademoiselle from Armentiers" (special lyrics by Moss), "White Christmas," and "I Can't Give You Anything But Love, Baby." A trio of guys in Andrews Sisters drag put a spin on "Pennsylvania Polka" and a flamboyant Carmen Miranda impersonator (who really *was* a Carmen Miranda impersonator) burned down the hangar with a hot rendition of "Chica-Chica-Boom-Chic."

Nothing, but nothing, was to interfere with the Air Corps itself or its conduct of the war, certainly not the budget, which the Pentagon declined to finance. Producer Gilbert Miller commandeered a sponsorship committee to fund the show. Miller's participation was guaranteed by Moss's promise to direct his production of Clare Boothe Luce's *Happy Marriage* as soon as *Winged Victory* was safely aloft. That never happened, but Moss's promise got Miller going. Fortunately for everyone, Miller included, he was married to Kitty Bache, daughter of Wall Street's Jules Bache. Miller placed personal calls to his father-in-law, Marshall Field (the department store heir and fellow Zilboorg alumnus who had been an investor in *Lady in the Dark*), Albert Lasker, William S. Paley, Robert Lehman, and Henry Luce among others, who put up $100,000 to get *Winged Victory* airborne. They could recoup their investment, Miller told them, but not a penny more. Patriotism was their reward, as it was for Moss, who waived his fees and percentages. All proceeds would go directly to the Relief organization. Cast, crew, orchestra, even box-office help would all be active military personnel receiving nothing more than their regulation army pay of $21 a month.

Lazar and Landis issued casting calls to military personnel with stage or entertainment experience, though none could be considered who were fit for combat and, ironically, no pilots or air cadets. This proved no handicap, as seven thousand men applied for what was surely the biggest cattle call in theater history. Lazar and Landis conducted field interviews and brought photos and résumés to Bucks County, where Moss narrowed his choices using the Selective Service system. Candidates were graded 1–A to 4–F and he culled some three hundred of them before he even finished writing.

By the time the full cast of 210, the orchestra of 45, the choral group of 50, and the stage crew of 70 were assembled, *Winged Victory* boasted the names of Lee J. Cobb, Karl Malden, Edmund O'Brien, Red Buttons (one of "The Andrews Sisters"), Gary Merrill, John Forsythe, Barry Nelson, Kevin McCarthy, Mario Lanza (né Alfred Cocozza), Ray Middleton, Peter Lind Hayes, and two future film directors, Don Taylor and Martin Ritt, all of them listed in the program with their military ranks. Their wives and sweethearts onstage were their real wives and sweethearts. Musicians were all government issue, too, rounded up by bandleader Glenn Miller before his plane was lost over the English Channel. M/Sgt. Joe Bushkin was at the piano, conducted by composer T/Sgt. David Rose, newly divorced from Judy Garland. Director of the fifty-man chorale was 2nd Lt. Leonard de Paur, late of the Hall Johnson Choir and Orson Welles's all-black production of *Macbeth*.

Broadway's lighting wizard Sgt. Abe Feder supervised the five switchboards and nine miles of cable for the 252 light cues; Sgt. Howard Shoup, direct from MGM's costume closet, was wardrobe manager. Writers Sgt. Ben Maddox and Pvt. Nat Hiken wrote publicity handouts and radio spots; future Broadway producer Pvt. Clinton Wilder was a personnel clerk; Pvt. Irving Schneider served (as always) as Moss's assistant; and a box-office assistant was future theater owner Pvt. James Nederlander.

Seventeen sets, including Mapleton, Ohio, and the South Seas island, were designed by Cpl. Harry Horner from *Lady in the Dark*. He employed five turntables this time, and built a section of the B-47 bomber bigger than the real thing as a prop. He designed backstage space, too, where more than three hundred people nightly dressed, made up, traded gossip, and listened for their cues.

Even with the $100,000 contributed by the sponsors, mounting the show would have been impossible without major concessions from vendors and suppliers. Someone calculated that when the show opened at top ticket prices of $4.40 and $5.50, a sold-out house could return only $35,000 a week for a show that, with actors on Equity contracts (then paying a munificent $20 a week during rehearsals) would have cost a weekly minimum of $50,000 just to raise the curtain.

Moss staged the play in a record seventeen days. "Every rehearsal was like an invasion," he said. "[I] managed to stay calm till I got to my bedroom at night, when I went crazy." It would have been impossible, he acknowledged, without military personnel accustomed to taking orders.

Just before leaving for the out-of-town tryout, Moss invited Gilbert Miller and the other civilian backers and their consorts to a private run-through. He stepped downstage to the footlights at the 44th Street Theatre and acknowledged polite applause. "I am reminded," he told his sponsors, "of the story of the acrobat who performed the death-defying feat of sliding on one foot from a wire stretched from the third balcony to center stage. After a heroic introduction followed by a tumultuous fan-fare, a little old man steps from the wings, his tights hanging loosely about his legs. He eyes the wire," Moss continued, "then scans the audience. Again his eyes travel up the length of wire, and then with a sigh, he turns again to the audience: 'If you really want to see an old Jew get killed, I'll do it!'" When the laughter was at its peak he interrupted it to announce, "Ladies and gentlemen, Act One, Scene One, *Winged Victory*." The performance left not a dry eye among the sharks and captains of industry who helped finance it.

Winged Victory tried out in Boston. Moss told a reporter it was "my attempt to put down the thing that *is* the Army Air Force, in terms of the men rather than the planes." But it was the planes that ended *Winged Victory*. The men onstage were dwarfed by a section of Horner's larger-than-life bomber revving up motors and deafening the audience. "Exhilarating," said Boston critic Elliot Norton, "but perhaps a little theatrical." Moss agreed it was a bit "Radio City Music Hall." Out went the bomber and in came the final scene of the pilot writing to the newborn son he may not live to see.

When the curtain rose in New York on November 2, 1943, it was to a celebrity audience that gave the show a fifteen-minute standing and weeping ovation. The reviews weren't reviews: they were testimonials. Typical of the critics was Howard Barnes in the *Herald-Tribune,* who thought it nothing less than "a great and profoundly moving war play" of "heroic proportions." Friends liked it, too. "Moss is a genius," Edna Ferber said after she saw it.

Not surprisingly for a show designed to appeal to patriotic passion, *Winged Victory* fails to survive the war that inspired it. In today's more cynical climate, it seems hopelessly sentimental and jingoistic, full of long speeches that were stirring in the heat of the moment, but now sound like windy commencement addresses. The airmen are so uniformly aw-shucks-noble they seem to be posing for recruiting posters or post-office murals, and their women make the Statue of Liberty look like an unpatriotic B-girl.

There were naysayers among the tearful. Wolcott Gibbs in *The New Yorker* found it "high-minded but vacant," though he acknowledged "it would be silly to review it as if it were intended to be a permanent contribution to the theatre." Gibbs observed "a great many fine things," but felt obliged to point out "one of the most peculiar lines I can remember." A young cadet refers to flying as "romantic" and adds "you don't hate yourself in the morning, either!" To Gibbs, "the idea of sex as inseparable from disgust, especially in a healthy young man who happens to be married, made me wonder just a little about the nature of Mr. Hart's researches into Army life."

Darryl F. Zanuck thought it was a swell rendition of Army life and paid $1 million for screen rights to underscore his enthusiasm, or so the 20th Century-Fox publicity drums thumped. The actual cost was $350,000 and a percentage of the gross, but it all went to Army Emergency Relief, as did Moss's screen salary and percentage, except for $10 he accepted as a quit claim.

The movie rights were purchased two months before *Winged Victory* opened, and Moss was not only to write the screenplay, but to direct the picture as well. He would later withdraw in favor of William Wyler, who had just made his documentary *The Memphis Belle,* about real airmen on real bombing missions. Wyler ducked the assignment in courteous "TERRIBLY SORRY" telegrams to Moss and Zanuck. The picture was turned over to Moss's old friend, George Cukor.

The movie's male cast was identical to the one on Broadway, with the exception of Cukor's discovery (as a choirboy in MGM's *Romeo and Juliet* in 1938), Lon McCallister, who now played a choirboy from Mapleton. Alonzo, as Cukor called him, was under contract to Fox and had attracted bobby-soxer interest a year earlier in *Home in Indiana* opposite contract player Jeanne Crain, who was added to the movie's cast as well. The most interesting newcomer to the cast was Judy Holliday as one of the wives. All but unknown outside of New York nightspots (studio documents refer to her as Judy Tuvim), she would make five more pictures with Cukor, including *Born Yesterday,* which made her a star on Broadway and won her an Academy Award in Hollywood.

Cukor's movie is watchable, but just barely. His biographer Patrick McGilligan calls it "laughably cornball," and Cukor scholar Gary Carey dismisses it as "adenoidal drivel." Their judgments are harsh, but not unduly so. Cukor and Moss would work together again—triumphantly— but the movie of *Winged Victory,* like the play it transcribes, is the artifact of a moment impossible to retrieve. Its virtues are those of Moss's skills at slick, entertaining topicality and its naïve and sentimental defects are his, too, however many handkerchiefs they dampened when the work seemed true and noble.

According to Kitty Carlisle, *Winged Victory* remained Moss's personal favorite among all his shows, "tied up with all those young men [in the show]," she explained, "whose lives he saved, because they didn't go overseas" (though none were eligible for combat duty). More likely it made up for avoiding the draft while others—even Cukor, at over forty— did their bits in uniform. Or maybe it was that *Winged Victory,* more than *Lady in the Dark,* was the show that finally established Moss as an above-the-title theatrical presence. *Time* pegged it "his first complete theatrical solo flight," and the ads, even for the movie, announced it as *Moss Hart's "Winged Victory."*

Cukor's directing the movie was almost accidental but has contributed to *Winged Victory*'s underground reputation as "a gay show." There were rumors about air cadets skinny-dipping on Santa Ana beaches for Cukor's cameras, and film director-to-be Martin Ritt told McGilligan he thought Moss and Cukor together created an "oppressively gay" atmosphere. Some asserted the show was gay just because it was Moss's. Principal tongue-clucker was choreographer Agnes de Mille, who didn't much like Moss and referred to him disdainfully as "a known homosexual," an odd remark from someone in the dance world. De Mille took pains to broadcast the complaint of one of her dancers who quit *Winged Victory* claiming that Moss "was openly carrying on with boys in the company who in turn flirted outrageously with him."

Any show employing three hundred actors and singers—or three hundred truckdrivers and machinists, for that matter—was bound to be partly gay, even in the military. One more or less openly gay member of the cast confirmed this. "We unmarried guys were billeted at the Narragansett Hotel way up at Ninety-third and Broadway (married men could live where they wanted) and, sure, there was stuff going on. They put us in rooms of three each, like boarding school. Then there was Sascha Brastoff, the flamer who played Carmen Miranda, and was *always* entertaining the troops in his room. There was an actor in the show called John Andes, who hung around a lot but didn't join in and we suspected him of being a 'spy' for Washington. We mentioned it to Peter Lind Hayes, who was in the show with his wife, and everyone—two hundred, three hundred people—boycotted him backstage, even the straights. Maybe that's why he changed his name to Keith Andes when he went to Hollywood."

Robert Cantell, another actor who lived at the Narragansett, recalled "stuff the War Department would have frowned at," but denied hearing rumors about Moss. "We revered him," Cantell recalled shortly after attending the fiftieth anniversary reunion of the *Winged Victory* cast. "Things happened. It was wartime and it was the theater, but if Moss was involved, no one ever heard about it. Moss was the general; we were his troops. Fraternization? I doubt it. Besides, what would Moss have been doing at the Narragansett? Have you ever *seen* the Narragansett?"

Which didn't mean that Moss was celibate or alone. He was keeping company with Paula Laurence, now in the Kurt Weill–Ogden Nash– Agnes de Mille musical *One Touch of Venus.* "Speaking of Moss Hart," Woollcott silkily told Ruth Gordon when recycling the old joke he may have forgotten was his, "I was entranced by the quoted comment of someone who saw him going into "21" with Edith Atwater's successor— a Miss Paula Laurence. 'There,' said this observer, 'goes Moss Hart with the future Paula Laurence.' "

Moss may have had the occasional dalliance during *Winged Victory.* "Apple Blossom Time in Puberty" may have had its temptations, but nothing in his Department of Defense records or FBI file indicates he was that indiscreet, and J. Edgar Hoover would surely have noticed. Moss would have risked Dr. Kubie's "rabbinical fury," too, something he was loath to do. And, anyway, there was a new "Moss's girl" on the scene— newer than Paula Lawrence—and this time he was serious.

19

New Stages

Moss's war was inescapably theatrical. Just before *Winged Victory* left for its out-of-town tryout, the official Army order came down that the company was to assemble Sunday morning at 0800 hours at the 44th Street Theatre and proceed on foot to Grand Central Station, there to embark at platform 23 for Boston. Moss futilely raised objections about keeping things under wraps, but right on schedule the company marched east on Forty-fourth Street and turned down Broadway in parade formation. Corporal Don Taylor recalled that "none of us noticed a civilian marching in our midst," but as they crossed Times Square "this civilian started singing 'Over There.' Slowly, the Company joined in, then the band followed, our pace quickened, soon everybody was singing at the top of their lungs, and then it happened. Traffic stopped, men waved their hats, women wiped their tears, saluting us with their damp handkerchiefs, children were hoisted to see the departing soldiers—not off to war, but merely catching a train to Boston for a tryout. Naturally, that civilian was Moss Hart!"

Moss won the Donaldson Award as Best Director for 1943–44 for *Winged Victory* and celebrated by writing to the parents of every American flyer awarded a Distinguished Flying Cross and enclosing a silver *Winged Victory* pin and two tickets to any performance of the show. If they couldn't make it to the 44th Street Theatre, the tickets were good in any of the thirteen American cities the show would tour before the end of the war.

By February he was in California working on the screenplay. Though reviewers had remarked on the play's cinematic flow, Moss still felt insecure with screen form and prevailed upon Zanuck to hire someone to prepare a screen treatment to which he could add dialogue and polish. Zanuck complied, scolding him for turning down the offer to direct and coaxing him to weekend at the Zanuck retreat in Palm Springs to discuss it further and play croquet, as competitive in the desert as in Bucks County. Moss usually won, even in the floodlit night games Zanuck preferred. When the mogul sponsored an East Coast vs. West Coast Croquet Tournament, Moss won yet again. Presented with a small trophy he indignantly told the crowd, "I did not come all the way to California to win this piddling little cup. I want something I can take home and really show around." Zanuck had a four-foot gold cup made that the victor accepted as his due.

He finished his work on the screenplay in three weeks and returned to New York, leaving his pages in the hands of Cukor, Irving Schneider, dialogue director Lee Strasberg, and Zanuck himself, all of whom contributed changes to the shooting script, though an uncredited John Larkin did the final draft.

Zanuck admired Moss's glamour, wit, and way with a croquet mallet and didn't give up on wooing him back to Fox. Nor did now Captain Irving Lazar let him. Lazar remained officially attached to *Winged Victory* for the military, and remained in California with Schneider and Harry Horner to oversee locations and logistics for Cukor.

Moss liked Lazar's chutzpah. He found him colorful, scrappy, and relentlessly creative in advancing his own and Moss's interests. The two shared their Jewish background, loved theater and "class," and thought of themselves in a curiously similar way. Moss often referred to himself as "Huckleberry Hart," while Lazar styled himself "the Huck Finn of Brooklyn." Lazar (whose real first name was Samuel; he thought Irving Paul "had a classy ring to it") had a law degree and wanted to establish his own agency after the war with Moss as his first client.

Moss hadn't needed an agent since his break with Frieda Fishbein over *Once in a Lifetime*. Fishbein had negotiated Moss's long-term contract with Sam Harris so well she could be dispensed with, and the partnership with Kaufman had been self-generating. The William Morris Agency had represented him for movies in the 1930s, but otherwise only Joe Hyman looked after him. Moss displayed a son's loyalty to Hyman's paternal constancy, so much more reliable than that of the Commodore, now permanently in Florida. Moss had even quietly nursed Hyman back to health from a nervous breakdown four years earlier.

With Harris dead, Moss was successful enough not to need an outside producer. He could attract blue-chip investors like the Luces, the Paleys, the Goldwyns, the Selznicks, and Marshall Field from his social contacts alone. For financial and legal matters Hyman would do. Hyman had a credit as Civilian Producer on *Winged Victory* and wanted to be more than a silent investor and business manager. Bernie, Moss's punster brother, wanted to be more than a stage manager and together Joe and Bernie—as Hyman & Hart—could provide Moss with the only production entity he needed.

It wasn't obvious what Lazar might actually *do* to represent him, but Moss agreed anyway. "You can call yourself my agent," he said, "but you can't deliver me." With Moss's introduction to Ira and Lee Gershwin, Lazar easily snared other clients, often with Moss acting as *his* agent. "What would you like for Christmas?" Moss asked him one year, and Lazar replied, "Cole Porter." He got Porter and, in time, Noël Coward, Edna Ferber, Yip Harburg, Maxwell Anderson, Garson Kanin, Betty Comden and Adolph Green, Rodgers and Hammerstein, and Lerner and Loewe, too. Then there were the ones he simply poached, like Truman Capote and Vladimir Nabokov, whose books he sold without permission, an innovative hustle that outraged them until they cashed the checks his initiative produced. He was a pint-sized pirate in outsized horn-rimmed glasses, bespoke tailoring, and handmade shoes that walked their own path over convention. He made himself the most colorful agent in Hollywood and, later, on Broadway, where his greatest coup would also be Moss's greatest triumph.

Insomnia and depression awaited Moss in New York. So did Kaufman. Moss was disturbed that since the end of their partnership and the Ferber project that had been delayed by *My Sister Eileen* Kaufman had not written a single full-length play. There had been wartime skits, but nothing more from a man who formerly turned out one or more plays a season. Kaufman had written Moss in California about a new show he might do for Billy Rose, adding, "if you have three days we might do a sketch and a half when you return."

The Billy Rose show was a revue called *Seven Lively Arts.* Moss thought Rose brash but courageous and was grateful for his having produced *We Will Never Die.* He quickly agreed to become involved for Kaufman's sake, if no other.

The first order of business was moving the new production firm of Hyman & Hart into the Paramount Building at 1501 Broadway, just around the corner from the New Amsterdam of Moss's youth. Hyman & Hart had optioned a play for late fall, and secured a director. To no one's surprise, it turned out to be Moss Hart, who publicized the tyro producers with a facetious piece in the Sunday *Times* titled "Let the Shuberts Be Warned."

The play was *Dear Ruth* by Norman Krasna, the playwright and screenwriter Moss had known off and on in Hollywood since the thirties. To anyone with a memory *Dear Ruth* was just *Junior Miss* revisited, with Judy Graves now sixteen and called Miriam Wilkins, and her sister Lois now twenty-two and called Ruth.

Their story went like this: Unknown to her Long Island family, Miriam has been writing letters to servicemen overseas as part of a school project. To add oomph and heart to her morale boosting, she has included a snapshot of Ruth and signed Ruth's name to every letter. A young pilot on twenty-four-hour leave arrives at the Wilkinses' front door to meet "Dear Ruth," who has never heard of him and has just decided to marry a stuffy banker. Miriam's literary impersonations are exposed and, to everyone's relief but the banker's, Ruth falls in love with her pilot. In the nick of time they are married in the living room by Ruth's father (he's a judge) before the pilot's leave expires. The curtain falls as the doorbell rings to announce the arrival of a sailor—looking for "Dear Ruth."

It was thin as a sheet of V-Mail and lacked the charm of *Junior Miss,* but was amusingly escapist and, like the earlier play, required only a living-room set and no stars. Moss again held readings for teenage actresses, this time in the basement of the Paramount Building. He found his Miriam in thirteen-year-old Stanja Lowe of Cleveland, Ohio. Lowe was young for Miriam, but had grown up acting and among actors at the Cleveland Play House, run by her father.

Lowe remembered Moss's forthright approach to directing and blocking, his courtesy and easy, jokey manner. "Stick with me, Kid," he used to tell her, "and I'll put you in mustard plaster." When he was tardy to rehearsals he explained jauntily, "Sorry I'm late. Had to get the Prez in," knowing that the teenager idolized FDR, whose unprecedented fourth-term election was imminent. Lowe was charmed by Moss and by handsome John Dall as Ruth's pilot-suitor, but in awe of Ruth herself (her wardrobe, anyway). Virginia Gillmore, who played the part (and was married to a young actor called Yul Brynner), arrived for rehearsal wearing a bold, diagonally striped suit from Valentina that seemed the epitome of chic to a teenager—and to Moss, who ordered it copied for the production.

Then Norman Krasna arrived from Hollywood. Krasna objected to Lowe as Miriam and insisted that Moss replace her with Lenore Lonergan, the froggy-voiced Fuffy of *Junior Miss.* Moss, as a member of the

Dramatists' Guild (and soon its president), knew that in the theater the writer was king and no director could override the author's wishes or make a line change without permission. He yielded to Krasna but couldn't bring himself to fire a thirteen-year-old. "I come from a long line of cowards," he liked to say when faced with unpleasant tasks. He asked her father to break the news, which was delivered gently in a long walk around the block. Fifty years later Lowe thought Moss's solution less cowardly than "just business," and remembered him as "a lovely, considerate man. I was kept on salary for a year and they later asked me to do the road company. By then I was ready to use the money I got for not acting to pay my way through Bennington."

Moss had not been late to rehearsals of *Dear Ruth* because of campaigning for "the Prez," but because he was seeing Kubie for an hour each morning and two and a half hours each afternoon, submitting to shock treatments every other day. Open as ever about his therapy, Moss discussed it shortly after D–Day over dinner and drinks at "21" with Lotte Lenya, a recital that lasted well into the night. Lenya was sympathetic, but stunned. The next day she wrote Weill in her imperfect English: "He talked nothing else except about his troubles. He is in an awful state. I am more than ever convinced that this Dr. of his is a great faker, if that is result of a seven ! years treatment, I must say it's a crime to do that to a person. He gets shock treatments now every other day. That means he gets an injection, which knocks him out completely and then his subconsciouess starts to talk! Good God. It aint human. I feel terribly sorry for him, but he believes so much in that guy that one has to be very careful what to say."

Moss believed in "that guy" because the success he was achieving in the theater was persuasive evidence that Kubie's influence was positive, however prolonged or painful it may have been, at least when treatment coincided with the upward phase of Moss's mood swings. How—or what—he might have written without Kubie is unknowable, but even friends who were privately appalled had to admit that the still bright marquees for *Lady in the Dark, Junior Miss,* and *Winged Victory* seemed to justify *something.*

If Moss's faith ever wavered, Beatrice Kaufman was there to prevent backsliding. She had gotten him into analysis in the first place and, according to Malcolm Goldstein, who had access to her private papers, Moss remained "the great but platonic passion of her life." He reciprocated her intensity, confiding in her as she did in him, and thought of himself as the "intimate companion" of "this rare and exceptional woman." He called their friendship "one of the most violent, stormy, but richly rewarding relationships of my life." It is more than likely that his romances with Edith Atwater, Paula Laurence, and others went nowhere because none of them could measure up to Beatrice.

Seven Lively Arts and *Dear Ruth* were both scheduled to open in December. While at Brooks Costume on a wardrobe search for *Dear Ruth,* Moss ran into Dora Sayers, an actress half Beatrice's age whom he hadn't seen since *The American Way,* in which she had played a small part opposite another newcomer, David Wayne. Before that she had been in *The Fabulous Invalid,* impersonating Ethel Barrymore, Eva Le Gallienne, and a burlesque dancer. She was a beautiful, doelike young woman from Toronto, still in her twenties, with a velvet voice and what a friend described as "startled brown eyes."

Kaufman cast her in *The Fabulous Invalid* after directing her in the touring company of *Stage Door.* She had recently understudied Katharine Hepburn in *The Philadelphia Story* and had just returned to New York from a tour of Noël Coward's *Private Lives* with Ralph Forbes (whom she would later marry) and Forbes's ex-wife, Ruth Chatterton.

She hadn't much liked Kaufman when she worked for him because of "that knife-like thing George had when directing." Moss, on the other hand, was "very humorous, very clever, and much more gentle." When he invited her for lunch at the Plaza, she accepted. Before long friends were referring to her as "Moss's girl" and wondering if she was or was not the future Miss Sayers.

Meanwhile, Moss prepared *Dear Ruth* and regretted he had ever agreed to work on *Seven Lively Arts.* Kaufman had argued with the always abrasive Billy Rose on the first day of rehearsals and Rose replaced him as director with Hassard Short and actor Philip Loeb. Almost everyone on *Seven Lively Arts* felt a victim of Rose's pretensions. Moss would take revenge on the page and the stage, but for now Rose's grandiosity was such that even Ziegfeld, whose mantle Rose trumpeted he was assuming, might have sniggered. Rose had gone so far as to buy the original Ziegfeld Theatre, which had fallen on evil days as a movie house, and was spending lavishly to restore it. He commissioned Salvador Dalí to paint new lobby murals when it turned out that Ziegfeld's scenic designer Joseph Urban hadn't painted the old ones after all. The original artist was available, but why restore the work of an unknown when Dalí was in town?

The show (its title borrowed from Gilbert Seldes's influential book about popular culture) was to demonstrate Rose's impresario mastery of comedy, drama, ballet, song and dance, swing, and any other art that occurred to him. To out-Ziegfeld Ziegfeld he hired Beatrice Lillie and

Bert Lahr to star, Cole Porter to write songs for them, Igor Stravinsky to compose ballet music, Anton Dolin and Alicia Markova to dance to it, Robert Shaw to conduct a chorale, Ben Hecht to write a loose narrative for delivery by stand-up comic "Doc" Rockwell (whose son, George Lincoln Rockwell, would later lead the American Nazi Party), Benny Goodman and his clarinet to swing, Norman Bel Geddes to design sets; and Moss and Kaufman to write sketches—separately as it turned out. The talent lineup sounded like the musical equivalent of the Tower of Babel and by the time the show previewed in Philadelphia Bea Lillie was rolling her eyes heavenward and referring to it as *Seven Deadly Arts.*

Lillie was probably the funniest woman in the world, but could hardly show it when submerged by Rose's more-is-more-and-expensive-is-better production. Any show that combined Porter, Stravinsky, and Goodman was inviting a musical identity crisis. Porter fought about his billing and contributed only one good song, "Ev'ry Time We Say Good-bye"; Goodman went lofty and insisted on wearing white tie and tails while swinging; and Stravinsky remained above-it-all on Olympus. From Philadelphia, Rose cabled him:

YOUR MUSIC GREAT SUCCESS STOP COULD BE
SENSATIONAL SUCCESS IF YOU WOULD AUTHORIZE
ROBERT RUSSELL BENNETT RETOUCH ORCHESTRATION
STOP BENNETT ORCHESTRATES EVEN COLE PORTER

To which Stravinsky dryly replied:

SATISFIED WITH GREAT SUCCESS

Moss wrote four sketches for the show, three for Lillie and one for Lahr. The unhappy Lahr rejected his because it involved being doused with cold water and Rose was cold water enough. The sketches for Lillie were almost as good as the ones Moss had written for her in *The Show Is On* in 1936. The best was one in which she tried, as a titled English-woman, to speak to American G.I.s in what she imagined to be their vernacular and startled them out of their wits with bawdy double entendres. Another had her trying to buy tickets for a ballet whose name she couldn't recall but thought might be "Sol Hurok." The final sketch came, oddly enough, from Moss's onetime friend and mentor, Lester Sweyd. Now eking out a living on the fringes of show business, Sweyd had suggested a parody of *Angel Street (Gaslight)* for Rose's ex-wife Fanny Brice when it was still thought she would star in the show with Groucho Marx.

Moss adapted Sweyd's idea, putting Lillie in the gaslit role of the wife, together with the leading characters of *Life With Father* and *Tobacco Road,* all of them now in heaven. There they gaslight critic George Jean Nathan, who had panned them mercilessly on Earth. The still-terrestrial version of Nathan was in the audience and found it all "hilarious."

Moss took Sayers to the opening on December 7, 1944, which Rose oddly billed as a "commemoration and denial of Pearl Harbor." Tickets were $24 at a time when orchestra seats for *Oklahoma!* could be had for $5.50 including tax. The evening began with a champagne reception at which Rose arrived with his swimming-star wife Eleanor Holm on one arm and Ziegfeld's widow Billie Burke on the other.

Moss and Sayers had to leave their seats to reenter the theater for photographers who hadn't caught them coming down the red carpet the first time, an omen suggesting that outside might be livelier than inside. Once seated they suffered through the bloated enterprise, noting that it was too highbrow for the lowbrows and too low for the high. Howard Barnes in the *Herald-Tribune* found Moss's sketches "inspired" but the rest of the show seemed "little more than a lavish night club exhibit." Advertising and relentless promotion kept it alive—if never lively—for 183 performances.

Dear Ruth opened six nights later at Henry Miller's Theatre on West Forty-fourth Street and did better. All the critics recognized how familiar and thin it was, and how effortlessly Moss's direction made it "seem fresh and genuine," according to the *Times.* It spun on for a highly lucrative 683 performances—exactly 500 more than *Seven Lively Arts*—and was made into a successful movie by Paramount that inspired two sequels, *Dear Wife* and *Dear Brat.*

Dear Ruth was light, but came as a relief to audiences suffering battle fatigue. Victory was in the air, before the nightmares of the Battle of the Bulge and the atomic bomb, and *Dear Ruth* put servicemen onstage—home again—for romance and comedy. Triviality, after years of grim headlines, was as welcome as hope. A furlough now felt like a future, not just a prelude to more heroism or tragedy, though the papers were still full enough of both.

It wasn't over, over there, and neither was Moss's war effort. Stateside benefits for civilians were important, but USO tours brought entertainment directly to the boys. In charge of the USO Dramatic Department was Franklin Heller, a veteran of Moss's Little Theater days in Newark and of both *You Can't Take It With You* and *The American Way.* Heller had been after Moss for some time to allow the USO to tour one of the comedies, and in early 1945 *The Man Who Came to Dinner* became USO

Show #453. Moss would direct it and fulfill his long-burning desire to play Sheridan Whiteside. Dora Sayers would come along as Maggie Cutler, at his side onstage and off. Moss and Heller between them persuaded the USO to allow Sayers to join the tour even though, as a Canadian, she was technically an alien.

Moss reduced the cast from thirty-five to fourteen, enlisting Janet Fox to reprise Miss Preen; his butler Charles Matthies to play the butler in Ohio; Dina Merrill, the nineteen-year-old daughter of Wall Street's E. F. Hutton, as the daughter; *Denver Post* heiress Haila Stoddard to glitter as Lorraine Sheldon; and Nedda Harrigan as Whiteside's hapless Ohio hostess.

Rehearsals began on February 1 in the attic of the Ziegfeld Theatre, courtesy of Rose, who traded the space for Moss's efforts to cut *Seven Lively Arts,* still lumbering nightly in the auditorium downstairs. A stream of visitors to the attic included Beatrice Kaufman; Dina Merrill's mother, cereal heiress Marjorie Meriweather Post ("acting very much like Margaret Dumont's dowager in the Marx Brothers movies," remembered Janet Fox); and Salvador Dalí, living rent-free in a hideaway office at the top of the theater where he painted, cooked on a hot plate, and slept on what was rumored to have been Ziegfeld's casting couch.

Life magazine came to call with photographers for a photo spread that never ran ("they were stockpiling pictures in case we got torpedoed," remembered Sayers), and no one knew what their itinerary would be until they were issued cotton khakis, which meant the theater of the Pacific. The company had two weeks for rehearsals, with tryout and shakedown performances at Camp Kilmer beginning February 16 prior to embarkation for ports unknown on February 27 via Seattle.

The Kaufmans gave Moss a going-away party, mainly to console Beatrice, who dreaded Moss's absence. Moss composed a long "farewell ode" for the occasion that concluded with bows to Beatrice as "the analysts' pin-up girl, Freud's favorite child."

Freud was a theme that evening. Kaufman had written a party sketch titled "Moss Hart at the Analyst's" in which he played Moss and actor Martin Gabel played Kubie. Part of it went:

KUBIE: *Tell me, Moss—have you forgotten that this is an anniversary?*

MOSS: *Anniversary?*

KUBIE: *You're beginning your 25th year of analysis today.*

MOSS: *You don't mean it? Twenty-five years! . . . What year is this?*

KUBIE: *This is 1945.*

MOSS: *1945, huh? I haven't slept since 1941.*

KUBIE: *On my records it mentions a nap you had in 1943.*

MOSS: *It does? . . . Oh, yes, while Max Gordon was talking.*

Also skewered were Moss's devotion to Joe Hyman; Moss's legendary personal extravagance; and Charles the butler, whose taste for showy luxe equaled his employer's. Kaufman's imaginary list of Moss's expenses included "Suit of clothes for Charles, three thousand dollars . . . gold navel for Charles, nine hundred dollars."

Just before Moss and Sayers left for Seattle, they met Lazar, now returned to the East Coast, for drinks at the Algonquin Hotel. Lazar ("he always behaved like Moss's puppy-dog," Sayers remembered) had in tow someone they both knew, the singer-actress Moss had once auditioned for *Jubilee*—Kitty Carlisle.

The meeting may have been awkward for Moss. He had been entangled that summer in attempts by Weill and Lenya to sabotage Carlisle's chances for a role in the new Weill and Ira Gershwin musical about Cellini called *The Firebrand of Florence*. Weill had written into the show an aggressively sexy singing duchess to serve as Lenya's Broadway debut. To his alarm, his former agent Arthur Lyons recommended a current client for the part, "his sweetheart Kitty Carlisle."

Gershwin had nodded that Carlisle seemed a good idea, to the dismay of Weill and Lenya. They were obsessed with denigrating Carlisle—"so impossible for the part"—and her romantic liaison with Lyons, a man once described as a Russian accent that was four foot three and weighed two hundred pounds. Weill and Lenya wanted Moss to direct the show and persuaded him to talk Gershwin out of Carlisle, but the lyricist said his remarks about her were meant "just to be nice." In the end, Lenya played the part and John Murray Anderson directed the show. It flopped.

Carlisle may or may not have known of all this, but it had been "just business" to Moss and failed to dampen the conviviality of cocktail chat about the upcoming USO tour. Moss stayed behind at the Algonquin with Lazar while the two women shared a taxi uptown. During the ride Carlisle put a curious question to Sayers. "Are you in love with Moss Hart?" she asked. Sayers was startled and remembered that Carlisle had "done an awful lot of twinkling in Moss's direction," but decided to ignore it. All she said was, "I don't know, but this trip will decide."

. . .

"Like all great adventures," Moss said once the tour was over, "it was wonderful and terrible," and terrible is how it began. At the last moment Nedda Harrigan decamped to marry director Joshua Logan and was replaced by Paula Trueman, who resented being a substitute and let everybody know it. Peter Boyne, cast in the Noël Coward part, began hitting the bottle and pinching servicemen in Seattle. He remained on probation and under threat of dismissal for the entire tour, though replacing him in the middle of the South Seas would have required Mandrake the Magician.

Seattle itself became a problem. Moss and his actors arrived there and waited—and waited—to ship out. The troupe was billeted in local hotels with nothing to do but wander from room to room kibitzing or complaining. Moss used the delay to grow a beard for his role as Whiteside, a handsome, neatly trimmed affair that added to his already Mephistophelean look. He and his cast mingled with G.I.s who were not always impressed by USO entertainers. Many of them resented the men for not being in uniform and the women for reminding them of what they were missing at home.

Sayers remembered that before embarkation she and Moss joined some others in one of the hotel rooms for a casual evening that grew tense, then ugly. After too many beers the servicemen who were there began taunting Moss, demanding to know why he wasn't in uniform. The atmosphere grew hostile. "They were challenging Moss and he was pretending to ignore it," Sayers recalled. "He kept staring at his drink until one of these young officers got louder and more obnoxious and I finally said to Moss, 'This is unbearable, you have to do something to defend yourself.' He mumbled, 'I can't. I hate any kind of violence.' He just pressed himself flat against the wall. Like wallpaper."

Sayers turned on the bullies and a donnybrook ensued. "I was furious with everyone—Moss, the soldiers, everyone. Somehow I burned someone with my cigarette and that shocked the room into silence. But Moss still didn't raise a whisper. He let me defend him. He didn't ask me to, but he couldn't or wouldn't stand up for himself."

The altercation was reported to the military provost in Seattle. "It was especially difficult for me because I was an alien and had some sort of special dispensation," Sayers recalled. "They dropped it finally. They had more important things on their minds than a private fracas, but it was an unsettling beginning for a three-month tour."

The tour finally got under way: Seattle to Hawaii, then on to the Marshall and Mariana Islands, with stopovers in Guam, Saipan, and assorted airfields and submarine bases with military code names.

Above: Mrs. Meshbesher (Mary Boland) arrives in court to *Face the Music.* (NYPL)
Below: "Soft Lights and Sweet Music," courtesy of Hassard Short and Irving Berlin (NYPL)

Above: Hassard
Short, Moss's *other*
collaborator (NYPL)
Right: Marilyn Miller
as Joan Crawford and
Clifton Webb as Douglas
Fairbanks, Jr., contemplate
divorce and their billing
in the publicity in *As
Thousands Cheer.* (NYPL)
Below: Ethel Waters
delivers the weather report
in *As Thousands Cheer:*
There's going to be a
"Heat Wave." (NYPL)

Above: The Prince of Wales (Thomas Hamilton) gets an earful about his "goodwill tour" from Queen Mary (Helen Broderick) and King George (Leslie Adams). (NYPL)
Below: The chandeliers starred in *The Great Waltz* —"beautiful but dumb." (NYPL)

Above: Catherine Conn in Hollywood and high heels, long before Moss (NYPL)
Below: The spectacular opening of *Merrily We Roll Along* as Althea (Jessie Royce Landis, center) makes her entrance, all in white and hell-bent on revenge (NYPL)

THE THREE HACKETTS

Above: The show-biz family in MGM's *Broadway to Hollywood* (Frank Morgan, Jackie Cooper, and Alice Brady). Here they are the Hacketts. Elsewhere Moss called them the Adrians, the Strausses, or the Booths. (NYPL) *Right:* Moss's confidante with the "granite face"—*Show Boat*'s Edna Ferber (NYPL)

FRANCONIA
LIVERPOOL

Above and Right: "Merrily We Sail Along"—Cole Porter and Moss promoting the *Franconia* and *Jubilee* at the same time (WHITE STAR–CUNARD)

Above: Karen Kane (June Knight) and a prince (future film director Charles Walters) "Begin the Beguine" in *Jubilee*. (NYPL) *Below:* "If he's the man I *think* he is, God Save the Queen!"—as played by Mary Boland in *Jubilee* (NYPL)

Above: A Pulitzer Prize for *You Can't Take It With You*, with Josephine Hull (far right) as Penny Sycamore and (just to her right) Jess Barker as Tony Kirby in the New York production

Above: Boston's Grandpa Vanderhof (standing) in *You Can't Take It With You* was Priestly Morrison, Moss's very first director; third to his left is Glen Boles as Tony Kirby. (NYPL) *Left:* Glen Boles, Moss's juvenile lead, onstage and off (NYPL)

Above: They'd rather be right: Kaufman, Lorenz Hart, Moss, and Richard Rodgers (NYPL) *Right:* The original "Yankee Doodle Dandy," George M. Cohan, as FDR, a man he detested (NYPL) *Below:* The Alexandria Theatre was the star of *The Fabulous Invalid,* but only the title survived. (NYPL)

This theater of war was the real thing, utterly different from anything Moss had experienced visiting training camps for *Winged Victory.* Entertaining combatants—so many of them, so young—who might not be there tomorrow was not uplifting: it was a burden and often grueling. These were not audiences to be satisfied by G.I.s in drag lip-synching to the Andrews Sisters. Some were grateful for any diversion; others were indifferent or hostile to intrusions of make-believe that seemed to belittle the daily struggle for survival. Performances on hastily constructed wooden platforms bare to the elements were a far cry from Broadway, even with the portable flats the USO transported for them from camp to camp. The closest they came to glamour was the candles guttering in beer cans that served as footlights at night.

Their first performance was in March on Johnson Island, directly following Maurice Evans's celebrated *GI Hamlet,* and the audience reception noisily echoed Seattle. For luck Moss had borrowed a silk smoking jacket embroidered with seagulls that Clifton Webb had worn as Whiteside in the Chicago company of the play. The elegant garment inspired hoots of derision from servicemen wearing shorts, dog tags, and sweat.

Moss was always a mannered actor and Janet Fox, onstage that night as Miss Preen, remembered him as especially tense and theatrical. "Moss was, well, *swishy* in that jacket, and the boys took one look at him onstage and began to whistle and hoot. They didn't know the play, they didn't know Alexander Woollcott, and they didn't know Moss. All they saw was this rather affected man in a beard and a silk jacket covered with seagulls. The play couldn't continue. Finally, Moss got out of his prop wheelchair and walked to the edge of the stage and said, 'Look, we've come here to do our duty and your duty is to let us do it. Save your boos for the end. If you don't like it then—fine. But let us do the job we came for.' It quieted them down. They seemed to respect him for standing up to them and in the end they liked the play. Moss toned down his mannerisms after that."

He had at last defended himself and his actors, but it had taken being onstage to make him do it and he never seemed comfortable mingling with G.I.s and officers in mess halls or canteens. He suffered from heat and mud and could never get the hang of washing in a helmet. He wrote Beatrice Kaufman that he contracted an ear infection and tropical fungus along the way, and that his view of exotic South Pacific palms was mostly framed by the windows of sick bay.

There were diversions, like South Sea beaches. On one of them Moss posed in a tan and a loincloth for Hollywood photographer Jerome Zerbe, beachcombing with his camera. In Guam they crossed paths with Tyrone Power ("and what a charming fellow he is!" Moss wrote Clifton Webb).

Power was on active duty and clowned onstage with the cast for a memorable one-night stand. Gertrude Lawrence turned up in Hawaii "in full regalia," Moss said, "with an Admiral and a three-star General on either arm."

By April the company was billeted in Honolulu at the Moana Hotel, most of them grousing about boredom in the hotel bar when Armed Forces radio announced that FDR had died in Georgia. "The place fell silent," Janet Fox remembered. "No one spoke. Moss said not a word. We felt so far from home." Performances were suspended and when the war ended in Europe three weeks later, the cast was still drydocked in Hawaii. V-E Day brought little joy. The rest of the world celebrated victory over Hitler, but forces in the Pacific felt like forgotten men.

During the tour Moss and Sayers were clearly together in spite of Seattle, and Fox thought Sayers appeared "full of love. She had only come along because of Moss and she was the steadiest one in the company. But not the toughest. She didn't have the steel, or the cynicism maybe, that got the rest of us through it."

Sayers's memory of the tour was colored by Seattle and her dismay at Moss's reluctance to join the others on their bedside visits to military hospitals. "He told me, 'I have learned to respect my fellow man as never before,' but he had to be forced to pay respect to the wounded. Some of those boys were disfigured or dying and he was frightened and repelled," she remembered. "We all were, but we did it."

The tour ended on June 12 after fifty-eight straight hours in Air Force planes from Oahu to New York that Moss could arrange because of *Winged Victory*. He wrote Webb that the "wonderful" part of the tour was "to see how well simple men behave in the face of despair, monotony, and death." The "terrible" part he shrugged off as "physical discomfit [*sic*] and emotional wear-and-tear." There was, he said, "a kind of cock-eyed majesty" to war, but he found it "difficult to remain aloof and objective to the utter waste and horror."

He was, he admitted, "emotionally exhausted," but mentioned not a word to indicate that the relationship with Sayers was over. He did not mention her at all.

"*I* ended it," she remembered. "I realized I couldn't depend on Moss. A man I couldn't depend on, I couldn't respect. And one I couldn't respect, I couldn't love." Though she held him in affectionate regard, the end of their affair didn't disturb her much. Nor, she thought, did it disturb Moss.

20

A New Life

I'm not married. I don't have any children.
I'm going to wind up like Sophie Tucker singing
"Some of These Days" in a café in Montana.

KITTY CARLISLE

"The show was a roaring success," Moss reported on reaching New York, "and I was, in a quiet way, superb." Showing off his rakish-looking beard and tropical tan, he reunited with the Kaufmans, noting that Beatrice was still overweight and smoking too much. He justified his own several packs of cigarettes each day by invoking the ungallant but obvious: He was forty; Beatrice was fifty and suffering from high blood pressure that she promised to lower by spending a dull summer with relatives in Rochester.

With Beatrice gone and no new "Moss's girl" in sight, he renewed old acquaintances. He had drinks with Glen Boles, now an officer in the Navy. Clifton Webb wrote from Hollywood, reveling in his reviews for *Laura,* in which he played the Waldo P. Lydecker version of Woollcott, who had died in 1943. He wanted Moss to write a play for him now that he was a movie star. Moss was only too willing, he said, but confessed that of ideas he had "not the slightest."

To take the place of ideas he had a playscript before him, a second Hyman & Hart production he had agreed to direct just before leaving for the South Pacific. It was a psychological thriller by John Turney called *The Secret Room.* Now that the tour was over it seemed less like the sure-fire successor to *Night Must Fall* and *Angel Street* than it had back in February when Haila Stoddard, eager to become a producer, gave it to him.

The play concerned an Italian concert pianist (Leda) who has barely escaped the Nazis with her life. She is treated in America by a psycho-analyst who arranges a job for her as a mother's helper in the home of a colleague. When she discovers that her analyst has revealed her tortured case history to her employers, she murders him, an act witnessed—but not understood—by the children. She explains the murder as a game and hides the analyst's incriminating records in a "secret room" the children use for play. She becomes ever more delusional and, when the children's mother becomes pregnant, tries to kill her and kidnap her young charges before being thwarted and institutionalized.

The most curious element of the plot is the psychoanalyst who betrays his patient, driving her to murder, but this may have been what appealed to Moss about it. Kubie was widely assumed to gossip about his famous patients and the play may have seemed a way to send a mischievous message to him before they resumed the regular sessions that had been interrupted by Moss's wartime travels. Or maybe it was just that psychiatry was coming into its own as a staple in thrillers, as Hitchcock and Ben Hecht would prove the following year with *Spellbound*. Forbidden secrets and hidden motives were too ripely suggestive for melodrama to ignore.

To give *The Secret Room* box-office appeal, Moss cast Hollywood's Frances Dee, wife of Joel McCrae, as the young mother. As the disturbed concert pianist, he selected German actress Eleonora von Mendelssohn, named for her godmother, Eleonora Duse. Mendelssohn was a former Max Reinhardt actress and mistress, who was, herself, an accomplished pianist only recently escaped from the Nazis, bringing with her nothing more than dark beauty and a secret morphine addiction.

Moss was in trouble and knew it early on. He had been "trapped," he said, and found himself rewriting the play to make it stage-worthy. "It's not a distinguished play, or even a very good play," he said, and "to make it seem better than it is will take every bit of theatrical shrewdness I can lay my hands on." Dramatists' Guild or no Dramatists' Guild, he was determined to save the play from its author, "a completely infuriating person to work with."

Theatrical shrewdness couldn't save a play that needed more than craft. Moss asked Kaufman to come with him to tryouts in Boston, where audience reaction ranged from bewildered to angry. Quoting Steinbeck's *Of Mice and Men* to Kaufman (who had adapted it for the stage), Moss meekly repeated simpleminded Lenny's confession, "George, I did a bad thing."

George and the critics agreed when it opened at the Royale in New York on November 7. Lewis Nichols in the *Times* thought it "a most improbable melodrama"; Ward Morehouse in the *Sun* referred to "the usually perceptive Moss Hart" as if he were a missing person. Frances Dee later admitted she had never quite known what it was all about, and Eleonora von Mendelssohn, no less unhappy than the woman she portrayed onstage, committed suicide—though not, as far as anyone could tell, as a direct result of the reviews.

The Hyman & Hart fiasco eked out a meager twenty-one performances. Moss had had disappointments before, but this was truly the "complete defeat" the *Times* said it was, his first unqualified failure in the fifteen years since *Once in a Lifetime*. It sobered and depressed him and sharpened his ambition to prove himself with serious drama.

He was still rehearsing *The Secret Room* when Beatrice Kaufman died. She had returned from Rochester in August to celebrate V-J Day in Bucks County. Her health had not improved, which failed to inhibit her social schedule in New York. On October 6 she planned lunch with Bennett Cerf's wife, Phyllis, who found her in bed, moaning, "I'm so sick, I'm so sick." She died of a cerebral hemorrhage that afternoon.

Moss—openly bereft—delivered one of several eulogies at a service two days later. The mourners made a gathering not unlike the one she had introduced him to in her living room fifteen years earlier, including the cream of publishing and the theater and two former New York City mayors, Jimmy Walker and Fiorello La Guardia.

Moss's sense of personal loss was acute, but he was concerned about Kaufman, too. Inviting him to Boston to look in on *The Secret Room* shortly after the memorial service was as thoughtful as it was futile. Kaufman had a production of his own in rehearsal at the time of Beatrice's death, and when it, too, flopped, the onetime partners sold the Lyceum to the Shuberts, loosening another of their professional ties, this one at a profit.

They might better have held on to it, for the Lyceum's next attraction would be its all-time longest-running hit. Fortunately they shared in the success by remaining loyal investors in each other's productions and those of friends like Max Gordon, whose new comedy by Garson Kanin was scheduled to open at the Lyceum just after the New Year but was now in trouble.

Born Yesterday was a vehicle for Hollywood's Jean Arthur. It took Billie Dawn, a featherbrained ex–chorus girl, to Washington with the rich but "not couth" junk dealer who keeps her in negligees and furs. To occupy her while he bribes Congress to approve a crooked war-surplus scheme, he hires a young reporter to show her around the Capitol. Billie learns about democracy, falls in love with her tutor, and declares her own independence by undoing the junk dealer's plot.

It was *Pygmalion*-on-the-Potomac or "Miss Dawn Goes to Washington," an offbeat vehicle for Arthur, who radiated intelligence on-screen and was a surprise delight onstage as an empty-headed chorine. New Haven reviewers sang her praises, noting only a few problems with the third act, whereupon Arthur succumbed to the pathological skittishness that would soon remove her from public view altogether. She missed performances, citing mysterious complaints, and finally had herself hospitalized, leaving Kanin and Gordon with an inadequate understudy and no alternative but to recast.

Moss and Kaufman helped Kanin doctor his third act and sat in on auditions of a young comedienne suggested by Jerry and Eddie Chodorov's agent sister Belle, who had worked with Moss at Camp Greater Utopia back in the twenties. The actress—Judy Holliday—got the part. In the film of *Winged Victory* she had made almost no impression, but as Billie Dawn she became a star.

As a perennial bachelor with no domestic ties Moss was considered objective about women and was, curiously enough, becoming something of a romantic arbiter. Norman Krasna thought so during rehearsals for *Dear Ruth*. Invited for a weekend to Fairview Farm, Krasna brought along a woman he was seeing, whose potential as a Hollywood wife he asked Moss to vet. The woman was Kitty Carlisle on a first visit to Bucks County. Apart from socializing with Moss's friends (renewing acquaintance with Dora Sayers and, for the first and only time, meeting Beatrice Kaufman), Carlisle was glumly aware that Moss seemed indifferent to her. He told Krasna she was the wrong choice for him, adding, "You see Kitty dressed in black velvet, sweeping down the stairs in your house to greet Louis B. Mayer, and she's not that kind of girl at all."

The kind of girl she was had been born Catherine Conn in New Orleans in 1910. Her mother, Hortense Holtzman, was the daughter of Shreveport's first Jewish mayor and moved to New Orleans as a young woman to marry a doctor from Mississippi named Joseph Conn—pronounced Kahn.

Hortense played bridge and the violin. She saw to it that her only child studied piano and other graces that would "furnish [her] mind" and enable her to "Be gracious!" anywhere and on any occasion. Young Catherine was dark, pretty, had a gift for music, wore braces, and was utterly dominated by her mother's artistic and social pretensions, summed up in her dictum that in life one should always "Go to the top."

When Dr. Conn died in 1920, his widow sold the family house as soon as a buyer appeared and bundled herself and her daughter off to

New York and then to Europe. School in Switzerland would polish Catherine until the braces came off, at which time she could attract a suitable husband, preferably a prince. "To marry European royalty," Hortense believed, "was not nearly so difficult for a Jewish girl" as marrying into high Jewish society in America, where money married money. European royals were too sophisticated to be anti-Semitic, and if they were, a girl could always "pass." A taxi driver is said to have asked her, "Is your daughter Jewish?" to which Hortense replied, "She may be, but I'm not."

Catherine—Kitty to her classmates—had no particular sense of being Jewish. As an adolescent who had never seen the inside of a synagogue, she briefly considered becoming a nun while in school in Switzerland; she didn't attend her first Seder until her mid-twenties, when George Gershwin took her to one in New York.

To keep globe-trotting while Kitty acquired more social graces, Hortense latched onto gentlemen who could finance visits to the Pyramids and other symbols of grandeur to which she could relate. Kitty learned languages in summer hotels while dealing with porters and waiters, following her mother to the Villa d'Este or Venice or the south of France, staying in the cheapest rooms in the best hotels. She was both princess-in-training and slavey to a mother who could be peremptory and unpredictable. At times overprotective, Hortense often seemed hardly aware of the awkward teenager struggling with the luggage and running the errands. When she was displeased, her harshness turned to raging withdrawals. She locked her daughter out both physically and emotionally, causing her to be "desperately afraid of any kind of rupture." This fear, she told Marie Brenner, writing about her for *The New Yorker* in the nineties, "has affected every area of my life."

Hortense's whims of iron were both curse and blessing. They forced Kitty to conceal vulnerability beneath a mask of self-confidence while "always pushing our way into places where we didn't belong." She learned to cope with being poor among the rich and a nobody among somebodies; later she would make the most of being known among the well-known. She learned to use charm as defense and entrée, to be amusing in order "to turn away my mother's wrath." Her entire persona was "passing," not as Gentile, but as poised, self-assured, and gracious. She might easily have become as selfish and grasping as Hortense; instead, she grew compassionate. She knew what it was to live on the fringes.

She prided herself on being the most attentive of listeners, a companion for whom confrontation and complaint were anathema. This may have been superficial, but survival depended upon it. So did denial, which became a social strategy and a credo. "I believe in denial," she told Brenner. "Denial is a marvelous thing."

Formal schooling ended when Kitty was fourteen or fifteen. Thereafter she was tutored haphazardly, mostly in Paris, where she and her mother relocated after Switzerland. On sojourns to Rome she developed schoolgirl crushes, tried not to appear an adventuress, and discovered singing. In New Orleans as a child she had seen and thrilled to Enrico Caruso. In Rome as an adolescent she observed Arturo Toscanini through the maestro's daughters, who were classmates, one of whom would marry Vladimir Horowitz and become, like Kitty, a sort of Kubie in-law.

The Crash of 1929 ended a nomadic life that had depended on a strong dollar and the stock market acumen of Hortense and her various beaux. By now Kitty's desire to sing was serious. She had encounters both encouraging and not with celebrated singers and teachers and accepted with concealed disappointment ("Be gracious!") their verdict that her pleasant soprano was better suited to operetta than opera.

In London she enrolled at the Royal Academy of Dramatic Arts, which Hortense pronounced "a ghastly mistake" after seeing her daughter onstage. The Depression forced a return to America but no admissions of defeat. Hortense told Kitty, "You're not the prettiest girl I ever saw, and you're not the best singer I ever heard, and you're certainly not the best actress I ever hoped to see—but if we put them all together, we'll find the husband we're looking for on the stage."

Kitty obediently searched the New York telephone book for a stage name and, after considering Vere de Vere, settled on Carlisle. So did her mother, who became Hortense Carlisle, widow of the prominent New Orleans physician Dr. Joseph Carlisle.

Kitty auditioned for and won the title role in *Rio Rita* at the Capitol Theatre in 1932. This tab (for tabloid) version of Ziegfeld's 1927 musical hit was presented in movie houses between shows in New York on the so-called subway circuit before going on national tour. The show was truncated and miked (even in 1932), but led to a Broadway role in pants as Prince Orlovsky in *Champagne Sec,* the adaptation of *Die Fledermaus* directed by Monty Woolley in 1933.

Champagne Sec attracted Hollywood attention. Paramount Pictures may have thought of her as a younger, darker version of Jeanette MacDonald, whom they had just lost to MGM. They cast her in *Murder at the Vanities* singing "Cocktails for Two." That was followed by *She Loves Me Not* and *Here Is My Heart,* both starring Bing Crosby. In the first (a critic found her "entirely charming") she sang "Love in Bloom," which later became Jack Benny's theme song. In the second she played a poverty-stricken but haughty Russian exile and warbled "June in January."

Paramount was underwhelmed and loaned her to MGM and the Marx Brothers for *A Night at the Opera.* "They told me I was to wear beautiful clothes and sing Grand Opera!" she later complained to George Axelrod. "*You are slumming,* I told myself again and again! How was one to know the wretched thing would become a classic?" Wretched or not, it gave her another hit song as she and Allan Jones sang "Alone."

To her disappointment, her movie career never took hold. There was something too composed about her on-screen; her impressive technique left too little room for spontaneity and personality. She was too grown-up to be an ingenue and too staid to be a glamour girl; too inexperienced to challenge MacDonald and too old to worry Durbin.

With no movie offers after *A Night at the Opera,* she returned to New York. She donned a dirndl for *The White Horse Inn* and looked through a lorgnette in *Three Waltzes.* Her one contemporary outing, *Walk With Music,* was a quick flop despite songs by Hoagy Carmichael and Johnny Mercer.

She kept going. Radio paid the bills with shows like "The Coca-Cola Song Shop" and "The General Motors Concert Hour." Privately there were suitors of varying intensity, including George Gershwin, novelist Sinclair Lewis, a dashing Brazilian diplomat, and her agent, Arthur Lyons. She was later to claim that the affair with Lyons was all in his Russian-immigrant head and in gossip column items he planted that damaged her reputation. Louella Parsons, for example, told her readers that Kitty was "one swell girl" whose "romance with agent Arthur Lyons is coming along nicely." Kitty demanded no retractions and when Lyons bought her jewels, she kept them.

If Lyons's appeal was debatable, his utility was not. He represented not only Kitty, but also Benny, Hedy Lamarr, Ida Lupino, Fred MacMurray, and others. In 1940 he decided to become a film producer and make Kitty the movie star she'd always dreamed of being. She returned with him to Hollywood, where he took a duplex apartment at the Sunset Towers on Sunset Boulevard. He formed a company called Producing Artists, Inc., and Kitty was soon back before the cameras. At Universal she was reunited with her *Night at the Opera* costar Allan Jones in a second-half-of-the-double-bill mistake called *Larceny With Music* that even at only sixty-four minutes was enough to end any movie career, and did.

She kept going. During the war she sang "The Star-Spangled Banner" in stateside camp shows and launched the occasional battleship at the

Brooklyn Navy Yard. She acted in summer stock and ritzed-up mob-controlled nightclubs, including the Chez Paree in Chicago, where she made backstage friends with Sylvia Fine and her husband Danny Kaye before *Lady in the Dark*. As the war neared an end she tried to change her luck by becoming what her publicity handouts described as a "pink blonde."

She kept going. It was a small career, but one that demanded all the stamina and resilience she had needed to survive her mother. Her work was not negligible, but would have merited only a line or two in *Variety* if she had given up, and the career was, she admitted, "really on a down-swing" by the end of the war.

One of her most admirable qualities was her sense of proportion. She was realistic about her gifts and stature as a performer. Her manner could be as grand as her gowns, but was seldom self-aggrandizing. She had seen Caruso, after all, and met Toscanini and broken bread with Gershwin. She knew that her talent was of a different order from the really big ones that seemed to come from nowhere and without conscious effort like, well, the high pianissimos she was never able to master. "Dose high pianissimos," she was told by voice teacher Madame Schoen-René (who also trained Risë Stevens), "come only from *Gott!*"

She respected talent greater than her own and understood that art's sources were finally a mystery. This awareness would make her in later life a highly effective arts advocate for everything from symphonies to circuses. It made her marvel in her youth at the seemingly effortless outpourings of "genius" (she called it that) that she had observed in George Gershwin and admired—at a distance—in Moss. She always thought, in fact, that they resembled each other.

Looking back, Dora Sayers was convinced that Kitty had quietly set her cap for Moss as early as the Bucks County weekend with Norman Krasna. Certainly she was prepared to renounce spinsterhood for him when the two women had shared their taxi from the Algonquin just before the USO tour. After the tour they bumped into each other at Bonwit-Teller and Sayers confirmed the end of her relationship with Moss. She was, as a matter of curious fact, now seeing (and would soon marry) screen and stage actor Ralph Forbes, with whom Kitty herself had been involved.

Kitty may have been pursuing Moss, but not for want of anything better to do in her romantic life. By war's end she was seriously involved with Irwin Swann, an advertising executive and sometime publisher. Swann was the widower of Tamara, the singer who died in an airplane crash during a USO tour after winning fame by introducing Jerome Kern's "Smoke Gets in Your Eyes" in *Roberta*.

If Kitty had eyes for Moss, there remained the fact that he seemed hardly aware of her. Then in July, shortly before V-J Day, there was a final war bond rally at Madison Square Garden where Kitty performed with Kaye and others. Lillian Hellman invited participants to a party after the rally, but Kitty decided she was too tired to attend and joined Swann at his apartment for a late supper. Hortense telephoned to remind her of the Hellman party, adding, "Your hero is going to be there." Kitty changed her plans.

She arrived unescorted just as Moss pulled up in a taxi with Edna Ferber and attached herself to them as if they were a trio. Once inside she did what she did best: She sang and she listened. "I wanted to rivet his attention," she admitted. "I looked at him as if it were the most important question in the world and I said, 'Moss, tell me about your trip to the South Pacific.' I knew I had riveted his attention. I knew that he had looked at me for the first time with a seeing eye."

Moss invited her to lunch at "21" to continue the conversation, and then to Bucks County for the weekend. She began to look like another "Moss's girl" that summer, but then Beatrice Kaufman died and *The Secret Room* flopped and she had singing jobs that took her out of town. At the end of the year she returned from an engagement in Montreal to find that Moss and Phyllis Cerf were giving a New Year's Eve party and she had promised to celebrate with Irwin Swann. "He [Moss] was furious that I would not break the date," she said. He followed her to Chicago on her next job and to Miami on the next.

Moss was, after the failure of *The Secret Room,* working on a new play of his own, the dramatic one he was always promising to deliver. He went to California with Lazar on a preliminary casting trip while Kitty sang in nightclubs and made plans for summer stock. Moss telephoned her often from California, and in one such call seemed to have suggested marriage in an offhand manner that was short of a proposal. "He wasn't ardent enough," she decided, and told him she didn't want to discuss it. She hung up and wondered what on earth she had done and why.

Carlisle believed in denial, which presupposed something to deny. She could not pretend ignorance of rumors about Moss, no matter how great a catch he might be. He had been dependent on Beatrice, who did "everything for him," and his other relationships with women had been "stormy." She knew Sayers, of course, and was friendly with Paula Laurence and knew about Edith Atwater. There had been "a lot of speculation" about his sexuality "always sort of floating around," she admitted years later. "He was obviously talked about a great deal," and in all kinds of ways. "I used to hear 'Moss Hart is living on the twenty-sixth floor of the Waldorf and he is suicidal!' "

Moss discussed his analysis with her, but theoretically, never specifics or symptoms. Kitty listened sympathetically and "whatever his problems were, I didn't know. And I didn't ask. Because I didn't want him to disappear," she said, sounding as if she were talking about her mother and her lifelong fear of abandonment.

But she *did* ask. "I asked him point blank. I said, 'Have you ever been a practicing homosexual?' And he said there was nothing to it. 'Absolutely not.' He said there had been a couple of people who had made passes at him. And that was it. I never gave it another thought."

Of course some of the talk she had heard was accurate. He *had* been suicidal on the twenty-sixth floor of the Waldorf, or so he told Schary at the time, and there had been more than a couple of people and a couple of passes. It seems clear that his sexuality had never been rigidly this or that and that he functioned sexually at various times in various ways. He enjoyed sex as a pastime readily available to him, but it never ruled his life. He once defined sex for Sayers as "the most fun you could have without laughing." Guilt, shame, fear, or confusion may have warred with impulse from time to time and made life difficult for partners; nevertheless, what he longed for was not a physical relationship so much as a satisfying emotional one.

What he said or didn't say to Kitty was less important than his taking a step into one kind of commitment and away from another and doing so willingly. It happened simply enough. In late July 1946, when he was almost forty-two and she was two months shy of thirty-six, Kitty was appearing at the Bucks County Playhouse for two weeks in *Tonight or Never*. Moss insisted she stay at Fairview Farm and there he helped her learn her lines. She later related that at some point in giving cues he said to her, "You are The One, the Only One for me," and she answered, "I will trust my life to you."

If the words sound undramatic and lacking in passion for a love match, they are. In a perhaps unguarded moment (or perhaps not), Carlisle told Barbaralee Diamonstein, then interviewing her for an oral history that can be read but not published during her lifetime, that she had not been in love with Moss when they married. Nor, she believed, was he in love with her. It was the right step for the right people at the right time. It was suitable. The love part could come later.

Moss was never so open about his motivation. The heart has its reasons, we know, and the degree to which Kubie and analysis contributed

to the decision to marry was surely sizable. At over forty Moss had a sufficiently wide range of experience to make a choice that was both practical
and meaningful, maybe even profoundly so. As he wrote Ferber in the
thirties, and as his pillow talk with Boles confirmed into the forties, it was
vital to him finally to commit emotionally to *some*one. Conventional
marriage was the kind of commitment that—passionately romantic or
not—could be openly celebrated and embraced, could provide companionship, and might even bring him something he felt he'd never really
had—a family.

On August 10 they were married in a five-minute single-ring ceremony in New Hope, Pennsylvania, in the parlor of eighty-six-year-old
Justice of the Peace John Simon. Kitty wore a red-and-white print dress
and a red straw hat that was a prop from her play. Moss shaved off his
beard at last and looked "jittery," a reporter said.

They had invited no guests, but Bernie, Joe Hyman, and Hortense knew of their plans and came down from New York uninvited.
Kitty remembered, "I was so nervous I didn't think it was all that wonderful. My mother was looking to one side as if she were witnessing a taxi
accident."

Locals from New Hope threw rice, exciting Moss's Old English
sheepdog, who kept trying to shake hands with his master at the reception that followed at Fairview Farm. Jerry and Rhea Chodorov, Kaufman, and weekenders from New York houseguesting at Barley Sheaf
Farm toasted the newlyweds and their future.

At some point Moss wandered from the house down to the pool,
where some of Kaufman's weekend guests were taking the sun, young
men mostly from the theater. Playwright Arthur Laurents was among
them and recalled years later how disconcerting, even embarrassing, it
was when Moss suggested, so soon after his wedding, that they take off
their suits because there were "no girls around."

Still, at about the same time Moss was making his poolside suggestion, Kitty was at the house, startled to realize that her groom had not
planned on separate bedrooms or even separate beds. "I was so miserable,"
she said later, "I called my mother and said, 'You have to tell Moss, I can't
sleep in the same bed with him!' And she said, 'I don't think that is
my role.' "

They spent the rest of their honeymoon at the Bucks County Playhouse acting in *The Man Who Came to Dinner*. Moss again played Whiteside and Kitty played Maggie Cutler. It was a hit.

21

Family Values and
Other Dramas

*Success is like anesthesia. You can increase the dosage and
increase it and finally it doesn't work.*

MOSS HART

"We were astonished that Moss wanted to marry and father children,"
Irene Selznick remembered, speaking for the Hollywood and New York
wives who doted on Moss, "but if that's what he wanted, we were prepared to support him." Not without comment, however. Selznick noted,
"We had seen Moss from time to time with women—usually just *dogs*.
He could have had any girl in the world if he really wanted one, and we
all thought—Kitty *Carlisle*?!"

The new Mrs. Hart was fearful all over again of pushing in where
others thought she didn't belong. She shrewdly styled herself "the new
kid on the block" and left the spotlight to Moss. She suffered graciously
Kaufman's acerbic manner and his disconcerting habit of rolling his
eyes whenever Hortense entered the room. She pretended not to have
heard—and never forgot—Atwater's wisecrack that Moss had only married her because she could speak French to the headwaiter.

She found Irene Selznick's imperial certainties "a particular trial" and
regretted being jealous of William Paley's wife, Dorothy, but she was.
Both women were or soon would be divorced from their famous husbands, adding to the threat they posed, though their chic was intimidating
enough. The other Dorothy, the wife of Richard Rodgers, seemed
"bristly and judgmental," and she suspected Phyllis Cerf of trying to put
some kind of "whammy" on her by sheer force of personality. She
deferred to these women, acknowledged the luster they added to New

York social and cultural life, and absorbed their accents and style of dis-
course as she had once acquired languages in other foreign lands. They
became devoted friends in time. As Selznick put it, "we accepted Kitty
because Moss wanted us to, but she turned out to be an intelligent, honest, loving woman and we accepted her for herself."

Winning their approval was no mean victory, not made simpler by
Moss's habit of treating her as a decorative accessory to a life no less self-
indulgent than bachelorhood had been, though it was a role she eagerly
accepted. "I had wanted to marry him for so long and I thought he was a
genius and I was perfectly happy to live his life," she said. "I loved his life."

It would be two years before she gave a dinner party on her own.
Until then Moss organized and cast dinners as if they were little plays. He
told her whom to invite, what to wear, and often purchased her wardrobe
for her, giving rise to the still-current (unsubstantiated) rumor that he was
a secret cross-dresser. It wasn't Norman Krasna who had visualized her
coming down the staircase in a velvet gown to greet the guests: it was the
master of Fairview Farm himself.

"Moss dressed me up a lot," she admitted. "He used to take me to
John-Frederics to make me wonderful headdresses that I would wear at
night to go to the theater." But the man who installed Liza Elliott at *Allure*
could be as autocratic as any fashion doyenne. "I remember once I
ordered a coat and it was pearl gray and it had silver fox all the way around
the bottom," Kitty reported. "I tried it on for him and he said 'Honey,
where are you going to wear that? To a parade?' "

A parade was just what their married life resembled, a flashbulb-lit
procession of dinners, theater visits, parties, and fashionable entrances
through fashionable—but conventional—doorways. Moss's exuberant
delight in success looked as indulgently high-spirited as when he had
been a bachelor, but the spotlight focused less ambiguously on two than it
had on one. Marriage hinted at settling down and stability and social
orthodoxy and the suggestion was not illusory. The public Moss dazzled
much as he always had, but the private Moss was moving from the mischievous iconoclasm of his youth to a more relaxed complacency of middle age.

He spent his final days of bachelorhood writing a play about family, a
subject more central to his thinking than Irene Selznick had guessed.
Outwardly his family was the theater. Apart from his aunt Kate (the first
Catherine in his life) and his brother Bernie, he had embraced no other.
It is easy to overlook how often his plays are *about* families. Sometimes
they are biological, like the father and son of *No Retreat* recycled in *The
Great Waltz* or the Sycamores and Kirbys of *You Can't Take It With You.*

More often they are, as in his own life, families by choice: the vaudevillians of *Once in a Lifetime;* the idealistic and then bitter companions of *Merrily We Roll Along*; the family of the famous in *The Man Who Came to Dinner.*

Theater itself, of course, is a paradigm of family life. Its members are a clan of insiders defending against outsiders, their ties formed by aspiration and affinity rather than genes. Egos and rivalries abound; love is fleeting, intimacy illusory. But the feeling of belonging is not less than tribal. Moss was as secure in that family as anyone on Broadway, but he felt unsure about more conventional arrangements; the play he wrote now was about a family ending. He was contemplating marriage and, as he did so, writing a play about divorce.

Christopher Blake centered on the dilemma of a child who must choose which of his divorcing parents he will live with. Originally titled "The World of Christopher Blake," the thematic focus was the boy's fears of abandonment and his feelings of guilt over his parents' failure in marriage. It was the dramatic play Moss had long promised to write, an intimate three-character piece—mother, father, son—that grew to fifty-three characters on another revolving turntable.

If, in his apprenticeship, Moss announced himself a candidate for the laurels of Ibsen, Shaw, and O'Neill, he settled early for his name in lights. The approval he found then came from audiences applauding what came easily to him and it brought him identity and fortune. Kaufman, for all his wit and expertise, was a mentor attuned to the gallery, not the ages, and—for publication at least—denigrated art as pretentious. To this day his best-known witticism is the one about satire closing on Saturday night. The box office was the standard Moss trusted, though seldom without misgivings.

He was an astute and sensitive barometer of changes in the Broadway climate. The season of 1946 first saw O'Neill's *The Iceman Cometh* and Arthur Miller's *All My Sons*. Recent seasons had featured Thornton Wilder's *The Skin of Our Teeth,* Elmer Rice's *Dream Girl,* Arthur Laurents's *Home of the Brave,* and Tennessee Williams's *The Glass Menagerie*. Moss saw these works, took notes on them in journals he kept, and admired most of them. They demonstrated that "though it seems to be irritatingly backward and laggard, the Theater is constantly changing."

The postwar audience was changing, too, but on some deep and immutable level being Moss Hart was inseparable from Broadway success, whatever his creative aspirations might have been. *Christopher Blake* presented him with a familiar dilemma: he wanted it to go beyond the standards of Broadway, but it had to succeed there first. Truth and art were fine and all that, but they had to *play*.

He had a near-unique control over his work as a writer-director and producer. When he directed the plays of others he had a kind of perfect pitch. He brushed up lines here and there in *Junior Miss* and *Dear Ruth*, but added only enough stage business to liven or sharpen the authors' words. It was Kaufman's directing method—"faster, louder, funnier"— adding the warmth that was part of his personality. As his own director, however, Moss placed himself in a kind of double jeopardy and could go off-key. The knowing showman, full of theatrical shrewdness, vied with the aspiring writer, full of uncertainties, and the showman often won before the writer ever set down his pen.

Moss was never a contemplative writer. The spontaneity and theatricality were where the fun was and is in his best work. His ideas came full-blown, bursting from his upswings of mood. Like most people affected with mood disorders, he found the upswings "so useful," creatively productive moods that are, to quote Kay Redfield Jamison again, full of "elation and vitality" and therefore "difficult to give up."

Moss described exactly this swing from depression to creative elation just as he began work on *Christopher Blake.* "One feels dry, empty, utterly without impulse or idea, then suddenly, while reading the newspaper, riding in the subway, sitting in the tub, eating breakfast—there it is, the germ idea, the nucleus, the jumping-off place." Time and again ideas burst with such immediacy that setting them down was a matter of only days or weeks of exhilarating creativity.

This made for brilliant moments, but limited his craft. "I don't rewrite," he admitted. "I don't know what people mean by a 'first draft' of a play. In rehearsal, yes . . . One readjusts in rehearsal. But drafting a play. No. It must go along steadily, page by page, sometimes fast, sometimes slow—but as nearly as possible in its final form."

Moss's composition of *Christopher Blake* began during his courtship of Kitty. It almost certainly coincided with one of those seductive highs Jamison talks about. He wrote neatly in student composition books, his handwriting flowing rapidly across the pages. A pause to collect his thoughts or find a word is filled by his "now is the time for all good men" scribble—never more than half a page—until inspiration races forward again.

The play's basic setting was the judge's chambers next to an unseen courtroom, where twelve-year-old Christopher, a cadet at (again) Mapleton Military Academy, meets with his father and mother to weigh their reasons for divorce and decide between them. But the play needed more than soulful or searching conversations to hold an audience, even at a time when divorce was still a topic of social controversy. Moss chose to dramatize the boy's fear and confusion in fantasies, exactly as he had Liza Elliott's dreams in *Lady in the Dark*. The structure was so similar that, even without songs, dubbing the new play "Boy in the Dark" was inevitable.

Christopher's fantasies were written separately from the main text, like *Lady*'s little one-act operas. The play begins with one, outside the White House. Christopher, attended by the Joint Chiefs of Staff, is decorated by President Truman for devising both a Super Atomic Bomb that can destroy an entire hemisphere and a peace plan to end war forever. At the high point of the ceremony Christopher shoots himself in the heart to protest his parents' divorce. Their promise to reconsider comes too late. "Now he belongs to the ages!" the president intones, and we adjourn to the judge's chambers.

In a later fantasy Christopher is a flamboyant, world-famous impresario/playwright. Like the Ghost of Christmas-Future, he stages for his parents the wretched fate awaiting a child of divorce. In another fever-dream, he revenges himself as a rich South American playboy. His *real* parents, he announces vindictively, are the kindly couple from Buenos Aires who took him in and showered him with love and pesos when his mother and father abandoned him. He loved his natural parents once "and some thanks I got for it." Now "I hate you—I hate you both. I hope you die!" At another moment Christopher fantasizes the offstage court-room complete with towering judge's bench. There his anxiety itself is on trial and, as the child who was never truly wanted, *he* is guilty of the failed marriage.

The fantasies ballooned the cast to fifty-three headed by Shepperd Strudwick and Martha Sleeper as the parents and Richard Tyler, a fourteen-year-old Boy Scout and professional child actor, as the boy whose role kept him onstage for most of the evening. Harry Horner's ingenuity with a turntable made the fantasies flow in and out of expressionistic sets meant to illustrate the boy's plight.

Hyman & Hart investors included loyal supporters of Moss's debut as a serious dramatist, including Kaufman, Gordon, Jerry Chodorov, Lazar, and Kitty—taking her first flight as a theatrical angel. Joe Hyman soberly advised her that such investment was a risk, but the play hinted at no risk at all when they saw it with an invited audience on a bare stage in New York, just before leaving for out-of-town tryouts in late October. "It was gripping, and it was moving, and it was terribly tight," Kitty remembered. Boston was another matter. Horner's turntable malfunctioned in dress rehearsal, chewing and grinding into the floor of the stage. Moss rushed down the aisle and fell facedown on the carpet, moaning and pounding the floor with clenched fists. For his bride it was "a terrible moment. Terrible."

Technical problems were solved and were the least of it. "Moss had a kind of lavishness about him," Kitty recalled. "He lived like an Indian potentate and that's the way he did the theater. He had ordered the most overblown, over-lavish, over-everything sets. There was one set that needed a telephone booth and there were twelve eighteen-foot-tall telephone booths all lined in orange velvet, which were left out in the alley because there was no room for them in the theater."

When the play opened at the Music Box on November 30 it drew painfully mixed reviews. *Time* declared it his "finest and maturest play to date," both "perceptive and powerfully moving." But Stark Young in the *New Republic* thought it marred by the "pretension of profundity" that had made *Lady in the Dark* "tedious and banal." *The New Yorker* got personal. Not for the first time, wrote Wolcott Gibbs, alluding to Moss's own bent for self-dramatization, he had written "a character so much more sensitive and vulnerable than the average member of the race that normal experience . . . can strike him only as outrageous tragedy, accompanied by full-stage delusions of highly ornamental pathos."

Negative reviews on *The Secret Room* hadn't mattered much. It wasn't Moss's play and he had known it was poor. But this was different. He had genuinely tried to imbue his characters with sensitivity and depth, forsaking even a conventional happy ending. It was just that *Christopher Blake* was a chamber play masquerading as a circus, its writer sabotaged by the director-producer looking over his shoulder.

In spite of his oft-repeated claim that he was unaffected by reviews, Max Gordon saw him as "gulping praise with an addict's avidity, suffering deeply over adverse criticism and failure." When John Chapman in the *Daily News* headlined his review of *Christopher Blake* "The Curse of an Aching Hart," and sniffed that the play must have been written "with misty eyes and a great big lump in his throat," Moss's façade fell. He was wounded and lashed out in print and on the radio, defending himself against Chapman's "sloppy writing and bad jokes," accusing him of "nasty and gutter journalism" that Moss felt qualified to judge because, he added archly, "I read you every day, religiously." Chapman answered calmly, "I think you ought to cancel your subscription."

Christopher Blake struck weak chords with audiences but Warner Bros. saw enough movie potential in the subject to pay $305,000 for the film rights with escalation clauses that would have earned Moss even more if anyone had seen it. When it was filmed with Alexis Smith as *The Decision of Christopher Blake* two years later, hardly anyone did.

No other play Moss wrote has suffered time so poorly. When revived in New York in 1983, it was called "soap-opera-ish" and "terribly dated." One critic thought it "virtually a disservice to Hart's witty and urbane memory to exhume this plodding 1946 drama."

True enough, but it may have served a private, even therapeutic purpose when he wrote it, dramatizing personal fears about love and marriage, and childhood wounds. Moss certainly wasn't Christopher, but the boy's strong mother and weak, self-indulgent father were emotionally very like what Moss thought of Lillie and Barnett. The play was a chance to throw old baggage overboard and smooth the transit to his immediate future. He dedicated the play to Kitty, "with all my love."

Moss and Kitty went to Bucks County for their first Christmas together after Moss restaged and rewrote in a vain attempt to keep *Christopher Blake* running, but it didn't help much. The play limped to a close after 113 performances, just about the time life contributed a drama of its own. Kitty was pregnant.

After the holidays Moss and Kitty traveled to California, where Lazar had persuaded Darryl F. Zanuck that Moss was ripe to become the screenwriter Zanuck wanted him to be and that *Gentleman's Agreement*, Laura Z. Hobson's best-seller about anti-Semitism, was the property to prove it.

Arthur Laurents later described *Gentleman's Agreement* as "the movie that said you better be nice to a Jew because he might turn out to be a Gentile." Others quipped that he might turn out to be Gregory Peck. But in 1947, *Gentleman's Agreement* was almost universally admired as a brave and outspoken denunciation of bigotry. It told of a magazine writer who poses as a Jew in order to experience and expose anti-Semitism in America, including the kind that thrives on well-meant silence.

Silence was just what greeted the subject in Hollywood. It was the movie Hollywood didn't want to make or see made. The exception among the moguls was Zanuck, the only Gentile studio head (a Protestant from Nebraska), who was unimpressed by the argument that non-Jewish moviegoers wouldn't care, or its sleeping-dog corollary that they might care too much. Protesting anti-Semitism might seem "pushy" and stimulate more of the same. Not only that; Hobson's book raised the issue of anti-Semitism among Jews.

Zanuck believed that in the wake of the Holocaust an exposé of homegrown prejudice was timely and good box-office. When Jack

Warner formally assembled the Jewish patriarchs of the industry to dissuade Zanuck from making the picture, Zanuck sent an articulate stand-in to the meeting: Moss. The picture went forward.

Zanuck had been alert to the commercial possibilities of social issues at Warner Bros. in the late twenties and early thirties, where he made gangster and "forgotten man" Depression pictures, and he continued at 20th Century-Fox with others like *Grapes of Wrath*. That *Gentleman's Agreement* was a best-seller indicated a large audience receptive to the subject, though perhaps only a Gentile could have made it without awakening charges of self-interest or special pleading.

Zanuck further neutralized such charges by assigning non-Jewish Elia Kazan to direct. There would be Jews in the picture, to be sure, to authenticate the Jewish experience. Sam Jaffe, the ancient high priest of Shangri-La in *Lost Horizon*, played a nonbelieving scientist who proudly calls himself a Jew because the world "makes it so hard to be one." John Garfield (né Jules Garfinkle) would be Dave, the reporter's army buddy, victimized by housing discrimination after his return from the war. June Havoc (Hovick), the onetime "Baby June" sister of Gypsy Rose Lee, took the picture's least attractive role as Elaine Wales (née Estelle Walinsky), a secretary passing as Gentile whose internalized anti-Semitism leads her to detest those she calls "the kikey ones."

The romantic stars were non-Jews. Delicate Dorothy McGuire was Kathy, the well-bred WASP from Darien who is the reporter's love interest and conceives of the masquerade to begin with. Peck, in the first full rush of movie stardom, was Philip Schuyler Green, who becomes Phil Greenberg for his research. Peck guaranteed a popular audience, but his playing the role ironically stimulated rumors that circulate to this day that he, too, was Jewish and pretending not to be.

Finally, there was Moss, the epitome of Broadway sophistication, who would write the screenplay, adding the wit and polish of literary New York. Moss was a nonobservant Jew, but never unmindful of his heritage. "I am a racial Jew," he liked to say, and friends took care to avoid any reminders of anti-Semitism around him. Robert Sherwood's wife Madeleine told of spending a weekend in Bucks County in 1938 and seeing to it that her luggage was scraped clean of German steamship labels, even to the point of damaging the distinctive Vuitton pattern they'd been pasted onto. Some thought Kitty's being Jewish had been a decisive factor in their marriage.

Just after the New Year, Moss and Kitty were houseguests of the Zanucks in Palm Springs, where Moss and Zanuck outlined the script before Kazan arrived from New York. While dressing for a star-studded

Zanuck dinner on their first evening in the desert, Kitty fell suddenly ill. "My body," she recalled, "which had always been my instrument, my means of support, and my joy; which had always done my mind's bidding, was playing me false." She was miscarrying and "in a rage."

Moss was panicked. He called Hortense in New York, who advised him, "Don't be an ass; call an ambulance and get her to a hospital." The ambulance arrived too late to save the baby, but got Kitty to the hospital without embarrassing her in front of Joan Crawford, Merle Oberon, or the other guests. Even in a life-threatening medical emergency, appearances counted.

The patient later implied that losing her baby had been caused partly by her distress at returning to Hollywood, a place where she had failed and that she still viewed as hostile to her. By the time they had settled into Otto Preminger's house in Beverly Hills, Moss adopted the role with Kitty that Kubie usually played with him. He made her face her never deeply buried feelings of humiliation at having failed in Hollywood, and the resentments at Hortense that went with them.

"He tried to explain that I had created a great cloak labeled Kitty Carlisle, which I had wrapped around myself because I believed that the real me . . . Catherine Conn, was nobody," she wrote in her memoirs. Moss insisted she establish her independence from her past, her mother, and even from him. "You can't depend on wrapping yourself in another cloak labeled Mrs. Moss Hart."

Kitty might well have responded that he was the one wrapping her in his mantle, but his adamancy stiffened her spine. She was forced to mingle and be gracious to the very people she imagined had twice sent her packing. She formed her first real bonds with Irene Selznick (packing up her own life in Hollywood) and other powerful industry wives like Virginia Zanuck, Frances Goldwyn, and Miriam Schary, while Moss went to work.

Zanuck was unfazed by Moss's insecurity about screenwriting. He knew Moss's aptitude was for gregarious collaboration, not for isolated writing in the studios Moss liked to call "the most beautiful slave-quarters in the world."

Moss's not knowing what others meant by a "first draft" was genuine. His writing process included getting his script on its feet with actors and improving it in rehearsal, not when the cameras were turning and lenses and microphones and technicians were doing whatever they did and it was too late to move a speech or improve a joke or rip the whole thing apart and begin again.

He loved the social glamour and luxury of Hollywood, but was shrewdly self-aware in avoiding it. He understood that his keenest distinction to Hollywood was that he was not in or of it. He was desirable because unavailable. Hollywood, he told a reporter, was "a totalitarian town and a very corrupt town," where "everything is soft and luxurious and dangerous. Here people have cars and homes and swimming pools. Deep down they know they don't deserve them but they're damn glad to have them. To hold on to them, they knuckle under. This corrupts."

The judgment sounded harsh coming from a connoisseur of sybaritic delights, but he may have realized that the potentate trappings were his own cloak of disguise and might be, to use his word, corrupting. They certainly hadn't helped *Christopher Blake* and neither had his directing. As for directing in Hollywood, he laughed as he told a reporter, "Lord knows, they don't need me to direct just another movie."

This wasn't quite true. Zanuck was even then negotiating a contract for Moss to write and direct at Fox and was willing to tutor him in storytelling for the screen, if that was what it took. Moss didn't see drama through a lens, constantly moving, advancing, receding, isolating, or enlarging; he saw it in a fixed rectangle that he viewed over the heads of hushed patrons clutching playbills, not popcorn. Zanuck knew this and prepared long memos on screenwriting technique, emphasizing the need for "a sense of movement within the scenes themselves." His most pointed and just criticism of Moss's work described "feeling that I am sitting in the front row of the theater and seeing only what takes place within the proscenium arch." Finally he stressed "the people and their relationships with one another." Dialogue didn't matter, star turns didn't matter, and curtain lines and technique didn't matter. "Unless the audience is touched by what happens to these people," he said, "it will not be a good picture."

Moss worked diligently, though not at the studio. He spent several days on Preminger's terrace with Laura Z. Hobson discussing changes from novel to film and she was relieved to find him "as anxious as I that it be an honest picture, that it be strong and challenging—and a hit." His problem was that Hobson hadn't written any kind of dramatic climax that would work on-screen. With the practicality of the born collaborator, he asked her to come up with one now. He loaned her a portable typewriter and sent her to the desert to find or invent one.

Hobson recalled a minor paragraph in her book in which Kathy was at a dinner party when a guest told bigoted jokes about "kikes and coons." In the novel she reacts with appalled silence, but thinks that "Not making fusses was also part of the gentleman's agreement [but to] rise and leave the room was not in her knees and muscles; to call him to account was not in her vocal cords."

Hobson turned Kathy's thoughts into what amounted to a new chapter no reader but Moss would likely ever see. She set it in a restaurant, where Kathy meets Phil's Jewish army buddy Dave. She mentions the dinner party and the bigoted jokes. As she tells him of her revulsion, it dawns on her that she had done nothing about it. Dave tells her, "There's a funny kind of elation about socking back, Kathy. I learned that a long time ago; Phil's learned it." Kathy listens hard. "And me? I haven't?" she asks, getting the point that paves the way for reconciliation with Phil, from whom she is momentarily estranged.

Hobson finished her new chapter and delivered it to Moss in Beverly Hills. He cut and trimmed it, put it in screenplay form, and left it otherwise word-for-word intact. It became one of the most effective scenes in the picture. Elia Kazan, who began working on the picture when the script was finished, credited Moss with this scene, calling it "the critical find, the one that made the film work." Only later did he notice that it played out the major theme of the picture between the heroine and the hero's best friend rather than between the principals themselves. Still, it's a scene that sticks in memory.

If Moss never told Kazan he hadn't written the scene, he did tell Zanuck, who offered to pay Hobson for it. She declined payment, but later published what she had written on Moss's typewriter in the desert, establishing her claim of authorship.

There's another part of Hobson's scene that Moss retained for the screenplay, a bit of wisdom about marriage that Moss thought worth retaining verbatim. "A man wants his wife to be more than just a companion," Dave tells Kathy, "more than his beloved girl, more even than the mother of his children. He wants a sidekick, a buddy to go through the rough spots with—and she's got to feel the same things *are* the rough spots, or they're always out of line with each other." He adds, sounding very much like Moss to his own wife: "You're not cast in bronze, sweetie; you're nice and soft and pliable and you can do anything you have to do—or want to do with yourself."

Of Moss's personal contributions to *Gentleman's Agreement,* the most interesting was a speech he wrote for Peck that was a vernacular echo of Shylock's "doth not a Jew" speech in *Merchant of Venice.* The most obvious was the old joke he first related after his world cruise with Cole

Porter, the one about the fatuous lady passenger who asked him, "Do you get your ideas first and then write, or do you write first and then get your ideas?" In the movie he put it in the mouth of a matron from Darien, a joke that characterized a buttoned-down mind in a buttoned-down town.

Gentleman's Agreement was a major success for everyone involved, though Kazan later decided it was "patronizing." Today it seems unbearably talky, but the talk seemed literate and hard-hitting in 1947. Moss received his second Academy Award nomination for the screenplay, but lost to *Miracle on 34th Street.* Zanuck won the Oscar for Best Picture, Kazan took Best Director, and newcomer Celeste Holm, the Ado Annie of *Oklahoma!,* won Best Supporting Actress as the stylish magazine editor who pines for Phil and gracefully loses him to Kathy. "She won," Kazan said, "because she had Moss Hart's wittiest lines."

By the time she said them for the cameras, Moss and Kitty were safely back in New York. Kitty was pregnant again. So was Moss. Another new play was brewing.

22

Magic Time

The lampshades at the Ritz in that suite I always
have are made of human skin. Mine.

MOSS HART

Moss embraced any change that involved decorating. Kitty's pregnancy cued a family-style apartment before the baby's arrival in January, and he found one in the converted Pulitzer mansion at 11 East Seventy-third Street, a dwelling of considerable limestone magnificence. Kitty had her things moved there from her old flat in the Madison Hotel, having long ago relinquished her pied-à-terre in the Ritz Tower to Hortense at Hortense's request. Park Avenue admirably suited Hortense's self-image, as did Moss's calling her "Hydrangea," the French for which is *hortensia*. Kitty was surprised that Moss got on so well with her mother, perhaps unaware that he was even then writing "Hydrangea" into a play not as a flower or Park Avenue matron but as a "pirate," "hoodlum," and "Dead End Kid."

Marital harmony in the new apartment survived Moss's swatches, paint chips, and his notion that Kitty's grand piano was just the place to display his antique candelabra with their many crystal prisms. Kitty informed him that her piano was not a prop in his personal stage setting, but a necessary adjunct to the vocal career she hoped to resume after the baby was born.

There were new rules in Bucks County, too. There would be no more nude sunbathing parties with the boys around the pool. Kitty determined that, whatever people whispered about Moss's past, his present would be beyond reproach. Sexually ambiguous associates, personal or professional, would have to go, or so the rumor went. Kitty denied it decades later to *The New Yorker,* causing one exile from Moss's bachelor days to pop out of the closet and claim he had indeed been banished on

Kitty's orders. He went to Hollywood, he wrote Marie Brenner, where he became a successful film producer.

Fatherhood, not fraternity, was on Moss's mind, a prospect that both "delighted and scared" him, he told Brooks Atkinson. To put his estate in order he had Fairview Farm evaluated by the Actual Appraisal Company of New York City. They certified its replacement value as $73,329.06, a very large sum in 1947, though considerably less than Moss claimed to have invested in it and a cautionary note for an expectant family man not famous for his frugality.

Husband and wife performed again that summer at the Bucks County Playhouse in *The Man Who Came to Dinner*, Kitty as Lorraine Sheldon, Moss repeating his version of the title role. Audience laughter was so warm and welcoming it inspired a return to lighter fare than *Christopher Blake* and *Gentleman's Agreement*. Moss wrote Atkinson in late August that he had finally started work on a new play. It was, he said, a "Shavian comedy"—not that he meant to compare himself to "the Old Boy," he added modestly. He merely hoped to deal "in terms of pure comedy" with "a fairly important kind of human behaviour." In other words, he was writing a play about the theater.

He wrote quickly at first, an almost certain sign of a mood upswing, completing and dating the first act on his forty-third birthday, October 24, 1947. Three days later he and Kitty joined Kazan and Hobson for a private look at the answer print of *Gentleman's Agreement,* the version Zanuck had blessed for release. The screening was a respite for Kazan from rehearsals of Tennessee Williams's new play, *A Streetcar Named Desire*. Kazan's producer was Irene Selznick, now relocated to New York, where Moss served as her personal theatrical adviser and Irving Schneider oversaw her office, working for someone other than Moss for the first time in fifteen years.

Moss hosted the black-tie premiere party for *Gentleman's Agreement* the following evening, standing in for Zanuck, who remained in California ducking New York process servers. As if to underscore the picture's point about the subtler forms of anti-Semitism, the wife of actor Raymond *(Abe Lincoln in Illinois)* Massey praised John Garfield's performance as Dave, referring to him repeatedly as "Julie Garfinkle," a name Garfield hadn't used in years. Finally Hobson grew tired of correcting her and asked why she didn't just go all the way and call him Julie Jewboy.

A week later Moss was elected to the first of five terms as president of the Dramatists' Guild, following which he and Kitty retired to Bucks County to await the baby's delivery. At the last minute Moss panicked in the country and insisted they return to the city and its more advanced medical facilities.

It was just as well. Christopher, the baby named after a play, was delivered by cesarean section on January 14, 1948. He inherited the coloring of his mother and father and looked, Irene Selznick recalled, "like a Persian prince. And that's exactly the way Moss treated him as long as he didn't need a bottle or his diapers changed. *That* was somebody else's department."

The prince was introduced formally to the world six months later in Bucks County. Kitty was appearing in Terence Rattigan's O *Mistress Mine* at the Playhouse and Moss concocted a bogus tradition that theatrical children had to be presented to an audience during a Saturday matinee. Christopher gurgled through his first ovation. Friends from the old days were there including Woollcott's editor and literary executor, Joe Hennessey, visiting Bucks County with his wife. Moss turned to Helen Hennessey during the baby's presentation. Savoring the applause, he told her, "Now they won't be able to say I'm gay anymore." Fifty years later Mrs. Hennessey still wondered, "Why did it matter to him? Who cared?"

Bucks County was the center of social and family life. Fairview Farm had always been a costly hobby, overseen almost entirely by Charles the butler, whose forte was not economy, as the elegance of his wardrobe attested. This had its advantages. When Moss and Kitty returned to New York after their wedding they discovered that Moss's bachelor digs had been thoroughly burgled during their honeymoon. Moss left the next day for *Gentleman's Agreement* meetings in California, wearing a wardrobe borrowed from Charles, whose taste and size were so similar to Moss's that no one noticed.

When it came to nickels and dimes, Charles was the master of all Moss surveyed, and it was not in Moss's nature to spend time going over the books. The responsibilities of married life demanded that someone do so and Kitty took on the chore as if checking her mother's hotel bills in Biarritz. Her motive may have been revenge, for Charles regularly beat her at gin rummy. But a close look at the household accounts revealed he had been taking the words "cash flow" so literally that the flow sometimes reached the pockets of his creditors instead of Moss's. Disbursement duties were taken from him, though he remained majordomo in Bucks County until he died of tuberculosis shortly thereafter. "Conspicuous consumption," someone joked.

Meanwhile, Moss's work on his "Shavian comedy" was slowed by distractions of marriage, fatherhood, the Dramatists' Guild, and mood downswings that defeated comedy. Certainly nothing about the play's milieu was holding him back. He knew the theater better than any other arena of life and its characters, too—most of them as insecure, self-dramatizing, narcissistic, and charming as he. Still, progress was fitful.

In the middle of his doldrums, he wrote a short lampoon of the same backstage world for Beatrice Lillie, his creativity stimulated perhaps by the Academy Awards collected by *Gentleman's Agreement*. The sketch he wrote for Lillie provided a moment of hilarity in Arthur Schwartz and Howard Dietz's musical revue *Inside U.S.A.*—"Suggested by John Gunther's Famous Book," as a program note read. It was the last of seven revues from Schwartz and Dietz before television made variety shows so available in the living room that the revue format was no longer viable on Broadway. *Inside U.S.A.* starred Lillie and Jack Haley (with onetime "Moss's girl" Paula Laurence understudying Lillie), but prominent in the cast were Herb Shriner, Carl Reiner, and Lewis Nye, all soon to become household names on the small screen.

Inside U.S.A. was Moss's third time writing for Lillie and maybe his best. Called "Better Luck Next Time," his sketch cast Lillie as a gossipy backstage maid named Gladys, who dotes on superstition, numerology, and the Ouija board that keeps her in touch with John Wilkes Booth. Her relentlessly perky observation of dressing room omens and the disasters they portend drives the leading lady she works for round the bend on opening night. The critics pegged it "savagely written" and it is as funny today as it was in 1948.

Moss continued working at his full-length play, dedicating it to the infant Christopher and calling it *Light Up the Sky*. The title came from a fake quotation Moss, Kitty, and Jerry Chodorov invented in a capricious mood: "Mad, sire? Ah, yes—mad indeed, but observe how they do light up the sky." This was attributed to "Old Skroob" in *The Idle Jest,* which sounded like something one might have once read or heard about. "Skroob" was an anagram of homage to Atkinson.

Though Moss finished the first act in a little over three months, the balance of *Light Up the Sky* took him three times as long, until July 31, a year after he had begun. He wrote Atkinson that it had been "a little bastard to write," and making it seem "effortless and easy" had been "downright infuriating." He noted ruefully that "Playwrighting is the only craft I know that gets no easier or more expert with practice," an observation that would come to seem absurdly understated in the months ahead.

Light Up the Sky concerned a play in trouble out of town, exactly what it would become. Its characters were the Broadway insiders assembled in a suite at the Ritz-Carlton Hotel in Boston before and after their new play's first performance. They include the leading lady, oozing graciousness; the idealistic young playwright, new to the theater; the overemotional director who weeps at the mention of greasepaint; and the vulgarian producer and his ice-skater wife, dripping furs and jewels. Also on hand are drunken Shriners on convention; the leading lady's wisecracking, gin-rummy-playing mother; a drab secretary transcribing the star's memoirs; a veteran playwright who drops by to dispense wise advice as the author's mouthpiece; and a talking parrot to punctuate the lulls.

Act one, just before the performance, is aglow with the approach of what the director swooningly calls "magic time." Act two, just after the performance, resembles a street brawl as everyone blames everyone else for the audience's having stampeded the exits before the final curtain. In act three, just before dawn, the morning papers arrive with notices heralding "a dazzling experiment in modern stagecraft" that needs a little work from the young playwright who, repulsed by the thuggish and vituperative backbiting of his colleagues, has already beaten a hasty retreat back to the Midwest. He is retrieved from the airport in the nick of time to whip his "dazzling experiment" into a hit. Wised-up, he takes charge with fervor and grit as the curtain falls.

Moss scheduled a November 4 opening at the Royale in New York to follow October tryouts in New Haven and Boston. He cast strong actors rather than stars (he was the star): Virginia Field as leading lady Irene Livingston; Barry Nelson (from *Winged Victory*) as the idealistic young playwright, Peter Sloan; Phyllis Povah as the leading lady's mince-no-words mother Stella; Sam Levene as loudmouthed producer Sidney Black; Audrey Christie as his ice-skater wife; and Philip Ober as the older, wiser dramatist, Owen Turner. Moss boasted to a reporter of "the best all-around cast I've had in years. It's like walking into a cage of lions; they know every trick. I always feel that I should go to a rehearsal with a whip and a revolver and a chair."

They knew every trick except how to prevent New Haven and Boston audiences from mimicking the one in the play. Reaction was so negative that Moss quickly postponed the New York opening and announced an emergency detour to Philadelphia for two more weeks of road repairs he later admitted "Damn near killed me." It was the midnight reworking and daytime restaging of *Once in a Lifetime* all over again, except that Moss was twenty years older, with no collaborator and acting as his own director and producer. The economics of the theater in Sam Harris's day had permitted tryouts, retreat for overhaul, more tryouts, and more rewriting before even committing to a New York opening, but that day was long gone, as Moss was painfully aware. "It takes time," he wrote, "to unravel the mechanism of a play without destroying its overall structure, time to think through and select the good and bad of audience reaction and friendly advice, and more time still to reach a fresh viewpoint or attitude on the work to be done if one is not to make the same mistakes all over again."

But time was money and the advice was not all friendly. "The wrecking crew" of visitors to New Haven and Boston, less aglow with "magic time" than with Schadenfreude, spread the word back in New York that *Light Up the Sky* was in trouble. The news was made tastier by pretour publicity Moss had orchestrated about his dramatis personae. His winks to the wise and coy denials to the press had hinted broadly that the play's characters were based on real-life models with whom he had battled wits or crossed swords in the past. The Shriners carousing at the Ritz-Carlton duplicated the noisy buffoons who had bedeviled him during the tryouts of *Christopher Blake*. The two playwrights—young and sincere Peter Sloan and sleekly tuxedoed Owen Turner—were obvious stand-ins for Moss-then and Moss-now, with Turner even made president of the Dramatists' Guild, a post everyone in the theater knew Moss held. No fear of lawsuits there, but the demanding leading lady in the play was *not* Gertrude Lawrence, Moss announced, which meant, of course, that she was. Her vulgarian producer and his ice-skating wife were anyone *but* Billy Rose and his swimming-star wife Eleanor Holm, just as the "swish director" (as *Variety* called him) was not at all Guthrie McClintic, husband of Katharine Cornell, who was emphatically *not* the offstage great actress–wife he telephoned with teary-eyed reports from the front. The star's gin-playing mother Stella was said to be based on some well-known person's mother, and she was—Kitty's. She was just a carbon copy of Althea Royce's backstage mother in *Merrily We Roll Along,* but updated with a dash of undiluted "Hydrangea Carlisle."

Moss put the most confident face possible on his New Haven and Boston debacle as he labored around the clock to save a play that audiences found confused and unfunny. Life was imitating art with a vengeance. He told reporters that what was going on onstage was just a "Shavian trick" of making "my own particular comment on the world we live in, in terms of the world I know best, the theater, and in terms of laughter."

It was the laughter that was missing. Moss, pacing at the back of the theater, could not tell if his play's comments were striking home when all he heard was silence or coughs, but the signs weren't good. He insisted that the audience, conditioned by years of Kaufman & Hart comedies and the dazzle of *Lady in the Dark,* resisted his vision of "the world we live in." He later asserted, "What I was trying to do was a kind of allegory on the United Nations." He was using some "rather sleazy" characters to make the point that "people behave terribly well in terms of crises and that the minute the crisis is over they behave miserably." This was, in fact, the reverse of what the play seemed to be saying. There, the milk of human kindness flowed in good times and turned toxic at the first hint of trouble. Moss's confused statement of his theme perfectly suggests the muddle he was in out of town.

He forever after maintained that *Light Up the Sky* contained "some of my finest writing," but that "in the second act I was getting a helluva lot of things off my chest and [people in the audience] were furious. The second and third acts [were] deadly." He forgave the audience, concluding that "they were right in a sense: if you want to write that serious play, write it serious."

This explanation was largely face-saving, though Moss may have believed it and it has become part of Broadway lore that *Light Up the Sky* got written "down" for Broadway and was originally "more philosophical." No existing version of the play bears this out. The "allegory on the United Nations" that opened in New Haven and Boston contained hardly more than a single speech suggesting anything of the sort. "Look at the way governments behave the moment national sovereignty is touched," wise Owen Turner tells young Peter Sloan when the fur begins to fly, adding that "governments and people behave no better than our friends here." Manuscript allusions to a world beyond the theater are few and generic, unlike the zingers about Broadway, including the drunken chorus of "There's No Business Like Show Business" that brought down the second-act curtain in New Haven.

Moss's describing the play as an "allegory" was curious, as the play-within-the-play was an allegory and as such was meant to skewer intellectual pretension. "This play is either an allegory or the biggest joke ever played on the City of Boston," a theatergoer remarks about the play-within-the-play before realizing, "By God—they're *not* joking—it *is* an allegory!" and dashing for the exit. (Peter Sloan's play is never seen, but we learn that it begins in the ruins of Radio City just after the bomb has fallen and ends—somehow—at Mount Rushmore.) Scorn is heaped on highfalutin allegory by tell-it-like-it-is Stella, who pronounces it "the biggest bunch of crap ever put on any stage."

The one character in Moss's first version of the play capable of appreciating allegory was Winslow Lorrimer, a caricature of playwright-novelist Thornton Wilder. He was a third writer figure, a pedantic contrast to Sloan's naïveté and Turner's savvy, a "bird-like little man with a professorial manner and a scholarly approach to life, love, and letters," who chirped on about the glories of Greek drama—in Greek—and the intricacies of Gregorian chant.

Moss's portrait of Wilder was mean-spirited and cut in New Haven. In a play obsessed with crowd-pleasing on Broadway, ridiculing a writer widely admired for the simplicity of *Our Town* and the originality of *The Skin of Our Teeth* (both of them better plays than this one) was gratuitous at best and dangerous at worst. It called to mind the kind of authentic theatrical aspiration unlikely ever to occur to anyone in *Light Up the Sky* except to cue a wisecrack. Dropped, too, was the lounge act "Benny and Flo," whose sole function was to burlesque Irving Berlin's show-business anthem at the end of act two.

This too-easy mockery suggested that Moss's real purpose in *Light Up the Sky* was to settle scores with postwar Broadway, especially its theater parties and the hit or flop economics he had been burned by, as had everybody else. In Moss's first version of the play Turner explains he is in Boston with no play of his own because he has asked himself "Why bother?" He is fed up with audiences, kibitzers, "friends" telling him "it needs work," and the *New York Times,* always insisting on details of activities it can't wait to disparage in print. He is sick to death of the whole thing. Tempering his cynicism is young Sloan, a former truck driver with "the body and face of a good-humored longshoreman, and the brooding deep-set eyes of a poet." The two playwrights are the least convincing characters onstage, but they embody the real theme: do-or-die professionalism. "Don't let the word professional scare you," the older playwright tells the younger, "it doesn't mean commercial—it means just what it says—professional—and the only word I'd watch out for if I were you is amateur. As a playwright or anything else."

The one professional who might have helped was George Kaufman, but he was in no position to offer help of any kind. He was in New Haven and Boston at exactly the same time with a troubled show of his own (and Edna Ferber's) called *Bravo!,* a title that failed to prevent a chorus of pans when it opened in New York.

The brutal truth was that Moss's first version of *Light Up the Sky* was badly structured and a jumble of scattershot effects in its second and third acts. In the final version the action revolves around the play the characters are putting on, but in the version that New Haven saw and rejected, the dramatic fireworks had almost nothing to do with the play—*or the United Nations. They were ignited by the discovery that Irene's memoir-in-progress tattletales that Stella and a missionary were once marooned for ten days by a tropical storm, thus inspiring Somerset Maugham's tale of Sadie Thompson and the Reverend Davidson. These characters weren't in Boston to work on the play so much as on each other. It was a comedy of bad manners punctuated by backstage jokes and soured by cynicism. Most startlingly, the young playwright returns to work on his play in the New Haven version only when goaded into it by Stella and the producer's wife, who confront him with, "We're talking about money. Dough! M-O-N-E-Y! Is that clear enough?"

"No one ever mentioned it before!" he says, coming to his senses thanks to "the two great realists of our time." He notes that "we've been talking for hours about human decency and hope and faith and self-interest and God knows what else—but these ladies have calmly put their fingers on the only self-interest there is!" It's not a triumph of professionalism or even show-must-go-on pragmatism. It's a triumph of greed.

The cynicism in that first version hinted again at Moss's awareness of the limitations of success. Success was a theme in almost all of his plays, but there was a shadowy side to it from *No Retreat* forward. It could be a sham for boobs as in *Once in a Lifetime,* or corrupting as in *Merrily We Roll Along,* or hollow and lonely as in *Lady in the Dark.* If Moss originally intended an unvarnished portrait of the theater's mercenary vanities, the portrait was not one Mr. and Mrs. First Nighter wanted to see or sit through. They were the suckers who were paying for it.

It is hard to argue that Moss did not pander in ending the play on a winking note of uplift for Broadway, but harder still to expect anything else. This world and these people, however "sleazy" they might be, had excited his imagination as a child and directed almost all of his adult life. He was one of them. Magic time might be sham and delusion, but it was what he had wanted and accomplished and very nearly all that he knew, no matter how bitter he might be or become. His monsters were, as someone caustically pointed out, "*swell* monsters." But they *were* swell— in show-biz terms, anyway; they had color and humor and passion and sometimes talent to justify their vanity. Maybe they couldn't light up the sky but—for their author—they could still strike sparks.

Light Up the Sky arrived on Broadway as a moderate hit. It stayed for six months and 216 performances, which reassured those who wished it well and even those who wished it ill: if Moss Hart couldn't make it on Broadway with a comedy, who could? The novelty of its insider look at backstage life was soon undercut by *Kiss Me, Kate,* Cole Porter's sensational musical hit that exploded in December and went backstage with style and

"Why Can't You Behave?" Ironically, Moss had seen a run-through of *Kiss Me, Kate* as a favor to the producers and, in a rare whopper of commercial misjudgment, had advised them to abandon it as "a sure failure."

No one thought *Light Up the Sky* any kind of triumph, "Shavian" or otherwise. Billy Rose, stung by Moss's lampoon-producer Sidney Black, had threatened a defamation-of-character lawsuit but settled for finger wagging in a pun-laden newspaper column. Moss—"the id-kid" and "Poor little Laddy in the Dark!"—had written a "fast, funny and phony show." After taking exception to the portrait of himself (in which he found more than a little of Moss Hart, producer), Rose noted with justice and common sense that the out-of-town history of *Light Up the Sky* featured no "cheap tantrums" like those in the play, and the company "did what professionals in the theater have been doing since there was a theater," digging in like pros and proving the hollowness of a "moss-covered plot."

The coolest, faintest praise came from director-critic Harold Clurman, writing in *The New Republic*. "To categorize Moss Hart's latest play," he wrote, "one has simply to say that it is a hit. This is not an evasion for there is a distinction between the play that becomes a hit through accident and a play that is a hit by design, a special order of playwriting. If *Light Up the Sky* had not come off, it would have been described as a hit that failed—for its aim is pointed only at the bull's-eye. . . . There is so little actual human substance or particularization that one cannot speak seriously of any theme, thesis or point of view."

Moss and Kitty achieved a domestic and professional rhythm that allowed time for shuttling between East Seventy-third Street and Bucks County while Moss was preparing *Light Up the Sky*. New butler John and nursemaid Ruth took care of Christopher while his parents worked. Kitty returned to summer stock and Broadway, appearing to good notices in a short run of Benjamin Britten's *The Rape of Lucretia*. Money wasn't the point: she got by on an allowance from Moss of $500 a month, an amount determined by Phyllis Cerf, because that was what her husband gave *her*.

Turning his comedy into even a nervous hit had so exhausted Moss that he swore never again to direct a show he had also written. Like many vows, this one would be honored in the breach, but it accounts for his signing on as director of a musical that looked to have *hit* written all over it—by Irving Berlin and Robert E. Sherwood, who would be Moss's coproducers.

Berlin's *Annie Get Your Gun* was only now winding down after four years on Broadway, but he was sixty-one and eager to prove himself against

the musical hits that had followed *Annie,* including *Kiss Me, Kate* and—
opening in April—Rodgers and Hammerstein's *South Pacific.* Sherwood
had suggested the new musical to him, which they called *Miss Liberty.*
The playwright had spent much of the war in England and when he
sailed back to the United States after V-E Day, was struck by the effect the
Statue of Liberty had on troops returning home. He knew that the statue,
the gift of the French to the people of America, had remained mostly in
packing cases on the New York docks until Joseph Pulitzer, publisher of
the New York *World,* conducted a fund-raising drive to pay for its
pedestal in the harbor. In Sherwood's version this causes James Gordon
Bennett, publisher of the New York *Herald,* to declare a circulation war
against the *World.* Horace, a young photographer fired from the *Herald,*
sails to France to find the model for the statue and get his job back. He
discovers Monique Dupont, a girl who might have danced directly out of
a Toulouse-Lautrec lithograph, living under the bridges of Paris with her
salty grandmother. He falls in love and brings both of them back to New
York so Monique can be the toast of the town, "Miss Liberty."

Robert E. Sherwood was, next to Eugene O'Neill, the most respected,
most honored playwright in the American theater. Tall (six foot six or
seven) and lean, he had been a wit in good standing at the Algonquin
Round Table and an editor of the original *Vanity Fair* before becoming
a playwright. His work in the theater was unmatched for audience and
critical approval, including such diverse fare as *The Petrified Forest,* in
which Humphrey Bogart found the gangster template that would carry
him to movie stardom, and *Abe Lincoln in Illinois,* with which Raymond
Massey would be identified for the rest of his life and for which Sherwood won a Pulitzer Prize. His most glittering successes were with the
Lunts, beginning with the high comedy of *Reunion in Vienna* (which put a
psychiatrist on Broadway a decade before *Lady in the Dark* did) and continuing with the antiwar *Idiot's Delight* and the militantly antifascist *There
Shall Be No Night,* both of which also won Pulitzer Prizes. During the
war he wrote speeches for FDR and a book-length history, *Roosevelt and
Hopkins,* for which he won an unprecedented fourth Pulitzer. His shelf of
awards also included an Oscar for writing Sam Goldwyn's *The Best Years of
Our Lives.* Almost the only thing he had never written was a musical.

It took no time at all to discover that the model for the Statue of Liberty was well known as the sculptor Bartholdi's mother, making short
work of the photographer-model love story. The focus shifted to the
rivalry between the two publishers, which interested Sherwood more,
anyway. With no experience at musicals and the kind of grueling rewriting that almost always went with them, Sherwood—with his clutch of

Pulitzer Prizes and his Academy Award—was not prepared to meet the needs of performers, choreographers, orchestras, or, for that matter, Berlin or Hart. Additionally he was unwell, suffering from trigeminal neuralgia, better known as *tic douloureux,* a nerve ailment that caused excruciatingly painful spasms in his facial muscles. He sought relief by self-medicating with copious amounts of scotch.

When asked to rewrite, he pointed to the enormous advance sale encouraged by the names Berlin, Sherwood, and Hart, and clung to his conviction that a newspaper circulation war elevated a mere musical beyond the trivialities of boy meets girl. Berlin was not greatly concerned. He persuaded himself that his tuneful score, made up of nostalgic and patriotic numbers like "Let's Take an Old-Fashioned Walk," "(There's) Just One Way to Say I Love You," and a musical setting of Emma Lazarus's poem "Give Me Your Tired, Your Poor" would carry the show, spiced by Parisian cancans and "The Policeman's Ball" choreographed by the brilliant young Jerome Robbins. From anyone else this score might have seemed richly satisfying, but after *Annie Get Your Gun* it seemed second-rate. The songs revolved around an increasingly marginalized love story, played not by stars but by talented and likable performers unlikely to carry the show or sell tickets by themselves. Eddie Albert, not seen on the musical stage since 1938 in *The Boys From Syracuse,* was cast as Horace, and newcomer Allyn (later Allyn Ann) McLerie, who had scored as Amy in Frank Loesser's *Where's Charley?* the previous season, was cast as Monique.

Berlin relied on Moss to handle Sherwood, but Sherwood was no tyro Moss could rewrite at will and he was a full producing partner in a show that had been, after all, his idea. Moss's respect for him and the rules of the Dramatists' Guild precluded his taking up a blue pencil himself. By the time *Miss Liberty* opened in Philadelphia, prior to a ballyhooed Fourth of July opening in New York, Sherwood was either falling-down drunk or on his knees forcing his amorous attentions on Allyn McLerie's toes. Moss threw up his hands and declared, "There goes the ball game."

McLerie was married to lyricist-librettist Adolph Green at the time and was no stranger to out-of-town tribulations. She coolly judged that the backstage failings were not exclusively Sherwood's. "They were all geniuses and they were so happy about being geniuses that they didn't get down to brass tacks." She recalled asking Moss if she couldn't smile occasionally to lighten the "lugubrious" book. "Yes, dear. Do that," he replied. "But *where?*" she asked. "I don't know," he said. "You'll find a way."

In contrast to life on the road with *Light Up the Sky,* Philadelphia audiences and critics showered *Miss Liberty* with praise and applause. Reviews heralded a show that "soared high into the musical comedy stratosphere," full of "imagination, invention and taste," all of it "brilliantly staged" with "style and gaiety." The Philadelphia run was completely sold out.

Still, opening night in Philadelphia had been half an hour too long. Sherwood was mostly in a stupor, allowing Moss to take charge of the show, cutting and tightening it by twenty minutes over the next three days. He extended the Philadelphia tryout to accommodate further changes that were mostly futile or worse. He added lines that critics later would complain stood out in vulgar relief from Sherwood's more literary style. Lines like "Horace, look, there's the new Brooklyn Bridge!" called attention to Oliver Smith's scenery or, at Monique's entrance in a ballgown, "Horace . . . You certainly spent that money where it shows," underlined the opulence of Motley's costumes, but did little to solve the problems of the book. Zingers like "And if my granddaughter weren't here, I'd tell you what you could do with that bridge," earned open derision from the New York critics directed at the likeliest culprit—Moss.

Meanwhile, the other creative partners gave interviews denying that their relations were less harmonious than Berlin's score. Sherwood sobered up sufficiently to tell the *Post* that there was "never an argument or dispute, never anything that would be characterized as ill feelings," a sure sign to many that acrimony reigned, but it didn't. It had all been too laissez-faire from the beginning, when hard questions and harsh remedies might have been advanced but were lost in the glow of the partners' mutual admiration.

Miss Liberty arrived tardily on Broadway on July 15 with an advance sale of half a million dollars, only to be met by nearly unanimous critical frowns, led by Atkinson in the *Times*. "To come right out and say so in public," he wrote, "'Miss Liberty' is a disappointing musical comedy. It is built on an old-fashioned model and it is put together without sparkle or originality."

The only unqualified praise for *Miss Liberty* went to Jerome Robbins for his choreography. But dances could not save a show that felt retrograde and irrelevant when compared to *Kiss Me, Kate* and *South Pacific,* the classics selling out down the block or around the corner. *Miss Liberty* ran for 308 performances, almost one hundred more than *Light Up the Sky,* but failed to repay the investment of $215,000 that had been advanced equally by its three producing partners. An artistic failure, *Miss Liberty* was a financial flop, too. It was a disheartening and expensive end to a decade that had begun with the dazzle of *Lady in the Dark* and seemed to be ending in slow, steady decline.

23

The Climate of
Broadway

Is this all? Good as it is—is this all it's to be—
just more of the same? For the rest of the years?

MOSS HART

"You never learn anything from a hit." Moss still liked to say it. What he meant, according to Jerry Chodorov, his closest friend in the forties and fifties, was that the most you could learn from, say, *Oklahoma!* or *Carousel* was how to make a perfect musical from *Green Grow the Lilacs* or *Liliom,* and since that had already been done, there was little to learn.

Failure was the real teacher, Moss believed, and now he could consider himself a student in good standing. He had not written a solid success since *Winged Victory. Light Up the Sky* did well enough to ensure its future in dinner and community theater and *Miss Liberty* hung on for almost a year, thanks to its advance sale. Its lessons included some to be learned again: laurels of the past don't guarantee those of the future and collaboration demands complete candor. He would apply these lessons in a few years and make theatrical history; he would then forget them and reap a bitter harvest. For now, however, he was disheartened enough to turn away from a Broadway that was "suicidal economically" and flirt with a more personal kind of profligacy.

Kitty was pregnant again. The baby was expected in June, giving Moss an excuse to seek more spacious shelter than the flat on East Seventy-third Street. His search yielded space he snapped up on first viewing without bothering to consult the expectant mother. It was a duplex apartment at

1185 Park Avenue, only a dozen or so blocks from the tenement on East 105th Street in which he'd been born. Opulence spread over fifteen rooms (seventeen, if you counted the pantries), with a separate wing for the children (Irene Selznick's pragmatic suggestion); live-in quarters for an upstairs maid, a downstairs maid, a butler, a cook, and a governess; an office-study for Moss; and a foyer-solarium from which a magnificent curving staircase rose that was, Kitty noted when she finally saw it, "perfect for trailing black velvet."

Floating down the stairs in hostess gowns would have to wait. Kitty would be forty in September and, after a brief postholiday vacation in California, spent the next four months in bed to avoid any risk of a miscarriage. Moss, meanwhile, decorated. After Catherine Carlisle Hart was delivered by cesarean section in June 1950, Kitty was allowed to descend the sweeping staircase for a sightseeing tour of the drawing room with its velvet sofa and French antiques; the paneled library with its leather-bound, gold-stamped volumes; and Moss's office with the display of pipes arranged in a sunburst pattern, trellises on the walls for climbing plants, shoji screens, and the working fountain that gurgled and splashed at the flip of a switch.

Moss's desk would later be adorned with a bust of George Bernard Shaw, the "Old Boy" keeping an eye on his disciple's discipline, which was negligible just now, as Moss seemed to be avoiding the theater entirely. On the California vacation he celebrated with Dore Schary, who had ascended to the Rajah's throne at MGM, having wrested control from Louis B. Mayer. Moss hoped Schary would use his freshly minted power to buy *Light Up the Sky* or *Miss Liberty* for the movies, but Schary had other plans. He wanted Moss to come up with an original screen story about Hollywood "which [would] do away with misconceptions."

Schary had struggled to get more realistic pictures made at MGM, like *Battleground,* his gritty World War II drama, and John Huston's *The Asphalt Jungle.* He now wanted to provide a corrective to the familiar caricature of Lotus Land that Moss had helped popularize with *Once in a Lifetime.* "I am not blinding myself to the glitter and the sham and the high pressure and sycophancy that exists [*sic*] in the picture business," Schary wrote Moss after he and Kitty had returned to New York, "but you and I also know that much of this exists in the theater among these people who use their little talent to get to far places." Moss should depict Hollywood, Schary said, as a place and an industry with a "decent, hard working, respectable side."

They agreed that Moss would draw on George Kelly's *The Flattering Word* ("which we both know so well," Schary reminded him), the one-act that had already served as a springboard for *The Man Who Came to Dinner*. In Moss's MGM reworking of it—which he titled *These Pretty People*—it is no mere actor or flamboyant radio personality who arrives to disrupt life and values in the provinces, but an entire movie company, hell-bent on filming Middle America in all its homespun honesty. The locals resist the arrival of the tinseled hordes from Sodom and Gomorrah. After many city-mouse, country-mouse complications, a freshly scrubbed boy and gingham-clad girl teach a Lana Turner–like star (who slouches along Main Street in red sequins) and her monomaniacal producer, Dick Stover (his name suggests a famous Yalie, but he may stand in for Dore Schary or David Selznick), about the simple verities of life, including true love. It managed to patronize both Hollywood *and* Middle America.

Schary sighed with regret and reassigned the project. He ordered up changes "under the heading of radical" from producer Arthur Hornblow, Jr., another old chum from the coffee-shop days of the 1920s and, with his novelist wife, Leonora, close to Moss still. *These Pretty People* was never made, but *The Bad and the Beautiful* was, the answer to Schary's enthusiasm for a behind-the-scenes Hollywood story. Made by Vincente Minnelli, it featured Lana Turner as a movie star and Kirk Douglas as a Selznick-like producer who was based in the source material on none other than Jed Harris.

Decorating, fatherhood, the Dramatists' Guild, and sessions with Kubie filled the hours while MGM's money paid the bills. Moss was ubiquitous at rehearsals and tryouts of other writers and producers to whom he generously gave advice and never asked for credit. He was regarded as a patron saint of young playwrights after helping to establish the New Dramatists' Guild for them within the protection of the larger guild over which he presided, and could often be found in New Haven, Boston, Philadelphia, or Chicago offering advice to shows in trouble. His rule was to be briskly frank—even brutal—when there was time to rescue an ailing show and to gush with cheerful insincerity when there wasn't. He was unstinting with suggestions for works-in-progress but wrote not a single word of his own for the theater for more than two years following *Light Up the Sky*.

Finally, in March 1951, he began and abandoned a comedy he called "The Nature of the Beast." He completed only one scene that, more than two years later, would be telecast "live" on the Ford Foundation's prestigious show *Omnibus*. Exposing it to television was the result of "the spinster quality I have about not wasting anything," he explained. "I'm a professional writer and I have to earn my living by the pen, and so I leave nothing in the trunk."

"The Nature of the Beast" took place in the hospital room of a celebrated writer (played by Mel Ferrer) suffering from amnesia after being hit by a Madison Avenue bus. His nurse (Audrey Christie from *Light Up the Sky*) intuits he's faking and confronts him. He admits it, but justifies his deception as a perfectly rational response to a midlife crisis: "Is this all? Good as it is—is this *all* it's to be—just more of the same? For the rest of the years?" He loves his wife and two children, but faking amnesia might allow him "a little time to . . . discover where *I* disappeared to, while all this was going on."

This opening suggested a quest into areas of marriage, fatherhood, and self. His abandoning it suggests that asking questions was more important than answering them. Or easier. Or maybe he chose to keep his answers to himself. Certainly he was wily enough to defeat speculation about autobiographical intentions. On the air with *Omnibus* host Alistair Cooke, he evaded probes by airily quoting Ibsen to the effect that the hardest part of playwriting was getting the actors on- and offstage.

Getting himself back onstage seemed of little urgency. Hollywood again rescued him from inactivity and insolvency, though not with *Light Up the Sky* or *Miss Liberty*, neither of which sold to the movies, unlike every full-length work he had written since *Once in a Lifetime,* except for *The Fabulous Invalid.* Even *I'd Rather Be Right* had turned up on-screen as part of *Yankee Doodle Dandy.* But if Hollywood wouldn't buy Moss's work any longer, it would buy *him,* as Schary had demonstrated. Zanuck had temporarily given up his efforts to make Moss a movie director but the door at 20th Century-Fox remained open. Similarly, Moss's relations with Sam Goldwyn had been carefully tended ever since *The Masquerader.*

In early 1951 Goldwyn asked Moss if he had any ideas for a writer for *Hans Christian Andersen.* Moss (who once exclaimed to himself within hearing of a reporter, "Moss, darling, you're the Hans Christian Andersen of your day.") modestly told Goldwyn that not a soul came to mind, but he'd think about it. Irving Lazar thought of Moss and worked out the deal with Goldwyn for the same $75,000 that Zanuck had paid him for *Gentleman's Agreement* and sweetened the deal with 5 percent of the profits.

Goldwyn had been working on the story of Denmark's most famous storyteller off and on since 1934. From the start ballet had seemed the way to pictorialize Andersen's fairy tales, and Goldwyn had hired writers in the thirties like Allan Scott (who had worked on the Astaire-Rogers pictures) and Jo Swerling (long before *Guys and Dolls*). In 1939 he and director William Wyler had scheduled tests with ballerina Vera Zorina and had hopes of persuading young James Stewart to play Andersen.

By 1948, however, his long-standing plan to use "The Red Shoes" as the story's centerpiece ballet was preempted by the worldwide success of the English film of that name. *The Red Shoes* only whetted Goldwyn's appetite for his Andersen picture, whose raison d'être now was Danny Kaye, who had been under contract to Goldwyn since *Lady in the Dark* and had become a major movie star. After the war, Goldwyn had hired a series of writers to fashion a script for Kaye, including Robert Ardrey, Don Hartman, Mel Shavelson, and Samuel Taylor. Still dissatisfied, he approached Robert Sherwood, Paul Osborn, and Garson Kanin and Ruth Gordon before getting around to Moss, who had made Kaye famous in the first place.

Kaye's broad and uninhibited comic style appealed strongly to children, as he would later prove in working for UNICEF. Taming his manic energy on-screen and making him credible as a gentle Dane was a challenge, but not one from which Goldwyn shrank. He snapped up Moira Shearer from *The Red Shoes* to be Kaye's costar, asked Rodgers and Hammerstein to write the songs, and insisted on George Balanchine to choreograph an as-yet-undecided Andersen story to take the place of "The Red Shoes."

Moss pointed out that since so little was known of Andersen the man, "his adventures in Copenhagen should have the same fairy-tale unreality of the man himself." A straight biography wouldn't do, but a fairy tale about a teller of fairy tales might work, some simple story within which Kaye could spin tales like "The Emperor's New Clothes," "The Ugly Duckling," and so on, some of them set to music. Rodgers and Hammerstein said they loved the idea but were immersed in their backstage musical *Me and Juliet*. Frank Loesser, whose *Guys and Dolls* was a sensation on Broadway (and would be filmed by Goldwyn), was signed to compose the score.

Balanchine became unavailable and Roland Petit flew from Paris to do the choreography. After almost a year of delays and Goldwyn's nagging her about her thinness, Moira Shearer bowed out of the project claiming pregnancy and *tour jetée*'d to MGM to do a ballet picture there. Roland Petit cried "Voilà!" and produced his première danseuse (and future wife) Renée Jeanmaire. Goldwyn dubbed her "Zizi" Jeanmaire (he had, after all, produced Zola's *Nana*) and would present her on-screen with an odd title card "introducing Jeanmaire, the famous French ballerina." Using "The Little Mermaid" for the big ballet had been Shearer's idea, but was good enough to keep without her.

Moss and Kitty flew to California with the children at the end of June, moving into 522 Ocean Front in Santa Monica, just down the sand from the Goldwyns' beach house. They spent time with Danny and

Sylvia Kaye and other Hollywood friends like George Cukor, the Horn-blows, the Ira Gershwins, and the Scharys. Their stay occasioned a possibly apocryphal Goldwynism. The producer is said to have told Sylvia Kaye, "I ran into Moss Hart the other day." "Where?" she asked. "At my house," he replied.

Moss quickly set down his fairy tale about a cobbler who told stories with "the unswerving belief of a child that all things are possible." Andersen is hounded from the village of Odense by a schoolmaster who objects to Andersen's filling the children's heads with dreams and goes to Copenhagen to see the city and the king. There he becomes enamored of a beautiful ballerina (Jeanmaire) and writes "The Little Mermaid" for her, which she dances for the king, though we see it only through Andersen's imagination. Gratified though unrequited in love (the ballerina is secretly married to her handsome, tyrannical ballet-master played by Farley Granger), he returns to Odense to spin stories for the ages.

Moss's script had charm and a tenderness that fatherhood seemed to explain. He found it easy to tailor a part for Danny Kaye, with whom the picture was a happy reunion. Dream sequences made Andersen's imagination visible, though Moss's originals were more sinister than what got filmed, featuring ballerinas who turned into icebergs or pillars of fire. He included a younger-man/older-man relationship that was, by now, something of a Moss signature, but here in reverse, with a boy acting as the voice of reason to the childlike Andersen. The most innovative aspect of Moss's script was Andersen's arrival in Copenhagen, which he wrote as a musical sequence to be sung through in mini-opera fashion before Frank Loesser had even been signed or written the lilting "Wonderful, Wonderful Copenhagen." Loesser's score would be the picture's greatest distinction with "Anywhere I Wander," "No Two People (Have Ever Been So in Love)," "Inch Worm," "Thumbelina," and "I'm Hans Christian Andersen."

The picture offered another reunion for Moss, one with the testy schoolmaster. The part was played by John Brown, who once followed Moss from Vermont to New York to become the only Gentile member of the Brooklyn Jewish Center. Brown was now well known to radio audiences as Digger O'Dell ("the friendly undertaker") on *The Life of Riley* and as Thorny on *The Adventures of Ozzie and Harriet*. He was, like Moss, married with children. Their crossing paths again via nineteenth-century Denmark was uneventful. "He seemed not to know me," Brown told a friend.

In the end Moss's 5 percent of the profits proved meaningful, as the picture made money, in spite of a then very high cost of $3 million. He hadn't cared deeply about the project, in spite of his fondness for Danny Kaye and Goldwyn. He allowed film director Charles Vidor to hire a writer named Lewis Meltzer to do the necessary cutting and rewrites before shooting began, though Goldwyn was scrupulous in asking Moss to approve every change.

The bitter pill Moss was forced to swallow was the "story by" credit that went to a writer he had never heard of. Miles Connolly had worked for Goldwyn as a screenwriter in 1938 and suggested then that the picture take the form of a fairy tale with a ballet and, in 1952, had the documents to prove it. Moss admitted reading the Sam Taylor and Jo Swerling scripts, but was unable to prove he hadn't read Connolly's. The Writers' Guild saw things Connolly's way and ordered credit for him on-screen, though not on posters or billboards. Lazar drew himself up to his full height of five feet three inches and thundered that it was "outrageous."

Moss was willing to leave the details of *Hans Christian Andersen* to others because, after almost three years, he found himself excited by a subject for the theater. It was a recently published English novel by Edgar Mittelholzer called *Shadows Move Among Them* and was radically different from anything he had ever turned his hand to.

The novel is set on the edge of the jungle in British Guiana, in and around the wooden house and church of an English missionary family. Moss had been enthralled by the tropics since he first sailed through the Panama Canal in the early thirties, but even without the setting he would have been attracted to the novel's most dramatic character, a playwright undergoing a breakdown.

The community between river and jungle is overseen by the Reverend Harmston, an unorthodox missionary for whom true religion is self-realization—"for in this life is the Kingdom of Heaven." He is a patriarch who rules his wife, two daughters, two sons, and his flock of native "children" with a stern but compassionate hand, blessing casual nudity and free love with no racial barriers. He metes out corporal punishment for transgressions of rules that seem arbitrary but are designed to bring order to chaos and create a "civilization without cynicism." He is philosopher-patriarch, magician, healer, and disciplinarian, and may also be Kubie.

The shadows of the title are those of the past haunting the present. The book is rich with contrasts of the primeval and the civilized, of flesh and the spirit, with allusions to *Hamlet,* the Bible, and especially to *The*

Tempest. Harmston is a Prospero figure and knows it. A misshapen native is nicknamed Caliban. Harmston's daughter Mabel suggests Miranda, while teenaged Olivia is a kind of Ariel.

Playwright Gregory Hawke comes to this isolated world, suffering from hallucinations that suggest he may have murdered his wife. Nineteen-year-old Mabel falls in love with him and leads him out of his personal shadows so he can "confess" the truth of his past, rendering it harmless. An uncertain but hopeful future beckons at the end.

The dramatic possibilities of the novel were clear—the exotic background, the unorthodox and theatrical lifestyle, a single set—and the pitfalls were just as obvious. Moss had never dealt with such complexities of character and theme. Here at last was the serious play he had always intended to write, one with a built-in, barely visible collaborator in the original author, and richly atmospheric, psychologically complex material that might allow him to compete with Tennessee Williams, Arthur Miller, Arthur Laurents, and others he admired, whose work he was convinced would be more lasting than his own. The novel "represented a challenge to me as a writer; a departure from anything I had ever done before; in style, in content, in my whole creative personality."

He acquired dramatic rights to the novel and began corresponding with Mittelholzer in England while still working on *Hans Christian Andersen.* In another of his astonishing bursts of creative energy, he completed a first draft of the play by November and titled it *The Climate of Eden.*

Apart from the title change and simplifying and compressing three hundred–plus pages into a playable three hours, he hewed to the novel with scrupulous fidelity. He made so few changes that those he did make were notable.

He moved the action from 1937 to the present to remove any political dimension from the story. This simplified Hawke but diminished him, too. In the novel he arrives after fighting on the Loyalist side in the Spanish Civil War. Eliminating that also removed the vaguely heroic air that made Gregory more than the sum of his demons.

Moss put distance between the character and himself by omitting any mention of Gregory's being a playwright, making him instead a novelist who paints on the side. Most strikingly, Moss removed the novel's indications that Gregory was bisexual. "There was a space in him waiting to be filled with someone's pity and love," Mittelholzer writes, "but if he found that someone . . . he would have to turn away from him or her with a shudder and a silent whimper."

Redefining Gregory's sexual nature made his apparent fear of women seem just melodramatic, heightening the possibility that he murdered his wife. He finally reveals in book and play that she committed suicide to escape the pain of his uncontrollable sexual promiscuity. In the book he confesses, "I've been promiscuous from my adolescence," hinting at male and female lovers. The play focuses on the more sensational and suspenseful "murder" theme, the first act ending with what seems to be Gregory's attempt to murder Mabel, later explained as a hallucinatory episode.

Both book and play trace two life passages. First, Gregory's: "What secret do you all possess?" he asks Mabel. "We love," she replies, granting him peace and redemption. The other is fourteen-year-old Olivia's transition from girlhood to womanhood. She is Ariel, creating mischief and magic, and Moss allows her to begin and end the play, perhaps a tribute to his daughter, Cathy, to whom he dedicated it.

Moss celebrated Christmas in Bucks County with Kitty and the children. He stage-managed decorations and festivities, having staked out Christmas as his preserve ever since trimming his first Bucks County tree in the thirties. Kitty was assigned the more mundane chores of coloring and hiding Easter eggs in the spring. Some of the Harts' Jewish friends looked askance at Moss's delight in Christmas and Easter, which bothered him not at all as they had no religious overtones to him. When Christopher reached adolescence Moss would not allow him to be Bar Mitzvah'd, maintaining it was a mistake to indulge in a ritual with no direct bearing on their family life, which remained unobservant. A Bar Mitzvah would just confuse the boy, he said, and that was that.

In late March Moss and Kitty flew to California courtesy of Goldwyn. Moss looked at the footage on *Hans Christian Andersen,* which had started shooting in January, and tried to write the picture's foreword informing the audience that what followed was not a biography, but a fairy tale about Andersen. Goldwyn insisted on seventy-five words or less, a limitation Moss couldn't meet. Frank Loesser took a stab, joking that it was the biggest project since Boulder Dam, and in the end Goldwyn wrote the opening statement himself with simplicity and grace.

After a month as houseguests of the Goldwyns, Moss and Kitty returned to New York, where Moss made plans for a November opening of *The Climate of Eden* at the Martin Beck Theatre. It would be a Hyman & Hart Production with Moss directing, despite his vow after *Light Up the Sky* never again to write and stage the same work.

As Moss prepared, Kitty rehearsed for a Cape Cod summer stock production of *Lady in the Dark*. She had never seen the original with Gertrude Lawrence, she later admitted to an interviewer, but Moss made up for that by coaching her through the play line by line and choosing her costumes and supervising the fittings. To ensure that "The Saga of Jenny" would be as effective as ever, he persuaded Lawrence, then on Broadway in *The King and I,* to demonstrate the bumps and grinds that had stopped the show in 1941. Lawrence wasn't much worried about Kitty erasing memories of her own legendary performance, for the "musical play" was being presented on the Cape by her husband, Richard Aldrich, in a minimalist production with a single piano instead of an orchestra. Kitty received superior notices, anyway, including an impressive one from the dean of Boston reviewers, Elliot Norton, invited by Moss. The review would aid him, he hoped, in finding a London producer to mount the show there. Starring Kitty.

They sailed to England immediately after Cape Cod so Moss could cast key roles in *The Climate of Eden* with English actors and set up *Lady in the Dark.* As it happened, *Lady in the Dark* would not be performed in London until 1997, fifty-six years after its Broadway premiere, when the Royal National Theatre did it as a period piece. It garnered respectful but mixed reviews.

Casting for *The Climate of Eden* seemed at first to go little better. Moss was less well known in London than in New York and many actors were cool to crossing the ocean for a no-star drama from an author-director best known for comedies and musicals. He saw seven hundred actors in ten days in auditions arranged by London's formidable impresario, Hugh "Binkie" Beaumont. Veteran character actress Isobel Elsom was cast as Mrs. Harmston and a youngster named Penelope Munday, who had been seen in Christopher Fry's *The Lady's Not for Burning,* displayed the fire and vulnerability to play Olivia. Moss was uneasy with his Gregory Hawke, a brooding, handsome young actor named Lee Montague who could convey neurotic melancholy but seemed to lack the spark of personality or sex appeal that would make the love affair with Mabel credible.

Mabel was his most serious concern. He needed a beautiful and sensitive young actress to supply the warmth he feared his leading man could not. He could find no one in London. Finally, Binkie Beaumont suggested he try the Birmingham Repertory Company. There he was struck by the look of a beautiful young woman accompanying a friend to the readings and insisted that she, too, audition. She was twenty-one, had been raised in India, and glowed with the luminous presence he had almost despaired of finding. Her name was Rosemary Harris. He persuaded her to come to America and play Mabel, and she has been mostly in America and mostly incandescent ever since.

Moss and Kitty returned to New York and the heat of the 1952 presidential race between Eisenhower and Stevenson, with Election Day scheduled for the same week as the opening of the play. Back on home ground Moss cast the smaller parts, including a dozen African American actors to play the natives in Harmston's care and, as one of the reverend's natural sons, a boy named Ken Walken, later better known as Christopher.

One young actor cast from open auditions was twenty-six-year-old Earle Hyman, who had appeared on Broadway with the American Negro Theater at the age of seventeen and had played *Hamlet* at Howard University. He read for the small part of a native boy who gives sonorous Bible readings in the mission church, but Moss asked him to read for the more conspicuous part of Logan too. Hyman remembered auditioning for Moss as "very, very pleasant" and was astonished when told on the spot that he could have his choice of parts. He chose Logan, the play's Caliban.

The most important role was Reverend Harmston, the master of this brave new world. Moss had failed to persuade Ralph Richardson to come to America to do the part and cast John Cromwell instead, the sixty-four-year-old American director of such films as *Of Human Bondage* with Bette Davis and *Anna and the King of Siam* with Irene Dunne and Rex Harrison. Cromwell's directing career had stalled in the wake of the House Un-American Activities Committee hearings and, rather than fight a blacklist, he had returned to his first profession of acting. He won a Tony in 1951 as best supporting actor in Paul Osborn's *Point of No Return,* setting an example for his actor son Jamie, well known today as James Cromwell, "father" of *Babe* and the chilling police chief of *LA Confidential*. Moss had crossed paths with John Cromwell many years before, though he may not have realized it. It was Cromwell, still working as an actor for William A. Brady, who had filmed the "illustrated intervals" shown during scene changes in *Life*, the first play Moss ever saw at the Bronx Opera House in 1911.

The tryout tour for *The Climate of Eden* was to include Washington, D.C., and Wilmington, Delaware, before the November 6 opening in New York. Rehearsals had gone exceptionally well under Moss's confident and relaxed direction, according to Hyman, who recalled the feeling that "we were working on a very important project which was going to be a big success." It came as a shock, Hyman said, to discover they were performing "something we believed in that had to do with man's humanity, mankind loving each other" in the theater of the Dupont Hotel, where the company was also billeted and which had a "whites only" policy. Also in the cast was Jane White, whose father Walter was president of the NAACP. According to Hyman, Moss and White convinced someone to convince "Mr. Du Pont, who owned Wilmington, that for the first time, blacks should live in that hotel." It was a different kind of shock to find there was virtually no advance sale on the road, white or black.

The confidence Moss showed his cast was inspiring but illusory. For support and advice he asked Kaufman to come to Wilmington for the first performance on October 9. The Delaware audience was small but attentive and respectful. Though the play had shape and atmosphere, it was too long and talky, with dialogue Moss had taken too faithfully from the novel and long passages quoting Ecclesiastes, among other sources.

The onetime collaborators spent the night in merciless cutting and the following morning Moss arrived at rehearsal, blue-penciled pages in hand. According to Hyman he told the company, "I have made some cuts. They will probably hurt some of you rather badly . . . but it has nothing to do with your brilliant acting ability. I'm grateful for last night's performance; the work was superb. But the cuts have to be made." Then, firmly: "*There will be no discussion whatsoever of any of these cuts.*"

The silence of Wilmington was duplicated in Washington. Moss tried to attribute the dismal ticket sales to the temporary distractions of "I Like Ike" or being "Madly for Adlai." He wanted to delay the New York opening for a week to avoid direct conflict with the election, but the costs of running the show scotched any such plan. After a matinee in Washington to an audience of no more than fifty, Bernie Hart tried to look on the bright side as he and Joe Hyman tallied the receipts. "Don't worry, Moss," he said. "We got out of Egypt—we'll get out of Washington."

Moss later berated himself for spending the weeks on the road with *The Climate of Eden* yielding to the pressure to "Broadway it up." He had cut poetic texture in favor of jungle sounds and exotic lighting that distracted from the characters. His great fear, he admitted, was "to be judged by the grotesque Broadwayese of success or failure," but it was exactly those terms to which he was most vulnerable. He later said he was "pushed" on *The Climate of Eden,* but the pressure had come from within, from his own anxiety.

Broadway's judgment was delivered with brutal clarity. He had been right about his Gregory Hawke and every critic said so, but they said, too, that the writing was faulty, that the oversimplifying had stripped the character of complexity and sympathy. The play had champions in Walter Kerr and John Chapman, but they were outnumbered. Even the tolerant and generous Atkinson seemed at a loss for words. He pointlessly reminded his readers of the "hilarity and showmanship" of Moss's past hits before discussing the present effort as "a serious drama with wistful overtones," a description all but guaranteed to shutter the box office, which is more or less what it did. *The Climate of Eden* eked out just twenty performances, the shortest run of Moss's career as playwright or director.

Publicly Moss took the failure stoically, avoiding the mistake of arguing with the critics as he had done after *Christopher Blake*. He said of *Climate* that he "watched it fail without a trace of bitterness," but no one close to him believed that. Max Gordon said he was "shattered" by the play's failure, and Moss admitted to Garson Kanin and Ruth Gordon that the only word to describe his feelings was "heartbreak." He echoed Adlai Stevenson's remark after losing the election to Eisenhower. "I am too big to cry," he told Kanin and Gordon, "but it hurts too much to laugh."

There would be another production of the play the following year, mounted in a small theater downtown by Center Stages, a group of young hopefuls nobody knew much about. Their production would get better reviews and run longer than Hart's. Atkinson reviewed that production for the *Times* and to his chagrin—and Moss's—now found the play "a beautiful piece of work—work of art, in fact." He stressed the "simplicity" on view downtown, so much less cluttered than Moss's overstaged production. Stripped of Broadway effects, the play revealed "sweetness, good humor and wonder."

Moss later overrated *The Climate of Eden,* calling it "by far the most interesting piece of work I have ever done for the theater." It wasn't. It was an adaptation that failed to create life on the stage, but as an experiment it had required courage. After absorbing the blows of the reviews, he dropped a note to Atkinson, sympathizing with him on the difficulty of writing a negative notice about a work that "made a valiant try" and—more difficult still—had been written by a friend. It was a gracious letter, but weary and resigned, and the critic felt "disconcerted" by it.

Atkinson knew as well as Moss how much the theater had changed since the twenties. The economics and the audiences were different. The financing of shows was no longer a matter of theatrical angels taking a flyer, but of businessmen demanding a return. The audience was decreasingly composed of regulars, those core reliables whose easy needs were now being met by television, which claimed their allegiance—or at least their time, which amounted to the same thing. Those who remained seemed more selective, more demanding, less easily satisfied, not only because ticket prices were constantly rising, but because the postwar world seemed to ask more from plays and playwrights than Broadway was used to delivering. It was becoming a more serious, more challenging, and maybe a more substantial place, but a less joyous one, too, for those used to relying on theatrical instinct or the old razzle-dazzle to get them through. The footing—and the rewards—were less secure.

As a playwright, Moss might have risen more confidently to the demands of the postwar theater if he hadn't assumed the roles of director and producer, too. Those multiple hats increased the odds against success, as *The Climate of Eden* seemed to prove. He always spoke gallantly about the play's failure as—of course—an opportunity for learning and for growth. But the lessons he learned as he neared fifty must have been harder than anyone could have guessed, for he would never finish another play.

Nor was growth a process without a price.

Pro

24

Surviving

Your last play shows up in your
next electrocardiogram.

MOSS HART

He was no longer the twinkling, devilish-looking youth, the "Wonder Boy" or "Byron of the Bronx." He was a seasoned veteran now and what had once been a dashing widow's peak had receded into deep bays and the glint in the hair was pewter. Though tailors and goldsmiths saw to his elegance and air of distinction, he looked haggard and weary when unguarded. Maybe sun would be a remedy. California almost always had a restorative effect on him, no matter what he said about it. If it didn't restore him emotionally or creatively, it did so economically.

When he flew west with Kitty and the children shortly after Thanksgiving and the closing of *The Climate of Eden,* he knew that—wounded or not by its failure—it had enhanced his stature on Broadway. To the envious, it humanized him. To friends and admirers, the grace with which he appeared to accept the critics' verdict elevated him in style. Most of all, he had aspired, and Broadway knew it without wondering what the inner cost had been.

Going to California at all was a sign that disappointment had not triggered one of his debilitating mood swings. He felt healthy enough to do without Kubie and the daily or twice daily psychiatric sessions, and had taken for the winter—or Lazar had taken for him—Frank Sinatra's house in Palm Springs, the rent paid by Warner Bros.

Before tinsel had been draped on Christmas trees in the desert, Judy Garland and her husband Sid Luft joined Moss and Kitty there, down from Los Angeles to discuss a remake with music of *A Star Is Born.* The original picture, starring Janet Gaynor and Fredric March, had been a huge success when David O. Selznick produced it in 1937. It told of the ascent of Esther Blodgett to movie stardom and the simultaneous descent of her husband and discoverer, Norman Maine, from stardom to alcoholic has-been. To prevent her throwing away her career to save him, he takes a fatal swim into the Pacific Ocean. Esther survives and greets her fans with tears in her eyes and one of the most romantic fade-out lines in movie history: "Hello, everybody, this is Mrs. Norman Maine."

Musicalizing the story was superficially just a matter of making Esther Blodgett a singer, but the assignment was more demanding than that. Creating a comeback vehicle for Garland, after the humiliation of her being publicly fired by MGM four years earlier, was a challenge far from routine.

Moss liked Garland. He admired her in pictures like *The Wizard of Oz* and *Meet Me in St. Louis* and had known her since 1945, when she and his old friend Vincente Minnelli honeymooned for three months in New York. He saw her from time to time in Hollywood, usually at George Cukor's elegant house in the hills, where he often joined her in after-dinner sing-alongs around the piano, singing surprisingly well and indulging his secret conviction that he would come back in a future life as a band singer.

He was intrigued, he said, by Garland's "curious instinct" as an actress that had "nothing to do with technique," but resembled "a great musician plucking the strings of a harp." Ellen Terry once called it that "something extra" that makes a star, and Moss would quote the line in *A Star Is Born,* making the words apply to both character and actress.

He sympathized with Garland's famously messy personal life (they had both logged hours on Dr. Ernest Simmel's couch), but he was wary. MGM—Schary, in fact—had fired her for being unprofessional from the only thing like a stable home she had ever had, and in the years since, the tabloids had been full of her suicide attempts, breakdowns, recoveries, and relapses. Then in 1952 she married Sid Luft, a man Hollywood mostly considered a racetrack opportunist, perhaps because he owned the movie rights to the life of Man O'War. ("Get me a horse that means something at the box office and you've got a deal," a mogul is supposed to have crowed.) But opportunist or not, Luft took charge of her career and the Garland shenanigans subsided. There was a comeback engagement at the London Palladium, and a bigger, more emotional one at the Palace in New York.

She brought back two-a-day vaudeville and demonstrated she was still one of the most talented performers alive and could be reliable after years of erratic and undisciplined behavior. With Luft as her producer, she signed with Jack Warner and Warner Bros. to make *A Star Is Born* as her comeback picture. Harold Arlen and Ira Gershwin would write the songs, Arlen having composed "Over the Rainbow" for *The Wizard of Oz* and Gershwin a longtime friend and favorite lyricist. Cukor would direct, and for the screenplay, "There's only one guy," Luft recalls Garland insisting. "Moss."

He would work from the original script by Dorothy Parker, Alan Campbell, and Robert Carson, based on the Academy Award–winning story by Carson and William Wellman, director of the 1937 version. Its characters and situations had evolved in part from an earlier Selznick picture directed by Cukor called *What Price Hollywood?* and in part from John Barrymore's fading alcoholic actor who commits suicide in *Dinner at Eight,* which Selznick and Cukor had also filmed. Cukor had turned down the first *A Star Is Born* because it was too similar to the pictures he had already made, but almost twenty years later the wheel had come full circle. Moss's screenplay would be finished by the time Cukor returned from Europe in March, but they would work as a mutually supportive unit for a year and a half after that, even when on separate coasts. It was a collaboration of affection that went back beyond Cukor's film of *Winged Victory* to the 1920s and Moss's office-boy days with Gus Pitou.

Moss had agreed to the project based on his fond memories of the original, but after seeing it again in a New York screening room, he was dismayed. He told Garson Kanin, "great sections of it are hopelessly old fashioned and I shall earn every penny of the huge sum they are paying me to write it."

The "huge sum" was $101,000, an increase over his fee from Goldwyn and—to Lazar, who negotiated the deal—a symbolic $1,000 more than Garland would be paid for playing Esther. However dated the first picture, Moss wanted to tread carefully "because the original was so famous and when you tamper with the original, you're inviting all sorts of unfavorable criticism." Nevertheless, "I had to say new things about Hollywood—which is quite a feat in itself as the subject has been worn pretty thin."

The dated script gave Moss a secure blueprint from which he could lift sequences and scenes that still worked and get rid of those that didn't. He outlined his script from fade-in to fade-out in just two weeks and in mid-January drove from Palm Springs to Beverly Hills to meet with Arlen and Gershwin to "spot" the musical numbers for the new version.

In setting the musical structure, he shaped the picture, updating it and making Garland's character credible at the same time. The 1937 version had begun in North Dakota, where Esther was a movie-struck farm girl with only a sympathetic grandmother to help her realize her dream of getting on a bus straight to Grauman's Chinese Theater where—suitcase in hand—she tries on for size the footprints of movie star Norman Maine, set in cement that turns to quicksand.

Moss reconceived Esther as a band singer with no Hollywood ambitions. If her scrapbook is slender, she's been around and knows deep down that her vague dream of a hit record someday is probably just kidding herself. With a single stroke Moss eliminated North Dakota and the grandmother, the bus ride to Hollywood, and most of the more wide-eyed clichés of 1937. He placed the first song right at the beginning, opening his screenplay (brilliantly shot by Cukor) with klieg lights raking the sky, limousines discharging precious cargo, and players large and small bumping into each other backstage in the chaos of a benefit at the Shrine Auditorium. It's a dark beginning in spite of the klieg lights and flashbulbs. Esther and the band are just puppets on the bill of one of Hollywood's homages to itself when she and her destiny collide—literally—with Maine, a charmer and a drunk.

Getting rid of North Dakota made Esther the product of no one and nowhere but show business. The role was for and *about* Judy, no longer an ingenue, but a grown-up weighted down by garish personal baggage the world knew too much about. "Here comes a big fat close-up," Moss would write for her to say, neatly defining the whole picture.

The most famous musical sequence would be the fifteen-minute "Born in a Trunk" production number from the movie-within-the-movie that makes Esther a star, turning her into Vicki Lester. She sings of being born backstage at the Princess Theater in Pocatello, Idaho, and warbles a sheaf of standards like "Swanee," "I'll Get By," and "Melancholy Baby" as if they were stations of the show-business cross. The number was added at great expense after the rest of the picture had been shot to justify an intermission; Moss didn't write it and Cukor didn't direct it, but it was Moss's Esther who sang it. This Esther was someone—like Moss—who had never heard of North Dakota except, perhaps, as another one-night stand. She was someone whose roots were wherever footlights were, which is what made "Born in a Trunk" so apt in a picture for which it was an afterthought.

Moss's change had another effect: it strengthened the love story of Esther and Maine. In the original, Esther sets out to become a movie star; that's her dream; he's her idol. In Moss's version she is less ambitious, more vulnerable. It is Maine who points out, after hearing her torch her way through a jam session, "You're a great singer." And then, astonished at her astonishment, "Hasn't anyone ever told you that?"

"You're better than you know," he tells her, persuading her to aim higher than a dream that asks "too little" of her ferocious talent. Every-thing that follows is Esther's fulfillment of *his* dream, not her own—because she loves him and love might yet save him, though it can't in the end. Vicki is his redemption, his "monument," Esther's gift and tribute to him. "Hello, everybody, this is Mrs. Norman Maine."

Moss's song spots remained almost exactly as he mapped them out for Arlen and Gershwin in January. "The 'Dive' song" became "The Man That Got Away" for Esther's jam session with the band at the Downbeat Club. The "Tour de Force" number—fully detailed in Moss's script—became "Somewhere There's a Someone," the picture's most innovative musical scene: Esther plays a rehearsal record of her "production number to end all big production numbers" and parodies its many locations—"It's an American in Paris, Brazil, the Alps, and the Burma Road!"—using just living-room props both to mock and to celebrate Hollywood style, cheering Maine, sidelined and trying to stay sober.

In dramatic sequences Moss retained whole chunks of the original script, leaving many scenes word for word as Parker, Campbell, and Carson had written them. Late in the picture, studio head Oliver Niles (Charles Bickford) visits Maine (James Mason) in a rehab sanitarium with a bit-part job offer Maine rejects; the scene is identical in both versions but for a single word referring to a prop. Esther and Maine's announcement to Niles that they are getting married, their run-in with the studio's bitterly resentful publicity head after they elope, Maine's fistfight with him at Santa Anita racetrack, his subsequent falling off the wagon, and the degrading night court scene that follows—all were retained from the first script virtually without change. Moss took pride in defending his fidelity to the original when disputes with Luft and Warner erupted during shooting. "I say this quite objectively," he could tell them, "for as you know I did not write this scene, I kept it in toto from the old picture, which is a fair measure of how right I thought it was."

When a scene needed more drama or character, he supplied it. At the end of the picture, after Maine's suicide and Esther's withdrawal from the world, she must be persuaded to return to the world (and the Shrine Auditorium). In 1937, Esther's crusty old grandmother gave her "gumption." But Moss had already eliminated her from the story and the obvious substitute was the studio head, delivering a Grand Old Man exhortation, the kind of thing Charles Bickford expected to get and thought he was good at. Moss argued that the speech would be more dramatic and less expected from Esther's onetime piano player (played by Tommy Noonan), a sidekick character, but the one who knew her "when" and called her a fool for believing in Maine. In the end he is

Maine's perceptive spokesman and triggers the most wrenching scene in the picture.

Maine is the most romantic of Moss's many mentor figures, but his doom is inherited from Parker/Campbell/Carson. So is the view of Hollywood, whose workaday world of cables, lights, soundstages, and back rooms Moss never knew well. But stardom, something he knew a great deal about, got a sober, ambivalent reading. Here it is a gift, something innate, something conferred, not something won by tooth and nail. Moss avoids all the ego, narcissism, and desperation that were the underlying truths of *Light Up the Sky,* but he brings a clear-eyed gravity, too, an acknowledgment of luck and limitations. "Talent isn't always enough," Maine tells Esther. "You need a sense of timing—an eye for seeing the turning point—or recognizing the big chance when it comes and grabbing it." And if talent alone is insufficient for a career, so is love for a life. "I thought *I* was the answer for Norman—but love isn't enough," Esther realizes when Maine hits bottom. "It isn't enough for him—and—I'm afraid of what I feel now—in myself." This is not Parker and the rest; it is a newly reflective Moss, doing the best screenwriting he ever did.

He had returned to New York by the time the picture started shooting in October. The production was notoriously troubled because Garland's weight yo-yoed up and down (it is apparent on-screen), and because she was often unable or unwilling to work except at night, incurring ruinous cost overruns. There had been problems at the very beginning of production, disputes over using the CinemaScope process owned by 20th Century-Fox or Warner Bros.' similar but inferior WarnerScope. Cukor won the quality battle to use CinemaScope only after shooting had begun, which meant starting from scratch.

A Star Is Born was as close to Jack Warner's personal production as he could make it, and as costs escalated so did his meddling. For all his egomaniacal crudeness, Warner was a more easily tolerated nuisance than "lovable Sid Luft," as Moss and Cukor privately called their producer, because the studio chief had more experience. When he interfered, Cukor caustically observed, "Apparently he doesn't think it enough that he's a great showman, very rich, a wonderful guy, besides a million laughs," but he had grudging respect for Warner's audience instincts and Moss was in no position to argue. Warner had, after all, made movies of *The Man Who Came to Dinner, George Washington Slept Here,* and *Christopher Blake.* Still, disputes escalated with the budget and, as always, the least disruptive thing to focus on during shooting was the script.

Through shooting and editing, Cukor deferred scrupulously to Moss in script matters, their often camp rapport defined by exchanges of letters and telegrams. "WAS IT SOMERSET MAUGHAM WHO SAID A WOMAN'S WORK IS NEVER DONE?" asked Moss in a cable when tired of rewriting. Cukor, hearing that Moss's back was ailing him, wrote, "I know what caused this illness—that back-bend of yours! . . . touching the floor with your head, at the same time waving that great big ostrich feather fan. To me it was the high spot of 'Rose Marie.' "

It wasn't all joking. When time came to shoot the scene between Esther and Maine at the Downbeat Club, Cukor discovered on the drive to the location that dialogue had been cut without his knowledge. Gone was the exchange in which Maine tries to define Esther's "something extra" with metaphors from boxing and fishing. "I'm trying to tell you how you sing," he explains. "You mean like a prizefighter, or a fish?" she asks. Then, trying to be helpful, she advises, "Try bullfighting."

Cukor called Luft from a gas station telephone booth in Laguna to read him the riot act. Later he described the scene to Moss as his playing of "the Big Scene from TROILUS AND CRESSIDA," saying, "I made a solemn vow—never again would I put up with any more of this crap." Moss cabled Luft and Warner at once from New York, leaving no doubt as to the importance he placed on characterizations—and on what was owed him as writer:

I WANT TO PROTEST AS STRONGLY AND VIGOROULY [sic] AS
I CAN AT THE WAY THIS SCENE HAS BEEN CUT. IT IS THEIR
BIG SCENE TOGETHER. THE SCENE THAT KICKS OFF THEIR
RELATIONSHIP AND THE SCENE THAT ESTABLISHES NORMAN
MAINE AS THE KIND OF PERSON HE REALLY IS. I WROTE IT
THAT WAY AND IT SHOULD STAY THAT WAY. WHOEVER CUT IT
HAS CALMLY PROCEEDED TO TAKE ALL THE CHARACTER AND
JUICE OUT LEAVING IT AS DULL AND CLICHE AS POSSIBLE
AND THAT IS EXACTLY THE WAY IT WILL PLAY IF YOU DONT
RESTORE THE CUT. FURTHER, IT SEEMS TO ME THAT SINCE YOU
ASKED ME CONSTANTLY TO RE-WRITE . . . YOU MIGHT RETURN
THE COURTESY BY LETTING ME KNOW WHEN THIS KIND OF
GROTESQUE AND HARMFUL CUTTING IS BEING DONE. I HARDLY
THINK I DESERVE THIS KIND OF DISMISSAL.

A Star Is Born finally became the most expensive picture Warner Bros. had ever made and was a triumph for Garland even though it failed to return its enormous investment. In one of Hollywood's paradoxical equations, it was both the pinnacle and the end of her career as a major screen star. The Oscar she was nominated for went instead to Grace Kelly's drab and dull performance in *The Country Girl,* the movie of Clifford Odets's play that was also a backstage story about a woman married to an alcoholic actor. Cukor was ignored by the Academy; so was Moss.

The three-hour-with-intermission version of the picture that opened in New York in September 1954 got the kinds of reviews that usually guarantee money, awards, and movie immortality. *Variety* headlined its review "Boffola box-office, period" and ended it "Fort Knox, move over." But the long version was too long or too special or too something, and was cut for general release from three hours to slightly over two by the studio, without Cukor's guidance or participation.

The legendary "lost" version that so impressed the critics and then vanished for thirty years was more or less reassembled in 1983 by Ron Haver of the Los Angeles County Art Museum, who assumed the daunting task of locating excised material that had been lost, damaged, or stolen over three decades of corporate neglect. The "restoration" (the only version currently available) is an approximation that awkwardly incorporates production stills, outtakes, and miscellaneous footage and audio tracks retrieved from private collectors and other sources. Haver's work was considerable, even heroic, but ironically restored material Moss had tried to convince Cukor and the studio to cut before the picture was ever released.

Luft remembers that Moss tried to persuade Cukor to shorten the picture and, when that failed, provided surreptitious coaching from the sidelines. "Cut the goddam thing, it's too long," he told Luft, or, "Make George think I made the cuts." He went so far as to approach Warner directly about "harmful and unnecessary length" he was hearing about from Elia Kazan, who had seen a rough cut. "I wonder if I might offer my services [in] suggesting some cuts," Moss wrote, an offer Warner politely ignored. As to the finished picture, Luft admitted, "Moss thought it was too long; I never did."

But Cukor had misgivings about the length, too. "I wish the picture were a little shorter," he told Moss after a preview that had been rapturously received by an ecstatic audience. "Neither the human mind nor the human ass can stand three and a half hours of concentration."

A Star Is Born was the best work of Cukor's long career, but it had been exhausting. When the end came he told Moss, "As for me, I think I'll be doing THE SHANGHAI GESTURE in the summer theatres this year, with me in the Mrs. Leslie Carter-Florence Reed part, because who better than I can read the famous speech, 'I survived . . .'?"

• • •

Moss had delivered his screenplay to Warner Bros. at the end of March. His duties were contractually finished and so was the lease on the house in the desert. Moss and Kitty bundled the children up and moved them from Palm Springs to Santa Monica, where Moss had rented Norma Shearer's beach house, the one she and Irving Thalberg occupied until his death in 1936. Moss knew the house from the thirties and Kitty had been there, too, on the arm of Oscar Levant at the time of *A Night at the Opera*. Now it was just a rental and their landlady a mostly forgotten ex–movie star who decorated the rooms with plastic flowers she insisted on changing weekly. The former queen of MGM collected rent that was being paid by the current sovereign of 20th Century-Fox.

Darryl Zanuck never fully suspended his efforts to make Moss a movie director. The studio had canceled his post–*Gentleman's Agreement* writing-directing contract when he signed on for *Miss Liberty,* but Zanuck hadn't abandoned his crusade. He still enjoyed competing at killer croquet with Moss and was certain Moss could direct pictures as well as write them. In 1953 he thought he had just the property to tempt him.

Prince of Players was the biography of Edwin Booth by Eleanor Ruggles that became a surprise best-seller that year. To anyone in the American theater, Booth's was and is a magic name. The Players' Club in New York occupies his former home, which his statue overlooks from its pedestal in the center of leafy Gramercy Park. He was the most celebrated tragedian of the American nineteenth century, whose *Hamlet* played one hundred consecutive performances in New York, a record until John Barrymore bettered it by one in 1923.

Booth's life was hardly less dramatic than his roles. His actor-father was a drunk who died insane; both his wives died young; and looming over all was his brother John Wilkes Booth's assassination of Abraham Lincoln in 1865, just months after Edwin's triumphant record run in *Hamlet*. The devastating aftermath of the assassination forced Edwin Booth's withdrawal from public life and the stage.

Zanuck intuited correctly that such a character and story would excite Moss's imagination. They excited Lazar's, too, who negotiated a deal that, in Hollywood's version of upward mobility, bettered the fee for *A Star Is Born* by another symbolic $1,000.

The story had everything for Moss: the theater, the historical background, dramatic incidents that needed no invention, and Shakespeare. The saga began with the patriarch, Junius Brutus Booth—father, drunk, and star actor. Moss wrote him with juicy bravura passages in which Falstaff's dialogue becomes drunkenly confused with his own, turning young Edwin into an unwitting Prince Hal. The father was one of those who raged against the dark, not unlike Grandfather Solomon perhaps, and Moss dipped into his trunk for a final retrieval of *No Retreat,* his durable actor-father/actor-son drama into which he had shoehorned the musical Strausses but that fit the Booths without a stretch.

The boy Edwin became his father's pupil, keeper, and rival, learning the great roles from the wings of opera houses, or in mining camps or on Mississippi steamboats when he wasn't rescuing his father from brothels, saloons, or creditors. He seized the Booth legacy by literally stepping into his father's shoes, displacing Junius on a night he was too drunk or psychotic to go on in *Richard III.* "The wrong Booth," someone cried from the audience, for the first and last time.

It was hard for Moss to ignore that Esther Blodgett and Edwin Booth had more in common than their initials. He overlaid the structure of *A Star Is Born* on the lives of the Booths after coloring the early scenes with the conflict from *No Retreat.* Shakespearean interludes were spotted in, like the musical numbers in *A Star Is Born,* structuring the drama with a "greatest hits" sampler—songs in the one, soliloquies in the other. Each picture had the protagonist delivering declarations of romantic emotion through roles in rehearsal; each provided extensive star turns; and each had, in an uncanny accident of casting, Charles Bickford. He was the sage studio head of *A Star Is Born* and the sage impresario of *Prince of Players,* filling identical plot functions in identical performances. Most strikingly, each leading character is affected by tragedy that forces withdrawal, culminating in a return to the public world with an assertion of identity that defies personal sorrow.

Esther does it from the stage of the Shrine Auditorium; Edwin does it with *Hamlet.* He mounts the stage to face an audience both curious and hostile. His fellow actors hang back as he steps to the footlights. Someone cries out "Murderer!" and a tide swells, a roar of taunts and curses.

Booth remains "utterly still," the screenplay tells us, as "the mob's cries reach a pitch, then gradually die down, and finally cease altogether . . . impressed by the courage of the man on the stage. . . . His eyes swimming with tears he comes to the footlights . . . cheers engulf him." He even has his "Hello, everybody . . ." moment. "The name is still Booth!" he thunders to anyone who might have forgotten.

Moss was pleased by his work on *Prince of Players.* He told friends that "it was a difficult job, and I think I did a good one." Others agreed. Richard

Zanuck, then working for his father at the studio, wrote an internal memo calling Moss's screenplay "one of the most beautifully written scripts that I have ever read." Zanuck père sent a copy of the memo to Moss with his own note attached: "This makes it official."

On the title page Zanuck penciled a note to studio underlings: "This is not a *regular* movie—this is *special material*." He added the words: "Moss direct."

Zanuck fairly spewed casting ideas, including Marlon Brando for Edwin and Tyrone Power for John Wilkes Booth. For Mary Devlin, Booth's doomed first wife, he suggested Elizabeth Taylor, Grace Kelly, or Jean Simmons. But his biggest star was CinemaScope, the wide-screen process he controlled that was revolutionizing film exhibition. The studio had just filmed Lloyd C. Douglas's faux-Biblical epic *The Robe* as its first CinemaScope release starring Richard Burton, the young Welsh actor who had been introduced to American audiences in the previous year's *My Cousin Rachel,* for which he had received an Academy Award nomination. Burton's role in the toga and breastplate of ancient Rome (not his last time in such garb) would contribute to *The Robe*'s box-office success and by the time *Prince of Players* was ready to go forward in the summer of 1954 Burton, with his Old Vic training, was a natural to play Edwin. Burton would indeed be directed by Moss, but not now and not in Hollywood and not as Booth.

Moss withdrew from *Prince of Players* shortly after turning in his script and returning to New York in mid-July. Zanuck admitted defeat and turned the picture over to a writer he was grooming as a producer, Philip Dunne, screenwriter of *How Green Was My Valley, Pinky,* and *The Robe.* The studio head told Dunne, "I think you will read one of the greatest scripts you have ever read in your life." Dunne agreed it was "a beautiful script and . . . Moss has never done anything finer," but he also thought it "much too long, talky, and diffuse."

Moss's recommendation to Zanuck that Cukor direct the picture was undone by delays on the not-yet released *A Star Is Born,* following which he was to direct for Columbia a film version of the John O'Hara/ Rodgers and Hart musical, *Pal Joey,* with Marlon Brando and Mary Martin. Cukor wanted Moss to write the screenplay, not knowing he had already said no. Moss explained he had always felt that, apart from songs like "Bewitched" and "Glad to Be Unhappy," *Pal Joey* was "highly overrated" and any adapter was begging to be accused of "spoiling" something "that was never very good in the first place."

With no director set for *Prince of Players* a year later, Dunne went to New York after the July 4 weekend to work on the final script with Moss.

He checked into the Plaza Hotel and, over drinks in the Oak Room, outlined changes he thought should be made. Moss cheerfully agreed and wished Dunne well in getting them on paper before dashing off, claiming a previous engagement. After four nearly identical meetings, Dunne realized Moss had no intention of doing any rewrites at all. After doing them himself, he conceded, "writing consists of ideas, not words" and "it didn't really matter which of us wrote down the actual words." Moss read Dunne's rewrite and approved the "shrewd craftsmanship" of "a first-rate job."

Still without a director, Zanuck abruptly named Dunne to the job on July 20. Dunne had worked with directors from John Ford to Elia Kazan and was willing to take up the megaphone, but wanted protection. He got it by persuading Eva Le Gallienne, cast to play Gertrude in the *Hamlet* scenes, to stay on as Shakespearean coach. Burton, however much experience he had at the Old Vic, was not a seasoned film actor, but looked brilliant next to young John Derek as John Wilkes Booth. Derek had the dash and looks of the assassin, but his performance suggested that the youngest Booth might have turned to assassination because he was such a wooden actor. The wistfully unhappy Maggie MacNamara played Booth's wife Mary Devlin with a suitably fragile air and Bickford—"Old Ironpants," Cukor called him—gave the performance he always gave. The surprise was Raymond Massey as Junius Brutus Booth. He roared and staggered his way through the lustiest performance of his career, confounding Moss's fears of disaster in having an actor so closely identified with Abraham Lincoln play the father of Lincoln's assassin.

The picture was shot in color and CinemaScope and was a tremendous "projection-room success." Everyone from the cop at the gate to the waitress in the commissary knew that the studio's one solid gold hit was *Prince of Players,* and forget about *How to Marry a Millionaire* with no one but Marilyn Monroe, Betty Grable, and Lauren Bacall. When *Prince of Players* was released in 1955, *Variety* agreed, calling it "a prince of a picture" and predicting it would be "sockeroo all over." But hardly anybody went to see it. *Prince of Players* became a footnote to film history as the first flop in CinemaScope and a turgid one at that. The speeches were Edwin's, but the action was his brother's. As Dunne ruefully acknowledged in hindsight, "What could poor Edwin do? He couldn't bring Lincoln back to life. . . . He could only give a performance of *Hamlet*."

Moss's relinquishing the chance to become a film director with *Prince of Players* had two causes. The first was simply that he didn't want to be one.

He had always said he didn't have the "camera eye," and Kaufman had tried to make the transition in 1947 and failed with a movie called *The Senator Was Indiscreet*. Warning enough.

A second and more urgent reason was that in October 1953, not long after he turned in his script and returned to New York, Kitty fell ill and was hospitalized in Columbia-Presbyterian Hospital. A friend called her illness "sudden and shocking" (though a more or less permanent veil was drawn over its nature), and her health was of intense concern until she recovered sufficiently for the Harts to begin entertaining at home again in early December.

In the meantime, Moss tried to find his way back into the theater while negotiating his own darkening mood swings, which may have prompted his leaving Hollywood when he did. His writing after his return to New York was meager, just two play outlines, one set in a Caribbean resort, the other in a drawing room. Neither got farther than a character list and a few notes before being abandoned.

He forced himself to stay busy. He saw Kubie once or twice a day, spoke daily with Kaufman on the telephone, and encouraged colleagues and competitors when they sought his help or judgment. Jerry Chodorov, for one, was enjoying huge success with his and Joe Fields's musical version of *My Sister Eileen*. Starring Rosalind Russell, *Wonderful Town* was a major hit, surviving a change of composers to arrive in New York with music by Leonard Bernstein and lyrics by Betty Comden and Adolph Green. Chodorov and Fields were working on still another musical and on a light comedy they asked Moss to look over now and then. Sam Behrman tried to interest him in writing and directing a musical based on *Serena Blandish* that Moss's old friend Leonard Sillman wanted to produce.

Moss turned from one project to the next, fastening finally on one he had discussed with Rodgers and Hammerstein at the time of *Hans Christian Andersen*. The notion was a musical based on Edna Ferber's *Saratoga Trunk,* which had been a successful novel and an absurdly overblown movie in 1946 with Gary Cooper and Ingrid Bergman. Moss persuaded Ferber to collaborate with him on the libretto, which, with Rodgers and Hammerstein's score, he would then direct.

Ferber was not an easy woman, as everyone acknowledged. Nor was she an easy collaborator, as Moss knew intimately from Kaufman, who once remarked, "I am fond of Ferber, but I don't like her." Moss did. He and she had formed close bonds during the thirties, when "Mossie" discussed his most intimate emotional concerns in correspondence that suggests more of a mother-son relationship than he had ever had with Lillie Hart. Indeed, Ferber called Moss "the son I never had" and, although he wondered for a moment if collaborating with her might not be "madness," he decided they could work happily together.

"I consider the fault to be mine," he told Garson Kanin and Ruth Gordon when the collaboration turned into an exploding cigar. "[I]t was idiotic and extremely pompous of me to think that I could 'handle' Ferber. I couldn't—and I consider it a blessing that I got the gypsy's warning at the very beginning."

Moss's version and Ferber's were different, but what is certain is that once they worked out a detailed outline for *Saratoga Trunk,* they sent it to Mary Martin, who Moss said was "more or less promised," and to Rodgers and Hammerstein, who were enthusiastic but not yet fully committed. They waited to hear while Kitty was in the hospital, both Hart children came down with the mumps, and Moss contracted a virus of his own.

On November 3 Rodgers and Hammerstein sent a detailed five-page letter responding in the friendliest way to the outline, adding that they had decided to devote their energies instead to John Steinbeck's new novel, *Sweet Thursday,* which would become *Pipe Dream.* According to Moss, Ferber's recriminations that they had "lost" Rodgers and Hammerstein combined with the stress of multiple illnesses and overwork to shorten his temper, resulting in a "bitter and graceless fight."

Ferber later claimed that their quarrel was completely unmotivated, but Moss said that when Rodgers and Hammerstein withdrew he suggested Harold Arlen as composer, and Ferber had hooted imperiously, *"Who?"* and sniffed, "Never heard of him." Moss grew impatient and snapped, "Oh, come off it, Edna." He left in something between a snit and a rage, washing his hands of Ferber and *Saratoga Trunk*—which would emerge on Broadway five years later as *Saratoga* with music by—of course—Arlen.

Moss was shaken by the incident (Kitty said he was "gray with fright"), but tried to smooth the waters and regain some dignity by returning a pile of books Ferber had loaned him for research. He delivered them to her Park Avenue doorman with what he thought was a "rather nice note" and "a bushelful of white chrysanthemums." Ferber replied the next day in a hand-delivered note that read, without salutation:

> *How pleasant of you to have sent me the flowers with books. Your note which I have here interests me. You wrote that "the books looked so naked alone." I wouldn't have found this so. I wondered out of my small store of psychiatric knowledge if perhaps this is one of those instances in which the*

*sensations or emotions of a human being are attributed by wish transfer-
ence to an inanimate object.* EDNA.

Moss replied: "Dear Edna: Do you think I ought to see a doctor?"

Ferber considered herself a friend to Kitty as well as to Moss and
called them "the most sustaining of friends." They visited her at Treasure
Hill, her country home in Connecticut, as often as she visited them at
Fairview Farm. All of that now lay in ashes not easily rekindled.

A full year went by in which she and Moss exchanged not a word.
Finally Kitty wrote her, trying to make peace. "In my long life," Ferber
wrote back, airing her side of the story, "I never had heard directed at me
(or at anyone) such undeserved vindicativeness [*sic*], such venom, as Moss
Hart hurled at my bewildered head. Horrified, I could only say, over
and over, as I did—but Moss, I don't know what you're talking about, I
don't know what in hell you're talking about! And I didn't know. And
I don't know to this day. . . . [H]e opened a barrage of the most savage and
uncalled-for abuse . . . [and] shouted (among other courtly statements)
that he was sick of looking at my granite face. . . . It was a saddening spectacle," she concluded. "I was, and am, ashamed for this man who was, I
had thought, a friend."

Ferber was famously sensitive about her severe, almost mannish appearance, and "granite face" was not a remark she was likely to forget or
forgive. Her biographer and grandniece Julie Goldsmith-Gilbert later
thought Moss might have said "granite-like" in response to Ferber's
annoying claim that she had never heard of Arlen, but Ferber's heart
remained as stony as what she decided Moss had called her face. Moss
tried to slough it off as "all rather graceless."

Shortly after their quarrel they found themselves at a matinee of *Peter
Pan,* the musical in which Mary Martin flew about on wires and sprin-
kled fairy dust on the audience. Moss was treating five-year-old Cathy to
the show and Ferber was doing the same with her five-year-old grand-
niece, Julie. The two adults caught sight of each other and turned away as
if on pivots.

After the show Martin received children of friends backstage where,
still in her Peter Pan costume, she would sprinkle fairy dust on them at
close range. Moss and Cathy arrived at her dressing room just as Ferber
and Julie did. The grown-ups ignored each other so ostentatiously that
the children couldn't help but be puzzled by the chill in the air.

"Who is that, Daddy?" Cathy asked, nodding in Ferber's direction.

"That, my dear," Moss replied, "is Captain Hook."

. . .

After Kitty recovered, Moss took the family to Florida for the holidays to visit "The Commodore," still going strong at almost ninety-one. He was particularly fond of Kitty, his only daughter-in-law (Bernie remained a lifelong bachelor), and had written one of his famous amateur songs about her, which made the holidays as fond as they were sunny and restful.

Florida was fine, but Moss missed decorating the tree in Bucks County. He made up for it on New Year's Eve by chartering a yacht to welcome in 1954. They left the dock at 10:30 in the evening and were grounded within minutes on a sandbar, where they remained until five o'clock the next morning. It was a farcical beginning to a year that would not be notable for laughter.

Moss's reunion with his father was not out of order for, whether stimulated by the row with Ferber or not, he had begun just after their quarrel to rummage around in his past. Over the Thanksgiving weekend he had started writing some autobiographical notes in a looseleaf note-book. On the first page he jotted *From the Bronx to Broadway* and then crossed out the "From" and added the date, November 24, 1953.

He confided to Garson Kanin and Ruth Gordon that "I have decided to do a theatrical memoir or autobiography. Do you think this is wrong? I have led quite a number of different kinds of lives, and I'd like to do some full length portraits of people like Sam Harris, and George, and Bea-trice,—as well as a definitive piece on Social Directing and the two kinds of Hollywood I knew from Thalberg to Cinemascope [*sic*]."

It was the same "book about the theater" he had told Schary he was going to write back in 1941, of which no word ever saw the light of day. Now, however, he had a brief burst of writing energy, and in longhand that looks never to have paused, filled twenty notebook pages with boy-hood reminiscences beginning with his first view of Times Square. After some lines about the magic of the theater, he began writing about Grand-father Solomon, but after describing the old tyrant's death, Moss put the pages aside for another day.

After returning to New York, Moss flew to California to see a rough assemblage of *A Star Is Born*. He stayed in Hollywood only five days, most of them at Warner Bros. discussing retakes with Cukor. He also met with Lazar, whom he was now calling "the Small Gatsby," because of the hugely lucrative screenplay deal the diminutive agent was extracting from Harry Cohn at Columbia. The subject was the life of pianist Eddie Duchin and his love affair and marriage with society figure

Marjorie Oelrichs, who died giving birth to their son Peter Duchin, a story Cohn was planning for Tyrone Power and Kim Novak. Moss had known both Duchin and Oelrichs and thought he could easily write the script, though he wanted to wait until the end of the year because he suddenly dreaded another extended stay in Hollywood. He found it "withered and dead," he said after his return to New York. "I usually enjoy Hollywood," he said, "and there are a great many people there I am fond of. But I just hated every moment of it this time."

Back in New York he yielded to Jerry Chodorov's urgent request to come to New Haven, where his and Fields's new musical, *The Girl in Pink Tights,* was in trouble. It was the second time in as many months that Moss had been to New Haven to diagnose a play and the second time for a Chodorov. In December he had been there with Jerry's older brother Eddie during tryouts for *Oh, Men! Oh, Women!,* a sex farce with Franchot Tone as a psychoanalyst. Working with the older Chodorov seemed to Moss no better organized an adventure than Camp Utopia in 1926. He thought Eddie was "both brilliant and idiotic, just the way he is in life and the play has some wonderful moments and some incredibly stupid moments." He insisted that Chodorov rewrite act two in New Haven, and returned to Philadelphia to insist he rewrite act three. The play arrived in New York enough improved to enjoy a healthy run of 352 performances.

Advising on *The Girl in Pink Tights* was less important to Moss, finally, than the comedy the younger Chodorov and his partner had been working on. He had decided to make it a Hyman & Hart production if only to "keep the office going" and give him something to direct after two years' absence from Broadway.

Anniversary Waltz was a script he had "been potching around with" for over a year, he told the Kanins. It was a domestic comedy he called "a trifle of a play," in the vein of *Junior Miss* and *Dear Ruth.* It concerned a couple celebrating their wedding anniversary, during which her parents and their two adolescent children learn that when engaged they had indulged in a year of happy and guilt-free premarital sex. Sex before marriage was still a titillating issue in 1954 and Moss thought the complications, including a subplot that required kicking in a series of television sets onstage, had a chance to be "funny and rather endearing."

It was a one-set play, easy to produce and cast. Macdonald Carey, absent from Broadway since *Lady in the Dark,* would play the husband opposite Kitty, on Broadway in a straight play for the first time.

Moss and Kitty carefully made clear to friends and the press that she had auditioned twice for the role independent of Moss and had won it by impressing the producers, Joe Hyman and Bernie Hart. Certainly the play required no bigger name than Kitty's, but it also seemed an ideal, even therapeutic opportunity for her to return to work after a serious illness, and may be the reason Moss took it on in the first place. He quipped that working together made them "feel like the Lunts, Jewish variety."

Kitty claimed "Lunt" neglected "Fontanne." She was reluctant to demand his attention during rehearsals, as the other members of the cast assumed she was getting direction at home, which wasn't the case. Finally, she recalled, "I cornered him one morning while he was shaving. 'I really need some direction on lines and timing, so if you'll read through the part aloud, I'll simply take your readings and be quite happy.' That is exactly what I did," she said, "imitating Moss."

Tryouts in New Haven, Boston, and Philadelphia were more stressful than Moss had anticipated. He was distracted by Cukor's daily cables about editing problems on *A Star Is Born* and preoccupied by attempts to get *The Climate of Eden* produced in London. Laurence Olivier had expressed interest in directing it and claimed to have interest from Ralph Richardson and Denholm Elliott to star.

Meanwhile, Moss found himself on the road with *Anniversary Waltz* while its authors were on the road with *The Girl in Pink Tights*. He claimed to be doing "all the rewriting and patching that has to be done" and called it "a damn nuisance to have to go home and re-write every night, instead of having the boys do it."

Anniversary Waltz opened at the Broadhurst Theatre on April 7 to reviews that found Kitty as delightful as Moss hoped she would be and found the play "a dull and tasteless little piece" that was "the season's high in tasteless hackwork." Atkinson called Moss's direction "swift, taut, and noisy," which was enough to encourage ticket buyers to line up at the box office for the next two years. This "trifle of a play" redeemed Moss's reputation as a director-producer with one of the surest commercial instincts on Broadway. It went on doing so for a phenomenal 615 performances, making it one of the longest-running hits of his career.

With Kitty playing eight shows a week at the Broadhurst, Moss spent most of the late spring and early summer with the children in Bucks County. John and Ruth helped, but Moss's sophisticated version of child psychology had admirable clarity. "I'm bigger than they are and it's *my* house," he announced, and it more or less got results. At the farm he got the news that there would be no London production of *The Climate of Eden* after all. Following a meeting with the English censors, who took official umbrage at Olivia's reference to her "bottom," Olivier's interest shifted to his film version of *Richard III*. "I am awfully sorry to have been such a damp squib," Olivier wrote from London. Moss resigned himself to this final disappointment with his most serious play.

In July he and Philip Dunne discussed the changes to *Prince of Players* that Dunne then put on paper. Moss returned to Bucks County with the children, telling Dunne he would remain available during production, a promise he would be unable to keep.

By the time *Prince of Players* started shooting in August and *A Star Is Born* finally had its premiere in September, Moss was fighting for his life in intensive care at Columbia-Presbyterian and Kitty, with the poise of an actress in a hit play, was telling everybody the whopper that he had slipped a disk.

25

Full Circle

My decision as to Pygmalion *is final:*
let me hear no more about it. This is final.

GEORGE BERNARD SHAW

Moss was three months shy of fifty when he had his first heart attack. He seldom bore physical discomfort in silence and, as Kitty allowed, could be "a master self-dramatist" about it, but he was alone in Bucks County with the children when the warnings came and he at first had no inkling that's what they were. He experienced no numbness or pain in the arm, none of the constrictions of the chest common to heart attack victims. The pain began in his jaw, suggesting another round in his lifelong bout with dental problems. When it became acute and traveled to the top of his head, he knew something else was occurring and whatever it was, was terrifyingly wrong.

The pain peaked on a Sunday before dawn. Kitty was sleeping, having arrived after midnight from New York on her weekend break from *Anniversary Waltz*. Moss was a famously late riser, but around six a.m. woke Kitty with his agitated pacing in the bedroom.

"I have a terrible pain at the top of my head," he told her. Alarmed, she called local doctors, who were mystified by his symptoms. His New York doctor ordered her to get him to the city at once for a thorough examination. John the butler laid him on blankets in the back of the Hart station wagon and Kitty tried to make him comfortable as John drove them to Columbia-Presbyterian.

Tests indicated he had had a coronary and required hospitalization until fully recovered. For a man of Moss's age, whose father was hale and hearty at over ninety, the diagnosis was shocking but the prognosis positive. There was every reason to believe he would recover and every reason to be cautious. He needed to slow down, the doctors said, to curb the pace of the very activities that had driven him for half his life and from which he made his living.

If he slowed down or didn't, news of his illness on the Broadway and Hollywood grapevines might bring about an enforced standstill he didn't want and couldn't afford. Inventing the story of a slipped disk was thus a practical matter for the newspapers and it worked with friends, too.

Cukor accepted it and wrote the jokey letter about the dangers of back bends with an ostrich-feather fan; Philip Dunne told Darryl Zanuck that "some mysterious back ailment" made Moss unavailable for *Prince of Players*. Jack Warner, Judy Garland, and Sid Luft were too preoccupied with details of the *A Star Is Born* premieres to question the story. Moss would miss the New York and Los Angeles galas and that was that.

Ferber believed the story, too. It was just after Moss was released from the hospital that Kitty wrote her, hoping for reconciliation now that a year had passed since their rupture. Ferber wrote back just days before Moss's fiftieth birthday, airing her bitter account of his behavior without a hint of concern for his health. Ignoring a heart attack would have been impossible for her, but reports of a bad back could not weaken her resolve to stay angry.

Kitty later said the quarrel with Ferber had been the direct cause of Moss's coronary and in her memory it may have happened that way, though the quarrel occurred in November and Moss's heart attack struck almost nine months later, in July. But the claim has a kind of emotional credibility, allowing for a variety of delayed reactions. It had been a wrenching upheaval and affected him so deeply, Kitty told Ferber's grand-niece, that every day he was in the hospital his first question on her arrival was "Has Edna called?" or "Have you heard from Edna?"

Another who wasn't informed of the true state of Moss's health was Harry Cohn. Lazar had concluded the deal with Columbia for the Eddie Duchin picture at $300,000, three times what Moss had received for his two last assignments and an almost unheard-of writing fee in the 1950s. In order to keep as much as possible from the IRS the $300,000 would be paid over five years with a first payment of $65,000 in January and gradually decreasing payments until 1960. It was not an unusual arrangement, but one that now took on an aspect of necessity, as it would provide continuity of income for Kitty and the children if anything worse should happen to him. He intended to fulfill the contract, doctors' orders or no doctors' orders.

After the first critical week, visitors were allowed to cheer the patient: old friends like Kaufman, slowing now with the onset of arteriosclerosis;

the always cheerful Jerry Chodorov with gossip of the Rialto; Bernie with the latest news from Sardi's; and Joe Hyman with box-office figures for *Anniversary Waltz*. Max Gordon came and heard Behrman urge, "You're a professional writer. You must write . . . write every day, even if it's only a diary." Marlene Dietrich arrived with her own record player to spin platters of her sensational cabaret debut at the Café de Paris in London. She spun them at such volume that the hospital accused her of disturbing the peace, and not just Moss's.

He was released after four weeks to continue recuperating at home. Convalescence required rest, supervised diet, slow walks around the block on Kitty's arm, and commonsense regimens to be observed for the rest of his life. He was a somewhat willful patient: easier than Sheridan Whiteside, but "not above demanding pity and concern from his friends," as Kitty told Marie Brenner. Though he had smoked up to three packs of cigarettes a day, he and Kitty had given them up after the first reports linking smoking and cancer. He now tugged only on his pipe, a writerly prop with a rim of gold around the bowl. Like Kaufman, he was a meat eater who turned up his nose at vegetables and fruits, but he would now make any accommodation to a recovery diet that he had to—as long as he could sneak in the occasional hot dog from Nathan's. The most wrenching adjustment was selling Fairview Farm after almost twenty years of remodeling inside and out. An estate auction in May would sell off the high-maintenance property and all the antiques Moss had collected to decorate it.

"If Bennett Cerf gets sick, he still gets paid. If I get sick, nobody pays me," Moss explained as he began work on the screenplay he titled "Music by Duchin," now more of a burden than a breeze. He managed to get thirty-eight pages on paper before the stress of writing caused a relapse shortly after the New Year. The doctors issued strict orders forbidding work of any kind for the next six months, forcing him to forgo the script and the fee that went with it. Lazar generously forgave the commission he was entitled to and Sam Taylor, author of *Sabrina Fair,* wrote *The Eddie Duchin Story* instead.

The sale of Fairview Farm only activated Moss's lust for real estate once he felt well enough to be up and about. In February Joe Hyman took him for a drive along the Jersey shore near Beach Haven, about seventy miles south of New York, where Hyman had a summer retreat. To hardly anyone's surprise, Moss returned to New York with a summer lease on the cottage across the way. "Summer is not summer," he announced, "unless you get sand up your ass."

It was a modest place, with a garage roomy enough for an upstairs studio that Moss could furnish with odds and ends from local tag sales and where he could contemplate the odds and ends of a career almost cut short. Maybe it was Behrman's "write every day" that did it, but the past had been on his mind and had crept into "Music by Duchin." His script introduced its hero as a young piano player at a down-at-the-heels summer camp that a disgruntled guest describes as "The Black Hole of Calcutta. Only with rain." Back in New York, young Duchin gets an interview with a big-time bandleader, who appears in the altogether, a carbon copy of Moss's first encounter with the nonchalantly nude Jed Harris. The partial screenplay's elements were transferred to the notebook pages Moss took up again in New Jersey. "The Bronx to Broadway" may have been therapeutic, but he was insecure about writing prose and once again he put the pages aside.

The Harts' summer rental was home base for Moss's excursions in search of something more spacious along the shore. The long spit of land with the Atlantic Ocean on one side and Barnegat Bay on the other was then almost barren except for seagulls and windblown cattails. When he came upon a large brown-shingled house with an ocean view from every room, he bought it.

He and the Kaufmans had made Bucks County fashionable and his presence made the Jersey shore a magnet for friends including Jerry and Rhea Chodorov; Joan and George Axelrod; husband and wife playwrights Augustus and Ruth Goetz; and composer-lyricist Harold Rome and his wife Florence. "Hydrangea" Carlisle visited, too, and grandly dubbed the area "Bèche Havenne."

Harold Rome was there mainly to work with Moss on his first project since the heart attack and relapse. They had worked together on *Sing Out the News!* when Rome was just starting out, but his career was now in high gear with *Wish You Were Here,* his 1952 musical about adult summer camps like those of Moss's youth, and *Fanny* with Ezio Pinza, based on stories by Marcel Pagnol. Now Moss and Rome were collaborating on "In the Pink," a title suggested by a line in *Time* magazine about the psychology of color that Moss quoted on his cover page: "Pink represents a mood of sentimentality, good times and luxury." The musical had more to do with consumerism and Madison Avenue than with moods or colors and featured a new tool of the business world that Moss spelled as the "computor."

"In the Pink" was meant to satirize advertising but spun off in a dozen different directions, taking potshots at television evangelists like Bishop Fulton J. Sheen, consumer manipulation, corporate (im)morality, and something very like virtual sexuality. Unfocused and overwritten, "In the Pink" was no more than a draft, a work-in-progress to provide a post–heart attack transition back to full activity.

Which it might have done, except that in late May or early June producer Herman Levin called—on behalf of Lerner and Loewe, he said. They were working on a musical based on George Bernard Shaw's *Pygmalion*, the one about the phonetics professor and the Cockney flower girl. Would Moss care to drop by the office and hear some songs?

Moss later admitted that he thought the project "a quite hopeless task" and a thoroughly "untenable proposition." He knew Levin slightly as a poker pal of Bernie's who had invested small sums in *Dear Ruth* and *Light Up the Sky*. Levin had produced such eclectic fare as Jean-Paul Sartre's *No Exit* and the musical of Anita Loos's *Gentlemen Prefer Blondes*. Moss's acquaintance with Lerner and Loewe was slighter still, though they had the same lawyer, Irving Cohen, who may have suggested they get together.

Alan Jay Lerner was the taut, intensely driven librettist-lyricist who had won an Academy Award for his screenplay for MGM's *An American in Paris* and had written, with composer Frederick Loewe, the Broadway hits *Brigadoon* and *Paint Your Wagon*. Lerner and Loewe were as odd as collaborative couples got: Loewe shrugged at any setback, while Lerner was so intense he picked and chewed at his hands and fingers and had to wear cotton gloves to keep from drawing blood.

Lerner was born to Park Avenue wealth in 1918 (his father founded the Lerner Shops that still bear his name). He attended private schools in New York and England before enrolling at Choate, where he co-edited the school yearbook with classmate John F. Kennedy. Blind in one eye from a boxing incident at Harvard, Lerner was 4–F and spent World War II writing for radio and learning his craft as a lyricist.

Loewe—called Fritz—was fifty-four, born in Berlin in 1901. Or maybe he was fifty-one and born in Vienna in 1904. His father was an operetta star cast as Prince Danilo in the first Berlin production of *The Merry Widow* and played the lead in the Berlin production of *The Chocolate Soldier,* the operetta Oscar Straus derived from Shaw's *Arms and the Man.* Loewe *fils* was precocious musically. He boasted of having been, at thirteen, the youngest piano soloist ever to play with the Berlin Symphony and, at fifteen, having written a song called "Katrina," about a girl with the prettiest legs in Berlin, a song so popular—he said—that it sold two million copies of sheet music. These tales may have been true. Then again, he also claimed to have had his first sexual experience before he was three and his first affair—with a governess—at nine. A lifelong gambler and Lothario, he was once asked (in the author's presence) while losing at roulette in London's White Elephant gambling club if there was any woman in the world he would not bed. He paused, appeared lost in thought and, after considering the possibilities, answered with a doubt-silencing no.

Loewe came to America in the early twenties because his father had a contract with David Belasco, or because of the ruinous inflation that devastated Germany following the armistice, or both. The young man expected to become a concert pianist in America, but by the early thirties his résumé included vagabond stints as a boxer, a cowboy, and a mail carrier in Montana. Ira Gershwin once remarked that the story of Loewe's life made him sound like a combination Paderewski, Tom Mix, and Baron Münchhausen. Whatever the truth (it remains unestablished), by 1933 he was playing piano in the pit for *Champagne Sec,* the Americanized *Die Fledermaus* that Monty Woolley staged with Kitty in her Broadway debut. Even then Fritz boasted about the day he would be a famous Broadway composer.

Lerner and Loewe met in 1942 and collaborated on a series of flops. *Life of the Party* opened and closed in Detroit the year they met; *What's Up?* did a quick fold shortly thereafter in spite of George Balanchine's direction; *The Day Before Spring* in 1945 attracted $250,000 of MGM's money, only to wind up on the shelf. Then in 1947 came *Brigadoon* and, in 1951, *Paint Your Wagon.*

Lerner was in Hollywood working on MGM's movie version of *Brigadoon* in 1952 when he was approached by the remarkable Gabriel Pascal. Pascal was a Romanian who claimed to be Hungarian and had spent years in Asia doing some of this and a little of that when not in India pursuing his passion to make a film about Mahatma Gandhi, whose sex life he claimed was a many-splendored thing. According to Lawrence Langner of the Theatre Guild, Pascal combined "all the astounding qualities of the oriental, the occidental, and the accidental." He was a promoter of fabulous schemes, one of which made him famous.

Pascal succeeded where great studios and mighty producers had failed: he persuaded George Bernard Shaw to entrust him with filming his plays. No one's works were more coveted by the movies than Shaw's or more problematic, for the author acted as his own agent and lawyer and would allow no alteration of his work. He regarded *The Chocolate Soldier* as a travesty and it soured him on adaptations of any kind, with or without music, no matter how much money was involved. Which made it even more remarkable that Pascal secured movie rights to his plays with hardly a penny to his name.

There are many versions of the fateful encounter, but Sam Behrman's is probably as reliable as any because Behrman knew them both and observed the irrepressible promoter and the ascetic playwright in the same room at the same time.

Behrman's version was that Pascal arrived at Shaw's residence at Number Four Whitehall Court in 1935, having borrowed five pounds from an acquaintance to get a shave and pay his taxi fare. On Shaw's doorstep he was asked who sent him. "Destiny," he replied, and with wild-eyed gypsy charm said he'd come for the film rights to the plays. Startled, Shaw asked, "How are you fixed for money? What is your capital?"

"Here, GBS, is my capital," Pascal announced, displaying the few shillings left from the five pounds he had borrowed and throwing them down with pride and contempt. "It is not enough to pay taxi fare back to my hotel."

Shaw, a shrewd judge of character at eighty, decided this was the first honest film producer he had ever met. "I just looked at him and handed him *Pygmalion*," he said. "The man is a genius: that is all I have to say about him."

Pascal filmed *Pygmalion* in 1938 with Anthony Asquith directing a screenplay credited to Shaw himself, for which Shaw won an Academy Award. Starring Leslie Howard (who shared director credit) as Professor Higgins and newcomer Wendy Hiller as Eliza Doolittle, the film was a worldwide success. Pascal then filmed (and directed) *Major Barbara* with Rex Harrison, Hiller, and the young Deborah Kerr; then came *Caesar and Cleopatra* with Claude Rains and Vivien Leigh. His plans to film *Saint Joan* were scuttled by World War II and the qualms of the British government about reminding their French allies of the bonfire they once lit under a peasant girl. Pascal was undeterred. He went directly to Charles de Gaulle to rally support for the film and cooled on the project only when it dawned on him that de Gaulle wanted to play the title role himself. Pascal returned to the Gandhi project dear to his heart.

Shaw, through Pascal, became rich. The playwright had demanded only two things of their partnership: a percentage of the box-office gross before studio accountants could start diddling the books (Shaw was a true genius) and absolute fidelity to his written word. Pascal, meanwhile, went broke, having ignored Shaw's advice to demand a gross percentage for himself. Instead, he plowed his fees back into the pictures when he unfailingly went overbudget, ending up with nothing but his eccentric reputation.

When Shaw died in 1950 at the age of ninety-four, the estate Pascal had done so much to enrich came under the control of a trustee. Sometime in 1951 Pascal got the idea of making a musical of *Pygmalion,* though almost everyone in the theater—anticipating Moss's reaction—thought it a lunatic idea. Binkie Beaumont, who would later make millions from the notion, admitted, "I thought it was absolutely *insane."* The play took its title from a Greek legend, was a talky drawing-room comedy about language and class that its author boasted was "intensely and deliberately didactic," and it had never run longer than six months on Broadway in any production.

Still, it was not the first time such a musical had been proposed. In 1921, just seven years after *Pygmalion's* first English production, *Merry Widow* composer Franz Lehár approached Shaw with the same notion. Shaw thundered back, "A Pygmalion operetta is quite out of the question." In the thirties he told the Theatre Guild that, after *The Chocolate Soldier,* "nothing will ever induce me to allow any other play of mine to be degraded into an operetta or set to any music except its own." In the forties he dismissed even the glittering Gertrude Lawrence, who successfully impersonated Eliza on Broadway after *Lady in the Dark.* "My decision as to [a musical version of] Pygmalion is final: let me hear no more about it," Shaw wrote Gertie in 1948. "This is final."

But now the great man was dead. Pascal pointed out to the Theatre Guild that the Shaw trustee, charged with maximizing the estate, might be less averse to adaptation than the deceased had been. Lawrence Langner of the Guild (who had known Shaw) agreed and recommended that Pascal meet Alan Jay Lerner while both were in Hollywood.

According to Lerner's autobiography, Pascal was not aware that he wrote the words and Loewe, then in New York, wrote the music. Pascal took this news in stride. After his lunch of three plates of spaghetti topped with raw egg, he and Lerner waited on the sidewalk for their cars. As they stood there, Lerner recalled, "without so much as a pause in his conversation, [Pascal's] hands moved toward the reproductive area and he opened his fly, extracted the contents, and proceeded to relieve himself. Everyone stared, but no one moved or said anything, including me, because no one could believe his eyes."

Shortly after this encounter Loewe came to California. Pascal told the duo with apparent sincerity that they were the only people in the world who could write *Pygmalion,* though Lerner knew Pascal had already approached and been turned down by Rodgers and Hammerstein, Cole Porter, Noël Coward, Frank Loesser, and Arthur Schwartz and Howard Dietz, to mention only the candidates he was sure of.

In March 1952—about the time Moss was polishing *The Climate of Eden*—Lerner and Loewe agreed to look at Pascal's film version of *Pygmalion*. After the screening they said they would get involved if they could interest Mary Martin, then in London with *South Pacific*. Finally, on October 28, they signed a nonbinding contract with Pascal and the Theatre Guild that was contingent on attracting Martin for Eliza.

Shortly thereafter, Lerner ran into Hammerstein at an Adlai Stevenson rally and mentioned *Pygmalion*. "It can't be done," Hammerstein declared. "Dick and I worked on it for over a year and gave it up." Rodgers and Hammerstein's having spent a year on the challenge indirectly confirmed its worth and appeal, but Lerner and Loewe were hesitant to rush in where giants declined to tread. They withdrew.

There were rumors that the collaborators had quarreled, for neither the first nor the last time. Lerner teamed with composer Arthur Schwartz on a musical version of Al Capp's comic strip *L'il Abner* for Herman Levin. The elegantly urbane Lerner was getting nowhere with Capp's hillbillies when he came across an obituary of Pascal in the summer of 1954. He asked Levin if he'd mind switching from Dogpatch to Mayfair. He smoothed things over with Loewe and *Pygmalion* was back on.

Oscar Hammerstein's "It can't be done" was neither offhand nor ill-considered. Musicals had been evolving from girls 'n' gags to works of more thematic heft ever since the 1920s, but had become notably more ambitious and accomplished in the mid-forties with *Oklahoma!, Carousel*, and *South Pacific*. Still, those achievements, for all their deserved stature, were built on familiar conventions: a foreground love story with a secondary (usually comic) romance as subplot or foil, with plenty of singing and dancing by as many boys and girls in as many colorful sets as the budget would allow. Rodgers and Hammerstein artfully integrated these elements to produce breakthrough musicals, but the basic ingredients were the same ones always deemed essential to the form or the box office.

Pygmalion had no surreys with fringe on top, no carnivals, clambakes, or choruses of sailors. It wasn't even a love story, but what Lerner aptly called "a non–love story." It was almost entirely talk about language and social class, almost all of it in Professor Higgins's study except for a brief opening scene at Covent Garden and two later scenes in the drawing room of Higgins's mother. There was no room for chorus or dance ensembles, and no romantic subplot, comic or otherwise.

Between 1952 and 1954 there were the conventional musical hits like *Can Can, Kismet,* and *The Pajama Game* but, in the emerging off-Broadway arena, innovative shows discarded or toyed with the conventions that had made Hammerstein declare, "It can't be done." Most notable were Weill and Brecht's corrosive *Threepenny Opera* that had opened and closed on Broadway in 1933; and John Latouche and Jerome Moross's *The Golden Apple,* a sung-through romp in turn-of-the-century America based on (of all things) *The Iliad* and *The Odyssey.* Audiences were restless with the conventions and ready to laugh at them. On Broadway, a faux-1920s musical from London called *The Boy Friend* was not only better than almost everything it parodied; it also demonstrated that you could build an entire show around kidding the old formulaic elements if you had a cast with enough charm and talent.

Lerner admitted questioning the conventions without knowing how to subvert them and retain George Bernard Shaw at the same time. He later wrote of Pascal with condescension, as if he were merely a crude but colorful amateur whose contribution to *My Fair Lady*—a title still two years away—was coming up with the idea. But Pascal all along held the key to transforming the play into a musical. It had eluded Rodgers and Hammerstein and would continue for almost two years to elude Lerner and Loewe.

Pascal's crucial contribution was his certainty that a musical *Pygmalion* needn't violate the Shavian qualities that made it distinctive and appealing if it were based on the movie—blessed and signed by Shaw—not on the play. He had already worked out a structure for the musical in the film, which is why he screened it for Lerner and Loewe in 1952. His point then seemed obscure, or maybe too simple to credit, but was the kind of idea that, once grasped, seems obvious, even inevitable. It was anything but.

Audiences familiar with *My Fair Lady* are often surprised when reminded that *Pygmalion* has no scenes of Eliza's struggle with English and her hard-won mastery and transformation. There are no scenes of Higgins's teaching methods. There are no scenes in the Cockney milieu of Eliza and her father (Covent Garden is only where she sells flowers). There is no Embassy Ball; no glimpse of Eliza alone with her young suitor, Freddy Eynsford-Hill; no return to Higgins's study at the end. All these now familiar scenes come not from the play, but they do come from the movie, right down to "the rain in Spain" falling "mainly in the plain" and "Hartford, Hereford, and Hampshire." The musical's structure, with the sole substitution of Ascot for Mrs. Higgins's parlor, is identical to that of the film.

It was much less than obvious that leaving well enough alone was the solution. Lerner admitted toying with scenes at Oxford full of singing and dancing undergraduates, but his earliest surviving outline, titled "Lady Liza" (not "My Lady Liza" as is usually reported), begins with Alfred P. Doolittle in Limehouse, surrounded by Chinese sailors and sinister denizens of the slums. Liza appears, sings a rude song about "Nobbies," is overheard by Higgins and Pickering (a "younger, wiser and more worldly" Pickering than Shaw's). Their presence causes Eliza to sing an anxious "I'm a Good Girl, I Am." Doolittle and his cronies then sing about "The Undeserving Poor" and Higgins and Doolittle have a side-walk debate about middle-class morality before Eliza has become any kind of dramatic connection between them. Other new locales—a flower shop, Windsor Park—are introduced to "open up" the stage, all of them later abandoned.

Not abandoned was the suggested romantic—and "un-Shavian"—ending to the story of Eliza and Higgins for which the musical is criticized to the present day. And it is true that Shaw went out of his way to reject a romantic future for the professor and the flower girl in his finger-wagging "sequel" to *Pygmalion,* a prose piece in which he insisted that Eliza spend the rest of her days with Freddy in a flower shop financed with a loan from Colonel Pickering.

But Shaw wrote that "sequel" because he had to. Interpreting *Pygmalion* as a "romance" (Shaw himself called it that) was standard ever since its English-language premiere in 1914 (it debuted in Vienna in German the previous year). Shaw wrote the play for Mrs. Patrick Campbell, the "perilously bewitching" actress who once posed for Moss's painter uncle, Solomon J. Solomon. Eliza is described as "perhaps eighteen, perhaps twenty, hardly older," though Mrs. Campbell was forty-nine when she first played Eliza opposite Sir Herbert Beerbohm-Tree as Higgins. That production was directed by the author, which didn't stop Sir Herbert from giving it a romantic turn at its very first performance.

"I writhed in hell," Shaw told his wife. "The last thing I saw," he raged, "was Higgins shoving his mother rudely out of his way and wooing Eliza with appeals to buy ham for his lonely home like a bereaved Romeo."

Mrs. Campbell rushed to Shaw's defense, but only until he was out of earshot, at which point she introduced a twist of her own. At the end of the play Higgins haughtily orders Eliza to buy him some ham, cheese, and a pair of gloves. Eliza announces her independence and, according to the text, sweeps out of Higgins's life forever. Mrs. Campbell sabotaged that by sweeping out and sweeping right back in with, "What size?"

Actor emendations—even from Mrs. Campbell—so annoyed Shaw that decades later he was still ranting, "I absolutely forbid the Campbell interpolation or any suggestion that the middle-aged bully and the girl of eighteen are lovers." But audiences—like actors—have almost always intuited or demanded that the play's emotional momentum be resolved romantically. *Pygmalion* seems to be a genuine instance of an author not fully understanding what he has written, or underestimating the attraction his opposites would have for one another. Their first encounter so perfectly suggests romance it might be a "meet cute" of screwball comedy decades before the genre was invented.

What was implicit in the ending of the play was made more or less explicit in the musical, which is, again, almost identical to Shaw's screenplay. The film ends with Leslie Howard as Higgins in his study listening to the recordings he made of Eliza's Cockney speech at the beginning. Wendy Hiller as Eliza enters the room silently, turns off the phonograph, and enunciates perfectly, "I washed my face and hands before I came."

Music swells. Higgins brightens, then regains his composure and sternly demands, "Where the devil are my slippers, Eliza?"

There it was on-screen: the "love story" ending to the "non-love story" that had vexed Lerner at the beginning. That ending would be incorporated into the musical with only two negligible changes: Eliza's line is delivered in her old Cockney accent. "I washed my face and hands before I come, I did," to which Higgins responds, "Eliza? Where the devil are my slippers?" The "un-Shavian" ending is virtually a word-for-word lift from Shaw himself.

In his study of Shaw's plays on film called *The Serpent's Eye,* Donald P. Costello points out that Shaw's dialogue script was based on a screen adaptation prepared by the experienced scenarist Cecil Lewis, with additional minor changes by W. P. Lipscomb and Ian Dalrymple (all of whom got adaptation Oscars of their own). Costello has meticulously traced the changes from play to screenplay to screen, where sound and image—Pascal's province of camera angles, editing, and particularly music—alter Shaw's intentions. Pascal filmed three different versions of the ending as insurance against the author's disapproval, but the one we know is the only one he ever screened for him. When the lights went up, Mrs. Shaw turned to Pascal and said, "This is the finest presentation of my husband's work." After a moment, according to Behrman, Shaw chimed in with, "You said it, Mother."

The Ascot scene is the only other change from play to film to musical, but Pascal may have suggested that, too. Few observers are aware that his *Pygmalion* was not the first or even the second film version. Shaw had previously permitted its filming in Holland in 1937 and, two years before that, in Germany. The Dutch version was for a local audience, but the German version of 1935 had ambition. It was directed by Erich Engel, director of the original stage production of *The Threepenny Opera*. Higgins was stylishly played by Gustaf Gründgens, the darling of the Third Reich who was the model for the opportunistic, Nazi-courting actor in Klaus Mann's 1936 novel *Mephisto* and the Oscar-winning film of 1981 based on it, a portrait so devastating that Gründgens sought and won a court order blocking publication of Mann's novel in Germany, a prohibition still in force.

Shaw sold the rights to the Germans together with his own screenplay, but was outraged when the result departed from his pages. "They spoiled every effect, falsified all the characters, put in everything I left out and took out most of what I had put in," he accused. One of the things they invented was Eliza at the racetrack, almost certainly suggesting the change of tea party locale from Mrs. Higgins's drawing room to Ascot. It is not known if Lerner ever saw the German film, but Pascal did and it taxes credulity to think he never mentioned it.

The basic shape of the musical was set shortly before it came to Moss's attention in 1955 as "Lady Liza," though much remained undone and his direct role remains a matter of conjecture. "Moss contributed very little to the book," remembered Lerner's longtime production associate Stone "Bud" Widney. But the text was evolving with the score and neither would become final until pre-Broadway tryouts in early 1956. Lerner, a perfectionist and procrastinator, admitted that Moss served as the most considerate of editors. "He did not intrude—he guided," Lerner said. "He was a superb constructionist," one who "could put his finger on the most subtle dramatic weakness." Widney recalls, "What he did was what a director *does*—sit and suggest what's working and what's not working. Moss could sometimes find solutions because he was a writer as well, but in the end they were Alan's solutions."

Widney's view is undoubtedly correct; it would have been out of character for Moss to wrest the pencil from the writer's hand, something he had done only once, on *The Secret Room*. Still, in late November 1955, almost half a year after Moss came on board and about six weeks before rehearsals began, Lerner's book was not yet finished and Moss firmly took control. "We're going to Atlantic City," he said, "and we're not leaving until you have finished the book and we have had time to discuss every scene together." They spent four days going over every scene, line, and word in what Lerner called "four of the most delightful days I have ever spent" that were creatively vital as well. "Moss was a writer who made you feel like a writer," Lerner said, one who "could say things that uttered by anyone else would have been answered with a broken jaw."

Moss's script guidance continued on the road. Reid Shelton, a member of the ensemble who would play Freddy on tour, remembered Moss's handling of Lerner and the rewriting out of town. "Alan would come into rehearsal," Shelton recalled, and "Moss would be directing some other scene or something, and he would read over [the new pages], and he would say, 'No, no try again, Alan.' And then a few days later, Alan would come in and he'd say, 'Oh, no, no, Alan, this would never work,' and so on. And then finally one day, without even saying 'Thank you, Alan, this is wonderful,' he said, 'Oh, yes, that's fine. We'll put it in tonight.' And that was that."

Pygmalion was, almost by definition, a star vehicle, and it had always attracted star actors. The economics of Broadway demanded star casting, as Lerner and Loewe understood when insisting on Mary Martin in 1952. Two years later Martin was sprinkling fairy dust over audiences as *Peter Pan*. She and her manager-husband, Richard Halliday, agreed in November 1954 to listen to the five songs Lerner and Loewe were ready to audition: Eliza's cheerfully spiteful "Just You Wait ('enry 'iggins)"; another Eliza song to precede the Embassy Ball called "Say a Prayer for Me Tonight" (later dropped); plus two songs for Higgins and, finally, "The Ascot Gavotte." Martin's husband reported her reaction as "those dear boys have *lost their talent*." Loewe deadpanned, "I guess they didn't like it."

After Martin's dismissal of their project, they attempted to attract a movie star whose studio might finance the show as part of a loan-out and pre-buy agreement. They approached Judy Holliday, who had a long relationship with Columbia.

"Alan then had a song for Eliza where she confesses she's falling in love with Higgins," remembered Widney, "and Judy said, 'She can't sing that; she doesn't *know* she's falling in love with him.' In that way Holliday helped instruct Alan and Fritz very early in what they were doing wrong. That's how dumb it was at the beginning," Widney says, "because it's always dumb until you've found your way. You do dumb, naïve things and the wonderful part about actors is that they approach character specifically from their perspective and an actor like Judy can say, 'Wait a minute!' So Alan threw that number out and began all over again."

Holliday committed instead to *Bells Are Ringing* by Jule Styne and Comden and Green. Lerner then turned to Paramount to negotiate a deal with the studio for an actress who was perhaps the most intriguing and surprising possibility of any. "With *My Fair Lady,* we were at one point thinking about Audrey Hepburn," Lerner confided to Ferber just after the musical opened in New York. "[W]e spent a good deal of time thrashing it all about with Paramount, who own her contract," he wrote, "until a strange report that she was pregnant reached our ears."

The report was strange only because it wasn't true. Hepburn had been trained as a dancer, was then one of the biggest stars in the world, had acquired stage and musical experience in England before entering American films in *Roman Holiday,* and had recently appeared on Broadway in *Ondine.* She had a small but expressive singing voice she would shortly use opposite Fred Astaire in *Funny Face,* Stanley Donen's Gershwin-based movie. She would in time have her chance to play Eliza and when she did would be almost universally criticized for "usurping" a role that might have been hers in the first place but for a pregnancy rumor that turned out to be false.

With no realistic star possibilities for Eliza, the focus shifted to casting Higgins. Lerner wrote in his autobiography that Rex Harrison had been everyone's first and only choice, but he wasn't. Lerner was writing when Harrison was still alive, still playing the part in revival, and still one of the most difficult actors anyone—including Moss—had ever encountered.

The only person involved with *My Fair Lady* who had wanted Harrison was Pascal and he was dead. Pascal had directed him in *Major Barbara* but his conviction that Harrison was right aroused little enthusiasm. He was not then anything like the star he would become through this very role; he was not a singer; nor was he an altogether sympathetic choice for a large general audience.

Harrison revered Shaw, whom he had known during the filming of *Major Barbara,* but he was more identified with the lighter works of Terence Rattigan and Coward (who is said to have told him, "After me, you're the best light comedian in the world"). He had been on the stage since 1924 at the age of sixteen and in movies since 1930, but only became a star at the end of World War II in David Lean's film version of Coward's *Blithe Spirit.* Soon after that he was in America playing opposite Irene Dunne in *Anna and the King of Siam* (from which a musical would be made without him). He starred in Preston Sturges's *Unfaithfully Yours* and other pictures in which he projected stylish elegance and dangerous charm.

Harrison's Hollywood career came to a standstill in 1948. Though married to Lilli Palmer, he had been having an affair with actress Carole Landis, who killed herself with an overdose of barbiturates because of him, it was said. Whether he was to blame for her death or not, gossip indicted him, making "sexy Rexy" cad non grata in Hollywood. He returned to the stage and Broadway success as Henry VIII in Maxwell Anderson's *Anne of the Thousand Days* and as the bewitched bachelor in John Van Druten's *Bell, Book, and Candle*. He starred in the latter in New York and in London opposite Palmer, whose patience with his escapades was monumental, but not limitless. Though Harrison had appeared in musicals in London in the early thirties and had even sung in them, his vocal abilities were minimal and mostly forgotten. Beyond Pascal's enthusiasm, there was no particular reason to reach for Harrison and—Lerner's memoirs notwithstanding—no one did.

Richard Maney, press agent on *My Fair Lady*, admitted that Harrison got the role "only after every other actor in England had been asked to play it, starting with Noël Coward and ending with John Gielgud." Coward was first choice. Having turned down Rodgers and Hammerstein's offer to play the king in *The King and I*, Coward kept his curiously wrongheaded record unblemished by turning down Higgins, too.

Others were considered, including David Niven, George Sanders, John Gielgud, and Michael Redgrave, who could sing and said yes. Herman Levin opened negotiations, but Redgrave balked at a two-year commitment on Broadway. Levin countered with one year, but Redgrave refused to sign for more than a six-month run. In December 1954 the offer to him was withdrawn.

Meanwhile, lawyer Irving Cohen had been negotiating with the Shaw trustee to resolve a legal issue that might have made Redgrave or anybody else a moot point by killing the project altogether. Shaw had always refused to license his plays for more than five years, which meant that no movie company would buy the rights to the musical with so little time in which to make and distribute a film. Levin and Lerner hoped the matter would be resolved in their favor (it was), but couldn't afford to wait. They decided to offer the project to television networks, whose broadcast needs were so demanding that the five-year restriction might not matter. If the show flopped, it might make a prestigious "live" broadcast of a Broadway musical. If successful, it could become a "Spectacular," as the splashy one-shot events promoting color were called, like Moss's *Lady in the Dark*, telecast on NBC in 1954, live and in color with Ann Sothern as Liza Elliott.

The *Pygmalion* musical was offered to NBC's Robert Sarnoff, a childhood friend of Lerner's, and to the head of CBS's Columbia Records, Goddard Lieberson, who more or less invented the long-playing original cast album (he had recorded both *Brigadoon* and *Gentlemen Prefer Blondes*). The offer included all rights in return for total financing, including album and broadcast rights and—if the five-year restriction were lifted—movie rights as well. Sarnoff never responded, but William S. Paley of CBS, friendly with everyone involved, did. He agreed to finance the entire show for $400,000 ($360,000 plus a 10 percent overcall, a form of contingency in the theater), which would eventually be repaid more than 2,000 percent, making it the single most lucrative investment in Broadway history.

Shortly after negotiations broke off with Redgrave, Lerner telephoned Harrison in London to ask if he might be interested. Harrison's reaction suggested "we had all gone around the bend," Lerner said. Still, the actor's long run in *Bell, Book, and Candle* had become a bore, especially since he and Palmer were speaking to each other only onstage and offstage he was deeply involved in an affair with actress Kay Kendall. When Lerner volunteered that they were willing to come to England with songs for him to hear, Harrison agreed to listen.

In January, while Moss was being readmitted to Columbia-Presbyterian after his relapse, Lerner and Loewe flew to London. There they played the same five numbers they had presented to Mary Martin, including the two songs for Higgins. In "Please Don't Marry Me" the professor expressed a mild sort of misogyny and in "Lady Liza," the (then) title song, he offered encouragement to his pupil before the ball.

Harrison's reaction was immediate. "I hate them," he said.

He was right, Lerner later conceded, and it is notable that of the five songs presented to Martin and Harrison only "The Ascot Gavotte" and "Just You Wait" survived. Eliza's "Say a Prayer for Me Tonight" would be dropped out of town, and Harrison's negative reaction forced a search for more character depth than "Please Don't Marry Me" delivered, yielding the deliciously self-justifying (and self-deluded) "I'm an Ordinary Man." "Lady Liza" was dropped altogether as superfluous.

Whatever Harrison's qualms, he consented to a singing—or nonsinging—audition so Loewe could judge his range and tailor songs to his abilities if it came to that. As Harrison vacillated, Lerner and Levin persuaded Cecil Beaton to design costumes, working with the already engaged scenic designer Oliver Smith. Stanley Holloway auditioned for Alfred P. Doolittle with a stentorian rendition of eight bars of "God Save the Queen" that rattled silverware and china in the dining room at Claridge's. Harrison continued to waver but suggested an old acting chum, Robert Coote, for Colonel Pickering and he, too, was cast.

Finally, in February Harrison agreed to play Henry Higgins during a wintry walk with Lerner in Hyde Park. It seemed clear by then that *Bell, Book, and Candle* would close before summer and these two talented and high-strung men were of a single stripe, both of them dedicated to serial matrimony. Lerner would marry eight times before he was through and Harrison six. ("Together we've supported more women than Playtex," Lerner is said to have quipped.) There is evidence that each thought himself—divorces and suicides notwithstanding—a compassionate expert in the care and handling of the female, not unlike the egocentric and oblivious Higgins. Lerner admitted that Harrison was as likely to address a wife—anybody's wife—with "You bitch!" as with any other endearment, which seemed part of Harrison's "unique approach to human relations." It followed that a chance remark by Harrison to Lerner inspired, almost word for word, Higgins's song "A Hymn to Him," sometimes called "Why Can't a Woman Be More Like a Man?"

With Harrison's signing on March 10, 1955, all the elements of the musical were in place except a leading lady and a director. Levin claimed that while in London they had auditioned "maybe fifty girls, including a nobody named Petula Clark." All were rejected and the search would resume in New York.

Harrison had approval of his leading lady and of his director. Levin had insisted in London that he preapprove directors in order to expedite things back in New York and Harrison agreed to: John Van Druten, author of *Bell, Book, and Candle* and director of *The King and I*; Alfred Lunt, the actor and recent director of Audrey Hepburn in *Ondine* (was she still a possibility for Eliza?); Robert "Bobby" Lewis, director of *Brigadoon*; Peter Glenville, director of Terence Rattigan's *The Browning Version* and *Separate Tables*; Tyrone Guthrie of Ontario's Shakespeare Festival; Cedric Hardwicke, director of Gertrude Lawrence's *Pygmalion*; Cyril Ritchard, Mary Martin's "Captain Hook" and recent director of Shaw's *Misalliance*; and Hume Cronyn, the Canadian actor who sometimes directed and, with his wife, Jessica Tandy, had recently starred on Broadway in *The Fourposter*, the movie version of which starred Harrison and Palmer.

According to Levin, Moss's name was raised offhandedly. Harrison remarked, "Oh, Moss Hart. He wouldn't be much good, would he?" The two knew each other casually through Darryl Zanuck and through Irene Selznick, who had produced *Bell, Book, and Candle* in New York. Harrison tepidly agreed to preapprove Moss as a fallback in the unlikely event no one else worked out.

In April Lerner and Loewe flew to California to meet with Van Druten, who was "not excited" by the idea, but might be in October, he said, whatever that meant. Ritchard announced that he was busy at the Met. Others were unavailable, found the project ill-advised, or were, like Lunt and Guthrie, not entirely right for a musical, or for Lerner or Loewe.

Which left Moss, recently ill and rumored to be working on a musical of his own with Harold Rome.

Casting Harrison as Henry Higgins relieved the pressure to cast a star as Eliza. She might even be a newcomer, like the girl in *The Boy Friend* over whom the New York critics had turned handsprings. Walter Kerr wrote in the *Herald-Tribune* that she was "a treasure," and John McClain in the *Journal-American* thought she was "all the musical comedy heroines you've ever seen, only more so."

No one ever disclaimed credit for "discovering" Julie Andrews—who had been singing professionally since childhood—but no one was quite sure who first suggested her for Eliza, either. Moss later thought it was Cy Feuer, producer of *The Boy Friend*. Bud Widney thought it might have been Lerner's agent. Lerner thought it was Lerner. Even Andrews was confused looking back on the whirlwind of events.

She was only nineteen, from an English village called Walton-on-Thames, engaged to a scenic designer–to–be named Tony Walton (no relation to the town), and she had grown up in show business. She later remembered first hearing about the *Pygmalion* musical in April 1955, but by then she had auditioned twice for Lerner and Loewe at the Majestic Theatre, across the street from the Royale, where *The Boy Friend* was playing. She had privately read acting scenes for Lerner. She had signed to appear opposite Bing Crosby in a CBS television musical based on Maxwell Anderson's *High Tor* that would also star Nancy Olson, who happened then to be Mrs. Alan Jay Lerner. She was under consideration by Rodgers and Hammerstein for their *Pipe Dream*. And on March 31 she had already signed a contract to play Eliza.

"What are these Americans going to do to poor George Bernard Shaw?" she wondered, while Broadway regulars wondered if the nineteen-year-old—however charming she was—was ready to hold her own with Harrison, Holloway, Coote, and Shaw.

Moss agreed in late May or early June to hear some songs, knowing that the "quite hopeless task" of a musical *Pygmalion* had already snared Harrison, Andrews, Holloway, Coote, Beaton, and Oliver Smith in addition to Lerner and Loewe. He knew that the show was fully financed by CBS (William S. Paley was a friend of his, too). Still, he went skeptically, prepared only to give a courtesy listen and then issue a "thumping no."

What he heard were four more or less completed songs: "Why Can't the English (Teach Their Children How to Speak)?," "Wouldn't It Be Loverly?," "The Ascot Gavotte," and an early version of "I'm an Ordinary Man." He realized, as he listened with an almost helpless elation, that "my goose was being cooked."

He had been struggling with a not very good musical of his own; he was still disheartened by the failure of *The Climate of Eden;* he was represented on Broadway only by a trivial comedy that pleased audiences and repelled critics; and he had had a recent brush with mortality. The songs he heard were not just the "few deft lyrical and musical strokes" he had expected. They were lifelines reconnecting him to the kind of aspiration that energized and sustained him. Which is why he agreed on June 21 to stage what would become *My Fair Lady.*

And when rehearsals began on January 3, 1956, they brought him back to the New Amsterdam Theatre on Forty-second Street, to the building in which he had begun his career more than thirty years before.

26

Loverly

> *. . . he kind of convinced the cast and crew before*
> *the curtain went up, that we were just marvelous and that*
> *if the audience didn't like it, well what did they know*
> *anyway? We were great. We really were.*

JULIE ANDREWS

Even after Moss said yes to *My Fair Lady,* he was uncertain enough about its prospects to insist that Herman Levin fund the ongoing development of "In the Pink" until it or the Lerner and Loewe musical went into rehearsal. He barely knew Lerner and Loewe, neither their score nor their book was close to completion, and the idea of a *Pygmalion* musical still caused widespread skepticism on the Rialto. Moreover, he was battling mood downswings intensified by the restrictions of a protracted physical recovery. As he recuperated, he saw Kubie in the city and tossed and turned with insomnia at the beach.

He took long, labored walks along the Jersey shore when serious depression set in. Kitty was often at his side, trudging through the sand with an umbrella raised against the elements, as if sheer doggedness could ameliorate his condition. She claimed ever after that she never questioned him directly about his analysis or Kubie's treatment, but it hardly mattered. Whether she did or didn't—or sympathized with or even understood the process—she was determined to provide support.

His emotional and physical states were worsened by lack of sleep. Kitty finally insisted he demand the then-new Librium or some other sedative from Kubie, but Kubie refused, perhaps aware that Moss had been relying on sleeping pills for more than thirty years. Besides, he said, the insomnia was useful for the psychoanalytic process and medication that alleviated sleeplessness might also "mask his symptoms."

Kitty was infuriated and confronted Kubie on the telephone from

Beach Haven. *"Mask the symptoms?"* she demanded. "The man has been in analysis for fifteen years and he's had a heart attack and he can't sleep. If you don't give me those tranquilizers I am going to come to New York and snatch you bald-headed."

Moss got his pills. More therapeutically, he got back to work in the theater.

After signing his contract in June, he focused on what he viewed as the emotional and dramatic heart of the show: Eliza's onstage transformation from flower girl to Cinderella literally on her way to the ball. He decided Eliza's preparations should provide the climax at the end of act one, giving the audience the Embassy Ball to look forward to after intermission. He was, in effect, determining structure. To build to the first-act curtain and provide choreographer Hanya Holms's dancers with something to do, Moss and Lerner borrowed what they called the "Decorating Eliza ballet" from the movie. Pascal had included a montage in which Eliza was mud-packed, manicured, pedicured, coiffed, and dressed for the ball while being taught to smile, curtsy, and behave regally enough to win Higgins's bet that he could pass her off as a duchess. Lerner wrote this as an extended ballet with "a dancing instructor from Vienna, a dressmaker from Paris, a physical culturist from Copenhagen," as well as "the best hairdresser in London" and "the Royal cosmetician." They and Eliza dance and pantomime the transformation to Cinderella over what Lerner decided was a three-month period between Ascot, Eliza's first appearance in society (livened in this version by her exhortation to a horse to "get the bloody cork out"), and the ball itself. The songs just before intermission included Higgins's cajoling "Come to the Ball" and Eliza's plaintive "Say a Prayer for Me Tonight." The second act would open with the Embassy Ball in full swing, with Eliza making her entrance in a dazzling Beaton gown as dancers whirled on double turntables under the electric shimmer of crystal chandeliers.

Moss's training in musicals had been almost entirely with Hassard Short, now retired and living in the south of France. Short taught him about size and brilliance of stage effects (and turntables) from *Face the Music* to *Lady in the Dark* and his influence continued after that, filtered through Harry Horner, with *Miss Liberty* the only musical Moss worked on without either of them until now. Short had given him tools to achieve effects that ranged from the subtlety of the sepia-glow of "Easter Parade" to the spectacle of Liza Elliott's Circus Dream, but Moss's weakness for overelaborate stage effects had damaged straight plays like *The American Way,* on which Short worked, and *Christopher Blake,* on which Horner realized the grandiose, perhaps fatal, schemes.

Now Moss could bring Short's taste for subtle beauties and his own for extravagant display to the ballet and the Embassy Ball, which were also the only scenes with finished songs that had been approved by everyone involved. The whole intermission-bracketing structure was technically feasible, lavishly executed, and would be discarded, songs and all, after a single performance on the road.

Rehearsals of *My Fair Lady* began at the New Amsterdam Theatre on January 3. Harrison's London run in *Bell, Book, and Candle* had been unexpectedly extended over the summer due to a surprise influx of American tourists riding high on a strong dollar. Harrison, still feuding with his costar wife and increasingly involved with Kay Kendall, was only too eager to be free of the comedy but was contractually bound to it until business fell below a certain point or until April 1956, whichever came first. Herman Levin, acting on expectations that the play would have closed before summer, had booked theaters in America for January, now an impossible date to meet unless Harrison was bought out of his London contract with Binkie Beaumont.

With no leverage, Levin yielded to Beaumont's demands for a cash payment of £25,000 and—to sweeten the deal—English and continental rights to the musical the English impresario had derided as "absolutely *insane,*" plus one and a half percent of the Broadway and touring company grosses. Beaumont was as shrewd as any producer on either side of the Atlantic and knew that, for the time being, the percentages were meaningless (100 percent of nothing is nothing), hence the demand for cash. He also knew that for no risk whatever he gained a percentage that—who knew?—might be worth something. In the event, the percentage of the touring companies alone would be worth millions. This windfall was shared indirectly by Irene Selznick as the original producer of *Bell, Book, and Candle,* making her one of the few individual beneficiaries of a show with no private investors. Another was Gabriel Pascal. The courts awarded him a posthumous coauthor credit with Shaw of the movie version of *Pygmalion,* an official *My Fair Lady* program credit, and a royalty equal to Shaw's own. Pascal, or his estate, would make money from his association with Shaw after all—millions, into perpetuity.

Julie Andrews, cast almost two months before Moss signed on to the show, remembers meeting him for the first time at the start of rehearsals. She appeared modest and at ease meeting the man who "really changed

Three producers:
Billy Rose, Max
Gordon, and
Moss, circa 1938
(NYPL)

The young and
beautiful (Canadian)
Dora Sayers in
The American Way,
before she became
"Moss's girl" (NYPL)

The inspiration for *The
Man Who Came to Dinner*
plays the part: Alexander
Woollcott as, well,
himself (NYPL)

Above: Monty Woolley on Broadway in *The Man Who Came to Dinner* with Gordon Merrick, "the handsomest man in New York," who would write a revealing book about his world (Charles Hulse) *Below Left:* Gertrude Lawrence meets Victor Mature, "a beautiful hunk of man," in *Lady in the Dark.* (NYPL) *Below Right:* Gertrude Lawrence as a *Lady in the Dark*, with an unidentified Danny Kaye at the far right, on the cover of *Time*

Happy thirty-eighth birthday backstage at *Junior Miss*. To Moss's right are one-time "Moss's girl" Paula Laurence and froggy-voiced Lenore Lonergan; to his left is Patricia Peardon, the "junior miss" herself. (NYPL)

The author presents *Winged Victory* to his cast and crew. (NYPL)

ONE OF THE 'LITTLE' PROBLEMS

Above: The brilliant young Harry Horner designed *Winged Victory* for Moss and the Army Air Force and kept a sketchbook diary of its "little problems"—like putting a bomber onstage. (Robert Cantell) *Below:* "The Andrews Sisters," featuring Red Buttons (center), doing something for the boys (Robert Cantell)

Above: Moss with his USO ladies (*left to right*): Dina Merrill, Dora Sayers, Paula Trueman, Haila Stoddard, and Janet Fox (Dora Caro) *Below:* Moss as Sheridan Whiteside in the South Pacific for the USO with (*left to right*) Tyrone Power, Dora Sayers, Dina Merrill, Janet Fox, and Haila Stoddard in *The Man Who Came to Dinner* (Dora Caro)

The "Moss's girl"
who became
"Moss's bride":
Kitty Carlisle
(NYPL)

"Boy in the Dark" meets judge in *Christopher Blake*. (NYPL)

Above: Bernie Hart and Joseph Hyman, Moss's partners, preparing to bite bullets, confer with their playwright-director on *The Climate of Eden.* (NYPL) *Left:* "Miss Liberty" raises her torch for a "Give Me Your Tired" finale. Eddie Albert and Allyn (Ann) McLerie are at the far left. (NYPL)

"Here comes a big fat close-up"—exactly what Moss wrote for Judy Garland (here with James Mason), in *A Star Is Born* (1954). This remains the most memorable of his three major screenplays, which include *Gentleman's Agreement,* Oscar's "Best Picture" of 1947, and *Hans Christian Andersen* for Sam Goldwyn and Danny Kaye in 1952. (AMPAS)

Above: Moss, Julie Andrews, and Rex Harrison before all hell broke loose on *My Fair Lady*, 1956 (NYPL)

Above: Julie Andrews becoming a star with "I Could Have Danced All Night" (NYPL)
Right: Eliza and Professor Higgins tearing at each other (NYPL)

my life" and was to become her personal Pygmalion. In truth, "I was simply terrified. Working with Rex Harrison and Stanley Holloway, and meeting a director I'd never worked with before." Moss told her how "enchanting" he had found her in *The Boy Friend* and privately thought her charmingly unspoiled and dismayingly unseasoned.

His early warning system began vibrating with alarm when she delayed flying to New York until the day rehearsals began. She insisted on spending New Year's in England with her fiancé Tony Walton, and her family. Moss wanted her to arrive a full week earlier, as Harrison had done, but she had promised to take her two young stepbrothers to a holiday pantomime and refused to break her promise. Her agent assured Moss that she was young and energetic enough to walk off the plane and directly into rehearsals with no jet lag.

Jet lag was not the point; professionalism was. She had been a great success in *The Boy Friend,* relying on charm and natural gifts, but the challenges of a 1920s lampoon were hardly comparable to the enormous ones facing her now.

She was unusually shy for a performer—and as a person, too—and there may have been an unspoken reason for her delay. After being released from *The Boy Friend* in August, she spent November in Hollywood filming *High Tor* opposite Bing Crosby. Crosby was notorious for his interest in younger women (he had made a conquest of Grace Kelly on *The Country Girl*) and found Andrews, just turning twenty, tasty enough to propose marriage to her. Whether heartfelt or a ploy, the proposal "knocked her sideways," as she reported to Walton. Remaining at home in Walton-on-Thames as long as possible helped postpone a professional situation full of unknowns, including another mature costar with a reputation as a womanizer even more lurid than Crosby's.

She arrived in New York on January 3 with her mother. They flew on BOAC, the airline that had a soft spot for young lovers and agreed to help her stay in touch with Tony Walton via courier pouch. The couple had Dictaphone machines on both sides of the Atlantic so Julie could dictate letters-in-sound to her fiancé and he to her, sometimes as many as five a day. The Dictabelts they made kept intimacy alive and inadvertently made a permanent diary of the day-to-day, sometimes hour-to-hour progress of the show.

What Lerner called Andrews's "dazzling array of gifts" promised to bring Eliza to fresh life. She was the first actress in memory who was the age of the character Shaw wrote. Her soprano voice was, as Lerner noted, "so flexible she could sing light opera and popular with equal ease." She had "immaculate diction." She "moved with grace." And "she was as pretty as any eye might decide her to be." She was, as the world would learn, all of those things. What she was not, was Eliza Doolittle.

Her acting experience had been a concern from the beginning, accounting for the multiple auditions. Lerner later allowed that "her first tryouts had not been very good," and he had given her a copy of Shaw's play to study over the summer and fall. Her modesty was a charming virtue and a handicap; even with her name in lights above the title of *The Boy Friend*, Lerner said, she "had no sense of being a star, none of the sense of obligation that a star has toward a play," an impression underlined by her late arrival in New York. The truth was she had little sense of herself onstage and never in her life had worked out a characterization of any greater depth than "the principal girl who," in her own description, "makes goo-goo eyes at Our Hero and gets him in the end."

Moss conducted the company's first read-through at the New Amsterdam Roof, where Ziegfeld produced nightclub shows in the teens and twenties. Company manager Samuel "Biff" Liff recalled the space as "very old, very dusty, very unappealing" but "it had a stage." The reading went forward in a flat, neutral manner with an unfinished score and a leading man who, as Reid Shelton remembered, "just mumbled in the script and you couldn't hear what he was saying." Flat first readings are the norm, but it was unsettling for actors to hear Loewe playing and Lerner singing unfinished numbers, from the still incomplete "Why Can't the English" at the beginning to "I've Grown Accustomed to Her Face" at the end, then just "a couple of couplets."

Moss's custom was to get a show on its feet as soon as possible and *My Fair Lady* was up and walking within four days. It was glaringly apparent that Andrews was learning on the job. "I got worse, not better," she admitted. "It was obvious to everyone that I was out of my depth, and the awful thing was that I knew it. It only made things worse."

But at twenty, she was a veteran and a trouper. She had made her professional debut with her pianist mother and tenor stepfather at ten, joining their vaudeville act with what she called "bastardized versions of operatic arias," standing on a beer crate to reach the microphone. She was a pigtailed child with unstraightened teeth and a grown-up voice of crystalline clarity that ranged up and down four octaves in perfect pitch. She soon became the headliner of the family act and breadwinner, too, appearing in the title roles of pantomimes like *Cinderella* and *Humpty Dumpty*. She even sang "God Save the Queen" in a Royal Command Performance that headlined Danny Kaye when she was only thirteen.

Now she was trying on a role identified with actresses like Mrs.

Patrick Campbell, Lynn Fontanne, Wendy Hiller, and Gertrude Lawrence, a far cry from *Humpty Dumpty*. "I didn't know what Eliza should be," she realized, "a whiny girl or a gutsy girl, a weak character or a strong one." She read and reread the play, saw and resaw the *Pygmalion* movie when Lerner screened it for her, and felt overwhelmed by the dawning sense of having taken on "a monstrous task." She felt secure enough with the singing but "When it came to acting, I was simply awful at first and terrified of Rex Harrison."

Harrison "hated the whole idea of working with this silly little girl," observers noted, especially when she arrived at the theater practicing her scales, something he as a nonsinger couldn't begin to do. Musical theater historian Miles Kreuger, then fresh out of Bard College and working on Lerner's office staff, remembered Harrison from rehearsal days as "one of the nastiest people one could ever want to meet—witty and stylish and marvelous when he was in a good mood, and cruelly cutting when he wasn't, and he often wasn't. He was very cruel with Julie Andrews. Not *to* her, but about her." Moss was seismographically sensitive to star tensions and conflicts of this kind, but even he admitted early on "she didn't have a clue about playing Eliza."

He vented his frustrations to Kitty after just five days of rehearsal. "If I were David Belasco," he said, "I would take Julie to a hotel for the weekend. I'd never let her out; I'd order up room service. I'd keep her there and *paste* the part on her." Kitty reminded him he had pasted parts on *her* and asked why he didn't do just that.

The situation was tense and growing volatile. Almost everyone in the company remembered that at some point in the first week Harrison threw down a prop—some remember a cane, others say it was his script—and announced in a voice that carried to both ends of Forty-second Street, "If that girl is here on Monday giving the same goddam performance, I am out of this show." Heads swiveled and froze. Kreuger remembered Harrison calling Andrews "that bitch," while Reid Shelton said the words were even bluer, but whatever they were, no one wanted to test Harrison's threat or argue the point. Moss decided to do what he thought Belasco would do.

He dismissed the company and closed the New Amsterdam Roof for the weekend to everyone but himself, Biff Liff, and Andrews. "It was the sort of thing you couldn't do in front of a company," Moss said, "without destroying a human being. We met in this silent, lonely dark theater and I told her, 'Julie, this is stolen time, time I can't really afford. So there can be no time for politeness and you mustn't take offense, because there aren't any second chances in the theater. There isn't time to sit down and do the whole Actors' Studio bit. We have to start from the first line and go over the play line by line.'" The trouper in her appreciated the situation. "He'd have to be ruthless and brutal, and I'd have to understand why," she remembered. "I felt as if I was going to the dentist to have a tooth pulled."

Moss worked with her after the morning costume fittings from two in the afternoon until six in the evening, broke for a meal, and resumed again from eight to eleven. Like a Henry Higgins in reverse, he dredged up Cockney-isms he had heard from his father in childhood and had once used playing Smithers in *The Emperor Jones* (she thought his accent "atrocious"); he helped her understand the play line by line, joke by joke or, if she didn't fully understand, *sound* like she did. She recalls his telling her bluntly, "You're playing this like a Girl Guide," or "You haven't any idea of how to play that," or "You're not thinking, you're just oozing out the scene," or "You're too light, much too light," or "I can't hear you. I want this louder. I want that angrier." Over two days, she said, "he bullied, cajoled, pleaded, scolded, encouraged." According to Liff, he also delivered an appeal to old-fashioned show-biz ambition. "You want to be a star," he told her, "you'd better *be* a star. And you're going to have to play as though you *are* a star. This is a starring role and you've got to stop being intimidated."

The only intimidating factor of the moment was Moss, using a canny psychological ploy in which he became a stern but benign version of the twin terrors she could not face down directly—Harrison and Shaw—in a setting that allowed her to fight back and grow or go down in defeat.

She remembered, "occasionally he would stomp up onto the stage to interrupt and show me exactly how he wanted it done," much as he had once done for Kitty. The man who had unhesitatingly given an entire performance for cast and crew as Gertrude Lawrence playing Liza Elliott was not hesitant to try Eliza Doolittle on for size in front of Andrews. "I remember when he snatched Eliza's purse from my hand and he hit out at an imaginary Higgins, to show me how he wanted it done," she said. "And then, I have a picture of him holding Eliza's teacup, very prim and proper with that ring finger extended. At times he actually became Eliza Doolittle and I just kind of stood back and watched.

"He was really the strongest force that I had ever come up against," she said. "I never had anything like it before. I just wanted to sit down and weep in despair. Or I got angry, at which time I yelled back at him, which was exactly what he wanted, of course. I think for a while I even hated him."

"Those two days made the difference," Moss said. "We were both absolutely done in, exhausted. But she made it. She has that terrible English strength that makes you wonder why they lost India." He praised her for being "neither affronted nor hurt. She was delighted."

She wasn't as delighted as all that. By her own account she was "infuriated, and scared and mad and frightened and in awe and full of an inferiority complex." But "I really did need a strong guiding hand," she admitted. "Moss supplied the route, the direction." She pauses. "He made me be Eliza."

"He dirtied her up," Bud Widney says. "There are two parts to Eliza: one she's a scruffy little street urchin and then she becomes a lady and while Julie was practicing the lady, she forgot the urchin. It was difficult for her to growl 'Aaaooowww'—that kind of stuff. Moss couldn't get her down to the street level and he had to have that if he wanted to get growth in the character. That was what was driving Rex crazy, whether she had the guts for it, the capacity as an actress."

While Moss was teaching the role to Andrews and holding Harrison's hand, Stanley Holloway decided to feel neglected and told Herman Levin he wanted out of the show. Moss sat him down, one old campaigner to another, and said, "Now look, Stanley. I am rehearsing a girl who has never played a major role in her life and an actor who has never sung on the stage in his life. You have done both. If you feel neglected, it is a compliment." The soft soap worked, though Holloway never warmed to Harrison and would later threaten a lawsuit when Harrison belittled him to the British press.

For now, however, Harrison's insecurities were painfully obvious and had to do with being faithful to Shaw and learning the ropes of the mystery he referred to as "musical com." He nagged Lerner incessantly to know where this or that speech came from. To verify fidelity to the original, he brought to every rehearsal a copy of the Penguin edition of *Pygmalion,* the standard edition ever since 1941 that, fortunately for Lerner, was Shaw's last revision and incorporated scenes from the screenplay that Lerner, in turn, had adapted. "Where's my Penguin?" Harrison would call out when dubious about a line or piece of business in order to check and verify. Finally Lerner tired of the constant challenges. He located a friendly taxidermist and the next time Harrison called out "Where's my Penguin?" rolled a genuine stuffed bird across the stage to him, dissolving the company in laughter, including the demanding star, who had a sense of humor after all. He liked the joke so much he told it on himself in his memoirs and the taxidermist's pride became a permanent companion in his dressing room.

Harrison's concern about his singing—he claimed to have a vocal range of a note and a half—was less easily handled. Loewe had taken the measure of his voice in London and composed songs for him that could be delivered in *Sprech-Stimme,* a manner of speaking rhythmically and on key that suggested singing. Still, as Widney recalled, "Rex was justifiably scared to death" with Holloway belting out his numbers like a brass band and Julie growing in assurance and maintaining her coloratura's perfect pitch.

Harrison was frightened and he was petty. Before the company left for tryouts in New Haven, he decided it was demeaning for him to remain passively onstage while Eliza sang her defiant "Without You" late in the second act, a song he didn't like anyway because it was at his expense. "I'm not going to stand up there and look like a cunt while this young girl sings a song at me," he announced, and walked off the stage.

He walked off every time the song was sung. Moss did nothing, giving him enough rope, he told Lerner, because "you can't fight every day of your life or you dissipate your strength and it becomes a way of life. In every play there's one battle you have to win, and when we're in the best position we will do battle."

The best position was a train seat on the way to New Haven. Moss sidled in next to Harrison and calmly but firmly confronted the issue. "I think you should at least give me the courtesy of seeing how I would like to stage it," he said, "because the song is going to get sung, don't make any mistake about that. It's going to be sung." Pause. "Now you can walk offstage while it's being sung and walk on again when it's over, but you will look like the biggest horse's ass in the history of the theater. So I would suggest that you at least come to the rehearsal and see how it could be staged."

Harrison bristled, but Lerner added a mollifying tag to the scene for Higgins after Eliza's song in which he could sing-chortle, "I did it. I did it. I said I'd make a woman and indeed I did." Harrison, having literally been given the last word, finally did as he was told.

He almost didn't do anything. The moment of crisis came not long after the technical rehearsal when Moss's turntables, true to form, didn't work. Finally light cues were set, revolving stages repaired, and all was in readiness for the actors to rehearse their songs backed by a full orchestra of thirty-two musicians rather than the rehearsal pianist who had been accompanying them. The experience, Lerner said, "blew Rex sky high." He heard nothing from the pit but a cacophony of instruments. He exploded at conductor Franz Allers (one such scene survives on an amateur film made during a rehearsal), demanding hysterically that the orchestra stop whatever it was doing and rewrite the orchestrations (by

Robert Russell Bennett and Phil Lang) on the spot before he would sing another note. Moss rehearsed him alone with the musicians and Allers finally designated a clarinet in the pit (an instrument Harrison liked and could hear) to carry the melody for Harrison from beginning to end of the performance. The clarinet accustomed him to "musical com" without fully allaying his fears.

On February 4, opening night in New Haven, the Shubert Theatre was sold out and a blizzard raged. Harrison, paralyzed with fear, refused to go on. No amount of persuasion by Moss, Lerner, Loewe, or Levin could overcome his terror. Radio announcements were hastily broadcast that the performance was canceled due to that familiar, all-purpose gremlin: "technical difficulties."

By six o'clock in the evening, lines were forming in the snow outside the theater. Ticket holders had left home early because of the blizzard and had missed the radio bulletins. The manager of the Shubert confronted the situation shaking with rage. "There will be a riot in this lobby at seven-thirty when I announce that there won't be any performance," he said. "You people leave here next week and move on, but I have to face this same audience every week." He threatened to announce from the stage the simple, ugly truth "that Rex Harrison refuses to go on."

David Hocker, Harrison's New York agent, arrived, went pale as he grasped the situation, and told his client he was likely never to work again if word got out, and he would personally see to it that word got out. The local theatergoers were, in any case, augmented by the usual New York "wrecking crew" (Lerner called them "dear shits"), most of them fairly aching to return to New York with reports of disaster. The combined threats persuaded Harrison he had no choice, but by this time his sense of terror had become contagious. Robert Coote as Colonel Pickering was, Widney remembered, "a basket case. He was more terrified than Rex, but he was getting his fear *from* Rex."

Finally the houselights dimmed around 8:45 that evening. Moss stepped before the curtain to announce stoically that the turntables weren't working and anyone who wanted a refund or exchange of tickets could apply at the box office. A few did and may still regret it. Harrison was greeted warmly by the audience on his entrance and managed to get through a wobbly "Why Can't the English" without betraying more than opening-night jitters. Then, according to Widney, "the combination of Moss's calm steady-at-the-helm captain and being suddenly confronted onstage with a terrific pro in Julie Andrews calmed Rex down. Julie sang 'Wouldn't It Be Loverly' with a sense of professional security confident enough to lend Rex the strength to get through it—in spite of his terror and his earlier skepticism about *her*. Then Stanley came on, a fearless old music hall pro, and did 'With a Little Bit O' Luck' and brought down the house. Rex was onstage with two old pros and their security *had* to register on him. They went through hell getting him past that fear on opening night, but once he did it, he did it."

The act progressed smoothly, growing in strength until Eliza's breakthrough with "the rain in Spain" and "Hartford, Hereford, and Hampshire." Harrison as Higgins began his rhythmic tango moves joined by Andrews and the evening's other terrified nonsinger, Coote. They sang and danced their way through an infectiously spirited "The Rain in Spain" that seemed to levitate the entire Shubert Theatre and at its climax collapsed on the sofa, just as Moss had staged it. They were engulfed by a swelling roar, a tidal wave coming at them from the auditorium. The New Haven audience had risen to its feet as one and, sharing the joy of Eliza's mastery of vowels and aitches, were cheering, laughing, screaming, stomping, whooping, and bringing the show to a standstill. Harrison and Coote had never experienced anything like this in drawing-room comedy and froze, dumbfounded. Finally Andrews grabbed the two of them and dragged them to the apron of the stage, where she led them in bows so the audience tumult could subside and allow them to get on with the show.

It was a once-in-a-lifetime moment in the theater, still remembered by those who stayed to see it. It was also the high point of an evening that, in the end, was at least twenty-five minutes too much of a wondrous thing. Harrison had been so much the focus of the evening's anxiety that, as the cheers faded into the night, he became the sole focus of relief. Andrews, whose support had done so much to get him through the performance, was virtually ignored. Suddenly Cecil Beaton rushed onto the stage, oblivious to the disaster that had almost befallen the evening, grabbed Andrews by the collar, dragged her across the boards to the quick-change booth, grabbed the brim of the yellow hat she was wearing, and turned it back-to-front saying, "Not like that, you silly bitch! Like *that!*"

Moss's most serious altercation with Harrison would come two years later in London, when Harrison had already made Henry Higgins the role of his life and decided he had no further need of Moss's direction or of rehearsals with Andrews or anybody else, including the new English members of the cast. The opening in London was probably the most highly publicized and anticipated premiere in English theatrical history, at least since Burbage opened in *Hamlet*. Harrison had already outraged the company by disparaging Holloway to the local press, then claimed to have been misquoted to avoid a lawsuit. When Moss told Harrison he was required to rehearse along with everybody else, including an uncomplaining Holloway, Harrison exploded.

"You Jewish cunt!" he screamed at Moss in front of the other members of the production, going on to make the outrageous claim, "If it hadn't been for me you would never have got this job directing the show in the first place."

Moss didn't flinch. A quarter-century of backstage squabbles and tantrums with everybody from Marilyn Miller to Gertrude Lawrence had stiffened his spine. "I'm a writer," he said quietly. "If we're going to get into this territory, I can do it a good deal better and more cruelly than you can." There followed a two-hour confrontation complete with screaming invective overheard by terrified and stunned wives, waiting in the next room to go out to dinner. Harrison was outnumbered by his London agent Laurence (Laurie) Evans, Binkie Beaumont, Lerner, Levin, and Moss.

Finally Beaumont told Harrison he would happily replace him with Michael Redgrave or John Gielgud, both of whom had already indicated they were more than willing to step into Higgins's slippers. Laurie Evans confirmed the reality of Beaumont's threat and Moss added, "Rex, please don't try any tricks, don't try to pull any fast ones." His very weariness suggested unflappable authority. Harrison, unprepared to move aside for Redgrave or Gielgud, agreed to report for rehearsals as ordered.

Later that evening at dinner, Evans told Moss, "Rex didn't mean any of those things." Moss lifted an eyebrow as he smiled. "I know Rex better than you, Laurie. He meant *everything* he said."

The only true casualties of opening night in New Haven were the ballet and Embassy Ball scenes Moss had so carefully fashioned to precede and follow the intermission. Higgins's song "Come to the Ball" and Eliza's "Say a Prayer for Me Tonight" received only polite receptions after the soaring and jubilant reaction to "The Rain in Spain" and almost equally thunderous applause for "I Could Have Danced All Night" and Freddy's comic serenade to Eliza, "On the Street Where You Live," that followed. The ballet—which the company referred to among themselves as "the thing ballet" because they never liked or understood it—seemed busy, pointless, and created the impression that Eliza was being manufactured by outsiders (not unlike the scenes in *A Star Is Born* in which "experts" prepare Esther Blodgett for her screen test).

After intermission the chandeliers flew in on their winches and the revolving stages stubbornly refused to turn; Eliza's entrance, revealing her for the first time fully transformed in her Beaton gown, went utterly unnoticed on a stage that was wall-to-wall costumes by Beaton, most of them flashing by in midwaltz. Worst of all, the complicated changeover from the ball scene back to Higgins's study seemed interminable, forcing the audience to sit impatiently in the dark waiting to discover if Eliza had been exposed as a fraud by Zoltan Karpathy, an obnoxious ball guest and former student of Higgins's.

Moss saw at once that all his planning, all the choreography, both of the songs, and the introduction of the transformed Eliza were simply wrong and had to go. He threw them out without hesitation or allowing any discussion from his stars ("Not a word, dear," he told Andrews) or his composer or lyricist, and they were never performed or seen again.

The cut—almost twenty-five minutes long—presented Lerner with the serious problem of bridging the gap that got Eliza from Ascot to the ball. Moss had seen that the ball must end the first act to avoid the long scene changeover that followed and could be better accomplished during intermission. The ball could play more or less as before, ending the first act on the question of Eliza's being unmasked as a fraud or not, but most vital was her transformation. It had fallen flat and had to be freshly invented.

Lerner needed almost two weeks to find a solution, during which time the play was performed in New Haven with no transition scene at all. "On the Street Where You Live" was a song that never quite fit anyway (Moss always called it "On the Street on Which She Lives"), so it acted as a kind of change of subject after Ascot that kept the audience from quite registering that there was a hole in the action. Finally Lerner delivered and Moss approved what became known as "the port wine scene."

Out had gone "Come to the Ball" and "Say a Prayer for Me Tonight." In went a very brief, very quiet dialogue scene between Higgins and Pickering as they wait in the study to escort Eliza to the ball. Pickering, a bundle of nerves, pours himself a glass of port while Higgins paces, as maddeningly complacent as ever. Without warning, Eliza appears on the landing at the top of the stairs, a vision in an Edwardian gown of silks and seed pearls, all the more radiant against the familiar book-lined background, now suddenly looking very drab and dusty. The audience—and

Higgins—had a moment in which to lose and regain breath, with no onstage competition to detract attention from Eliza except Higgins's hasty pouring of a glass of port, a bit of business that neatly suggested the impact on him of the transformed Eliza and seeded emotion to flower at evening's end.

The scene was put in place in Philadelphia on February 15, by which time word had circulated for almost two weeks in New York that a sensation was on its way to town. The expectations encouraged the inevitable skepticism among Broadway professionals. Could the show be that good? Really that good? Even Moss didn't know, as he admitted to Kitty when they prepared to truck the scenery to New York and the Mark Hellinger Theatre. "It's some kind of a hit. I don't know how big."

The cast knew. Miles Kreuger remembers that the afternoon of opening night, March 15, 1956, he was in Lerner's office and realized that the gypsies in the show were holding their own cast party at somebody's loft before the curtain ever went up. "They were toying recklessly with theatrical superstition, I suppose, but very little. *My Fair Lady* was that much of a sure thing after New Haven and Philadelphia."

The critics knew. Brooks Atkinson began his review in the *Times* acknowledging as much. "Bulletins from the road," he wrote, "have not been misleading. *My Fair Lady* . . . is a wonderful show." Walter Kerr told his readers in the *Herald-Tribune*: "Don't bother to finish reading this review now. You'd better sit right down and send for those tickets."

Within hours, it seemed, everyone in America knew. The world knew.

It was not only the biggest hit of Moss's life, but also the biggest hit in the lives of everyone connected with it. No one, not even Andrews, would ever again enjoy such unqualified, overwhelming success. Nor, it can be argued, would they have the opportunity to achieve as much as they had on the stage of the Mark Hellinger.

The performances were definitive and remain so for anyone who ever saw them. The physical beauty of the production was the result of many hands, from Beaton and Oliver Smith to lighting designer Abe Feder and the ghost of Hassard Short ("I would have sworn that Hassard Short had come in," a former assistant of his declared), but the very modesty of Shaw's original scheme and Lerner's fidelity to it had guided Moss's hand, forcing a light and subtle touch that was instantly recognized as a high-water mark of taste in the Broadway theater. The book Lerner fashioned is brilliantly effective even half a century later, and it is hard to imagine a corner of the world where Loewe's score is not being sung by somebody, in some language, at this or any other moment—even "On the Street on Which She Lives."

The work of the creators meshed like the cogs and wheels of a precision timepiece and Moss's role was vital in winding that watch and setting it to ticking perfectly. His hand was everywhere present and everywhere unobtrusive. He later wrote that "the best-directed play is the one in which the hand of the director remains unnoticed . . . the custodian of the proceedings on the stage, not the star of them." He was not describing *My Fair Lady,* but might as well have been.

My Fair Lady became a spectacular success, a phenomenon, the best-known and most-admired musical of its era, the most widely performed and translated operetta since *The Merry Widow* at the beginning of the century. It would surpass *Oklahoma!* as the longest-running musical on Broadway by almost 500 performances, registering a spectacular 2,717 curtains until the final one fell in September 1962, almost seven years after it had first gone up. Tickets were so hard to come by on Broadway (and later, in London) that editorial and magazine cartoons regularly made fun of frustrated theatergoers, like the masked matron in *The New Yorker,* clutching her purse and holding a gun on the box-office vendor, demanding "Two!" for any performance. The story went around about the woman at a matinee shortly after the opening who used the empty seat next to her for her coat. Richard Maney, the legendary press agent, was so nonplussed at seeing an empty seat he asked for an explanation. "It was for my husband, but he couldn't come," she said. Maney asked why she hadn't given the ticket to a friend. "I couldn't," she explained. "All our friends are at my husband's funeral."

Records fell everywhere. The film rights were sold to Warner Bros. for a then-record $5.5 million. The original cast album, recorded monaurally, became the number one album in the nation and the best-selling album in the history of Columbia Records, a feat repeated by the London cast album, recorded later in the then-new stereo process, which became the *new* best-selling album in Columbia's history, relegating the first album to the number-two position on the hit parade after an almost three-year reign as number one. Even more remarkably, original cast albums in Spanish, German, Italian, Portuguese, Hebrew, and other languages topped local charts as productions proliferated around the world.

There have been three revivals on Broadway to date, in 1975, 1981, and 1993. International productions show no signs of abating almost fifty years later, particularly in Europe, where it has entered the permanent repertory of opera houses in Germany and Austria. The most recent estimate of aggregate earnings topped $800 million and may yet reach $1 billion.

There is general agreement that *My Fair Lady* was the culmination and the end of the musical era it perfected, partly because Broadway exploded in every direction the following year with *West Side Story* and its innovative, vernacular musical genius (though it, too, was based on the work of a British playwright). But the legacy of *My Fair Lady* continued to influence musical theater for decades, if only through the sources of material it suggested to enterprising librettists, lyricists, composers, and producers. Shaw's trunk was raided again for *Androcles* and then for *Her First Roman* (based on *Caesar and Cleopatra*). Everyone from Jane Austen with *First Impressions (Pride and Prejudice)* to Oscar Wilde with *Ernest in Love (The Importance of Being Earnest)* to Terence Rattigan with Noël Coward's *The Girl Who Came to Supper* (*The Sleeping Prince*) turned up on Broadway—to mention only a few—all of them more or less inspired by what Lerner and Loewe, Moss, and Gabriel Pascal had set in motion.

My Fair Lady won the Tony Award as Best Musical and Moss won for directing it. Oliver Smith won for his settings, Cecil Beaton for his costumes, Franz Allers for his musical direction, Hanya Holm for her choreography, Lerner for his book, Loewe for his music, and Harrison for his performance. Hardly anyone remembers today that Andrews lost to Judy Holliday for *Bells Are Ringing*.

All that success made it inevitable that Lerner and Loewe and Moss would want to work together again and they resolved to do so as soon as possible. They wouldn't need a producer, they decided, but could produce their next show themselves, and would do exactly that, perhaps knowing they were tempting Fate.

There was a small, easily overlooked footnote. On December 23, 1957, Harrison gave his last performance of the original Broadway run. It was his 750th, and to commemorate the occasion Kay Kendall, his bride of six months, went onstage unannounced as the queen of Transylvania in the Embassy Ball scene that now ended the first act. Her escort—also unannounced—was Moss. It was his last appearance on a Broadway stage, but far from his last hurrah.

27

"The Darling of Everyone There"

Everything is apple pie.

MOSS HART

Moss and Kitty left New York two days after the opening of *My Fair Lady* for a holiday in Barbados as houseguests of Sir Ronald and Marietta Tree. Moss joked that he was "off to learn the lingos of pink flamingos, way out on the coral where nothing's immoral, just Kitty and me and the Caribbian [*sic*] and the rest of the world can kiss my ass." When they returned four weeks later Moss found a place for the opening-night gift that had pleased him most, a white plaster bust of George Bernard Shaw from Herman Levin. He placed it on the desk in his study/office at 1185 Park Avenue, where the "old boy" smiled enigmatically at tropical vines and the gurgle of Moss's indoor fountain. He may also have inspired Moss's first writing of consequence since the failure of *The Climate of Eden* four years earlier.

Levin and his wife, Dawn, were an early audience for Moss's new work during the Philadelphia tryout of *My Fair Lady*. Moss had asked if he might drop by their suite at the Warwick Hotel and read a few pages aloud of some prose he'd been working on. Levin remembered Moss's tightly clutched sheaf of yellow handwritten pages and how lively and vivid they were. Julie Andrews was "enchanted" when she heard them and found them funny and touching, as did Tony Walton when his turn came, or any of the other friends who listened—often enthralled—as Moss read his growing manuscript aloud with brio and precisely gauged dramatic pauses. The circle of listeners expanded as his confidence grew and the pages mounted until whole dinner parties laughed out loud or froze with suspense at a narrative whose outcome they already knew, or found their eyes glistening at dark and unsentimental details of youthful hardship. No audience cheered him on more than Phyllis and Bennett Cerf, who heard and then read his manuscript in installments and offered detailed suggestions. Later, when depression halted his pen, it was Phyllis who devotedly urged him to finish no matter what, knowing that Random House was waiting.

He had returned to what he had titled in 1953 "The Bronx to Broadway." He said he was just setting down tales he recited on long nights ruled by insomnia when Kitty urged him to talk himself to sleep by telling her about the parts of his life she had missed. But now he wrote knowing he was back on top after fearing the theater and success—maybe even life—had passed him by. Money and kudos were flowing in, the ideal circumstance for nostalgic reflection. His lifelong habit of reminding everyone how far he'd come had always had an incantatory quality to it, as if by acknowledging hardship and struggle he could conjure away their recurrence. Or could silence envy and resentment of the success he wore as flamboyantly as his much-talked-about mink-lined raincoat, tossed over his shoulders with movie-star panache, an ostentation forgivable in one who'd once had nothing. He understood and respected luck and, according to Kitty, often burst out, "Isn't it wonderful how far I've come in the world," not only in words, but also in everything he wore, bought, and displayed. It wasn't gloating; it was frank acknowledgment of the journey.

There was nothing new about any of this. He had been using the material since his first fame in 1930. It is startling to look back at those giddy, loquacious press interviews and realize they tell exactly the same story he was retelling now, the same one he had once tried to fashion as a musical with Kaufman and again as his "book about the theater."

He had broken off after Thanksgiving 1953 and didn't begin writing again in earnest until June 23, 1956 (he dated his pages). The oft-told story detailed the grinding poverty of his childhood and his early days in the theater with Gus Pitou and *The Beloved Bandit,* the hated summers of social directing, and the saga of working with Kaufman on *Once in a Lifetime.* In expanding old anecdotes to book length he enriched them with theatrical lore and, as a writer will, improved them artfully and consciously.

He had begun in longhand with his first impressions of Broadway. His earliest version told of being sent to Manhattan on a music-store errand by Pop Levenson and emerging from the subway for a forbidden glimpse of Times Square in the middle of a confetti-strewn, brass-band celebration. His teenager's sense of wonder mistook the gaiety for every-day life in and around the theater. He discovered later, he wrote, that the streamers and music were celebrating Armistice Day in 1918, but he changed it for the final version to the presidential election of 1916, scaling back the moment for youth and verisimilitude.

He had put his handwritten manuscript aside after writing about the death of his grandfather Solomon and picked it up again with his adventures in the same New Amsterdam Theatre where he'd just rehearsed *My Fair Lady*. He maximized the horrors of his work in the fur company vaults and omitted any mention of the National Cloak and Suit Company and his impresario grandeur there with "Miss Melody," "Miss Plot," and "Miss Jazz." He left out any mention of Eddie Eliscu as coauthor of *The Beloved Bandit,* or of *Jonica* or *No Retreat,* and turned his four years of summer camps into six whose truth was not that of the calendar, but of remembered struggle. He was the boy Cinderella with a fairy godmother named Kate whose magic wand was just a ticket to the upper balcony where he might observe the ball. He let her fold laundry and die when youth needed the comedy to turn poignant. This Kate set no fires, carved no crosses. She had turned his world from a pumpkin to a footlit stage and he righted her fate on the page.

He fictionalized, he improved, he used himself as the vehicle to express the thrill of Broadway, the desperation for success that would make him "somebody else," and fashioned what was everywhere acknowledged as the warmest, most moving memoir of being stagestruck ever written in America. It didn't matter whether or not it was literally true; it rang with what George Abbott had called that "Truth-ier Truth."

Bennett Cerf and Random House published it in late 1959 as *Act One*. Cerf changed "The End" to "Intermission" as the book's final word, implying there would be an *Act Two* and maybe an *Act Three*, books Moss only halfheartedly discouraged the press from anticipating, and he might have written them, had he had time. The public made *Act One* a runaway best-seller on the *New York Times* list for almost a year and number one for twenty-two weeks.

Sam Behrman, Moss's old friend who had been disapproving of him on occasion, reviewed *Act One* on the front page of the *Times Book Review,* calling it "the best book on 'show business' as practiced in this country in our time that I have ever read." Walter Kerr in the *Herald-Tribune* called it "emotionally fastidious" and "accurate where accuracy counts most," which meant "about happiness and despair, about poverty and money, about talent and luck."

Moss was always hungry for praise and carefully clipped his best reviews, but went farther with *Act One*. He sent out dozens of inscribed copies of the book before publication and asked the recipients to put their appreciations in writing and, when they forgot, was not shy about nudging them to fulfill his request. He built a fat file of letters whose autographs alone would have been worth fortunes to collectors, including, among many others, Alfred Lunt and Lynn Fontanne, Gielgud, Tallulah Bankhead, Coward, Garland, Lauren Bacall, Leonard Bernstein (writing on music paper), Abbott, Spencer Tracy, Richard Burton, Jerome Robbins, and William Inge. The literati were heard from, too: W. Somerset Maugham, Truman Capote, Herman Wouk, and Upton Sinclair (asking if Moss would mind reading his play). Then came Henry Luce, Jean Kerr, Oscar Hammerstein II, the Sam Goldwyns, Richard Avedon, Bernard Baruch, and Irene Selznick mingling their voices with some from the past: Ziegfeld's aging but still salty secretary Goldie; Mrs. Henry B. Harris, who had financed *The Beloved Bandit;* and boyhood chum George Steinberg, who opened the door to Aunt Bea and Gus Pitou. There were hundreds of letters from "civilians" who never suspected how they had dreamed of the life Moss lived until they saw it excerpted in *Life*. He grew so accustomed to the praise that when he ran into Jessica Tandy at the theater and insisted she put her admiration in writing, Hume Cronyn protested, telling him fondly but firmly, "Now stop that."

Lillian Hellman was a spoilsport. Moss was wounded and lashed out at her faint praise in what she called "the most incredible letter I have ever had . . . the snide Woollcott kind of blow." She said, "Yes, I did have reservations about the book" because "I don't see the theater as you do, or the people in it." Neither did Kenneth Tynan, writing in *The New Yorker*. He complained that *Act One* was a collection of "autobiographical clichés" without a single sentence or sentiment that addressed the art of the theater. "For [Hart]," Tynan wrote, "a success is a success is a success and any price is worth paying to ensure it." Not entirely untrue, perhaps, but excessively harsh for a book about the realpolitik of Broadway and its audience. Tynan wanted a different kind of book, from a different kind of man.

So did Lester Sweyd and Frieda Fishbein, voices from the past that shrilly damned him for figments of the imagination and withholding credit where it was due. They wrote at furious length and copied Bennett Cerf and Brooks Atkinson for good measure, men of the world who allowed the angry voices to fade away in the files.

Cerf preferred a good story and liked to tell the one about Moss's having signed his copyright over to the children before publication. Cerf had estimated that a good theatrical memoir might make its author as much as $25,000 and the amount seemed about right as a modest advance against college and the future. With *My Fair Lady* spinning money Moss could afford to give away the income from *Act One,* but when the book rocketed upward on the best-seller lists and Warner Bros. paid a healthy $125,000 for the movie rights, he claimed to be outraged at Cerf's faulty judgment. He began referring to eleven-year-old Christopher and eight-year-old Cathy as "the Lear kids." He blamed Cerf that "the Lear kids are getting all of this dough" and harangued him with, "You dog. You told me it would never be a real best seller."

Cerf planned a combination book party and fifty-fifth birthday celebration for Moss and three hundred friends on October 23, 1959, the day before his real birthday, at Mama Leone's, the theatrical restaurant on Forty-eighth Street. The party was supposed to be a surprise and Moss made sure it would be a good one by taking charge of the entertainment. Cerf remembered it as so star-studded that "if something had happened to that restaurant that night, the theater would have ended in New York."

Marlene Dietrich was there (with Tynan), and so were Claudette Colbert, Truman Capote, Gielgud, Ed Sullivan, Lerner, Yves Montand, Simone Signoret, Ethel Merman, Alec Guinness, Rosalind Russell, and José Ferrer just for starters. Phil Silvers was master of ceremonies for skits that included Betty Comden and Adolph Green performing various ways in which *Act One* might be disastrously adapted by the movies. Moss had ordered from Arthur Schwartz and Howard Dietz a musical based on his book with an everything-including-the-kitchen-sink ballet like the one he cut from *My Fair Lady*. It included a parody of "The Rain in Spain" in which young Moss was advised by Eddie Chodorov (played by Melvyn Douglas) and Dore Schary (played by Ralph Bellamy) that his posh English accent would never go over on Broadway. To teach him diction comprehensible in Shubert Alley, they drilled him to pronounce perfectly "De Oily Boid Desoives De Oily Woim," to a tune derived from Fritz Loewe. As a finale, there was a song for Kitty to perform called "It Only Happens Once in a Lifetime."

Another act involved a quartet of cleaning women, one each from Doubleday, Random House, Simon and Schuster, and Little, Brown. They carried mops and wore skirts and babushkas beneath which they sharply resembled Bennett Cerf, Adolph Green, Martin Gabel, and the guest of honor. Following the mop brigade, Kitty, Florence Rome, Phyllis Cerf, and Arlene Francis sang a Cole Porter song for which Moss wrote special lyrics in praise of himself that went, "He's the top! He's a Lindy waiter. He's the top! He's a borscht potato."

The evening's funniest skit was performed by Mel Brooks, with Mel

Tolkin standing in for Brooks's cowriter Carl Reiner, who was doing television in California. Tolkin was an interviewer quizzing Brooks as a celebrated psychoanalyst (a graduate of the "Vienna School of Good Luck") who had become rich and famous treating Moss. The analyst was shocked at the kind of smut his patient—"a nice Jewish boy"—talked, all about Greeks with designs on their mothers ("with a Jew, you don't do a thing like that even to your wife, let alone your mother") and other such degrading and disgusting stuff "that makes me want to puke," so "I walk straight out of the room, I climb up a stepladder, and I toss in aspirins through the transom."

Moss had accomplished an almost unique triple-play: *Act One* was at or near the top of every best-seller list in America, he had directed the biggest musical hit in Broadway history, and it had become, in its London version, the biggest thing to hit the West End since the blitz. Crossing home plate was a simple—and excruciatingly difficult—matter of finding and mounting a new show "as though *My Fair Lady* did not exist," he said. "It may sound like a joke, but your next show could be a complete artistic and financial success, yet if it ran only two or three years you'd hear the comment, 'They're slipping.'"

While he finished *Act One,* Lerner and Loewe had gone to Hollywood to make *Gigi* for MGM, based on the novel and play by Colette, another sensational hit that won the Best Picture Academy Award and further raised expectations for their Broadway encore. The trio, now producers as well as creators, searched for a subject, flirting with a musical version of Marcel Carné's film *Les Enfants du Paradis,* the inspiration of producer Alain Bernheim, and toyed with a Sherlock Holmes musical with Billy Wilder. They turned down, together or separately, projects like Meredith Willson's *The Music Man,* which Moss assured producer Kermit Bloomgarden was too homespun ever to succeed on Broadway.

Moss published *Act One.* Loewe had a serious heart attack from which he recovered so he could play roulette with *My Fair Lady* money. Lerner played it with wives and came up with—of all things—a beautiful French lawyer who would prove unable to differentiate between *c'est l'amour* and *c'est la guerre.*

Finally, Bud Widney read a review of a book by T. H. White called *The Once and Future King* and placed it on Lerner's desk just as Moss telephoned that his curiosity had been aroused by the same review. The subject was King Arthur and Queen Guenevere and her love affair with Lancelot that brought an end to the age of chivalry and the Round Table.

Lerner and Moss were beguiled from the start, though Loewe, when he heard the idea, was appalled. "You must be crazy," he told them. "That king was a cuckold. Who the hell cares about a cuckold?"

Audiences cared, and for centuries. From medieval troubadours to Alfred Lord Tennyson to Twain the story had worked and survived a seemingly infinite variety of approaches. Why not as a lavish musical, a magical-tragical romance based on a world-famous legend with Julie Andrews as Guenevere?

White's book was in four parts, one of which, "The Sword and the Stone," had already been sold to Walt Disney. The book might be called postmodern today, interweaving Arthurian legend with anachronistic allusions to Robin Hood, the Declaration of Independence, Freud, and Einstein. White's Lancelot du Lac was not the "parfit knight" but the "Chevalier Mal Fet—the Ill-Made Knight," ugly as Quasimodo, bereft of any sense of self-worth. "It is so easy to make young children believe that they are horrible," White wrote, which may have been the single sentence that most reverberated for Moss and Lerner.

Guenevere's betrayal of Arthur with a psychologically damaged Lancelot seemed the key to a fresh telling of a familiar tale and inspired a first title, "Jenny Kissed Me." It also shifted the focus away from Arthur and suggested obvious casting problems for Lancelot. The play would end as the book did, with King Arthur alone and preparing for battle, charging a young boy with spreading the story of a place called Camelot. The boy was Tom from Warwick, White's version of Sir Thomas Malory of Warwickshire whose *Le Morte d'Arthur* is the primary literary source of Arthurian legend, though the real Malory wrote it in 1485, almost a millennium after Camelot and all that it stood for had vanished.

It was said that Lerner at first suggested he and Moss write the libretto together but then changed his mind. Kitty remembered telling Moss, "You're well out of that," on the grounds that, no matter how good, "Jenny Kissed Me" could never "be as good as *Fair Lady* and you'll be the one who gets the blame. Just do what you did on *Fair Lady:* direct it, and help as much as you can."

Bud Widney remembered no such willingness on Lerner's part to share responsibility for the book, and it is not immediately obvious what Moss might have contributed to a story so distant in setting, tone, mood, and theme from anything he had ever attempted. Lerner's ego had grown monumental, in any case, and he had never submitted to the give-and-take of collaboration Moss had enjoyed with Kaufman, not even with Loewe. But Lerner had been to Choate and Harvard, had tamed Shaw and Colette, and was certain he could handle T. H. White and Lancelot.

"As I began thinking about the dramatization of this monumental tale," he wrote, "it seemed to me that the play demanded, almost depended upon, finding a reason [that Arthur forgave the adultery], and that once found it had to be the turning point in the drama." It proved the drama's undoing instead, for Lerner's solution was that Arthur and Guenevere both loved Lancelot—one paternalistically, one romantically—whom Lerner transformed from the "Chevalier Mal Fet" to the impossibly handsome and pompous narcissist who presents himself with a hallelujah chorus of self-adoration, "C'est Moi!" As love object Lancelot diminished them all dramatically, a problem neither Lerner's book nor Loewe's music nor Moss's direction could ever fully overcome, though in hindsight it was a minor problem among so many.

Julie Andrews had always been Guenevere and Moss suggested Richard Burton, his onetime Edwin Booth in *Prince of Players,* for King Arthur. Burton was no more known for singing than Rex Harrison had been, but later said that "Lerner and Loewe came to Hollywood to pick up their twenty-five Oscars or whatever it was they got [for *Gigi*], and they called and said they'd like me to be in their new musical. So I said I'd be enchanted, of course. I said, 'But what about singing?' And they said, 'Oh, we know you can sing.' And I said, 'How?' They said, 'Because we heard you sing at Ira Gershwin's at a party, we heard you sing a duet with Laurence Olivier.' And I said, 'You did?' And they said, 'Yes.'

"Well, Sir Laurence happened to be staying with me at the time, so I went home, and I said, 'Have we ever sung a duet together?'

"And he said, 'Not as far as I know, dear heart.'

"So I said, 'Lerner and Loewe think I have, that we did sing together, and they want me to be in a musical.' And he said, 'Say nothing and carry on.'

"So I said nothing and carried on."

English-born Roddy McDowall begged Lerner to include Arthur's bastard son Mordred in the libretto so he could play him and won both the argument and the role. Robert Coote from *My Fair Lady* rejoined the team to play King Pellinore. Adrian, a Hollywood friend of Moss's who had designed costumes at MGM for Garbo and Joan Crawford, was charged with designing lavish costumes assisted by Tony Duquette. Oliver Smith was given twenty stage scenes to design, from throne room to bedroom to battlefield. Choreographer Holm, lighting director Feder, and musical conductor Allers were enlisted to ensure continuity from *My Fair Lady*. A search began for a Lancelot who was beautiful and could sing.

On the final day of auditions, Moss and Lerner and Loewe had almost given up on ever finding a suitable singer-actor for the role and were walking up the aisle and out of the theater when a young man in blue jeans (or white ducks, in another account) walked onstage and began to sing, stopping them in their tracks. Loewe asked the handsome young man to sing again. Following the song he recited some Shakespeare and, responding to questions, informed them he had been born in Lawrence, Massachusetts, but had grown up in Canada. He had been trained at the Toronto Conservatory of Music and was on his way back to Toronto, where he was working mostly in radio and television. The unknown Robert Goulet was signed to play Lancelot on the spot.

Casting was virtually complete by the summer of 1959 when, just before the publication of *Act One,* Moss and Kitty traveled to the south of France. Loewe was gambling in Cannes and Lerner had rented a château at Antibes, where he and Moss were to work on revising the libretto. When the Harts arrived they learned that Lerner had gone to Capri on his yacht, an ominous foreshadowing of elusiveness and procrastination that would get worse.

After *Act One* was securely launched and winter arrived, Moss joined Lerner and Loewe to work on the book in Palm Springs, where Loewe had recuperated from his heart attack and would spend much of the rest of his life. By now the title had become *Camelot* and in March, on the fourth anniversary of the opening of *My Fair Lady,* the Sunday *Times* ran a huge ad initiating ticket sales and announcing a New York opening in November. Within a month *Camelot* sold $750,000 in tickets, exceeding the $650,000 CBS was paying to finance the show, as they had financed *My Fair Lady.*

Lerner had yet to produce a workable book by summer, a year after the abortive trip to Antibes. He took a house at Sands Point, Long Island, and invited Moss to join him there and at last get down to work. Marital warfare with his French wife, Micheline, was an incessant distraction until she took their young son, Michael, to Europe for a holiday.

Lerner used the calm to resume writing until halted by the devastating news that Micheline was leaving him and keeping their son in Europe with her. "I felt torn, trapped, and helpless," he admitted. "I lost all control of my tear ducts and other bodily functions." Moss got the name of a Long Island psychiatrist from Kubie, who prescribed what Lerner called "medication with a capital *M,*" and within two days he was back at work. It was, Lerner realized, "the last day of July, rehearsals were to begin on September third, and I had not written page one of the second act."

Within three days his medication had helped him get to the end of a script that looked long, but complete.

Moss, no stranger to difficulties in book writing, remained heroically patient with Lerner and officiated over the first day of rehearsals in an unusually buoyant mood, perhaps aware that, as Bud Widney remembered, "the cheer and confidence factor went up enormously the minute Moss arrived."

He invited to the first reading the husbands, wives, boyfriends, and girlfriends of the cast. Tony Walton was there, now married to Andrews, and remembered Moss's establishing the tone. "Here's what you're in for," he told them. "You'll get all the agonies and tears on your shoulders, so you have the right to know what's about to disrupt your lives. But remember—we're all successful, we're all very good, and we all know what we're doing." He brought out the champagne and continued, "It's going to be a happy experience. So let's all drink some champagne and do a toast. God Bless Us Every One and screw Tiny Tim."

It was the last carefree moment most of them could remember.

The troubles started early. Costume designer Adrian was the first casualty, dying before he finished his costume sketches, which were taken over by Tony Duquette. The husband of the wardrobe mistress died. Flu swept through the company. A dancer contracted blood poisoning from stepping on a needle. Even as the champagne flowed there was trouble. Moss arranged to have Oliver Smith's set designs on display for the first reading, which Lerner described with alarm as "more scenery than Switzerland." The direst signal was that the first unembellished reading of the book lasted well over three hours.

Moss put his cast into a five-week rehearsal period in New York before they moved out of town to Toronto, where *Camelot* would open the new 3,200-seat O'Keefe Center, named for the division of Canadian Breweries, Ltd., that built it. The use of a new theater presented challenges. Technical equipment was new. Every rope, chain, switch, cog, and wheel was untested and a potential booby trap. There was no backstage crew familiar with the building's nooks, crannies, and idiosyncrasies. Sound conditions were unknown or hostile. "The walls of a theatre," Lerner fretted, "are quasi-human. They need to absorb life in order to become alive. It is a well-known fact that when one plays a theatre that has been dark for a long period, it is difficult to induce laughter for at least three performances." And these walls were new, vast, and cold.

There was the additional factor of opening a much-publicized new theater in full view of the national presses of both the United States and

Canada. Lerner had agreed to the O'Keefe, he said, "on one condition. And that is that no critics come up," which was naïve to the point of lunacy. Moss knew, if Lerner didn't, that keeping critics and wrecking crews out of Toronto was a fantasy after *My Fair Lady* and the phenomenal advance sale mounting daily at the Majestic box office in New York.

The truth is that Moss and Lerner and Loewe as producers had leaped at what was an enormous economic coup, an unprecedented no-cost deal for the use of the theater arranged by Alexander Cohen, the Broadway producer who was acting as consultant and booker for the O'Keefe.

"I had the right to book anything into the theater that I wanted to book," Cohen told Gene Lees, biographer of Lerner and Loewe, and "I had to have that show." To get it, Cohen and the theater owners agreed to offer the O'Keefe to *Camelot* for no rent and zero percent of the gross. It was a deal that "hadn't been done before and it hasn't been done since," Cohen said, and had not been done in order to hide the O'Keefe or its opening attraction under a bushel. "My interest was the theater and in showing people this majestic piece of work," Cohen said. "And so we had marching bands, we had grandstands, we flew a plane from New York, with a full load, we flew another from London, with sixty or seventy people." Instead of being far enough from New York to work out the problems of *Camelot* in peace and privacy, Toronto became a new subway stop on the New York and London transit lines.

Lerner's marital problems worsened, aggravated by his painful withdrawal from the capital *M* medication (capital *A* for amphetamines) that had given him the energy to finish a sprawling book badly in need of major surgery. Nothing had brought the length under control and the rehearsal period at the O'Keefe, compounded by the technical shakedown of the theater, was grueling and increasingly without clear direction.

Moss had been uneasy with Goulet because of his inexperience and because he found himself resentful of Goulet's (quite oblivious) sex appeal, but McDowall was an experienced actor as well as an old friend and recalled Moss's direction as "adorably flirtatious but aimless." He remembered Moss's telling him, " 'Enter from stage left, go to center stage, look around, then exit stage right. Now enter stage right, go to center stage, look around, and then exit stage left.' Finally I asked what I was supposed to be looking around for. Moss said, 'Nothing, dear boy. I just like to watch you walk and twinkle your ass!' That was flattering, I suppose, and Moss was a charmer through and through, but it didn't help me much with my character."

One observer told Gene Lees it "was a hell of a struggle. It wasn't in shape, it was so long, and it floundered, it waffled, and they didn't seem to be able to get a grasp on it. . . . Lerner was a man of tremendous ego. And such people cannot admit to the areas in which they don't function well. . . . It was logistically a terribly difficult subject to make into a musical [and you] could see it in that month they were struggling through it at the O'Keefe . . . like men playing tennis in the dark. They were all on edge, trying to get a four-hour-and-more show down to two and a half."

Opening night in Toronto was October 2 and every one of the 3,200 seats in the O'Keefe was sold, many of them to kibitzers from New York and London. Moss came out before the curtain and made one of his announcements.

"*Camelot* is lovely," he told them. "*Camelot* is going to be glorious. *Camelot* is long. You're going to be a lot older when you get out of here tonight."

The first performance ran four and a half hours. The curtain didn't come down until almost one o'clock in the morning. The audience was more dazed than dazzled, causing Lerner to observe sourly, "Not since Rodgers and Hammerstein's first failure had I seen so many smiling faces."

A reporter described Moss on the morning after the opening as "dark and flinty-eyed in the spanking new backstage quarters." He brushed away difficulties by stressing, "All the good things are there. It only needs tightening." The reporter's eyebrows lifted, wondering how you tightened almost two hours out of a show. He also noted that Kitty was looking at Moss "as if she would like to take him and give him a sedative."

Three days later Lerner was strapped onto a gurney and wheeled into Wellesley Hospital in Toronto with a bleeding ulcer. Earlier that same day Moss had received news that his father—"the Commodore"—had died in Miami at the age of ninety-seven, cheerful and active until the end, when his heart simply stopped.

Moss had not left California when Lillie died twenty years earlier and he did not leave Canada to go to Florida. Bernie, working as assistant stage manager on *Camelot,* was dispatched to Miami Beach to arrange matters for their father much as Joe Hyman had once done for their mother.

The *Camelot* company understood Moss's burdens on the show, weightier than ever with Lerner confined to his hospital bed, and most were frankly relieved that he stayed with them in Toronto. They were only dimly aware of his lifelong resentment of Barnett because those notes had been so muted in *Act One.* As a result, his composed response to his father's death seemed more stoic than lacking in feeling. He offered something like a benediction when he ordered Bernie to "make it a simple casket for a simple man." Only later did they realize it was a casket for cremation at Miami's Riverside Memorial Chapel.

Lerner's bleeding ulcer was not helped by his incomplete withdrawal from drugs and doctors ordered him to remain in bed for two full weeks. That time might have given Moss a chance to cut the four-hour libretto by himself but he, too, was flat on his back at the Royal York Hotel suffering from what he told Dore Schary was "a bad case of flu and complete nervous exhaustion." He mentioned Barnett's death in passing and added, "I suppose I shall survive this and live to fight another day although, at the moment, there is not too much fight left in me."

Bernie returned from Florida on October 14, the day Lerner's ulcer stopped bleeding and he was released from hospital supervision. As Lerner waited with a nurse for an elevator, he noted with curiosity that a bed was being rolled into the very room he had just vacated. The nurse informed him that the room was being readied for someone else who was in town working on *Camelot*. Perhaps he knew Moss Hart? Unable to stay away from the theater, Moss had gone to rehearsals that morning, gone back to his rooms at the Royal York Hotel, and collapsed with a coronary thrombosis.

Bernie heard the news on the taxi radio on the way in from the airport. When he arrived at the hospital, the elevator doors opened to reveal what he described to Tony Walton as "a paraplegics' convention." He doubled over with laughter, wondering if things could possibly get any more disastrous.

Kitty heard the news on her car radio, too, and, after reassuring the children, rushed to Moss's bedside. When she got there he ordered her, "Go immediately to Alan's room and tell him to take over the direction of the play until I'm well enough to come back, and not to look for anyone else."

Fortunately for Moss, his doctors turned deaf ears to his wishes and, to avoid the relapse that had sent him back to the hospital after his first heart attack, refused to allow him out of bed or out of their care until they decided he was well enough, which was four weeks later. He was hors de combat and perhaps lucky to be.

Camelot moved on to Boston with Lerner attempting to direct the show, though he was still an outpatient under doctors' care himself. Loewe stepped into the breach, according to Widney, and told the cast, "Relax, everybody. Both Moss and Alan are down but we're sold out, we've got plenty of time to fix this, and we'll take our time and we'll get there." What Loewe didn't say was that he was adamantly opposed to Lerner's directing actors when the book needed his full attention and he was clearly in no condition to do both.

They finally agreed that if any director were to take over for Moss on an interim basis it should be José Ferrer, whose recent list of directing credits included the musical *Oh, Captain!* and *The Andersonville Trial.* Ferrer proved unavailable and Lerner's insistence on directing resulted in a breach with Loewe that was never to heal. Even Lerner recognized, he said, understating the case, that "the seams of our collaboration had begun to pull loose."

McDowall claimed that "after Moss went into the hospital no directing got done at all. Richard brought his acting teacher Philip Burton over from England and all the dear man could do was remove all the musical elements Moss had put in. Richard was the one who finally held everybody together, aided by Julie and the tea and sympathy she poured backstage while the rest of us floundered. The book was never properly trimmed or fixed and the show was so unsettled that one of Julie's major songs, 'I Loved You Once in Silence,' went into the show the night before we opened in New York. You couldn't tell, of course, because Julie was so professional, but still . . ."

Moss missed the opening at the Majestic on December 3. He sent Kitty as his representative and read the reviews, which praised the costumes and settings and songs and cast and were almost uniformly disappointed that what wags on the street were calling "Costalot" had taken such a toll in manpower and delivered so little in the way of theatrical magic. Kerr in the *Herald-Tribune* absolved Moss of responsibility, pointing out that "the secure, precise hand that guided *My Fair Lady* was so early and so unluckily withdrawn."

Moss's return to health was slow, painful, and incomplete. Doctors cautioned him that if he wanted to survive he would have to relinquish a pace that had twice required a major coronary to slow him down. Chastened and frightened, he took Kitty and the children to Palm Springs, site of Loewe's recovery, where his recuperation continued until he felt well enough to return to New York and see *Camelot* for himself.

By February, conditions at the Majestic were bleak and no one expected the show to stay open beyond May. Not even an advance sale that had finally amounted to a phenomenal $3 million could keep a show running that sometimes had as many as two or three hundred walkouts in the course of a single performance.

Moss saw the play with the grim determination of one with no time for tact or nonsense. He had been away long enough to see its lineaments clearly and knew, if anybody did, how to listen to an audience. He ordered the kind of major, ruthless cuts he might have made on the road if not for his health. Lerner gratefully did as he was told, making major cuts and even removing two songs, finally bringing the play down to size.

The cuts and shaping resulted in what Lerner later called the "miracle." On the fifth anniversary of the opening of *My Fair Lady,* the *Ed Sullivan Show* planned a Lerner and Loewe tribute and allowed the honorees the right to program it themselves. That the popular Sunday evening show was on CBS, which had financed both *My Fair Lady* and *Camelot,* was more than coincidence, but not even William S. Paley himself could program audience reaction.

Before the broadcast, the *Camelot* company rehearsed a full week for the Sullivan show under Moss's direction, not neglecting the cuts and changes he had insisted on for the stage. The night of the broadcast Goulet sang "If Ever I Would Leave You," Andrews sang "Where Are the Simple Joys of Maidenhood?," Burton sang "Camelot," and Burton and Andrews together sang "What Do the Simple Folk Do?" The songs were presented in costume against sets that suggested the show and the result foreshadowed a revolution in the electronic selling of Broadway.

"The following morning," Lerner recalled, "I was awakened by a phone call from an excited manager at the Majestic Theatre. 'You better come down here,' he said, 'and look at this.' "

What he saw were lines at the box office. Television viewers had forgotten the reviews and were charmed by what they had seen and heard in their living rooms. That night they came to see what the *Ed Sullivan Show* had told them was wonderful and a hit and what they saw was the version critics hadn't seen, the one Moss had cut and rehearsed and so vastly improved the week before. He had begun on Broadway saving *Once in a Lifetime* at the eleventh hour and, thirty years later, he saved another show. *Camelot* was a hit.

That summer Moss sold the house at Beach Haven, put the apartment at 1185 Park Avenue on the market, and prepared to move himself and his family to the house he had bought in Palm Springs the previous winter. He hoped to slow his pace and write there, perhaps taking advantage of Hollywood's proximity to turn out the occasional screenplay. He had earned a rest, some time in the sun.

The previous year he had given some guest lectures at Yale and Harvard and the University of Denver had invited him to teach a seminar in theater during the coming school year, which he accepted with pride, reminding friends that the professor-to-be had not made it through the eighth grade.

He had begun writing again in the hospital and had the beginnings of a comedy he wanted to work on in the desert. He called John Cullum, who was standing in for Burton in *Camelot,* and asked if he and musical comedy actress Gretchen Wyler would come to his office and go over some pages. They did and later walked through the scenes on the stage of the Majestic. Cullum, who found Moss "such an elegant man [with] tremendous presence," remembered "a scene where a lady gets locked out. It's about a couple who live, who shared a vestibule in one of those very expensive places and there's an apartment on both sides of the vestibule and . . . the woman gets locked out and has to spend the night with the man and . . . all I remember is the situation was very funny . . . she gets locked in the vestibule and the only place she can stay is in the apartment next to hers and she goes in to stay and as the door closes behind her, her son comes home from college and knocks on the door. And that's the end of the first act."

There wasn't much more than that and even that disappeared.

Moss's saddest chore, the one with the most finality, was not selling the apartment or the beach house but saying good-bye to old friends, none older or more cherished than George S. Kaufman. His mentor and collaborator had been in ill health for several years and had withdrawn to a cranky, even bitter reclusion that puzzled and saddened visitors who still remembered him as the lethal wit of the Round Table or the energetic Lothario of the mournful countenance. On June 2 he died, attended only by a nurse, and Moss paid his last respects by delivering the eulogy.

"We all sat at his feet," he said. "My own debt to him is incalculable, but he would be astonished and disbelieving even now if he were told that the theatre, too, is in his debt. . . . The people who worked with him in the theater and all of us, his friends, owe him a different kind of debt, a very special one. He was a unique and arresting man, and there are few enough unique people in anyone's time. Nature does not toss them up too often. And part of our loss is that we will not know again the uniqueness and the special taste and flavor that was George. But part of our solace is that we were lucky to have known him—that he lived in our time. Thank you, George, and farewell."

. . .

Maybe with two fathers gone, the real one and the one of choice, it was easier to leave New York, though no one who had ever watched him struggle and thrive there could imagine his leave-taking was anything but an ordeal, however jaunty his manner, even at the going-away cocktail party he and Kitty threw for themselves and friends on November 9. Afterward, Kitty stayed behind in New York to finish her obligations on *To Tell the Truth,* the television panel show on which she appeared, while Moss went ahead to Palm Springs, to the house he had bought at 467 Via Lola, an address that Edna Ferber thought "doesn't sound respectable." Ferber had long since forgiven the quarrel of years before and wanted to know "Lola who? Montez? Brigida?"

Moss spent some of his California time talking with Warner Bros. about the movie version of *Act One.* Joshua Logan had won the right to produce and direct it and had persuaded George Axelrod to write the screenplay. In mid-December, for reasons never made clear, Logan left the project and *Act One* and Axelrod's script fell into development limbo. Eventually, the project went to a character *in* it to write, direct, and produce for the movies: Dore Schary. He would cast Jason Robards, Jr., as Kaufman, George Hamilton as Moss, and Sam Groom as himself. It was a box-office disaster when it was released in 1963, and maybe it's just as well Moss missed it.

The deeper hours of desert solitude he spent with "one of my heroes"—Eugene O'Neill—devouring the galleys of the playwright's biography by Arthur and Barbara Gelb. He knew the Gelbs, Arthur as the junior drama critic in Atkinson's office at the *New York Times* and his wife, Barbara, as the stepdaughter of Sam Behrman, and wanted to write them an enthusiastic and affectionate blurb. On December 15 he wrote Russel Crouse (who had known O'Neill) that he was reading their work "with enormous satisfaction." But he was measuring his own days and achievements against those of his idol as he read and that may have accounted for what he admitted to Crouse was "a good deal of sadness" as the pages turned.

The move to Palm Springs was final when Kitty arrived with the children in time for the holidays. On the balmy evening of December 20, Moss and Kitty went window-shopping beneath the Christmas lights strung in the palm trees lining Palm Canyon Drive. They had quarreled during the day over how to handle Christopher, who had been frightened by the sonic boom of a jet breaking the sound barrier, and they welcomed the distraction, at dinner and on their walk, of Laurence Harvey, the Hungarian-born English actor who would play King Arthur in the London production of *Camelot*. As Harvey was leaving he asked, "How are you feeling now, Moss?" and Moss answered serenely, "Everything is apple pie."

The next morning he rose at dawn, complaining that his teeth—those teeth that had plagued him since childhood—ached. Kitty called his dentist, who agreed to squeeze him into a busy schedule. While Kitty got the car, Moss waited at the side of the driveway. She pulled the Cadillac convertible out of the garage and heard a thud. She realized what it was when she saw Moss lying on the grass, motionless and still. It was his third coronary and his last. He was only fifty-seven.

28

Joie de Vivre

. . . if enjoying every minute of being alive is a way of being grateful—
well, I guess that's what I'm really trying to say—just
"thank you"—only it doesn't seem enough.

MOSS HART

Tributes poured in. Moss was a household name because of *My Fair Lady* and *Camelot* and *Act One* and his death struck those who knew him only from the page or the stage as some kind of personal loss. He had been in their living rooms, after all, laughing with Edward R. Murrow on *Person to Person,* and his wife got all dressed up to visit them once a week on *To Tell the Truth.*

First came the official obituaries, shocked and frankly emotional. Brooks Atkinson wrote in the *Times* that he was "devastated" by the news and paid homage to Moss's "unconquerable enthusiasm for life." He noted that Moss had hoped to finish the comedy about the woman in the vestibule that Cullum had read, and claimed that Hyman & Hart had already scheduled a production for "early next season." He didn't mention that Moss had written him a cheery note from Palm Springs about finally getting down to work and had signed it "Huckleberry Hart."

There were memorial services in New York at the Music Box Theatre, site of his first great success, and in Palm Springs at the Temple Isaiah. Both were SRO and the standees represented a who's who of American show business.

The New York service was on January 9 and Howard Lindsay presided, introducing Atkinson, Schary, Ferber, Lerner, and Bennett Cerf, each of whom spoke with loving intimacy to the crowd that included Kitty and Bernie. Atkinson stressed the "joy" of having known him and Schary his sense of independence and style. Ferber called him "the son I never had" and Lerner spoke of him as the essence of theater and glamour and courage. Cerf spun the words that Moss's memory brought to mind: "gaiety, warmth, understanding, laughter, gusto, loyalty, integrity, delight."

No one made exaggerated claims for him as a playwright, for that seemed both too formal and too limited and was beside the point now. It was the man they wanted to remember. Each had an anecdote or two to relate and each nodded knowingly at what Cerf called "the periodic attacks of almost unbearable depression" that had been the hidden cost of being Moss Hart.

The *un*hidden costs had always been extravagant, and when his will was probated, the estate was estimated at $500,000, surprisingly modest for a man who had earned so lavishly over so many years. He left Bernie the income from a trust of $50,000, but Bernie would enjoy it for less than three years, dying as Moss had of a heart attack in 1964. The oldest of Moss's debts, the one that went back to Vermont, he repaid with an outright gift of $25,000 to Joe Hyman, who continued to look over the estate until he, too, died in the late sixties. The children already had *Act One* and Moss left Kitty $100,000 and all the other copyrights, the legacy that would continue.

The best of the plays would be revived again and again in the decades that followed: *Once in a Lifetime* and *Light Up the Sky* less often than *You Can't Take It With You* and *The Man Who Came to Dinner*. The topicality that once seemed so fresh and bright has, as Frank Rich points out, "wilted," but the best contain zany or endearing or outrageously vain behavior that can still produce smiles of recognition or explosions of laughter. Of the movies, *A Star Is Born* remains powerful and moving and the sentiments of *Gentleman's Agreement* continue to command respect. The lesser-known musicals and revues—especially those of the thirties—are treasures waiting to be discovered.

It happened that when Moss died, the January 1962 issue of *Esquire* was on the stands with a light and chatty "Self-Portrait" he had written a few months earlier. "I wanted to be an actor," he wrote, "but I would have been, at best, an adequate performer; and adequate is a damnable word in the theatre." He allowed that in thirty years his work had satisfied him only twice (he didn't say when), and he reiterated his persistent fear that "every success was a combination of luck and a modicum of skill, and that with each new play the luck is bound to run out." He claimed that "only two things matter in a man's life: Love and Work. It is possible to live without one, but not without the other," he said, and added that he was hoping "to get together enough money some day to give up work."

No one who knew him believed that. Love and work for Moss had always been synonymous or at least inseparable. That's the great secret of the theater for those lucky enough to make their lives in it: love and work are one.

It was *Camelot* that proved it, the show that may have killed him, but not before he climbed back on the stage of the Majestic Theatre to fix it— not for the critics, or for Ed Sullivan, or the press, or even for the box office. He'd done it to get it right because that was what he knew how to do and loved doing and did.

Such caring was too audience-friendly, too posterity-be-damned to please a Kenneth Tynan. And as times change and audiences evolve, that kind of caring may come to seem an almost quaint sort of accomplishment, the kind that blurs as the playbills gather dust. But if one wants to know what New Yorkers and Americans were like from the twenties to the sixties and beyond, there are worse questions to ask than what made them laugh and what made them sing. Moss captured much of that in *Act One*, especially the yearning that theater can inspire, the sense of refuge from an otherwise inhospitable world it can provide. He detailed a road map to the glittering, transforming world he so splendidly personified in life, and if that world has altered in its details and become almost unrecognizable, the spirit that sends talent in search of it has changed hardly at all.

MOSS HART: THE PLAYS AND FILMS

Moss Hart wrote countless sketches, parodies, and early pastiche works for amateur productions while still in his teens and early twenties, almost all of them now lost if they were ever, in fact, put on paper. Many were "revisions" of works by others, compiled for summer camps like the Flagler, while others were devised for amateur groups in New York, Newark, and Brooklyn.

The following chronological listing records the significant titles and does not attempt to include more than the obvious major credits.

THE PLAYS

THE "NATIONAL" REVUE

Written and directed by Moss Hart for the National Cloak and Suit Company, New York, Monday, June 26, 1922.

THE HOLD-UP MAN
A/K/A THE BELOVED BANDIT

Comedy by "Robert Arnold Conrad" [Moss Hart and Edward Eliscu]; staged by Priestly Morrison; produced by Augustus Pitou, Jr., and Mrs. Henry B. Harris as *The Hold-up Man;* first performance November 23, 1924, Lyceum Theater in Rochester, New York, closed at the Adelphi Theatre in Chicago, December 27, 1924.

Reopened as *The Beloved Bandit* "by Moss Hart," first performance Youngstown, Ohio, September 17 or 18, 1925. Approximately 45 performances.

ANYTHING MIGHT HAPPEN

One-act version of *The Beloved Bandit,* first version (of several) performed by the YMHA Masquers Junior Group, Brooklyn, New York (339 Eighth Street), directed by Moss Hart; Monday, May 28, 1927. Numerous productions, 1927–29.

JONICA

Musical comedy by Dorothy Heyward and Moss Hart based on *Have a Good Time, Jonica* by Dorothy Heyward. Music by Joseph Meyer, lyrics by Billy Moll; additional numbers by William B. Friedlander (producer and director). Opened at the Craig Theatre on April 7, 1930. 40 performances. Cast: Nell Roy, Joyce Barbour, Jerry Norris.

NO RETREAT

Drama by Moss Hart. Produced by Bela Blau for the Hampton Players, July 16, 1930, East-hampton, L. I.; directed by Hank C. Potter. Major cast: Albert (Dekker) Van Decker, Sally Bates, H. C. Potter. 5 performances.

ONCE IN A LIFETIME

Comedy by Moss Hart and George S. Kaufman; staged by Kaufman; produced by Sam H. Harris at the Music Box Theatre, New York, September 24, 1930. Cast: Jean Dixon, Hugh O'Connell, Grant Mills, Spring Byington. 305 performances.

FACE THE MUSIC

Revue with book by Moss Hart, songs by Irving Berlin. Directed by Hassard Short and George S. Kaufman. Presented by Sam H. Harris at the New Amsterdam Theatre on February 17, 1932. Songs include "Let's Have Another Cup o' Coffee" and "Soft Lights and Sweet Music." Cast: Mary Boland, Hugh O'Connell, J. Harold Murray. 165 performances.

AS THOUSANDS CHEER

Revue with sketches by Moss Hart and songs by Irving Berlin; staged by Hassard Short; presented by Sam H. Harris at the Music Box Theatre on September 30, 1933. Songs include "Easter Parade," "Heat Wave," "Suppertime," "How's Chances." Cast: Marilyn Miller, Clifton Webb, Helen Broderick, Ethel Waters. 400 performances.

THE GREAT WALTZ

Book by Moss Hart, based on *Waltzes from Vienna;* lyrics by Desmond Carter; music by Johann Strauss, Sr., and Johann Strauss, Jr.; direction by Hassard Short. Presented by Max Gordon at the Center Theatre on September 22, 1934. Cast: Guy Robertson, Marion Claire, Marie Burke. 298 performances.

MERRILY WE ROLL ALONG

Drama by George S. Kaufman and Moss Hart. Directed by Kaufman. Presented by Sam H. Harris at the Music Box Theatre on September 24, 1934. Cast: Jessie Royce Landis, Mary Philips, Kenneth McKenna. 155 performances.

JUBILEE

Musical with book by Moss Hart, music and lyrics by Cole Porter. Direction and lighting by Hassard Short; dialogue direction by Monty Woolley. Presented by Sam H. Harris and Max Gordon at the Imperial Theater, October 12, 1935. Songs include "Begin the Beguine," "Just One of Those Things," "Me and Marie," "Why Shouldn't I?" Cast: Mary Boland, Melville Cooper, Charles Walters, Montgomery Clift. 169 performances.

YOU CAN'T TAKE IT WITH YOU (PULITZER PRIZE)

Comedy by Moss Hart and George S. Kaufman; directed by Kaufman; presented by Sam H. Harris at the Booth Theatre on December 14, 1936. Cast: Josephine Hull, Henry Travers, Margot Stevenson, Jess Barker. 837 performances.

THE SHOW IS ON

Revue with sketches by David Freedman and Moss Hart. Songs by Arthur Schwartz and Howard Dietz, Hoagy Carmichael and Stanley Adams, Vernon Duke, Ted Fetter, Richard Rodgers and Lorenz Hart, George and Ira Gershwin, Harold Arlen and E. Y. Harburg, et al. Directed by Vincente Minnelli. Presented by the Shuberts on December 25, 1936, at the Winter Garden. Cast: Beatrice Lillie and Bert Lahr. 237 performances.

I'D RATHER BE RIGHT

Musical by George S. Kaufman and Moss Hart; music by Richard Rodgers; lyrics by Lorenz Hart; directed by Kaufman. Presented by Sam H. Harris at the Alvin Theatre on November 2, 1937 (moved to the Music Box Theatre in May 1938). Songs include "Have You Met Miss Jones?" Cast: George M. Cohan. 290 performances.

SING OUT THE NEWS

Revue with sketches by Charles Friedman and Kaufman and Hart (uncredited); music and lyrics by Harold Rome. Presented by Max Gordon with George S. Kaufman and Moss Hart at the Music Box Theatre on September 24, 1938. Songs include "FDR Jones." Cast: Philip Loeb, Hiram Sherman, Mary Jane Walsh, Will Geer, Rex Ingram. 105 performances.

THE FABULOUS INVALID: A CAVALCADE OF THE THEATER

Drama with interpolated songs by Moss Hart and George S. Kaufman; directed by Kaufman. Presented by Sam H. Harris at the Broadhurst Theatre, on October 8, 1938. 65 performances.

THE AMERICAN WAY

Drama by George S. Kaufman and Moss Hart. Directed by Kaufman; lighting and technical direction by Hassard Short; music composed and conducted by Oscar Levant. Presented by Sam H. Harris and Max Gordon at the Center Theatre on January 21, 1939. Cast: Fredric March, Florence Eldridge, David Wayne. 244 performances.

THE MAN WHO CAME TO DINNER

Comedy by Moss Hart and George S. Kaufman. Directed by Kaufman; the song "What Am I to Do?" by Cole Porter. Presented by Sam H. Harris at the Music Box Theatre on October 16, 1939. Cast: Monty Woolley, Edith Atwater, Mary Wickes. 739 performances.

GEORGE WASHINGTON SLEPT HERE

Comedy by Moss Hart and George S. Kaufman. Directed by Kaufman. Presented by Sam H. Harris at the Lyceum Theatre on October 18, 1940. Cast: Jean Dixon, Ernest Truex. 173 performances.

LADY IN THE DARK

Play with music by Moss Hart; music by Kurt Weill; lyrics by Ira Gershwin. Directed by Moss Hart; production, lighting, and musical sequences directed by Hassard Short; settings by Harry Horner. Presented by Sam H. Harris at the Alvin Theatre on January 23, 1941. Songs include "The Saga of Jenny," "This Is New," "My Ship." Cast: Gertrude Lawrence, Macdonald Carey, Danny Kaye, Victor Mature. 467 performances.

JUNIOR MISS

Comedy by Jerome Chodorov and Joseph Fields, based on stories by Sally Benson; directed by Moss Hart; produced by Max Gordon on November 18, 1941, at the Lyceum Theatre in New York. 246 performances.

WE WILL NEVER DIE

"Memorial: Dedicated to the Two Million Jewish Dead of Europe," by Ben Hecht; music by Kurt Weill; directed by Moss Hart; produced by Billy Rose; sponsored by the Committee for a Jewish Army of Stateless and Palestinian Jews. First performed at Madison Square Garden on March 9, 1943. Cast: Paul Muni, Edward G. Robinson, Luther Adler, Burgess Meredith, John Garfield, Jacob Ben-Ami, Ralph Bellamy, Frank Sinatra, Sylvia Sidney, and a choir of five hundred voices. Touring performances.

WINGED VICTORY

Written and directed by Moss Hart. Produced by the U.S. Army Air Force. Opened at the 44th Street Theatre on November 20, 1943. National tour began October 9, 1944, in Los Angeles, followed by Pittsburgh, Detroit, Philadelphia, Washington, Baltimore, Richmond, Denver, Kansas City, San Francisco, St. Louis, Chicago, Cincinnati, and Cleveland. Cast: United States Army Air Corps, including Barry Nelson, Lee J. Cobb, John Forsythe, Edmund O'Brien, Gary Merrill, Don Taylor, Martin Ritt, Red Buttons, Sacha Brastoff, Mario Lanza, Peter Lind Hayes, Kevin McCarthy.

SEVEN LIVELY ARTS

Revue produced by Billy Rose; directed by Hassard Short; sketches by George S. Kaufman, Moss Hart, et al. [and Ben Hecht]; songs by Cole Porter; ballet music by Igor Stravinsky; orchestral composition by William Schuman. Cast: Beatrice Lillie, Bert Lahr, Dolores Gray, Benny Goodman. Opened on December 7, 1944, at the Ziegfeld Theatre in New York. 183 performances.

DEAR RUTH

Comedy by Norman Krasna; directed by Moss Hart; produced by Hyman and Hart; opened on December 13, 1944, at Henry Miller's Theatre in New York. Cast: Virginia Gillmore, John Dall. 683 performances.

THE SECRET ROOM

Drama by Robert Turney; directed by Moss Hart; produced by Hyman and Hart in association with Haila Stoddard; opened on November 7, 1945, at the Royale Theatre. Cast: Frances Dee, Eleonora von Mendelssohn. 21 performances.

CHRISTOPHER BLAKE

Drama written and directed by Moss Hart; produced by Hyman and Hart; production designed by Harry Horner. Opened on November 30, 1946, at the Music Box Theatre. Cast: Shepperd Strudwick, Martha Sleeper, Richard Tyler. 114 performances.

INSIDE USA

Revue produced by Arthur Schwartz; book by Arnold Auerbach, Moss Hart, and Arnold B. Horwitt; music by Arthur Schwartz, lyrics by Howard Dietz. Opened on April 30, 1948, at the New Century Theatre in New York. Songs include "Haunted Heart." Cast: Beatrice Lillie and Jack Haley. 399 performances.

LIGHT UP THE SKY

Comedy written and directed by Moss Hart; produced by Hyman and Hart; opened November 18, 1948, at the Royale Theatre. Cast: Sam Levene, Barry Nelson, Virginia Field, Phyllis Povah, Audrey Christie. 216 performances.

MISS LIBERTY

Musical with book by Robert E. Sherwood (and Moss Hart); music and lyrics by Irving Berlin; directed by Moss Hart; choreography by Jerome Robbins; settings and lighting by Oliver Smith; presented by Berlin, Sherwood, and Hart. Songs include "Let's Take an Old-Fashioned Walk," "(Just One Way to Say) I Love You," "You Can Have Him." Cast: Eddie Albert, Allyn (Ann) McLerie, Mary McCarty, Tommy Rall. Opened July 15, 1949, at the Imperial Theatre. 308 performances.

THE CLIMATE OF EDEN

A drama written and directed by Moss Hart, based on the novel *Shadows Move Among Them* by Edgar Mittelholzer; presented by Hyman and Hart at the Martin Beck Theatre, New York, November 13, 1952. Cast: John Cromwell, Rosemary Harris, Earle Hyman. 20 performances.

ANNIVERSARY WALTZ

Comedy by Jerome Chodorov and Joseph Fields; directed by Moss Hart; produced by Hyman and Hart at the Broadhurst Theatre on April 7, 1954. Cast: Kitty Carlisle and Macdonald Carey. 615 performances.

IN THE PINK

Book by Moss Hart; music and lyrics by Harold Rome. Unproduced.

MY FAIR LADY

Musical by Alan Jay Lerner based on George Bernard Shaw's *Pygmalion;* music by Frederick Loewe; lyrics by Alan Jay Lerner. Directed by Moss Hart; presented by Herman Levin at the Mark Hellinger Theatre on March 15, 1956. Cast: Rex Harrison, Julie Andrews, Stanley Holloway, Robert Coote. 2,717 performances.

CAMELOT

Musical play by Alan Jay Lerner based on T. H. White's *The Once and Future King;* music by Frederick Loewe; lyrics by Alan Jay Lerner. Directed by Moss Hart (and Lerner). Presented by Lerner, Loewe, and Hart at the Majestic Theatre on December 3, 1960. Cast: Richard Burton, Julie Andrews, Robert Goulet, Roddy McDowall. 873 performances.

FILMS

Almost all of the Kaufman and Hart plays were made as movies, though neither playwright was directly involved in any of them. The filmography below includes only films based on Hart's direct work on the motion picture and the credits are limited to major contributors.

FLESH—1932

MGM; directed by John Ford; story adaptation by Leonard Praskins and Edgar Allan Woolf from an original story by Edmund Goulding; dialogue by Moss Hart. Premiere: December 8, 1932. Running time 95 minutes. Starring Wallace Beery.

THE MASQUERADER—1933

Samuel Goldwyn presents *The Masquerader*, based on the novel by Katherine Cecil Thurston. Adaptation and screenplay by Howard Estabrook, dialogue by Moss Hart; directed by Richard Wallace. Running time 75 minutes. Cast: Ronald Colman, Elissa Landi. Released through United Artists.

BROADWAY TO HOLLYWOOD—1933

MGM. Directed by Willard Mack; produced by Harry Rapf; screenplay by Willard Mack and Edgar Allan Woolf (and Moss Hart). Running time 90 minutes. Cast: Alice Brady, Frank Morgan, Jackie Cooper, Russell Hardie, Madge Evans, Mickey Rooney, Eddie Quillan, Jimmy Durante.

FRANKIE AND JOHNNIE—(1934 TO) 1936

RKO Radio Pictures, 1934; released by Republic Pictures, May 1936. Produced by William Saal; directed by Chester Erskine [and John H. Auer, uncredited]. Screenplay by Moss Hart and Lou Goldberg, based on a story by Jack Kirkland. Running time 70 minutes. Cast: Helen Morgan, Chester Morris, Florence Reed, Lilyan Tashman (unbilled).

BROADWAY MELODY OF 1936—1935

MGM; produced by John Considine; directed by Roy del Ruth; screenplay by Jack McGowan and Sid Silvers; story by Moss Hart; costumes by Adrian; dance direction by David Gould; dream ballet by Albertina Rasch; cameraman Charles Rosher; songs by Arthur Freed and Nacio Herb Brown: "Broadway Rhythm," "You Are My Lucky Star," "I've Gotta Feelin' You're Foolin'," "Sing Before Breakfast," "All I Do Is Dream of You," "On a Sunday Afternoon." Released 1935. Running time 103 minutes. Cast: Jack Benny, Eleanor Powell, Robert Taylor, Sid Silvers, Buddy and Vilma Ebsen.

WINGED VICTORY—1944

20th Century-Fox in association with the U.S. Army Air Forces; produced by Darryl F. Zanuck; directed by George Cukor; screenplay by Moss Hart. Running time 130 minutes. Cast: Lon McCallister, Jeanne Crain, Edmund O'Brien, Mark Daniels, Judy Holliday, Lee J. Cobb, Barry Nelson, Karl Malden, Red Buttons.

GENTLEMAN'S AGREEMENT—1947

20th Century-Fox. Produced by Darryl F. Zanuck; directed by Elia Kazan; screenplay by Moss Hart, based on the novel by Laura Z. Hobson. Running time 118 minutes. Cast: Gregory Peck, Dorothy McGuire, John Garfield, Celeste Holm, Anne Revere, Jane Wyatt, June Havoc.

HANS CHRISTIAN ANDERSEN—1952

Produced by Samuel Goldwyn; directed by Charles Vidor; screenplay by Moss Hart, based on a story by Miles Connolly; songs by Frank Loesser, including "Wonderful, Wonderful Copenhagen," "No Two People (Have Ever Been So in Love)," "Inch Worm," "Anywhere I Wander." Running time 112 minutes. Cast: Danny Kaye, Zizi Jeanmaire, Farley Granger, John Brown. Distributed by RKO.

A STAR IS BORN—1954

A Transcona Enterprises Production for Warner Bros.; produced by Sidney Luft; directed by George Cukor; screenplay by Moss Hart, based on the Dorothy Parker, Alan Campbell, Robert Carson screenplay, from a story by William A. Wellman and Robert Carson. Running time 181 minutes. Cast: Judy Garland, James Mason, Charles Bickford, Jack Carson, Tommy Noonan. Premiered at the RKO Pantages in Hollywood, September 29, 1954.

PRINCE OF PLAYERS—1955

20th Century-Fox; produced and directed by Philip Dunne; written by Moss Hart from the book by Eleanor Ruggles. Running time 102 minutes. Cast: Richard Burton, Raymond Massey, Maggie MacNamara, Charles Bickford, John Derek, Elizabeth Sellars, Eva Le Gallienne.

NOTES

Eliscu and Fisk David Eliscu and Merlin Fisk
EYH "Yip" Harburg
FB Frederic Bradlee
FF Frieda Fishbein
FTM *Face the Music*
GA George Abbott
GB Glen Boles
GBS George Bernard Shaw
GC George Cukor
GK George Kelly
GS George Steinberg
GSK George S. Kaufman
GWSH *George Washington Slept Here*
GZ Gregory Zilboorg
Hahn Collection The Hahn Collection, Dallas, Texas
HBH, Mrs. Mrs. Henry B. Harris
HCA *Hans Christian Andersen*
HL Herman Levin
HL Papers Herman Levin Papers
HW Herman Wouk
IMS Irene Mayer Selznick
int. interview
JC Jerome Chodorov
JF Janet Fox
JGG Julie Goldsmith-Gilbert
JLW Jack L. Warner
Jones *The Emperor Jones,* O'Neill
KCH Kitty Carlisle Hart
Kitty *Kitty: An Autobiography* by Kitty Carlisle Hart
KM Karl Menninger
Laura Z. *Laura Z.,* by Laura Hobson
LCL Billy Rose Theater Collection, Lincoln Center Library of the Performing Arts, New York Public Library
LS Lester Sweyd
LSK Lawrence S. Kubie
LUTS *Light Up the Sky*
LZH Laura Z. Hobson
MB Marie Brenner
MCNY Museum of the City of New York
MFL *My Fair Lady*
MG-LCL Max Gordon Collection, LCL
MGM-USC MGM Collection, University of Southern California
MH Moss Hart
MH Papers, Wisc. Moss Hart Papers, Wisconsin
m.s. manuscript
MW Monty Woolley
MWRA *Merrily We Roll Along*
NOTB "The Nature of the Beast"
NYC New York City
NYH-T *New York Herald-Tribune*
Nymph *The Constant Nymph*
NYPL New York Public Library

NYT   *New York Times*
OIAL   *Once in a Lifetime*
Phil.   Philadelphia Free Library
PM   PM newspaper
R&H tape Rodgers & Hammerstein Collection
RC   Robert Cantrell
RH   Random House
RLD/RD   Ronald L. Davis/Reid Shelton
RM   Richard Madden
RR   Richard Rodgers
SB   author
SG   Samuel Goldwyn
SG-Academy Samuel Goldwyn Collection, Academy
Six Plays *Six Plays by Kaufman and Hart*
SJS   Solomon J. Solomon
SMU   Southern Methodist University Oral History Program
SNB   Sam Behrman
Song   *With or Without a Song,* Eliscu
TGW   *The Great Waltz*
TMWCTD   *The Man Who Came to Dinner*
UA   United Artists
USC   University of Southern California, *A Celebration of Moss Hart: USC Friends of the Libraries, 12 April 1970* (Los Angeles: University of Southern California, 1970)
WB   Warner Bros.
Wisc.   State Historical Society of Wisconsin, Madison, Wisconsin
WMA   William Morris Agency
WWD   *Women's Wear Daily*
YCTIWU   *You Can't Take It With You*

INTRODUCTION: "HUCKLEBERRY HART"

xii "Truth-ier Truth": letter, GA to MH, 10 Sept. 1959; "shocked": letter, LS to MH, 18 July 1959; "Chapter and Verse": letter, EE to MH, 30 July 1959. GA and EE: MH Papers, Wisc. Sweyd: LCL.

PART I: OUTSIDE

1: BROADWAY BABY

3 E. B. White: *Here Is New York,* pp. 9–10.
   Fifth Avenue: the line appears often. See for instance, *Time,* 29 Nov. 1943, p. 43.
   "the Darling of": letter, MH to GK, "Monday," c. Nov. 1953, Hahn Collection.
4 Yakima: Hart, AO m.s., Box 15, folder 1, [p. 3], MH Papers, Wisc.
   Birthdate and place: Certificate of Birth 49583 (1904), State of New York, City of New York.
   "Shabby gentility": Hart, AO, p. 9.
   "enormous . . .": ibid., p. 15. Birth: Death certificate, Barnett Solomon, 2 Jan. 1911. State of New York Certificate and Record of Death, NYC Municipal Records.
   Solomon family history: Holland: Barnett Solomon's death certificate (see above) gives Holland as birthplace for both his mother and father.
   Further on Solomons: mostly from Phillips; plus int. CF [Finkelstein], 4 Feb. 1995; letters, CF to SB, 5 Feb. 1995; letters BF to SB, Mar. 1995. Mrs. Forsyte, first

cousin to Lillie Hart, prepared for my use a handwritten abstract of reminiscences and family connections. BF was a second cousin of MH, a Solomon descendant through the Bentwich family.

5 Solomon as painter: Phillips and Pery.

Mischa Elman: this was Margery Bentwich: int. CF.

SJS: (1860–1927) SJS was the second Jew ever elected to the Royal Academy; the first, oddly enough, was a painter called Solomon Hart, no relation to anyone in this story. SJS was also first president of the Maccabeans, the still extant society of Anglo-Jewish leaders for social and charitable activities.

Shaw: Phillips, p. 29.

". . . a record!": ibid, p. 219.

Re Barney Solomon: int. CF, as cited.

"cast off to El Dorado": int. SB/CF. Barnett Solomon's death certificate gives his stay in America as "about 50 years," though no shipping logs or other records reveal a definite date. The date of his naturalization was 10 Oct. 1883. File #S455, vol. 336: National Archives—Northeast region, New York.

Kate and Lillie's birthdates: Lillian Solomon was born 17 February 1870: Death certificate, State of New Jersey Office of Registrar of Vital Statistics, City of Asbury Park, Monmouth County.

Lily [sic] Solomon's death certificate states that she was born in New York City, but MH birth certificate (cited above) gives her birthplace as England, as does her marriage license (cited below). New York is evidently an error by the clerk recording her death or by Joseph M. Hyman, who represented MH on the occasion of her death in 1937.

6 Gompers may actually have been a distant relative: the family name of brother Joseph's wife Helena had been Gomper (or Gomperz or Gompers) before it was changed to Liechtenstadt in the Napoleonic era: Phillips, p. 14.

briefcase story: AO, p. 8.

locked . . . closet: AO m.s., Box 15, folder 1 [p. 11].

7 "transparent": CF, as cited.

Lillie "buxom" and Kate "wizened": ibid.

Barnett Hart: his birthdate in London was 24 Apr. 1863: Certificate of Death, State of Florida Office of Vital Statistics, Dade County, Miami Beach, Florida. The witness to this certificate was his second son, Bernard Hart.

8 Marriage of MH's parents: 27 Nov. 1901, in New York, registered on 2 Dec. 1901. New York City Department of Records and Information Services, Municipal Archives.

West 118th Street: marriage license, as above. East 105th Street, MH birth certificate, cited above.

Name of MH: Barnett Hart's father was named Moss Hart, too, according to the marriage license; his mother's name had been Rebecca Rosenheim.

"monstrous": AO, p. 15.

14 East 107th Street: Public School Records (Moss Hart), New York City Board of Education. Death certificate of Barnett Solomon, as above, also gives this address in 1911, indicating a basement apartment that was superintendent lodgings.

eczema: int. SB/CF, as cited.

"unruffled . . .": AO, p. 12.

9 "sole and . . .": ibid., p. 13.

Literary Society: ibid.

"drabness": ibid., p. 18; "poverty": p. 8.

"a cry from the heart": ibid., p. 344.

2: POOR RELATIONS

10 Behrman: *People in a Diary,* p. 6.

Solomon's death: death certificate as cited. The attending physician noted his age as "77 years, 11 months." MH was mistaken when he wrote that his grandfather was seventy-nine at his own birth: AO, p. 12. He was equally incorrect in dating his brother's birth in the same week as Solomon's death.

Bernard Hart's birth and withered arm: int. CF. Also, *Variety,* 19 Aug. 1964, LCL.

school records: here and later, New York City Board of Education records covering Manhattan P.S. 171, Bronx P.S. 10, Bronx P.S. 51. For health and absences: at P.S. 171 in his first term (1A), which began Oct. 24, 1910, he was present thirty-one days and absent twelve by the time he was withdrawn. His second enrollment in 1A was little better, with fifty-eight days attended and thirty-two missed, but he finished the term, going on to 1B in Jan. of 1912, where his record continued at a rate of fewer than one-third of the term's days in attendance.

11 name, accent, etc.: AO, p. 19.

MH's voice and pronunciation: hear, for instance, "Moss Hart" on Spoken Arts, where Yakima is heard; "orche*ster*" etc., USC, p. 9; "*zollo*phone" from Goldstein, p. 471.

"squalor": USC, p. 9; AO, p. 26.

"iron": ibid., p. 16.

"faintly . . .": ibid.; "shrewd . . .": pp. 16–17.

12 blackmail: ibid., p. 17.

"new babe" and Mrs. Bentwich in NY: int. CF. Mrs. Bentwich was CF's mother. She was the grandmother of BF.

First theater experience: Anon., "Moss Hart," *Current Biography,* 1940, p. 369; also Goldberg, "Merry-Maker for 'Jubilee.'" MH thought the prolific Owen Davis wrote the play, but he was in error. The author was Thompson Buchanan. All citations and details are from programs and advertising materials, LCL.

13 Alhambra pronunciation: Spoken Arts Distinguished Playwright Series #725 (audio recording), *Moss Hart Reads.*

"lifelong infection": AO, p. 5.

"the art" and "to be loved . . .": ibid., p. 6.

14 dressing up and impersonating: Gardner.

"insanely jealous": int. CF.

Kate and Barnett: int. CF.

15 "pathological": AO, p. 16.

New Yorker: Harriman, p. 82.

hexes, warnings, arson: Harriman discusses this; corroboration and elaboration are from int. SB/CF. The outbreak of arson in the theater occurred in 1935, when MH's *Jubilee* was in rehearsals.

Home for Immigrant Girls: MH gets this wrong in AO, calling it the "Home for Working Girls."

hexes, etc.: MH does not refer to any of this in AO. See Harriman, who was permitted to draw the conclusion that Lillie may have been responsible, as the incidents ended around the time of her death. Both Barnett and Bernie Hart seem to have cooperated in this version. That Aunt Kate was responsible is confirmed by CF, who cited her pathological nature.

"I did not like her": AO, p. 25.

"battle-ax": int. SB/Walter Bernstein, 30 Nov. 1995.

Lillie and library books: letter, Feuerstein to MH, as above; "warm-hearted . . .": int. CF.

"jewelry": int. CF, who remembered witnessing this activity.

16   wedding photograph: it belongs to the bride, who was CF and supplied details of the wedding.

"deeply disturbed": AO, p. 6.

tennis racket: letter, Benjamin Feuerstein to MH, 17 Nov. 1959. Colman's: letter, Syd Hoff to MH, 23 Oct. 1959, both MH Papers, Wisc.

17   Ho and Ko: letter Feuerstein to MH as above, and GS to MH, 24 July 1959, MH Papers, Wisc.

Poe, not Dreiser: ibid.

Friedlander family, summers, gifts: int. CF; letters, BF to SB, 2 Apr. 1995; 13 July 1995; int. SB/BF: 9 June 1995.

speech: included in the MH Papers at Wisc.

quotations from the speech: as above.

18   certificate of illness and leaving school: see above for school records sources.

diplomas: U.S. Bureau of the Census, Historical Statistics of the United States to 1879, Bicentennial Edition, part 2, p. 379. The graduation rate was not quite 12 percent.

"staggeringly selfish": AO m.s., Box 15, folder 1, p. 17a; this harsh judgment was deleted from the finished book, possibly because MH's father was still living at the time it was published.

Friedlander job help: int. CF; int. SB/BF, as above.

Neuburger Furs: In AO, MH calls this firm "A.L. Neuburger" and says it was on Fourteenth Street. There is no listing for such a firm, though there was a "Max Neuburger Furs" at 151 Fifth Avenue, which moved to Twenty-third Street in 1920. New York City Telephone Directories, 1916–24.

3: "THAT DAMN KID"

19   AW epigraph: While Rome Burns, p. 167.

"National Revue": all details from program, Scrapbook, MH Papers, Wisc.

20   GS, AO, p. 37ff.

21   Aunt Bea and Aunt Belle and George: letter, GS to MH, 24 July 1959, Wisc. MH made errors in AO about the story of the aunts and GS corrected him.

Burston: his early career is covered in Slide, pp. 244–45, 370–71, and 390. Also, Motion Picture Studio Directory: 1920, in which Burston took a full-page ad for his then-company, Films Incorporated.

Oscar Wilde and Burston: "'Oscar Wilde' Latest is New Drama by Moss Hart and Lew Burston Will Produce It," Brooklyn Eagle [n.d., n.p.], Scrapbook, MH Papers, Wisc. Burston died 4 April 1923: Variety, 6 April 1923.

22   Follies of 1922: Green, Broadway Musicals Show by Show, p. 40.

AP, Jr.'s colon: letter, EE to MH, 30 July 1959, MH Papers, Wisc.; also, letter, EE to SB, Aug. 1995.

23   "You never learn": MH quoted to SB by JC, c. 1974.

"gift of banter . . .": Eliscu, Song m.s., p. 93.

24   GC: Lambert, On Cukor, pp. 24–25; GC in USC, p. 20; letter, GC to MH, 22 Sept. 1959, GC Collection, Academy.

Sillman: Sillman, p. 52.

EE on MH: "theater mad" and "fantastic appetite," letter, EE to MH, as cited, gap-toothed," Song, p. 93.

"Ziggy": letter, Mrs. R. E. Clough [Goldie] to MH, 18 Jan. 1960, MH Papers, Wisc.

"Mouse" or "Marcy": MH claimed in AO that AP, Jr. called him "Mouse," but in all correspondence the producer writes "Marcy," as do others at the same period. It is an ambiguous nickname.

25 "Irish Robin Hood" and following: EE and MH, first draft m.s., *Lad O'Laughter,* courtesy David Eliscu and Merlin Fisk [c. 1924]. This unique [?] draft is two acts, annotated in hand by MH and EE. Other drafts, which appear to be production drafts with pencil annotations regarding casting, etc., are at LCL and in MH Papers, Wisc. None bears an author credit.

"toothpaste": *Song,* p. 96.

AP, Jr., letter, here and hereafter: AP, Jr., to "Robert Arnold Conrad," 24 Sept. 1924, p. 3. Courtesy Eliscu and Fisk.

26 "sawed . . .": *Song,* p. 96.

EE on MH's dialogue: *Song,* p. 96.

"royalties": AO, p. 63.

"Our jerry-built . . .": *Song,* p. 96.

MH's terms: letter, AP, Jr., to Lincoln Osborne, 10 Oct. 1924. Courtesy Eliscu and Fisk.

27 Mrs. Harris: MH gets this wrong in AO, p. 65, in which he refers to her theater as the Hudson on Forty-fourth Street. The Fulton was on West Forty-sixth Street and had been built by Harris and Jesse Lasky in 1911.

letters from the road: all courtesy David Eliscu and Merlin Fisk. The series of seven letters and two postcards begins 20 Nov. 1924, and continues through 15 July 1925, with a single postcard dated 1930 and one undated letter that may be post-1925. There is also a long poem by MH of appreciation to EE of some 150 lines, undated. References to sleep are from MH to EE, 20 Nov. 1924.

sidelines: EE was in Washington, D.C., with a play called *Quarantine,* starring Sidney Blackmer. "Scorched and scalded" is from EE's letter to MH, 30 July 1959.

reviews: MH Scrapbook, Wisc.

28 Joseph Regan and "wind": letter, EE to MH, 30 July 1959, Wisc.

MH on Chicago: letter, MH to EE, 6 Dec. 1924, as above.

Ashton Stevens: the Chicago Historical Society turned up no such review as MH quoted in AO, p. 87. Stevens wrote for the *Herald* and the *Examiner* and was a force in Chicago.

reviews: headline, *Tribune,* 1 Dec. 1924; "too awful" is Amy Leslie.

Chicago reviews and "heart-sick": MH to EE, 3 Dec. 1924.

"Funny, isn't it": MH to EE, 6 Dec. 1924.

money on the road: MH to EE, 6 Dec. 1924.

29 "booming . . . surprise . . .": MH to EE, 6 May 1925.

rehearsal hall: letter, LS to MH, 18 July 1959, LCL.

For the record: *The Beloved Bandit* played the Park Theater in Youngstown, the Majestic Theater in Fort Wayne, and the Grand Opera House in Dubuque. Source: MH Scrapbook, Wisc., plus Wolfe Collection, LCL.

"a fascinating play . . .": Fort Wayne, Ind., *Journal Gazette,* 18 Sept. 1925. Wolfe Collection, LCL.

30 "Fantabulous": letter, Mrs. Henry B. Harris to MH, 14 July 1959; MH Papers, Wisc.

4: MOUNTAIN GREENERY

31 Mankiewicz: *All About Eve,* pp. 47–48.

Costs: MH's reckoning is sketchy and confusing, but on 3 Dec. 1924, he claimed to EE that the week prior to the original Chicago opening had resulted in a loss of

$7,943.64 with another $3,103.46 in bills unpaid. These figures would have been offset by box-office revenues. Letter, as cited, courtesy Eliscu and Fisk.

31 Theatre Guild costs: Langner, p. 119.
Ziegfeld and musical costs: Bordman, *Revue,* p. 46; Theatre Guild and *Methuselah:* Lynes, p. 190.

32 numbers of productions: Douglas, p. 60; Lehman Engel: quoted in Lynes, p. 158.
AW: quoted in Green, *Ring Bells:* p. 32.
hardships at home: EE wrote MH after AO was published, "You must have concealed them [hardships] very proudly": letter, EE to MH, 30 July 1959. EE did not dismiss the possibility of exaggeration to heighten dramatic effect in AO. EE to SB, as cited.
MH's wardrobe: DS mentions it often in the Flagler newsletters he edited, DS Papers, Wisc. Also, int. SB/Celeste Holm, Nov. 9, 1995.

33 LS: he was born in Holland on 23 Sept. 1892, and died in Englewood, N.J., in Nov. of 1978: *Variety,* 12 Dec. 1978. His vast theater collection is partly at Lincoln Center and partly at Queens College.
Chu Chin Chow: letter, LS to MH, 8 Aug. 1958, LCL.
Maurice Burke: letter, MH to LS, "Summer, 1929," Flagler Hotel, Fallsburg, N.Y., LCL; "dangerously . . .": [n.p.] *Worchester Evening Post,* 18 June 1927, Burke File, LCL; "masculine sex-appeal": letter, Burke to LS, c. 1927, Ambassador Hotel, Chicago. Burke admitted he had been fired as the juvenile lead from his current show for being insufficiently masculine, LCL. "darling": letter, Burke to LS, 12 Feb. 1937, LCL.
photograph and scrapbook: the scrapbook is in the MH Papers, Wisc. "Here's that picture" is from a letter, MH to LS, dated "Summer 1929," from the Flagler Hotel in Fallsburg, N.Y.: Sweyd Cage File, LCL.

34 EC and EE: EE felt MH gave EC too much credit in AO for pointing him in the direction of Little Theater and went on record that "one Eddie was given credit which was due another Eddie": letter, EE to MH, 30 July 1959, Wisc. EC and *Abie's Irish Rose:* Chodorov clipping file: LCL.
Perlman [not Perleman, as in AO]: his plays on Broadway included *My Company* in 1926 and *Broken Chain* in 1929. He was later involved in the Federal Theater Project.
Ghosts: Lynes, p. 177; Mantle, 1932–33, p. 498. Oddly, *Ghosts* had its world premiere in Chicago in 1882 in a production in Norwegian.

35 Mae West: Leider, pp. 168, 172. Also, AT, p. 87.
Kelly: *The Flattering Word,* p. 13. MH's first production of the play was 28–29 Jan. 1926 at the Labor Temple.
GK: his printing his address—"3665 Midvale Avenue"—was highly unusual. GK sent MH a telegram on the opening of OIAL, four years later. It read: "THINKING OF YOU AND WISHING YOU BEST OF LUCK TONIGHT": Scrapbook, Wisc.

36 American Co-Optimists: press release by Roland Wallace, 2 May 1926. Scrapbook, Wisc.
opening bill: the Wilde play was the first American presentation of "A Florentine Tragedy," and the GK was "Finders Keepers." Johnson's "Water Boy" was a premiere. The evening appears to have gone unnoticed by all standard sources, if—in fact—it ever took place.

37 *Garrick Gaieties:* MH mentions the show specifically in the m.s. to AO, but the reference was deleted from the book: Box 15, folder 2, p. 138B5, Wisc.
"a la Chodorov": letter, MH to LS, #3 summer 1929 from the Flagler; LCL.
"If Men Played Cards as Women Do": originated in the *Music Box Revue of 1923,*

where the players were called George, Bob, Marc, and John and were under-stood by playgoers to be surnamed respectively Kaufman, Benchley, Connelly, and Toohey.

38   soliciting bookings: MH wrote letters soliciting rental of the theater at $100 per night. One such letter is dated 8 Mar. 1927. Scrapbook, Wisc.

letter re Perlman: MH to "The Drama Critic" BA, 29 Aug. 1926. BA Collection, LCL.

O'Neill on Gilpin: Douglas, p. 80.

"greatest": ibid., p. 87.

Provincetown production of *Jones:* it opened 16 Feb. 1926. Except for Gilpin, the cast was entirely different at the Mayfair in November of that year.

Reviews of *Jones:* undated clips; Scrapbook, Wisc.

Intimate Theater: clips, Scrapbook, Wisc. "inner violence": AO, p. 98.

39   *Nymph:* it opened at the Selwyn on 9 Dec. 1926, while Jones was still running. MH may have hoped to get out of the latter.

"tragedy": AO, p. 105.

"magic of": ibid.

40   "six damnable years": ibid., p. 170. MH's arithmetic was off or he was exaggerating for effect.

Geller's: Harriman, *Take Them Up,* p. 87. The CCC is called "Half Moon Country Club" in AO. George Gold there is called "Mr. Axeler."

41   course offerings, etc.: CCC brochure, Scrapbook, Wisc.

Gross: unsourced obituaries, LCL. Gross was innovative in the field. He founded the Thalians in 1918 and put on new plays as well as standards of the Little The-ater repertoire. His groups regularly won awards. There have been suggestions that MH acted with the Thalians while still working with AP, Jr., but there is no evidence for such an involvement.

Dannemora and Sacco and Vanzetti: int. CF; letter, CF to SB, 9 Feb. 1995. CF was then Mrs. Finkelstein.

HW: HW's novel is *City Boy* and takes place partly at the camp: letter, HW to MH, 31 Oct. 1959, Wisc. Letter, HW to SB, 8 Apr. 1996. The children's camp was called the GKG: G for Gold, G for Philip Gross, and K for an absentee partner named Kufeld.

42   "woeful tale": letter, Harold Korzenik to MH, 15 Dec. 1959, in which Korzenik quotes Gross. Korzenik's brother had been a counselor at CCC, too. Wisc.

John Brown: int. CF, 4 Feb. 1995; letter, CF to SB, 14 Feb. 1995.

"budding John Barrymore": from an informal program biography Hyman wrote in the 1940s. Hyman File, LCL. "gorilla": int. SB/Walter Bernstein, 25 Nov. 1995.

"cross between": MH, "Let the Shuberts Be Warned," NYT, 17 Dec. 1944.

43   Hyman's loan: in AO it is $200. In "Let the Shuberts Be Warned" it was $100. Hyman said "several": affidavit to the Surrogate Court in New York in 1963 [he represented MH's estate]: "I advanced several hundred dollars to [MH] and also gave employment in my business to his father and younger brother." Other details: "An Educated Illiterate," *San Francisco Chronicle,* 18 Nov. 1945.

"Anything Might Happen": Typical was the Brooklyn YM-YWHA on 9 May 1928. Scrapbook, Wisc.

master of ceremonies at hotel ballroom: the event was held on 31 Mar. 1928, in the Louis XVIth ballroom of the Hotel Manger at Fifty-first Street and Seventh Avenue. Second season in Vermont: year-end [May 1928] YMHA New Leader, Brooklyn YMHA. Scrapbook, Wisc.

play titles: undated clips, Scrapbook, Wisc.

depression, etc.: AO, pp. 213–14; AO m.s., p. 242. On pp. 242–65 of the m.s. MH writes an account of a canoeing trip at CCC to offset these spells. The twenty-page passage was deleted before publication, but its highlight was a storm on Lake Champlain and it resembles in detail the trip to Dannemora described by CF.

44   "golden yawn": Cary Grant to SB, in conversation, c. 1975.

Serlin: letter, Allen Boretz to MH, 1959. MH Papers, Wisc.; *Song,* pp. 94–96.

"procrastination": letter, LS to MH, 18 July 1959, LCL.

45   *Panic:* MH alluded to but never acknowledged this play, which is not among his official papers and he may have thought it destroyed. The copy cited here is in the Katharine Cornell Manuscripts Division of Lincoln Center Library in New York. The account here and to follow is taken from the m.s. and from other papers in the LS File, plus letter, LS to MH, 18 July 1959. LCL.

The Center Follies: 6 April 1929.

New Jersey Federation Dramatic Contest: 14 April 1929.

King: AO, p. 233.

MH's salary: Bellamy, p. 80. The figure is cited by DS, who is the source for his own salary figure of $400.

Flagler: mostly from Flagler Hotel brochures and the DS Papers, Wisc. The DS Papers, Wisc., include a complete set of the camp newspaper, the *Flagler News,* with a day-to-day record of the summer. This account relies heavily on them.

46   *Flagler News:* see note above.

LS: the letters to LS are not part of the MH papers, but of the LS File at LCL. All are written from the Flagler.

48   RM: letter, RM to LS, 22 July 1929, Scrapbook, Wisc.

"the glittering": the phrase is Wouk's in letter, HW to SB, 8 Apr. 1996.

"It looks like": Flagler letter, #3, MH to LS, as above, LCL.

title: MH gave his original m.s. to LS when it was still titled *Once to Every Man;* letter, LS to MH, 18 July 1959, LCL. The scrapbook has a title page on which *Every Man for Himself* is crossed out and *Once in a Lifetime* substituted.

5: ONCE IN A LIFETIME

49   Kean quotation: traditional.

"most fierce . . .": AO, p. 254.

50   first reading: letter, LS to MH, 18 July 1959, LCL. In AO, MH claimed that LS came later into the process than was the case, confirmed by FF (see below), who challenged MH's published version in many particulars. All details regarding Silvernail, Merlin, readings, etc., come from the LS letter of 18 July 1959.

"that night": in intro., *Six Plays,* p. xxi. In AO he sees the play after completing a draft.

June Moon: the reading was on 7 Oct. and *June Moon* opened at the Broadhurst on 9 Oct.

Merlin: *Hobo* opened and closed at the Morosco in Feb. 1931.

51   citations from the first draft: from the versions at Wisc. and LCL, as cited above.

typist: for the record, her name was Sally Simon, LS to MH as above.

poet: the text is:

> For Lester:—A SLIGHT TRIBUTE TO AN OLD FRIENDSHIP [.]
> *Beautiful and rich to me is an old friendship.*
> *Grateful to the touch as ancient ivory,*
> *Smooth as aged wine or sheen of tapestry,*
> *Where light has lingered long.*
> *Full of tears and warm is an old friendship*
> *That asks no longer deeds of gallantry*

> *Or any deeds at all . . . save that the friend*
> *shall be*
> *Alive and breathing somewhere, like a song.*

LS File, LCL. "Marcella Hartowitz": Scrapbook, Wisc.

51 reading: those present at the reading included Marc Loebell, Martin Shulman, Roy Lloyd, and Denton Vane.

52 WALL STREET: *Variety,* 30 Oct. 1929, p. 1.

FF: LS's original copy of the play bore a title page reading "please return to Moss Hart" and giving his address as Twenty-first Avenue in Brooklyn. The Wisc. copy bears FF's name and office address as the official representative. Other details from letter, FF to MH, 4 Aug. 1959, BA Files, LCL.

Jed Harris's name: Gottfried, p. 41.

"I'm a master . . .": Behrman, *People,* p. 40.

producers: misc. clips re Woods and others, Scrapbook, Wisc. Re Belasco et al., letter, FF to MH, 4 Aug. 1959, BA Files, LCL.

"hear the laughs": Irving Drutman, "From Office Boy to Producer," Max Siegel Files, LCL.

53 Berlin and Harris in Hollywood: Bergreen, pp. 288–90.

MH to Max Siegel: AO, p. 263.

"aghast," "furious," "my courage": AO, pp. 263–64.

FF and LS and "figment": letter, FF to MH, 4 Aug. 1959, and LS to MH, 31 July 1959, both in BA Files, LCL. FF and LS felt betrayed by MH in AO, which minimized their efforts. FF's address as official agent is on early m.s. copies of the play. She later copied BA at the *Times* with her letters to MH. BA made them part of his files at LCL.

age: all press releases at the time of OIAL gave MH's birthdate as 1906. He was the source of the error and it persisted even in the m.s. to AO.

54 "secret illusion": AO, p. 264.

GSK quote: ibid., p. 268.

"compulsively devious": Gottfried, p. 102.

Ben Hecht: "Not All Plays By Unknowns Are Sent Back," unsourced clip, MH Cage File, LCL. Harris quote re Hecht: "Moss Hart Didn't Mind Being Rewritten—by the Right Man," unsourced clip, Scrapbook, Wisc.

55 $1.69: the contract is a straight option agreement with no mention of collaboration. The typist spelled the names incorrectly: "Fischbein" and "Siegal." Contract top sheet, LS Cage File, LCL.

Harris and *No Retreat:* quote is from LS, LS to MH, 9 Aug. 1959.

"Shoot her": Connelly, p. 75.

56 "fat Jewish whore . . .": Gottfried, p. 100.

Peggy Hopkins Joyce: int. SB/Connie Rosenbloom, 8 Jan. 1997; Meredith, p. 426.

"baring of the teeth": the employee was BA, intro., *Six Plays,* p. xi.

Twain: Goldstein, p. 7.

57 BA: op. cit., p. xiii.

Billy Rose: Goldman, p. 148, and Scrapbook, Wisc. Heyward, here and later, Scrapbook; both also letter FF to MH, as above.

Ryskind quote: Maslon, p. 30.

Joseph: Goldstein, p. 171.

June Moon on the road: *June Moon* Scrapbook, LCL.

"faster . . .": the phrase is JGG's.

Kelly: see *The Flattering Word,* p. 38ff.

58 Vail's line: the original line cited "Mr. Dahlberg" instead of "anybody." OIAL first draft, LCL.

58 collaboration contract: LS, diary, 9 May 1930. The contract seems to have coincided with official casting. LCL.

59 Flagler: DS Papers, Wisc.; see below.

Brice and "Babykins": Goldman, p. 148.

Reviews: NYT, 26 Mar. 1930; "smart cracks," J. J. Farrell; "high voltage," E. F. Smith, *Atlantic City Press,* 2 Apr. 1930; *Variety,* dateline 1 Apr. 1930. Scrapbook, Wisc.

reviews: Winchell, 8 Apr. 1930. *Jonica* file, Museum of the City of New York. William B. Friedlander produced and staged the show and contributed to the score. He may have rewritten it without credit, too, in which case MH's claim that he had little to do with the show would be buttressed. No script is known to survive.

60 Jessel: unsourced clips, Scrapbook, Wisc.

61 GSK's withdrawal: AO, pp. 367–68.

Grand Hotel: MH saw it on the desk and claimed later to have advised GSK against it. Ibid., p. 364.

"scribbled" and changes: ibid., p. 363.

62 MacMahon and Dixon: Goldstein, p. 182, for Dixon. For MacMahon, CF reported being present for a "bitter" argument about MacMahon in Brighton Beach: int. SB/CF, 4 Feb. 1995. In the AO m.s., MH stressed that MacMahon had been his idea: AO m.s., Box 15, folder 4, pp. 378a, 378b.

"lack of . . .": intro., *Six Plays,* p. xii.

63 "this new boy": quoted by John O'Hara in *Colliers,* 25 May 1956.

Copake: int. SB/Walter Bernstein, as before. MH was hired for Copake for the summer of 1931, but didn't have to take the job. Bernie Hart and the rest of the family went anyway.

"Baby Snooks": Goldman, as before. David Freedman eventually wrote Baby Snooks.

Flagler: in AO, MH invents a sentimental journey to the Flagler with a last impersonation of Fanny Brice, but the DS/MH correspondence makes clear it never happened. MH begged off on 19/20 July 1930, "Tuesday—2[:]35 a.m." DS Papers, Wisc.

Bolitho: his *Overture* became a posthumous *success d'estime.* Mantle, 1930–31, p. 256ff.

No Retreat: details, quotes, AP, Jr., from clippings, Scrapbook, Wisc.

trip to the Hamptons with LS: letter, LS to MH, 19 July 1959, LCL. Also, MH to DS, as above, DS Papers, Wisc.

64 Dunne: clip in Scrapbook. Interestingly, the headline accidentally ran "ONCE IN A LIFETIME" [*sic*] HAS GERM OF FINE PLAY, BUT NEEDS SOME TINKERING.

jelly doughnuts, etc.: AO m.s., pp. 461, 465. Passages dropped from m.s.

65 BK's party: AO, pp. 293–96.

Thanatopsis members: AO m.s., p. 469, passages deleted from book.

AW's island, Kahn estate: letter MH to DS, as above.

"days of terror": MH used the phrase often. Anon., *Current Biography, 1940,* p. 369; intro., *Six Plays,* p. xxii.

five-year deal with Sam Harris: FF to MH, 4 Aug. 1959, FF to BA, 17 Sept. 1959, BA File, LCL.

66 GSK and *Times:* Teichmann, *Kaufman,* p. 87. His letter of resignation was dated Aug. 16, two weeks before the Philadelphia opening. "corpulent": intro., *Six Plays,* p. xii.

Jean Dixon: quoted in Goldstein, p. 182.

Philadelphia reviews: OIAL Scrapbook, LCL.

67 Harris: AO, pp. 391–92.

67 Two versions: see MH "Men at Work," p. xxvi, and AO, pp. 392–93. In the first it is a carousel; in the second it is swings.

BK: MH "Men at Work," p. xxv.

Dinty Moore's: AO m.s., p. 531, deleted from book.

telegrams: Scrapbook, Wisc.

70 GSK's speech: AO, p. 427. Contemporary accounts quote GSK as having said 75 percent (*The New Yorker*, 4 Oct. 1930) or two-thirds (Burns Mantle).

Lillie and Macy's: Eells, *Life*, p. 123.

PART II: INSIDE

6: "AND WHO, PRAY TELL, IS MOSS HART?"

73 Jed Harris: quoted in Gottfried, p. 66.

GSK: for instance, the *New York Telegram* of 9 June 1930, had a headline reading KAUFMAN'S NEW PLAY GIVES HOLLYWOOD TRUTHS IN CALCULATED DIGS, p. 10. This was typical.

reviews: OIAL Scrapbook, LCL; MG-LCL.

74 BA and Mantle: clips, OIAL Scrapbook, LCL.

75 season statistics: Mantle, 1930–31, p. v.

royalties: for instance, Sam Harris announced the gross for the week of 29 Dec. 1930 as $31,122. MH's 60 percent of a 10 percent gross royalty would have been approximately $1,867. The amount varied weekly, but would grow with touring company and movie sale income and continues to the present day.

"Money Box": AO, p. 443.

Ansonia: int. SB/CF, as above. Re opera: KCH to Barbara Diamonstein, Columbia University Oral History, p. 444.

76 decorating: Harriman, *Take Them Up*, p. 91; black walls, floors, curtains for insomnia: int. SB/CF, as above. black divan: Gardner, p. 11.

money: Goldstein, p. 185.

clothes: confidential source; int. SB/Celeste Holm, 9 Nov. 1995.

77 "success poisoning": AO m.s., pp. 429, 434. The term was deleted in favor of the quite different "success modesty": AO, p. 343. queasiness: letters to DS, as below, in which he expresses medical concern.

78 "capacity for enjoyment": letter, MH to DS, "en route" on Twentieth Century Limited, c. Dec. 1930. change: letter, MH to DS, Palm Springs, Calif., c. Feb. 1931. MH refers to DS's silence and a widespread feeling among their friends that success had changed him; "money-grubbing": same source. MH specifically mentions Brooklyn and Newark in this regard. DS Papers, Wisc.

FF: letter, FF to MH, 4 Aug. 1959. FF's letter(s) mentioning her lawsuit and bitterness were prompted by AO. She asked to be portrayed accurately in the book or deleted from it. She told BA that she had "never received an answer" to her letter to MH. BA Files, LCL.

Grauman: Florence Lawrence, "Grauman's Ability to Aid Stage," unsourced, Scrapbook, Wisc.

Schenck and Berlin: see Barrett, throughout. Schenck as partner: Bergreen, p. 178.

79 UA: this may have been a Schenck-Harris cabal to help the sale of movie rights. Press releases regarding MH's travel to California were issued not by Grauman, but by UA.

Louella Parsons: "Merry-Go-Round," 24 Jan. 1931, unsourced, Scrapbook, Wisc.

MH on Hollywood: "Mr. Hart Reports on Hollywood," NYT, 7 Dec. 1930, section IX, p. 1.

Thalberg and Harris: AO, p. 257.

80 fashions: Jean Loughborough, "Fashion Show of Notables at Mayan," Scrapbook, Wisc.

influenza, etc.: clips, OIAL Scrapbook, LCL.

"weak and wasted," Fairbanks, etc.: letter, MH to DS, c. Feb. 1931, El Mirador Hotel letterhead, Palm Springs. Also letter en route to Palm Springs, "The Apache" (Southern Pacific RR letterhead). DS Papers, Wisc.

81 "fearful depression": MH to DS, as above.

7: FACING THE MUSIC

82 Jean Dixon: to Malcolm Goldstein, in Goldstein, pp. 184, 471. Also, int. SB/Goldstein, 13 Feb. 1995.

"swishy": int. SB/JF Goldsmith, 20–21 Mar. 1995.

"Chinese actor": Harriman, p. 86. Harriman's piece was originally a *New Yorker* profile.

Wind Up, Cavalcade: "On a Hart and Its Beat," NYT, 4 Oct. 1934, sec. 10, p. 3; Talmey, "Biography of a Play," *Stage,* Nov. 1934, pp. 18–22.

Coward and *Cavalcade:* Morley, *A Talent,* pp. 182–85. Cable, p. 184. Hart's stories about *Wind Up an Era* all date from 1934, two years after the fact.

83 "sheer impossibility": "On a Hart . . ." as above.

Marx Brothers: cables, GSK to MH, Dec. 1930/Jan. 1931; Scrapbook, Wisc. Also, unsourced clips, LCL.

"Up in the dumps": quoted by Goldstein, p. 190.

84 "But not on the lot": Lloyd Thompson, "Moss Hart Has Some Undeniably Emphatic Ideas on Hollywood," San Francisco clip, OIAL File, LCL.

"gone dry," "rock bottom": Barrett, pp. 82, 89.

"fiasco": ibid., p. 88.

"dry spell": ibid., p. 82ff. Berlin as old hat: Bergreen, p. 290.

85 Sardi's: MH in "Men at Work" put the period of their working together at a full twelve months. They began in June, according to all sources, and the show opened in Feb., eight months later.

BA on *Band Wagon:* NYT, 4 June 1931, p. 31.

Harris quote: Goldstein, p. 197.

"fear of failure": Bergreen, p. 309; false starts: Barrett, pp. 91–92. Also, Percy Stone, NYH-T, 23 Feb. 1932.

Insomnia and "Buddha": "Men at Work" m.s., pp. 17–18.

86 Camp Copake: int. SB/Walter Bernstein, as cited.

Authorship: Berlin biographers usually credit him with uncredited work on the book. The same is true for those writing about GSK. Even Morrie Ryskind is cited in some accounts, but no one ever officially claimed credit but MH. For Ryskind: NYH-T, 16 Oct. 1932.

August: Barrett, p. 92. Barrett also cites her father's lead sheet of "Soft Lights and Sweet Music" as 13 Aug. 1932, by which time work seems to have been progressing well: p. 113.

BA: as above. Reviews noted Walker's uncomfortable presence at the opening.

87 citations: from FTM m.s., Wisc.

never open: see, for instance, Gilbert W. Gabriel, *NY American,* "New Stage, Screen Plays," 18 Feb. 1932.

"best he's": *Variety,* 8 Feb. 1932, out-of-town review.

88 elephant: Barrett, p. 205; BA, NYT, 18 Feb. 1932. Ziegfeld prop: *World Telegram,* 10 Mar. 1932; Sederholm, p. 361.

88 budget: Bergreen, p. 311. Sederholm says $125,000, which was still a huge figure in 1932: Sederholm, p. 374.

program note in full: "All the production and lighting effects, including the mirrors, created by Hassard Short and are patented and protected." Another note concerned a song. It read: "Acknowledgment is made to the 'New Yorker' for permission to use the phrase 'I Say It's Spinach.' "

staging: admiration for "Rhinestone" number: NYH-T, 1 Mar. 1932; 27 Mar. 1932; mirror number: *Stage,* Jan. 1934; the "crinoline number" had originally been written as a nudist number set in Sweden, which seemed out of place: "Scene Revised at Tryout Put Zest in Revue," FTM Scrapbook, LCL. Also, FTM m.s., Wisc., in which the original "Nudity Song" lyrics remain. Chorus boy "mooning": Sederholm, p. 360.

89 Brown on Boland: as cited, 18 June 1932.

90 Harris's loss: Sederholm, p. 375.

Mrs. Berlin: Barrett, p. 149; Short's background: Leiter, p. 266ff.

"folderol": unsourced clips, MH folder, MCNY.

Porter: meeting through Hale, Schwartz, p. 139; house, Stephen Citron, "Cole Porter at 13 rue Monsieur," *Architectural Digest,* p. 84ff; also Eells, p. 72.

91 MH on Linda Porter: MH's introduction to *The Cole Porter Songbook,* here quoted from m.s., p. 5, Wisc.

"terrible in their grandeur": Harriman, *Take Them Up,* p. 145.

The Porters: mostly Schwartz, pp. 50–54. Painful: I thank Porter biographer William McBrien for sharing information and insights based partly on recently discovered papers now housed at Yale.

Benay Venuta: McBrien m.s., p. 264.

"Do more, say less": Watson, pp. 195–96.

marriage quote: Goldberg, "Merry . . ." *Jubilee* Scrapbook, MG-LCL.

92 itinerary: "British Audiences Impress Mr. Hart Very Favorably," unsourced clips, MH Cage File, LCL.

8: HOLLYWOOD TO BROADWAY

93 Hecht quote: Gary Herman, p. 63.

94 Eisenstein: Seton, p. 186.

Variety: 13 Dec. 1932.

reviews: "severe disappointment": John S. Cohen, Jr., *NY Sun,* 12 Dec. 1932, Academy Library.

Tugboat Annie: letter, MH to DS, 12 Oct. 1932. DS Papers.

95 Crawford photo: Van Damm Collection, LCL. Addresses: letter, MH to DS, as above; postcard [n.d.] giving new address as 1625 Sunset Plaza Drive. DS Papers.

Dancing Lady fragment: MH script dated 20 Oct. 1932, MGM-USC.

96 "brittle": Thorton Delehanty, *NY Post,* SG-Academy.

"yesteryear": Regina Crewe, American: *Masquerader* File, SG-Academy.

Kohlmar and Goldwyn: Berg, p. 235; Hornblow: SG-Academy; BK and SG: Berg, p. 268.

97 Bernie: telegram, MH to SG, 29 May 1933. SG's office answered two days later on May 31st, SG-Academy.

Wizard of Oz: telegrams, MH to SG, SG to MH, both 18 Oct. 1933; telegram Irving Berlin to SG, 16 Dec. 1933, SG-Academy.

"March of Time" here and later: memos, drafts, other miscellany, MGM-USC. Also, Barrios, pp. 338–41, 395–96.

98   Harburg: John Lahr, "The Lemon-Drop Kid," *The New Yorker,* 30 Sept. 1996, p. 73.
dialogue: MH draft screenplay for "March of Time," p. 27, dated 4 Jan. 1933. MGM-USC.

writers: between MH's draft of 4 Jan. 1933, and the start of shooting in June of that year, the following writers are listed in the MGM files: William A. Grew, Zelda Sears, Eve Greene, Albert Hackett and Frances Goodrich, Bradford Ropes, Harlan Thompson, and Albert M. Ottenheimer, in addition to director Willard Mack and Edgar Allan Woolf, whose script was submitted to Rapf on 24 May and okayed by him on 31 May, MGM-USC.

Broadway to Hollywood writers and credits: though MH received no screen credit, *International Photographer* listed production credits including "author, Moss Hart" in "On the Firing Line," by Helen Boyce, Aug. 1933, p. 34, when the picture was editing. The final version was substantially based on the MH screenplay of 4 Jan. 1933.

Broadway to Hollywood is now part of Ted Turner's film library and turns up on television now and then, minus any color sequences, though comparison to the dialogue cutting continuity prepared four days before the original release indicates it is dramatically intact. Trade paper reports of the period alluded to short-subject use of remaining footage. Dialogue cutting continuity: 26 August 1933, MGM-USC.

99   MH to SG: interoffice memo, 9 Oct. 1944, SG-Academy.

100 "If . . .": Hart, "Before Thousands Cheered," *Stage,* July 1935, p. 16.
"mutual consternation": Harriman, *Take Them Up,* p. 170.

101 RR: *Musical Stages,* p. 157.

102 Mayer and MacDonald: Higham, p. 207. Also, Philip K. Scheuer, *Los Angeles Times,* "Hollywood's Traducer Now Its Booster," 19 Feb. 1933, LCL.
angel: Nolan, pp. 173–74; Green, *Broadway Musical,* p. 102.
MH on Hollywood: "Before Thousands Cheered," as before, p. 16.

9: CHEERS

103 Mantle: 1932–33, p. 3.
"great rally": ibid., p. v.
statistics: ibid., p. 3.
money: MH admits to borrowing in "Before Thousands Cheered," p. 17.

104 Berlin loan: Bergreen, p. 313.
title announced: NYH-T, 25 Dec. 1932. MH Cage File, LCL. statistics: Mantle, 1932–33 and 1933–34.
Man Bites Dog: opened on 25 Apr. 1933, for seven performances.
Parker and Barry: unsourced clip, Philadelphia Theater Collection, Phil. Barry was writing a play for Lillian Gish called *The Joyous Season,* which lasted only sixteen performances on Broadway. See Chapter 10, re Barry and "Richard Niles" in *Merrily.* Also Parker and "Julia Glenn."
Short in Bermuda: Sederholm, p. 378; "There . . .": "And Now Rests the Weary Hart," ATC Scrapbook, MG-LCL, LCL.
ATC: the handwritten m.s. is in the MH Papers, Wisc. Some sketches were published in Oliver [see Bibliography], but unless so noted, reference is to the annotated m.s.

105 *Broadway to Hollywood:* MH had specified "several amusing stock shots of Easter Parades of that period [1909]" to introduce a major scene in his script.
"Easter Parade" and MGM: Bergreen, p. 475.
names: "Fifty Celebrities Have a Couple of Authors Worried," unsourced clip, ATC Scrapbook, MG-LCL.

105 "Heat Wave": Bergreen, p. 317.
106 Montauk: Barrett, pp. 116–19.
    IMS: int. SB/IMS, 26 Nov. 1985.
    GSK and Berlin: Meredith, p. 75; Bergreen, pp. 310–11. Berlin quote: Teichmann, *Kaufman,* p. 92; GSK quote: "Memoir," *The New Yorker,* 11 June 1960.
    Berlin and GSK swap: Meredith, p. 465.
107 "I've never missed": Bergreen, p. 318.
    MH on Marilyn Miller: "Hart Realizes One Dream of His Late Youth," unsourced clip, ATC Scrapbook, MG-LCL.
    Mordden, BB, p. 56.
108 "my blemish": inscription on a photograph of MH signed to CW, courtesy Judith and Erik Hahn, Hahn Collection.
    MH on Broderick: "Before Thousands Cheered," p. 19.
    Boland: Harris at one point announced Edna May Oliver for the part Broderick played, and an early additional casting choice had been W. C. Fields: *NY World-Telegram,* 8 June 1933, MG-LCL.
    "dusky": quoted in Bergreen, p. 317.
    "*hot* stage": Garson Kanin, quoted by Mordden, BB, p. 57.
109 English protest: "British Objecting to Portrayal of Royal Family in Revue Here," *Philadelphia Public Ledger,* 20 Sept. 1933.
    stage manager quote: John Kennedy, quoted in Sederholm, p. 393. Hamilton discovery: "Showmen Find Their Prince at Soda Fountain," NYH-T, 21 Jan. 1934, and Bernard Sobel, "Thomas Hamilton Is a Ringer for Prince of Wales," *NY Daily Mirror,* MG-LCL.
    MH on Hamilton: Lucius Beebe, "Berlin and Hart Look Over Their Revue and Find It Good," NYH-T, 1 Oct. 1933, LCL.
    Berlin: quoted in Sederholm, p. 386.
110 contemporary lynchings: Green, *Ring Bells,* p. 86.
    Waters and "underworld": Waters, p. 219; "Supper Time," p. 222.
    Brown: *NY Post,* 2 Oct. 1933; BA, *Broadway,* p. 321.
    backstage in Philadelphia: "Before Thousands Cheered," pp. 16–19.
    curtain-call story: quoted in Jablonski, *Berlin,* p. 159.
    reviews: all 2 Oct. 1933, MG-LCL.
111 short staging: Sederholm quoting assistant stage manager Jerome Whyte, pp. 383–85.
    MH's work: Percy Hammond found MH's jibes "thoughtless" and directed at easy targets. BA found his portraits occasionally "venomous and vindictive," MG-LCL.
    plagiarism suit: NYT, 7 Jan. 1934.
    "Happy Birthday": *Time,* 27 Aug. 1934; NYH-T, 15 Aug. 1934, MG-LCL. The suit was a landmark, originally brought against *Fox Movietone News* because of a newsreel in which the song was sung to FDR in the White House and was audible on the soundtrack. The case is a classic oddity in copyright law.
112 Coward reference and *Wind Up:* NYT, 12 Nov. 1933, LCL.
    illness: unsourced clips, MH Cage File, LCL.
    "city of dreadful night": "And Now Rests the Weary Hart," as cited.
113 "Miss Pamela . . .": treatment by MH dated 28 Apr. 1934. In it MH specifies Davies. MGM-USC.
    Liebmann: the ultimate fate of Liebmann has long been a mystery. His German version of MH's story was dated 7 Jan. 1935, and the final screenplay emerged 4 Mar. 1935. MGM-USC.
    GSK and MH: they may have traveled from N.Y. together. The NYT reported on 30 Jan. 1934, that they would leave for Palm Springs on 12 Feb. Goldstein claims that GSK joined MH there in mid-March. Goldstein, p. 230.

114 BK: Goldstein, p. 35. Goldstein worked from her unpublished autobiography and
        letters.
      GSK's impotence: Goldstein, p. 49.
      Goldstein quote: ibid.
      GSK and AW: ibid.
      Oppenheimer: "Overture to a Reader," in Oppenheimer, p. 6.
      MH on BK, "intimate,": AO m.s., folder 15, file 4, pp. 356–57, 447a, MH Papers,
        Wisc. MH deleted passages referring to the turbulence of his relationship with BK.
      BC: Meredith, p. 592. BC made the remark at BK's funeral.
115 GZ: int. SB/Dr. Richard Isay, 16 Nov. 1996; also Farber and Green, pp. 62–65.
      Gershwin quote: quoted by Rouben Mamoulian in "I Remember," in Armitage,
        p. 57; also in Jablonski, p. 71.
      Kay Swift: Jablonski, *Gershwin Remembered,* p. 71.
      "criminal intentions": KM, *The Selected Correspondence of Karl A. Menninger,
        1919–1945* (New Haven: Yale, 1988), p. 357.
      GZ: ibid., pp. 342, 352.
116 "dangerous and vicious": ibid., p. 257, in a letter from KM to GZ, 7 Feb. 1942.

10: BROADWAY MELODIES

117 BA: NYT, 15 Oct. 1933, sec. IX, p. 1.
      Short and *Roberta:* Sederholm, pp. 415–19.
      Hitchcock: Taylor, *Hitch,* p. 118.
      MH for humor: Sederholm, p. 427.
118 "stupendous" and "clean": Gordon, pp. 188–89.
      "mad": ibid., p. 189; the following mostly from pp. 182–92.
      "Rosemarie": "Strausses End Hart's Dodging of Operettas," NYH-T, 23 Sept. 1934.
      Frankie and Johnny: NYT, 18 Feb. 1934.
119 *Variety:* 27 May 1936.
      RKO: *Motion Picture Herald,* 25 June 1935; *Variety,* as above.
      Russian countess: Gordon claimed that MH invented the Russian countess, but she
        was present in the London production.
      dialogue: TGW m.s., p. 39, MH Papers, Wisc.
      parallel speeches: Kenneth Adrian in *Panic* [*No Retreat*] m.s., p. 3, LCL; Johann
        Strauss in TGW, as cited.
120 Mae West joke: Gordon, p. 188.
      "nine hundred": Richard Maney, quoted in Oppenheimer, p. 375.
      Rockefeller costs: *Variety,* 1 June 1935.
      chandeliers: *Boston American,* 13 Sept. 1934.
121 production details: mostly Sederholm, pp. 428–38.
      "You never saw" and "The Great Waste": Gilbert Gabriel, *NY American,* 30 Sept.
        1934.
      Barnett Hart: quoted by John Chapman, *Daily News,* 26 Oct. 1934. Also in Ager.
      "integrity": ATC m.s. [n.p.], Wisc.
122 rowboat: letter from MH dated Aug. 1934 on AW's Bomoseen letterhead refers to
        working there on the play. Judith and Erik Hahn Collection.
      "Don't ask": "Hart Conceived Play 'in Reverse' When But a Boy," unsourced clip,
        MWRA Scrapbook, MG-LCL.
      "Hartacade": Talmey, p. 19.
123 Elmer Rice and GSK's *Going Up:* Goldstein, pp. 36–37.
      Akins: her play opened on Broadway in Dec. 1921. Elmer Rice: BA, *Broadway,*
        pp. 273–74.

123 dialogue: *Six Plays,* p. 140.
124 MH on chronological order: Talmey, p. 19.
     BA: NYT, 1 Oct. 1934, p. 14.
     BA: ibid.
125 Garland: MWRA Scrapbook, MG-LCL.
     "If you have a message": BA, *Broadway,* p. 242.
     "I'm a genius": act 2, scene 3 [quoted from m.s., Wisc.].
126 "you like him . . .": act 3, scene 1 [m.s.].
     Mankiewicz: the version here is from BA, *Broadway,* though it is quoted in many
        different versions.
     ten best: Mantle, 1934–35.
127 BA's reassessment: *Broadway,* p. 235. The later judgment was not published until
        1970, when both authors were dead.
     MH on Mary Astor: letter, MH to DS, Feb. 1931, El Mirador, Palm Springs. DS
        Papers, Wisc.
     Astor in MWRA: Goldstein, pp. 237–39.
128 "Pale Irving": confidential source.
     Niles's dialogue: *Six Plays,* p. 140.

11: CRUISING

129 Wilde: quoted by Brown, *Art of Playgoing,* p. 88.
     F for Freud: the joke was ubiquitous. Oscar Levant used it in his *Memoirs of an
        Amnesiac* and MH and Herman Mankiewicz used it, too. Its origin is impossible
        to trace.
130 CP on MH: Hubler, p. 19.
     CP and boredom: Oppenheimer, p. 497.
     Lindsay and Crouse: Skinner, pp. 153–55.
131 London, Morocco: unsourced clip, *Jubilee* Scrapbook, MG-LCL. See also below, re
        "Men at Work."
     versions: MH told two: one is in "Men at Work," which acknowledges Morocco as
        a goal; the other is in MH's introduction to *The Cole Porter Song Book.* CP said
        that MH approached him with the whole idea: Hubler, p. 31.
     Cunard: *Stage,* Nov. 1935, featured a full-page advertisement about the trip, with
        lengthy quotes from CP and MH, as well as MW, who would direct *Jubilee,* pub-
        licizing both line and show.
     Re Powell: McBrien m.s., p. 270.
132 Coward and Bombay: unsourced clip, *Jubilee* Files, LCL.
     MH investment: int. SB/Malcolm Goldstein, 13 Feb. 1995.
     Sherwood: quoted in Oppenheimer, p. 228.
133 Abbott: this was related to me by Bella Spewack, one of the authors of *Boy Meets
        Girl.*
     MGM: *Hollywood Reporter,* 15 Oct. 1935, refers to *Jubilee* in a front-page article as a
        joint venture of Harris-Gordon-MGM, predicting it would be "MGM's first big
        hit picture of 1936–37." It was, of course, never made.
     Fun: Eells, p. 120.
     Beebe quote: "Moss Hart, World Traveler, Shows His Album," LCL.
     MH's photographs: the album is part of the MH Papers, Wisc., as are the ship's itin-
        erary and other miscellany used as source material here.
134 "Samoan manhood": from *My Trip,* quoted by McBrien m.s., pp. 278–79.
     Porter's baggage: Eells, p. 119.
     Powell and Hanna: Schwartz, p. 138.

134 Powell's rooms: Grant, p. 157.
  AW: "The First Mrs. Tanqueray," in AW, *While Rome Burns,* p. 139. AW spelled his name "Sturgis," as do others. According to McBrien, "Sturges" is correct.
  Sturges: Schwartz, pp. 58ff and 138–39. CP and Sturges not lovers: McBrien m.s., p. 110.
  Sturges quote: Gill, *Cole,* p. 50.
  MW: "the Beard" and later, Maloney, p. 25ff.
  MW: mostly Maloney.

135 "Miss Linda's . . .": Kimball, *Cole,* p. 128.
  CP and MH as lovers: confidential sources, plus McBrien m.s., p. 270.
  CP and MW cruising: see Schwartz, who details several episodes.
  diary: KCH would not allow McBrien access to the diary. McBrien agrees that there is no reason to draw conclusions. MH donated the diary—without reader restrictions—to Wisc. in his lifetime, and it is unlikely he would have done so if it contained information embarrassing to him or others.
  McBrien: m.s., p. 144.
  Linda Porter's manner: McBrien m.s., p. 100.
  Linda Porter incident: Eells, *Life,* p. 121.
  "Begin the Beguine" story: KCH, in Columbia University Oral History [Diamonstein], vol. 3, p. 578.

136 MH to CP: letter, MH to CP, 28 Feb. 1961, Wisc., donated by CP.
  "My Trip . . .": LS's copy bore the inscription "For Lester—Who is about to find that the world is his oyster, too. Moss Hart." This copy came into the possession of Helen Broderick, who presented it to Hart's children in the 1950s. It is now part of the MH Papers, Wisc.
  Ball of Wax: these materials are part of the *Jubilee* files, Wisc.

137 dialogue: quoted in *Stage.* The m.s. is in the MH Papers, Wisc.
  "tireless tugboat": Harriman, *Take Them Up,* p. 143.
  Linda and Elsa Maxwell: McBrien m.s., p. 171.
  song for Maxwell: ibid.

138 title: MH, "All at Sea," *Jubilee* Scrapbook, MG-LCL.
  Lillie Hart meeting Mrs. Porter: Eells, *Life,* p. 123.
  Aunt Kate: Lloyd Shearer, "I Cover Hollywood," 28 June 1935.

139 KCH anecdote: *Kitty,* pp. 74–75.
  unwritten song: KCH reported that she sang, among others, "Just One of Those Things," which would not be composed until later that summer.
  Fire Island and the Gershwins: Ewen, *Journey,* p. 259.

140 "Gossamer": Eells, *Life,* p. 128.
  Short and "unscathed": George Ross, "So This Is Broadway," clip [n.d.], *Jubilee* File, LCL.
  war: *Time,* 21 Oct. 1935, p. 51.
  vandalism and Boland: Eells, *Life,* pp. 126–29.
  Aunt Kate: AO, pp. 91–92, plus Eells, *Life,* and int. SB/CF, 14 Feb. 1995. No search could locate definitively Aunt Kate's death records in New York. Records of the Clara de Hirsch Home for Immigrant Girls (which merged with the 92nd Street Y in 1962) are incomplete. Int. Lee Armitage/Steven Siegal, Librarian, the De Hirsch Residence at the 92nd Street Y; 15 Mar. 1996.

141 reviews: *Jubilee* Scrapbook, MG-LCL; *Theatre Arts,* Dec. 1935, p. 901.
  Bermuda: Eells, *Life,* p. 129.

142 Agnes de Mille: quoted in McBrien m.s., p. 188.

12: HEART

143 "[T]he way to live . . .": letter, GSK to BK, in Goldstein, p. 271.
GSK at the Harts': Goldstein, p. 257.
Maurizius: numerous references, including *Stage,* Nov. 1935, and program for *Jubilee.*

144 Bernstein and *Maurizius:* int. SB/Walter Bernstein, as cited. (The letter from MH to Harold Ross hangs today in Bernstein's New York apartment.)
house and dogs: souvenir program, YCTIWY.
KM letters: pp. 349–50. As late as 1941 KM was lobbying on Simmel's behalf for a license to practice, withholding of which was largely a matter of internship required under California law but not in Berlin, where Simmel had enjoyed considerable eminence until the Nazis came to power.
Simmel: Merryman, p. 198ff. Behrman discusses Simmel in *People in a Diary,* misnaming him "Samuel," pp. 254–55. Elsewhere he called him "Semel" and left him unindexed. It is unclear, but the misnomers may be intentional. Edward Jablonski in *Gershwin Remembered,* pp. 158–9, notes that Simmel, finally thinking the illness might be organic, referred Gershwin to an internist.
GSK letter: quoted in Goldstein, p. 270. Goldstein dates it 31 May 1936. GSK arrived in California two days earlier.
GSK on Trumbo: Goldstein, p. 270.

145 Solomons: int. SB/CF, as cited.
GSK and pip: Goldstein, p. 269.
"the Hart play": ibid., p. 271. title: Michener Museum, Doylestown, Pa., Kaufman-Hart exhibit.

146 "Chekhovian": Sheridan Morley, in conversation.

147 grace: in *Six Plays,* p. 318.
Original ending: ibid.

148 Rheba and Mary Campbell: Nolan, p. 101.
Russian prince: souvenir program.
Other sources: ibid.
"How many . . .": *Six Plays,* p. 315.
Barnett Hart to Berlin: the story is ubiquitous. Here quoted from Harriman, *Take Them Up,* p. 83.

149 GSK to BK: Goldstein, p. 271.
Reviews: YCTIWY Scrapbook, MG-LCL.
Fadiman: *Stage,* "Comedy With Errors," Mar. 1937, pp. 41–44.

150 Morrison: Boston souvenir program.
Abie's price: *NY Telegraph,* 12 Feb. 1941.
Capra and AW: McBride, p. 328.
Shangri-La reference: by Otis Ferguson, quoted in Maland, p. 101.
Capra: in Capra, p. 241.

151 McBride: McBride, pp. 380–82.
The Women: Sylvia Jukes Morris, *Vanity Fair,* May 1997, p. 187.
GSK and MGM and *The Women:* Goldstein, p. 301.
Show Is On: mostly Bordman, *American Musical Revue,* p. 103ff.

152 EYH: letter, EYH to MH, dated "Thanksgiving Week '59," AO File, MH Papers, Wisc.

153 letter to DS: MH to DS, Waldorf-Astoria stationery, undated. The date is sometime in 1938, shortly after MH took up residence in the hotel and after he returned to New York from California. DS Papers, Wisc.
MH to CW: three letters, 15 Mar., 7 Apr., 17 Apr. 1937. All courtesy the Hahn Collection.

154 Gershwin's death: Ewen, *Journey,* p. 300.

154 fork in ear story: letter, Joan Peyser to the NYT, 4 Oct. 1998, "Arts and Leisure,"
p. 4. Peyser quotes MH here.
Behrman: *People,* p. 255.
Dietrich and Webb: SB, p. 273.
Dietrich musical: Goldstein, p. 290.

156 genetics: see Jamison, *Unquiet Mind,* as below. For his grandfather, see AO.
Jamison: p. 217.
Jamison: both citations, p. 128.

157 Bi-polar: Jamison, p. 181.
Ferber: JGG, Ferber's grandniece and biographer, examined and copied MH's letters to Ferber (Edna Ferber Papers, Wisc.), but was not allowed by MH's widow
to quote from them in her Ferber biography. She discussed them with SB in
numerous interviews, 1995–98.
Jess Barker: int. SB/Fred Walker, Thanksgiving, 1996.
GB: Int. SB/GB, 29 Mar. 1995; 5 Apr. 1995.

158 de Mille and Holm: de Mille, McBrien m.s., p. 270; Celeste Holm, Farber and in
conversation with author.
Merrick: p. 143. I am indebted to GSK's biographer, Malcolm Goldstein, for calling
Merrick's book to my attention.

159 Further Merrick quotes: "chappie," p. 151; analyst, p. 147.
Hulse citations: letters, Charles Hulse to SB, 6 Oct. 1995; 18 Jan. 1996; 8 Feb. 1996;
plus telephone int., June 1996.
"We wanted work . . .": int. SB/Otis Bigelow, 16 Mar. 1998.
Robert Goulet: int. SB/GB, as cited.

13: GREASE PAINT

160 tennis: RR, letters to Dorothy, p. 236.
RR letter: ibid., p. 224.

161 "most daring": RR, *Musical Stages,* p. 183.

163 pale: ibid.
RR on *Phantom President:* ibid., p. 154.
RR on Cohan: ibid., p. 183.

165 MH singing: ibid., p. 185.
Cohan and FDR: ibid., p. 186.
FDR speech: quoted here from Mason, p. 229.

166 "You!": MH, *I'd Rather Be Right,* p. 121.
long run: Bordman, *American Musical Comedy,* p. 141.
Lillie Hart's death and Hyman: death certificate, State of New Jersey Office of Registrar of Vital Statistics, City of Asbury Park, Monmouth County, 6 Sept. 1937.
"I did not like her": see Chapter 1.

168 Schneider: Goldstein, p. 303.
Nothing Sacred: Lardner, p. 253.

169 AO as a musical: Goldstein, pp. 301–32.
quotations from Dramatists' Play Service text. Here, pp. 1-18.

170 Bill's dialogue: pp. 49–50.
musical numbers: quoted from copyright notice in souvenir program.
Dora Sayers: int. SB/Dora Sayers, 15 June 1995.

171 Orson Welles speech: pp. 11-28.
John Mason Brown review: *Fabulous Invalid* Clipping File, LCL.

172 Loeb: Bernstein, *Inside Out,* p. 185.
Brown: 26 Sept. 1938.

173   "Swing Out the Jews": letter, MH to DS [n.d.], Waldorf-Astoria letterhead, c. winter 1938, DS Papers, Wisc.

14: AMERICANA

174   GSK on MH: "Forked Lightning," in Six Plays, p. xxix.
       apartment decorator: Ager.
       farm: details mostly from Michener Museum, Doylestown, Pa., plus Aronson, p. 170ff. The toothbrush quote is from Oppenheim, p. 31.
175   fireplace: "Look calls on Moss Hart," Look, Mar. 1940.
       MH quotes: Aronson, pp. 170, 265; BA: "Gold-plated Hart," Six Plays, p. xiii; "Whenever . . .": "Country Manners," NYT, 27 Oct. 1940.
176   inventory: sale catalog, 9 May 1955, Pennypacker Auction Centre, Reading, Pa., MH Papers, Wisc.
       "Baby Pandas": letter, MH to DS, summer 1940, DS Papers, Wisc.
       cost: low: Gardner, Saturday Evening Post; high, Look.
       trees quote: ibid., p. 265; number, Gardner.
       "Jewish Ethan Frome": MH to DS, summer 1940, as above.
177   "what God would do" origin: BC, Try and Stop Me, p. 27. GB, int. SB/GB, as cited. Most frequent attribution is to GSK.
       Barnett and women: int. SB/JF, as before.
178   "black blob": int. SB/GB, as cited.
       "peace": letter MH to DS, c. Jan. 1938. "enchantment" and "happy": as before, c. early 1938, both DS Papers, Wisc.
       "publicly": MH to DS, Sept. 1938, Waldorf Towers, as above.
       "good or not": letter, MH to DS, late summer–early fall 1938. As before.
180   "the English Moss Hart": Goldstein, p. 311.
       re White Horse Inn: Willela Waldorf, NY Post, [n.d.], LCL.
182   financials: Variety, 24 Jan. 1939.
183   Rutland, Vermont: John Peter Toohey, "How Noel Coward Spoiled Hart's Appetite," LCL. [Toohey was the press agent for The American Way.]
185   Winchell: Daily Mirror, 23 Jan. 1939; box office: Variety, as above.
       Broun: World-Telegram, 24 Jan. 1939.
186   "I have got everything . . .": The American Way, in Six Plays, p. 398.
       freedom: ibid.
       movie price: NY Telegraph; 12 Feb. 1941, LCL.
       Mantle: 11 Sept. 1939.
187   Variety: MG-LCL.
       GSK quote: "Kaufman Shy," unsourced clipping, MG-LCL.
       AW to Fontanne: AW, Letters, p. 271.
       letter: MH to DS [n.d.], DS Papers, Wisc.

15: PRINCE CHARMING

188   AW quote: AW, Letters, p. 322.
       Thurber: p. 243.
       Ross: quoted in Thurber, p. 246.
       Ferber: quoted in Adams, p. 2.
       "Fabbulous Monster": ibid., p. 3.
189   "God's big brother": ibid., p. 77.
       Brown: quoted in Chatterton, p. 42.
       "grows delirious": Chatterton, p. 72.

189   "rubbish": ibid., p. 89.
     "cape flowing": Margaret Case Harriman, quoted by Thurber, p. 247.
     "Louisa May": Gill, *Here at the New Yorker,* p. 202.
190   "incurable triviality": Chatterton, p. 135.
     "amiable . . .": ibid., p. 131.
     Behrman character description: Adams, p. 173.
191   reviews: quoted in ibid., p. 174.
     AW: MH, "How A.W. Came to Dinner," NYT, 29 Oct. 1939, and "Mr. Woollcott
        Comes to Lunch," m.s., Wisc.; also Goldstein, p. 318; the actual guest book is at
        the Michener Museum in Doylestown, Pa.
192   AW quote: AW, *Letters,* p. 321. AW refers to both Behrman plays in a letter to Lady
        Colefax.
     "exhibitionism" and "central part": ibid.
     AW and GSK and MH: mostly from MH, NYT, as above.
193   "Dowager Empress": ibid., m.s. p. 4.
     "slum gutter" etc.: ibid., m.s. pp. 4–5.
     "as different . . .": AW, *Letters,* p. 321.
     plagiarism suit: from MH's testimony, "Vincent O'Conner vs. George S. Kaufman,
        Moss Hart, et al.," p. 107. GSK and MH won the lawsuit. MH Papers, Wisc.
194   "guilty-looking": AW, *Letters,* p. 321.
     Whiteside description: TMWCTD in *Six Plays,* p. 416.
     "I was . . .": AW, *Letters,* p. 321.
     "I thought . . .": ibid., p. 322.
     "alienating and offensive . . .": ibid.
     Barrymore: ibid.
195   dedication: TMWCTD, p. 405.
     re Eugene Tesh: Kelly, p. 4.
     That's Gratitude: Mantle, *1930–31,* p. 7.
     jingle: Brackett, p. 42; in TMWCTD, p. 247.
     GBS anecdote: AW, *While Rome Burns,* p. 313.
196   "Acky Wooky": Goldstein, p. 287.
     "Suppose": TMWCTD, p. 456.
     "cobra": ibid., p. 413.
     "mercy killings": ibid., p. 452.
     "spared": ibid., p. 419.
     "jelly": ibid., p. 417.
     Quotes re Maggie: ibid., pp. 439, 440.
197   Rich: Rich, p. 27.
198   Nurse Preen's speech: TMWCTD, pp. 492–93.
     Maggie's speech: ibid., p. 485.
     "good turn": ibid., p. 486.
     reviews: Scrapbook, LCL.
199   Atwater: int. SB/JF, 21 Mar. 1995.
     time: Scrapbook, LCL. The remark is quoted in the magazine's original review of
        the play.

16: PROPERTY

200   Lindsay: quoted in Barrett, p. 289.
     movie money: *NY Telegraph,* 12 Feb. 1941, LCL.
     bungalow neighbors: Adams, p. 335.
     "completely loathsome": ibid.

201   "amateur company": letter, MH to DS, c. May 1940, DS Papers, Wisc.
      "pansy": letter, AW to GSK, c. Dec. 1939, GSK Papers, Wisc.
202   Lyceum purchase: Goldstein, p. 336; Bordman, *Oxford,* p. 446. Gordon's associate
         Marcus Heiman was also involved in the purchase.
      letter: MH to DS, c. May 1940, DS Papers, Wisc.
      lecture tour: ibid.
      menu: Adams, p. 336.
      White House letters: AW to GSK, as above.
203   "Evil": letter, MH to DS, c. 14–15 May 1940, DS Papers, Wisc.
      Sherwood musicalization: Nolan, p. 272.
      HUAC: Hart's FBI file contains numerous such anonymous reports. Department of Jus-
         tice, FBI file # NY 100–105631, obtained under the Freedom of Information Act.
      barbershop notion: "How to Write a Play: Forget Your Big Idea," NYH-T, 3 Nov.
         1940, GWSH Scrapbook, LCL.
      "stress of emotion": MH to DS, as above.
204   "Way down upon": Ben Bagley, in "The Decline and Fall of the Entire World as
         Seen Through the Eyes of Cole Porter Revisited," Columbia Records.
      "a very simple . . .": letter, MH to DS, c. July 1940, DS Papers, Wisc.
      BA: NYT, "Country Manners," 27 Oct. 1940.
      "average man": GWSH, p. 6.
      BA: op. cit.
205   Dixon quote: *New York Post,* 26 Oct. 1940.
206   "You know . . .": GWSH, p. 39.
      BA: NYT, 27 Oct. 1940; Mantle: *Daily News,* 19 Oct. 1940; "dated" and "remote":
         George Freedly, *Morning Telegraph,* 20 Oct. 1940.
      "riotously funny": Freedly; "real level . . .": John Anderson, *Journal-American,*
         19 Oct. 1940.
207   Connelly: quoted in Meredith, p. 557.

PART III: SOLO

17: GOING IT ALONE

211   BA: *Broadway,* p. 444.
      GSK and Gordon: Goldstein, p. 339.
      Gordon and *My Sister Eileen:* mostly from Meredith, p. 577ff.
212   "pure torture": letters, MS to DS, c. mid-May 1940, DS Papers, Wisc.
213   play dedication: *Lady in the Dark* is dedicated to "L.S.K.," Kubie's initials.
      Bradlee: int. SB/FB, 15 Nov. 1997. Also, conversations re LSK with Christopher
         Mankiewicz, Celeste Holm, and LSK's daughter, Mrs. Ann Rabinowitz. See
         also *Haywire* by Brooke Hayward.
214   Homosexuality and the APA: Loughery, p. 345. The APA's diagnostic list of mental
         disorders was established in 1952.
      Horowitz and Williams: see Farber and Green, plus Hayman, *Tennessee Williams*
         (New Haven: Yale University Press, 1993), pp. 170–71 and Williams-St.Just, *Let-*
         ters (London: Andre Deutsch, 1991), p. 144.
      Rabinowitz: int. SB/Ann Rabinowitz, 28 Nov. 1995.
      LSK and the new play: Robert Rice int. with MH, "Rice and Old Shoes," *PM,*
         3 Feb. 1941, p. 22.
215   shock treatments and dismayed friends: Weill and Lenya discuss both. See Kowalke,
         p. 405.
      "rabbinical fury": int. SB/FB, as above.
      GB quotes: as above.

215 LSK letters: LSK to MH, 7, 14, 20 May 1954: series of letters with copies of LSK's
      correspondence with Anna Freud. Part of the MH Papers, Wisc.
      on marriage: letter, MH to DS, summer 1941, DS Papers, Wisc.
      "Work . . .": letter, MH to DS, summer 1940, DS Papers, Wisc.
216 GB "it grew . . .": as above.
      inscription: courtesy Glen Boles.
      re Cornell: Hart, "The Saga of Gertie," and Goldstein, pp. 331–32.
      Weill: details mostly from Sanders, pp. 292–309. Other specifics as noted below.
      MH quotes re Weill and musical theater here and below: MH, introduction to
      Piano Score *Lady in the Dark* [unpaginated], Chappell.
217 "new technique . . .": ibid.
218 Ira Gershwin: Kimball, *Complete Lyrics,* pp. 279–82.
      Weill quote: Jablonski and Stewart, *Gershwin Years,* p. 272.
219 Sharaff to Weill: Kowalke, p. 216.
220 "irrevocable": The *Times* piece was called "The Saga of Gertie" and appeared
      2 Mar. 1941. The m.s., housed at Wisc. among the MH Papers, is titled "Life
      With Gertie." When different, citations are labeled "Saga" or "Life." Both accounts
      call Lawrence the "irrevocable" choice.
      title: MH in "Life" hints that Lawrence came up with the title.
      Percy Hammond: quoted in Gene Brown, p. 64.
      Van Druten: quoted in Hyland.
221 Cornell's reaction: all from "Life."
      MH on Holtzmann: "Life."
222 MH telegram: "Saga"; Coward: Morley, *A Talent to Amuse,* p. 258.
      "my farm . . .": Hart, "Saga."
      Lawrence contract: signed on 25 July 1941. Courtesy MCNY.
      Golden anecdote and quote: "Life."
224 re Kaye, here and later: radio interview of MH by BA, c. 1957, courtesy James
      Gavin.
      "I give that lecture": *I Am Listening* m.s., act 1, scene 4, MH Papers, Wisc.
      Variety and "pansy": 29 Jan. 1941.
225 "hysterical": Kowalke, p. 365.
      "punish Gertie": Kowalke, p. 365.
      Gershwin quote: Kimball, *Lyrics of . . . ,* p. 291.
      "bordello blues": Sanders, p. 307.
      Lawrence and "Jenny": BA radio interview, as above.
226 "Tschaikowsky" and Lawrence: Kimball, as above.
      "Jenny" reception: BA radio interview; Gershwin, as above.
      Time: cover and article "Gertie the Great" are dated 3 Feb. 1941, p. 53ff.
227 New York press: NYT, 1 Jan. 1941.
      Williams: Elinor Hughes, *Boston Herald,* 5 Jan. 1941.
      Globe: 31 Dec. 1940.
      importing critics: Kowalke, p. 274.
228 "the greatest performance": Danny Kaye, USC, 12 Apr. 1970 [the author was
      present].
      BA and reviews that follow: all 24 Jan. 1941, except Freedly, who is 25 Jan. and *PM,*
      which is 25 Jan. and 2 Feb. 1941.
      Peggy Ann: Ewen, *Rodgers,* p. 325.
      Marietta: see Green, *Show by Show,* p. 113; Mordden makes the same point in BB.
229 Santos's dialogue: *Lady in the Dark* m.s., act 2, scene. 4, MH Papers, Wisc.
230 "From the technical": LSK, intro., *Lady in the Dark,* p. viii.
      "the license": ibid., p. xiv.

230 Croce: p. 143.
"Right now": Rice, op. cit.

18: TAKING WING

231 Epigraph: MH quoted in Meredith, p. 556.
"Just a few days": Meredith, p. 556.
"every success": MH Q&A column in *Esquire,* Jan. 1962.
LSK: see, for instance, Whipple.
"toughest one": see for instance, Rice.
"I have no . . .": letter, MH to DS, 20 May 1941, DS Papers, Wisc.
"book about the theater" and "excellent director": ibid.
232 "concentration camp": ibid.
draft exemption: Department of Justice; FBI file / NY 100–105631, obtained under the Freedom of Information Act.
AP, Jr.: 9 Jan. 1942, quoted in Farmer, p. 65. See also Valentine, NYT *Magazine.*
"defiance": MH to DS, op. cit.
Man in Bucks County: Goldstein, pp. 352–53.
233 pool: Kaiser, p. 58.
"They had to be": Irving Lazar, USC.
234 Serlin in Village: Oppenheimer, p. 380.
"play-giarized": *Variety,* 26 Nov. 1941.
JC quote: letter, JC to Patrick Farmer, 14 Feb. 1980, in Farmer, p. 152.
JC: conversations, SB/JC, 1970s.
235 "Everything I know": Ward Morehouse, "Broadway After Dark," c. 1947, LCL.
"hidden hand": AO, p. 315.
Schneider: Farmer, p. 160.
Lonergan: see Gibbs, below.
Gordon: Gordon, p. 256ff.
236 BA: NYT, 19 Nov. 1941; Gibbs, *The New Yorker,* 29 Nov. 1941, p. 35.
Variety: 26 Nov. 1941.
Movie sale: undated clip, LCL.
"War committees": letter, MH to DS, as above.
237 Hecht dinner: Taylor, *Strangers,* p. 277ff. Also, Sanders, pp. 318–19; NYT, 9 Feb. 1943, sec. 1, p. 5; Hecht, *Child,* pp. 550–57.
Hecht quote: Taylor, *Strangers.*
lunchtime: NYT, "Whistle While You Work," 23 June 1942, sec. 1, p. 22.
238 Lazar: from MH, "One World . . . One Trip . . . One Play," souvenir program, *Winged Victory.*
239 MH quotes here and below: ibid.
"the boss": *Time,* 29 Nov. 1943, p. 43.
Intimidation by atmosphere: int. SB/JF, as cited. JF was present with MH on a USO tour. Also, int. SB/Dora Sayers, 15 June 1995.
cost of show: John Chapman, "Winged Victory All Yours" [n.d.], LCL.
rehearsals: *Time,* 29 Nov. 1943, p. 43.
"I am reminded": Edmond O'Brien, USC, p. 39.
240 "Winged Victory is": Valentine.
242 Norton: "Broadway's Cutting-Room Floor," in Oppenheimer, p. 218.
243 Ferber: letter, 3 June 1943, Ferber Papers, Wisc.
20th Century-Fox: price from Fox legal department memo, 20 Mar. 1944, George Wasson to Felix A. Jenkins. MH signed for $10 on 14 Apr. 1944. Ref: Fox legal Records Coll. 095 mc 4834861 FX-LR-1136, courtesy UCLA.

243 Wyler telegrams: Herman, p. 266.
244 McGilligan: p. 179; Carey: p. 100.
KCH: int. Patrick Farmer/KCH, Jan. 1980, Farmer, p. 88.
Time: as above.
Santa Ana: Letters, Lon McCallister to GC, 9 Oct. and 15 Nov. 1980, courtesy Cukor Collection, Academy.
Ritt: conversation with Patrick McGilligan, 1995.
De Mille: quoted in McBrien m.s., p. 270.
245 morals spy and below: confidential source, int. with SB, Feb. 1995.
RC: int. SB/RC, New York, 13 Mar. 1995.
AW: letter to Ruth Gordon, 28 Sept. 1942. AW, *Letters.*

19: NEW STAGES

246 Cyril Connelly: quoted by Anthony Lane, "A Most Untypical Man," *The New Yorker,* 29 Jan. 1996, p. 88.
"none of us noticed": Don Taylor, USC, p. 40.
tickets and letters: Gordon, p. 288.
247 treatment: The writer was Jerry Cady. Fox legal files: FX-LR-1136, 4 Feb. 1944, courtesy UCLA.
"I did not": anecdote courtesy Judith Hahn, Hahn Collection.
screenplay pages and Larkin: Fox legal files, as above, 14 June 1944, UCLA.
"Huck Finn of Brooklyn": Tapert, *Swifty,* p. 15.
Lazar's name: ibid., p. 27.
WMA: WMA letters: Goldwyn Collection, Academy, courtesy Sam Goldwyn, Jr.
Hyman breakdown: letter, MH to DS, c. 1940, DS Papers, Wisc.
248 "You can": conversation, JC to SB, c. 1974.
CP story: Tappert, "Swifty's A-List Life," *Vanity Fair,* Apr. 1994, p. 158. See also *Swifty.*
GSK to MH: Goldstein, p. 377.
249 *Times:* "Let the Shuberts Be Warned" appeared on 17 Dec. 1944.
"Cowards" line: see, for example, *Esquire,* Jan. 1962. Also: MH tape, Dramatists' Guild Tapes, Rodgers and Hammerstein Collection, NYPL, LCL.
Lowe: int. SB/Stanja Lowe, 11 and 22 Mar. 1999.
250 shock treatments: Kowalke, p. 405.
Lenya: letter, Lenya to Weill, 29 July 1944, in Kowalke, p. 405.
Goldstein quote: p. 350.
"intimate" and "rare . . .": AO deletion; in m.s., p. 357. Folder 15, file 4, MH Papers, Wisc.
"one of the most": ibid.
251 "startled brown eyes": JF, int. as cited.
Sayers: int. SB/Dora Sayers [Caro], 15 June 1995 and 27 May 1999. Lee Armitage conducted supplemental interviews in Feb.–Apr. 1999.
murals: letter, Kindred McLeary to Billy Rose, 7 Aug. 1944. Billy Rose Cage File, LCL.
252 telegrams: AMR, p. 126.
Lahr: John Lahr, *Cowardly Lion,* p. 230.
Lillie skit: AMR, op. cit.
LS: letter, LS to Billy Rose, 23 Apr. 1944. Rose Cage File, LCL.
253 Nathan: *Theater Book of the Year 1944–45,* p. 188.
Barnes: NYH-T, 8 Dec. 1944; NYT, same date.
USO tour: details in TMWCTD USO file, LCL.

254   Sayers: int. SB/Dora Sayers, as cited.
        Ziegfeld attic: ints. SB/JF; SB/Dora Sayers, as cited.
        BK and party: in Goldstein, pp. 384–85.
        dialogue: quoted in Goldstein, as above.
255   re Charles: ibid.
        "his sweetheart": letter Kurt Weill to Lotte Lenya, 17 July 1942, op. cit., p. 392.
        "just to be nice": ibid.
        KCH and Sayers: int. LA/Dora Sayers, Mar. 1999; SB/Dora Sayers, 27 May 1999.
256   "Like all . . .": letter, MH to CW, summer 1945, courtesy Hahn Collection.
        itinerary: Dora Sayers kept a scrapbook during the tour, which she generously
            shared.
257   opening anecdote: int. JF, as cited.
        ear infection and fungus: Goldstein, p. 368.
        power: letter to CW, as above.
258   re Lawrence: to CW, as above.
        FDR's death: int. SB/Dora Sayers, 22 Mar. 1999.
        Sayers quotes: int. SB/Dora Sayers, as cited.
        To CW, letter as above.
        end of the affair: int. SB/Dora Sayers.

20: A NEW LIFE

259   KCH quote: KCH, in Brenner Ts; KCH quote: in Brenner, "The Art of Mrs.
        Hart," *The New Yorker,* 5 July 1993, p. 46. Note: Brenner shared her interview
        transcripts for the referenced article with SB. When citing from the transcript,
        spelling and punctuation are corrected. If not designated "Ts," a Brenner refer-
        ence is to the published article.
        "The show was . . .": letter, MH to CW, summer 1945, Hahn Collection.
        Boles: int. SB/GB, as cited.
        "not the slightest": letter MH/CW, as above.
        plays: Farmer, p. 108.
        LSK gossip and suspended therapy: KCH in Brenner, pp. 46–48.
260   Von Mendelssohn: Reinhardt, pp. 12–15, 401.
        "trapped" and "to make it better . . .": letter, MH/CW, as above.
        Steinbeck line: USC, pp. 26–27.
        Frances Dee: int. SB/Frances Dee, July 1995.
261   BK's death: Goldstein, p. 389ff.
        Sale of Lyceum: Meredith, p. 571.
262   "You see": *Kitty,* p. 105.
        "Furnish": ibid. p. 105; "Be gracious!": p. 43.
        "Go to the top": ibid., p. 19.
263   marrying royalty: ibid.
        taxi driver story: Brenner, p. 42.
        Passover Seder: *Kitty,* p. 78; becoming a nun: p. 19.
        unpredictable: Brenner, p. 43.
        "every area of my life": ibid.
        "always pushing": ibid.
        denial: ibid., p. 40.
264   "ghastly mistake": *Kitty,* p. 46.
        "You're not": NYT, 23 Apr. 1985, p. 16.
        Rio Rita miked: Burns Mantle review, KCH Clipping File, LCL.
        The critic was Richard Watts, Jr.

265 to Axelrod: quoted in McDowall.

Louella Parsons: syndicated column, 11 Dec. 1943, Lyons Clipping File, LCL.

Lyons and KCH: See Diamonstein. This Columbia University Oral History may not be quoted directly during KCH's lifetime and remarks are, therefore, paraphrased or summarized here; references to the Lyons affair and the jewels he gave her occur in vol. 1 on pp. 219–22.

Lyons: Lewis Funke, NYT, "The Lyons' Leap from Minsk to Hollywood," "Producing Artists, Inc. Has an Idea," LCL. *Larceny With Music:* KCH Clipping File, LCL. Other details from Diamonstein, as above.

266 "pink blonde": A. H. Weiler, NYT, 15 Oct. 1944.

downswing: Brenner Ts, p. 3.

"only from Gott!": *Kitty,* p. 47.

"genius": Brenner Ts. KCH uses the term about MH throughout.

KCH and Ralph Forbes: Diamonstein, KCH Oral History, p. 262ff.

267 Hortense's remark: Brenner Ts, p. 35.

Ferber: int. KCH/JGG, courtesy JGG.

"I wanted": Brenner Ts, p. 31.

"he was furious": ibid., p. 31.

telephone proposal: *Kitty,* p.117.

"everything . . .": Brenner Ts, p. 32.

"stormy": ibid., p. 31.

268 sexuality and suicidal quotes: ibid., p. 14.

"whatever his problems were . . .": ibid., p. 58.

"I asked him": ibid., p. 56; also Brenner, NY, p. 49. I have here combined the transcript version and the published version.

MH to Sayers: SB/Dora Sayers, as cited.

proposal: *Kitty,* p. 117.

269 Hortense at wedding: Brenner Ts, p. 29.

Arthur Laurents anecdote: *Original Story By,* p. 73.

bed anecdote: Brenner Ts, p. 19.

21: FAMILY VALUES AND OTHER DRAMAS

270 epigraph: quoted in Meredith, p. 556.

Selznick: int. SB/IMS, 23 and 26 Nov. 1985.

"new kid": Brenner Ts, p. 46.

Atwater's crack: KCH refers to it numerous times in her conversations with MB.

Women's attitudes to KCH: Brenner Ts, pp. 33, 41, 46, 49.

271 Selznick: int., as above.

"I had wanted": Brenner Ts, p. 3.

Cross-dressing: int. SB/CB, 1996. According to CB, the playwright and male actress, the rumor is widespread in cross-dressing circles.

dressing Kitty: Brenner Ts, p. 23.

272 MH quote on theater: intro. to COE, RH, p. x.

273 "so useful": Brenner Ts, p. 13.

Jamison quotes: Jamison, *Unquiet Mind,* pp. 211, 128.

ideas and writing: Gilder, "The Fabulous Hart," *Theatre Arts,* Feb. 1944, p. 92.

dating the play: the m.s. is in a series of composition books, and at the end of the first act includes a letter dated "June 1946." CB m.s., MH Papers, Wisc.

274 Truman dialogue: CB, RH, p. 13.

dialogue: ibid., pp. 76–77.

KCH on CB out of town: Farmer, p. 178.

275   reviews: CB Clipping File, LCL. All 1–4 Dec. 1946.
Gordon: Gordon, p. 203.
Chapman: the m.s. of the piece is in the MH Papers. It was read on the radio program "Broadway Talks Back," Mutual Broadcasting Company, 9 Dec. 1946. I
am indebted to James Gavin for furnishing me with the tape of this broadcast.
Warners: the contract called for an additional 20 percent of the box-office gross
after breakeven, an astonishingly rich deal. Letters to and from WB [Jacob Wilk]
and Joe Hyman, 6 and 16 Dec. 1946, MH Papers, Wisc.
revival reviews: NY Tribune; "so terribly dated," Marilyn Stasio in the Post, 1 Aug.
1983; "one critic" was WWD, 26 July 1983. CB, RH Clipping File, LCL.
276   dedication: CB [n.p.]
Laurents: in his play Jolson Sings Again. Cited by Ben Brantley, NYT, 20 Mar. 1999.
Jack Warner meeting: Kazan, p. 272.
Peck as Jewish: Peck was under contract to Selznick, whose son Jeffrey maintained
to Selznick biographer DT that Peck was, in fact, Jewish. Int. SB/DT, Mar. 1999.
277   Madeleine Sherwood: Sally Bedell Smith, p. 115.
Jewishness: Malcolm Goldstein, GSK's biographer, told me that, based on the unpublished memoirs of BK, he thought it important to MH that his wife be Jewish.
278   KCH on miscarriage: Kitty, p. 139.
KCH on MH and Hollywood: ibid., p. 141.
slave-quarters: Bob Thomas, Hollywood Citizen-News, 27 June 1947.
279   MH on Hollywood: Scheuer, "Moss Hart Hits Hollywood," MH Clipping File,
LCL.
"Lord knows": ibid.
DFZ notes: the comments cited are taken from conference notes with MH on
16 Feb. 1944 and an internal Fox memo from DFZ dated 13 May 1944. They
concern the screenplay for Winged Victory, but illustrate DFZ's method and convictions about screenwriting as expressed to MH. Source: Fox Files, UCLA.
LZH quotes: Laura Z., pp. 29–30.
novel scene: ibid., p. 34.
280   Kazan quote: Kazan, p. 354.
MH to DFZ re LZH: Laura Z., p. 39.
Dave's speech: ibid., p. 34, 318.
281   "patronizing": Kazan, p. 355.
Kazan re Holm: ibid., p. 354.

22: MAGIC TIME

282   epigraph: MH, quoted by KCH to Patrick Farmer, 12 Jan. 1980.
Hortense in play: KCH affirmed that Hortense was the model for Stella in LUTS,
Diamonstein, KCH Oral History, p. 695; for descriptions see LUTS, p. 11.
piano and antiques: Kitty, p. 144.
pool parties: Kaiser, p. 58.
KCH and gay associates: on the rumors, Ronald Alexander and Fred Walker among
others. Hollywood producer: int. SB/MB, 29 Nov. 1995. Confidential at MB's
request.
283   "delighted and scared": letter, MH to BA, c. late Aug. 1947, BA Cage File, LCL.
BA's reply to this letter is dated 3 Sept. 1947.
appraisal: statement, 1 Mar. 1947; Actual Appraisal Company, MH Papers, Wisc.
Shavian comedy: MH to BA, as cited.
parties and "Julie Jewboy": Laura Z., pp. 72–75.
284   "Persian prince": int. SB/IMS, as cited.

284 "Now they won't be able to say": int. SB/Helen Hennessey, 3 Aug. 1994. When
    questioned, Mrs. Hennessey confirmed that "gay" was the word MH had used.
    Charles and accounts: the rumors were widespread in MH's circle. KCH confirmed
    them to Diamonstein, pp. 332–35.

285 "Savagely written": *Times*, 1 May 1948, sec. 1, p. 19.
    dedication prank: *Kitty*, p. 136; see title page, LUTS.
    BA: letter, MH to BA, c. spring 1948. BA Cage File, LCL.

286 "dazzling experiment . . .": LUTS, p. 54.
    MH on cast: to Ward Morehouse, "Broadway After Dark," LUTS Clipping File,
    LCL.
    "Damn near killed me": from "New Dramatists Series," tape, NYPL R&H tape,
    [n.d., 1959?].

287 "It takes time . . .": AO, p. 362.
    "Shavian trick," etc.: quoted in "The Men Who Came to Supper—Hart and
    Rose," *New York Post*, 16 Nov. 1948, LCL.
    MH on LUTS: New Dramatists/R&H tape, as cited.

288 "finest writing": ibid.
    "in the second act," etc.: ibid.
    "philosophical comedy": Bordman, *Oxford*, p. 429.
    "Look at the way": LUTS m.s., act 2, p. 54, MH Papers, Wisc.
    allegory speech: LUTS, DPS, p. 29.
    "bunch of crap": LUTS, DPS, p. 13.

289 "bird-like . . .": LUTS m.s., act 1, p. 55ff. Some of his dialogue was retained but
    transferred to other characters.
    Turner's "Why bother?" and ff: LUTS m.s., act 1, pp. 19–20.
    Sloan: LUTS, DPS, p. 13.
    "Don't let the word professional": LUTS m.s., act 3, p. 3.

290 "Money" and "self-interest" speeches: LUTS m.s., act 3, pp. 54 and 60.

291 MH on *Kiss Me, Kate:* int. SB/Arnold Saint Subber.
    Billy Rose column: LCL.
    Clurman: "Light Up the Box Office," *The New Republic*, 29 Nov. 1948, pp. 37–38.
    Phyllis Cerf and allowance: KCH, Oral History, Columbia, p. 393.

293 Sherwood's ailment: Jablonski, *Irving Berlin*, p. 258.
    "There goes": Barrett, p. 252. McLerie's toes: Bergreen, p. 488.
    McLerie: quoted in Bergreen, p. 493.
    McLerie and MH: ibid., p. 488.
    Philadelphia reviews: Edwin Schloss, *Miss Liberty* File, LCL.

294 cuts in Philadelphia: "The Making of a Musical: Fast Pace Disconcerts Robert
    Sherwood," NYH-T, 10 July 1949, LCL.
    "Horace, look": cited by Mel Gussow, NYT, 29 July 1983 (revival of the show).
    "Horace . . . spent": quoted in Jablonski, *Irving Berlin*, p. 264.
    scorn: Wolcott Gibbs, "The Mountains in Labor," *The New Yorker*, 23 July 1949,
    p. 28.
    Sherwood to *Post:* Vernon Rice, 15 July 1949, LCL.
    BA: NYT, 16 July 1949.
    costs: Bergreen, p. 496.

23: THE CLIMATE OF BROADWAY

295 epigraph, "Is this all?": MH, NOTB, m.s., p. 17, MH Papers, Wisc.
    "You never learn": quoted by JC to SB, 1974.
    "suicidal economically": MH in Dramatists Guild, R&H tape as cited above.

296 "black velvet": *Kitty,* p. 146.
    KCH bedridden and cesarean delivery: Diamonstein, KCH Oral History, as cited above.
    DS quote: letter, DS to MH, 5 June 1950, DS Papers, Wisc.
    DS quote: letter, DS to MH, 5 June 1950, DS Papers, Wisc.
    "which we both know so well": letter, DS to MH, 5 June 1950.

297 Ardrey and Hornblow: letter, MH to DS, 16 Oct. 1950, DS Papers, Wisc. "radical": letter, DS to MH, 23 Oct. 1950, DS Papers, Wisc.
    The Bad and the Beautiful: the source material is George Bradshaw's short story "Memorial to a Bad Man."
    NOTB m.s. is dated 11 Mar. 1951, MH Papers, Wisc. The *Omnibus* broadcast was 13 Dec. 1953. MH Papers, Wisc.
    "spinster": MH, Dramatists Guild R&H tape.

298 "is this all?": NOTB m.s., p. 17; "where I disappeared to": p. 19.
    MH and Alistair Cooke: *Variety,* 16 Dec. 1953.
    "Moss, darling, you're . . .": MH quoted in Ager.
    MH and SG: letter, MH to SG, 22 Jan. 1951, and cable, Irving Lazar to SG, 19 June 1951; also legal file #904: all SG-Academy, courtesy Samuel Goldwyn, Jr.
    Goldwyn and writers: all from SG-Academy.

299 MH on Andersen: letter, MH to SG, 22 Jan. 1951, SG-Academy.
    "Little Mermaid" and Shearer: letter, Moira Shearer to Frances (Mrs. Sam) Goldwyn, 29 Oct. 1951, SG-Academy.

300 Goldwynism anecdote: *Kitty,* p. 161.
    "unswerving belief . . .": letter, MH to SG, 22 Jan. 1951, SG-Academy.
    Brown told a friend: she was Carmel (Finkelstein) Forsyte. Int. SB/CF, as cited.
    profits: a statement from Goldwyn legal file 904 records a payment to MH's estate of almost $38,000 in 1962, a year after MH died.

301 Connolly: primarily letters, Connolly to SG, 1 May 1952, Lazar notes 20 June 1952, dictated by Saul Rittenberg, all SG-Academy.
    "Kingdom of Heaven": COE, RH, p. 84.

302 "a challenge . . .": MH, intro to COE, RH, p. viii.
    "There was a space": Mittelhölzer, p. 12.

303 "I've been promiscuous": Mittelhölzer, p. 96.
    "What secret": COE, RH, p. 138.
    Bar Mitzvah story: Diamonstein, p. 407.
    foreword to HCA: many drafts exist in the HCA files, SG-Academy.
    KCH had never seen *Lady in the Dark:* Diamonstein, p. 276.

304 Cape Cod production: program, courtesy Warren Enters.
    "hoped to set up *Lady*": *Variety,* [n.d., 1952], LCL.
    Moss feared: MH, R&H tape, LCL.
    Rosemary Harris: Farmer, p. 124.

305 Earle Hyman: quoted in ibid., p. 144.
    "we were working": ibid., p. 164.
    "something we believed" and "Mr. Dupont, who owned Wilmington": int. Patrick Farmer/Earle Hyman, 6 Jan. 1980.

306 "I have made some cuts": Farmer, pp. 164–65.
    "Don't worry": KCH, *Kitty,* p. 160. Herman Levin also tells this story.
    "to be judged": COE, RH, p. xi.
    "pushed" on COE: R&H tape, LCL.

307 BA: NYT, "Life in a Jungle," NYT, 16 Nov. 1953, sec. 2, p. 1.
    "watched it fail": COE, RH, p. vi.
    "shattered": Gordon, p. 233.

307 "heartbreak": letter, MH to Kanin and Gordon [n.d.], courtesy Hahn Collection.
BA rereview: NYT, 23 Nov. 1953, p. 11.
"by far the most": COE, RH, p. viii. Repeated in *Theater Arts,* May 1954, p. 32.
"made a valiant try": letter, MH to BA, and "disconcerted": reply, BA to MH. Both
in BA File, LCL.

PART IV: PRO

24: SURVIVING

311 epigraph: MH, quoted by Celeste Holm, int. SB/CH, 9 Nov. 1995.
312 MH as band singer: KCH, Columbia Oral History, p. 352.
"curious instinct": quoted in Haver, p. 165.
All Luft quotations: int. SB/Sidney Luft, 16 Nov. 1995. The studio did not sign GC
until February: WB memo, Steve Trilling to MH, 16 Feb. 1953.
313 to Garson Kanin: letter, MH to Kanin and Ruth Gordon, 15 Dec. 1952, courtesy
Hahn Collection.
MH's fee: WB budget memo, 14 Oct. 1953, GC Collection, courtesy AMPAS.
"because the original": Haver, p. 45.
315 "I say this": letter, MH to GC [n.d., c. Sept. 1953]. GC Collection, AMPAS.
316 "Talent isn't": MH, *A Star Is Born* script, 21 Oct. 1953, GC Collection, AMPAS.
"love isn't enough": MH, *A Star Is Born* script, 21 Oct. 1953, GC Collection,
AMPAS.
"lovable Sid Luft": letter, MH to GC, 16 Feb. 1954, GC Collection, AMPAS.
"Apparently it isn't enough": letter, GC to MH, 17 Aug. 1954, GC Collection, AMPAS.
317 Maugham joke : MH to GC, 17 Sept. 1953. GC Collection, AMPAS.
"I know what caused . . .": letter, GC to MH, 18 Aug. 1954. GC Collection,
AMPAS.
"the Big Scene" and "I made a solemn vow": letters, GC to MH, 11 and 18 Feb.
1954, GC Collection, AMPAS.
cable: MH to JLW, GC, and SL: 10 Feb. 1954, GC Collection, AMPAS.
never made money: int. SB/ SL, 16 Nov. 1995.
318 *Variety:* 24 Sept. 1954.
"Cut the": quoted in Haver, p. 175; "Make George think": int. SB/SL, 16 Nov.
1995.
"harmful": quoted in Haver, p. 193.
"Moss thought": ibid., p. 214.
"Neither the human mind": letter, GC to MH, 18 Aug. 1954, GC Collection,
AMPAS.
"As for me": letter, GC to MH, 24 Feb. 1954, GC Collection, AMPAS.
319 DFZ and writing-directing cancellation: Fox Files, letter, Fox legal department to
Irving Lazar, 12 Mar. 1949, UCLA.
another symbolic one thousand: *Prince of Players* budget memo, 23 Aug. 1954, stat-
ing scenario costs at $102,200. 20th Century-Fox Files, UCLA.
320 "utterly still" and subsequent *Prince of Player* quotes: MH, draft screenplay, 1 July
1953, Fox Files, UCLA
"a difficult job": letter, MH to Garson Kanin [n.d., c. Nov. 1953], Hahn Collection.
321 DFZ memos: Richard Zanuck to DFZ, 20 Aug. 1953, Fox Files, UCLA.
"This is not" and "Moss direct": cover notes on draft screenplay, 1 July 1953, Fox
Files, UCLA.
"I think you will read": memo, DFZ to Philip Dunne, 7 June 1954, Fox Files,
UCLA.

321 "a beautiful script": memo, Philip Dunne to DFZ, 8 June 1954, Fox Files, UCLA.
 "much too long": Dunne, *Take Two,* p. 269.
 "highly overrated": letter, MH to GC, 11 May 1954, GC Collection, AMPAS.
322 "writing consists": Dunne, *Take Two,* p. 270.
 "shrewd craftsmanship": letter, MH to Philip Dunne, 17–21 July 1954, Fox Files, UCLA.
 "projection-room success": Dunne, *Take Two,* p. 271.
 Variety: 5 Jan. 1955.
 "What could poor Edwin": Dunne, *Take Two,* p. 273.
323 "sudden and shocking": letter, Edna Ferber to KCH, 3 Oct. 1954, Ferber Papers, Wisc.
 two slender play outlines: they are untitled, but located as loose sheets in Box 12, folder 2 of the MH Papers, Wisc. Clipped to the top is "Original Notes 'Climate of Eden' N.Y." This may indicate a prior use of the title for the Caribbean work. Otherwise there is no similarity and the outlines seem unconnected to COE except by proximity in filing.
 "I am fond": int. SB/JGG, as cited.
 "their correspondence is witness": Ferber Papers, Wisc. Permission to quote from these letters has been withheld by KCH, even to Ferber's biographer and literary executor, JGG. Int. SB/JGG, as cited.
 "the son": eulogy, reprinted in USC testimonial.
324 "madness": letter, MH to Garson Kanin [n.d., c. Oct. 1953], Hahn Collection.
 "I consider": letter, MH to Garson Kanin [n.d., c. Nov. 1953], Hahn Collection.
 "more or less promised": letter, MH to Garson Kanin [n.d., c. Nov. 1953], Hahn Collection.
 "bitter and graceless": letter, MH to Garson Kanin [n.d., c. Nov. 1953], Hahn Collection.
 "Who?": int. SB/JGG, as cited.
 "Oh, come off it" and "gray with fright": int. JGG with KCH, 1977, courtesy JGG.
 Ferber flowers, letter, and MH's reply: letter, MH to Garson Kanin [n.d., c. Nov. 1953], Hahn Collection.
 "the most": cable, Edna Ferber to MH [n.d., c. 1947], Ferber Papers, Wisc.
325 "In my long life": letter, Edna Ferber to KCH, 3 Oct. 1954, Ferber Papers, Wisc.
 "all rather graceless": letter, MH to Garson Kanin, 9 Dec. 1953, Hahn Collection.
 Captain Hook anecdote: int. SB/JGG, as cited.
326 yacht story: letter, MH to Garson Kanin, 6 Jan. 1954, Hahn Collection.
 "From the Bronx": MH, AO m.s., MH Papers, Wisc.
 "I have decided": letter, MH to Garson Kanin [n.d., c. Nov. 1953], Hahn Collection.
327 "withered and dead": letter, MH to Garson Kanin, 1 Feb. 1954, Hahn Collection.
 "both brilliant and": letter, MH to Garson Kanin, 1 Feb. 1954, Hahn Collection.
 "keep the office": letter, MH to Garson Kanin [n.d., c. 20 Nov. 1953], Hahn Collection.
 "a trifle" and "funny and endearing": letter, MH to Garson Kanin, 1 Feb. 1954, Hahn Collection.
328 "feel like the Lunts": letter, MH to Garson Kanin, 1 Feb. 1954, Hahn Collection.
 "I cornered him": *Kitty,* p. 170.
 rewriting *Anniversary Waltz:* letter, MH to Garson Kanin, 16 Feb. 1954, Hahn Collection.
 "dull and": *The New Yorker,* 17 Apr. 1954, p. 61; "hackwork": Kronenberger, *Best Plays,* p. 348.
 BA: NYT, 8 Apr. 1954.

328 "I'm bigger": letter, c. 1959, T. H. White to MH, White quoting Julie Andrews quoting MH, courtesy Tony Walton.

329 "I am awfully sorry": letter, Laurence Olivier to MH, 22 June 1954, MH Papers, Wisc.

25: FULL CIRCLE

330 GBS: letter to Gertrude Lawrence, Dan Laurence, *1926–1950*, p. 817.
"a master": KCH to MB, courtesy MB.
"I have a terrible": *Kitty*, pp. 171–73.

331 "some mysterious back ailment": letter, Philip Dunne to DFZ, 30 July 1955, Fox Files, UCLA.
"Kitty later said": to Diamonstein, KCH Oral History, p. 277.
"Has Edna called": int. SB/JGG, as cited.
Duchin deal: various trade accounts, *Variety* and *Hollywood Reporter*, AMPAS.

332 "You're a professional": quoted in Gordon, p. 234.
"not above": KCH to MB, courtesy MB.
"If Bennett Cerf gets sick": KCH to MB, courtesy MB.

333 "Summer": quoted in Lerner, *The Street Where I Live*, p. 79.
"The Black Hole": MH, *Music by Duchin* m.s., p. 5, MH Papers, Wisc.
Beach Haven house: *Kitty*, pp. 174–76. Mother's pronunciation: Florence Rome to MB.
Time, title page of "In the Pink" m.s., MH Papers, Wisc.

334 "quite hopeless" and "untenable": MH, untitled m.s. [MFL], p. 2, MH Papers, Wisc.
Loewe: early life details, Lees, pp. 9–25.

335 silencing "No": the author was present on this occasion.
Ira Gershwin: quoted in MFL souvenir program.
MGM purchase: Lees, p. 46.
"all the astounding qualities": Langner, p. 410.

336 "How are you fixed" and anecdote: Behrman, *The Suspended Drawing Room*, pp. 69–71.
"I just looked" and "The man": quoted in Pascal, frontispiece.
de Gaulle as St. Joan: Pascal, p. 84.

337 Beaumont quote: Huggett, p. 480.
"intensely": Shaw, *Pygmalion* preface, p. 9, Penguin edition.
"a Pygmalion operetta": in Laurence, *1911–1925*, pp. 730–31.
"nothing will ever": in Laurence, *1926–1950*, p. 528.
"My decision": see epigraph and note.
"While we stood": Lerner, *Street*, p. 32.

338 In March and Martin as condition: ibid., p. 239.
contract with Pascal and Theatre Guild: Pascal, p. 241.
"It can't be": Lerner, *Street*, p. 38.

339 Screening in 1952: Pascal, p. 239.

340 "younger, wiser" and following: AJL, "Lady Liza" draft m.s. and outline, MH Papers, Wisc.
"I writhed in hell": Laurence, *1911–1925*, p. 227.

341 "What size?": Lerner, *Street*, p. 37.
"I absolutely forbid": Laurence, *1926–1950*, p. 815.
screenplay extract: quoted in Costello, pp. 187–88. The screenplay was published only in paperback by Penguin in the UK in 1941, a Shaw-authorized edition

from which Costello quotes and which is the text subsequently used by the MFL company in rehearsals, int. SB/Miles Kreuger, 15 Nov. 1995.

341   excerpt from MFL: Lerner, MFL, p. 186.

"This is the finest": Behrman, p. 73.

Shaw's statement: quoted in Costello, p. 42.

342   "Moss contributed": int. SB/Stone Widney, 29 Nov. 1995.

"He did not": Lerner, Street, p. 76.

"He was": ibid., p. 72.

"What he did": int. SB/Stone Widney, as above.

"We're going": Lerner, Street, p. 88.

"four of": ibid., pp. 88–89.

343   "Moss was": ibid., p. 75.

"could say": ibid., p. 74.

"Alan would come": letter, Reid Shelton to Patrick Farmer, 15 Feb. 1980, Farmer, p. 153.

"those dear boys": Lerner, Street, p. 51.

"I guess": ibid.

"Alan had a song": int. SB/Bud Widney, 29 Nov. 1995. Correspondence between Lerner and producer HL discusses "Judy" in the early stages of preparing the show, HL Papers, Wisc.

344   "With My Fair Lady": letter, AJL to Edna Ferber, 9 Apr. 1956, Ferber Papers, Wisc. Ironically, the letter from Lerner to Ferber was written to explain why he and Loewe were backing out of the musical of Saratoga Trunk three years after Moss and Ferber's blowup over the same project.

"After me": Eyles, Rex Harrison, p. 46.

345   "only after every other actor": Maney made the remarks in the Toronto Globe and Mail and is quoted in Lees, p. 95.

HL and Redgrave: letter, HL to Michael Redgrave, 1 Dec. 1954, HL Papers, Wisc.

346   "we had all": Lerner, Street, p. 49.

"I hate": ibid., p. 58.

347   "You bitch!" and "unique approach": ibid., pp. 56–57.

Harrison contract: HL Papers, Wisc.

"maybe fifty": int. Patrick Farmer/HL, 10 Jan. 1980.

"Oh, Moss Hart.": int. Patrick Farmer/HL, 10 Jan. 1980.

"not excited": int. Patrick Farmer/HL, 10 Jan. 1980.

Cyril Ritchard: letter, HL to Laurence Evans, 1 Apr. 1955, HL Papers, Wisc.

348   quotes re Boy Friend: all 1 Oct. 1954, LCL.

Pipe Dream: Windeler, p. 39.

Julie Andrews's contract: HL papers, Wisc.

"What are": Windeler, p. 39.

"thumping no": MH, MFL m.s., p. 2, MH Papers, Wisc.

349   "my goose": ibid., p. 3.

"a few deft": ibid.

26: LOVERLY

350   Julie Andrews quote: in USC, p. 33.

Levin and In the Pink: contract, 21 June 1955, MH and HL, HL Papers, Wisc.

"mask his symptoms": KCH to MB, courtesy MB. "Librium" is from Diamonstein, p. 320.

351   "Mask the symptoms?": KCH to MB, TS., p. 14.

351   "a dancing instructor": AJL, unpublished m.s. scene for MFL, act one, scene 9,
          p. 66; HL Papers, Wisc.
      "get the bloody": AJL, unpublished outline for MFL, HL Papers, Wisc.
      "courtiers" etc.: AJL, unpublished outline for MFL, HL Papers, Wisc.
352   deal with Beaumont: Huggett, p. 460.
      "really changed my life": Julie Andrews, USC, 12 Apr. 1970, p. 32. [The author was
          present.]
353   "enchanting": int. SB/Miles Kreuger, 15 Nov. 1995.
      Re Crosby: int. SB/Tony Walton, 15 Nov. 1995.
      "a dazzling": Lerner, Street, p. 52.
      "so flexible": ibid., p. 52.
354   "Her first tryouts": Windeler, p. 11.
      "had no sense": ibid., p. 11.
      "Principal girl": ibid., p. 27.
      "just mumbled": int. RLD/RS, SMU, p. 20.
      "a couple": int. RLD/RS, SMU, p. 21.
      "I got worse": Julie Andrews, USC, p. 32.
      "bastardized": Julie Andrews in Back on Broadway, PBS, 1995.
355   "I didn't know": Julie Andrews, USC, p. 32.
      "a monstrous": Windeler, p. 40.
      "When it came": ibid.
      "hated": ibid.
      "one of the nastiest": int. SB/Miles Kreuger, 15 Nov. 1995.
      "it seemed": Windeler, p. 41.
      "If I were": Kitty, p. 178.
      "It was the sort": Windeler, p. 41.
356   "He'd had to be": Julie Andrews, USC, p. 32.
      "I felt as if": ibid.
      "atrocious": ibid., p. 33.
      "You're playing": this is an amalgam of Windeler, pp. 41–42; Julie Andrews, USC,
          pp. 32–33; and Julie Andrews in Back on Broadway, PBS, 1995.
      "You want to be": int. Biff Liff/Patrick Farmer, 9 Jan. 1980.
      "occasionally" and "I remember": Julie Andrews, USC, p. 33.
      "He was really": Julie Andrews, USC, p. 33.
      "he bullied," etc.: Windeler, pp. 41–42.
357   "infuriated": ibid., p. 42.
      "I really did": ibid., pp. 42–43.
      "He dirtied her up": int. SB/Bud Widney, 29 Nov. 1995.
      "Now look, Stanley": Lees, p. 128.
      "Where's my Penguin?": Harrison, p. 131.
358   "I'm not going to": Lees, p. 129.
      "You can't": Lerner, Street, p. 100.
      "I think": Lees, p. 129.
      "blew Rex": Lerner, Street, p. 103.
359   "There will be": Lees, p. 130.
      "a basket case": int. SB/Bud Widney, as cited.
      A few did: Arthur Zigouras, NYT, 26 Dec. 1993, p. 2 [letter to the editor; the
          writer was a student at Yale Drama and an usher at the first performance].
      "the combination of Moss's calm": int. SB/Bud Widney, as cited.
360   "Rain in Spain" incident: Suskin, p. 471.
      "Not like that": int. SB/Tony Walton, 5 Nov. 1995.

361 "You Jewish cunt!": Huggett, pp. 464–65. Huggett claims that Lerner personally
        vouched for this story.
     "I'm a writer": int. SB/Tony Walton, 5 Nov. 1995.
     "Rex, please don't": Huggett, p. 466.
     "Rex didn't mean": ibid., p. 466.
     "the thing ballet": Shelton, SMU, p. 21.
     "On the Street on Which": AJL, USC, p. 31.
363 "It's some kind": Lees, p. 133.
     "They were tempting": int. SB/Miles Kreuger, 15 Nov. 1995.
     "Bulletins": BA, NYT, 16 Mar. 1956.
     Walter Kerr's "Don't bother" and following: Suskin, pp. 469–70.
     "I would have sworn": Eric Brotherson, in Sederholm, pp. 543–44.
364 "the best-directed": AO, p. 316.
     Maney anecdote: *Saturday Evening Post,* 2 May 1959, p. 110.

27: "THE DARLING OF EVERYONE THERE"

366 epigraph: USC, quoted by Laurence Harvey, p. 35.
     "off to learn": letter, MH to HL, 18 Mar. 1956, HL Papers, Wisc.
     "enchanted": int. SB/Tony Walton, 15 Nov. 1995.
367 Cerf suggestions: letter, Phyllis Cerf to MH, 27 Jan. 1957, MH Papers, Wisc.
     "Isn't it wonderful": quoted by KCH to Patrick Farmer, 12 Jan. 1980, courtesy
        Patrick Farmer.
368 1916: the original handwritten m.s. is in the MH Papers, Wisc.
     "Truth-ier Truth": letter, GA to MH, 10 Sept. 1959, MH Papers, Wisc.
     "the best book": NYT, 20 Sept. 1959.
     emotionally fastidious: Walter Kerr: NYH–T, 20 Sept. 1959.
369 Hume Cronyn: letter, Hume Cronyn to MH, 25 Sept. 1959, MH Papers, Wisc.
     "the most incredible": letter, Lillian Hellman to MH, 11 Aug. 1959, MH Papers,
        Wisc.
     Tynan on AO: "Miles and Miles and Miles of Hart," *The New Yorker,* 28 Nov. 1959.
     "I'm bigger": letter, T. H. White to MH, 4 Apr. 1960, MH Papers, Wisc.
370 "the Lear kids": *At Random,* pp. 262–63.
     "one of the": ibid., p. 263.
     Guest list: Tynan, *Show People,* p. 189.
     "De Oily Boid": Dietz, pp. 330–33.
     "He's the top!": *At Random,* p. 263.
371 "nice Jewish boy" etc.: Tynan, *Show People,* pp. 191–92.
     "as though": NYH-T, 2 Oct. 1960.
372 "You must be": Lerner, *Street,* p. 190.
     "It is so easy": quoted in Lees, p. 174.
     "You're well out": *Kitty,* p. 196.
373 "As I began": Lerner, *Street,* p. 191.
     "Lerner and Loewe": Burton quoted in Lees, pp. 174–76.
     McDowall and Mordred: int. SB/Roddy McDowall, 3 Nov. 1997.
374 "I felt torn": Lerner, *Street,* p. 204.
     "medication": ibid., p. 205.
     "It was now": ibid.
375 "the cheer": int. SB/Bud Widney, 29 Nov. 1995.
     "Here's": int. SB/Tony Walton, 15 Nov. 1995.
     "more scenery": Lerner, *Street,* p. 206.

375 "the walls": ibid., p. 212.
376 "on one condition": Lees, p. 183.
    "I was": ibid., pp. 184–85.
    "Enter from": int. SB/Roddy McDowall, 3 Nov. 1997.
    "was a hell of a": Lees, p. 191.
377 "*Camelot* is lovely": ibid., p. 188.
    "not since": Lerner, *Street,* p. 214.
    "All the good": Lees, pp. 189–90.
    "Make it": int. SB/Tony Walton, 15 Nov. 1995.
378 "a bad case": letter, MH to DS, 9 Oct. 1960, DS Papers, Wisc.
    "paraplegics' convention": int. SB/Tony Walton, 15 Nov. 1995.
    "Go immediately": *Kitty,* p. 202.
    "Relax": int. SB/Bud Widney, 29 Nov. 1995.
379 Ferrer: int. SB/Bud Widney, 29 Nov. 1995.
    "the seams": Lerner, p. 219.
    "after Moss": int. SB/Roddy McDowall, 25 Nov. 1992.
    "the secure": Walter Kerr, NYH–T, 4 Dec. 1960.
    Two or three hundred: Lerner, p. 244.
380 "The following morning": ibid., p. 245.
381 "such an elegant": Cullum, quoted in Farmer, p. 168.
    "a scene": Cullum, quoted in Farmer, p. 172.
    eulogy: quoted in Meredith, pp. 648–49.
382 "doesn't sound": letter, Ferber to MH, 25 Apr. 1961, Ferber Papers, Wisc.
    "with enormous satisfaction" and "sadness": letter, MH to Russell Crouse, 15 Dec.
        1961, MH Papers, Wisc.
    sonic boom quarrel: KCH to MB, Brenner Ts, p. 57.
383 "How are you": USC, p. 35.

28: JOIE DE VIVRE

384 "…if being": MH, *Music by Duchin* m.s., p. 32a, MH Papers, Wisc.
    BA: NYT, 21 Dec. 1961, BA Cage File, LCL.

SELECTED BIBLIOGRAPHY

FULL-LENGTH WORKS BY MOSS HART

Act One: An Autobiography. New York: Random House, 1959.

The American Way (with George S. Kaufman). New York: DPS.

As Thousands Cheer (with Irving Berlin). See Oliver, Donald. *The Greatest Revue Sketches*.

The Beloved Bandit (also known as *The Hold-up Man* and as *Lad O'Laughter*), with Edward Eliscu. Unpublished. Wisconsin Historical Society.

Christopher Blake. New York: Random House, 1947.

The Climate of Eden. New York: Random House, 1953.

The Fabulous Invalid (with George S. Kaufman). New York: Random House, 1938.

Face the Music (m.s.) (with Irving Berlin).

George Washington Slept Here (with George S. Kaufman). New York: DPS.

I'd Rather Be Right (with George S. Kaufman, music by Richard Rodgers and lyrics by Lorenz Hart). New York. Random House, 1937.

Inside U.S.A. (with others). See Oliver, Donald, below.

Lad O'Laughter (see *Beloved Bandit* above), with Edward Eliscu. Unpublished m.s., 1924, property David Eliscu, courtesy Merlin Fisk.

Lady in the Dark (music by Kurt Weill, lyrics by Ira Gershwin). New York: Random House, 1941.

Light Up the Sky. New York: DPS.

The Man Who Came to Dinner (with George S. Kaufman). In *Six Plays*.

Merrily We Roll Along (with George S. Kaufman).

My Trip Around the World. Unpublished; privately bound and distributed by MH.

No Retreat (or *Panic*). Unpublished playscript; 1929/30; NYPL/LCL.

Once in a Lifetime. Unpublished playscript; 1929; Wisconsin Historical Society, Madison, Wisconsin.

Once in a Lifetime (with George S. Kaufman). New York: Farrar and Rinehart.

Sing Out the News. See Oliver, Donald, below.

Six Plays by Kaufman & Hart (intro by Brooks Atkinson, "Men at Work" by Moss Hart, "Forked Lightning" by George S. Kaufman). New York: Modern Library (Random House), 1942.

Winged Victory: The Air Force Play. New York: Random House, 1943.

You Can't Take It With You (with George S. Kaufman). In *Six Plays*.

SHORTER WORKS BY MOSS HART

"Dream On, Soldier" (with George S. Kaufman), short play, DPS (also published in *Theatre Arts*, September 1943).

"The Ladies," DPS.

"The Paperhanger" (with George S. Kaufman), short play, DPS.

SELECTED ARTICLES BY MOSS HART

"An Adventure in Creation." *YMHA New Leader,* Brooklyn, May 1928.

"Advice to Breathless Thespians." *New York Times Magazine,* June 5, 1960.

"All at Sea: So 'Jubilee' Was Named Amid Cups and Cheers." LCL

"Before Thousands Cheered." *Stage,* July 1935, pp. 16–19.

"Confessions of a Dying Dramatic Director." Newsletter of "The Stagers," Newark YMHA
   (n.d., c. 1929).

"Decentralize the Play." *Theatre Arts,* October 1948, p. 55.

"A Devil's Dictionary of the Theatre" m.s., Wisconsin Historical Society.

"East-West Croquet." *Life,* July 22, 1946, pp. 28–29.

"Foreword." *The Cole Porter Songbook.* New York: Simon & Schuster, 1959.

"A Graduate Academy." *Theatre Arts,* April 1950, pp. 54–55.

"How a Lady Kept a Playwright in the Dark," *Theatre Arts,* November 1952, pp. 80–82.

"How A.W. Came to Dinner, And Other Stories." *New York Times.*

"A Jew Approaches Greatness." *Jewish Center Bulletin,* Brooklyn (n.d., circa 1928).

"Let the Shuberts Be Warned." *New York Times,* December 17, 1944.

"Men at Work." *Stage,* November 1936, pp. 58–62. (Revised version in *Six Plays,* Random
   House, 1942. Ms. at Wisconsin Historical Society.)

"Moss Hart." *Esquire,* January 1962, p. 102.

"Moss Hart's Farewell to His Famous Partner." *Life,* June 9, 1961.

"Mr. Hart Reports on Hollywood." *New York Times,* December 7, 1930.

"No Time For Comedy . . . Or Satire: My Most Interesting Work." *Theatre Arts,* May 1954,
   pp. 32–33 (abridgment of: "A Playwright's View," see below).

"A Playwright's View." *New York Times,* November 2, 1952.

Preface to *Lady in the Dark* vocal score, untitled. New York: Chappell & Co., March 18, 1941.

"The Saga of Gertie." *New York Times,* March 2, 1941 (reprinted in Oppenheimer, *Passionate
   Playgoer*).

"Why I Will Vote for Franklin D. Roosevelt." *The Independent,* September 21, 1944, vol.1,
   no.1, p.1.

"A Winged Victory." *New York Times,* November 14, 1943.

SELECTED FULL-LENGTH SOURCES

Abbott, George. *Mister Abbott.* New York: Random House. 1963.

Adams, Samuel Hopkins. *A. Woollcott: His Life and His World.* New York: Reynal & Hitchcock,
   1945.

Aldrich, Richard Stoddard. *Gertrude Lawrence as Mrs. A: An Intimate Biography of the Great Star.*
   New York. Greystone Press. 1954.

Anderson, John Murray (as told to Hugh Abercrombie Anderson). New York: Library, 1954.

Atkinson, Brooks. *Broadway.* New York: Macmillan, 1970.

Atkinson, Brooks, Bennett Cerf, Edna Ferber, Alan J. Lerner, Howard Lindsay, Dore Schary:
   A Memorial Tribute to Moss Hart (pamphlet) New York: Random House, 1962.

Bach, Steven. *Marlene Dietrich: Life and Legend.* New York: Da Capo, 2000.

Barrett, Mary Ellin. *Irving Berlin: A Daughter's Memoir.* New York: Limelight, 1996.

Barrios, Richard. *A Song in the Dark: The Birth of the Musical Film.* New York: Oxford, 1995.

Beaton, Cecil. *Self Portrait with Friends: The Selected Diaries of Cecil Beaton 1926–1974* (ed.,
   Richard Buckle). London: Weidenfeld & Nicolson, 1979.

Behrman, S. N. *People in a Diary: A Memoir.* Boston: Little, Brown, 1972.

———. *The Suspended Drawing Room.* New York: Stein & Day, 1965.

Bellamy, Ralph. *When the Smoke Hits the Fan.* Garden City, N.Y.: Doubleday, 1979.

Benson, Sally. *Junior Miss.* New York: Knopf, 1941.

Bentwich, Margery, and Norman Bentwich. *Herbert Bentwich:The Pilgrim Father.* Jerusalem: Gersher, 1940.

Berg, A. Scott. *Goldwyn: A Biography.* New York: Knopf, 1989.

Bergreen, Laurence. *As Thousands Cheer:The Life of Irving Berlin.* New York: Viking, 1990.

Berkman, Edward O. *The Lady and the Law:The Remarkable Story of Fanny Holtzmann.* Boston: Little, Brown, 1976.

Bermel, Albert. *Farce: A History from Aristophanes to Woody Allen.* New York: Simon and Schuster, 1982.

Bernstein, Walter. *Inside Out: A Memoir of the Blacklist.* New York: Knopf, 1996.

Block, Geoffrey. *Enchanted Evenings: The Broadway Musical from Show Boat to Sondheim.* New York: Oxford, 1997.

Bordman, Gerald. *American Musical Comedy: From Adonis to Dreamgirls.* New York: Oxford, 1982.

———. *American Musical Revue: From the Passing Show to Sugar Babies.* New York: Oxford, 1985.

———. *American Musical Theatre: A Chronicle* (second ed.). New York: Oxford, 1992.

———. *Oxford Companion to the American Theatre* (second ed.). New York: Oxford, 1992.

Brackett, Charles. *Entirely Surrounded.* New York: Knopf, 1934.

Brown, Gene. *Show Time: A Chronology of Broadway.* New York: Macmillan, 1997.

Brown, John Mason. *The Art of Playgoing.* New York: Norton, 1936.

———. *Dramatis Personae.* New York: Viking, 1963.

———. *The Ordeal of a Playwright: Robert E. Sherwood and the Challenge of War* (ed. Norman Cousins). New York: Harper & Row, 1970.

———. *The Worlds of Robert E. Sherwood: Mirror to His Times 1896–1939.* New York: Harper & Row, 1965.

Capra, Frank. *The Name Above the Title.* New York: Macmillan, 1971.

Carey, Gary. *Cukor & Co.The Films of George Cukor and His Collaborators.* New York: Museum of Modern Art, 1971.

Cerf, Bennett. *At Random.* New York: Random House, 1977.

———. *Try and Stop Me.* New York: Simon and Schuster, 1945.

Chatterton, Wayne. *Alexander Woollcott.* Boston: Twayne, 1978.

Chauncey, George. *Gay New York: Gender, Urban Culture, and the Making of the Gay Male World 1890–1940.* New York: Basic Books, 1994.

Chodorov, Jerome, and Joseph Fields. *Anniversary Waltz.* New York: DPS. 1957.

———. *Junior Miss.* New York: Random House. 1942.

Clurman, Harold. *The Collected Works of Harold Clurman* (ed. Marjorie Loggia and Glenn Young). New York: Applause, 1994.

———. *The Fervent Years.* New York: Harvest, 1975.

Connelly, Marc. *Voices Offstage: A Book of Memoirs.* New York: Holt, Rinehart and Winston, 1968.

Cornell, Katharine (as told to Ruth Woodbury Sedgwick). *I Wanted to Be an Actress.* New York: Random House, 1939.

Costello, Donald. *The Serpent's Eye.* South Bend, Ind.: University of Notre Dame Press, 1966.

Crawford, Cheryl. *One Naked Individual: My Fifty Years in the Theatre.* New York: Bobbs-Merrill, 1977.

Croce, Arlene. *The Fred Astaire and Ginger Rogers Book.* New York: Outerbridge & Lazard, 1972.

Diamonstein, Barbaralee. "Columbia University Oral History: Kitty Carlisle Hart." New York: Columbia University. Unpublished.

Dietz, Howard. *Dancing in the Dark.* New York: Quadrangle, 1974.

Douglas, Ann. *Terrible Honesty: Mongrel Manhattan in the 1920s.* New York: Farrar, Straus, and Giroux, 1995.

Drutman, Irving. *Good Company: A Memoir Mostly Theatrical*. Boston: Little, Brown, 1976.

Dunne, Philip. *Take Two: A Life in Movies and Politics* (rev. ed.). New York: Limelight, 1992.

Eells, George. *The Life That Late He Led: A Biography of Cole Porter*. New York: Putnam, 1967.

———. "Introduction." In Jean Howard and James Watters, *Travels With Cole Porter*, (New York: Abrams, 1991.)

Eliscu, Edward. "With or Without a Song: A Memoir. 1999: unpublished m.s. Courtesy David Eliscu and Merlin Fisk."

Ewen, David. *A Journey to Greatness: The Life and Music of George Gershwin*. New York: Henry Holt, 1956.

———. *Richard Rodgers*. New York: Henry Holt, 1957.

Eyles, Richard. *Rex Harrison*. London: W. H. Allen, 1985.

Farber, Stephen, and Marc Green. *Hollywood on the Couch*. New York: Morrow, 1993.

Farmer, Patrick Alan. *Moss Hart: American Playwright/Director*. Kent, Ohio: Kent State University, 1980.

Ferber, Edna. *A Kind of Magic*. Garden City, N. Y.: Doubleday, 1963.

———. *A Peculiar Treasure*. New York: Doubleday Doran, 1939.

Fink, Naomi Zimmer. "A Biography of Dore Schary: His Contribution to the Motion Picture Industry and Theatre of the United States of America." Unpublished thesis, University of Miami: Coral Gables, Florida, 1967.

Fordin, Hugh. *The World of Entertainment: Hollywood's Greatest Musicals*. Garden City, N. Y.: Doubleday, 1975.

Fowler, Gene, and Rowland Brown. *What Price Hollywood?* New York: Frederick Ungar, n.d.

Gershwin, Ira. *The Complete Lyrics of Ira Gershwin* (ed. Robert Kimball). London: Pavilion, 1994.

Gilbert, Julie Goldsmith. *Ferber: A Biography*. Garden City, N. Y.: Doubleday, 1978.

Gill, Brendan. *Cole: A Biographical Essay* (ed. Robert Kimball). New York: Holt, Rinehart & Winston, 1972.

———. *Here at The New Yorker*. New York: Berkley, 1975.

———. *A New York Life: Of Friends and Others*. New York: Poseidon, 1990.

Goldman, Herbert G. *Fanny Brice: The Original Funny Girl*. New York: Oxford, 1992.

Goldstein, Malcolm. *George S. Kaufman: His Life, His Theater*. New York: Oxford, 1979.

Gordon, Max, with Lewis Funke. *"Max Gordon Presents."* New York: Bernard Geis/Random House, 1963.

Gottfried, Martin. *Jed Harris: The Curse of Genius*. Boston: Little, Brown, 1984.

Grafton, David. *Red, Hot, and Rich! An Oral History of Cole Porter*. New York: Holt, 1987.

Grant, Jane. *Ross, The New Yorker and Me*. New York: Reynal and Company, 1968.

Green, Stanley. *Broadway Musicals Show by Show*. Milwaukee: Hal Leonard Books, 1985.

———. *Ring Bells! Sing Songs! Broadway Musicals of the 1930s*.(intro. by Brooks Atkinson). New York: Galahad Books, 1971.

Gurlock, Jeffrey S. *When Harlem Was Jewish, 1870–1929*. New York: Columbia University Press, 1979.

Hamm, Charles. *Irving Berlin—Songs from the Melting Pot: The Formative Years, 1907–1914*. New York: Oxford, 1997.

Harriman, Margaret Case. *Take Them Up Tenderly*. New York: Knopf, 1944.

———. *The Vicious Circle: The Story of the Algonquin Round Table*. New York: Rinehart & Co., 1951.

Harris, Jed. *A Dance on the High Wire*. New York: Crown, 1979.

Harrison, Rex. *A Damned Serious Business: My Life in Comedy*. New York: Bantam, 1991.

Hart, Kitty Carlisle. *A Broadway Memory: Stories and Songs of the American Musical Theater*. Audio. New York: Airplay Audio Publishing, 1997.

———. *Kitty: An Autobiography*. New York: Doubleday, 1988.

Haver, Ronald. *A Star Is Born: The Making of the 1954 Movie and Its 1983 Restoration.* New York: Knopf, 1988.

Hayman, Ronald. *Brecht: A Biography.* London: Weidenfeld & Nicolson, 1983.

Hecht, Ben. *Charlie: The Improbable Life and Times of Charles MacArthur.* New York: Harper & Brothers, 1957.

———. *A Child of the Century.* New York: Primus, 1985.

———. *1001 Afternoons in New York.* New York: Viking, 1941.

Herman, Gary. *The Book of Hollywood Quotes.* New York: Omnibus, 1979.

Herman, Jan. *A Talent for Trouble.* New York: Putnam, 1995.

Higham, Charles. *Merchant of Dreams: Louis B. Mayer, MGM, and the Secret Hollywood.* London: Pan, 1994.

Hobson, Laura Z. *Laura Z: A Life* (intro. by Norman Cousins). New York: Donald I. Fine, 1986.

Howard, Jean, and James Watters. *Jean Howard's Hollywood: A Photo Memoir.* New York: Abrams, 1989.

———. *Travels With Cole Porter* (intro. by George Eells). New York: Abrams, 1991.

Hoyt, Edwin P. *Alexander Woollcott: The Man Who Came to Dinner.* New York: Abelard-Schuman, 1968.

Hubler, Richard G. *The Cole Porter Story.* Cleveland and New York: World, 1965.

Huggett, Richard. *Binkie Beaumont: Eminence Grise of the West End Theatre 1933–1973.* London: Hodder & Stoughton, 1989.

Hyland, William G. *Richard Rodgers.* New Haven: Yale University Press, 1998.

Isay, Richard. *Becoming Gay: The Journey to Self-Acceptance.* New York: Pantheon, 1996.

———. *Being Homosexual: Gay Men and Their Development.* New York: Farrar, Straus & Giroux, 1989.

Jablonski, Edward. *Gershwin: A Biography.* New York: Doubleday, 1987.

———. *Gershwin Remembered.* London: Faber & Faber, 1992.

———. *Harold Arlen: Happy With the Blues.* New York: Da Capo, 1986.

———. *Irving Berlin: American Troubadour.* New York: Henry Holt, 1999.

Jamison, Kay Redfield. *An Unquiet Mind.* New York: Vintage, 1997.

Kaiser, Charles. *The Gay Metropolis 1940–1996.* New York: Houghton Mifflin, 1997.

Kanin, Garson. *Remembering Mr. Maugham.* New York: Atheneum, 1966.

Kaufman, George S., et al. *George S. Kaufman and his Collaborators* (intro by Anne Kaufman Schneider). New York: Performing Arts Journal Publication, 1984.

Kazan, Elia. *A Life.* London: Pan, 1989.

Kelly, George. The Flattering Word *and Other One-Act Plays.* Boston: Little, Brown, 1925.

Kerr, Walter. *God on the Gymnasium Floor and Other Theatrical Adventures.* New York: Simon and Schuster, 1971.

———. *Tragedy and Comedy.* New York: Simon and Schuster, 1967.

Kimball, Robert, ed. *Cole: A Biographical Essay.* New York: Holt, Rinehart & Winston, 1972.

———, ed. *The Complete Lyrics of Ira Gershwin.* London: Pavilion, 1994.

Kowalke, Kim H., and Lys Simonette, eds. *Speak Low (When You Speak Love): The Letters of Kurt Weill and Lotte Lenya.* Berkeley, Calif.: University of California Press, 1996.

Kramer, Dale. *Ross and* The New Yorker. Garden City, N. Y.: Doubleday, 1952.

Krasna, Norman. *Dear Ruth.* New York: Random House, 1945.

Kubie, Lawrence S., M.D. *Neurotic Distortion of the Creative Process.* Lawrence, Kan.: University of Kansas Press, 1958.

———. *Practical and Theoretical Aspects of Psychoanalysis.* New York: International Universities Press, 1950.

Lahr, John. *Light Fantastic: Adventures in the Theatre.* New York: Dial, 1996.

———. *Notes on a Cowardly Lion.* New York: Knopf, 1969.

Lambert, Gavin. *Norma Shearer*. New York: Knopf, 1990.

———. *On Cukor*. New York: Capricorn, 1973.

Langner, Lawrence. *The Magic Curtain*. New York: E. P. Dutton, 1951.

Lardner, Ring, Jr. *The Lardners: My Family Remembered*. New York: Harper Colophon, 1977.

Laufe, Abe. *Broadway's Greatest Musicals* (rev. ed.). New York: Funk & Wagnalls, 1977.

Laurence, Dan H., ed. *George Bernard Shaw: Collected Letters 1911–1925*. New York: Viking, 1985.

———*George Bernard Shaw: Collected Letters 1926–1950*. New York: Viking, 1988.

Laurents, Arthur. *Original Story By: A Memoir of Broadway and Hollywood*. New York: Knopf, 2000.

Lawrence, Gertrude. *A Star Danced*. Garden City, N. Y.: Doubleday, 1945.

Lees, Gene. *Inventing Champagne: The Worlds of Lerner and Loewe*. New York: St. Martin's Press, 1990.

Leider, Emily Wortis. *Becoming Mae West*. New York: Farrar, Straus Giroux, 1997.

Leiter, Samuel L. *The Great Stage Directors*. New York: Facts on File, 1994.

Lerner, Alan Jay. *Camelot*, in *Great Musicals of the American Theatre*, vol. 2 (ed. Stanley Richards). Radnor, Penn.: Chilton Book Company, 1976.

———. *The Musical Theatre: A Celebration*. New York: McGraw-Hill, 1986.

———. *My Fair Lady*. New York: Coward-McCann, 1956.

———. *The Street Where I Live*. New York: W. W. Norton, 1978.

Levy, Emanuel. *George Cukor: Master of Elegance*. New York: Morrow, 1994.

Loughery, John. *The Other Side of Silence: Men's Lives and Gay Identities. A Twentieth Century History*. New York: Holt, 1998.

Lynes, Russell. *The Lively Audience: A Social History of the Visual and Performing Arts in America 1890–1950*. New York: Harper & Row, 1985.

Maland, Charles J. *Frank Capra*. New York: Twayne, 1995.

Mander, Raymond and Joe Mitchenson. *Revue: A Story in Pictures*. New York: Taplinger, 1971.

Mantle, Burns. *The Best Plays* [of the Season]. Annual series. New York: Dodd, Mead and Co., 1931–1935.

Marx, Harpo, with Roland Barber. *Harpo Speaks!* New York: Freeway Press, 1961.

Marx, Samuel. *A Gaudy Spree: Literary Hollywood When the West Was Fun*. New York: Franklin Watts, 1987.

Marx, Samuel, and Jan Clayton. *Rodgers and Hart*. New York: Putnam's, 1976.

Mason, Jeffrey D. *Wisecracks: The Farces of George S. Kaufman*. Ann Arbor, Mich.: UMI Research Press, 1988.

McBride, Joseph. *Frank Capra: The Catastrophe of Success*. New York: Simon and Schuster, 1992.

McBrien, William. *Cole Porter*. New York: Knopf, 1998.

McDowall, Roddy. *Double Exposure: Take Two*. New York: William Morrow, 1989.

McGilligan, Patrick. *George Cukor: A Double Life*. New York: St. Martin's Press, 1991.

Meredith, Scott. *George S. Kaufman and His Friends*. Garden City, N.Y.: Doubleday, 1974.

Merrick, Gordon, and Charles E. Hulse. *The Good Life*. New York: Alyson, 1997.

———. *The Lord Won't Mind*. New York: Avon, 1970.

Meryman, Richard. *Mank: The Wit, World, and Life of Herman Mankiewicz*. New York: Morrow, 1978.

Meyers, Jeffrey. *Hemingway: A Biography*. New York: Perennial, 1986.

Miller, Arthur. *Timebends: A Life*. New York: Grove, 1987.

Minnelli, Vincente, with Hector Arce. *I Remember It Well*. Garden City, N.Y.: Doubleday, 1974.

Mitgang, Herbert. *Dangerous Dossiers*. New York: Ballantine, 1989.

Mittelhölzer, Edgar. *Shadows Move Among Them*. New York: Lippincott, 1951.

Mordden, Ethan. *The American Theatre*. New York: Oxford, 1981.

————. *Better Foot Forward: The History of American Musical Theatre*. New York: Grossman/ Viking, 1976.

————. *Broadway Babies: The People Who Made the American Musical*. New York: Oxford, 1983.

Morley, Sheridan. *Gertrude Lawrence*. New York: McGraw-Hill, 1981.

————. *A Talent to Amuse: A Biography of Noël Coward*. Middlesex: Penguin, 1975.

Morris, Lloyd. *Curtain Time: The Story of the American Theater*. New York: Random House, 1953.

Moses, Montrose, and John Mason Brown, eds. *The American Theatre as Seen by Its Critics 1752–1934*. New York: Norton, 1934.

Mosley, Leonard. *Zanuck: The Rise and Fall of Hollywood's Last Tycoon*. Boston: Little, Brown, 1984.

Nathan, George Jean. *Art of the Night*. New York: Knopf, 1928.

————. *Encyclopaedia of the Theatre*. New York: Knopf, 1940.

————. *The Magic Mirror* (ed. Thomas Quinn Curtis). New York: Knopf, 1960.

————. *The World of George Jean Nathan* (ed. Charles Angoff). New York: Knopf, 1952.

Nolan, Frederick. *Lorenz Hart: A Poet on Broadway*. New York: Oxford, 1994.

Oliver, Donald. *The Greatest Revue Sketches*. New York: Avon, 1982.

Oppenheimer, George, ed. *The Passionate Playgoer: A Personal Scrapbook*. New York: Viking, 1962.

Paley, William S. *As It Happened: A Memoir*. Garden City, N. Y.: Doubleday, 1979.

Pascal, Valerie. *The Disciple and His Devil*. New York: McGraw-Hill, 1970.

Pery, Jenny. "Solomon J. Solomon, RA." Exhibition Catalogue, Ben Uri Art Gallery, London, 1990.

Phillips, Olga. *Solomon J. Solomon: A Memoir of Peace and War*. London: Herbert Joseph, n.d. (c. 1933).

Porter, Cole. *The Cole Porter Songbook*. New York: Simon & Schuster, 1959.

Rabinowitz, Ann. *Bethie*. New York: Macmillan, 1989.

Reinhardt, Gottfried. *The Genius: A Memoir of Max Reinhardt by His Son*. New York: Knopf, 1979.

Rice, Elmer. *The Living Theatre*. New York: Harper & Brothers, 1959.

Rich, Frank. *Hot Seat: Theater Criticism for* The New York Times, *1980–1993*. New York: Random House, 1998.

Rodgers, Richard. *Musical Stages*. New York: Random House, 1975.

Rollyson, Carl. *Lillian Hellman: Her Legend and Her Legacy*. New York: St. Martin's Press, 1988.

Ruggles, Eleanor. *Prince of Players*. New York: Norton, 1953.

Sanders, Ronald. *The Days Grow Short: The Life and Music of Kurt Weill*. New York: Holt, Rinehart and Winston, 1980.

Schary, Dore. *Heyday*. New York: Little, Brown, 1979.

Schickel, Richard. *Cary Grant: A Celebration*. London: Pavilion, 1983.

Schwartz, Charles. *Cole Porter: A Biography*. New York: Da Capo, 1979.

Sederholm, Jack P. *The Musical Directing Career and Stagecraft Contributions of Hassard Short, 1919–1952*. Unpublished dissertation, Wayne State University, 1974.

Seton, Marie. *Sergei M. Eisenstein*. New York: Grove, 1960.

Shapiro, Doris. *We Danced All Night*. New York: Morrow, 1990.

Shaw, George Bernard. *Pygmalion* (published together with text of Alan Jay Lerner's *My Fair Lady* adaptation). New York: Signet, 1975.

Sheehy, Helen. *Eva Le Gallienne: A Biography*. New York: Knopf, 1996.

Sillman, Leonard. *Here Lies Leonard Sillman: Straightened Out at Last*. New York: Citadel, 1959.

Skinner, Cornelia Otis. *Life With Lindsay & Crouse*. Boston: Houghton Mifflin, 1976.

Slide, Anthony. *The American Film Industry: A Historical Dictionary*. New York: Limelight, 1990.

Smith, Sally Bedell. *In All His Glory: The Life of William S. Paley*. New York: Simon and Schuster, 1990.
Suskin, Steven. *Opening Night on Broadway*. New York: Schirmer Books, 1990.
Tapert, Annette. *Swifty*. New York: Simon & Schuster, 1995.
Taylor, John Russell. *Hitch*. New York: Pantheon, 1978.
———. *Strangers in Paradise*. London: Faber, 1985.
Teichmann, Howard. *George S. Kaufman: An Intimate Portrait*. New York: Atheneum, 1972.
———. *Smart Aleck: The Wit, World and Life of Alexander Woollcott*. New York: Morrow, 1976.
Thomas, Bob. *King Cohn*. New York: Putnam's, 1967.
Thomson, David. *A Biographical Dictionary of Film*. New York: Knopf, 1994.
———. *Showman: The Life of David O. Selznick*. New York: Knopf, 1992.
Thurber, James. *The Years With Ross*. New York: Ballantine, 1957.
Tynan, Kenneth. *Profiles*. London: Walker, 1989.
———. *Show People*. New York: Simon & Schuster, 1979.
———. *The Sound of Two Hands Clapping*. New York: Holt, Rinehart and Winston, 1975.
———. *Tynan Right & Left*. New York: Atheneum, 1967.
University of Southern California. *A Celebration of Moss Hart: USC Friends of the Libraries, 12 April 1970*. Los Angeles: University of Southern California, 1970.
Vickers, Hugo. *Cecil Beaton: The Authorized Biography*. London: Weidenfeld & Nicolson, 1985.
Waldau, Roy S. *Vintage Years of the Theatre Guild: 1928–1939*. Cleveland: Case Western Reserve University Press, 1972.
Wassermann, Jakob. *Der Fall Maurizius*. Munich: Langen/Müller Verlag, 1928.
Waters, Ethel, with Charles Samuels. *His Eye is on the Sparrow*. Garden City, N.Y.: Doubleday, 1951.
Watson, Steven. *Prepare for Saints: Gertrude Stein, Virgil Thomson, and the Mainstreaming of American Modernism*. New York: Random House, 1999.
Wharton, John F. *Life Among the Playwrights*. New York: Quadrangle, 1974.
White, E. B. *Here Is New York*. New York: Harpers, 1949.
Windeler, Robert. *Julie Andrews: A Biography*. New York: Putnam's, 1970.
Woollcott, Alexander. *The Letters of Alexander Woollcott* (ed. Beatrice Kaufman and Joseph Hennessey). New York: Viking, 1944.
———. *Long, Long Ago*. New York: Bantam, 1946.
———. *While Rome Burns* (intro. by Sheridan Morley). London: Simon and Schuster, 1989.
Wouk, Herman. *City Boy: The Adventures of Herbie Bookbinder*. New York: Little, Brown, 1992.

SELECTED ARTICLES

Ager, Cecilia. "Moss Hart Merrily Chatters On." *Variety*, November 1934, LCL.
Anon. "A Bit of Constitutional Fun." *Stage*, December 1937, pp. 56–59.
———. *"The Great Waltz."* *Stage*, November 1934, p. 9.
———. "Moss Hart." *Current Biography*, 1940.
———. "Moss Hart." *Current Biography*, 1960.
———. "The Secretary-Dramatist." *New York Morning Telegraph*, 12 July 1925.
Aronson, Steven M. L. "Broadway Legends: Moss Hart—The Playwright's Fairview Farm in Pennsylvania." *Architectural Digest*, November 1995, p. 170ff.
Atkinson, Brooks. "Introduction." In *Six Plays by Kaufman & Hart*. (New York: Modern Library [Random House], 1942).
Beebe, Lucius (photographs by Jerome Zerbe). "Going to It." *Stage*, December 1937, pp. 60–65.
Brenner, Marie. "The Art of Mrs. Hart." *The New Yorker*, 5 July 1993.
Brubaker, Howard. "Utopia '37." *Stage*. Privately bound, Moss Hart Papers, Wisconsin.
Carlisle, Kitty. "Why I Love My Man, Moss." *Cosmopolitan*, November 1960.
Cerf, Bennett. "Broadway's Double-Play Boys." *Liberty*, 29 July 1944.

————. "A Few Words About Moss Hart, By His Publisher, Bennett Cerf." M.s., Wisconsin State Historical Society.

Cooper, Wyatt. "Whatever You Think Dorothy Parker Was Like, She Wasn't." *Esquire,* July 1968, p. 57ff.

Doll, S/Sgt. Bill. "On Filming 'Winged Victory.'" *New York Times,* 17 December 1944.

Drake, Silvie. "Son Paying Homage to Moss Hart." *Los Angeles Times,* 7 March 1987, part VI, pp. 1, 4.

Fadiman, Clifton. "Comedy With Errors." *Stage,* March 1937.

Gardner, Mona. "Byron from Brooklyn." *The Saturday Evening Post,* 18/25 November 1944.

Gilder, Rosamond. "The Fabulous Hart." *Theatre Arts,* February 1944.

Gill, Brenda. "Pursuer and Pursued: The Still Untold Story of Cary Grant." *The New Yorker,* 2 June 1997, p. 84ff.

Goldberg, Isaac. "Merry-Maker for 'Jubilee.'" LCL.

Hecht, Ben. "1001 Afternoons in New York: Nude On Rocks." *PM,* 1941.

Horner, Harry. "Designer in Action." *Theatre Arts,* April 1941, pp. 265–75.

————. "'It's Never Work': *Winged Victory* in Production." *Theatre Arts,* February 1944.

Kaufman, George S. "Forked Lightning." In *Six Plays by Kaufman & Hart.* (New York: Modern Library [Random House], 1942).

————. "How I Became a Great Actor." *Theatre* magazine, December 1930, p. 46.

————. "Memoir." *The New Yorker,* 11 June 1960.

Kissell, Howard. "Early John Ford." *Women's Wear Daily,* 18 August 1975.

Maloney, Russell. "It's De-Lovely!" *The New Yorker,* 20 January 1940, pp. 25–29.

Maslon, Lawrence. "George S. Kaufman: The Gloomy Dean of American Comedy." Liner notes, "Strike Up The Band," Roxbury Recordings, 1991.

Motherwell, Hiram. "What Is the Play About?" *Stage,* November 1934, p. 23.

Oppenheim, Beatrice. "Wonder Boy of Broadway." *Reader's Digest,* March 1944.

Powell, William B. "Da Capo Round the World." *Stage,* November 1935.

Pryor, Thomas M. "By Way of Report." *New York Times,* 8 September 1940.

Richards, Stanley. "A Visit with Moss Hart and Kitty Carlisle." *The Theater,* August 1960, pp. 2–3.

Scheuer, Philip K. "Hollywood's Traducer Now Its Booster." *Los Angeles Times,* 19 February 1933.

————. "Moss Hart Hits Hollywood as Totalitarian, Frightened." *Los Angeles Times,* 2 March 1947.

Smith, Cecil. "Next: 'Act Two' From the Pen of Moss Hart." *Los Angeles Times,* 19 June 1960.

Talmey, Allene. "The Biography of a Play." *Stage,* November 1934, pp. 18–22.

Valentine, Elisabeth-R. "Moss Hart: A Drama in 3 Acts." *New York Times Magazine,* 31 October 1943.

Vandamm. "Hassard Short—Who Is Master of the Revue." *Theatre* magazine, January 1931, p. 45ff.

"M. W." "Moss Hart and His Success." *Newark News,* 1 November 1934, LCL.

Woollcott, Alexander. "The Deep, Tangled Kaufman." *The New Yorker,* 18 May 1929, pp. 26–29.

ACKNOWLEDGMENTS

Preparing these pages began in earnest fifteen years ago and, like most biographers, I had help right from the beginning.

I had just written and published a first book in 1985 and intended this as my second. I confided my plans to a shrewd and sympathetic friend who insisted on taking time from the novel she was writing to organize a small New York luncheon where I might meet Kitty Carlisle Hart. Our hostess sat me on Mrs. Hart's left, giving me the opportunity to mention casually my desire to write these pages. On *my* left, sharply alert to my theme, was Irene Mayer Selznick, that formidable woman pegged by David Thomson as "actress and spell-binder." Mrs. Selznick—noting Mrs. Hart's apparent indifference to my topic—shortly there-after informed me she had doted on Moss Hart since before I was born and appointed herself godmother to this book. It was an offer I could not refuse, certainly not in Cézanne-hung digs high in the Hotel Pierre, though I failed to conceal a certain sense of intimidation. I finally relaxed when, in my presence, she dismissed whatever it was her friend Katharine Hepburn wanted to impart, telling her that Hart and I were—at that moment, anyway—of far greater interest and importance. Mrs. Selznick's guidance and tough standards are, I hope, justified here. I miss her challenging presence as much as I am grateful to her, but I would still like to know what Hepburn wanted to say.

A few months later—months of research and interviewing—I put the project, still unblessed by Hart's widow, temporarily aside to write a biography of Marlene Dietrich, then in her late, loquacious eighties and not likely to last forever. It happened that I finished the manuscript of that book exactly two days before Dietrich died, but in the interim there had been the occasional intersection between the worlds of Dietrich and Hart, in which research and sources overlapped. This included an interview at home with Mrs. Hart, who was warm, witty, and forthcoming about Dietrich, though her cooperation on the one subject did not extend to the next. Compensation came from the enthusiasm and kindness of many others who livened and perhaps even deepened my experience of writing.

No biographer goes to press alone. I got there in the company of many generous people, some of whom remain (as they requested) unnamed here. They shared their time, memo-ries, and insights in a spirit unfailingly patient and friendly to my subject and me. Some made vital, long-term contributions and I single them out now:

The Internet and Rollerblades delivered Lee Armitage to me, fresh from her stint on Stephen Sondheim's *Passion,* and passion is what she glowed with and brought to every research challenge that came her way. Marie Brenner's largeness of spirit (always evident in her writing) made life easier; her generosity with transcripts and acuity of insight made pages richer. Dr. Patrick Farmer, professor of theater at the University of the Ozarks, shared original research for his Kent State doctoral dissertation without restriction: notes, tapes, letters, and interview transcripts. James Gavin took time from his writing in New York to provide (I have no idea how) miracles on audio- and videotape ranging from obscure radio programs of the thirties and forties to a black-and-white kinescope of Ann Sothern's live television outing in

Lady in the Dark. Julie Gilbert's friendship is a many-splendored (and durable) thing and her help permeates these pages, as does—I hope—her wisdom. Judy and Erik Hahn of Dallas opened wide their unique collection of first editions, letters, photographs, and holographs associated with the Algonquin Round Table crowd at Wit's End, their secluded West Texas retreat that hospitably houses the collection and the occasional grateful guest. Thanks, too, to Annabel Davis-Goff, for reasons she knows and some she doesn't. And finally, to the greatly missed Roddy McDowall—who gave me a title by calling Moss Hart "a dazzler"—and for too many fond reasons to enumerate or articulate.

I also sincerely thank:

Ronald Alexander, Alain Bernheim, Walter Bernstein, Otis Bigelow, Betsy Blair (Reisz), Dr. Glen Boles, Frederic Bradlee, Kate Buford, Charles Busch, Robert Cantrell and Carl Edwards, Dora (Sayers) Caro, Alexander Cohen, Elliot J. Cohen, Ronald L. Davis of Southern Methodist University, Robert Dawidoff, Frances Dee, David Eliscu, Edward Eliscu, Warren Enters, Stephen Farber, Merlin Fisk, Catherine Flye, Carmel Forsyte, Benjamin Friedlander, Robert Fryer, Arthur Gelb, William Goldman, Janet (Fox) and Henry Goldsmith, Malcolm Goldstein, George Hamilton, Helen Hennessey, Philip Hoare, Celeste Holm, Jan-Cristophe Horak, Dr. Joan (Mrs. Harry) Horner, Dr. Arnold Horwell, Jean Howard, Charles Hulse, Albert Innaurato, Dr. Richard Isay, Patricia Johnston, Garson Kanin, James Kirkwood, John and Barbara Kohn, Miles Kreuger, Robert Lantz, Wayne Lawson, Leo Lerman, Robert "Bobby" Lewis, Stanja Lowe, Sidney Luft, Scott Manning, Joseph McBride, William McBrien, Patrick McGilligan, Iris Montagu, Sheridan Morley, Eric Myers, Ann (Kubie) Rabinowitz, Dr. Bernard Rabinowitz, Dr. Francine Rasco, Karel Reisz, Frank Rich, Ruby Rich, Carrie Rickey (and Cora), Connie Rosenbloom, Charles Russell, Reid Shelton, Peter Stone, Annette Tapert, David Thomson, Hugo Vickers, Fred Walker, Tony Walton, Shelly Wanger, Julia Weiner, Stone "Bud" Widney, and Herman Wouk.

I received invaluable aid from: David Bartholomew, Rod Bladel, and Jeremy Megraw of the Billy Rose Collection at the Lincoln Center Library for the Performing Arts (New York Public Library), Charles Silver of the Film Studies Center at the Museum of Modern Art, Martin Jacobs at the Museum of the City of New York, and the staff at the Museum of Broadcasting. Also in New York, Ronald J. Grele, director of the Oral History Research Collection at Butler Library of Columbia University, was a knowledgeable, sophisticated, and witty archivist and guide. In Philadelphia, Geraldine Duclow was unceremoniously generous with information and material at the Philadelphia Free Library Theater Collection, as was Rosemary Haines at the Library of Congress in Washington, D.C.

In Los Angeles I enjoyed (not for the first time) the exceptional generosity of Ned Comstock at the University of Southern California's Cinema and TV Archives. (When a patron saint of researchers is recognized he will surely be called "Saint Ned.") At the Louis B. Mayer Library of the American Film Institute I was befriended by Alan Braun and Alan Gevinson; at UCLA Brigitte Kueppers opened for me the 20th Century-Fox Collection.

At the Margaret Herrick Library of the Academy of Motion Picture Arts and Sciences in Beverly Hills, I am indebted to Linda Harris Mehr for her exceptional staff, Val Almendarez, Warren Sherk, and especially Sam Gill, all of whom steered me to sources I didn't know existed or helped me negotiate those I did. Sam Goldwyn, Jr., graciously opened the riches of the Sam Goldwyn Collection to me.

The State Historical Society of Wisconsin in Madison houses not only the Moss Hart and Kitty Carlisle Papers, but also those of Dore Schary, Edna Ferber, George S. Kaufman, Herman Levin, and other figures central to these pages. Maxine Fleckner Ducey was notably friendly there, and Harry Miller was indispensable in navigating the collections and their occasional mysteries. Thanks, too, to Michael Walsh and Teresa Becker for their help during and after my two extended stays in Madison.

None of this book would have been possible without Robert Lescher, friend and agent. He brought me to Robin Swados, who found a home for me at Knopf, where Sonny Mehta provided welcome and where Jonathan Segal has been an exemplary editor and friend: meticulous, sophisticated, patient, and unflappable. I suspect that he relies as gratefully on the warmth and aid of Ida Giragossian as I have learned to.

Also at Knopf, production editor Kathleen Fridella has been dauntingly efficient and had the wisdom and good luck to enlist the aid of Muriel Jorgensen in checking my commas and semicolons, though any remaining errors should be laid at my doorstep and no one else's. The handsome design of the book is Ralph Fowler's and the jacket is the inspiration of Megan Wilson. Grateful thanks to both of them, as well as to Roméo Enriquez, the master of photo reproduction and other printing matters.

Finally, during all the research and writing there have been those who contributed to the process without suspecting they were crucial to the day's pages or the scrivener's sanity. For such sustenance (and good times) I thank, in addition to those named on the dedication page, Dr. Anke Heiman, Stephen Hollywood, James Kellerhals, Else and Werner Röhr, James Cresson, Daniel Roth, and—still prompting from whatever wings she now inhabits—Miss Cecilia McGrath: my own Aunt Kate.

INDEX

Povah, Phyllis, 286
Powell, Eleanor, 113, 141
Powell, William B., 131, 134
Power, Tyrone, 172, 257–8, 327
Power, Tyrone, Sr., 45
Prince of Players, 319–23, 329, 331
Private Lives, 75, 83, 251
Provincetown Playhouse, 38
Pulitzer, Ralph, 65
Pulitzer Prize, 35, 74, 89, 181, 292
  You Can't Take It With You, 149, 156, 167,
    231
Pygmalion (Shaw), 17, 334, 338–41, 357, 363
  Dutch and German film versions of, 342
  Pascal's 1938 film version of, 336, 338–42,
    351, 352, 355
  Pascal's idea for musical version of, 337–8,
    339
  see also My Fair Lady

Rabb, Ellis, 151
Radio City Music Hall, 120
Rains, Claude, 39, 336
Random House, 115, 169, 367, 368
Rape of Lucretia, The, 291
Rapf, Harry, 97–8, 99, 100, 105
Rasch, Albertina, 219
Rattigan, Terence, 344, 347
Reader's Digest, The, 136
Redfield, Billy (later William), 235–6
Red Shoes, The, 299
Reiner, Carl, 285, 371
Reinhardt, Max, 34, 216, 218–9, 260–1
Rice, Elmer, 272
Rich, Frank, 197, 385
Richardson, Ralph, 305, 328
Rio Rita, 264
Ritchard, Cyril, 347
Ritt, Martin, 241, 244
RKO Pictures, 182, 186, 187, 212
Robards, Jason, 151, 382
Robbins, Jerome, 293, 294, 369
Roberta, 117, 118, 267
Robeson, Paul, 38
Rockefeller family, 82, 105, 120, 121, 180,
    182
Rodgers, Dorothy, 127, 143, 164, 270
Rodgers, Richard, 127, 130, 156–7, 160, 180
  collaboration with Lorenz Hart, *see*
    Rodgers and Hart
  -Hammerstein collaboration, *see* Rodgers
    and Hammerstein

Rodgers and Hammerstein, 248, 292, 299,
    323, 324, 338, 339, 345, 348
Rodgers and Hart, 27, 30, 95, 101–2, 152,
    155, 172, 203, 228, 233
  I'd Rather Be Right and, 161–3, 164, 165
Rogers, Ginger, 75, 108, 230
Rome, Harold, 171, 333, 348
Rooney, Mickey, 100, 178, 233
Roosevelt, Franklin D., 103, 105, 155, 236–7,
    258, 292
  I'd Rather Be Right, 160–7
Rose, Billy, 53, 57, 59, 63, 78, 237, 248,
    251–3, 254, 287, 291
Ross, Harold, 65, 86, 134, 144, 188, 189, 190
Ruggles, Eleanor, 319
Russell, Rosalind, 75, 323, 370
Ryskind, Morrie, 54, 57, 83, 89, 122, 132–3,
    143

Saratoga Trunk, 323–5
Sarnoff, David, 345, 346
Sartre, Jean-Paul, 334
Saturday Review, 213
Sayers, Dora, 170, 215, 251, 253, 254, 255,
    256, 258, 262, 266, 267
Schary, Dore, 137, 202, 300, 326, 370, 378,
    382, 384
  Academy Award, 178
  on Flagler Hotel staff, 46, 63
  friendship and correspondence with Moss,
    51, 64, 65, 77–8, 80, 94, 127, 153, 156,
    178, 187, 203, 208, 212, 215, 229, 231,
    236, 268, 296
  as head of MGM, 296–7, 298, 312
Schary, Miriam, 278, 300
Schenck, Joseph, 78–9
Schneider, Irving, 127–8, 168, 235, 241, 247,
    283
Schurr, Louis, 110
Schwartz, Arthur, 83, 107, 285, 338, 370
Scott, Allan, 298
Secret Room, The, 259–60, 267, 342
"Self-Portrait," 385
Selznick, David O., 95, 98, 106, 160, 168,
    247, 311, 313
Selznick, Irene, 106, 113, 157, 160, 270, 271,
    278, 283, 284, 296, 347, 352, 369
Serlin, Oscar, 44, 51, 234
Seven Lively Arts, 248, 251–3, 254
Shadows Move Among Them (Mittelholzer),
    301–2
Shakespeare, William, 32, 103, 320

462 INDEX

Wouk, Herman, 41, 369
Writers' Guild, 301
Wyler, Gretchen, 380
Wyler, William, 243, 298

Yankee Doodle Dandy, 163, 233, 298
You Can't Take It With You, 144–51, 157, 199, 208, 271, 385
 Pulitzer Prize, 149, 156, 167, 231
Young, Stark, 275

Zanuck, Darryl, 182, 243, 246–7, 276–7, 281, 283, 298, 319, 321, 322, 331, 347
Zanuck, Richard, 320–1
Zanuck, Virginia, 277, 278
Ziegfield, Florenz, 22, 24, 87, 88, 107, 167, 251, 264, 354
 assistant Goldie, 24, 33, 369
Zilboorg, Dr. Gregory, 115–6, 129, 143, 154, 156, 213, 241
Zorina, Vera, 102, 298

A NOTE ABOUT THE AUTHOR

Steven Bach was born in Pocatello, Idaho. He was a theatrical and film producer before heading worldwide production at United Artists, where he was involved in such films as *Raging Bull, Manhattan, The French Lieutenant's Woman, La Cage aux Folles,* and *Heaven's Gate,* about which he wrote his first book, *Final Cut.* He is also the author of *Marlene Dietrich: Life and Legend.* He teaches at Columbia University and Bennington College and divides his time between Europe and the United States.

A NOTE ON THE TYPE

This book was set in a version of the well-known Monotype face Bembo. This letter was cut for the celebrated Venetian printer Aldus Manutius by Francesco Griffo, and first used in Pietro Cardinal Bembo's *De Aetna* of 1495. The companion italic is an adaptation of the chancery script type designed by the calligrapher and printer Lodovico degli Arrighi.

Composed by Creative Graphics, Allentown, Pennsylvania
Printed and bound by Berryville Graphics, Berryville, Virginia
Designed by Ralph Fowler